# The Business of Analytics

This comprehensive textbook explores the fundamental intersection of business principles and analytical methodologies. Each chapter systematically builds upon core business concepts while integrating essential statistical frameworks and analytical approaches.

Designed for universal application across undergraduate, postgraduate, and professional settings, this text bridges theoretical knowledge with practical implementation. Readers will benefit from:

- Real-world case studies demonstrating successful analytics integration across industries
- Interactive learning elements that reinforce key concepts through hands-on application
- Industry insights from leading professionals who leverage analytics daily
- Practical applications showcasing how analytical frameworks solve authentic business challenges

The text addresses critical statistical concepts while providing a road map for organizations to enhance communication, foster inclusion, and develop data-driven leadership. Students will learn how to develop working analytical models that eliminate decision-making biases, improve cross-functional collaboration, and drive measurable business outcomes.

This essential resource prepares future business leaders to champion statistical literacy in the workplace, transforming organizational culture through evidence-based practices and analytical thinking.

**Jamey M. Long** is a professor within the Costello College of Business at George Mason University, USA; an educator for public schools; and a small business owner.

**Joseph A. Pisani** is the senior doctoral dissertation chair at Grand Canyon University and a doctoral adjunct faculty/LDFM at Marymount University, USA; an educator for public schools; and a small business owner.

# THE BUSINESS OF ANALYTICS

## An Introduction to Statistical Analysis in the Business Environment

Jamey M. Long and Joseph A. Pisani

Routledge
Taylor & Francis Group
NEW YORK AND LONDON

Designed cover image: Getty Images

First published 2026
by Routledge
605 Third Avenue, New York, NY 10158

and by Routledge
4 Park Square, Milton Park, Abingdon, Oxon, OX14 4RN

*Routledge is an imprint of the Taylor & Francis Group, an informa business*



ISBN: 978-1-041-04740-7 (hbk)
ISBN: 978-1-041-04507-6 (pbk)
ISBN: 978-1-003-62965-8 (ebk)

DOI: 10.4324/9781003629658

Typeset in Times New Roman
by Apex CoVantage, LLC

Access the Instructor and Student Resources: www.Routledge.com/9781041045076

# Contents

# Notes From the Authors

In today's data-driven world, the ability to interpret, analyze, and act on information is no longer a luxury. It has become a necessity. For business students, understanding business analytics and statistics is not just about passing a course; it's about preparing for a future where data is the guiding force and universal language of decision-making.

Whether you're aspiring to lead a marketing campaign, streamline operations, manage financial portfolios, or drive strategic initiatives, your success will center on your ability to obtain new insights from all available data sources. Business analytics provides students with the tools to ask the right questions, uncover hidden patterns, and make evidence-based decisions. As a result, statistics provide the foundation for understanding variability, assessing risk, and validating results of an assessment.

This book is more than a guide to analytics and statistical formulas and software. It is a road map to becoming a competent, data-driven strategic leader. It bridges the gap between theory and practice by showing how analytical thinking can resolve real-world business problems. As you progress through this course and into your career, the skills you develop here will empower you to interpret the numbers while also providing a narrative of the story behind them. Congratulations! You are now on your way to leading with confidence in an increasingly complex global environment by becoming a business analyst.

We welcome you to the future world of business that begins with analytics.

Dr. Jamey M. Long
Dr. Joseph A. Pisani

# Preface

Understanding business analytics and statistical analysis is essential in academic settings because it prepares students with the necessary statistical tools to make data-driven decisions. In a global environment where there is information overload, the ability to interpret and analyze this information is a key differentiator in both academic learning and practical business applications. Business analytics provides an outline for identifying trends, forecasting outcomes, and maximizing strategies, which are essential skills in fields such as business, management, marketing, finance, accounting, operations, and information technology.

Statistical analysis, as a foundational component of business analytics, enables students to thoroughly test hypotheses, validate models, and make reliable conclusions from data. It develops critical thinking and enhances problem-solving abilities by encouraging a structured approach to uncertainty and variability of the researcher. Through statistical methods, students learn to quantify risk, assess performance, and support arguments with empirical evidence, which are essential competencies in both academic learning and professional practice.

The integration of business analytics and statistics into academic curricula prepares students for the changing demands of the workforce. Employers increasingly seek graduates who can not only understand data but also translate it into actionable insights by making data-driven decisions. Academic programs that emphasize these skills help bridge the gap between theoretical knowledge and real-world application to develop a new generation of professionals who are analytically minded, strategically conscious, and capable of driving innovation through data. Some practical examples of how business analytics is applied across different domains using statistical data:

1. **Customer Segmentation in Marketing.** Companies use business analytics to segment their customer base based on purchasing behavior, demographics, and engagement levels. For example, an e-commerce platform might analyze customer data to identify high-value customers and tailor marketing campaigns specifically for them. This helps in improving customer retention and increasing sales through personalized experiences.
2. **Financial Forecasting and Budgeting.** In finance, business analytics is used to predict future revenue, expenses, and cash flow. A retail chain, for instance, might use historical sales data and seasonal trends to forecast demand and optimize inventory levels. This

minimizes overstock or stockouts of inventory and ensures efficient allocation of financial resources.

3. **Operational Efficiency in Supply Chain Management.** Analytics helps businesses streamline operations by identifying bottlenecks and inefficiencies. A logistics company might analyze delivery times, fuel usage, and route data to optimize delivery schedules and reduce costs. Predictive analytics can also be used to anticipate equipment failures and schedule maintenance proactively.

CHAPTER 1

# Introduction to Business Analytics

## DEFINITION AND SCOPE OF BUSINESS ANALYTICS

In today's global and dynamic market, businesses have increasingly become part of a data-driven environment. This situation causes organizations to continuously find new ways to use data analytics to gain a competitive advantage. Business analytics is responsible for the transformation within all companies that enables them to make better-informed decisions that are founded in data analysis, evaluation, and data interpretation. Next, business analytics is the systematic use of statistical analysis, modeling, data mining, and other methods used to analyze data to make informed business decisions. Third, business analytics relies on a variety of systematic processes that convert raw data into actionable information. This situation provides organizations with the ability to fully understand past trends, to predict future outcomes, and to optimize their performance levels. Finally, business analytics enables organizations to make decisions based on data and statistics instead of only relying on experience or personal intuition.

There are many different components to business analytics. Each department or function within a business will use business analytics in three main ways. The first way to use business analytics is with descriptive analytics. *Descriptive analytics* is the analyzing of historical data to gain a better understanding of what happened in the past. Next, descriptive analytics relies on systematic techniques that include the aggregation of data, statistical analysis, data reporting to determined trends, and looking for patterns or anomalies within the business environment. The second way business analytics will be used within an organization is through predictive analytics. Predictive analytics uses Oracle data and combines machine learning algorithms to forecast future events and possibilities that can occur. Next, predictive analytics will help organizations anticipate market trends, operational challenges, new opportunities, and consumer behavior.

The final way organizations use business analytics is with prescriptive analytics. Prescriptive analytics is the most advanced form of analytics. The main goal of prescriptive analytics is to provide the organization with the recommendation for decisions or actions that are based only on the analysis of the collected data. This strategy will use tools such as optimization and simulation to help guide the decision-making process. So organizational leaders can determine the best possible outcome. As a result, prescriptive statistics enable organizations

DOI: 10.4324/9781003629658-1

to determine the most effective and efficient business strategies for new campaigns, allocating resources, and making improvements to their processes.

## Exploring the Fundamentals of Business Analytics

It is important to understand that the essentials of business analytics are necessary for an organization to improve its potential and competitive advantage in the marketplace. There are several primary components contained in the framework of business analytics that include data collection preparation, data analysis, visualization and reporting, decision-making support, and ethics and compliance. The first step in business analytics is data collection and preparation. This process involves gathering data from various sources, which can include internal databases, web analytics, consumer feedback, and market research. Next, data preparation is also important and involves sanitizing and transforming data into a usable format. Data preparation includes methods like normalization, managing missing values, and data integration to ensure the quality and reliability of the statistical analysis.

The second step is data analysis. Data analysis involves the use of descriptive, predictive, and prescriptive analytics. Business analytics will rely on a variety of statistical and quantitative methods to interpret data by providing a range of functionalities for visualizing and interpreting data. The third step is visualization and reporting. Effective communication of findings is critical in business analytics. Visualization tools enable statistical analysts to provide data insights in a clear and understandable format. As a result, the clear reporting of findings through dashboards, charts, PivotCharts, and graphs allows stakeholders to comprehend complex data interpretations and support a data-driven decision-making process.

The fourth step is decision-making support. The main purpose of business analytics is to support informed, data-driven decision-making. Organizational decision-makers rely on perceptions produced from analytics to create innovative strategies and act. This strategy involves collaboration between analysts, leaders, managers, and departments to ensure that all viewpoints are translated into practical business actions. The fifth step is continuous improvement. Business analytics is not a one-and-done process; instead, this process is cyclical and will require organizations to continually improve their analytics capabilities and strategies based on feedback loops and key performance indicators (KPIs).

The last step is ethics and compliance. With the increase in data collection requirements, ethical considerations involving data privacy and compliance have become critical. Organizations must ensure that their data collection and analysis practices align with legal regulations and ethical standards. Finally, this process includes the protection of sensitive consumer information while also being transparent about how data is used. As a result, business analytics represents an essential component of modern organizational management and strategy. The ability to convert data into meaningful information and actionable strategies enables the organization to improve performance, innovation, and competitive advantage. Organizations willing to embrace business analytics will not only address industry trends but also increase their competitive advantage, which will determine their future in the business environment.

Business analytics has become an important piece of the organizational strategy of modern companies in all market segments. The ability to change vast amounts of data into specific and useful information has enabled organizational leaders and managers to give more meaning to decisions and actions. This strategy has helped increase performance, drive innovation, redefine the organizational culture, and provide a new competitive advantage in the marketplace. When an organization is willing to implement business analytics as part of its strategy and decision-making process, it will be able to better predict and forecast their future results and actions. As the global business environment continues to change and expand, business analytics will continue to play an important role in determining the success of the organization, by making data-driven choices based on the analysis of data available.

## HISTORICAL EVOLUTION OF BUSINESS ANALYTICS

With the development and integration of information technology, today *business analytics* has become synonymous with *critical thinking* in the decision-making process. In that the goal of an organization is to achieve high levels of effectiveness, efficiency, profitability, and competitiveness, the situation that has caused organizational leaders to heavily rely on data to make more informed decisions as part of their business strategies. While this process seems commonplace today, it was not always that way. In the beginning, merchants only used simple methods of recordkeeping and mathematics to make decisions. The only statistical tools that were used were inventory management and the forecasting of sales.

However, during the 19th and 20th centuries, the formation of business analytics began to take place during the Industrial Revolution due to the increased level of competition in the market. Businesses and merchants began to see the importance of data and how it can be used to improve their business strategies. Frederick Taylor recognized the importance of analytics by studying individuals and processes to determine the necessary level of efficiency in the production process. This new approach forever changed the way analytics would be used in the business environment. As a result, organizations could analyze larger datasets more efficiently and effectively. This situation led to quantitative methods as a formal systematic process within the business environment. Statistical analysis and mathematical models were used to solve complex and diverse business problems. Next, forecasting models and linear programming were used during the decision-making process within various industries to help predict sales and success.

During the 1980s and 1990s, business analytics underwent another evolution and business intelligence was created. Business intelligence systems (BI) enabled organizations to collect, store, retrieve, and analyze data efficiently when making decisions. Databases and data warehousing technology created a centralized location for businesses to store their historical data so they could use it to conduct a more detailed and sophisticated analysis. Finally, during this time frame, other analytical tools were created that provided reporting, online analytical processing, and data mining (OLAP) to provide organizational leaders with a high level of statistical analysis so they could transform decisions into positive actions while mitigating risk.

During the 21st century, business analytics focused on "big data" and advanced analytics. Big data was developed due to the advancements in digital technologies, the Internet of Things (IoT), and social media. With these new resources, organizations found that they had an inordinate amount of data available to them from a variety of sources. This situation provided both opportunities and challenges for business analytics, and there was a need for advanced analytical tools to help provide real-time data processing and predictive modeling. As a result, advancements in artificial intelligence (AI), machine learning, and cloud computing were created to enable companies to use advanced algorithms to analyze unstructured data and to turn it into useful information in real time, so leaders and managers can make proactive decisions based on predictive analytics instead of being reactive within their environment.

## TRACING THE DEVELOPMENT AND ADOPTION OF ANALYTICS IN BUSINESS

Today, business analytics involves the use of three main models. These models are verbal descriptions, visual representations, and mathematical or equation models. Each business analytic model has a specific purpose, to enable organizations to understand data and communicate the information gained from its analysis. The first model is the *verbal description* model. This model relies on the use of language and the development of a narrative to communicate the viewpoint of the analysis of data. This strategy is necessary in making business analytics understandable to all stakeholder groups who may not understand the technical background of the data analysis. When data is communicated using a shared language or narrative, the results of the analysis can be communicated more effectively and efficiently.

The second business analytics model is the visual model. With this model, there is a strong reliance on graphical representations to communicate information using charts,

**TABLE 1.1** Verbal Description Model

**Previous Quarter of Sales Data from a Company**

| Month | Product A Sales | Product B Sales | Total Sales |
|---|---|---|---|
| January | $10,000.00 | $8,000.00 | $18,000.00 |
| February | $12,000.00 | $7,000.00 | $19,000.00 |
| March | $14,000.00 | $9,000.00 | $23,000.00 |

**Verbal Description**

Over the last quarter, the sales figures showed a positive trend. In January, total sales amounted to $18,000, predominantly driven by Product A, which generated $10,000. Product B contributed $8,000 to the overall income.

In February, the company experienced a slight increase in total sales to $19,000, with Product A sales rising to $12,000, while Product B encountered a decrease, falling to $7,000. This indicates that while Product A increased, Product B's performance started to decline.

March showed the strongest performance of the quarter, with total sales reaching $23,000. This increase can be attributed to the increased popularity of Product A, which achieved sales of $14,000. However, Product B saw a slight recovery with sales of $9,000.

Overall, the company experienced an upward trend in total sales across these three months, with Product A leading as the primary contributor. However, it is necessary to develop a new strategy to improve Product B's sales to ensure balanced growth going forward for the company.

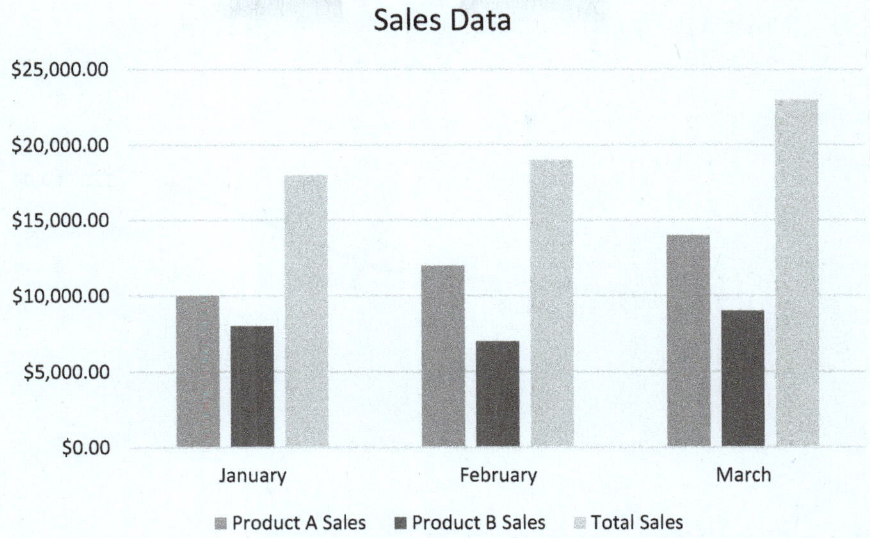


**FIGURE 1.1** Visual model.

graphs, and dashboards. These methods will illustrate patterns, relationships between variables, and trends through a logical and intuitive method. Next, the visualization of data enables all stakeholder groups to quickly understand complex information and to identify the results quickly and efficiently. As a result, the visual model improves the understanding and retention of information, enabling organizational leaders to make important data-driven decisions.

The third model and business analytics is the mathematical or equation model. This model relies on equations and algorithms to show the relationships among different variables. This strategy enables organizational leaders to make predictions and to optimize their resources to ensure success. Examples of mathematical or equation models include linear regression, time series forecasting, and logistic regression. As a result, historical data is used to make predictive forecasts for the future and to ensure that the organization can meet the changing demands of consumers and all stakeholder groups.

There has been a historical evolution of business analytics within the strategic decision-making process for organizations. As organizations continue to rely on new and innovative technology, business analytics will be required to understand the complexities and impacts of each decision and action. Next, "big data" will continue to expand given the new resources made available within the business environments to collect data. Today, organizations have more capabilities than ever to analyze patterns, improve operational efficiency and effectiveness, and predict future trends. This situation is due to the integration, in combination, of the verbal description model, the visual model, and the mathematical or equation model. As organizations look to the future, they will need to integrate the evolution of business analytics to help transform their current operation so they can maintain a competitive advantage in the future.

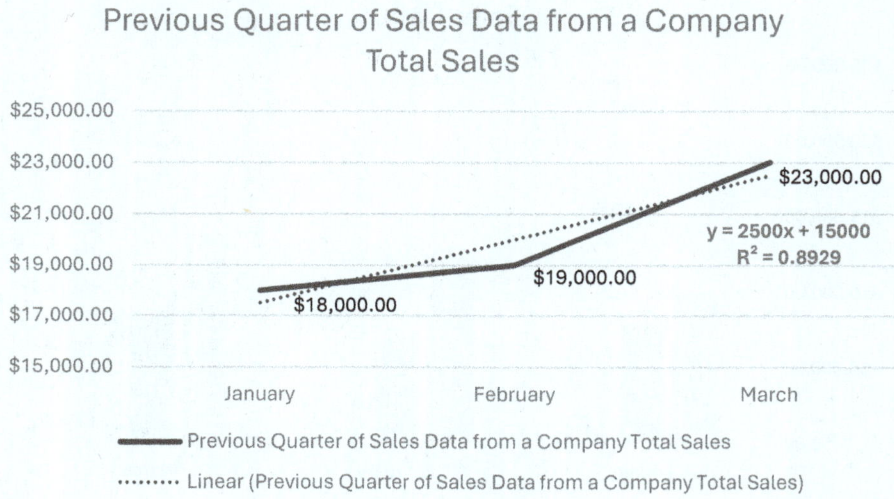


**FIGURE 1.2** Mathematical or equation model.

## Importance of Data-Driven Decision-Making

In a globally diverse business market, there is a high level of importance in data-driven decision-making. Organizations are increasingly relying on data-driven decision-making to guide their leadership and management strategies to best support their business operations. This situation will require the use of data analytics to make informed choices, minimize confusion, and enhance the overall effectiveness of making decisions or acting. As a result, there is a change from relying on your "gut" feeling and focusing on data-centric strategies based on business analytics to achieve the objectives and goals of the organization.

One of the main benefits of data-driven decisions is the improvement in accuracy. When decisions are based on data, they will become more objective than those made only on the intuition of the decision-maker. This situation will lead to improved operational efficiency through the streamlining of business operations. The use of data will provide the organization with the information necessary to make specific and direct changes to improve its workflow. As a result, the organization will be able to reduce operational costs, increase productivity, and strengthen stakeholder return on investment (ROI).

Another benefit of data-driven decisions is to improve the understanding of consumer needs and wants. With the analysis of data, organizations can analyze the preferences and purchasing patterns of consumers within their market. Consumer feedback is also used to enable the organization to develop more customized and personalized products or services to meet their changing demands. As a result, organizations can strengthen their marketing strategies to produce a higher level of consumer engagements and satisfaction. Data-driven decision-making will reduce the risk of the organization through the evaluation and analysis of historical data and using it to make predictions and forecasts to overcome potential challenges within their environment. This strategy will lead to a proactive and forward-thinking process to help minimize risk and uncertainty to help the business maintain a competitive advantage in the future.

The business will experience continuous improvement as part of its organizational culture. When data is constantly collected and analyzed, the organization can quickly assess the effectiveness of its current strategy and operations. This situation will lead to timely improvements and adjustments so the organization can be responsive to the changing needs of the market. When data analytics are used within the strategy of the organization, it will be better positioned for long-term success. If an organization does not embrace business analytics, it will fail to recognize the changes and will be unable to accurately forecast what to expect in the future and will lose its competitive advantage to its competitors.

## UNDERSTANDING THE VALUE OF ANALYTICS FOR INFORMED CHOICES

The value of business analytics is important when supporting informed decision-making. This process extends beyond the interpretation of data. Business analytics will give an organization the power it needs to use its knowledge and insights to make impactful decisions and informed choices. Understanding the value of business analytics is essential for all organizational leaders and managers, so they can lead in the operational effectiveness and strategic growth in their business environment. Next, informed choices can only be made when raw data is transformed into useful information that can be used to make decisions or actions. This situation will provide clarity in the decision-making process in enabling organizational leaders to analyze all potential outcomes with confidence in their choices. Finally, business analytics will create a culture of transparency and trust in the decision-making process between the organizational leaders and all other stakeholder groups.

## DESCRIPTIVE, PREDICTIVE, AND PRESCRIPTIVE ANALYTICS EXPLAINED

There are different types of business analytics used to take advantage of complex sources of data and make informed decisions. Business analytics is a combination of descriptive analytics, predictive analytics, and prescriptive analytics. Each type has a unique purpose and implements various techniques to ensure that organizations can effectively analyze past performance, forecast future outcomes, and recommend actions for optimization. Descriptive analytics focuses on the summarization of historical data to provide insights into what has happened in past events. Second, descriptive analytics provides a framework to allow organizational leaders to fully understand current business performance using various techniques and tools, include the following.

### Data Visualization

Data visualization is important for transforming raw data into a visual context and making it easier to identify trends, patterns, and outliers. Visualization tools like dashboards, charts, graphs, and heat maps help communicate complex information in an accessible method. By presenting data visually, stakeholder groups can quickly understand the viewpoint without having to explore complex datasets. This situation clarity facilitates more meaningful discussions around performance metrics and decision-making.

### Descriptive Statistics

Descriptive statistics use statistical techniques to summarize and organize data into meaningful patterns. This analysis includes measures such as mean (average), median (middle value), mode (most frequently occurring value), range, variance, minimum value, maximum value, skew, kurtosis, and standard deviation. These summary statistics provide a comprehensive overview of data distributions and reveal the typical trends and central tendencies within a dataset.

### Probability Distribution

Probability distributions represent how data points are spread over a range of values. Understanding probability distributions helps organizations evaluate uncertainty and variability in data. Common distributions, which include normal, binomial, and Poisson distributions, enable various analyses and allow businesses to evaluate risks and make decisions.

### Data Modeling

Data modeling involves the creation of mathematical representations of data to assist analysis. By structuring data into defined associations, organizations can better understand data interactions and dependencies. Data models help identify trends and correlations and provide the foundation for advanced analyses.

**TABLE 1.2** Descriptive Statistics

| Dataset | *Dataset* | |
|---|---|---|
| 1 | | |
| 2 | Mean | 4.222222222 |
| 3 | Standard error | 0.640697922 |
| 4 | Median | 5 |
| 5 | Mode | 5 |
| 5 | Standard deviation | 1.922093766 |
| 5 | Sample variance | 3.694444444 |
| 6 | Kurtosis | –0.547458873 |
| 7 | Skewness | –0.402912753 |
| | Range | 6 |
| | Minimum | 1 |
| | Maximum | 7 |
| | Sum | 38 |
| | Count | 9 |
| | Confidence level (95.0%) | 1.477452057 |

### Sampling and Estimation

*Sampling* is the process of selecting a descriptive subset of a population to make inferences about the entire population. Estimation techniques including point estimates and confidence intervals will enable organizations to generalize their findings from a sample to the entire population. Effective sampling and estimation allow for more competent data collection without compromising accuracy.

### Statistical Inference

Statistical inference involves the drawing of conclusions about a population based on the sample data. Techniques like hypothesis testing enable organizations to evaluate assumptions and make decisions grounded in empirical evidence.

Predictive analytics go beyond just analyzing historical data to forecast future outcomes. Next, predictive analytics implements various statistical and machine learning techniques to predict trends and behavior that allow organizations to anticipate changes within the environment. The primary components of predictive analytics include the following.

### Trendlines and Regression Analysis

Trendlines denote data trends over a specified period and are crucial for visualizing changes. Regression analysis, especially linear regression, helps the organization analyze the relationship between independent and dependent variables.

### Forecasting Techniques

Forecasting incorporates various methods for predicting future values based on historical data. Forecasting techniques like moving averages, exponential smoothing, and autoregressive integrated moving average (ARIMA) models enable an organization to estimate future performance. Accurate forecasting allows businesses to plan resource allocation effectively, change strategies, and meet consumer demand more efficiently and effectively.

### Data Mining

Data mining involves the exploration of large datasets to uncover hidden patterns and relationships. Techniques like clustering, classification, and association analysis enable businesses to segment consumers, identify market trends, and detect unexpected perceptions.

### Simulation and Risk Analysis

Simulation techniques allow organizations to assess the impact of uncertainty on outcomes by modeling various scenarios. Risk analysis involves identifying potential risks and quantifying their impact. This situation enables an organization to develop risk mitigation strategies.

Prescriptive analytics is the most advanced form of business analytics. Prescriptive analytics is focused on recommending actions to optimize outcomes based on analyzed data.

Finally, this method of analytics combines the viewpoints of both descriptive and predictive analytics to guide organizational decision-makers in using these techniques.

### Linear Optimization

Linear optimization, or linear programming, involves optimizing an objective function subject to a set of linear constraints. Organizations can maximize profits or minimize costs while ensuring resource constraints are respected.

### Integer and Nonlinear Optimization

Integer optimization is a specific form of linear programming where decision variables must be whole numbers. This method is often used in logistics when scheduling deliveries or assigning employees to shift schedules. Nonlinear optimization is used when the objective function or constraints are nonlinear, to allow for more complex relationships between variables. This strategy finds applications in areas such as portfolio optimization, where relationships may not be linear.

### Optimization Analytics

*Optimization analytics* refers to a broader application of optimization techniques to various problem domains. Optimization analytics uses algorithms and models to analyze scenarios and to determine the best choice. Next, this method acts as a valuable tool in various market segments, which include logistics, supply chain management, and financial planning.

As a result, the three types of business analytics – descriptive, predictive, and prescriptive – all play an important role in leading organizations toward effective decision-making. Next, descriptive analytics helps organizations understand past performance through data visualization and various statistical techniques. However, predictive analytics accesses historical data to forecast future outcomes and trends. Finally, prescriptive analytics examines the results from both previous phases to recommend optimal strategies for organizational leaders and decision-makers. By implementing these analytical methods, organizations can improve their operational efficiency and strategic planning while also gaining a competitive edge in an increasingly data-centric business environment.

### Tools and Technologies in Analytics

Over the years, there have been many advancements in the tools and technologies used in analytics that allow organizations to make data-driven decisions. Business analytics has been assisted by the various tools and technologies that enable an organization to collect, process, analyze, and present data so the information can be visualized by the stakeholders. Next, these analytical tools fully empower and engage organizational leaders to gain a heuristic perspective of the situation, optimize their business processes, and increase their performance levels. As a result, business intelligence tools (BI) use several different types of software in the business environment. It is important to know what these tools are, their unique features, application, and suitability to the needs of the organization.

BI tools are necessary for reporting and visualization to help convert raw data into useful information for the stakeholder groups using an easy-to-understand format. Examples of BI tools include the following.

## BUSINESS INTELLIGENCE TOOLS (BI)

### Tableau

**Features:** Interactive visualizations, dashboards, drag-and-drop interface, extensive connectivity to data sources

**Applications:** Suitable for real-time analytics, ad hoc analysis, and sharing of insights across functions or departments

**Strengths:** Highly intuitive, strong community support, robust visual capabilities

### Power BI

**Features:** Comprehensive data modeling capabilities, integration with Microsoft applications, real-time data updates, and AI analytics

**Applications:** Ideal for organizations heavily using Microsoft products; supports self-service analytics

**Strengths:** Affordable, user-friendly, excellent for integrating with other Microsoft services

### QlikView/Qlik Sense

**Features:** Associative data indexing, self-service visualization, embedded analytics, and mobile accessibility

**Applications:** Good for organizations requiring quick reporting and visual discovery

**Strengths:** Fast and flexible; allows users to explore data intuitively

## DATA ANALYTICS PLATFORMS

### SAS Analytics

**Features:** Comprehensive suite for advanced analytics, predictive modeling, and data management

**Applications:** Used widely in industries such as finance, health care, and marketing for in-depth statistical analysis

**Strengths:** Extensive analytical capabilities; strong support for a variety of data types; established reputation

### IBM SPSS

**Features:** Statistical analysis, predictive analytics, survey research tools, and reporting
**Applications:** Commonly used in academia and research for its powerful statistical capabilities
**Strengths:** User-friendly interface; strong support for qualitative and quantitative research

### R

**Features:** Open-source programming language for statistical computing, with a wide range of packages for advanced analytics
**Applications:** Used extensively in academia and industries for statistical analysis, data visualization, and machine learning
**Strengths:** Highly customizable and extensible; strong community and resource availability; suitable for complex statistical modeling

## DATA MANAGEMENT AND EXTRACT, TRANSFORM, LOAD (ETL) TOOLS

### Talend

**Features:** Open-source ETL, data integration, and data quality tools
**Applications:** Suitable for organizations looking for affordable ETL solutions; good for integrating multiple data sources
**Strengths:** Cost-effective; strong community support; flexible integration options

### Apache Nifi

**Features:** Data integration and automation; flow-based programming model; real-time data integration
**Applications:** Great for organizations requiring robust data flow management across platforms
**Strengths:** Highly configurable; robust real-time capabilities

### Informatica PowerCenter

**Features:** ETL tools, data governance, and data quality management
**Applications:** Used by large enterprises for complex data integration tasks
**Strengths:** Comprehensive tools; well-established in the industry; strong support for cloud integration

## CLOUD-BASED ANALYTICS

### Google Analytics

**Features:** Web analytics, tracking and reporting user behavior, conversion tracking

**Applications:** Ideal for businesses looking to analyze website and app usage patterns
**Strengths:** Free version available; ease of integration with other Google services

**Microsoft Azure Synapse Analytics**

**Features:** Integrated analytics service; data integration; big data and machine learning capabilities

**Applications:** Suitable for businesses requiring large-scale data preparation, exploration, and analytics

**Strengths:** Scalable; seamless integration with other Azure services; supports both SQL and NoSQL data storage

**AWS Analytics (Amazon Web Services)**

**Features:** Comprehensive suite for big data processing, data warehousing, and machine learning integration.

**Applications:** Commonly used by enterprises for scalable analytics solutions in cloud environments.

**Strengths:** Highly scalable; supports a wide array of analytics services; strong security and compliance capabilities.

## COLLABORATION AND DATA SHARING TOOLS

**Microsoft Teams**

**Features:** Collaboration platform integrated with Office 365, supporting chat, videoconferencing, and file sharing.

**Applications:** Ideal for teams to collaborate on analytics projects, integrating insights from different departments.

**Strengths:** Seamless integration with Microsoft applications; supports real-time collaboration.

**Slack**

**Features:** Messaging platform with integration capabilities, allowing teams to communicate and share files easily.

**Applications:** Great for teams requiring constant communication and collaboration around analytics tasks.

**Strengths:** User-friendly; supports integration with many analytics and data visualization tools.

**Trello**

**Features:** Project management tool utilizing boards, lists, and cards to organize tasks.

**Applications:** Suitable for teams managing analytics projects and tasks, facilitating visibility and accountability.

**Strengths:** Simple to use; visually intuitive; effective for tracking project progress.

Deciding on the right combination of tools can significantly enhance an organization's ability to generate actionable decisions from data and ensure that stakeholders make informed decisions that drive growth and efficiency. By effectively using these analytical technologies, organizations will increase their competitive advantage as they continue to operate in a data-driven market environment.

## OVERVIEW OF SOFTWARE AND TOOLS COMMONLY USED IN ANALYTICS

To effectively use business analytics, various types of data must be analyzed and used by the organization. The different types of data sources can be categorized into two distinct categories, namely, internal data and external data. *Internal data* sources are found within the organization. *External data* sources are collected from outside of the organization. The combined methods and use of these sources is necessary to provide an organization with a transparent and true evaluation of the situation based on the analytical analysis of this data.

### Internal Data Sources

Internal data sources address the information generated and collected from within the organization. This data is typically aligned with the organization's operational activities and functions.

**Transaction Data.** Collected from sales, bookings, financial transactions, and operational processes.

**Customer Relationship Management (CRM) Systems.** Data related to customer interactions, sales processes, and customer feedback.

**Enterprise Resource Planning (ERP) Systems.** Data across multiple business processes, including finance, HR, supply chain, and manufacturing.

**Financial Records.** Includes income statements, balance sheets, and cash flow statements.

**Employee Data.** Information related to employee performance, attendance, and HR metrics.

**Marketing Campaign Data.** Data collected from marketing efforts, such as campaign performance metrics, customer engagement, and lead generation.

**Website and App Analytics.** Data on user behavior, traffic sources, page views, and engagement metrics, typically gathered through tools like Google Analytics.

*Advantages and Disadvantages of Internal Data Sources*

**Advantages**

- **Relevance.** Data is closely aligned with the organization's operations and business objectives, making it highly pertinent for analysis.
- **Control.** Organizations have complete control over the collection, storage, and management of internal data.

- **Consistency.** Since this data comes from established processes and systems, it tends to be reliable and standardized.
- **Historical Perspective.** Internal data provides a historical record of operations, customer behavior, and performance metrics.

**Disadvantages**

- **Limited Scope.** Internal data may lack broader contextual insights as it does not include external factors influencing the industry or market.
- **Potential Bias.** Organizations may focus on data that confirms existing beliefs or practices, leading to confirmation bias.
- **Data Silos.** Different departments may have their data systems leading to fragmented data that is difficult to integrate.
- **Resource-Intensive.** Collecting, managing, and analyzing large volumes of internal data can require significant human and technological resources.

## External Data Sources

External data sources incorporate data collected from outside the organization. This data can provide context and meaning that complement internal information.

**Market Research Reports.** Studies conducted by research firms that provide insights into industry trends, customer behavior, and competitive analysis.

**Publicly Available Data.** Data from government databases, trade organizations, and nonprofit entities covering various sectors and demographics.

**Online and Social Media Data.** Viewpoints collected from online and social media platforms that reflect customer sentiment, brand perception, and engagement trends.

**Third-Party Data Sources.** Companies that specialize in collecting and selling data, such as demographic data, economic indicators, and consumer behavior analytics.

**Customer Reviews and Surveys.** Feedback collected from customers through reviews, surveys, and focus groups, often found on websites or feedback platforms.

**Competitor Data.** Information about competitors, such as pricing, marketing strategies, and product offerings, that are derived from various open sources.

**Web Crawling.** Gathering data from websites, including competitor prices, product descriptions, and customer reviews using automated tools.

*Advantages and Disadvantages of External Data Sources*

**Advantages**

- **Broader Viewpoints and Perspectives.** External data can provide context and highlight trends that internal data may not disclose, increasing understanding of the market.
- **Benchmarking.** Organizations can compare their performance with those of competitors and industry standards using external data.
- **Diverse Perspectives.** External data sources often include information from different stakeholders, providing a more well-rounded view.

- **Real-Time Information.** Many external data sources, especially social media, provide real-time insights that can rapidly inform business decisions.

**Disadvantages**

- **Quality Issues and Concerns.** External data may vary in quality, and organizations must critically assess its reliability and relevance.
- **Accessibility Issues.** Some external data sources may be behind paywalls or require specific permissions, complicating access.
- **Interpretation Challenges.** Integrating and interpreting external data with internal data can be difficult and possibly lead to misinterpretations if handled incorrectly.
- **Potential for Overload.** The sheer volume of data available can overpower organizations and make it challenging to extract actionable knowledge.

As a result, internal and external data sources have an important role in business analytics. While internal data offers an inclusive view of the performance of the organization, external data provides additional context and information about consumer preferences and market trends. When internal and external data sources are combined, organizational leaders can make better-informed and data-driven decisions. By understanding the benefits and challenges of each source of data, the organization can effectively use business analytics to understand past events, forecast future events, and conduct simulations to optimize their resources by understanding the complexity of the information in its entirety.

## SIMULATION SOFTWARE

Business analytics simulation software plays an important role in enabling organizations to determine the best course of action in a diverse and complex business environment. By relying on advanced modeling techniques, these analytical software tools will duplicate real-world actions and systems. This situation will enable businesses to visualize the impacts of potential decisions before implementing them as part of prescriptive analytics. *Prescriptive analytics* is a part of advanced analytics that focuses on recommending actions based on data-driven decisions. Next, prescriptive analytics combines various techniques that include optimization, simulation, and algorithms to determine the outcomes of different what-if scenarios.

Business analytics simulation software plays an important part in this process and provides the framework for businesses to explore a variety of scenarios, analyze possible outcomes, and make more informed analytical decisions based on these simulations. The first benefit of business analytics simulation software is scenario planning. Simulation software allows businesses to create a variety of potential future scenarios, helping them understand how different variables interact and influence outcomes. The second benefit is risk assessment. By simulating various situations, organizations can identify risks and develop strategies to mitigate negative impacts, thus enhancing their decision-making processes.

The third benefit is resource allocation, which enables managers to test different resource allocation strategies to determine the most efficient ways to utilize resources for maximal benefit. The fourth benefit is cost–benefit analysis, where businesses can simulate the financial implications of various decisions and help them weigh the costs against potential benefits before proceeding with a project. The final benefit of simulation software is performance optimization, which allows companies to optimize their operations by modeling processes, identifying bottlenecks, and implementing solutions.

There are many different examples of business analytics simulation software. Following are five examples of the leading software packages and their characteristics and benefits:

## EXTENDSIM

### Characteristics

- **Flexibility.** ExtendSim offers a modular design that accommodates a range of simulation types, from discrete event simulation to continuous and system dynamics.
- **Graphical Interface.** The intuitive drag-and-drop interface simplifies model building and data visualization.
- **Data Integration.** Supports integration with various data sources, enabling the use of real-time data.

### Benefits

- **Comprehensive Analysis.** Users can analyze complex scenarios across different systems.
- **Customizability.** Allows users to tailor models to fit specific needs and scenarios, enhancing adaptability.
- **Decision Support.** Offers robust tools for testing assumptions, thereby supporting better decision-making.

## ARENA

### Characteristics

- **Visual Modeling.** Arena uses a flowchart-based approach that simplifies the creation of simulation models.
- **Discrete Event Simulation.** Primarily focused on discrete event simulation, making it ideal for modeling processes with distinct events.
- **Integration with Excel.** Facilitates data import/export from Excel, enhancing usability.

### Benefits

- **Industry Versatility.** Applicable across various industries, including manufacturing, health care, and logistics.
- **Data-Driven Insights.** Provides detailed reports and dashboards for performance analysis and continuous improvement.
- **Rapid Model Development.** Enables quick model building, which accelerates the simulation process.

## ANYLOGIC

### Characteristics

- **Multi-Paradigm Approach.** Supports discrete events, agent-based, and system dynamics modeling within a single platform.
- **Real-Time Simulation.** Capable of conducting real-time simulations for dynamic environments.
- **3D Animation.** Provides 3D visualizations to enhance model presentation and analysis.

### Benefits

- **Comprehensive Modeling.** Users can choose the most suitable modeling approach based on their specific requirements.
- **User-Friendly Interface.** Encourages user engagement through its intuitive design, allowing users of different skill levels to develop simulations.
- **Collaboration Features.** Enables sharing of models with stakeholders for collaborative decision-making.

## SIMUL8

### Characteristics

- **Discrete Event Simulation.** Focused on discrete event processes, making it highly effective for operations management.
- **Drag-and-Drop Modeling.** Provides a user-friendly drag-and-drop interface for easy model development.
- **Integrations.** Offers straightforward integration with existing business systems.

### Benefits

- **Fast Modeling.** Facilitates quick changes and adjustments to simulations, speeding up the modeling process.
- **Comprehensive Reporting.** Delivers detailed analysis outputs, aiding in performance tracking and optimization.
- **Effective Resource Management.** Helps businesses optimize resource allocation and workflow efficiency.

## ANYLOGIC PERSONAL LEARNING EDITION

### Characteristics

- **Free for Personal Use.** Offers a free edition for students and learners, making it accessible for educational purposes.

- **Agent-Based Modeling.** Specialized in agent-based simulations, suitable for modeling complex interactions.
- **Cloud Deployment.** Supports cloud simulations, making the tool accessible from anywhere.

**Benefits**

- **Skill Development.** Provides a platform for users to learn simulation modeling without financial commitment.
- **Rich Learning Resources.** Comes with extensive learning materials and tutorials, benefiting users in their educational journey.
- **Community Support.** Offers access to an active community of users and experts, allowing for knowledge sharing and troubleshooting.

As a result, business analytics simulation software is a necessary tool that empowers businesses to weigh data for improved decision-making through prescriptive analytics. By enabling scenario planning, risk assessment, resource allocation optimization, and detailed cost–benefit analysis, these analytical simulation tools assist in the development of a comprehensive process for strategic planning. Whether it is through flexible modeling approaches, intuitive interfaces, or real-time simulations, professionals across all industries can use the power of analytical simulation software to identify the complex challenges and make improvements to their operational efficiency and effectiveness.

Finally, the strategic implementation of analytic simulation tools will improve an organization's ability to make data-driven decisions, optimize workflows, and ultimately achieve a competitive advantage in their specific markets and environments. Following is an example of a problem scenario of a fictional company using analytical simulation software:

## Problem Scenario: Inventory Management in a Retail Warehouse

*Background*

A retail company is experiencing challenges with its inventory management. The warehouse is frequently overstocked with certain products while understocked with others. This situation has led to increased holding costs and stockouts, respectively. The company has decided to use analytical simulation software to model the inventory management process and optimize their stocking strategy to better align supply with customer demand.

**Simulation Objectives**

1. **Identify Demand Patterns.** Analyze historical sales data to determine demand fluctuations over different time periods (daily, weekly, monthly, yearly).
2. **Optimize Inventory Levels.** Develop a simulation model that helps identify optimal inventory levels for various products to minimize costs related to overstocking and stockouts.

3. **Evaluate Ordering Strategies.** Test different ordering strategies for reorder points and order quantities to assess their impact on inventory costs and customer satisfaction.
4. **Assess Lead Times.** Consider the impact of supplier lead times on inventory management and stock availability.

**Steps in the Simulation Process**

1. **Data Collection**
   a. Gather historical sales data, including average daily sales, peak sales periods, and seasonality effects.
   b. Collect information on current inventory levels, restocking lead times, and associated holding costs.
2. **Model Development**
   a. **Building the Model.** Create a visual flowchart representation of the warehouse operations, including processes for receiving, storing, and fulfilling orders.
   b. **Defining Parameters.** Input data parameters, such as demand rates, inventory holding costs, stockout costs, and lead times.
   c. **Creating Logic for Inventory Management.** Implement logic for reorder points and order quantities, simulating how inventory is monitored and how new stock is ordered.
3. **Running Scenarios**
   a. **Baseline Scenario.** Simulate the current inventory management process to benchmark performance.
   b. **Variable Adjustments.** Modify parameters such as reorder points, lead times, and safety stock levels to evaluate their effects on inventory management.
   c. **Scenario Comparison.** Compare the outcomes of different approaches to identify which yields the best balance of cost and service level.
4. **Analysis of Results**
   a. Use reporting tools to generate summaries of key performance indicators (KPIs):
      i. Average inventory levels
      ii. Stockout frequencies
      iii. Total holding costs
      iv. Customer satisfaction metrics
   b. Analyze the results to determine which inventory management strategies effectively minimize costs while maintaining adequate product availability.

**Example of Potential Results**

- **Baseline Scenario:** Results may show high holding costs due to excess inventory, with a stockout rate of 25% during peak buying seasons.

- **Modified Scenario A:** Introduction of reorder points based on forecasted demand may reduce average inventory by 30% but results in a stockout rate of 20%.
- **Modified Scenario B:** Implementing a just-in-time inventory approach leads to a 20% reduction in holding costs and a stockout rate of 15% during high-demand periods.

### Conclusion

With business analytics simulation software, the retail company can simulate various inventory management strategies to optimize their operations. This simulation enables them to make data-driven decisions on how to manage and control inventory levels effectively while reducing costs and improving service levels. Finally, the outcome of this simulation not only assists in immediate inventory optimization but also provides an adaptable and flexible approach that can adjust to future changes in consumer demand or supply chain conditions.

## COMMON OBSTACLES AND CHALLENGES IN THE IMPLEMENTATION OF BUSINESS ANALYTICS

When implementing business analytics as part of the organizational culture, companies can experience various challenges that can impede their success. The most common challenges of implementing business analytics are the following:

#### Data Quality and Integrity

**Challenge:** One of the most significant obstacles is ensuring the quality and integrity of the data being analyzed. Data that is inaccurate, incomplete, or outdated can lead to flawed perceptions and misguided decision-making.

**Impact:** Poor data quality can result in lost opportunities, inefficient operations, and a lack of trust in analytical outputs. Organizations may find themselves making decisions based on imperfect or misleading information, which could have serious consequences.

**Solution:** Implementing strong data control practices can help organizations establish standards for data quality. Regular data cleaning and validation processes improve accuracy, and developing a culture of accountability for data management can encourage employees to prioritize data quality.

#### Integration of Data Sources

**Challenge:** Businesses often operate with data spread across various systems, departments, and formats. Integrating these unrelated data sources into a cohesive analytics framework can be complex and time-consuming.

**Impact:** Data silos can lead to inconsistencies and limit the scope of analysis. If different departments or functions rely on dissimilar data sources, it can be challenging to achieve a unified view of performance and insights.

**Solution:** Developing a comprehensive data integration strategy that includes extract, transform, load (ETL) tools can assist in the consolidation of data. Organizations may also consider adopting data warehouses to store integrated data to make it easier to access and analyze.

### Skills Gap and Training Needs

**Challenge:** A skills gap exists in many organizations, where employees may lack the necessary knowledge and expertise to effectively use analytics tools. Trained professionals in data analytics, statistics, and related fields are in high demand and often make it difficult for organizations to find appropriate candidates.

**Impact:** Insufficient skills can lead to underutilization of analytics tools, reducing the potential benefits. Employees who lack training may have difficulty interpreting and applying analytical findings appropriately.

**Solution:** Investing in training programs and professional development for existing employees can help bridge the skills gap. Collaborating with academic institutions or providing access to online courses can improve the capabilities of the current workforce.

### Executive Buy-In and Organizational Culture

**Challenge:** For analytics initiatives to succeed, they need the support of executive leadership and a culture that values data-driven decision-making. Resistance to change from leadership or employees can delay progress.

**Impact:** A lack of buy-in can limit the allocation of resources and budget for analytics initiatives. If the organizational culture is not aligned with data-driven practices, employees may be reluctant to embrace analytics.

**Solution:** Engaging organizational leaders and managers in the vision and goals of analytics initiatives is critical. Communicating the potential benefits of data-driven decision-making, supported by case studies or pilot projects, can help secure executive support. Developing a culture that encourages curiosity, data exploration, innovation, and collaboration can lead to greater acceptance of analytics.

### Technology and Infrastructure Limitations

**Challenge:** Many organizations face limitations in their existing technology infrastructure that inhibit effective analytics implementation. Legacy systems may not support advanced analytics tools, and outdated technology can negatively impact adaptability, flexibility, and scalability.

**Impact:** Poor infrastructure can lead to performance bottlenecks, slower data processing, and challenges in handling large datasets. Organizations may struggle to extract insights in a timely manner, reducing the relevance of analytics efforts.

**Solution:** Conducting a thorough assessment of current technology systems can help identify gaps and opportunities for improvement. Investing in cloud-based solutions and analytics platforms can provide greater scalability, flexibility, and performance. This strategy will support real-time data processing and visualization.

### Change Management

**Challenge:** Implementing business analytics often requires significant changes in processes, workflows, and employee roles. Change management is essential to minimize disruption and ensure a smooth transition.

**Impact:** Resistance to change can lead to confusion and setbacks. If employees or stakeholders do not understand new processes or feel overwhelmed by new tools, and adoption may be inconsistent, causing an undermining of the success of the analytics initiative.

**Solution:** A structured change management framework can support the transition. Communicating the reasons for changes, providing guidance and support, and involving employees in the implementation process can help reduce or mitigate resistance to change. Focused training sessions and resources can ensure that employees feel equipped to navigate new tools and processes.

### Security and Compliance Concerns

**Challenge:** With the increase of data, organizations face increasing scrutiny regarding data privacy and compliance with regulations. Ensuring the security of sensitive client and organizational data is important and must be handled with integrity and transparency.

**Impact:** Breaches in data security can lead to significant reputational damage and financial penalties. Concerns about data handling practices may also impede employee and customer trust in all analytics initiatives.

**Solution:** Establishing strict data governance and security policies is essential. Implementing encryption, regular audits, and compliance training can ensure that all stakeholders understand their responsibilities in maintaining data security and compliance.

### Measuring Success and Return on Investment (ROI)

**Challenge:** Organizations often find it challenging to measure the success of analytics initiatives and demonstrate a return on investment (ROI). Without clear performance metrics and defined objectives, it becomes difficult to assess effectiveness.

**Impact:** A lack of quantifiable results can lead to uncertainty regarding the value of analytics, making it harder to secure ongoing investment and support.

**Solution:** Establishing clear KPIs (key performance indicators) and goals before introducing analytics projects can help organizations track progress. Regularly reporting on outcomes and aligning analytics with business objectives can provide tangible measures of success.

Finally, implementing business analytics can present an organization with a wide range of unique challenges that must be addressed to maximize their potential. Organizational leaders will need to ensure data quality and the integration of business analytics into its culture to overcome technological limitations and to create a collaborative environment within its strategic planning process. By understanding these challenges and implementing proactive solutions, organizations can effectively apply business analytics to lead its decision-making and to improve its operational level of performance.

CHAPTER 2

# Economics and Business Analytics

## THE ROLE OF ANALYTICS IN ECONOMIC ANALYSIS

Business analytics plays an important role in the economic evaluation of an organization by providing the necessary tools and methods required to interpret data and identify new trends in making data-driven decisions across various markets within the business environment. These various market segments include retail, finance, health care, and manufacturing, which rely on business analytics to help gain valuable knowledge and insight to improve their effectiveness, efficiency, stakeholder profitability, and return on investment (ROI) and to achieve sustainable and new growth.

In finance, business analytics assists in making risk assessments and management decisions. Financial institutions will use business analytics and predictive modeling tools to analyze market trends and consumer behavior patterns. The strategy will enable financial institutions to make more informed investment decisions and to manage and enhance their diverse portfolios. As a result, the use of business and predictive analytics will help predict and detect fraudulent behavior and activities by identifying any unusual pattern in the transaction of data.

In the health-care industry, business analytics has also become a necessary part of its strategic management process, with the amount of data health-care institutions must access, large datasets that include patient information. Health-care providers must use this information to improve the outcomes of patients by understanding and examining their operational efficiencies, resource allocation, and the effectiveness of the administered treatments. As a result, predictive analytics in the health-care industry is necessary to allow for proactive measures to address outbreaks, crises, pandemics, and patient care strategies. Finally, predictive analytics will help health-care institutions reduce their expenses and increase their cost savings while providing better health care to all patients.

Within the retail sector, business analytics is used to improve consumer experience and to manage product inventory levels. When predictive analytics are used, retail companies can analyze consumer purchasing behavior and customize their marketing strategies and promotions to meet the unique and specific needs of their target market. Next, business analytics will improve the supply chain management process by predicting consumer demand fluctuations, ensuring timely availability of all products, and reducing the overstocking of items in stores.

DOI: 10.4324/9781003629658-2

In the manufacturing industry, business analytics will be used. To develop streamlined production processes to reduce costs and improve efficiency for companies, when data is analyzed, the results can be related to machine performance, supply chain, logistics, and employee productivity. As a result, business and predictive analytics will play an important part in the development of future quality control measures and key performance indicators (KPIs) that will enable manufacturing companies to reduce waste, mitigate risk, and maintain high productivity standards while improving their bottom line for all stakeholder groups.

Finally, business analytics is directly tied to the macroeconomic environment. Economists and policymakers will use business analytics and aggregated data from all industrial sectors to better understand the economic environment. As an example, unemployment trends can provide data and knowledge on economic growth and consumer spending policies that will influence new regulations and policies that will directly impact the monetary and fiscal strategies of the local, state, and federal governments. When business analytics transform data into real-world decisions and actions, organizations in all industries can improve their strategic processes, maximize their daily operations, and improve their competitive advantage, in the respective markets. As the global environment continues to expand, business analytics will play a more important role in understanding all opportunities and challenges that will arise, so organizational leaders can make data-driven decisions that will be used to shape the future of all policies, regulations, and strategies.

## USING ANALYTICS FOR ECONOMIC FORECASTING AND MODELING

In economics, industries use business analytics to improve their forecasting and predictive models. This situation helps companies in all industries make data-driven decisions and actions. The more accurate the data, the more informed predictions and strategies can be implemented. This situation requires the analysis and use of data to better understand historical information and patterns, current and new trends, and other economic indicators that include finance, retail, health care, and manufacturing.

In the finance industry, business analytics has become a critical component of economic forecasting. First, financial institutions use statistical modeling, algorithms, and business analytics to predict market trends and interest rates and mitigate investment risks. When the historical movement of price elasticity and other economic indicators is analyzed, organizations can make more accurate and precise predictions about economic cycles and the performance of investment stocks. Examples of how the finance industry uses business analytics include time series events and regression analysis, in improving investment strategies, enhancing risk management, and forecasting the changing market trends in the global economy.

Next, the retail industry market relies on business analytics to forecast and better understand sales trends and consumer behavior. For retailers, it is advantageous to analyze data that includes seasonal trends, past sales performance, and other economic factors to enable them to predict the future demand of products based on the fluid changes of consumer behavior. Next, retailers rely on machine learning and algorithms to identify patterns in consumer purchasing behaviors so they can maximize their inventory levels and customize their marketing campaigns and strategies. While this approach helps reduce the level of stockouts, it also helps improve the customer satisfaction rate by guaranteeing that all products and services are directly aligned with the demand of consumers based on analysis of the data.

Third, health-care organizations implement business analytics to conduct economic forecasts to improve their resource allocation and the management care of patients. Influential health-care industry trends that are analyzed include treatment outcomes, health-care costs, and patient admissions so providers can predict the future demands of health care. As an example, predictive analytics for health care will be used to forecast the spread of future diseases. The data that is gathered is then used to assist in the staffing decisions of hospitals and for the inventory management of medical supplies and resources. As a result, this information becomes invaluable to policymakers within the health-care system in managing resources and budgets.

For the manufacturing industry, forecasting and economic modeling are necessary for strategic planning and efficiency. Manufacturing companies must analyze data for production, supply chain logistics, and economic indicators so they can forecast the demand for their products and services. This situation is achieved with the use of advanced analytical tools that include predictive analytics and simulation models. The use of these advanced analytical tools enables manufacturing businesses to determine the impact of the cost of raw materials of their production process and the level of demand of its consumer market. As a result, business analytics is required in the manufacturing industry to improve the supply chain and to manage production schedules, by determining the critical path to eliminate risk and waste.

Finally, business analytics and forecasting are used in various industries within the global market. Next, business analytics allows organizations to conduct "what if" and scenario analysis so leaders and managers can determine the potential outcomes of the multiple and diverse conditions of the economy. When various scenarios can be simulated, industrial organizations can better prepare and make data-driven decisions to prepare for changes in the economy and market environment. This situation will promote a stronger strategic planning process. As a result, business analytics and forecast modeling will enable organizations to use data to make more knowledgeable choices to enhance their business operations, and predictive capabilities to maximize growth, efficiency, and market share within their industrial environment.

## Market Structures and Consumer Behavior Analysis

Business analytics has an important role in understanding the various market structures and consumer behavior that combine to make up the global economy. When data-driven methodologies are implemented, organizations can understand and become more aware of every dynamic within their environment. These dynamics include purchasing patterns, consumer preferences, and strategic decision-making strategies of organizational leaders. When discussing market structures and consumer behavior analysis, the industries that use business analytics the most are retail, finance, telecommunications, and automotive.

First, the retail industry relies on business analytics to study the structure of its market. Retail companies analyze data that include consumer demographics, market trends, and sales transactions daily. This information is needed to help retailers determine their present market share and the chances to increase their competitive advantage within the market.

One statistical technique that retail companies use is cluster analysis. This statistical method enables organizations to segment their market based on consumer preferences and behavior. Next, cluster analysis enables retailers to customize their marketing strategies to directly connect with their consumer market. As an example, retail companies can better identify their high-value consumer segments so they can customize specific promotions to increase sales in their specific categories based on their unique preferences. As a result, predictive analytics will enable retail organizations to forecast their inventory needs based on historical data and purchasing patterns so they can improve the supply chain management system.

When looking at consumer behavior, business analytics can determine the purchasing decisions and preferences of consumers over time. Next, when transaction data is analyzed, retail companies can uncover the hidden patterns that are related to the seasonality of products or services, promotional awareness, and the product life cycle of an item. The situation allows retailers to create targeted marketing strategies and campaigns that directly connect with the consumer. As a result of this strategy, retailers can use business analytics to improve brand loyalty, increase sales, and improve efficiency. Finally, retailers can use business analytics to understand sentiment analysis based on the responses from online platforms and social media that contain consumer reviews. With consumer reviews, there are customer perceptions that will lead to future product developments and better branding strategies.

Second, the finance industry uses business analytics to understand its market structure. Financial institutions use analytics to evaluate their competitive advantage and to understand market behavior. Market behavior within this industry includes price movements and trading volumes of stocks and other monetary resources. Next, financial institutions rely on machine learning algorithms that can identify anomalies and new trends in stock prices in real time to maximize the investments of the investor. This situation will help provide the finance industry with better risk management and investment strategies. As a result, when investor behavior and market sentiment are analyzed with business analytics, financial institutions maximize their trading strategies and improve consumer engagement.

The third industry to use business analytics to understand market structures and consumer behavior is telecommunications. Within the telecommunications industry, business analytics enables organizations to analyze market structures and to determine the turnover and retention rate of consumers. When a telecommunications firm uses predictive modeling, it can identify all factors that influence consumer loyalty and those that lead to turnover. This strategy requires a telecommunications company to segment its consumer base, based on preferences and usage patterns. As a result of this strategy, telecommunications companies can develop specific and targeted retention strategies, products, and service offerings to its consumer base that will ultimately lead to a higher satisfaction rate and reduced turnover.

Finally, the automotive industry uses business analytics to analyze the behavior of its customers. Automotive firms must examine data that is collected from sales transactions, online interactions, and consumer surveys. Based on the information gathered, automotive companies can determine the trends that are directly related to consumer preferences based on design elements, safety features, vehicle attributes, and fuel efficiency. As a result of this information, automotive manufacturers can then customize their product offerings to meet the changing demands of the market and improve their effectiveness, to maintain a competitive advantage over their competitors. The ability to analyze and interpret consumer preferences and market structure with the use of business analytics will be necessary to enable businesses to respond effectively to changes in the market conditions and to maintain sustainability and growth in the future.

## HOW DATA INFLUENCES UNDERSTANDING OF MARKET DYNAMICS

The economics industry uses business analytics as an important tool to influence the understanding and interpretation of data as it relates to market dynamics of all industries. When analytical techniques are applied, the various sectors that make up the global environment can gain new insight and knowledge to develop new strategies and daily operational protocols that enable the organizations to quickly respond to the changing conditions of the economy. The data of market dynamics can best be seen within the financial services industry, retail industry, health-care sector, manufacturing industry, and telecommunications industry.

In the financial services industry, company organizations use business analytics to analyze large datasets to help identify trends in the market behavior in consumer preferences. Financial institutions must use predictive modeling to forecast market fluctuations, investment risk, and interest rates. When creating a forecast, it is necessary to analyze historical data of enough economic indicators that go into these decisions. This situation requires organizations to develop new strategies to help manage diverse portfolios and mitigate risk. An example of the situation is when a bank uses regression analysis within the macroeconomic environment that includes unemployment rates and inflation when conducting a credit risk assessment.

Next, the retail industry will heavily rely on business analytics to understand marketing strategies and consumer behavior. Retail stores will analyze consumer demographics, inventory levels, and sales data to create demand forecasts and customized marketing promotion plans. Various techniques that are used include determining the associations between products so retailers can develop a cross-selling strategy based on the purchasing patterns of consumers. When the market dynamics are understood by analyzing the data, retailers can modify their product offerings and promotional strategies to improve the alignment with consumer trends. As a result of this strategy within this industry, retailers will experience maximized profits and consumer satisfaction levels.

Third, the health-care sector uses business analytics to gain knowledge that is used to help organizations understand the diverse dynamics within the market. Health-care organizations and providers constantly analyze patient data, operational efficiencies, and treatment outcomes to improve the delivery of products and services. Predictive analytics plays an important part in this process. With predictive analytics, health-care providers can better understand health trends in the population that will enable them to properly allocate resources more effectively and efficiently. As an example of the analysis of data, health-care companies can develop targeted intervention strategies related to patient readmissions and properly serving at-risk populations based on patient care and cost forecasts.

Within the manufacturing industry, business analytics provides real-time data that enables companies to quickly adapt to the changing conditions in the market and provide new solutions to improve the efficiency of the supply chain management process. When historical production data and external market trends are analyzed with business analytics, manufacturers can begin to forecast production schedules and consumer demand so they can maximize their profits and reduce their risk. One statistical technique that is used within this industry is simulation modeling. Simulation modeling provides manufacturing firms to determine the impact of all factors within the market, which include the costs of raw materials, the availability of labor, and the economic shifts impacting their daily operations. As a result, business analytics and a data-driven approach improve supply chain efficiency and ensure that manufacturers can meet the changing demands of the market on a recurring basis.

Finally, the telecommunications industry uses business analytics to understand market competition and consumer usage patterns. Data that is analyzed with business analytics includes consumer feedback, market share, and call data. Based on the state of the global economy, telecommunications companies can make more informed decisions about the products and services they offer. Next, telecommunications companies can develop an effective pricing strategy that best meets the needs of the consumer market. Predictive analytics will identify risks that can lead to consumer turnover and will also enable organizations to implement new retention strategies so companies can maintain or increase their level of brand loyalty. As a result, organizations in all industries benefit from business analytics, since it allows for improvement in the decision-making process, optimizes daily operations, and provides flexibility and adaptability within the constantly changing global environment.

## Supply and Demand Forecasting

Business analytics enables organizations in various industries in market segments to make more informed decisions that improve the operational efficiency and profitability of companies around the world. When data is thoroughly analyzed, organizations can accurately predict the level of future demand for their products and services and can effectively manage their supply chain with reduced costs and risks. In the retail industry, business analytics is critical in conducting demand forecasting. For demand forecasting to occur, retail organizations must analyze seasonal trends, consumer behavior, and sales data to determine the future purchasing patterns of customers. The situation requires time series analysis and predictive modeling to enable retailers to create accurate forecasts about the demand of products and services. An example of a time series analysis is the analysis of promotional events or seasonal sales that can be used to predict how the current initiative will influence consumer behavior in the future. When anticipated demand fluctuations are determined, the retailer can maximize its inventory level by reducing stockouts. This situation will minimize costs and excessive inventory, which will ultimately improve the satisfaction of customers and the profitability of the company.

The manufacturing industry will use business analytics and supply and demand forecasting. Data analytics will be necessary to evaluate production capabilities, the availability of raw materials, and market trends for the manufacturer. Through the analysis of historical data production and other external factors that include industry trends, manufacturers can then develop a forecast that will meet the demand of the consumer market more effectively and accurately. By developing an accurate forecast model, manufacturers can adjust their production schedules and become proactive in managing and allocating the resources more efficiently. As a result, manufacturers can prevent overproduction from occurring and reduce costs by understanding peaks of seasonal demand throughout the year.

In the food and beverage industry, business analytics is required to manage perishable goods more effectively. Food and beverage companies analyze sales data, consumption patterns, and environmental factors to help create a demand forecast for fresh products in the future based on consumer need. Analysis of data gives food and beverage companies predictive capability in reducing waste and maximizing their supply chain process. Next, predictive analytics will enable food and beverage companies to determine the optimal timing for inventory replacement and to ensure products are available when consumers need them most and before they expire.

In the health-care industry, business analytics supports supply and demand forecasting and inventory management of pharmaceuticals and other medical supplies. When patient admission rates, treatment protocols, and seasonal illness trends are analyzed, health-care companies can forecast the demand for specific medications and supplies to meet the changing needs of patients. This situation helps health-care providers reduce costs, optimize their levels of inventory, and guarantee that the required supplies are constantly available, all while minimizing excess stock items.

Finally, the telecommunications sector of the global market uses business analytics to create demand forecasts through the analysis of consumer behavior and their usage patterns. Next, telecommunications companies combine internal data with external market trends. This strategy enables the organizational leader of the telecommunications firm to become empowered to anticipate changes in service demand, whether it is based on products and services offered by competitors or the introduction of new technologies. Demand forecasting and business analytics enable telecommunications companies to adjust their resource allocation and capacity levels in real time so they can increase the efficiency of their daily business operation. As a result, business analytics plays an essential part in demand forecasting across various economic industries that make up the global environment.

## TECHNIQUES FOR PREDICTING MARKET TRENDS

There are techniques used in business analytics for predicting market trends within the economic environment. These techniques help enable organizations across all sectors within the global market to make more informed decisions that provide sustainability, growth, and a competitive advantage within their sector. When large quantities of data are analyzed, organizations everywhere can discover new patterns, identify trends, and anticipate potential changes in consumer behavior to help improve their strategic planning process. Industries that will be discussed include the financial sector, retail industry sector, technology sector, health-care industry sector, and the telecommunications industry sector.

First, the finance sector uses business analytics in predicting market trends through modeling and quantitative analysis. *Quantitative analysis* is a systematic approach that focuses on quantifying data and applying various statistical techniques to analyze and interpret numerical information. It is most used in finance, economics, and market research. There are four main components to quantitative analysis. The first component is data collection, which is the gathering of numerical data through experiments, existing databases, or surveys. The second component is statistical analysis, which involves the use of mathematical formulas to test hypotheses, summarize data, and explore the different possible outcomes. The third component is modeling, which is the development of mathematical models to characterize real-world events and to predict the outcomes based on the analysis of data. The final component of quantitative analysis is interpretation, which involves making conclusions from the business analytics to identify trends and ultimately make data-driven decisions.

Financial institutions will use business analytics to develop advanced statistical models and algorithms that are used to study interest rates, market data, and economic indicators. Regression modeling and time series analysis are some of the techniques used to help financial companies understand the volatility and price movements in different classes of financial assets within the market. As an example, financial institutions that manage hedge funds will use predictive analytics to determine the level of risk so they can optimize their investment strategies based on the anticipated conditions of the market. This situation enables the financial institution to take advantage of new potential opportunities while reducing the level of risk and exposure to the negative impacts of the market.

The retail industry uses business analytics to predict consumer preferences and trends within the market. Data that is analyzed includes consumer demographics, point-of-sale data, and online purchasing habits. Based on these datasets, retailers within this industry can develop new models that forecast future sales and market demand of consumers. The strategy is made possible using machine learning algorithms that are used to improve the capabilities of the retailer by identifying the complex patterns in consumer shopping behaviors. As a result of this analysis, retail companies can begin to make proactive decisions about inventory management, promotional strategies, and marketing campaigns.

Next, the technology sector of the global environment uses business analytics to identify consumer preferences and trends of new technologies and services. By analyzing online reviews and consumer feedback, technology companies can gain qualitative data through qualitative analysis that is necessary to understand the interests of consumers and the changes in the market. Qualitative analysis is a research method dedicated to understanding concepts, experiences, and social phenomena from the perspective of the subject. Next, qualitative analysis attempts to understand deeper meanings and insights through the use of non-numerical data. There are four main aspects to qualitative analysis. The first aspect is data collection, which is the gathering of non-numerical data through various methods, which include observations, focus groups, open-ended surveys, and interviews. The second aspect is thematic analysis, which is the identification and interpretation of themes, patterns, and trends within the data to understand the underlying meaning. The third aspect is contextual understanding, which is the collection of data to understand the meaning, cultural, and social factors that influence the response of the person. The final aspect of qualitative analysis is descriptive and narrative reporting, which is used to present the findings of the data in a narrative form that focuses on the unique perspectives and experiences of the individual. As a result of qualitative analysis, telecommunications companies can make more informed decisions about the development of new products and the use of marketing strategies that will ensure a stronger alignment between the company and their target market.

In the health-care industry, business analytics is used to support the prediction of trends for the analysis of data as it relates to the outcome of treatments, patient care, and other public health indicators. When predictive analytics are used, health-care organizations and providers can identify new trends in the health sector that include changes in patient preferences for treatments and the spread of communicable diseases. As a result, predictive analytics provides health-care organizations with new knowledge and information to help improve the allocation of resources and to develop an effective strategic plan for long-term growth and success.

Finally, the telecommunications industry will benefit from business analytics in the prediction of trends. This situation will require telecommunications firms to analyze subscription data, market competition, and customer usage patterns. Once this data has been analyzed and cross-referenced, telecommunications companies can better anticipate future changes in the dynamics of the market and in the level of demand for services and products. Next, predictive models will help telecommunications companies make decisions about future investments in infrastructure and new service and product offerings based on the anticipated trends of the market. Using business analytics, telecommunications companies and other industrial sectors within the global market will be able to maintain a competitive advantage and achieve long-term success within their environments.

## Price Optimization Techniques

Business analytics plays a critical role in the development of the optimization of pricing in all economic industries within the global environment. Next, business analytics provides organizations with the ability to establish prices that maximize profits, increase profitability, and strengthen their competitive advantage within their market sector. When data-driven predictability models are used, organizational leaders will become more empowered to make more informed decisions that directly influence consumer behavior, market conditions, product cost, and pricing strategies.

In the retail industry, price optimization is important in enabling a business to maintain profitability while attempting to gain new consumers within their existing or new markets. Next, retailers use business analytics to study pricing strategies of their competition, demand patterns of consumers, and past sales data. When analyzing these datasets, retailers can implement elasticity modeling to determine how the changes in a product or service will directly or indirectly influence the consumer's purchasing behavior. As an example, a retail store might determine that a small reduction in price on a single product can lead to a large increase in the volume of overall sales. This situation would lead the retail store to implement a new strategic pricing policy that adjusts prices during peak shopping hours or seasons to maximize its profits. Finally, retailers can implement dynamic pricing strategies based on data-driven analysis of the various datasets to adjust prices in real time based on the demand of the market and inventory levels.

In the hospitality and travel industry, business analytics are needed for price optimization. Hotels and airline companies will need to analyze past data, external marketing factors, and seasonal trends when creating a competitive pricing strategy. This situation will require the use of yield management and "what-if" scenarios that involve the adjustment and modification of prices based on current supply and demand, necessary for increasing the revenue associated with each room or seat. For instance, an airline will rely on predictive modeling to forecast the demand of travel during peak times in a year. This strategy would enable the airline company to increase prices during peak travel times based on the projected volume of passengers while also ensuring that the company will remain competitive with other airlines.

Within the automotive industry, business analytics will use price optimization techniques to study competitor pricing and consumer purchasing habits. Automotive dealerships and manufacturers analyze various features that include buyer preferences, vehicle features, and market trends to help create a pricing strategy that attracts new buyers while maintaining their current profit margin. When data is used effectively, regional preferences and consumer demographics can be better understood and applied to future decision-making and actions as they relate to targeted pricing strategies or the company.

For the telecommunications industry, price optimization is a critical component of business analytics. Subscriber patterns, competitive products and services, and consumer demographics and psychographics are important to understand when a company develops a pricing plan to strengthen its consumer retention rates and acquisition of new clients. As an example, consumer responsiveness must be identified to develop various service bundles and pricing levels. As a result, telecommunications companies can create effective pricing structures that improve consumer satisfaction and minimize consumer turnover rates.

Finally, the health-care industry implements business analytics to optimize the price of pharmaceuticals and medical services. After analytics have been conducted, health-care companies can use this data to study patient demographics, costs of treatment, and the impact of competitor products and services from other health-care providers. With the help of business analytics, health-care providers can set new price points that include the realities of the market along with the perceived and actual value associated with the product or service. The health-care provider can ensure that there is a consistent level of high-quality service while increasing its return on investment (ROI). As a result, we will create an effective pricing strategy for all sectors within the global environment that can improve consumer demand, improve revenue, and increase the level of competitive advantage.

## USING ANALYTICS TO ADJUST PRICING STRATEGIES EFFECTIVELY

As part of the global economy, the economics industry uses business analytics and statistical analysis to adjust pricing strategies effectively across different market segments within the business environment. When statistical modeling is used, organizations can analyze consumer behavior, competitors, and the diverse changing condition of the market in real time. This situation enables organizations within the economics industry to effectively adjust prices to maximize their revenue and return on investment while ensuring that their products and services remain desirable to the consumer market. The various economic industries that constantly adjust pricing strategies using business analytics include the retail sector, travel and hospitality, automotive, health care, and telecommunications.

The retail sector uses business analytics and statistical analysis to study past sales data and the elasticity of demand. One of the main methods used is regression analysis. Regression analysis enables retailers to understand the direct relationship between consumer purchasing behavior and changes in price. When the sensitivity of price is identified for different products, the retailer can then implement an effective pricing strategy that maximizes its sales revenue and volume within the market. As a result, the use of business analytics and statistical modeling provides retailers with the ability to forecast how the adjustments of price will influence sales so they can then develop an effective promotional pricing and markdown strategy in real time.

The travel and hospitality industry sector of the global market uses business analytics and statistical modeling to improve its pricing strategies through yield management. As an example, let's take the airline industry. We use statistical modeling to study booking patterns, competitor pricing, and seasonal demand of travel for the consumer market. When travel and hospitality companies use time series analysis, they can forecast the fluctuations in demand and adjust their ticket prices accordingly to match the changing needs of the market. As a result, business analytics enable the travel and hospitality industry to maximize revenue by travel seat time and locations and adjust their prices to the optimal level during peak travel throughout the year.

Within the automotive sector of the global market, business analytics also plays an important role in pricing strategies. Manufacturers must constantly analyze data as it relates to sales trends, conditions of the regional market, and consumer preferences. Statistical models that are used include conjoint analysis and cluster analysis. With these methods, automotive companies can identify consumer segments in their ability and willingness to pay for specific features. Next, the statistical tools and methods used by the automotive companies will provide useful and accurate forecasts that directly impact the pricing changes on sales volumes that will guide the overall pricing strategies of the organizations.

Next, the health-care industry uses business analytics and statistical modeling to improve its pricing strategies for all pharmaceutical products and medical services. The main use of business analytics is to study treatment costs, patient data, and the reimbursement rates of insurance. The situation requires health-care organizations to use analytics to determine the optimal pricing structure for all patient services. One of the main statistical methods used is cost volume profit analysis which directly impacts operational efficiency and patient access to health care. As a result, using a data-driven method will allow health-care providers to set prices that are aligned with the current market conditions while also ensuring that they cover all associated costs and maintain a high level of profitability.

Finally, the telecommunications industry uses pricing strategies as part of its business analytics method to make informed decisions about market share, turnover rates, and consumer usage patterns. This strategy enables telecommunications companies to understand the regression of logistics and survival within this sector of the global market. When the analytics of this sector are understood, telecommunications companies can then create customized and targeted pricing plans that maximize new acquisition of customers in the retention of existing consumers. As a result, telecommunications companies can analyze how different pricing levels can influence consumer turnover rate and therefore adjust pricing and product offerings accordingly to maintain a competitive advantage within the market. When business analytics is used correctly, organizations in all sectors of the global market maximize pricing based on market conditions, competitive dynamics, and consumer behavior to improve the growth of revenue and increase its competitive advantage.

## Measuring Economic Performance With Analytics

Business analytics plays an important part in determining economic performance across various sectors of the global market by providing data-driven decisions and methodologies that improve the understanding of operational efficiencies, market dynamics, and other economic indicators. When business analytics is used, organizations in all sectors can determine performance levels and how they relate to industrial benchmarks to make better-informed decisions, ensure sustainability, and maximize the potential for growth.

Within the manufacturing sector, business analytics will be used to evaluate economic performance using key metrics that include production costs, productivity, and efficiency of supply chain management. Charts and dashboards will be used to consolidate data that study the efficiency of labor, product output rates, and equipment usage. Next, statistical modeling will require process mining and root cause analysis to determine if the organization can properly identify inefficiencies in the production process and to implement corrective actions to reduce risk and cost. As a result of this process, business analytics will improve operational performance while also enabling manufacturing companies to increase profitability and reduce operational expenses.

Third, the retail industry will use business analytics in measuring economic performance through the analysis of consumer behavior, inventory turnover, and sales data to better understand their operational effectiveness and position within the market. With business analytics, retailers will be able to forecast trends in consumer demand and sales. The situation will enable retailers to optimize stock and inventory levels to improve consumer satisfaction rates. As a result of this process, the data-driven approach enables retailers to make logically informed pricing decisions that will lead to successful marketing campaigns that increase the overall revenue of the organization.

The health-care industry uses business analytics to measure its economic performance based on its operational efficiency, financial sustainability, and patient care. The metrics in the health-care industry include treatment costs, readmission rates, and patient satisfaction scores. When statistical modeling is used, to report the performance of business analytics, health-care companies can monitor key indicators of economic performance that are directly related to reimbursement of goods and services along with service delivery. As a result, business analytics supports effective resource allocation and strategic planning that contribute to an improvement in patient care while maintaining an affordable cost structure.

Finally, the telecommunications industry relies on business analytics to determine its economic performance, which includes consumer turnover rates, growth of subscribers, and average revenue per user (ARPU). Various datasets are used by telecommunications companies, which include market trends and consumer usage patterns, to understand its position within the market. When using statistical modeling, a telecommunications company can accurately identify all factors that impact the retention of subscribers and allow them to adjust the pricing and service offerings to increase revenue and profitability.

## KPIs AND METRICS THAT MATTER

Business analytics and statistical modeling play a critical role in developing key performance indicators (KPIs) and metrics that provide for organizations in various sectors of the global markets to understand and measure their level of performance effectively so they can achieve their long-term strategic goals. When statistics are used, organizational leaders can make data-driven decisions and identify the most important KPIs that are directly aligned with their short-term objectives and long-term goals. As a result, business analytics and statistical modeling will primarily focus on key metrics that provide data-driven decisions and actions that lead to the improvement of performance.

For retailers, business analytics will identify KPIs that include consumer acquisition costs, inventory turnover rates, and sales growth. Next, retailers will study consumer feedback, market trends, and historical sales data to determine which metrics are required to best reflect their level of performance in the market. When business analytics tools are used, retailers can calculate the customer lifetime value (CLV) and judge the long-term profitability impact of their loyal consumer base. As a result, business analytics and KPIs will be used to support targeted marketing strategies and management of inventory to improve the overall performance of the organization.

In the financial services sector, companies rely on business analytics and KPIs to determine their financial and operational well-being. Financial companies will analyze data that is related to return on equity (ROE), cost-to-income ratios, and profit margins. When statistical modeling is applied, financial companies can accurately identify outliers and trends in their key performance metrics. One method is for financial companies to conduct stress testing. Stress testing analysis helps a financial institution assess their level of risk and exposure under different and changing conditions of the market. As a result, the findings of the stress test analysis will enable organizational leaders to make data-driven decisions about the allocation of capital and developing new policies and practices for its risk management strategies.

Third, the manufacturing industry relies on business analytics and KPIs to focus on quality control, productivity of the workforce, and efficiency of production. Key metrics include defect rates, overall equipment effectiveness (OEE), and production yield to understand the operational performance level of the company. When datasets are used to study the supply chain and production floor, manufacturers can quickly identify slowdowns and bottlenecks within the manufacturing process to determine areas for immediate improvement to reduce work stoppage and to maximize its usage of resources.

In the health-care sector, business analytics and KPIs are used to determine the outcome of patients and operational efficiency. Key performance metrics include treatment cost per patient, patient readmission rates, and patient satisfaction levels. With these metrics, the health-care organization can better understand its quality of care and usage of resources to support its strategic initiatives. When data analytics are used, health-care companies can identify patterns and trends and areas that need improvement. As an example, a hospital can use business analytics to track infection rates within a local area so it can improve its infection control protocols, which will ultimately improve the safety of the patient while reducing the overall costs to the institution.

Finally, telecommunications companies use business analytics and KPIs to study operational efficiency and consumer satisfaction rates. Key performance metrics include turnover rates, the performance of the network, and the average revenue per user (ARPU). The combination of these metrics is used as a guide and indicator for assessing the overall performance of the organization. When usage patterns in consumer data are analyzed, business analytics support telecommunications companies in the ability to address potential concerns and risks and to optimize their product and service offerings to maximize the retention rate of their consumers.

As a result, the use of business analytics and the monitoring of KPIs enable all market sectors to determine performance levels and make data-driven decisions and lead to a continuous improvement process that is responsive to the changing conditions of the market environment.

## Impact of Global Economic Factors on Business Decisions

Business analytics is used to understand the impact of global economic factors on business decisions across all sectors within the global environment. When data analytics are implemented, companies can understand the complexities of the global market environment, by assessing the potential for risk and optimizing their strategies accordingly. New information and trends gained from the use of business analytics and statistical modeling allow organizations to adapt in real time to the changing economic conditions of the market.

In the financial sector, business analytics is necessary for organizations to understand the impact of global economic factors on all decisions within various industries. Next, business analytics helps financial organizations understand macroeconomic indicators, which include inflation, changes in currency prices, and interest rates. When business analytics and statistical modeling are applied, financial companies can evaluate and determine the potential impact of these factors on lending practices, investment portfolios, and risk management strategies. When there is a downturn or when the economy is uncertain, financial institutions can use business analytics to conduct stress test to analyze their financial models to ensure that they can survive the negative conditions of the market. As a result, business analytics enables financial institutions to become proactive in their decision-making and allocation of capital to reduce risk based on the ability to make data-driven choices.

The manufacturing industry uses business analytics to determine the impact of global economic factors affecting its reduction planning and supply chain management. The datasets that are analyzed by manufacturing firms include labor costs, the prices of raw materials, and the development of geopolitics within a specific location. It is important to understand each of these areas so the manufacturing company can then defy any possible potential disruption in their supply chain management system. Using business analytics to determine the impact of global economic factors will help manufacturers forecast changes in demand that can arise from the changes in the global economic market. This situation allows manufacturers to adjust their production schedules and optimize their levels of inventory based on the changing need of the consumer market. As a result of this data-driven approach, manufacturers can minimize their level of risk, eliminate the chance of overproduction or stockouts, and become more operationally sustainable within a diverse and constantly changing environment.

In retail, companies will use business analytics to understand global economic trends that influence the behavior of consumers. It is important for retail organizations to monitor international economic indicators, which include exchange rates, consumer confidence levels, and economic growth rates, within their market segments so they can adjust their pricing and marketing strategies. When business analytics determines a decline in consumer confidence levels within a region, the retail organization can change its level of inventory and streamline its marketing campaign efforts to reduce its financial losses. Finally, retail organizations can use business analytics to improve their analysis of the market by better understanding purchasing patterns that develop during changing conditions within the economy.

In health care, providers will use business analytics to determine how global economic conditions impact health-care spending and patient demand for products and services. Key economic factors include health-care reforms, unemployment rates, and income levels. Each of these factors will directly impact the behavior and choices of patients. When health-care data is analyzed, demographic information on patients can be developed, which enables the health-care provider to adapt and change product and service offerings, along with the redistribution of resources, to effectively meet the changing needs of the market.

Finally, the telecommunications industry uses business analytics to understand how global economic factors directly influence the competitive dynamics and the demand for service by consumers. Telecommunications companies must analyze consumer usage patterns and the conditions of the macroeconomic environment so they can maximize their pricing strategies and invest their resources to support an infrastructure that enhances their ability to deliver services. As a result, business analytics will reveal new opportunities for growth and current and emerging markets where demand may increase due to the economic development of the location. The new capabilities that come from using business analytics will enable organizational leaders to make informed decisions that ensure sustainability and long-term growth in a dynamic and changing global business environment.

## ANALYTICS IN NAVIGATING GLOBAL ECONOMIC CHANGES

The economics industry within the global business environment uses business analytics to provide data-driven decisions that enable companies across all sectors to make better-informed choices and to adapt their production to the changing conditions of the market. When large amounts of data are analyzed, organizations will have the ability to better understand the implications of the trends in the economy, to anticipate new challenges, and to take advantage of new opportunities that at once did not exist to increase their competitive advantage.

First, the finance industry uses business analytics to understand and respond to fluctuations in the global economy. It is important for all financial institutions to analyze the risks associated with currency exchange rates, interest rates, and other economic indicators. Banks and other investment firms will use business analytics to determine how global events, which include changes in monetary policy or geopolitical differences between countries, impact their investment portfolios. When conducting stress test or scenario analysis, financial companies can evaluate the potential outcomes of their choices and can adjust their investment strategies to meet the new needs of the market despite the threat of volatility and uncertainty.

For manufacturers, business analytics will be used to understand global economic changes, which include production planning and supply chain optimization. Global economic changes in the economy include the fluctuation of the prices of raw materials and the changes in consumer demand. Each of these economic changes directly impacts the operation of a manufacturing firm. When data is analyzed using various datasets, manufacturing firms can forecast the trends in demand and identify potential disruption to its supply chain management system. When there is a shortage of raw materials due to natural disasters or geopolitical events, the use of business analytics enables companies to re-evaluate their sourcing strategies and inventory management. As a result, manufacturing firms can become proactive in their approach to mitigate risks and to support the continuity of their daily business operations within a volatile or uncertain global environment.

Next, the retail sector of the global market uses business analytics to respond to global economic changes by understanding and tracking consumer spending patterns, international trends, and other economic indicators so these companies can change their marketing and pricing strategies. As an example, business analytics may indicate a slowdown or reduction in consumer spending in specific regions or locations. When this situation occurs, a retail company can adjust their product offerings and develop new targeted marketing promotions to maximize sales using sentiment analysis. This situation enables retailers to understand and evaluate the perceptions and behaviors of consumers. As a result, retail companies can adjust their strategies to better align with the evolving and changing dynamics of the global market.

In health care, business analytics will study the implications of global economic changes on the allocation of resources and on patient care. Economic conditions within the sector include income levels and unemployment rates, which will influence access to health care and future demand for services. It is important for health-care organizations to analyze the demographics of their patients and to determine the trends in the usage of health care so each company can adjust its product and service offerings along with allocating resources effectively and efficiently. If there is a slowdown in the economy, business analytics will help health-care organizations identify communities or locations that need additional support services or preventative care. As a result, the use of analytics will enable health-care organizations to respond appropriately to the status situation of the economy.

Finally, the telecommunications sector of the global environment uses business analytics to determine how the dynamics of the market impact the demand for service and its level of competitive advantage within the market. Telecommunications companies must analyze data related to market trends, consumer behavior, and other economic indicators. When this data is analyzed, telecommunications companies can make informed and data-driven decisions about investments in infrastructure, the pricing of services, and marketing strategies. As a result, the use of business analytics enables telecommunications companies to be flexible and adaptable to the changing needs of consumers and economic climates across the world while ensuring sustainability and long-term growth.

## BUSINESS ANALYTICS FUNCTION FOR ECONOMICS USING MICROSOFT EXCEL

In the business environment, there are many business analytical terms mentioned that play a critical role in making informed and data-driven choices to drive decisions, optimizing daily operations, and developing strategic actions and initiatives. Various statistical concepts play an important role in economics and business analytics by providing essential tools for data analysis and decision-making. Here's a detailed overview of their definition and importance and how to conduct this statistical analysis using Microsoft Excel.

### Average Revenue Per User (ARPU)

This metric provides understanding of the revenue generated by each consumer and allows organizations to evaluate performance levels and set pricing strategies effectively and efficiently.

Formula: ARPU = Total Revenue/Number of Users

**Steps:**

1. Input total revenue in one cell (e.g., A1), and number of users in another (e.g., B1).
2. In a new cell (e.g., C1), type the formula =A1/B1 and press Enter.

### Averages

*Averages* are a fundamental statistical tool for summarizing data that enables companies to understand typical performance and make comparisons across different markets.

Formula: Average = SUM(range)/COUNT(range)

**Steps:**

1. List your values in a column (e.g., A1 to A10).
2. In an empty cell, use the formula =AVERAGE(A1:A10), and press Enter.

### Charts

Visual representations of data help identify trends, patterns, and outliers and make complex information clearer for stakeholders.

**Steps:**

1. Select the data range you want to visualize.
2. Go to the Insert tab and choose a chart type (e.g., column, line, pie, scatter).
3. Customize the chart as needed using the Chart Tools.

### Cluster Analysis

This technique groups similar data points that assist organizations in identifying consumer segments, optimizing marketing strategies, and personalizing product and service offerings.

**Steps:**

1. Prepare your data in columns (e.g., sales data, customer demographics).
2. Use Excel's Data Analysis ToolPak (enable it via File > Options).
3. Select Clustering option if available, or use Excel's k-means clustering through formulas and PivotTables.

## Conjoint Analysis

By evaluating consumer preferences, this method helps companies in understanding how different features impact purchasing decision and guide product development and pricing strategies.

**Steps:**

1. Prepare a survey with product features and preferences.
2. Input response data into Excel.
3. Use regression analysis: Go to Data > Data Analysis > Regression, and run your model.

## Cost Volume Profit Analysis

This analysis helps companies understand the interaction between costs, sales volume, and profits to enable improved budgeting, pricing decisions, and financial forecasting.

**Steps:**

1. Create a table with fixed costs, variable costs, and sales price per unit.
2. Set up formulas to calculate total costs (fixed + variable) and profit (total revenue − total costs).
3. Use a data table to analyze different volumes.

## Customer Lifetime Value (CLV)

CLV estimates the total revenue a consumer can generate over their lifetime while providing insights into long-term profitability and guiding investment in consumer acquisition strategies.

Formula: CLV = Average Purchase Value × Purchase Frequency × Customer Lifespan

**Steps:**

1. Calculate average purchase value and purchase frequency.
2. Multiply the three components in a new cell using the formula.

## Dashboards

These tools combine and present key performance indicators (KPIs) using a visual method and allow decision-makers to monitor business performance and respond quickly to changes.

**Steps:**

1. Organize key metrics and KPIs in a comprehensive table.
2. Use charts and tables linked to the data.
3. Use the Insert Slicer option under PivotTables for interactivity.

## Data Validation

Guaranteeing data accuracy and consistency is essential for reliable analysis and leads to more informed decision-making and mitigating risks associated with imperfect data.

**Steps:**

1. Select the range for which you want to apply validation.
2. Go to Data > Data Validation.
3. Set criteria (e.g., list, whole number).

## Demand Forecasting

By predicting future consumer demand, organizations can maximize inventory management, production planning, and resource allocation to enhance overall operational efficiency.

**Steps:**

1. Organize past sales data in columns.
2. Use Forecast Sheet (found under the Data tab) to create future demand predictions.

## Filtering Data

This process allows business analysts to focus on relevant information by improving the clarity and relevance of insights derived from large datasets.

**Steps:**

1. Select your data range.
2. Go to Data > Filter.
3. Use the dropdowns in the header cells to filter data based on your criteria.

## Logical Functions

Using logical functions in data analysis helps companies make complex decisions based on specific conditions and improve analytical capabilities.

**Steps:**

1. Use the formula =IF(condition, value_if_true, value_if_false) in a new cell to return results based on specific conditions.

## Lookup Functions

These functions simplify data retrieval from large datasets and provide efficient access to essential information for decision-making and analysis.

**Steps:**

2. Use the formula =VLOOKUP(lookup_value, table_array, col_index_num, [range_lookup]) in a cell to find data from a specified table.

### Overall Equipment Effectiveness (OEE)

OEE measures manufacturing productivity by assessing availability, performance, and quality. This analysis helps identify inefficiencies and areas for improvement in production processes.

Formula: OEE = Availability × Performance × Quality

**Steps:**

1. Input your availability, performance, and quality metrics in cells.
2. Multiply them in a new cell using =A1*B1*C1.

### Pareto Analysis

This technique is based on the 80/20 rule, which helps companies prioritize issues by identifying the most significant factors contributing to problems and allows for effective resource allocation.

**Steps:**

1. Organize your data in descending order (e.g., causes of problems).
2. Create a cumulative percentage column.
3. Use a bar chart and overlay a line chart for cumulative percentages.

### PivotTables

PivotTables allow users to summarize and analyze large datasets flexibly and make them instrumental in data exploration and reporting.

**Steps:**

1. Select your data range.
2. Go to Insert > PivotTable.
3. Drag and drop fields into Rows, Columns, and Values areas to summarize data.

### Return on Equity (ROE)

ROE measures a company's profitability relative to its equity and provides knowledge into financial efficiency and effectiveness related to shareholder funds.

Formula: ROE = Net Income/Shareholder's Equity

**Steps:**

1. Input net income and shareholder's equity in cells.
2. In a new cell, use formula =A1/B1 to calculate ROE.

### Return on Investment (ROI)

ROI assesses the profitability of investments and assists in resource allocation and strategic planning by evaluating the financial benefits of each initiative.

Formula: ROI = (Net Profit/Cost of Investment) × 100

**Steps:**

1. Input net profit and cost of investment in cells.
2. Use the formula =(A1/B1)*100 in a new cell to calculate ROI.

### Simulation Modeling

This method models complex systems to predict outcomes under various scenarios and assists organizations in risk assessment and strategic planning.

**Steps:**

1. Set up your model with inputs in cells.
2. Use Excel's Data Table feature (under What-If Analysis) to simulate various scenarios.

### Sorting Data

Efficiently organizing data supports clearer analysis and interpretation and provides quicker response times to challenges and opportunities for the company.

**Steps:**

1. Select the data range you want to sort.
2. Go to Data > Sort and choose the sorting criteria (i.e., ascending or descending).

### Time Series Events

Analyzing data over time enables organizations to identify trends, seasonal patterns, and cyclical behaviors to make more informative, accurate forecasts and strategic plans.

**Steps:**

1. Organize your time series data in a column (dates in one column, values in another).
2. Create a line chart by selecting the data range and going to Insert Chart.

## REAL-WORLD EXAMPLES OF ECONOMIC INSIGHTS DRIVING BUSINESS SUCCESS

In today's global business environment, companies are increasingly relying on economic knowledge and analytics to improve their business strategies and drive success. By successfully using data analytics and understanding the dynamics of the market, organizations can make more informed decisions that improve their operational efficiency, improve customer satisfaction, and ultimately increase profitability of the stakeholder, as demonstrated with the following examples.

### Ford Motor Company

Ford Motor Company has been increasingly dependent on economic data to lead its strategic decisions in the automotive industry. The company uses extensive data analytics to assess market trends, consumer preferences, and economic indicators that impact vehicle sales. By analyzing data such as fuel prices, consumer income levels, and demographic shifts, Ford can develop targeted marketing campaigns and adjust its product offerings to directly align with market demand. For example, as consumer preferences have shifted towards electric and hybrid vehicles, Ford has used economic insights to inform its investments in electric vehicle technology. By understanding the growing demand for sustainable transportation options, Ford has positioned itself to compete effectively in this constantly changing market segment. This strategic change has improved Ford's product lineup but also aligns the company with broader economic trends focused on sustainability and environmental responsibility. Finally, Ford's use of data analytics extends to its production processes. The company analyzes data related to supply chain logistics, manufacturing efficiency, and cost structures to optimize production schedules and reduce waste. By employing just-in-time manufacturing techniques informed by real-time market data, Ford can respond quickly to changes in consumer demand to ensure that its production aligns closely with sales trends. As a result, this efficiency not only reduces costs but also increases the company's agility in a competitive automotive market.

#### Question 1

How has Ford Motor Company leveraged economic data to make informed decisions regarding electric and hybrid vehicle development?

Answer: The Ford Motor Company has effectively used economic data to make strategic decisions regarding the development of electric and hybrid vehicles, aligning its product offerings with shifting consumer preferences and broader market trends. By analyzing various economic indicators, such as fuel prices, environmental regulations, and consumer income levels, Ford has gained important knowledge into the growing demand for sustainable transportation options. As public awareness of environmental issues has increased and fuel prices have fluctuated, consumer interest in electric and hybrid vehicles has grown. Ford recognized this trend early on and used economic data to inform its investments in electric vehicle (EV) technology and infrastructure. This strategic focus allowed Ford to compete in the rapidly evolving automotive market, also demonstrating the company's commitment to sustainability and environmental responsibility. Finally, Ford's investment in electric vehicles is supported by data-driven marketing strategies that highlight the benefits of EVs, which include lower operating costs and reduced emissions. By associating its EV offerings with positive economic and environmental impacts, Ford is positioned to gain a significant share of the sustainable vehicle market. As a result, the integration of economic data into Ford's product development strategy improves its competitiveness and responsiveness to emerging trends.

**Question 2**

Discuss the significance of data analytics in Ford's production processes and how it contributes to operational efficiency.

Answer: Data analytics plays a critical role in the Ford Motor Company's production processes and greatly contributes to operational efficiency and cost-effectiveness. By analyzing data related to supply chain logistics, manufacturing efficiency, and cost structures, Ford can maximize its production schedules and minimize waste. This analytical strategy enables the company to gain knowledge of various aspects of its manufacturing processes, from raw material procurement to delivery timelines. One significant application of data analytics at Ford is its implementation of just-in-time (JIT) manufacturing techniques. By using real-time market data and historical performance metrics, Ford can coordinate its inventory management more efficiently and effectively. This strategy minimizes excess inventory and reduces carrying costs and allows the company to respond immediately to changes in consumer demand.

Finally, data analytics enables Ford to identify bottlenecks, slowdowns, or inefficiencies within the manufacturing process. By continuously monitoring production metrics, the company can detect issues in real time and implement corrective measures quickly and accurately. This strategy enhances the workflow more efficiently but also reduces the downtime and optimizes labor utilization. As a result, Ford's use of data analytics in its production processes supports improved operational performance and strengthens the company's competitive advantage within the automotive industry.

**Question 3**

How does Ford's understanding of economic indicators shape its targeted marketing campaigns, and what are the implications for consumer engagement?

Answer: Ford's understanding of economic indicators significantly models its targeted marketing campaigns and allows the company to improve its consumer engagement and drive sales effectively and efficiently. By closely monitoring economic data, such as consumer income levels, spending habits, and demographic shifts, Ford can customize its marketing strategies to connect with specific market segments and address consumer needs. For example, during periods of economic growth with increasing consumer confidence, Ford may emphasize its premium truck and SUV models and highlight features such as advanced technology, luxury finishes, and performance capabilities. However, in declining economic conditions, marketing strategies can change towards more budget-friendly vehicles that focus on fuel efficiency and affordability to attract cost-conscious consumers. Finally, Ford employs data analytics to segment its consumer base more effectively. By understanding regional preferences and economic factors, the company can create targeted promotions and advertisements that appeal to specific demographics. For example, marketing campaigns focused on younger and environmentally conscious consumers may highlight Ford's electric vehicle offerings since they are centered on the benefits of sustainability and lower operational costs.

## JPMorgan Chase

In the financial services sector, JPMorgan Chase is a prime example of how economic data can lead to business success. The bank uses a combination of data analytics and economic modeling to understand market conditions, mitigate risk, and inform investment strategies. By analyzing a wide range of economic indicators that include interest rates, employment data, and GDP growth, JPMorgan can make informed decisions about lending practices, investment opportunities, and asset management. One specific use of this approach is in the bank's risk assessment processes. By implementing predictive modeling techniques, JPMorgan can determine the chance of loan defaults under various economic scenarios. This situation allows the bank to adjust its lending criteria and develop strategies for mitigating potential risks. Next, by understanding macroeconomic trends, JPMorgan can offer customized financial products that meet the evolving needs of its clients and further enhance its market position.

### Question 1

How does JPMorgan Chase utilize economic data and modeling to enhance its risk assessment processes?

Answer: JPMorgan Chase uses economic data and modeling to improve its risk assessment process by implementing predictive modeling techniques to evaluate the likelihood of loan defaults across various economic situations. By analyzing a wide range of economic indicators, such as interest rates, employment levels, and GDP growth, the bank can gain insights into potential risk factors that might impact borrowers' ability to repay the loans.

Next, JPMorgan's complex risk assessment strategy involves continuously monitoring economic conditions and trends that allow the bank to adjust its lending criteria in real time. For example, if data suggests an impending economic downturn depicted by rising unemployment rates, the bank may tighten its credit standards to mitigate the risk of defaults. However, when economic indicators signal growth, JPMorgan may relax its lending criteria to capitalize on increased consumer and business borrowing. Finally, predictive analytics empowers JPMorgan to segment its loan portfolio effectively, identifying at-risk borrowers and customizing its risk mitigation strategies accordingly. This proactive approach allows the bank to minimize potential losses while ensuring that its lending practices remain aligned with the prevailing economic market. By integrating economic data into its risk assessment processes, JPMorgan improves its decision-making capabilities and strengthens its financial position.

### Question 2

Discuss how an understanding of macroeconomic trends informs JPMorgan Chase's investment strategies and product offerings.

Answer: An understanding of macroeconomic trends plays a critical factor in informing JPMorgan Chase's investment strategies and product offerings. By closely monitoring economic indicators, such as inflation rates, interest rates, and overall economic growth,

JPMorgan can make more informed, data-driven decisions about where to allocate resources and how to structure its investment products to meet client demands. For example, during periods of low interest rates and economic expansion, JPMorgan may focus on promoting equity investments and growth-oriented funds, capitalizing on improved consumer spending and corporate profitability. However, if macroeconomic data indicates rising inflation or economic uncertainty, the bank may shift its strategy to emphasize more defensive investments, such as bonds or commodities, which can act as protection against inflation risks. Finally, by analyzing consumer behavior and economic indicators, JPMorgan can customize its financial products to better align with the evolving needs of its clients. For example, in response to increasing demand for sustainable investment options, JPMorgan can design products that focus on environmental, social, and governance (ESG) criteria. As a result, this alignment between macroeconomic insights and product development not only enhances the bank's market relevance but also allows it to maintain a competitive edge by meeting the diverse needs of its clients.

**Question 3**

How does JPMorgan Chase leverage economic data to develop customized financial products for its clients?

Answer: JPMorgan Chase leverages economic data to develop customized financial products that align with the specific needs and preferences of its diverse clientele. By utilizing comprehensive market research and analytics, the bank can gain knowledge into various economic trends and consumer behaviors, enabling it to identify gaps in the market that its products can fill.

For instance, by analyzing demographic data and economic indicators, JPMorgan can recognize emerging market segments, such as young professionals seeking investment opportunities or retirees looking for income-generating products. This situation enables the bank to design customized financial products that serve the specific requirements of these groups, enhancing client satisfaction and strengthening long-term relationships. Next, JPMorgan utilizes predictive analytics to assess client preferences and tailor services accordingly. For example, if data indicates a growing interest in digital banking solutions, the bank might accelerate the development of user-friendly mobile apps or customized investment platforms that provide clients with personalized investment advice based on their financial goals. Finally, the integration of economic data helps JPMorgan anticipate changes in consumer needs due to changing market conditions.

## Procter & Gamble

Procter & Gamble (P&G) is a global leader in consumer goods and demonstrates how economic knowledge and data can improve market strategies and product offerings. The company employs extensive market research and data analytics to understand consumer needs and preferences across various demographics. By analyzing trends and economic indicators, P&G can identify opportunities to innovate its product lines or introduce new brands suited to the needs of specific market segments. For example, P&G's use of predictive analytics enables the company to forecast consumer demand for different products based on macroeconomic factors, including income levels and consumer confidence indexes. This capability enables P&G to perfect its marketing strategies, focusing on products that are likely to resonate with consumers during specific economic conditions. By aligning its product development and marketing efforts with economic insights, P&G has maintained its competitive position in the consumer goods industry.

**Question 1**

How does Procter & Gamble utilize market research and data analytics to better understand consumer preferences and enhance product development?

Answer: Procter & Gamble (P&G) leverages extensive market research and data analytics to gain insights into consumer preferences that guide its product development processes. The company employs a combination of surveys, focus groups, and consumer feedback to collect qualitative and quantitative data on consumer needs across various diverse demographics. By analyzing this data, P&G can identify new patterns and trends that support the innovation of new products and enhancement of existing ones. Next, P&G uses advanced analytics to segment its customer base more effectively. This segmentation strategy enables the company to customize its marketing campaigns and product offerings to meet the specific preferences of different target groups. For example, P&G may analyze geographic trends to understand regional preferences for certain personal care products or household items. Through this systematic approach to data collection and analysis, P&G can align its product offerings with consumer expectations but also reduces the risks associated with new product launches. Finally, by using data gathered from data analytics, P&G continually improves its product development strategies and maintains its majority share position as a leader in the consumer goods industry.

**Question 2**

Discuss how P&G's use of predictive analytics enhances its marketing strategies and helps the company respond to changing market conditions.

Answer: Procter & Gamble's integration of predictive analytics into its marketing strategies has enabled the company to strengthen its responsiveness to changing market conditions and consumer demands. By analyzing macroeconomic factors such as income levels, consumer confidence indexes, and purchasing behaviors, P&G can forecast demand for various products more accurately to better meet the needs of their consumers. Next, this predictive capability enables P&G to anticipate changes in consumer preferences and adjust its marketing strategies accordingly. For example, during periods of economic downturn, when consumer spending decreases, P&G can focus on promoting value-oriented products that connect with cost-conscious consumers. However, in a growing economic environment, the company might change its focus to offer premium products that cater to consumers willing to spend more for quality and innovation. Finally, by utilizing predictive analytics to optimize marketing expenditures and campaign timing, P&G can dedicate resources more effectively to ensure that budgetary investments are maximized. The result of this strategic alignment with economic indicators is an improved ability to connect with consumers on appropriate messaging while improving overall marketing ROI. As a result of this data-driven approach, P&G successfully navigates market fluctuations and fortifies its competitive edge within the consumer goods sector.

**Question 3**

What are the strategic advantages of aligning product development and marketing efforts with economic insights for P&G in the consumer goods industry?

Answer: Aligning product development and marketing efforts with economic data provides Procter & Gamble (P&G) with various strategic advantages that strengthen its position in the consumer goods industry. One main advantage is improved consumer relevance. By understanding the economic factors that drive consumer behavior, P&G can develop products that meet the changing needs and preferences of its target audiences. This alignment ensures that new and existing products resonate with consumers, reducing the chance of unsuccessful product launches. Finally, this strategic alignment allows P&G to identify and gain new market opportunities. By closely monitoring economic trends, the company can innovate its product lines and introduce new brands that cater to specific demographic needs. Aligning its marketing efforts with economic data equips P&G to optimize its promotional strategies effectively. By timing campaigns and focusing messaging on particular economic conditions that include emphasizing affordability during tough economic times, P&G improves its marketing effectiveness and level of consumer engagement.

## Walmart

Walmart is the world's largest retailer. The company uses economic data and knowledge to improve its supply chain and pricing strategies. Next, the company uses a combination of data analytics and econometric modeling to analyze market trends, consumer preferences, and competitor pricing. This data-driven approach enables Walmart to implement new dynamic pricing strategies that adjust to changes in consumer demand and competitive pressures. For example, during peak shopping seasons or local events, Walmart can quickly adjust prices in real time to stay competitive and attract cost-conscious consumers. This strategy not only maximizes sales but also helps in maintaining market share among online retailers within the market. Finally, Walmart's extensive supply chain analytics help the company identify inefficiencies and cost-saving opportunities to improve overall operational efficiency and effectiveness. Finally, by focusing on economic data, Walmart continues to thrive in a highly competitive retail landscape.

**Question 1**

How does Walmart utilize data analytics to refine its pricing strategies and improve its competitive positioning in the retail market?

Answer: Walmart employs a complicated blend of data analytics and econometric modeling to refine its pricing strategies and improve its competitive positioning in the retail market. By using data gathered from various sources, which include sales transactions, consumer behavior, and competitor pricing, Walmart can develop a better understanding of current and future market conditions. One main aspect of Walmart's pricing strategy is dynamic pricing, which allows the company to alter product prices in real time in response to changes in supply and demand. As an example, during peak shopping seasons or local events, Walmart analyzes real-time data to adjust prices on popular items to ensure they remain attractive to price-sensitive consumers. This responsive strategy maximizes sales during crucial buying periods while also strengthening consumer loyalty by reinforcing Walmart's image as a low-cost leader.

**Question 2**

Discuss the role of supply chain analytics in Walmart's operational efficiency and how it contributes to cost savings.

Answer: Supply chain analytics plays an important role in improving Walmart's operational efficiency and identifying cost-saving opportunities. By using advanced data analytics across its supply chain, Walmart can monitor and analyze various components that include inventory levels, transportation logistics, and supplier performance. This comprehensive strategy enables the company to pinpoint inefficiencies that affect overall productivity. One of the main benefits of Walmart's use of supply chain analytics is the optimization of inventory management. By analyzing sales trends and seasonal demand patterns, Walmart can ensure that stock levels are aligned with consumer needs while reducing the risks associated with overstocking or stockouts. Next, Walmart leverages supply chain analytics to streamline logistics operations. By analyzing data related to transportation routes and delivery schedules, Walmart can optimize its distribution network to guarantee that products reach stores in a timely manner while minimizing transportation costs. As a result, these efficiencies culminate in reduced operational costs, which allows for a greater return on investment (ROI) and operational efficiency.

**Question 3**

Evaluate the impact of Walmart's economic data focus on its competitive advantage in the retail industry.

Answer: Walmart's emphasis on economic data has significantly impacted its competitive advantage in the retail industry by informing strategic decisions and enhancing overall business performance. The company's extensive use of data analytics supports pricing and supply chain optimization while also improving its understanding of consumer preferences and market dynamics. By analyzing economic indicators and consumer trends, Walmart can customize its product offerings and marketing strategies to better meet the needs of its customer base. For example, Walmart's ability to identify shifting consumer preferences allows it to stock relevant products and execute effective promotional strategies. This proactive approach in catering to consumer demand helps Walmart maintain its reputation as a retail leader and reinforces consumer loyalty and encourages repeat visits. Finally, Walmart's investment in technology and data-driven initiatives positions the company strongly against growing online competition. By understanding market trends and consumer behavior through data, Walmart can integrate both its physical stores and e-commerce platforms to create a seamless shopping experience. This omni-channel approach attracts a broader customer base while supporting Walmart's commitment to innovation in the retail sector.

## CASE STUDIES ON ECONOMIC SUCCESS THROUGH ANALYTICS

### Business Success Through Business Analytics

Business analytics plays a crucial role in understanding economic trends and consumer behavior that enables organizations in the economics industry to make more data-driven and informed decisions. Following are three examples of how economic data and knowledge are translated into business success using analytics.

### Example 1: Retail Sector Forecasting

A major retail chain implemented advanced predictive analytics to anticipate consumer demand and optimize inventory levels. By analyzing historical sales data, socioeconomic trends, and seasonality, the retailer could predict which products would be in demand and when. This approach reduced instances of overstock and stockouts, significantly cutting down operational costs and improving customer satisfaction. The retailer used regression models to examine various economic indicators that included employment rates and disposable income levels, which influenced shopping habits. By integrating this new knowledge into their supply chain management, they achieved a 15% reduction in logistics costs and a 25% increase in effective inventory turnover.

### Short-Response Questions:

1. What method did the retail chain use to predict consumer demand?
   Answer: The retail chain used advanced predictive analytics and regression models to forecast consumer demand.
2. What were the economic indicators analyzed by the retailer?
   Answer: The retailer analyzed employment rates and disposable income levels as part of their predictive analytics strategy.
3. What were the outcomes in terms of logistics costs and inventory turnover?
   Answer: The retailer achieved a 15% reduction in logistics costs and a 25% increase in effective inventory turnover.

### Example 2: Financial Services Risk Management

A large financial services firm turned to business analytics to improve its risk management framework. By using machine learning algorithms to analyze credit scores, transaction histories, and external economic data, the firm could more accurately assess the creditworthiness of loan applicants. The firm reduced default rates significantly while expanding its client base. Finally, the knowledge gained enabled the firm to identify emerging market trends, such as shifts in consumer borrowing patterns linked to changing interest rates. By promptly adjusting their lending policies based on these insights, the firm increased its loan approvals by 30% while maintaining a low-risk profile.

### Short-Response Questions:

1. How did the financial services firm assess the creditworthiness of loan applicants?
   Answer: The firm used machine learning algorithms to analyze credit scores, transaction histories, and external economic data.
2. What specific changes did the firm make to its lending policies?
   Answer: The firm adjusted its lending policies based on knowledge from emerging market trends related to consumer borrowing patterns and interest rate changes.
3. What was the increase in loan approvals while maintaining a low-risk profile?
   Answer: The firm increased its loan approvals by 30% while maintaining a low-risk profile.

### Example 3: Manufacturing Efficiency Optimization

A global manufacturing company used business analytics to streamline its production processes. By analyzing production line data, equipment performance metrics, and labor costs, the company identified underperforming machines and inefficiencies in labor allocation. Through this analysis, they implemented predictive maintenance schedules to reduce machine downtime and reorganized labor to maximize productivity. The new information and knowledge from the data led to a 20% increase in overall production efficiency and a 10% reduction in operational costs. Finally, the company used economic indicators like global supply chain stability to make strategic decisions about sourcing materials, which optimized both quality and cost.

### Short Response Questions:

1. What data did the manufacturing company analyze to optimize its production processes?
   Answer: The company analyzed production line data, equipment performance metrics, and labor costs.
2. What were the results of implementing predictive maintenance schedules?
   Answer: Predictive maintenance schedules resulted in a 20% increase in overall production efficiency and a 10% reduction in operational costs.
3. How did economic indicators influence the company's material sourcing decisions?
   Answer: Economic indicators like global supply chain stability guided the company in making strategic decisions about sourcing materials, optimizing both quality and cost.

---

## CASE STUDY: ASTUTE ECONOMICS INC.

Astute Economics Inc. is a consulting firm that specializes in providing economic analysis and forecasting to businesses across various market sectors that include retail, manufacturing, and financial services. Established a decade ago, the company has grown rapidly due to its use of a data-driven approach that implements cutting-edge business analytics to empower clients with actionable information and knowledge. The company's primary services include market research, economic forecasting, and specialty consultation focused on helping businesses manage economic complexities effectively and efficiently.

As competition increased and market dynamics became more challenging, Astute Economics Inc. recognized the need to further improve its forecasting capabilities to provide clients with real-time insights. This initiative led the company to invest in advanced analytics tools that enable deeper analysis of economic trends, consumer behavior, and financial performance. The goal was to improve internal decision-making processes while also improving service offerings to clients. This situation would ensure that they could remain ahead of their competitors within their respective markets.

Last year, Astute Economics Inc. experienced a decline in client engagement and satisfaction that was attributed to inaccurate economic forecasts and a lack of integration of useful data analytics in their models. The leadership team decided to conduct a comprehensive review of their forecasting methods by focusing on improving both their quantitative and qualitative data sources. Finally, by analyzing internal sales performance data alongside broader economic indicators, the company attempted to enhance the accuracy and reliability of its economic predictions.

## Data Tables for Business Analytics Calculations

**TABLE 2.1** Historical Sales Data

| 1 | A | B | C | D | E | F |
|---|---|---|---|---|---|---|
| | Year | Q1 Sales | Q2 Sales | Q3 Sales | Q4 Sales | Total Sales |
| 2 | 2020 | $150,000 | $170,000 | $180,000 | $660,000 | |
| 3 | 2021 | $160,000 | $180,000 | $190,000 | $700,000 | |
| 4 | 2022 | $170,000 | $190,000 | $200,000 | $740,000 | |
| 5 | 2023 | $180,000 | $210,000 | | | |

**TABLE 2.2** Economic Indicators

| 1 | A | B | C | D |
|---|---|---|---|---|
| | Year | Unemployment Rate (%) | GDP Growth Rate (%) | Consumer Confidence Index |
| 2 | 2020 | 10.50 | –3.40 | 75.00 |
| 3 | 2021 | 8.00 | 5.70 | 85.00 |
| 4 | 2022 | 6.00 | 4.00 | 95.00 |
| 5 | 2023 | 5.00 | | 100.00 |

### Forecasting and Accounting Analytics Problems

1. *Forecast Q3 and Q4 sales for 2023.* Use the year-over-year growth rate from the previous years to forecast sales for Q3 and Q4 for 2023. Calculate the average growth based on Q1 and Q2 sales data from prior years.
2. *Calculate total yearly sales for 2023.* Based on your answers from problem 1, calculate the total sales for the year 2023.
3. *Determine the average growth rate.* Calculate the average year-over-year growth rate for total sales over the years 2020, 2021, and 2022.
4. *Evaluate the impact of economic indicators on sales.* Correlate the unemployment rate and GDP growth rate with the total sales of the company for the years 2021 and 2022. Discuss any observable trends.
5. *Forecast GDP growth rate for 2023.* Using historical GDP growth rates, forecast the GDP growth rate for 2023 based on the trend from previous years.
6. *Determine sales elasticity relative to consumer confidence.* Calculate the sales elasticity concerning the changes in the consumer confidence index from 2020 to 2022 and predict how changes in 2023 may impact sales.

### Answer Key

1. *Forecast Q3 and Q4 sales for 2023.*
   Q3 sales for 2023: Assume a growth rate of 5% based on previous trends from Q3 (170,000 to 200,000). Q3 = $210,000. Q4 sales for 2023: another 5% growth. Q4 = $220,500.
2. *Total yearly sales for 2023.*
   Total Sales = Q1 + Q2 + Q3 + Q4 = $180,000 + $210,000 + $210,000 + $220,500 = $820,500.
3. *Average growth rate.* Average growth rate = [(700,000 − 660,000)/660,000 + (740,000 − 700,000)/700,000]/2 = 0.075 or 7.5%.
4. *Impact of economic indicators on sales.*
   A decrease in the unemployment rate from 10.5% to 6.0% that correlates with sales increasing from $660,000 to $740,000 suggests that lower unemployment positively impacts sales.
5. *Forecast GDP growth rate for 2023.*
   Assuming a consistent trend and averaging the previous year rates (5.7%, 4.0%), you may expect a rate of 3.5% growth for 2023.
6. *Sales elasticity relative to consumer confidence.*
   Sales increased by $100,000 (from $660,000 to $740,000) as consumer confidence increased from 75 to 95. Sales elasticity = (100,000/660,000)/(20/75) = 1.14, indicating a strong positive correlation.

## CASE STUDY: SUNTAINABLE ENERGY INC.

SUNtainable Energy Inc. is a start-up founded that specializes in sustainable packaging solutions. With eco-conscious consumers rising and businesses increasingly wanting to reduce their environmental impact, SUNtainable Energy entered the market to provide innovative biodegradable packaging alternatives to existing products and services. Their product line includes compostable bags, plant-based wraps, and recycled paper solutions. The goal of SUNtainable Energy's product line is to capitalize on the growing market trend where businesses are transitioning from traditional plastic packaging to greener options to meet sustainability goals and regulations for the communities it serves.

SUNtainable Energy's entrepreneurial journey began with a team of environmental science graduates who recognized the often-overlooked packaging industry as a significant contributor to pollution. They successfully secured seed funding from investors who shared their vision that enabled SUNtainable Energy to conduct research and develop prototypes that focused on durable and compostable items. During their first year, SUNtainable Energy managed to collaborate with 30 small to medium-sized businesses and gained a strong percentage of market share to establish its brand reputation around sustainability and quality.

In the following year, SUNtainable Energy faced critical decisions on scaling their operations and expanding their consumer and client base. An analysis of sales data from the past year showed promising growth but contained inconsistencies within their operations. Potential market saturation also raised questions about various strategic plans. The leadership team needed to implement business analytics to assess their performance metrics, consumer feedback, and sales trends to make data-driven and more effective decisions about product development and marketing strategies. With a concentration on using data-driven insights, SUNtainable Energy attempted to develop a comprehensive strategy to strengthen consumer retention and identify potential new markets.

### Business Analytics Data

#### Monthly Sales Data

**TABLE 2.3** Sales Data (January–December 2023)

| 1 | A | B | C | D |
|---|---|---|---|---|
| | Month | Total Sales ($) | New Customers | Return Rates (%) |
| 2 | January | 15,000 | 5 | 10 |
| 3 | February | 20,000 | 8 | 5 |
| 4 | March | 30,000 | 12 | 3 |
| 5 | April | 25,000 | 7 | 4 |
| 6 | May | 35,000 | 15 | 6 |
| 7 | June | 40,000 | 20 | 2 |
| 8 | July | 45,000 | 25 | 3 |
| 9 | August | 50,000 | 30 | 2 |
| 10 | September | 55,000 | 35 | 1 |
| 11 | October | 60,000 | 40 | 4 |
| 12 | November | 70,000 | 50 | 5 |
| 13 | December | 80,000 | 55 | 3 |

**TABLE 2.4** Customer Feedback and Response

| 1 | A | B | C | D |
|---|---|---|---|---|
| | **Feedback Category** | **Count** | **Positive Feedback (%)** | **Negative Feedback (%)** |
| 2 | Product quality | 200 | 85 | 15 |
| 3 | Customer service | 150 | 80 | 20 |
| 4 | Delivery time | 100 | 70 | 30 |
| 5 | Pricing | 120 | 65 | 35 |
| 6 | Overall experience | 180 | 90 | 10 |

## Analytics Problem Using Excel

SUNtainable Energy wants to identify which feedback category needs immediate attention and which product had the highest sales. Using the provided feedback and sales data, perform the following tasks in Excel to present in a report to the leadership team:

1. Sort the sales data to identify the month with the highest sales.
2. Create a Pareto analysis of customer feedback to highlight the major causes of customer dissatisfaction.
3. Filter the data to show only the months when the return rate was above 4%.
4. Use logical functions (IF statements) to determine if the negative feedback in any category was above 30%.
5. Apply lookup functions to connect customer feedback with sales data.
6. Create charts to visualize the trends in sales and customer feedback over the year.
7. Utilize PivotTables to summarize feedback counts by category and percentage breakdowns.
8. Implement data validation controls to ensure that the new feedback data entered about product quality is within acceptable parameters (0–100%).

## Answer Key

1. After sorting, the month with the highest sales is December, with $80,000.

   Step 1: Open your Excel workbook that contains the sales data table.
   Step 2: Click anywhere in the "Total Sales ($)" column (column B).
   Step 3: Navigate to the Data tab in the toolbar.
   Step 4: Click on the Sort Largest to Smallest button. This will sort the data by sales amount in descending order.
   Step 5: The month with the highest sales will now be at the top of your table.

   *Sales data sorting* gives you a clear view of your top-performing months, which is necessary to understand your best sales periods.
2. The Pareto analysis shows that negative feedback is primarily due to pricing and delivery time, suggesting how focusing on these areas can significantly enhance customer experience.

   Step 1: Calculate cumulative percentages for negative feedback.
   Step 2: Add a new column next to "Negative Feedback (%)" called "Cumulative Negative Feedback (%)."

Step 3: In the first row of this new column (let's say row 2), use the formula to start calculating the cumulative percentages. For example, if negative feedback starts in cell D2, the formula would be =D2.

Step 4: For the second cell (D3), use the formula =D3 + Cumulative Negative Feedback for the previous entry. This will continue to build on previous percentages.

Step 5: Create a bar chart for "Negative Feedback (%)" using the Insert tab, followed by choosing the Bar Chart option.

Step 6: Add a line chart for the cumulative percentage of negative feedback on the same graph for easy comparison.

*Pareto analysis* identifies key issues within customer feedback and allows you to prioritize solutions that will have the most significant impact

3. Filtering data reveals that April, June, and July are the months with return rates above 4%.

Step 1: Select the entire sales data table.

Step 2: Navigate to the Data tab and click on Filter.

Step 3: Click on the drop-down arrow in the "Return Rates (%)" column header.

Step 4: Select Number Filters and then Greater Than, entering 4. Click OK.

Step 5: Excel will now display only the rows where the return rate is above 4%.

*Data filtering* is a quick way to focus on specific metrics and allows for a more focused analysis on return rates.

4. Logical functions identify that the feedback for pricing criteria had a concerning 35% negative feedback, exceeding the threshold.

Step 1: Next to the "Negative Feedback (%)" column, create a new column named "Need Attention."

Step 2: In the first cell (e.g., E2), enter the following formula: =IF(D2 > 30, "Yes", "No"). This checks if negative feedback is above 30%.

Step 3: Drag the fill handle down to apply this formula to all rows.

*Logical functions* help in easily selecting areas that need immediate attention based on set criteria.

5. A lookup function allows linking customer feedback to specific months by finding corresponding sales in the sales table.

Step 1: Create a new table to use VLOOKUP or INDEX & MATCH for connecting sales data with feedback categories.

Step 2: In a new column, you could use =VLOOKUP(B2, FeedbackTable, 3, FALSE), where *FeedbackTable* refers to your customer feedback table.

Step 3: Adjust column numbers to retrieve the desired values based on the data tables.

*Lookup functions* enhance your ability to correlate sales data with customer feedback, adding depth to your analysis.

6. Charts display a visual representation of monthly sales and a bar graph for customer feedback, illustrating overall trends and categories that may require action.

Step 1: Prepare your data. Open Excel and enter your data in a worksheet. Make sure to organize it clearly, usually in two columns: one for the categories (e.g., names of items), and the other for the values (e.g., sales numbers).

Step 2: Select your data. Click and drag to select the range of data you want to include in your bar chart, including the headers.

Step 3: Insert the bar chart. Go to the Insert tab on the Ribbon at the top of Excel. In the Charts group, look for the Bar Chart icon. It may show several types of bar charts. Click on the Bar Chart icon and choose the type of bar chart you want (e.g., clustered bar, stacked bar, etc.).

Step 4: Customize your chart. After inserting the chart, you can customize it. Click on the chart to display the Chart Tools on the Ribbon, which include Design and Format tabs. Use the Design tab to change the chart style and layout and switch rows and columns if needed. Use the Format tab to change the fill color, outline color, and effects for your chart components.

Step 5: Add chart elements. Click on the chart and you'll see a + icon at the top right of the chart. Click this to add chart elements like chart title, axis titles, data labels, and legends.

Step 6: Adjust the chart size. Click and drag the edges or corners of the chart to resize it as needed.

Step 7: Finalize your chart. Once you're satisfied, click anywhere outside the chart. Save your Excel worksheet to retain your changes.

*Charts* visualize trends for better comprehension and presentation of data.

7. The PivotTable summarizes customer feedback counts by category, showing the number of responses, and calculates the percentage of positive and negative feedback for each.

Step 1: Select the dataset for customer feedback (in both count and feedback percentages).

Step 2: Navigate to the Insert tab and select PivotTable.

Step 3: In the PivotTable Field List, drag Feedback Category to the Rows area and Count to the Values area.

Step 4: Right-click on the count column in the PivotTable and select Value Field Settings, then choose Show Values As and select % of Grand Total.

Step 5: Your PivotTable should now summarize the feedback percentages by category.

*PivotTables* quickly summarize large sets of data, giving insight into the effectiveness of customer satisfaction based on category feedback.

8. Data validation controls are implemented to ensure feedback percentages for product quality falls within the range of 0–100, preventing erroneous data entry.

Step 1: Select the new feedback column for product quality.

Step 2: Go to the Data tab and click Data Validation.

Step 3: In the dialog box, under Settings, choose Whole Number and set the range between 0 and 100.

Step 4: Add an error alert message to prevent users from entering invalid data.

Step 5: Click OK, ensuring that entries in this column adhere to your specifications (0–100%).

*Data validation controls* ensure data integrity, enhancing the overall reliability of the analytics derived from these entries.

CHAPTER 3

# Entrepreneurship and Business Analytics

Entrepreneurship is an accelerator for innovation and job creation within organizations across various sectors of the global environment. Entrepreneurs work to identify gaps in the market and then introduce new products and services to meet the unmet needs of the consumer. When creativity and risk-taking are encouraged, competition will increase within the market. As a result, this situation will lead to an improvement in quality and lower prices for customers. Various industries rely on entrepreneurship, including technology, retail, and health care. Within these markets, entrepreneurs have improved traditional business models by introducing disruptive technologies and innovations that redefine how our products and services are delivered to consumers.

Entrepreneurs would not be successful without the use of business analytics. Business analytics supports entrepreneurship by developing methodologies and tools that are necessary for the entrepreneur to make informed decisions. Within the global environment, entrepreneurs constantly face uncertainty and challenges when launching new products or service ideas. It is this situation that requires business analytics to help reduce the amount of risk by using knowledge gained from data-driven research. By using statistical analysis, data visualization, and predictive modeling, entrepreneurs can successfully identify consumer preferences, market trends, and future challenges within the market sector. As a result, business analytics and statistical analysis enable the entrepreneur to make logical choices that improve the profitability and efficiency of the organization.

In the retail industry, business analytics is used by entrepreneurs to improve their inventory management system and enhance consumer experience. When retailers can study the purchasing behavior of the consumer, they can customize their marketing strategies to retain and attract new customers. This situation will ultimately increase sales and return on investment for the company. In health care, business analytics will determine slowdowns or bottlenecks so the organization can improve the delivery of patient care while also maintaining a low-cost structure. As a result, the ability to take advantage of statistical data will greatly improve the competitive advantage of one company over the rest within the market sector.

Next, there is a collaboration between entrepreneurship and business analytics within the technology industry. In this industry, products and services that are data-driven are critical to being successful within the constantly changing and growing environment. This situation makes it necessary for entrepreneurs to use business analytics to innovate and improve their product and service offerings on a regular basis. As an example, an entrepreneur in the

DOI: 10.4324/9781003629658-3

technology environment will use statistical analysis to develop powerful algorithms that will further personalize and customize user experience for the consumer through streaming services and social media to improve engagement and long-term loyalty.

Third, business analytics and entrepreneurship are necessary in identifying challenges within the economy. Small and medium enterprises (SMEs) will greatly contribute to the creation of new jobs and economic growth. When business analytics is integrated into the daily operation of the company, the business will operate more efficiently, gain a competitive advantage, and respond and adapt to changes in the market environment. As a result, business analytics enables entrepreneurs to improve innovation to drive economic growth while enabling leaders and managers to make data-driven decisions to create a sustainable internal and external environment within the global market.

## THE IMPORTANCE OF ANALYTICS FOR START-UPS

Business analytics is important for start-up companies by creating an environment for sustainable growth. In today's global environment, start-ups must use business analytics to lead their strategies, to improve their efficiency, and to make data-driven decisions that will directly impact their presence within the market. First, entrepreneurs are required to operate in market sectors that are full of uncertainty and risk. This situation makes data analytics a necessary component to success. With business analytics, the entrepreneur can enable the start-up to change raw data into knowledge and information. As a result, the entrepreneur can better understand consumer behavior, operational performance, and market trends.

For entrepreneurs in the technology sector of the market, start-ups will use statistical analysis to improve their product offerings and consumer experiences. When data is analyzed, the entrepreneur can identify the lack of features of their product, maximize the user interface, and develop new solutions that are customized to the unique needs of the consumer. As an example, a start-up software company can use consumer feedback and data usage to determine the success of a product and to make sure that it remains strategically aligned with the demands of the market. In the health-care sector, start-ups will face issues and challenges when operating in regulatory environments while attempting to deliver innovative solutions to consumers. The situation will require entrepreneurs to use business analytics to analyze patient data and use the results to improve the outcomes of patients and the efficiency of the organization. An example of the situation is when a start-up uses business analytics to forecast the admission rates of patients to enable the health-care facility to dedicate the right resources and to reduce waiting times.

Within the retail industry, start-ups will experience transformational changes due to the use of business analytics. Start-up companies will study and analyze consumer purchase patterns that will allow them to create customized marketing campaigns that are targeted to improve consumer engagement and retention. This situation is necessary for the start-up to generate revenue and a highly competitive and volatile market. Finally, start-ups in the finance sector will rely on business analytics to identify new market opportunities and assess the level of risk associated with them. A financial start-up company can create new algorithms for credit scoring and provide accurate assessments of the financial services it offers to its consumers. As a result, the financial start-up company can improve the acquisition of new consumers while also promoting responsible lending practices to reduce the overall risk to the business, demonstrating how entrepreneurship and business analytics must work together to create empowerment for the start-up and to use information for growth and sustainability.

### How Start-Ups Can Leverage Data for Growth

Entrepreneurs will use business analytics and start-ups to leverage data for growth. By using data analytics, entrepreneurs will discover new information and knowledge that will be used to inform the company about competitive positioning, product development, and entry into new sectors. Entrepreneurs are constantly facing uncertainty in dynamic market environments. This situation will require entrepreneurs to use business analytics tools to convert large amounts of data into useful knowledge and information to successfully recognize changes in consumer preferences and emerging trends in the market. This situation makes business analytics the primary tool for entrepreneurs within the technology, health-care, retail, and finance sectors.

First, entrepreneurs in the technology sector use business analytics to determine gaps or holes in the market. The situation is achieved by the entrepreneur studying the unmet needs of the consumer, and their behavior patterns, and anticipating the demand for new product features that will provide necessary solutions that directly connect for current and potential consumers. Second, the health-care sector uses business analytics to enable entrepreneurs to identify areas for improvement and inefficiencies in the daily business process. Entrepreneurs will need to examine the operational metrics and outcome of patients so they can determine new opportunities for products and services to improve the delivery of care to patients. An example is a health-care start-up company that analyzes patient data and focuses on the demographics that are not being supported in developing a targeted outreach program of services to address their needs.

Third, the retail industry sector requires start-ups to use business analytics to identify market opportunities through the trend analysis of its consumers. When the purchasing behavior of consumers is conducted, start-up companies can better understand the preferences and sustainability of products, subscription models, and personalized shopping experiences. As a result, a new retail start-up can analyze the sales of data across different geographic locations to identify the untapped markets and look for potential areas of expansion to maximize the distribution of their inventory.

Start-ups in the finance sector will rely on business analytics to uncover unidentified areas in traditional banking and credit services. This situation is achieved by the start-up examining the patterns in services and consumer complaints about existing products. Once all deficiencies have been determined, the start-up can begin to develop new products that are customized to meet the needs of specific market segments that include underserved communities or SMEs. As a result, business analytics enables entrepreneurs to analyze the effectiveness of their competitors. When the effectiveness of competitors is analyzed, a start-up company can determine new performance metrics, market share, and consumer feedback so they can improve their strategic position based on their product offerings to gain new market share. The use of business analytics will ultimately allow the start-up to make improved decisions on pricing models, marketing strategies, and product differentiation.

## IDENTIFYING MARKET OPPORTUNITIES WITH ANALYTICS

Entrepreneurs will use business analytics to identify new market opportunities. When entrepreneurship is combined with business analytics, start-ups will be able to position themselves strategically for long-term sustainability, growth, and innovation through the identification of gaps in the market. By using data-driven information, entrepreneurs can identify the undetermined needs of the consumer and the competitive weaknesses of other companies and adapt to the emerging trends within the market sector. Next, entrepreneurs will use business analytics to conduct market research to gather and interpret data related to consumer preferences and behaviors. This situation will enable the entrepreneur to discover the product features that consumers want but are not currently available. As a result of this insight, entrepreneurs can develop new and innovative product enhancements that directly address the unmet needs of the consumers.

Retail entrepreneurs will use information gained from consumer and sales data to conduct comparative analyses to expose unserved demographics or to create a niche market. As an example, an entrepreneurial start-up company can use statistical analysis to determine the consumer segment of the market that only supports eco-friendly products but does not have access to them. By collecting this information, start-ups can create and introduce sustainable products that are designed to meet the needs of this market. Health-care entrepreneurs will use business analytics to study service delivery, patient care, and feedback from patients, outcome from treatments, and operational workflows to determine any inefficiencies within the operation. An example is when the entrepreneur studies patient satisfaction scores and wait times for elder care patients to create online or virtual care options to reduce the level of inefficiencies and improve consumer satisfaction. As a result, new and customized telehealth options will be created to improve access and patient engagement for all elder care patients.

Financial entrepreneurs all benefit from the use of business analytics by identifying issues in financial services, which include a lack of credit options for individuals and small businesses, and eliminating the barriers that traditional financial companies currently suffer, from reducing access to monetary funding and resources to their potential clients. As a result, business analytics enables entrepreneurs to determine the competitiveness of the market. Once the viability of the market has been determined, the entrepreneur can begin to create benchmarks based on key performance indicators (KPIs) compared to their competition. The entrepreneur can identify the weaknesses and threats of the product and service offerings of the competition. As a result, the entrepreneur can gain a competitive advantage by exploiting the shortcomings of their competitors by offering new innovations to gain consumer loyalty, sustainability, and service quality.

Finally, it is important for start-ups to combine entrepreneurship and business analytics to correctly locate and identify holes in the market throughout the multiple industries within the global environment. It is important for the entrepreneur and start-up to take full advantage of business analytics and statistical analysis to improve its operational efficiency and effectiveness and identify new consumer preferences and weaknesses and threats to its competitive position. As a result, business analytics will support the entrepreneur by enabling the start-up to create new product and service offerings and to become a leader in innovation to meet the changing needs of the market, while also positioning them for long-term success and growth within the competitive environment.

## RISK ASSESSMENT IN NEW VENTURES

Entrepreneurship and business analytics play an important role in risk assessment in new ventures. Business analytics helps the entrepreneur make knowledgeable and data-driven decisions to reduce the risk or threat of potential weaknesses within its daily operation. Next, it is important for the entrepreneurial start-up company to understand the risks that can impact the rate of survival of long-term sustainability in the global environment. When data-driven information is used to make decisions, the entrepreneur will be more equipped and prepared to identify, analyze, and reduce the level of risk across the various industries within the economic environment.

When a start-up is first developed and undertakes a new venture, the entrepreneur is faced with a high level of uncertainty that is associated with the demands of the market, competition, and daily operational challenges. This situation makes business analytics a critical tool for systematically evaluating these uncertainties. In the technology sector, entrepreneurs starting a new venture will gather and study data based on the beta tests of a new product with its users. The information collected will enable the new venture to identify a lack of functionality and potential drawbacks to the product that may cause a disconnect with its primary users. When these issues or threats are identified within the early stages of the new venture, the entrepreneur can reduce the level of risk when it is time to officially launch the new product so it does not fail to meet the expectations of the market.

Within the retail sector, new ventures will rely on business analytics to assess and understand their supply chain and distributor risks. It is necessary for new ventures or start-ups to study the past data associated with fluctuations in demand, the reliability of suppliers, and the level of inventory. By analyzing this historical data, the new venture can create a strong and efficient supply chain and distributor strategy to reduce the risk associated with stockouts or the overstocking of products. As an example, a technology e-commerce start-up can use statistical analysis to predict the demand of specific products while guaranteeing that the new venture maintains the required level of inventory without incurring additional costs to its daily operation.

In the health-care sector, a new venture will also experience risks and challenges in its assessment of its position within the market. This situation is particularly evident when dealing with regulatory compliance and government mandates about patient safety and compliance. This situation makes it important for entrepreneurs to implement business analytics to evaluate and determine the risk to its operation and to ensure that their products and services meet current industry standards. As an example, a new health-care venture would use business analytics to monitor operational metrics and the success of outcomes for patients. When the areas for improvement have been determined using statistical analysis, the new venture can implement the required changes necessary to improve patient care, while also reducing the amount of risk associated with the delivery of poor services to its clients.

In the finance market, new ventures rely on business analytics to determine the market and credit risks to its long-term growth and sustainability. With the implementation of business analytics, the new venture can gain new information and knowledge of market conditions and consumer behavior patterns. This situation will enable the start-up to develop a model for risk assessment by analyzing the transaction patterns and credit histories of the target market.

Next, the new venture can improve its product and service offerings through the innovation and customization of new products that better align and identify with the risk profiles of clients. As a result, the use of business analytics does not just provide the new venture with improved lending decisions but also reduces the risk of default payments by consumers within a volatile market.

Finally, business analytics enables new ventures to effectively evaluate the risk of competition by conducting an analysis of the market. Once the risks have been assessed, the new venture can develop benchmarks for their product and service offerings compared to their competition. As a result, statistical analysis provides the new venture with the potential opportunities and threats that will enable the entrepreneur to improve their strategic plan and to reposition themselves more strongly in the market due to the reduction of risk associated with competition and the saturation of the market. By being proactive through the use of predictive analytics, the new venture can create a solid foundation for innovation and sustainable growth.

## Evaluating Potential Risks Using Analytical Frameworks

Entrepreneurs use business analytics to evaluate potential risks using analytical frameworks. Analytical frameworks enable the entrepreneur to methodically assess various risks associated with different economic industries and to make informed decision-making and strategy development. One of the main analytical frameworks used in the evaluation of risk is the SWOT analysis. The SWOT analysis includes strengths, weaknesses, opportunities, and threats associated with the decisions of an entrepreneur. Next, the SWOT analysis provides the entrepreneur with the necessary tools required to accurately identify the internal capabilities and the external factors that can occur. As an example, a company in the technology sector of the market can use SWOT analysis to determine the innovative capabilities or strengths, compared to the threats, or solutions, of their competitors. When the internal factors are linked with the dynamics of the market, the entrepreneur can identify the areas that require a greater level of strategic focus or risk mitigation.

The second type of analytical framework is the PESTEL analysis. PESTEL studies the political, economic, social, technological, environmental, and legal factors of the market. Using the PESTEL approach is especially important in the health-care industry since there is mandatory regulatory compliance and new advancements in technology that can directly impact the operations of the business. When these factors are analyzed, the health-care entrepreneur can acknowledge all potential risks associated with the changes in the economy, government mandates, and changes in consumer behavior. As a result, the PESTEL analysis will enable the entrepreneur to develop new strategies to mitigate risk and avoid conflicts in the market.

The third analytical framework is scenario analysis. *Scenario analysis* is a useful tool for evaluating the potential of a risk and the implications it has for a given choice or action. Next, scenario analysis begins with the concept of a hypothetical situation that is based on different variables. Based on these variables, the entrepreneur must determine how the change in market conditions or consumer preferences will impact their business operation. An example is in the retail industry, when an entrepreneur establishes a start-up scenario analysis that involves supply chain disruptions or consumer spending habits. As a result, scenario analysis will enable the entrepreneur to accurately identify the threats and weaknesses of the company so they can prepare new ventures based on various outcomes that provide more adaptable and flexible responses.

The fourth analytical framework includes quantitative risk assessment tools. Quantitative risk assessment tools include Monte Carlo simulations, which are used to statistically evaluate uncertainties and risks. This strategy allows entrepreneurs to develop a comprehensive understanding of the probability of the different risks that occur and their potential impact on the success of the company. As an example, Monte Carlo simulations are used in the financial sector of the market to assess the level of risk associated with the defaulting of loans of clients based on various economic situations.

The final analytical framework is the use of key performance indicators (KPIs). KPIs are used to monitor and determine the level of risk over time. When the entrepreneur establishes important benchmarks and KPIs, they can accurately monitor operational performance and point out any deviation from the standard that might indicate an emerging risk. An example of this situation is a technology company that uses KPIs to track consumer retention rates. If the technology company notices a significant drop in the use of a specific product, it could be determined to be a result of a product failure or an innovation from a competitor that will require real-time corrective action. As a result, there are many different methods and analytical frameworks available for entrepreneurs to make data-driven decisions.

**TABLE 3.1** Comparing Analytical Frameworks for Business Analytics

| Analysis Type | Purpose | Components | Focus | Usage |
|---|---|---|---|---|
| **SWOT analysis** | To evaluate internal and external factors affecting an organization | Strengths, weaknesses, opportunities, threats | Internal and external | Strategic planning, identifying competitive position |
| **PESTEL analysis** | To analyze external macro-environmental factors affecting an organization | Political, economic, social, technological, environmental, legal | External | Strategic planning, understanding market dynamics |
| **Scenario analysis** | To assess potential future outcomes based on different scenarios | Best-case, worst-case, base-case scenarios | External | Risk management, strategic planning, investment strategy |
| **Quantitative risk assessment** | To numerically evaluate the impact of risks on project objectives | Probability, impact, expected monetary value, sensitivity analysis | Internal and external | Project management, decision-making, risk mitigation |
| **Key performance indicators (KPIs)** | To measure and track performance against specific goals | Financial KPIs, customer KPIs, process KPIs, employee KPIs | Internal | Performance measurement, strategic management, operational improvement |

## BUSINESS MODEL INNOVATION THROUGH DATA INSIGHTS

Entrepreneurs rely on business model innovation through data insights, which enables organizations to adapt to changes in market conditions, improve the experience of consumers, and identify new streams of revenue. When data is collected and analyzed, the entrepreneur can recreate their business model despite the industry, leading to improved short-term performance and a long-term competitive advantage. The main way that business analytics and entrepreneurship support business model innovation is through the capability of making data-driven decisions. Next, entrepreneurs can use business analytics to develop a higher level of understanding of consumer preferences, behaviors, and trends.

Within the retail industry, data analytics allows retailers to divide their consumers into groups based on purchasing patterns. Through the analysis of data analytics, retailers can identify new strengths and opportunities to diverge from the traditional sales model to the innovative subscription-based and direct-to-consumer-based methods. As a result of this change, the retailer can create brand loyalty and establish new sources of revenue. In the technology industry, entrepreneurs will rely on knowledge gained from data analysis to reform their product and service offerings and to create new business models for future success and sustainability. Software-as-a-service (SaaS) companies will study user engagement performance metrics to discover undervalued features. Based on the results of the analysis, SaaS companies can change from a freemium pricing model to offering basic services free of charge while also charging for premium features. As a result, SaaS companies will develop consumer loyalty and a higher rate of return on investment (ROI).

In health care, business analytics provide entrepreneurs with the ability to innovate their business models by using data to improve operational efficiency and patient care. Next, business analytics will identify problems or missed opportunities in the delivery of services. This situation will result in the development of new telehealth solutions, virtual care, and personalized health-care plans. A health-care entrepreneur can analyze the demographics of patients and the outcomes of treatments to create a new wellness program. As a result, the development of new wellness programs has transformed traditional care models into a data-driven analytical model.

In the finance sector, business analytics play an important role in forming the business model innovation. Financial companies rely on analytics and statistical analysis to create customized financial products that are based on the individual preferences and behaviors of consumers. Next, when spending patterns are analyzed, the financial company can develop new budgeting tools that are specifically designed to meet the needs of consumers. As a result, this process will change the current-most from a one-size-fits-all approach to a more personal advisory financial service.

Next, business analytics will lead to the development of collaborative business models that enable entrepreneurs to create strategic partnerships that improve the creation of value. When data and information are shared with other partners, companies can begin to develop complementary products and services that meet the wider range of consumer needs. As an example, a technology company can collaborate with a logistics company to offer real-time delivery updates with the goal of improving the overall experience of the consumer. As a result, it is important for data and information to be analyzed and for the results to be shared with all collaborators so new business models can be implemented to enable the company to remain competitive in a competitive and diverse global environment.

## Enhancing Business Models With Analytics

Entrepreneurs can enhance business models with analytics. Entrepreneurs and business analytics improve existing business models through the integration of data-driven knowledge as part of the decision-making process. First, this approach supports innovation and new product development. Second, analytics enables organizations to adjust and adapt to the changes in the market to improve their efficiency and effectiveness in all industries. The main benefit of using analytics in entrepreneurship is to better understand the preferences and needs of the client. In the retail sector, it is beneficial for the retailer to study the historical purchases made by consumers to identify behaviors, preferences, and trends. As a result, using a data-driven approach provides retailers with new personalized selling techniques, marketing plans, and product assortment to improve sales and enhance their business model.

In the field of technology, business analytics supports product development and duplication. Entrepreneurs can use the collected feedback from users and establish performance metrics to determine how every consumer interacts with their products. Next, entrepreneurs can implement A/B testing using a split test philosophy to compare two versions of a product to determine which one performs better. With the result of A/B testing, the tech company can uncover the features that provide the most value for the users of the product. With the new knowledge, the tech company can develop new products and enhancements that are more in line with the demand of consumers and value creation.

In the health-care industry, business analytics is integrated into entrepreneurship to allow them to develop patient-focused business models. It is important to analyze information related to demographics, treatment paths, and patient outcomes so health-care entrepreneurs can better identify unidentified areas in service delivery. This situation leads to the creation of customized solutions that include personalized treatment plans for patients, telehealth, and virtual care services that address the needs of specific patients. However, the development of these new services will shift the traditional business model of a fee-for-service to a new model that focuses on patient outcomes and quality of care that will appeal to both providers and consumers.

In the finance sector, changes and transformations occurred due to the incorporation of business analytics into entrepreneurship. The financial company will use data analytics to better understand credit risk more accurately and to create financial products that meet the unique needs of their consumers. Through the analysis of consumer spending, income patterns, and credit histories, financial companies can provide customized loans and investment options. This fitted method improves value proposition and differentiates them from the current traditional banking model.

Finally, business analytics allows entrepreneurs to use key performance indicators (KPIs) to monitor performance. By using KPIs, companies can identify problem areas in real time to make improvements for potential market opportunities. As an example, a subscription-based service has the capability to determine consumer turnover rate and to implement new retention strategies and to adjust its business model to better focus on the satisfaction and experience of customers. By using data analytics to better understand consumer behavior, companies in all industries can improve existing products and optimize business operations.

## FUNDING OPTIMIZATION STRATEGIES USING ANALYTICS

Funding optimization strategies using analytics is important for entrepreneurial start-ups so they can make more informed, finance-based decisions that are strategically aligned with their short-term objectives and long-term goals. When data-driven information is used correctly, the entrepreneur or start-up can succeed in various industries in the global market. This situation is made possible by the enhancement of funding strategies, the efficient forecasting of return on investments, and the development of a sustainable growth model.

One of the main ways business analytics supports funding optimization is with financial forecasting. Financial forecasting allows the entrepreneur to use analytical models to help estimate future cash flow, funding requirements, and revenue growth. As an example, a technology start-up company can analyze previous customer retention rates, sales data, and market trends to develop more accurate forecast models. With this new information based on analytics, the entrepreneurial start-up company can establish the necessary time to secure funding, determine the amount of capital to raise, and invest in the right sources of funding to minimize the level of risk of under- or over-capitalization.

Within the health-care industry, funding optimization is critical in preparing for the high-cost structures associated with development, research, and governmental regulatory compliance standards. Business analytics will enable entrepreneurial health-care start-ups to determine the need for potential funding opportunities by studying data associated with the availability of investment trends, philanthropy, and grants. This strategy is based on the funding levels required to fund the mission and vision of the company. As a result, the health-care start-up can maximize their use of resources to secure the required capital to support future innovations for the start-up.

For entrepreneurial retailers, business analytics can optimize their strategy for inventory financing. First, the start-up retailer must analyze its past consumer purchasing patterns, inventory levels, turnover rates, and sales history. With this statistical analysis, the retailer can make more accurate predictions and decisions to manage case flow and inventory requirements for optimal performance. As an example, a retail start-up would have the capacity to identify specific products that constantly perform at high levels during precise seasons throughout the year. With this new information, the start-up retailer can optimize its management and funding of purchasing new items, having the right levels of inventory, and mitigate all risks to daily business operations.

Next, the finance industry will use business analytics to support entrepreneurship through the evaluation of, or by determining, effective funding sources. Financial start-up companies will need to analyze consumer behaviors associated with different financial products to identify which product offerings are more likely to yield the highest rate of return on investment. By determining consumer credit history and spending patterns, financial start-up companies can optimize their allocation of capital and develop strategies to gain the necessary investments with the highest potential yield for profitability while also managing all risks associated with the lending process. The situation is made possible with scenario analysis that allows entrepreneurs to evaluate various funding strategies that include alternative financing, debt, and equity financing that will directly impact financial projections in the future. As a result, financial start-ups develop a comprehensive understanding and strategy that will allow them to choose the correct funding model that aligns with their long-term goals.

## Analyzing Funding Needs and Sources

Entrepreneurship and business analytics will help in the determination of funding needs and sources for the company. The first stage in analyzing funding involves an assessment of the company's current financial situation and projections for future growth. Entrepreneurs will use financial modeling techniques that include budgeting and cash flow forecasts to understand the required capital needed for sustainability and growth. As an example, companies in the technology sector of the market will need to perform a detailed analysis of their projected revenues, anticipated market growth, and operational expenses. This statistical analysis will enable the company to identify specific funds that are needed for product development, marketing campaigns, and the scaling of the business operation.

Next, business analytics will enable the entrepreneur to determine the timing and level of funding requirements needed for success. By studying historical performance data, the entrepreneur will have access to new data that can be used. To support additional financing initiatives within the retail industry, there are seasonal patterns that must be identified by the entrepreneur and then be used to indicate when more capital is needed to purchase a new inventory before the peak sales periods begin. By anticipating the needs of the company, the entrepreneurial retailer can ensure the necessary funding in advance and avoid any challenges or threats to the cash flow of the business.

After the necessary funding needs have been identified, the next step for the entrepreneur is to analyze potential funding sources for future growth. This situation is achieved by the entrepreneur using statistical analysis to determine all financing possibilities, which include venture capital, grants, equity financing, and debt financing. This situation is most seen in the health-care market. Health-care entrepreneurs will need to analyze trends in venture capital investments to identify current or potential investors. This strategy will require the entrepreneur to evaluate the investors' area of focus and portfolios, which include health-care technology and biotechnology. However, in the finance sector of the market, the entrepreneur will need to simulate various scenarios to understand how the dilution of equity or debt repayment will impact future cash flows of the company. An example of the situation is a financial company that uses a model scenario based on the changing interest rates and repayment terms of the loan that will allow them to make informed decisions about the future of financing any amounts required for sustainability and growth.

Next, data-driven decisions will improve the ability to negotiate terms with future lenders and investors for a company. When a thorough financial analysis has been conducted, accurate forecasts and projections by the entrepreneur can be used to demonstrate their understanding of funding needs through a credible growth strategy model. As a result, business analytics will improve the chances of the entrepreneur to gain the necessary funding with better negotiated terms that align with the organization's mission and vision while reducing risk to the daily operation. Through a systematic approach, entrepreneurship, combined with business analytical strategies, will guarantee that the organization can effectively secure the necessary capital required to grow in the current market or expand into new and emerging market sectors.

## INNOVATION TRACKING AND MEASUREMENT

Innovation tracking and measurement is another aspect of business analytics that supports entrepreneurship. One of the main functions of business analytics and innovation tracking is to develop key performance indicators (KPIs) that measure the outcomes of all innovations for the company. KPIs can include metrics like revenue earned from new initiatives, new product developments, and the time required to bring new innovations into the current market. An example is a technology company that uses analytics to monitor their product development life cycles. Through data analysis, the market response and timeline of development can be identified to enable the company to make the required adjustments necessary to improve its operational efficiency and effectiveness against its competitors.

Next, entrepreneurship relies on innovation tracking and measurements to determine how their innovations impact market performance in consumer satisfaction. Within the retail industry, companies can use consumer feedback analytics that include surveys and online analysis to determine how their products and services meet the expectations and requirements of the customer. In the automotive industry, tracking innovation is important for companies to remain ahead of the competition by investing in technological advancements and the changing demands of consumers. An entrepreneurial automaker will use statistics to determine the effectiveness of new vehicle designs and features through consumer feedback and testing. By studying consumer preferences, safety concerns, and driving habits, the automotive company can drive new innovations that directly connect with their consumer base and will ultimately improve market share and brand loyalty.

There are financial implications when business analytics are used in innovation tracking and measurements to determine financial models that are associated with marketing, production, and research and development. In the biotechnology industry, companies will need to heavily invest in research and development to create new drugs for patients. The situation will require the company to use business analytics to determine future return on investment for their various innovative projects and to use the data to guide the allocation of resources within the strategic planning process.

Finally, innovation, tracking, and measurements will expand beyond the internal metrics of the company and will also include external benchmarking requirements within the market environment. With business analytics, the entrepreneur will have the capability to compare their performance of innovation against their competitors' and the industry standards. The situation will provide valuable perspective for evaluating their current progress compared to the rest of the market. With this comparative analysis, the entrepreneur can identify the best practices and areas for improvement to improve the overall innovation capabilities of the company. As a result, innovation, tracking, and measurement, combined with KPIs, will benefit companies in technology, retail, automotive, biotechnology, and other industries within the diverse and constantly changing global market.

## Metrics for Evaluating Innovation Impact

Metrics for evaluating innovation impact will benefit entrepreneurship using quantitative and qualitative metrics to determine how their innovative efforts connect with their consumer market, influence market performance, and provide long-term growth for companies in all economic industries within the global market. The first metric for evaluating innovation impact is the revenue generated from new products or services by a company. Within the technology sector, companies will use the revenue generated from incremental software updates or new product features that are launched throughout the year. Data from sales from before and after the innovation was introduced will be analyzed by the entrepreneur to quantify the financial benefits to the company based on the innovation initiative. As a result, this revenue analysis will offer the required proof of market acceptance or rejection of the innovation for the entrepreneur.

The second metric is consumer feedback. Entrepreneurs will need to use metrics such as the customer satisfaction score (CSAT) or the net promoter score (NPS) to determine the reactions of customers to new products or service offerings. This situation is seen primarily in the retail industry. Within this industry, retailers will use customer reviews and surveys to collect information on how well new products meet their expectations and requirements. When these metrics are analyzed, the entrepreneur can improve their products and service offerings based on the input from consumers and guarantee that all innovations are aligned with the needs of the market.

The third metric for evaluating the impact of innovation is market share growth. To determine market share growth due to the impact of innovation, the entrepreneur will need to analyze the company's market share before an innovative solution is introduced, along with the change in market share after the introduction of the new product innovation. Based on the results of this analysis, the entrepreneur can determine if sales increased and if consumers improved their loyalty to the brand based on the specific innovation initiative. In the food and beverage industry, the company can introduce a new health-conscious product line. Once this new product line has been introduced, the entrepreneur can monitor changes in market share and determine how well the innovation positioned the brand against their competitors and determine the percentage of the acquisition of new consumers.

The fourth metric for evaluating innovation impact is time to market. Entrepreneurs must study how fast they can bring innovative products or services to the market compared to the current benchmarks established within the industry. This situation can best be seen in the automotive industry, where technological advancements occur rapidly in the market. This situation makes it important for an entrepreneurial automaker to update its vehicles with new technology to maintain a competitive advantage against their competitors. As a result, there must be a short time to market to enable the company to capitalize on new trends and the changing consumer demand if the company wants to position itself as an industry leader.

The final metric for evaluating innovation impact is return on investment (ROI). ROI is important to the entrepreneur when they are determining the financial practicality of their innovative enterprises. The entrepreneur must compare all associated costs related to marketing, production, and research and development. These costs must then be compared to the revenue generated from new products, so the entrepreneur can quantify the level of success of their innovation. In the field of biotechnology, new drugs are constantly being developed. With each new drug that is developed, there is a high cost associated with its creation and time to market. To remain competitive, the entrepreneur of the biotechnology company will need to evaluate the ROI of the new drug development to help the company prioritize its investments in future research opportunities.

## BUSINESS ANALYTICS FUNCTION FOR ENTREPRENEURSHIP USING MICROSOFT EXCEL

In the business environment, there are many businesses analytical terms mentioned that play a critical role in making informed and data-driven choices to drive decisions, optimize daily operations, and develop strategic actions and initiatives. Various statistical concepts play an important role in entrepreneurship and business analytics by providing essential tools for data analysis and decision-making. Here's a detailed overview of their definition, their importance, and how to conduct this statistical analysis using Microsoft Excel.

### Chebyshev's Theorem

Chebyshev's theorem helps entrepreneurs understand the dispersion of data and the expected variability within any given dataset, which allows for more informed risk assessment and data-driven strategies despite the shape of the distribution.

Formula: $P(|X - u| \geq sigma) \leq (1/k^2)$

Where:

- *P* is the probability,
- *X* is a random variable,
- *u* is the mean of the distribution,
- *sigma* is the standard deviation, and
- *k* is the number of standard deviations from the mean.

**Steps:**

1. Calculate the mean: =AVERAGE(data_range).
2. Calculate the standard deviation: =STDEV.P(data_range) or =STDEV.S(data_range).
3. Decide on *k* and use the formula to determine the percentage of data within that range.

### Coefficient of Variation

Coefficient of variation provides a standardized measure of risk per unit of return that enables entrepreneurs to compare the relative variability of different investment options or key business performance metrics.

Formula: CV = (Standard Deviation/Mean)*100

**Steps:**

1. Population = STDEV.P(data_range)/AVERAGE(data_range)*100.
2. Sample = STDEV.S(data_range)/AVERAGE(data_range)*100.

### Constructing Frequency Distributions Using PivotTables

Constructing frequency distributions using PivotTables allows for the efficient organization and summarization of large amounts of data, making key information more accessible and actionable, and ultimately supports data-driven decision-making.

**Steps:**

1. Select your data range.
2. Go to the Insert tab and choose PivotTable.
3. Drag your categorical or numerical variable into Rows and Values (to count frequency).
4. For numerical data, you may want to group them by right-clicking on the row labels and selecting Group.

### Correlation and Covariance

Correlation and covariance are critical for understanding the relationships between different variables. Entrepreneurs can identify potential partnerships, market trends, and operational efficiencies by analyzing how changes in one variable affect another.

**Correlation Steps:**

1. To calculate correlation coefficients: =CORREL(array1, array2).
2. This function returns the correlation between two sets of data.

**Covariance Steps:**

1. Population covariance: =COVARIANCE.P(array1, array2).
2. Sample covariance: =COVARIANCE.S(array1, array2).

### Cumulative Relative Frequency Distribution

Cumulative relative frequency distribution provides collective knowledge into large datasets, which helps businesses assess where they stand in relationship to the market or competition over time.

**Steps:**

1. Create a frequency distribution first, then add a cumulative frequency column.
2. To find cumulative relative frequency, divide each cumulative frequency by the total number of data points.

## Empirical Rules Theorem

Empirical rules theorem assists in projections regarding data distributions to enable organizational leaders to make accurate assumptions about market behaviors and performance measures.

**Steps:**

1. Use the standard deviation and mean calculated earlier to evaluate what percentages fall within 1, 2, and 3 standard deviations.

## Frequency Distribution for Categorical Data

Frequency distribution for categorical data helps in analyzing consumer preferences, segmenting markets, and using demographic information to improve strategically targeted marketing practices.

**Steps:**

1. This can be achieved using PivotTables, as described earlier, summing counts of each category.

## Frequency Distribution for Numerical Data

Frequency distribution for numerical data provides knowledge of numerical performance metrics that include sales figures that allows for better forecasting and inventory management.

Formula: =FREQUENCY(data_range, bins_array)

**Steps:**

1. Define bins (calculated ranges), and then use =FREQUENCY(data_range, bins_array).
2. Can be determined using PivotTables.

## Grouped Frequency Distribution

Grouped frequency distribution simplifies complex datasets for clear interpretation that are required for identifying trends and patterns in large quantities of information.

**Steps:**

1. Use PivotTables to group numerical data into specified ranges directly by right-clicking the values in the row labels area and selecting Group.

## Interquartile Range, Percentiles, and Quartiles

Interquartile range and variances such as percentiles and quartiles are necessary for measuring statistical dispersion and identifying outliers to support entrepreneurs in evaluating key performance metrics and customer behavior.

*Quartiles*

Formula: =QUARTILE.INC(data_range, quart) or =QUARTILE.EXC(data_range, quart)

**Steps:**

1. Use =QUARTILE.INC(data_range, quart) or =QUARTILE.EXC(data_range, quart), where *quart* can be 0 (minimum), 1 (Q1), 2 (median), 3 (Q3), or 4 (maximum).

*Interquartile*

Formula: =QUARTILE.EXC(data_range, 1) and =QUARTILE.EXC(data_range, 3)

**Steps:**

1. Calculate the first quartile: =QUARTILE.EXC(data_range, 1).
2. Calculate the third quartile: =QUARTILE.EXC(data_range, 3).
3. The interquartile range (IQR) is the difference between Q3 and Q1: =Q3 − Q1.

*Percentiles*

Formula: =PERCENTILE.EXC(data_range, k)

**Steps:**

1. Calculate percentiles using =PERCENTILE.EXC(data_range, k), where *k* is the desired percentile (like 0.9 for the 90th percentile).

## Relative Frequency Distribution

Relative frequency distribution highlights the share of each category within a specific dataset and is helpful in determining market analysis and competitive benchmarking.

**Steps:**

1. Calculate relative frequency using =Frequency Count/Total Count for each category or interval.
2. This can be accompanied by a frequency table.

### Standard Values With Z-Scores

Standard values with z-scores allow businesses to compare data points relative to the mean of a dataset that leads to the evaluation of performance and the assessment of risk in the business environment.

**Steps:**

1. In Excel, use the formula =(data_point − AVERAGE(data_range))/STDEV.P(data_range).
2. Calculate z-scores using the formula Z = (X − Mean)/Standard Deviation.
3. In Excel, use the formula =(data_point − AVERAGE(data_range))/STDEV.P(data_range).

## REAL-WORLD EXAMPLES OF ENTREPRENEURSHIP INSIGHTS DRIVING BUSINESS SUCCESS

### Amazon

Amazon has become a dominant force in the e-commerce industry by leveraging advanced business analytics to better understand consumer behavior and preferences. The company used data from millions of consumers to power its recommendation engine that suggested products based on past purchases and browsing habits. This personalized experience increased conversion rates and consumer satisfaction scores. Next, Amazon implemented predictive analytics to optimize its supply chain and inventory management system. By accurately forecasting the market demand for products, Amazon ensured timely restocking and reduced its excess inventory costs, which led to improved operational efficiency and higher profitability for its shareholders.

**Question 1**

How has Amazon's recommendation engine powered by business analytics influenced consumer behavior and purchasing decisions?

Answer: Amazon's recommendation engine, built by sophisticated data analytics, has significantly influenced consumer behavior and purchasing decisions by creating a personalized shopping experience. By analyzing large amounts of data that include past purchases, browsing habits, and even what other customers in similar profiles have bought, Amazon can suggest relevant products customized to the interests of the individual. This level of customization improves the shopping experience and makes it more enjoyable for users as they discover products they might not have found otherwise. These recommendations increase conversion rates, as consumers are more likely to purchase items that align with their personal preferences. The effectiveness of this strategy can be seen in the statistics surrounding Amazon's sales, where a significant portion of revenue has been credited to products recommended through this engine. Finally, the recommendation system creates new consumer loyalty, encouraging repeated visits and purchases, and ultimately supports Amazon's dominance in the e-commerce market.

**Question 2**

Discuss how predictive analytics has contributed to Amazon's supply chain optimization and inventory management.

Answer: Predictive analytics has been a main factor in Amazon's ability to optimize its supply chain and manage inventory effectively. By leveraging historical sales data, market trends, and seasonal buying patterns, Amazon can accurately forecast demand for various products with remarkable accuracy. Next, this predictive capability enables Amazon to proactively manage inventory levels to ensure that popular items are restored in a timely manner while minimizing excess inventory costs. For example, by analyzing data from multiple sources that include consumer behavior and external factors like holidays and promotions, Amazon can determine which products are likely to see increased demand to improve its responsiveness to meet that demand. This situation results in reduced costs associated with storage and markdowns and maximizes customer satisfaction by ensuring that products are available when needed. Finally, the integration of predictive analytics into supply chain processes has led to improved operational efficiency, higher profitability, and a strengthened competitive advantage for Amazon in the e-commerce market.

**Question 3**

How has Amazon's strategic use of business analytics affected its overall profitability and market share in the e-commerce industry?

Answer: Amazon's strategic use of business analytics has significantly impacted its overall profitability and market share in the e-commerce industry by enabling data-driven decision-making and operational excellence. The incorporation of advanced analytics into various aspects of the business that include marketing and product recommendations to supply chain management has enabled Amazon to differentiate itself in a crowded marketplace. By improving consumer experience through personalized recommendations and ensuring product availability through predictive analytics, Amazon has attracted a large consumer base that frequently returns to the online platform. Next, precise inventory management reduces costs associated with excess stock and stockouts to contribute to higher profit margins. As a result, the combination of increased sales conversions and cost efficiencies has strengthened Amazon's profitability to enable the company to invest further in technology, infrastructure, and customer service. This continuous cycle of data-driven improvement has advanced Amazon to control a superior market share and to solidify its position as a leader in the global e-commerce market.

## Netflix

Originally a DVD rental service, Netflix transformed its business model by implementing data analytics to understand viewer preferences and behavior. By analyzing consumer data, Netflix developed a recommendation algorithm that suggests shows and movies based on individual viewing patterns. This new analytical approach not only improved user engagement but also strengthened data-driven content creation decisions by the company. As a result, Netflix successfully produced original series, which contributed significantly to subscriber growth and transformed the company into a leading global streaming service.

### Question 1

How did Netflix's use of data analytics contribute to its transition from a DVD rental service to a leading streaming platform?

Answer: Netflix's transition from a DVD rental service to a leading streaming platform was mainly driven by its innovative use of data analytics. By collecting and analyzing large amounts of consumer viewing data, Netflix gained new knowledge into viewer preferences, habits, and trends. This information enabled the company to develop a sophisticated recommendation algorithm that personalized the user experience by suggesting content aligned with individual viewing patterns. The improved viewer engagement resulting from these personalized recommendations encouraged consumers to stay longer on the platform. Next, the new knowledge from data analytics informed Netflix's content creation strategy to enable the company to produce original series and films that connected with its subscribers. This strategic shift not only attracted new subscribers but also developed a loyal viewer base to set Netflix's position as a leader in the global streaming industry.

### Question 2

What role did Netflix's recommendation algorithm play in enhancing user engagement, and what impact did this have on the company's growth?

Answer: Netflix's recommendation algorithm played a crucial role in enhancing user engagement by providing personalized content suggestions that accommodated to the individual's viewing preferences. The algorithm analyzed user behavior, such as previous watch history, ratings, and even the time of day when users typically watch content. By developing a customized viewing experience, Netflix made it easier for subscribers to discover new shows and movies while also encouraging longer streaming sessions. This increase in engagement translated into higher subscriber retention rates, which was essential for a subscription-based model. Finally, as users became more invested in the platform due to appropriate content recommendations, Netflix experienced significant subscriber growth and revenue increases, further solidifying its position in the competitive streaming market.

### Question 3

In what ways did data-driven content creation decisions contribute to Netflix's competitive edge in the entertainment industry?

Answer: Data-driven content creation decisions significantly contributed to Netflix's competitive edge by allowing the company to align its productions closely with viewer preferences and market demands. By leveraging knowledge gained from viewing patterns and consumer feedback, Netflix could identify trends and gaps in content offerings to enable them to develop original series and films that appealed to specific audience segments. Examples include investing in genres or themes that garnered high viewer interest, ensuring that production budgets were allocated to projects with the highest potential for success. Next, by analyzing the success of released content, Netflix continually refined its strategy to make data-driven decisions about renewals and new acquisitions. This evidence and data-driven approach to content creation and curation not only differentiated Netflix from traditional broadcasters but also accelerated its growth trajectory to attract a diverse global audience and establish the platform as a powerhouse in the entertainment industry.

## Starbucks

Starbucks used business analytics to improve customer engagement and its operational efficiency. The company used data to analyze customer buying patterns, preferences, and purchasing behaviors across its various locations. By tracking these key performance metrics, Starbucks identified new opportunities to personalize its marketing efforts that included offering customized promotions through its online store and app. Data-driven decisions also allowed Starbucks to optimize its menu offerings and adjust its optimal level of products within its inventory management system. This approach has resulted in increased consumer loyalty and higher sales to demonstrate the power of business analytics in improving an already well-established brand.

### Question 1

How has Starbucks utilized business analytics to enhance customer engagement, and what specific methods have they implemented?

Answer: Starbucks has effectively utilized business analytics to enhance customer engagement by analyzing data related to customer buying patterns, preferences, and purchasing behaviors. By leveraging the knowledge gathered from their loyalty program and mobile app, Starbucks can segment their customer base and understand the unique preferences of different market demographics. This information allows for the customization of marketing efforts that include personalized promotions and targeted advertising campaigns that resonate with specific customer segments. For instance, Starbucks can send special offers on a customer's favorite beverage or promote seasonal products that align with consumer tastes. Next, Starbucks uses techniques such as A/B testing on promotions and menu offerings to determine which campaigns yield the highest engagement rates. This analytics and data-driven approach develops a stronger connection with consumers and ultimately leads to an increase in loyalty and satisfaction.

### Question 2

In what ways has data-driven decision-making improved Starbucks's operational efficiency, particularly regarding inventory management and menu offerings?

Answer: Data-driven decision-making has significantly improved Starbucks's operational efficiency, particularly in inventory management and menu offerings. By analyzing purchasing data across its various locations, Starbucks can identify trends and predict consumer demand for specific products. This strategy enables the company to adjust its inventory levels to ensure that popular items are adequately stocked while minimizing excess inventory of less popular products. Next, data analytics enables Starbucks to enhance its menu offerings based on consumer preferences and seasonal trends. For example, if data indicates an increase in demand for cold beverages during warmer months, Starbucks can focus on promoting those items and adjusting its supply chain to meet increased demand. This proactive approach not only reduces waste and operational costs but also improves consumer satisfaction by guaranteeing that popular products are constantly available when consumers want them most.

**Question 3**

Discuss the impact of personalization in marketing strategies on consumer loyalty for Starbucks, and provide examples of how this is achieved through business analytics.

Answer: Personalization in marketing strategies has a major impact on consumer loyalty to Starbucks since it makes customers feel valued and understood. Through comprehensive data analysis, Starbucks can customize its promotional strategies to meet the unique preferences of individual consumers. For example, the Starbucks Rewards program uses data to track consumer purchases and deliver personalized offers that include discounts on frequently bought items or birthday rewards to develop a sense of appreciation among customers. Next, personalized emails and app notifications that highlight new products based on past purchases create a more engaging experience for users. By consistently using knowledge from data and business analytics to personalize marketing efforts, Starbucks builds a stronger emotional connection with its consumers that results in increased loyalty, repeat visits, and higher overall sales. The effectiveness of this data-driven approach demonstrates the importance of personalization in driving customer engagement and loyalty in today's competitive market.

## Airbnb

Airbnb relies on business analytics to improve their user's experience and to optimize pricing strategies for hosts. By analyzing data on booking patterns, seasonal travel trends, and consumer reviews, Airbnb provides host recommendations on pricing adjustments to maximize occupancy rates for each location. This data-driven approach enables hosts to meet market demand effectively while boosting their earning potential. Next, Airbnb uses business analytics to identify which areas are experiencing increased travel interest to help create direct-target marketing strategies. The result has been a significant growth in platform usage and an expansion of global market share for Airbnb.

**Question 1**

How has Airbnb leveraged business analytics to enhance the experience for both guests and hosts, particularly in terms of pricing strategies?

Answer: Airbnb has used business analytics to enhance the user experience for both guests and hosts by implementing data-driven pricing strategies that boost occupancy rates. By analyzing booking patterns, seasonal travel trends, and consumer feedback, Airbnb can deliver actionable knowledge and strategies to hosts about how to price their listings competitively. For example, the online platform provides recommendations based on historical data that includes peak travel seasons and local events that enable hosts to adjust their rates dynamically. The adaptability and flexibility help hosts capitalize on increased demand during busy periods while maintaining favorable pricing during off-peak times. As a result, guests benefit from more appropriately priced accommodation to improve their overall experience. This reciprocal relationship between hosts and guests facilitated by business analytics not only maximizes earning potential for hosts but also ensures that guests find suitable options that meet their budgets and preferences.

### Question 2

In what ways does Airbnb utilize business analytics to identify emerging travel trends and consumer preferences, and how does this influence their marketing strategies?

Answer: Airbnb uses business analytics to identify emerging travel trends and consumer preferences through the analysis of various data points that include booking histories, search queries, and demographic information. By assessing which locations and types of accommodations are gaining popularity, Airbnb can pinpoint specific areas experiencing increased travel interest. This strategy allows the platform to develop targeted marketing strategies that specifically address these market segments. For example, if data reveals a rising interest in eco-friendly stays in a particular region, Airbnb can promote listings that emphasize sustainable practices in that market. Next, Airbnb can use predictive analytics to predict future travel patterns to enable proactive marketing campaigns that emphasize trending destinations or seasonal attractions. Finally, this data-driven approach not only enhances Airbnb's relevance in the market but also establishes a deeper connection with travelers seeking unique experiences and ultimately drives platform usage and expands the company's market share.

### Question 3

Discuss the impact of Airbnb's data-driven approach on its overall growth and competitive positioning within the hospitality industry.

Answer: Airbnb's data-driven approach has had a significant impact on its overall growth and competitive positioning within the hospitality industry. By effectively relying on business analytics to understand customer behaviors, market trends, and pricing dynamics, Airbnb has distinguished itself from traditional hospitality providers. This dependence on data enables the platform to deliver personalized recommendations and dynamic pricing options that enhance the user experience and maximize the revenue opportunities for hosts. Next, the new knowledge gained from analytics supports strategic decision-making when entering new markets or adjusting marketing efforts to ensure that Airbnb remains flexible and responsive to changes in consumer demand. The company's ability to use data effectively has enabled it to innovate continuously, maintaining its appeal to both travelers and hosts even in a competitive environment. As a result, Airbnb has expanded its global market share while also strengthening its position as a leader in the hospitality industry, attracting a diverse range of users and fostering brand loyalty in an increasingly digital global environment.

## Zillow

Zillow is an online real estate marketplace. The company employs sophisticated business analytics to provide new insights into the housing market and property valuations of various locations. By gathering and mining large amounts of data that include property prices, historical sales, market trends, and demographic information, Zillow analyzes all the economic indicators that affect the housing market. Next, Zillow uses predictive modeling to estimate home values through its Zestimate feature. By breaking down data geographically and regionally, the analytical program provides users with an exact understanding of real estate trends.

Homebuyers, sellers, and real estate agents can use these data-driven insights when making informed decisions, improving market transparency and trust in the home-buying process.

**Question 1**

How has Zillow's use of sophisticated business analytics transformed the way users engage with the real estate market?

Answer: Zillow's implementation of advanced business analytics has profoundly transformed user engagement with the real estate market by providing accessible and actionable data-driven knowledge. By collecting and analyzing extensive datasets that include property prices, historical sales, market trends, and demographic information, Zillow prepares home-buyers, sellers, and real estate agents with comprehensive tools to manage the complexities of real estate transactions. The introduction of features like the Zestimate provides users with estimated property values based on predictive modeling that enables them to estimate market conditions more accurately. This high level of transparency allows users to make informed decisions, whether they are buying, selling, or investing in properties. Next, Zillow's geographic and regional data segmentation helps users understand local market distinctions to further improve their level of personalized engagement with the platform. As a result, users are more empowered in their decision-making processes, and Zillow can create a stronger amount of trust and confidence in operating the real estate market.

**Question 2**

Discuss the role of predictive modeling in Zillow's Zestimate feature and how it impacts homebuyers and sellers.

Answer: Predictive modeling plays a critical role in Zillow's Zestimate feature that enables the platform to provide highly informed estimates of home values. By applying advanced algorithms to a wide range of data inputs that include historical sales data, property characteristics, and current market trends, Zillow can forecast property values with a high degree of accuracy that assists both the homebuyer and seller. This feature assists homebuyers in assessing whether a property's asking price aligns with market value and allows them to make educated offers or negotiate better deals. For sellers, Zestimate can guide pricing strategies to ensure properties are competitively priced to attract buyers while maximizing sale potential. Next, the transparency provided by this predictive modeling improves market trust since homebuyers and sellers can base their decisions on data rather than speculation. Finally, the Zestimate feature empowers users by thoroughly explaining the valuation process and facilitating more informed transaction decisions.

**Question 3**

In what ways does Zillow's approach to data analysis improve market transparency and trust among real estate stakeholders?

Answer: Zillow's data-driven approach significantly enhances market transparency and developing trust among real estate stakeholders, which include buyers, sellers, and agents. By collecting and analyzing large amounts of data from a diversity of sources, Zillow presents an accurate picture of market conditions and property values and eliminates much of the confusion generally associated with real estate transactions. Next, the availability of interactive data visualizations and knowledge into market trends assists users in understanding local dynamics and empowers them to make informed, data-driven decisions based on facts rather than guessing. Finally, the Zestimate feature promotes transparency by providing estimated home values established in detailed statistical analysis that can be verified against actual sale prices. This open access to information not only levels the playing field between buyers and sellers but also enhances the credibility of real estate professionals who leverage Zillow's data in their practices. Finally, the prioritizing of transparency through comprehensive data analysis enables Zillow to create a trusted environment that encourages productive interactions and relationships among all real estate stakeholders.

## Zara

Zara is a leading fast-fashion retailer headquartered in Spain. The company has thrived by using data analytics to streamline its supply chain and product offerings. The company collects real-time data from store sales, consumer feedback, and market trends to support data-driven decisions about inventory and styles. By analyzing this data, Zara quickly adapts its product line based on data from consumer demand and allows time for new and quick design and manufacturing cycles. This flexibility ensures that Zara maintains its competitive advantage by delivering trendy products that better align with consumer preferences and will ultimately increase profitability and brand loyalty.

### Question 1

How has Zara's use of data analytics contributed to its ability to respond quickly to changing consumer preferences and market trends?

Answer: Zara's use of data analytics has been fundamental in allowing the company to respond quickly to changing consumer preferences and market trends. By collecting real-time data from store sales, online feedback, and social media, Zara has gained real-time insights into what customers prefer and want. This data-driven approach enables the company to track which styles are selling well or not to allow for just-in-time inventory adjustments. Next, the analysis of consumer feedback helps Zara identify new trends and preferences that may not be immediately known from sales data itself. This adaptability and responsiveness are complemented by Zara's vertically integrated supply chain, which allows for immediate design and manufacturing cycles. As a result, Zara can introduce new products in a matter of weeks rather than months, to guarantee that its product offerings are always reflecting the current trends, and maintain a high level of consumer interest and engagement.

### Question 2

In what ways has Zara's data-driven approach to inventory management enhanced its operational efficiency and profitability?

Answer: Zara's data-driven approach to inventory management has significantly enriched its operational efficiency and profitability. By leveraging data analytics, Zara can accurately forecast demand for different products based on real-time sales data, market trends, and consumer behavior patterns. This strategy allows the company to optimize inventory levels and minimize excess stock while also ensuring that popular items are easily available. This level of precision prevents lost sales opportunities due to stockouts and reduces the costs associated with overstocking and clearance sales for the company. Next, data analytics enables Zara to customize its inventory to specific geographic markets that align product offerings with local tastes and preferences. This strategic alignment improves profitability since it increases the probability of sales while decreasing company waste. Finally, Zara's effective inventory management, powered by data analytics, leads to improved consumer satisfaction and higher profit margins.

**Question 3**

Discuss how Zara's ability to adapt its product offerings based on data analytics influences brand loyalty among consumers.

Answer: Zara's ability to adapt its product offerings based on data analytics plays a critical role in influencing brand loyalty among consumers. By constantly analyzing data from sales, customer feedback, and market trends, Zara can stay attuned to the evolving preferences of its target audience. This commitment to responsiveness results in a product line that repeatedly reflects the latest fashion trends and entices consumers to return for new arrivals. Next, Zara's emphasis on quality design and stylish options develops a sense of exclusivity and desirability that improves the overall consumer experience. When consumers understand that Zara not only listens to their feedback but also acts upon it, this situation creates trust and loyalty toward the brand. The ability to continuously deliver popular, relevant products ensures that consumers feel valued and are directly connected to the brand. As a result, this situation establishes their long-term loyalty and encourages repeat business in a highly competitive retail environment.

## CASE STUDIES ON ENTREPRENEURSHIP SUCCESS THROUGH ANALYTICS

### Business Success Through Business Analytics

Business analytics plays a crucial role in understanding entrepreneurship trends and consumer behavior, which enables organizations in the entrepreneurship industry to make more data-driven and informed decisions. Following are three examples of how entrepreneurship data and knowledge are translated into business success using analytics.

### Example 1: TechGuru Solutions

TechGuru Solutions specializes in developing cutting-edge software tools for small businesses. By using advanced business analytics, TechGuru has been able to identify emerging trends and customer needs while allowing them to create products that are both innovative and highly relevant. TechGuru uses data analytics to gather information from consumer feedback and market trends. This approach enables them to customize their software solutions to meet the specific needs of their target audience, ensuring high customer satisfaction and loyalty. Next, the company uses a flexible business model that allows for rapid duplication and deployment of new features. By analyzing user data, they can quickly adapt their offerings to changing market demands, maintaining a competitive edge. Finally, TechGuru uses predictive analytics to identify potential markets for expansion by analyzing demographic and economic data to strategically enter new markets with a high chance of success.

*Short-Response Questions*

1. What approach does TechGuru use to ensure their products meet customer needs?
2. How does TechGuru maintain a competitive edge in the market?
3. What tool does TechGuru use to identify potential markets for expansion?

### Example 2: WaveVerde Enterprises

WaveVerde Enterprises is a company focused on sustainable energy solutions. By integrating business analytics into their operations, they have successfully positioned themselves as leaders in the renewable energy sector. WaveVerde uses analytics to measure the environmental impact of their products. This data-driven approach helps them improve their sustainability practices and appeal to eco-conscious consumers. Next, by analyzing supply chain data, WaveVerde identifies inefficiencies and implements strategies to reduce costs and improve delivery times, enhancing overall operational efficiency. Finally, WaveVerde uses advanced analytics to segment their customer base, allowing for targeted marketing campaigns that increase conversion rates and customer engagement.

*Short-Response Questions*

1. How does WaveVerde improve their sustainability practices?
2. What benefit does WaveVerde gain from supply chain optimization?
3. What strategy does WaveVerde use to enhance their marketing efforts?

### Example 3: Healthy Innovations

Healthy Innovations is a company that develops wearable health devices. By employing the power of business analytics, they have revolutionized the way consumers monitor their health. Healthy Innovations uses analytics to collect data from their devices, enabling continuous product improvements and personalized user experiences. Next, by analyzing health and wellness trends, Healthy Innovations can anticipate consumer needs and develop products that align with emerging health priorities. Finally, Healthy Innovations uses analytics to identify potential partners in the health-care industry, facilitating collaborations that enhance their product offerings and expand their market reach.

*Short-Response Questions*

1. How does Healthy Innovations ensure continuous product improvement?
2. What does Healthy Innovations analyze to anticipate consumer needs?
3. How does Healthy Innovations expand their market reach?

## CASE STUDY: FLYTHECOOP SOLUTIONS

FlytheCoop Solutions is an entrepreneurial company dedicated to providing eco-friendly home improvement products and services. The company focuses on sustainable living and offers a range of items from solar panels and energy-efficient appliances to biodegradable home goods. FlytheCoop serves environmentally conscious homeowners and businesses by promoting a greener lifestyle through education and innovative products. In just over a year, FlytheCoop has gained considerable market share with a growing consumer base and an increasing positive reputation as a trusted provider of green solutions.

In its first year, FlytheCoop Solutions achieved impressive sales figures. The company generated $1.5 million in revenue and expanded its consumer base to over 1,000 satisfied clients. FlytheCoop secured funding through a combination of angel investors and a successful crowdfunding campaign totaling $750,000. These funds were strategically invested in product development, marketing, and creating partnerships with local eco-friendly suppliers and distributors. As environmental concerns prevail more globally, the demand for sustainable products continues to rise and places FlytheCoop favorably for additional market share and growth.

However, despite its initial success, FlytheCoop Solutions currently faces challenges in understanding consumer behavior, effectively managing inventory, and expanding its marketing campaigns. To manage these challenges, the company is focused on leveraging business analytics and statistics to gain new insights from consumer data, sales trends, and product performance. By focusing on data-driven decision-making, FlytheCoop wants to refine its product offerings, improve consumer experience, and effectively strategize for long-term growth in the competitive eco-friendly market environment.

### Business Analytics Data Tables

**TABLE 3.2** Monthly Sales Data

| 1 | A | B | C | D |
|---|---|---|---|---|
| | Month | Total Sales (USD) | Number of Transactions | Average Transaction Value (USD) |
| 2 | January | $150,000 | 250 | $600 |
| 3 | February | $180,000 | 300 | $600 |
| 4 | March | $200,000 | 350 | $571 |
| 5 | April | $220,000 | 400 | $550 |
| 6 | May | $250,000 | 450 | $556 |
| 7 | June | $300,000 | 500 | $600 |
| 8 | July | $280,000 | 550 | $509 |
| 9 | August | $320,000 | 600 | $533 |
| 10 | September | $340,000 | 700 | $486 |
| 11 | October | $360,000 | 750 | $480 |
| 12 | November | $380,000 | 800 | $475 |
| 13 | December | $400,000 | 850 | $471 |

**TABLE 3.3** Customer Satisfaction Ratings

| 1 | A | B | C | D |
|---|---|---|---|---|
| | **Customer ID** | **Product Purchased** | **Satisfaction Rating** | **Purchase Frequency** |
| 2 | 1 | Solar panel | 5 | 2 |
| 3 | 2 | LED bulb | 4 | 3 |
| 4 | 3 | Biodegradable bags | 5 | 1 |
| 5 | 4 | Energy-efficient oven | 3 | 2 |
| 6 | 5 | Compost bin | 5 | 1 |
| 7 | 6 | Rainwater collector | 4 | 1 |
| 8 | 7 | Reusable straws | 4 | 4 |
| 9 | 8 | Solar charger | 5 | 3 |
| 10 | 9 | Eco-friendly paint | 3 | 1 |
| 11 | 10 | Insulation material | 5 | 2 |
| 12 | 11 | Energy-efficient fridge | 4 | 4 |
| 13 | 12 | Smart thermostat | 5 | 2 |
| 14 | 13 | Bamboo toothbrush | 4 | 4 |
| 15 | 14 | Water filter | 5 | 1 |
| 16 | 15 | Eco-friendly toilet | 5 | 3 |
| 17 | 16 | Rechargeable batteries | 3 | 1 |
| 18 | 17 | Organic fertilizer | 4 | 2 |
| 19 | 18 | Electric lawn mower | 5 | 2 |
| 20 | 19 | Recycled shower curtain | 4 | 3 |
| 21 | 20 | Indoor air purifier | 5 | 1 |

## Analytics Problems Using Excel

FlytheCoop wants to refine its product offerings, improve consumer experience, and effectively strategize for long-term growth in the competitive eco-friendly market environment. Using the information provided, perform the following task in Excel to present in a report to the leadership team:

1. *Frequency of customer ratings of FlytheCoop.* Create a frequency distribution of customer satisfaction ratings (1–5) based on Table 3.2. Excel Functions: Use the FREQUENCY function or create a PivotTable.
2. *Distribution of purchases per customer of FlytheCoop.* Calculate the frequency distribution for purchase frequency among customers. Excel Functions: Use the COUNTIF function or a PivotTable to summarize the purchase frequencies.
3. *Sales distribution analysis of FlytheCoop.* Construct a histogram for total sales per month from Table 3.1. Excel Functions: Use the Histogram Chart option in Excel.
4. *Average satisfaction rating of FlytheCoop.* Determine the average satisfaction rating across all customers. Excel Functions: Use the AVERAGE function to compute this from Table 3.2.

5. *Sales variability calculation of FlytheCoop.* Analyze the variability of total sales using standard deviation. Excel Functions: Use the STDEV.P function to calculate standard deviation for sales.
6. *Visualization of sales trends of FlytheCoop.* Generate a line chart displaying the sales trend over the 12 months. Excel Functions: Create a line chart from the monthly sales data.

### Answer Key

1. *Frequency of customer ratings: FlytheCoop.* Use FREQUENCY to show counts for ratings 1 through 5.
2. *Distribution of purchases per customer: FlytheCoop.* Calculation using COUNTIF might yield:

   Frequency 1: 8 customers
   Frequency 2: 4 customers
   Frequency 3: 4 customers
   Frequency 4: 4 customers
3. *Sales distribution histogram: FlytheCoop.* Creating a histogram will create a visual representation of the distribution of total sales across the 12 months.
4. *Average satisfaction rating: FlytheCoop.* Output = AVERAGE(Range of Satisfaction Ratings) = 4.2.
5. *Sales variability calculation: FlytheCoop.* Output = STDEV.P(Total Sales from Table) = $74,385.
6. *Sales trends visualization: FlytheCoop.* A line chart is generated to visually represent the sales growth, illustrating trends, peaks, and troughs over the year.

CHAPTER 4

# Marketing Analytics

## UNDERSTANDING CUSTOMER SEGMENTATION

Marketing analytics is an important component of business analytics since it provides data-driven information and results in the organization's understanding of promotional strategies, consumer behavior, and gaining a competitive advantage in the environment. With marketing analytics, an organization can combine the techniques of large-scale data mining, predictive modeling, and statistical analysis to accurately determine the performance of the market and enable organizational leaders and managers to implement a data decision-making culture within their internal and external environments. With the information gained from marketing analytics, a company can implement the correct processes that are essential for ensuring effective consumer segmentation, focusing on target and niche markets, and developing new promotions and strategies that will increase market share by meeting the diverse needs of various groups of stakeholders.

Next, marketing analytics is required for an organizational leader to examine and disseminate large amounts of data to identify underlying trends and patterns that include the analysis of purchasing preferences and behaviors of customers. Next, market analytics will use descriptive statistics to gain knowledge and information into the past performance of the company to help the business better understand what was successful and to identify areas of improvement. Diagnostic analytics will also be used to help leaders and managers understand the true meaning and outcome of these situations by providing a logical explanation for marketing strategies and consumer behavior patterns. Predictive analytics is used within marketing analytics to make accurate predictions and forecasts about the success of the company based on historical data and previous trends. Finally, marketing analytics will use the statistical technique of prescriptive analytics. Prescriptive analytics provides knowledge on actionable solutions and recommendations based on data instead of intuition to improve organizational efficiency and effectiveness.

With the combination of these various techniques, marketing leaders can use analytics to segment the consumer market and focus on their core group of clients based on purchase history, in-person and online transactions, and demographics. Once the consumer profile has been identified, the leadership team can begin incorporating marketing analytics using technology that includes machine learning and artificial intelligence (AI) to improve the

DOI: 10.4324/9781003629658-4

decision-making process. Machine learning and AI will possess the ability to process and analyze large amounts of datasets and to gain meaning and insight. As a result of marketing analytics and technology, marketing leaders will ultimately be able to develop more effective marketing strategies and consumer segmentation to develop long-term engagement, sustainability, and growth and increase the return on investment (ROI).

## Techniques for Dividing Customers Into Actionable Segments

In marketing analytics, there are techniques for dividing customers into actional segments. *Marketing analytics* is a discipline that requires the systematic analysis of data and information associated with marketing performance. The marketing analytics process uses various strategies and technologies that are used to collect information that is used to improve the overall effectiveness of the business operation. The main goal of marketing analytics is to determine the best way to measure and improve the influence of marketing promotions that ensure that organizational resources are dedicated to ensuring success with their segmented target market. As a result, consumer segmentation enables companies to customize their marketing messages and promotions to meet the various and unique needs of the customer to improve the longevity of engagement and the conversion of new clients.

For marketing analytics and consumer segmentation to be successful, there are different methods that can be used to divide customers into groups. The first method is demographic segmentation. This method requires the categorization or placing of consumers based on demographic factors that include ethnic background, income, education, gender, and age. When these characteristics are analyzed, the organization can develop more precise targeted marketing strategies that identify with the choices and preferences of each demographic group.

The second method is geographic segmentation. Geographic segmentation analyzes and focuses on the location of each customer. The location of the customer is important since it will directly influence their personal purchasing preferences and behaviors. With this technique, the company can become more flexible and adapt their marketing strategies to focus on cultural preferences, regional trends, and climate needs to ensure that the message contained within their promotion is effective and relevant to the market segment.

The third method is psychographic segmentation. This strategy enables businesses to understand the values, interest, personalities, and lifestyle of each market segment. It is important for companies to know what factors motivate their consumers beyond the typical and broad demographics so they can develop a more personalized message that establishes connection on a deeper level. The fourth method is behavioral segmentation. Using this approach includes the analysis of consumer behavior objectives, such as product usage, purchasing patterns and preferences, and short- and long-term engagement, through marketing campaigns. Next, behavior segmentation enables segmentation of the consumer market based on how customers interact with a brand. As a result, this strategy allows organization to accurately identify priority consumers, potential customer turnover, and the opportunities to upsell or cross-sell products and services.

The fifth method is recency, frequency, and monetary analysis (RFM). RFM is a business analytics technique that uses a quantitative method that segments consumers based solely on

**TABLE 4.1** Consumer Segmentation Techniques

| Segmentation Method | Description | Advantages | Disadvantages |
|---|---|---|---|
| **Demographic segmentation** | Divides the market based on age, gender, income, education, etc. | Easy to collect data; straightforward to implement | May overlook individual differences; can be too broad |
| **Geographic segmentation** | Divides the market based on location such as country, region, city, etc. | Useful for regional marketing; easy to collect data | May ignore other important factors; can be too broad |
| **Psychographic segmentation** | Divides the market based on lifestyle, values, interests, etc. | Provides deeper insights into consumer behavior; can be very targeted | Harder to collect data; more complex to implement |
| **Behavioral segmentation** | Divides the market based on consumer behavior, such as purchase history, usage rate, etc. | Highly relevant to marketing strategies; can be very targeted | Requires detailed data; can be complex to analyze |
| **RFM analysis** | Evaluates customers based on recency, frequency, and monetary value of purchases | Helps identify high-value customers; data-driven | Requires detailed transaction data; may not capture all customer behaviors |
| **Cluster analysis** | Uses statistical methods to group customers based on similarities | Can reveal hidden patterns; highly customizable | Requires advanced statistical knowledge; complex to implement |

their purchasing behaviors. Next, the *recency* in RFM takes into consideration how consumers make recent purchases. *Frequency* focuses on how often consumers make a purchase. Third, *monetary* refers to the amount of money consumers spend on purchases. As a result, this technique enables marketing leaders to properly identify their loyal consumers, potential support, and how to re-engage with previous clients.

The final method is cluster analysis. Cluster analysis relies on techniques that require data mining and analyzing the results of consumers based on their similarities and other various factors. Next, cluster analysis identifies and focuses on the true segments that are found within the consumer base of the market. This situation enables companies to recognize specific and distinct consumer groups that may have been overlooked or ignored. As a result, when these various consumer segmentation methods are used, organizations can benefit from a new understanding of their customer base and how to create new effective marketing strategies to improve engagement, develop long-term brand loyalty, and increase profitability.

## DATA-DRIVEN CAMPAIGN STRATEGY DEVELOPMENT

Marketing analytics plays an important role in the development of data-driven campaign strategies while providing organizations with the knowledge necessary to make informed data-driven decisions that are strategically aligned with consumer preferences and the demand of the market. Next, marketing analytics will systematically evaluate data that was collected from various sources, which include consumer transactions, website performance, and interactions on social media platforms. As a result of this analysis, businesses in various sectors can gain a more comprehensive understanding of the behavior and preferences of their target market.

In the retail industry, data-driven campaign strategy development supports marketing analytics to track consumer interactions across multiple avenues. In the e-commerce sector, marketing analytics will enable the optimization of online shopping experiences. Companies have the capability to collect and study all data associated with website traffic, conversion metrics, and the abandonment of online cart products. With the availability of this information, the business can identify all potential barriers to consumer purchasing and then implement new improvements to boost the shopping experience. One method is to implement focused email promotions with product recommendations to specific market segments. Another method is to use A/B testing so e-commerce companies can test the effectiveness of different marketing messages and measure the yield of each variation sent to consumers.

Organizations in the technology sector will rely on marketing analytics to allow businesses to effectively engage with clients more effectively with the use of focused messages that relate to the specific consumer segment. As an example, a start-up software company can analyze its user data to identify the preferred features and problem areas. Once these areas have been pinpointed, the software company can create new marketing messages that emphasize the changes and solutions to the stated problems. As a result of this approach, the software company will have implemented a data-driven approach that ensures all communication channels are important, an increase consumer loyalty, and long-term brand engagement.

Next, the use of predictive analytics in marketing analytics is a main component of data-driven campaign strategy development. By understanding and using historical data to forecast anticipated trends, the organization can better predict the preferences and needs of the consumer while becoming more proactive in designing effective marketing campaigns. Finally, effective marketing analytics will result in new data-driven strategies that are more aligned with the needs of the customer while also becoming more flexible and adaptable to changes in the conditions of the market. When the environment changes, businesses that rely on data-driven decisions will become better positioned to gain market share, enter emerging markets, and develop long-term satisfaction and brand loyalty.

### Analytics in Designing Effective Marketing Campaigns

Marketing analytics is the process of measuring, analyzing, and managing market performance to maximize promotions and campaigns to increase return on investment (ROI) for the organization. This process involves collecting and analyzing data from different marketing channels to enable the leader or manager to gain better insight into the behavior and preferences of the consumer to determine the overall effectiveness of the marketing strategies of the company. The primary focus of marketing analytics is to gather data from various sources that include consumer feedback, online interactions, social media, and email messages. The data that is collected is quantitative in nature and includes information such as sales figures and click-through rates. However, qualitative data is also collected, including survey responses and consumer reviews of products and services. As a result, analyzing this information allows marketers to identify trends, assess marketing campaign performance, and understand the underlying factors that drive consumer engagement and conversion processes.

There are several ways to use marketing analytics to design effective marketing campaigns to ensure that all company resources are used efficiently and effectively. Next, marketing analytics will be used to ensure all messaging channels directly connect with the target audience or market. There are several methodologies used within this process that include consumer segmentation, A/B testing, predictive analytics, performance tracking, attribution, and modeling. Consumer segmentation is achieved through the analysis of customer data so businesses can segment their audience into distinct groups based on factors that include preferences, behaviors, and demographics. With this segmentation, the organization can develop campaigns that are customized to meet the needs of consumers and will ultimately result in higher rates of engagement and improved client conversion within the market.

Next, A/B testing is a method that involves creating two variations of market elements in comparing their performance to each other. A/B testing enables marketers to identify which version connects more effectively with the target audience. As a result, the company will gain the ability to make better data-driven decisions for maximizing future marketing campaigns. Third, predictive analytics uses historical data to enable organizations to forecast future trends and consumer behaviors. Through the understanding of knowing which factors influence purchasing decisions, marketers can become proactive in designing campaigns and promotions that single out potential customers more effectively while also increasing the chance of conversion.

*Performance tracking* is the continuous monitoring of campaign performance that is necessary for us to determine marketing effectiveness. With marketing analytics, performance tracking will monitor key performance indicators that include conversion rates, return on ad spending, and click-through rates. As a result of this real-time feedback, marketing leaders can adjust campaigns and promotions to improve the overall performance of the marketing strategy. Finally, *attribution modeling* is used to determine how different marketing channels assist with the conversion of consumers necessary for maximizing the allocation of resources and budgeting. With attribution modeling, marketers will understand the process consumers take before making a purchase and can allow for more strategic investment in high-performing marketing channels when attempting to meet the needs and engage with the consumer market.

## MEASURING MARKETING ROI

Marketing analytics plays an important role in improving the effectiveness of marketing strategies in measuring ROI for all marketing activities within an organization. The data is systematically analyzed and collected from various marketing channels to enable organizations to make informed decisions that lead to improving performance in the maximization of resources. The knowledge that is gained through marketing analytics is invaluable to marketing industries throughout the global environment, which include retail, e-commerce, technology, and consumer goods.

The main function of marketing analytics is to evaluate the performance of marketing using reliable metrics. KPIs that include consumer acquisition costs, conversion rates, and consumer lifetime value enable the company to determine the effectiveness of their marketing strategies. As a result, measuring marketing ROI provides a clear understanding of what works and what does not. The situation allows organizations to improve and refine the marketing strategies to enhance the overall results of the business.

Measuring marketing ROI is necessary to the marketing analytics process. ROI enables businesses to determine their financial effectiveness of all marketing investments. A positive ROI will indicate that marketing strategies are creating a higher level of revenue, and the costs incurred. However, a negative ROI will indicate that the marketing strategies will need to be reassessed to allow for optimization and maximization in all marketing efforts. In the retail sector, marketing analytics provides companies with the ability to analyze consumer purchasing behaviors and preferences. This information helps marketers develop customized marketing campaigns that connect with specific consumer segments and ultimately lead to an increase in sales revenue.

In the e-commerce sector, marketing analytical tools allow companies to track user interactions on their websites, including product reviews and abandoned online shopping carts. Through the analysis of this data, e-commerce companies can create more personalized experiences through targeted email promotions and develop ads that re-target consumers to improve engagement and conversion rates. Third, marketing analytics in the technology sector helps businesses determine the impact of their promotional strategies on product adoption and consumer satisfaction. By using A/B testing, these companies can maximize their messaging techniques and reach the correct audience more effectively and efficiently. Finally, consumer goods companies will benefit from the use of marketing analytics by adapting their current strategies based on new market trends and emerging consumer preferences. With the use of social media analytics and surveys, these companies can better gauge the perception of their brand and then customize the marketing strategies as necessary.

## Frameworks for Evaluating Campaign Success

Marketing analytics requires frameworks for evaluating campaign success. In marketing analytics, there is a structured approach that contains various key components that include data collection, performance measurement, and actionable insights or knowledge. First, data collection is the foundation of an effective marketing analytics framework. Next, data collection involves the collection of data from various sources, including social media platforms, website analytics, online shopping carts, email marketing tools, and customer relationship management (CRM) systems. When this data is collected and aggregated, companies can create a comprehensive understanding of consumer interactions and engagement with their marketing strategies and campaigns.

The second framework is creating objectives and KPIs. To thoroughly evaluate the campaign success of an organization, it is necessary to define clear objectives and key performance indicators ahead of time. Objectives will include boosting sales conversions, improving website traffic, increasing brand awareness and loyalty. However, KPIs will include diversion rates, ROI, and consumer acquisition costs to provide quantifiable metrics for determining whether these objectives are achieved.

Third, performance management involves the analysis of collected data against established KPIs to determine the effectiveness of the marketing campaign. This situation requires multiple analytical tools to be used, including descriptive analytics, to summarize past performance measures, along with predictive analytics, to forecast future outcomes based on historical data. As a result, these methods allow marketers to properly identify patterns and trends in consumer behavior and help the company understand what was successful and what failed.

Fourth, *attribution modeling* is the process of understanding how different marketing channels contribute to consumer conversion rates that are important in evaluating the success of a campaign. Next, attribution modeling provides insight and knowledge into which channels are most effective in driving results through the marketing process. As a result, this process helps marketers allocate their budgets more efficiently and optimize future marketing campaigns.

Fifth, actionable insights and information are critical to marketing analytics to help support data-driven strategies in the future. Through identification directly connected with consumer markets in which they were not connected, marketers can make data-driven decisions to develop future marketing strategies. As a result, actionable insights and knowledge are part of the iterative process necessary for continuous improvement within the organization.

Finally, reporting and communication involve sharing findings with all stakeholder groups through clear and concise reports. This process helps to strategically align all team members and to communicate the successes and areas for improvement. Within reporting and communication, visualization tools and dashboards should be used to help improve the level of understanding and engagement with the data using charts and graphs for easy comprehension by the stakeholders. As a result, using a data-driven approach will help ensure future marketing campaigns are more effective, targeted, and strategically aligned with the needs of the consumer, ultimately improving the success of the company.

## PREDICTIVE ANALYTICS FOR CUSTOMER BEHAVIOR

Marketing analytics will rely on predictive analytics to determine customer behavior. One of the main components of marketing analytics is predictive analytics. Predictive analytics uses machine learning techniques, statistical algorithms, and data mining to forecast future consumer behaviors based on past data. This strategy enables companies to anticipate consumer needs and preferences, which ultimately results in a greater competitive advantage within the market. This strategy can be seen in various marketing industries, including retail, e-commerce, and telecommunications.

In the retail industry, predictive analytics enables companies to understand patterns of consumers' purchasing behavior, which include past sales data, peak shopping times, popular product categories, and seasonal trends. With this information, companies can customize promotions and improve their inventory management to strategically align with the predicted level of demand and to improve consumer satisfaction while increasing ROI. In the e-commerce industry, predictive analytics is used to create targeted marketing campaigns and personalized shopping experiences and to analyze consumer behavior on websites through the study of browsing habits, previous purchase history, and click-through rates. New marketing campaigns can include dynamic pricing strategies, re-targeted ads based on user interests, and personalized product recommendations.

In the telecommunications industry, predictive analytics are used by companies to study consumer data and to predict turnover rate while identifying at-risk situations. Through predictive analytics, companies can understand the factors and situations that lead to consumer attrition, which enables the company to implement new strategies focused on retaining their targeted market.

Finally, the financial services industry uses predictive analytics to understand consumer credit risk and behavior patterns. Through the analysis of historical transaction data, banks and other financial institutions can create models to predict loan defaults or potential for fraud. As a result of this knowledge, companies can become more responsible in their lending practices and focus on the marketing of financial products that directly align with correct customer profiles. This strategy allows marketing analytics to combine with advanced technologies, such as AI, to create predictive models so the company can continuously learn from new data and continually improve their prediction strategies in real time.

## Anticipating Consumer Actions Through Data Models

Marketing analytics is necessary for anticipating consumer actions through data models. First, marketing analytics requires a systematic collection and analysis of data from various sources, including sales history, social media engagements, online purchasing behavior, and consumer interactions. Once this information is collected, marketing analytics will rely on statistical and machine learning models to enable businesses to identify patterns and trends in data that correspond with the decisions and actions of customers. The situation relies on predictive modeling, which uses historical data to forecast future behaviors of consumers.

As an example, regression analysis can provide companies an understanding of the factors that influence purchases, while clustering techniques will segment customers into groups based on similar behaviors. With the use of these models, marketers can predict which consumers are more likely to respond to specific marketing campaigns or promotions, to ultimately develop a more precise targeted marketing strategy. Next, cohort analysis can be used to examine the behavior of groups of customers over time. This strategy involves determining how different cohorts interact with products and services so marketers can identify trends that may determine the shift or changes in consumer preferences or behavior. As a result, cohort analysis can inform marketers about product development strategies, consumer retention efforts, and promotional tactics required for the engagement and retention of consumers.

In the retail and e-commerce sectors, marketing analytics is important for understanding and anticipating the actions of customers. The situation will require the analysis of shopping patterns and purchase history of consumers so retailers can develop personalized recommendations for consumers. Next, retailers and e-commerce companies will need to develop advanced recommendation systems that are powered by AI and algorithms to enable the business to suggest products that will be properly aligned with the customers' past purchasing behavior and improve the chance of conversion of new consumers.

In the technology and telecommunications sectors of the market, marketing analytics will be used to predict the churn rate of consumers. This situation is achieved by studying the patterns associated with consumer feedback so organizations can identify customers that are at risk and to immediately implement new retention strategies. As a result of the situation, companies that offer customized promotions or improved service plans will ultimately reduce the rate of attrition and successfully address the concerns of consumers. Finally, the use of AI and marketing analytics will improve the ability to predict the actions of customers. AI algorithms will analyze complex and large-scale datasets to determine new insights that may not have been available or apparent through traditional human analysis. This new information will allow companies to adjust their marketing strategies in real time and respond to changes in consumer behavior and preferences dynamically within the global market.

## EMPLOYING SOCIAL MEDIA ANALYTICS

Marketing analytics employs social media analytics, which involves the analysis of data collected from online social media channels, which include TikTok, Facebook, Instagram (IG), LinkedIn, and Twitter. Next, the data collected from social media analytics contains performance metrics, such as shares, comments, likes, dislikes, growth of followers, and click-through rates. When these metrics are analyzed, organizations can determine and evaluate how their current content connects with their target audiences and can make the necessary refinements in their marketing messages and engagement strategies.

One of the main benefits of using social media analytics is the ability to track brand opinion. This situation is achieved through the analysis of reviews, comments, and user-generated content that organizations can use to determine the perception of the public of their brand while identifying potential areas for improvement. Opinion analysis relies on natural language processing to categorize sentiments expressed in all social media interactions and to help businesses understand whether their target audience feels positively, negatively, or neutral about their brand name. As a result, this information becomes invaluable in managing the reputation of the brand and in addressing all the concerns of the consumer in real time.

Next, engagement metrics are also used within social media analytics. Engagement metrics evaluate how users interact with online posts through comments, likes, dislikes, or shares, which marketers will then use to determine which types of content perform the most effectively. This information is used to lead to the creation of content strategies and to allow companies to focus on topics and formats that connect the best with their target market audiences. Third, social media analytics plays an important role in consumer segmentation. Through the analysis of behavioral and demographic data, companies can develop a detailed profile of their social media followers. With this segmentation, businesses can create more targeted advertising campaigns and guarantee that their messages reach their intended consumers. As a result, tracking campaign performance in real time with the assistance of social media analytics will empower companies to adapt their marketing strategies quickly and effectively. Marketers would determine the effectiveness of their marketing ads and content and make the necessary changes based on the results of the performance metrics.

### How Social Media Platforms Influence Consumer Insights

Marketing analytics and social media platforms will influence the insights of consumers. Social media platforms are powerful methods for communication and interaction between brands and customers. Next, social media platforms generate large amounts of data through comments, posts, likes, dislikes, and shares that enable marketers to accurately track consumer thoughts, sentiment, and preferences in real time. Once this information is collected, marketing analytics is used to decode and decipher the data to provide companies the ability to make data-driven and informed decisions based on the interactions of consumers.

The main way social media platforms influence customer insights is through sentiment analysis. Using natural language processing techniques, businesses can analyze user-generated content that includes reviews and comments to determine the overall sentiment or opinion toward a certain product or brand. This situation enables the analysis to help companies gauge the perception of the target market and enables them to address any negative thoughts or opinions proactively, along with taking advantage of all the positive feedback that is received to increase their brand reputation.

Next, marketing analytics provides the segmentation of consumer markets based on their interactions on social media. The situation requires the analysis of interest, demographic information, and online behavior for companies to develop a detailed customer profile. With this segmentation, marketers can customize content and campaigns to engage with specific audience groups, while ensuring the message remains relevant and increases the likelihood of long-term connections in support of the brand of the product or service.

Third, social media analytics produces new information and insight into emerging topics and consumer interests. The situation requires the monitoring and observation of keywords, conversations, and hashtags that are used in social media platforms to enable marketers to identify changes in the preferences and behaviors of consumers. With this information, businesses can help their brand stay ahead of the market trends by adapting their product or service offerings accordingly to ensure they are meeting the needs and wants of the target market.

Finally, marketing analytics is used to measure the effectiveness of marketing campaigns on social media. The situation will require the analysis of engagement metrics that include shares, conversion rates, and click-through rates. With the collection of this information, companies can determine which campaigns connect most effectively and efficiently with their target audience. As a result, this new information and this data allow for the maximization and optimization of future marketing campaigns. Marketers will also be able to focus their resources on marketing strategies that lead to the highest level of consumer engagement and ROI.

## MARKET BASKET ANALYSIS

Another important component in marketing analytics is market basket analysis. *Market basket analysis* involves the study of transaction data to identify patterns in consumer purchasing behaviors. The main goal of market basket analysis is to determine and identify which products or services are frequently bought together, to enable businesses to better understand the habits and preferences of consumers. The situation will require the use of algorithms like association rule and mining to provide businesses the ability to determine connections and associations between products and services not previously available.

In the retail sector, market basket analysis is important in recognizing the associations that enable the retailer to design strategic merchandising tactics that include product placement, bundled promotions, and offering discounts on related items. While this approach not only improves the shopping experience of the consumer but also increases the average value of each purchase transaction, in the e-commerce sector, market basket analysis is used to improve the online shopping experience. Through the analysis of consumers' browsing and purchasing histories, e-commerce companies can divide customized and personalized product recommendations. As a result, this personalized experience will significantly increase the conversion rates and satisfaction levels of the consumer market.

Within the consumer-packaged goods sector, market basket analysis helps in maximizing promotional strategies for the company. Company brands can analyze sales data to determine which products or services complement each other and develop bundled offers for customers. This situation enables a business to run joint promotions through marketing campaigns to increase sales and brand visibility based on new information and knowledge gained from marketing analytics.

Finally, market basket analysis assists with inventory management and supply chain optimization of companies. Through an understanding of which products are frequently purchased together, companies can improve shelf stocking practices and ensure that items related to the product are available at the same time. This strategy will reduce the level of stockouts while improving the level of consumer satisfaction. As a result, consumers are more likely to find all the items they wish to purchase on one shopping trip, which will increase sales and ROI.

## Techniques for Analyzing Purchasing Patterns

There are various techniques for analyzing purchasing patterns as part of the methodology within marketing analytics. Since marketing analytics is a systematic process of studying data related to marketing performance in consumer behavior, it will require the use of various analytical techniques so companies can gain new information and knowledge and make data-driven and informed strategic decisions to increase the effectiveness of their marketing strategies. One of the main areas of marketing analytics is the study of purchasing patterns by consumers. Understanding consumer purchasing patterns will enable companies to customize their marketing strategies to maximize their product offerings and improve the level of engagement with customers. As a result, there are several techniques used in marketing analytics to study purchasing patterns effectively.

The first technique is descriptive analysis. Descriptive analysis provides knowledge into key performance metrics that include frequency of purchases, product preferences, and sales volume. By studying past purchasing behavior, companies can gain a better understanding of the overall consumer trend in the market while improving future marketing strategies. The second technique is market basket analysis. Market basket analysis is used to identify the relationship between products that are purchased together. This strategy relies on the use of algorithms to uncover purchasing patterns in past transaction data. As a result, market basket analysis improves the shopping experience while increasing sales by encouraging complementary products to go with the original item.

The third technique is customer segmentation. Customer segmentation requires the division of customers based on their purchasing behaviors to businesses of the different groups. The situation enables marketers to design targeted and focused marketing campaigns that are aimed at specific market segments to increase the likelihood of engagement and conversion through clustering techniques and RFM (recency, frequency, monetary) analysis. The fourth technique is predictive analytics. Predictive analytics require the use of historical data to predict future consumer behaviors. Regression analysis and machine learning models are used to influence consumer purchasing choices while enabling companies to anticipate which products will sell more successfully in the future.

The fifth technique is time series analysis, which is used to analyze data points that are collected or recorded at different intervals or time. Next, time series analysis helps companies identify cyclical patterns, changes in purchasing behavior over time, and seasonal trends. As a result, companies will be able to understand temporary patterns and enable businesses to adjust their marketing campaigns and inventory management levels to strategically align with the cycles of consumer demand.

The final technique is A/B testing. A/B testing is a new technique that enables companies to compare variations of the marketing factor to determine which performs better. By analyzing purchasing patterns resulting from each variation of the factor, businesses can make data-driven and informed decisions to maximize the effectiveness of their marketing campaigns and strategies. This situation makes marketing analytics an important component

**TABLE 4.2** Techniques for Analyzing Purchasing Patterns

| Analysis Type | Description | Purpose | Key Metrics/ Methods | Applications |
|---|---|---|---|---|
| **Descriptive analysis** | Summarizes historical data to understand past behavior and trends | Provides insights into what has happened | Mean, median, mode, standard deviation, etc. | Sales reports, performance analysis, etc. |
| **Market basket analysis** | Identifies products frequently bought together | Helps in understanding product associations | Association rules, support, confidence, lift | Cross-selling, product placement, etc. |
| **Customer segmentation** | Divides customers into distinct groups based on specific criteria | Tailors marketing strategies to different segments | Demographic, behavioral, psychographic data | Targeted marketing, personalized offers, etc. |
| **RFM analysis** | Evaluates customers based on recency, frequency, and monetary value of purchases | Identifies valuable customers | Recency, frequency, monetary value | Loyalty programs, customer retention strategies |
| **A/B testing** | Compares two versions of a variable to determine which performs better | Optimizes marketing campaigns and user experiences | Conversion rates, click-through rates, etc. | Website optimization, email marketing, etc. |

in analyzing the purchasing patterns of consumers through various techniques. It is important for companies in all industries to use descriptive analytics, market basket analysis, customer segmentation, predictive analytics, time series analysis, and A/B testing to better understand the patterns of behavior of the consumer market. As a result, market analytics will improve consumer satisfaction and will also increase the success and competitive advantage of the company.

## BUSINESS ANALYTICS FUNCTION FOR MARKETING USING MICROSOFT EXCEL

In the business environment, there are many business analytical terms mentioned that play a critical role in making informed and data-driven choices that drive decisions, optimize daily operations, and develop strategic actions and initiatives. Various statistical concepts play an important role in marketing and business analytics by providing essential tools for data analysis and decision-making. Here's a detailed overview of their definition and importance and how to conduct this statistical analysis using Microsoft Excel.

### Bernoulli and Binomial Distributions

These distributions are essential for modeling binary outcomes in marketing campaigns that include success or failure that help organizations understand consumer behavior and the effectiveness of strategic campaigns.

Formula: =BINOM.DIST(k, n, p, FALSE) or =BINOM.DIST(k, n, p, TRUE)

**Steps:**

1. Use the formula =BINOM.DIST(k, n, p, FALSE) for the probability of exactly *k* successes, or =BINOM.DIST(k, n, p, TRUE) for cumulative probability.

### Chi-Square Goodness-of-Fit Test

This test evaluates how well-observed data fits an expected distribution and enables marketers to assess the effectiveness of segmentation and targeted marketing strategies.

Formula: = CHISQ.DIST.RT

**Steps:**

1. Enter your observed frequencies in one column and your expected frequencies in another
2. Calculate the chi-square statistic using =SUM(((observed − expected)^2)/expected).
3. Use the CHISQ.DIST.RT function to find the p-value: =CHISQ.DIST.RT(chi_square_statistic, degrees_of_freedom).

## Combinations and Permutations

These models are necessary in analyzing different ways to combine marketing strategies and tactics and in enabling marketers to optimize resource allocation and campaign strategies.

*Combinations*

Formula: =COMBIN(n, k)

**Steps:**

1. Calculate the number of combinations (*n* choose *k*).
2. Use the formula =COMBIN(n, k).

*Permutations*

Formula: =PERMUT(n, k)

**Steps:**

1. Calculate the number of permutations (nPk).
2. Use the formula =PERMUT(n, k).

## Conditional Probability

Conditional probability allows marketers to evaluate the chances of consumer actions based on assumed conditions to improve personalization and effectiveness.

Formula: =P(A and B)/P(B)

**Steps:**

1. Calculate conditional probability, P(A|B).
2. Use =P(A and B)/P(B).
3. You will need to calculate P(A and B) and P(B) first.

## Discrete Probability Distribution

A modeling scenario involving discrete outcomes that are frequently important in market response forecasts, consumer choice analysis, and inventory management.

**Steps:**

1. Generate a probability distribution table by listing all possible outcomes and their corresponding probabilities.

## Expected Value in Decision-Making

A calculation that anticipates the various outcomes of different marketing strategies and is used to lead organizations in selecting choices with the highest potential return on investment (ROI).

Formula: =SUMPRODUCT(outcomes, probabilities)

**Steps:**

1. Create a table with outcomes and their probabilities.
2. Use the formula =SUMPRODUCT(outcomes, probabilities).

## Exponential Distribution

When analyzing time until an event occurs, this distribution helps companies predict and manage consumer retention strategies.

Formula: =EXPON.DIST(x, lambda, TRUE)

**Steps:**

1. Calculate the probability of an event in a time frame.
2. Use the formula =EXPON.DIST(x, lambda, TRUE) for the cumulative probability.

## Joint and Marginal Probabilities

These probabilities enable marketers to understand the relationships between different variables that include the correlation between customer demographics and purchasing behavior.

*Joint Probabilities*

**Steps:**

1. Calculate joint probabilities by multiplying the individual probabilities if they are independent.

*Marginal Probabilities*

**Steps:**

1. Compute marginal probabilities from joint probabilities by summing the probabilities across the relevant dimension.

## Normal Distribution and Standard Normal Distribution

Many marketing metrics, including consumer satisfaction scores and sales figures, typically follow a normal distribution that is used in the facilitation of data analysis and hypothesis testing.

*Normal Distribution*

Formula: =NORM.DIST(x, mean, standard_dev, FALSE) or =NORM.DIST(x, mean, standard_dev, TRUE)

**Steps:**

1. Use the formula =NORM.DIST(x, mean, standard_dev, FALSE) for the probability density function.
2. Use the formula =NORM.DIST(x, mean, standard_dev, TRUE) for cumulative distribution.

*Standard Normal Distribution*

Formula: =NORM.S.DIST(z, TRUE)

**Steps:**

1. Use =NORM.S.DIST(z, TRUE) for the cumulative distribution function (CDF) of the standard normal distribution.

## Poisson Distribution

This statistical tool is used in modeling the number of events occurring in a fixed interval of time or space to allow organizations to predict occurrences such as consumer inquiries or sales.

Formula: =POISSON.DIST(k, lambda, FALSE) or =POISSON.DIST(k, lambda, TRUE)

**Steps:**

1. Calculate the probability of *k* events in a fixed interval.
2. Use the formula =POISSON.DIST(k, lambda, FALSE) for the probability of exactly *k* events or =POISSON.DIST(k, lambda, TRUE) for cumulative probability.

## Probability and Probability Rules and Formulas

Knowledge of probability principles that is used to support risk assessment, mitigation, and decision-making in uncertain environments that is used in everyday, common scenarios in marketing.

**Steps:**

1. Calculate probabilities based on the counts of favorable outcomes over total outcomes by using the formula = favorable_outcomes/total_outcomes.

### Random Variables

Random variables enable marketers to quantify uncertainties within a sector and predict various outcomes based on distinct market factors.

**Steps:**

1. Construct a table defining random variables and their probabilities.
2. Analyze expected value or variance as needed.

### Standard Normal Distribution Tables

Provide quick references for probabilities associated with the standard normal distribution that support the statistical analysis for marketing metrics.

Formula: =NORM.S.DIST(z, TRUE)

**Steps:**

1. Use =NORM.S.DIST(z, TRUE) for the cumulative distribution function (CDF) of the standard normal distribution.
2. Prepare your spreadsheet by creating a header row and labeling the first two columns as follows: A1: Z-score and B1: cumulative probability.
3. Enter Z-scores. In column A, starting from cell A2, enter the Z-scores you want to include. For example, you might want Z-scores from −3.0 to 3.0 in increments of 0.1.
4. Calculate the cumulative probabilities by using the formula =NORM.DIST(A2, 0, 1, TRUE) for the Z-score in cell A2 using a mean of 0 and a standard deviation of 1.
5. Create a chart to provide a visual representation of the Z-scores and cumulative probabilities using a scatter chart with smooth lines.

### The Norm.INV Function

This function is used in predictive modeling to determine the value associated with a specified probability within a normal distribution to improve the accuracy of forecasting future events or results.

Formula: =NORM.INV(probability, mean, standard_dev)

**Steps:**

1. To find a value from a normal distribution, use =NORM.INV.
2. Identify the cumulative probability for which you want to find the corresponding value. It must be between 0 and 1.
3. Determine the arithmetic mean of the normal distribution.
4. Find the standard deviation of the normal distribution.

### Triangular and Uniform Distributions

These distributions are applied in marketing scenarios with limited data to create estimations or when simplifications are necessary for modeling consumer behavior.

**Steps:**

1. To calculate probabilities in a triangular distribution, use the simulation approach or formulas.
2. You can use a random number generator along with the triangular distribution formulas.

### Uniform Distribution

*Uniform distribution* is a probability distribution where all outcomes are equally likely within a defined range, and it can be calculated using the =UNIFORM.DIST function for probabilities and the =UNIFORM INV function for finding values corresponding to given probabilities.

Formula: =UNIFORM.DIST or =UNIFORM.INV or =RAND()

**Steps:**

1. Use the formula =UNIFORM.DIST, =UNIFORM.INV, or =RAND() for a uniformly distributed value between 0 and 1, and adjust it to the desired range.

### Variance of a Discrete Random Variable

Understanding variance helps marketers determine the risk and variability of their strategies and allows for better inventory, resources, and budget management.

Formula: =SUMPRODUCT((outcomes − expected_value)^ 2)$^2$, probabilities)

**Steps:**

1. To calculate variance, create a table of outcomes and their probabilities.
2. Use the formula =SUMPRODUCT((outcomes − expected_value)^ 2)$^2$, probabilities).

## REAL-WORLD EXAMPLES OF MARKETING INSIGHTS DRIVING BUSINESS SUCCESS

### HubSpot

HubSpot's success in marketing is an indication of the power of the knowledge of business analytics. By implementing data-driven strategies, the company transformed its approach to consumer engagement. One example is HubSpot's highlighting of inbound marketing that uses knowledge from consumer behavior to personalize content and create focused campaigns. This approach has gained more traffic while also improving lead generation. Next, HubSpot's business analytics tools enabled companies to track performance metric and allowed for real-time modifications to their marketing strategies. An example is their use of A/B testing for email campaigns that resulted in significant expansions in open and click-through rates. Through these business analytics metrics, HubSpot refined its marketing efforts while also providing instrumental resources to its users that helped them achieve their own marketing goals. As a result, their commitment to data-informed decision-making has solidified HubSpot's position as a leader in the marketing technology market.

#### Question 1

How has HubSpot used inbound marketing to enhance consumer engagement, and what role does consumer behavior play in this strategy?

Answer: HubSpot has effectively used inbound marketing to improve consumer engagement by focusing on the personalization of content and the creation of targeted campaigns. This strategy is founded in understanding consumer behavior that allows HubSpot to customize its marketing efforts to meet the specific needs and preferences of its users. By analyzing data on consumer interactions and preferences, HubSpot can develop content that connects with potential customers and increases engagement. This personalized approach attracts more traffic and improves lead generation since consumers are more likely to respond positively to content that is relevant and customized to their interests. Finally, inbound marketing serves as a useful tool for HubSpot to connect with consumers on a deeper level that develops long-term relationships and drives business success.

#### Question 2

In what ways have HubSpot's business analytics tools contributed to the optimization of marketing strategies for both the company and its users?

Answer: HubSpot's business analytics tools have been important in optimizing marketing strategies by providing valuable knowledge into key performance metrics. These tools enable both HubSpot and its users to track key indicators, such as website traffic, conversion rates, and customer engagement, in real time. One example is the use of A/B testing for email campaigns, which allows marketers to experiment with different versions of emails to determine which one performs better in terms of open and click-through rates. This data-driven approach facilitates informed decision-making, which allows for real-time modifications to marketing strategies based on empirical evidence. As a result, HubSpot and its users continuously refine their marketing efforts, ensuring that they remain effective and aligned with their goals. Finally, the ability to adapt quickly to changing market conditions and consumer preferences is a significant advantage provided by HubSpot's analytics tools.

**Question 3**

Discuss the impact of data-informed decision-making on HubSpot's position in the marketing technology market.

Answer: Data-informed decision-making has had a major impact on guaranteeing HubSpot's position as a leader in the marketing technology market. By prioritizing data-driven strategies, HubSpot has been able to make informed decisions that improve its marketing efforts and deliver high-quality results. This approach has allowed the company to stay ahead of industry trends and adapt to the evolving needs of its customers. The focus on data has also enabled HubSpot to develop innovative tools and resources that empower its users to achieve their marketing objectives. As a result, HubSpot has built a reputation for reliability and effectiveness by attracting a loyal customer base and establishing itself as a trusted partner in the marketing technology environment. The commitment to leveraging data for strategic decision-making has not only driven HubSpot's success but also establishes a benchmark for excellence in the industry.

## Warby Parker

Warby Parker uses business analytics to revolutionize the eyewear industry. By using data analytics, the company has gained a better understanding of consumer preferences and shopping behaviors. One of their main initiatives is the Home Try-On program, which enables consumers to select five frames to try at home. This strategy is supported by extensive analysis of consumer feedback and purchasing patterns, which has led to a significant increase in conversion rates.

Finally, Warby Parker uses advanced analytics to maximize their supply chain and inventory management by ensuring popular styles are always available while minimizing excess stock. Their commitment to data-driven decision-making extends to their marketing strategies, where they use segmentation analysis to target specific demographics effectively. By continually using analytics, Warby Parker has enhanced consumer experience while also setting its brand as a leader in direct-to-consumer eyewear by demonstrating the transformative power of data in marketing analytics.

**Question 1**

How does Warby Parker utilize business analytics to enhance consumer experience through their Home Try-On program?

Answer: Warby Parker leverages business analytics to significantly enhance consumer experience with their innovative Home Try-On program. By analyzing consumer preferences and shopping behaviors, the company identifies the demand for a more personalized and convenient eyewear shopping experience. The Home Try-On program allows consumers to select five frames to try at home, a strategy that is informed by extensive analysis of consumer feedback and purchasing patterns. This data-driven approach not only increases conversion rates but also empowers consumers to make informed decisions in a comfortable setting. The success of this program underscores the importance of using analytics to tailor services to meet consumer needs, ultimately leading to a more satisfying shopping experience.

**Question 2**

In what ways does Warby Parker apply advanced analytics to optimize their supply chain and inventory management?

Answer: Warby Parker applies advanced analytics to optimize their supply chain and inventory management by closely monitoring consumer demand and purchasing trends. Through data analysis, the company is able to predict which styles will be popular and ensure that these are always available, thus minimizing the risk of stockouts. Simultaneously, analytics helps in reducing excess inventory by aligning production with actual consumer demand. This strategic use of data not only improves operational efficiency but also reduces costs associated with overproduction and storage. By maintaining a balance between supply and demand, Warby Parker ensures that they can meet consumer expectations promptly, further solidifying their reputation as a leader in the direct-to-consumer eyewear market.

**Question 3**

How does Warby Parker's use of segmentation analysis contribute to their marketing strategies?

Answer: Warby Parker's use of segmentation analysis plays a crucial role in their marketing strategies by allowing the company to effectively target specific demographics. By analyzing data on consumer demographics, preferences, and behaviors, Warby Parker can create tailored marketing campaigns that resonate with different segments of their audience. This targeted approach ensures that marketing efforts are more relevant and engaging, leading to higher conversion rates and customer loyalty. For instance, by understanding the unique needs and preferences of different consumer groups, Warby Parker can craft personalized messages and offers that appeal directly to each segment. This data-driven strategy not only enhances the effectiveness of their marketing campaigns but also strengthens their brand presence in the competitive eyewear industry.

## Red Bull

Red Bull's success in marketing is attributed to its innovative use of business analytics. The company carefully tracks consumer behavior and engagement patterns, which enables it to develop campaigns that connect with its target audience. One primary example is Red Bull's strategic sponsorship of extreme sports events that is supported by data showing a correlation between youth culture and adventurous activities. This approach not only improves brand visibility but also strengthens emotional connection with their customers. Next, Red Bull uses social media analytics to monitor trends and maximize content strategy. By analyzing real-time engagement metrics, the brand customizes its messaging to strategically align with audience interests and preferences while ensuring maximum impact to its stakeholders. The legendary "Red Bull Stratos" project, where Felix Baumgartner jumped from the stratosphere, demonstrates data-backed marketing. This strategy not only captivated millions but also reinforced Red Bull's association with audacity and innovation. Finally, through these analytical practices, Red Bull has successfully created a distinct niche in the competitive energy drink market environment.

### Question 1

How does Red Bull utilize business analytics to enhance its brand visibility and emotional connection with its target audience?

Answer: Red Bull leverages business analytics to enhance its brand visibility and emotional connection with its target audience by strategically sponsoring extreme sports events. This decision is informed by data that shows a strong correlation between youth culture and adventurous activities. By aligning its brand with these events, Red Bull not only increases its visibility but also strengthens its emotional ties with consumers who identify with the thrill and excitement of extreme sports. This data-driven approach ensures that Red Bull's marketing efforts resonate deeply with its audience, fostering brand loyalty and engagement.

### Question 2

In what ways does Red Bull use social media analytics to optimize its content strategy?

Answer: Red Bull employs social media analytics to optimize its content strategy by monitoring real-time engagement metrics. This allows the company to track trends and understand audience preferences, enabling it to tailor its messaging to align with current interests. By analyzing data on how users interact with their content, Red Bull can adjust its strategy to maximize impact, ensuring that its messaging is both relevant and compelling. This approach not only enhances the effectiveness of their campaigns but also ensures that Red Bull remains at the forefront of consumer attention in the digital space.

### Question 3

Describe how the "Red Bull Stratos" project exemplifies Red Bull's data-backed marketing strategy.

Answer: The "Red Bull Stratos" project is a prime example of Red Bull's data-backed marketing strategy. This ambitious endeavor, where Felix Baumgartner jumped from the stratosphere, was not only a feat of human achievement but also a meticulously planned marketing campaign supported by data analytics. By analyzing audience interests and engagement patterns, Red Bull identified a unique opportunity to captivate millions worldwide. The project reinforced Red Bull's brand association with audacity and innovation, capturing the imagination of viewers and solidifying its position as a leader in the energy drink market. The success of this campaign highlights Red Bull's ability to use data to create impactful, memorable experiences that resonate with its audience.

## Patagonia

Patagonia uses its analytical knowledge in marketing to show its commitment to environmental sustainability. The company continually analyzes consumer preferences and values that lead to campaigns that connect with environmentally conscious consumers. One example is its "Don't Buy This Jacket" campaign, which encourages consumers to consider the environmental impact of their purchases. This new bold approach increases brand loyalty while also aligning with the company's core values. Next, Patagonia uses data analytics to track consumer engagement with its initiatives. By measuring the impact of campaigns like its Worn Wear program, which promotes recycling and repairing gear, the company has gained valuable insights into consumer behavior and preferences. Finally, Patagonia monitors social media analytics to improve messaging while ensuring it effectively communicates its environmental mission. Through these business analytic strategies, Patagonia has built a strong community of loyal consumers who share its commitment to sustainability, which drives both brand success and meaningful change in the industry.

**Question 1**

How did Patagonia's "Don't Buy This Jacket" campaign reflect its commitment to environmental sustainability, and what impact did it have on consumer behavior?

Answer: Patagonia's "Don't Buy This Jacket" campaign was a bold move that directly addressed the environmental impact of consumerism. By urging consumers to reconsider their purchasing habits, Patagonia aligned its marketing strategy with its core value for sustainability. This campaign not only increased brand loyalty among environmentally conscious consumers but also sparked a broader conversation about responsible consumption. The campaign's success lay in its ability to resonate with consumers who prioritize sustainability, thereby strengthening Patagonia's brand identity and fostering a community of like-minded individuals committed to environmental stewardship.

**Question 2**

In what ways did Patagonia utilize data analytics to enhance its Worn Wear program, and what insights were gained from this initiative?

Answer: Patagonia leveraged data analytics to track consumer engagement with its Worn Wear program, which promotes the recycling and repairing of gear. By analyzing consumer interactions and feedback, Patagonia gained valuable insights into the preferences and behaviors of its target audience. This data-driven approach allowed the company to refine its messaging and improve the program's effectiveness. The insights gained highlighted a strong consumer interest in sustainable practices and reinforced the importance of offering initiatives that align with these values. As a result, Patagonia was able to enhance its brand reputation as a leader in sustainability while fostering deeper connections with its customers.

**Question 3**

How does Patagonia's use of social media analytics contribute to its environmental mission, and what are the benefits of this strategy?

Answer: Patagonia uses social media analytics to monitor and improve its messaging, ensuring that it effectively communicates its environmental mission. By analyzing engagement metrics, such as likes, shares, and comments, Patagonia can gauge the impact of its campaigns and adjust its strategies accordingly. This approach allows the company to stay attuned to consumer sentiment and preferences, enabling it to craft messages that resonate with its audience. The benefits of this strategy include increased brand visibility, stronger consumer relationships, and the ability to drive meaningful changes by inspiring others to adopt sustainable practices. Through social media analytics, Patagonia not only amplifies its environmental message but also reinforces its position as a leader in the sustainable business movement.

---

## CASE STUDIES ON MARKETING SUCCESS THROUGH ANALYTICS

### Business Success Through Business Analytics

Business analytics plays a crucial role in understanding economic trends and consumer behavior that enable organizations in the marketing industry to make more data-driven and informed decisions. Following are three examples of how marketing data and knowledge are translated into business success using analytics:

### Example 1: Thoughtful Innovations Inc.

Thoughtful Innovations Inc. is a marketing company that specializes in data-driven marketing strategies. The company has created a niche for itself by using advanced analytics to understand consumer behavior and preferences. By employing machine learning algorithms, they analyze large amounts of data from social media, online reviews, and purchasing patterns to create highly personalized marketing campaigns. The company has developed a proprietary analytics platform called "MarketPulse," which integrates data from various sources to provide real-time insights into consumer trends. This platform allows Thoughtful Innovations to segment their audience more effectively and customize their marketing messages to specific demographics. As a result, their clients have seen a significant increase in engagement and conversion rates. By leveraging these insights, Thoughtful Innovations has helped its clients achieve a 30% increase in return on investment (ROI) from their marketing campaigns. The company's ability to predict market trends and consumer preferences has positioned it as a leader in the marketing analytics space.

#### *Short-Response Questions*

1. What is the name of the proprietary analytics platform developed by Thoughtful Innovations Inc.?
2. By what percentage did Thoughtful Innovations' clients see an increase in ROI?
3. What types of data does Thoughtful Innovations analyze to create personalized marketing campaigns?

### Example 2: Creative Optics Co.

Creative Optics Co. is an agency that focuses on creative marketing solutions powered by data analytics. The company excels in transforming raw data into exciting visual stories that connect with audiences. The company uses a tool called "VisualizeNow," which transforms complex datasets into easy-to-understand infographics and interactive dashboards. This tool helps clients understand their market position and identify opportunities for growth. By presenting data in a visually appealing manner, Creative Optics Co. enables clients to make informed marketing decisions quickly. Next, Creative Optics Co. has helped its clients increase brand awareness by 40% through visually driven marketing campaigns. Their ability to simplify complex data into actionable insights has made them a preferred partner for businesses looking to enhance their marketing strategies.

### *Short-Response Questions*

1. What is the name of the tool used by Creative Optics Co. to create visual stories?
2. By what percentage did Creative Optics Co.'s clients increase their brand awareness?
3. What is the primary benefit of using data visualization in marketing according to Creative Optics Co.?

### Example 3: Data Dynamics Ltd.

Data Dynamics Ltd. is a company that specializes in predictive analytics for marketing. The company uses advanced statistical models to forecast market trends and consumer behavior, allowing clients to stay ahead of the competition. The company developed a predictive analytics tool called "TrendPrediction," which analyzes historical data to identify patterns and predict future market movements. This tool helps clients allocate their marketing resources more efficiently and target the right audience at the right time. Data Dynamics Ltd. has enabled its clients to achieve a 20% increase in market share by anticipating consumer needs and adjusting their marketing strategies accordingly. Their expertise in predictive analytics has established them as trusted advisors in the marketing industry.

### *Short-Response Questions*

1. What is the name of the predictive analytics tool developed by Data Dynamics Ltd.?
2. By what percentage did Data Dynamics Ltd.'s clients increase their market share?
3. What is the main advantage of using predictive analytics in marketing according to Data Dynamics Ltd.?

## CASE STUDY: BRILLIANT MARKETING SOLUTIONS (BMS)

Brilliant Marketing Solutions (BMS) is a marketing agency that specializes in digital advertising services. The agency has quickly gained popularity among small to medium-sized businesses due to its data-driven approach and innovative strategies. Recently, SMS had a customer base of 200 clients and reported a revenue growth of 45% compared to the previous year. The marketing agency primarily uses social media marketing and email campaigns to reach potential customers. Finally, the management team at SMS conducted an analysis to understand customer engagement rates and predict future marketing success.

### Business Analytics Data Tables

**TABLE 4.3** Customer Engagement Metrics

| 1 | A | B |
|---|---|---|
| | **Engagement Type** | **Count** |
| 2 | Email open rates | 150 |
| 3 | Social media likes | 200 |
| 4 | Website click-throughs | 100 |
| 5 | Conversion rates | 80 |

**TABLE 4.4** Campaign Results

| 1 | A | B | C | D |
|---|---|---|---|---|
| | Campaign Type | Successes | Total Attempts | Conversion Rate (%) |
| 2 | Email marketing | 60 | 150 | 40 |
| 3 | Social media ads | 90 | 200 | 45 |
| 4 | SEO optimization | 40 | 100 | 40 |

## Analytics Problems Using Excel

1. Using the BINOM.DIST function, calculate the probability of exactly 40 successful conversions out of 150 email marketing attempts, assuming a success rate of 40%.
2. Apply the CHISQ.TEST function to determine if the distribution of successful marketing campaigns across the three types (email, social media, SEO) fits a uniform distribution.
3. Estimate the expected value of customer engagements using the discrete probability distribution, considering the possible outcomes based on the engagement metrics.
4. Using the NORM.INV function and the normal distribution of customer engagement data, find the number of engagements corresponding to the 90th percentile.
5. Perform a chi-square goodness-of-fit test for the campaign outcomes to see if they conform to expected distributions based on past performance.

## Answer Key

1. *Calculating probability of successful conversions.*
   Formula: =BINOM.DIST(40, 150, 0.4, FALSE)
   You should find the probability of getting exactly 40 successes in 150 attempts, with a success rate of 40%.
2. *Chi-square test for uniform distribution.*
   Observed counts: (60, 90, 40)
   Expected counts for uniform distribution while assuming 50 each if total attempts is 200: (66.67, 66.67, 66.67)
   Formula: =CHISQ.TEST(A2:A4, B2:B4), where *A2:A4* is the range of observed data and *B2:B4* is the expected data.
3. *Calculating expected value of customer engagements.*
   Expected Value (E) = Σ (x * P(x))
   Create a probability distribution by dividing each engagement metric count by the total.
   Calculate E using the formula: =SUMPRODUCT(range_of_engagements, range_of_probabilities).
4. *Finding the 90th percentile using NORM.INV.* Use the average and standard deviation of the engagement data.
   Formula: =NORM.INV(0.9, AVERAGE(range), STDEV.P(range))
   Replace range with the actual engagement data ranges.

5. Chi-square goodness-of-fit test for campaign outcomes.
Observed marketing outcomes: (60, 90, 40)
Expected marketing outcomes based on equal distribution might be (66.67, 66.67, 66.67).
Formula: =CHISQ.TEST(range_of_observed, range_of_expected)
Assess if the result shows significant deviation from the expected uniform distribution.

## CASE STUDY: MARKETBRAINS INC.

MarketBrains Inc. is a marketing consultant company that specializes in digital marketing strategies for small and medium-sized enterprises (SMEs). The company has grown rapidly and uses data-driven strategies to help clients maximize their marketing campaigns. Recently, MarketBrains Inc. began a project for a client in the e-commerce sector seeking to increase their online sales through targeted advertising and personalized email campaigns. To measure the effectiveness of their strategies, MarketBrains Inc. collected data on the client's website traffic, conversion rates, and customer demographics for over six months. The data was analyzed to identify patterns and trends that could inform future marketing efforts. The following tables summarize key findings from the project:

**TABLE 4.5** Website Traffic and Conversion Rates

| 1 | A | B | C | D |
|---|---|---|---|---|
| | Month | Website Visits | Conversions | Conversion Rate (%) |
| 2 | January | 50,000 | 1,250 | 2.5 |
| 3 | February | 55,000 | 1,375 | 2.5 |
| 4 | March | 60,000 | 1,500 | 2.5 |
| 5 | April | 65,000 | 1,625 | 2.5 |
| 6 | May | 70,000 | 1,750 | 2.5 |
| 7 | June | 75,000 | 1,875 | 2.5 |

**TABLE 4.6** Customer Demographics

| 1 | A1 | B1 |
|---|---|---|
| | Age Group | Percentage of Customers |
| 2 | 18–24 | 15% |
| 3 | 25–34 | 35% |
| 4 | 35–44 | 25% |
| 5 | 45–54 | 15% |
| 6 | 55+ | 10% |

### Analytics Problems Using Excel

1. *Chi-square goodness-of-fit test.* Is there a significant difference between the observed and expected customer age distribution?
2. *Combinations and permutations.* How many different ways can a marketing team of three be formed from a group of ten employees?
3. *Conditional probability.* What is the probability that a randomly selected customer is aged 25–34, given that they made a purchase?
4. *Discrete probability distribution.* Calculate the probability distribution of conversions per month.
5. *Exponential distribution.* Determine the time between website visits if the average rate of visits is 2,000 per day.
6. *Joint probability.* What is the joint probability of a customer being aged 25–34 and making a purchase in May?
7. *Normal distribution.* Assuming the conversion rates follow a normal distribution, what is the probability of achieving a conversion rate above 3%?
8. *Poisson distribution.* Calculate the probability of receiving exactly 1,500 conversions in a month.
9. *Random variables.* Define the random variable for the number of conversions per month, and calculate its expected value.
10. *Standard normal distribution tables.* Find the z-score for a conversion rate of 2.5%, and interpret its significance.
11. *Uniform distribution.* If website visits are uniformly distributed, what is the probability of receiving between 60,000 and 70,000 visits in a month?
12. *Variance of a discrete random variable.* Calculate the variance of the number of conversions per month.

### Answer Key

1. *Chi-square goodness-of-fit test.* Enter the observed and expected frequencies in two columns. Use the CHISQ.TEST function to calculate the p-value. Interpret the p-value to determine if there is a significant difference.
2. *Combinations and permutations.* Use the COMBIN function for combinations: =COMBIN(10, 3). Use the PERMUT function for permutations: =PERMUT(10, 3).
3. *Conditional probability.* Calculate the probability using the formula P(A|B) = P(A and B)/P(B). Use the COUNTIF function to find the relevant counts.
4. *Discrete probability distribution.* List the number of conversions and their probabilities. Use the PROB function to calculate probabilities.
5. *Exponential distribution.* Use the EXPON.DIST function: =EXPON.DIST(x, lambda, cumulative).
6. *Joint probability.* Multiply the individual probabilities of the events.

7. *Normal distribution.* Use the NORM.DIST function: =NORM.DIST(x, mean, standard_dev, cumulative).
8. *Poisson distribution.* Use the POISSON.DIST function: =POISSON.DIST(x, mean, cumulative).
9. *Random variables.* Define the random variable and use the SUMPRODUCT function to calculate the expected value.
10. *Standard normal distribution tables.* Use the STANDARDIZE function to find the z-score: =STANDARDIZE(x, mean, standard_dev). Use the NORM.S.DIST function to find the probability.
11. *Uniform distribution.* Use the UNIFORM.DIST function: =UNIFORM.DIST(x, a, b, cumulative).
12. *Variance of a discrete random variable.* Use the VAR.P function to calculate the variance: =VAR.P(range).

CHAPTER **5**

# Ethics in Business Analytics

## ETHICAL CONSIDERATIONS IN DATA COLLECTION

In business ethics, there are ethical considerations in data collection. Organizations in the global environment are increasingly relying on data-driven decisions. The ethical implications of those choices are based on how data is gathered, used, and disseminated throughout the internal and external environment. The situation requires business analytics to not only support the decision-making process but also be effective in aligning their current business processes with ethical standards and compliance regulations. One of the main responsibilities of business analytics is to guarantee that data collection methods are ethical with respect to maintaining the privacy and the consent of the individual.

This situation requires companies to implement policies and procedures that protect all sensitive information and follow regulations like the California Consumer Privacy Act (CCPA) and the General Data Protection Regulation (GDPR). CCPA is a state statute that gives California residents the ability to access, delete, and control the sale of their personal information collected by businesses, while the GDPR is responsible for improving the person's control over their personal data with data privacy laws under European Union Law. As a result, organizations must be truthful and transparent about their data collection practices. The situation will require a business to inform users how they will use our data and give the option to opt out the process if they desire.

Ethics in business analytics can be found in berries industries in the global market. Various industry sectors include health care. Within the health-care industry, it is important for companies to maintain ethical standards in data collection. Patient confidentiality must be protected by regulations like the Health Insurance Portability and Accountability Act (HIPPA). HIPAA requires organizations to guarantee that data is provided anonymously, securely. The situation requires organizations to use business analytics to develop ethical practices that lead to the improved outcome of patients without compromising the privacy of the individual. As a result, health-care companies will need to use business analytics tools to utilize large datasets while following strict ethical guidelines.

In the finance sector, companies will also rely on ethical considerations in collecting and analyzing data. In this industry, there are large amounts of personal and financial information. The situation will require companies to ensure that their data collection practices do not lead

DOI: 10.4324/9781003629658-5

to unfair treatment or discrimination against the consumer. As a result, business analytics strategies will help identify potential biases, using advanced machine algorithms used for cutting lending in scoring that will enable businesses to correct any disparities and maintain the necessary ethical standards.

Finally, the retail and e-commerce industries are faced with ethical dilemmas when it comes to collecting data that concerns the tracking of consumer preferences and behaviors. While retail and e-commerce companies can benefit from the new assist in purchasing patterns, these businesses must respect the privacy of consumers while balancing their need for data collection. This situation will require ethical business analytics to allow retailers and e-commerce companies to personalize marketing campaigns without infringing on consumer rights. When ethical business analytics are used, long-term relationships will be developed and there will be transparency and trust between the consumer and the business.

As a result, business analytics is important in guaranteeing that ethical considerations are fully integrated into the data collection process. Next, it is important for business analytics professionals to be aware of all ethical considerations in all industries within the global environment. When transparency, data protection, and consent are prioritized, companies can use business analytics to increase value while also maintaining a high level of standards. As a result, the combination of business analytics with ethics will develop trust among all stakeholder groups and provide a positive benefit for both the business and the consumer.

## Addressing Privacy Concerns and Data Ownership

Business analytics can be used to address privacy concerns and ownership of data. Ethical companies will use business analytics to address any privacy concerns about data ownership. Recognizing the importance of the ethical elements of data collection is necessary in gaining consumer trust, and also in complying with government regulations. When business analytics and ethics are used effectively, organizations can ensure that ethical standards are upheld in data collection and analysis. This situation can be seen in various industries in the global environment.

The first industry that I must address concerning privacy concerns and data ownership is health care. Within the sector, data ownership and privacy are critical to the business. Healthcare companies must process and analyze patient data following strict regulations, such as HIPAA. The situation will require the business to use complex analytical tools to enable health-care providers to identify patterns and trends to improve patient care without compromising confidentiality and sensitivity of the data. Next, health-care providers must ensure that data is collected anonymously and filtered through advanced encryption models to guarantee that patient data is kept confidential and secure. As a result of this process, positive outcomes will be developed while ensuring that the rights of the individual have not been infringed upon.

The second industry that must address privacy concerns and ethics is finance. The financial services industry deals with issues relating to privacy in data ownership on a regular basis. Next, financial institutions must use business analytics to determine and assess credit risk, detect fraudulent activity, and provide personalized offerings to the consumer. Ethical considerations will be used within the business analytics process to help companies collect and analyze data effectively and transparently. This situation will require financial companies to implement consumer data consent management systems to guarantee that consumers have a clear understanding of how information is being used, while also giving them the ability to control how it is used. Transparency and data collection must respect the privacy rights of the consumer. However, transparency and ethical considerations will also be used to build a strong foundation of trust that is necessary for long-term relationships and success between the lender and the borrower.

The third industry is education. Within the education sector, business analytics and ethics are used to improve the outcome of students while following privacy concerns. Strict regulations such as the Family Educational Rights and Privacy Act (FERPA) must be followed. FERPA is a federal law that protects the privacy of student education records and permits parents or students the right to access, modify, and control the disclosure of their records. Next, educational institutions collect data on student performance and engagement levels. This process will require ethical practices to manage the data that is being collected responsibly to avoid any issues. It is important for educational institutions to use business analytics to guarantee that data remains anonymous and secure while still enabling them to determine new trends in order to develop focused interventions to problems without compromising the privacy of students. As a result of this approach, educational organizations will be able to make informed data-driven decisions based on reliable information while also respecting the rights of families and students.

Finally, nonprofit organizations, which include human rights and social services, experience difficult challenges related to the privacy and ownership of data. Nonprofit companies will need to use business analytics to determine the effectiveness of programs and to improve the delivery of services, while also considering all ethical considerations related to the data collection process. The situation will require nonprofits to prioritize the overseeing of data practices by emphasizing transparency and ethical usage of data. As a result of this process, nonprofit organizations can benefit from business analytics to ensure a positive outcome of events that support and respect the privacy of the individuals they serve. With the implementation of transparency, data security, and consent management, all these industries can become responsible in using business analytics to improve their operations while developing long-term trusting relationships with various stakeholder groups.

## BIAS AND FAIRNESS IN ANALYTICS

Inherently, there are bias and fairness issues in business analytics. Since there is an increased need for companies to rely on data-driven information to lead to their decision-making process, there is an increased potential for bias in the result. This situation makes it important for all businesses to ensure transparency and fairness in their business analytics practices and that they do not need any potential inequalities or inequities in the results. One of the main functions of business analytics is to identify and reduce bias in large datasets and machine algorithms. Unfortunately, bias can be found in various sources, including historical data, which reflects the prejudice of society at that time, along with models used to collect flawed data. This situation makes it necessary for companies to examine the data used in models for any potential or inherent bias, and then to implement all corrective measures to guarantee a fair outcome or result. As a result of this proactive process, industries, such as finance, health care, and human resources, where bias analysis has had negative consequences in the past can be corrected in real time.

First, the financial services industry uses business analytics to assess lending decisions and the creditworthiness of clients. With machine algorithms developed and trained on biased data, the results may overly deny credit to certain demographic groups or clients. When fairness and where algorithms and regular audits of lending processes are implemented, financial companies can better identify and rectify any potential bias. This strategy will ensure the equitable and fair treatment of all consumers. As a result of this approach, financial service companies will fully comply with regulatory requirements while also improving the business's reputation and trustworthiness with the consumer market.

Next, the health-care industry uses business analytics to guide the treatment process and allocation of resources while also accounting for fairness and bias. If predictive models studying health-care analytics are not checked for bias, underrepresented populations may receive inadequate or subpar care. The situation makes it important for companies to use methods like stratified analysis to examine treatment outcomes across different demographic groups. The situation well ensures that analytical models will promote equitable and fair health-care delivery to patients. By acknowledging and addressing bias, health-care companies can improve patient outcomes and guarantee fairness in accessing medical services.

Third, the human resource industry relies on ethical business analytics to prioritize fairness and equity. When hiring, recruiting algorithms can accidentally favor certain individual profiles over others. This situation can create a lack of diversity and inequity in the workforce. Human resource companies must use business analytics to audit and monitor their hiring practices to ensure that their machine algorithms do not discriminate against candidates based on gender, race, or other personal identifiers or characteristics. As a result, ethical business analytic processes focus on fairness in acquiring new employee talents and in guaranteeing that companies comply with regulations in developing a more inclusive workplace.

In the education industry, ethics in business analytics is used to analyze student performance and achievement gaps. Next, ethical consideration will be used to determine how educational institutions use business analytics to support equitable and equal access to opportunities and resources. The situation will require educational institutions to address bias within the interpretation of data so they can recognize and correct any shortcomings or disparities in the fair treatment of all students. As a result of this process, the combination of ethics in business analytics will create equitable outcomes and hold companies in all industries to a high level of ethical standards to promote fairness and increase their level of trust with stakeholders.

## Recognizing and Mitigating Bias in Data Interpretation

It is important for companies to recognize mitigating bias in data interpretation when using business analytics. Ethical industries rely on business analytics to recognize and reduce risk in interpretation of data and to ensure that their decision-making process supports integrity and fairness. In the health-care industry, it is important for health-care providers to accurately interpret patient data to provide health equity and treatment. Next, health-care providers use business and like tools to study large datasets for potential biases that develop from historical patterns and other socioeconomic factors. By using machine algorithms that can detect and look for anomalies and disparities in treatment fairness, health-care providers can identify biases in data interpretation among different demographic groups. As a result, implementing fairness and ethical models helps guarantee that all patient demographics receive equitable and fair treatment and care due to the safeguarding of ethical standards.

In the financial services industry, ethical awareness must be given consideration to address the challenges of bias in data interpretation in assessing insurance premiums and creditworthiness of clients. Ethical financial institutions have been found to use business analytics to study their algorithms and collection of past data for any potential biases that could impact future decisions. Through conducting regular audits of loan approval processes in using key performance metrics that look for disparities in outcomes across different demographic groups, financial institutions can identify and correct biases within their practices. As a result, the commitment to equitable treatment by financial institutions will improve trust and transparency to help maintain long-term consumer relationships.

Within the education industry, institutions use business analytics to guarantee fairness in interpreting data related to student performance. Next, educational institutions study data on student achievement to identify emerging trends. However, if this analysis does not look for bias, there can be a negative influence on the decision about support services in the allocation of resources. This situation makes it important for educational institutions to use business analytics tools that allow educators to determine performance gaps and to provide a targeted intervention strategy based on the overall comprehensive view of the needs of the students to ensure everyone receives equitable and equal opportunities.

Finally, the nonprofit industry uses business analytics to address issues related to social justice. Nonprofits that are focused on human rights for community development will use data to monitor the effectiveness of programs while also ensuring that all services are equal and equitable to the community. When biases in the data interpretation of program outcomes are recognized, nonprofits can improve the meeting of needs of the diverse communities they serve. As a result, ethical industries rely on business analytics to emphasize fairness and accountability within the analytical process. By using advanced analytic techniques, industries can maintain a strong commitment to ethical standards and guarantee that the use of data that is being collected only promotes equitable outcomes and builds trust with all stakeholder groups.

## TRANSPARENCY IN ANALYTICS

Business analytics and ethics play an important role in the transparency in analytics in various industries within the global environment. In the financial services sector of the market, transparency is necessary due to the sensitive nature of financial and personal information. Next, financial institutions will rely on ethical practices in business analytics to develop a clear perspective of credit scoring, loan approvals, and investment decisions. When financial companies can use business analytical tools in their decision-making process and to visualize large datasets, they can help their consumers better understand how their collected data is used, and the logic behind the decisions that were made. This situation creates open channels of communication that are used to create a positive brand reputation, develop trust, and support all ethical standards and required regulations.

In the health-care industry, transparency in business analytics is critical to the success of companies. Patients have the right to know how their health-care data is collected, analyzed, and used in making clinical decisions. Business analytics must be used by health-care providers to establish transparency by providing patients with clear expectations of how their data supports treatment plans and other public health initiatives. An example is a health-care provider using business analytics to identify trends and patient outcomes and how the health-care provider communicates the results effectively about the safety of treatments. As a result, health-care companies can improve their engagement with patients while also supporting their obligations to ethics as they relate to autonomy and patient consent.

Next, the tech industry uses business analytics and transparency in their algorithms and decision-making process. Today, many tech companies use AI in machine learning for multiple applications and purposes. The situation requires ethical implications of these technologies to be addressed openly with consumers. This situation causes business analytics to play an important role in enabling companies to audit their algorithms to guarantee that they are operating fairly and without potential bias. Next, businesses' transparent analytics provide the disclosure of data sources and methodologies that are used to help the user understand the potential limitations and associated risks with automated decisions, so the company can remain committed to remaining responsible in future innovations.

Finally, the nonprofit industry has benefited from business analytics and transparency as it relates to determining the effectiveness of programs and its impact on the community. Nonprofits rely on business analytics to evaluate the success of programs and how to correctly allocate resources. When nonprofits share data and analysis results transparently with stakeholders, which include community members and donors, they can demonstrate credibility and accountability with their stakeholders. As a result, the use of transparency in business analytics creates an ethical practice that improves the trust of stakeholders while also encouraging the ongoing collaboration and support of the community members they serve. The situation demonstrates the importance of transparency and how it is necessary for the responsible usage of data along with the long-term success of industries within the global environment.

## The Importance of Clear Communication of Analytical Results

Business analytics combined with ethics must focus on the importance of clear communication of analytical results. Clear and effective communication leads to transparency and ensures that informed decision-making is taking place to ultimately build trust with stakeholders. This situation can be seen in various sectors of the global market. First, health-care companies rely on clear communication of their statistical results for patient care and safety. Next, health-care providers must use business analytics to study patient data, operational efficiencies, and the outcome of treatments. However, the knowledge gained from business analytics must also be translated into understandable formats for both patients and professionals. When data is presented clearly and effectively, health-care providers can empower patients to make better-informed and logical decisions about their health care while also enabling health-care professionals to customize their treatment plans based on the new information gained from the analysis.

Second, financial service companies require clear channels of communication of analytical results to their stakeholders. Financial companies rely on complex algorithms and models to determine and assess the level of risk. This result is used to determine investment advice and the eligibility of receiving a loan. To guarantee customers understand their financial options, financial companies will need to communicate their assumptions, logic, and methodologies used in their analysis. Next, business analytic tools are also used in creating reports that break down key performance metrics, expected outcomes, and potential risks in a straightforward and easy-to-understand manner. This situation creates a level of transparency that helps consumer trust the financial institution since they feel more informed and aware about their financial decisions.

Third, educational institutions require effective communication of data and analytics when addressing student performance and achievement gaps. Educational institutions must analyze data related to attendance, engagement, and student learning to assist in the formation of effective instructional practices. When business analytics is clearly communicated to teachers, students, and parents, improvements to the original process can be made. Finally, when educational institutions can easily interpret the results of the analysis, they can begin to customize their approach to meet the diverse learning needs of students and other community members, which will ultimately lead to improved educational outcomes.

Finally, nonprofits depend on clear communication channels of their analytical results to share the effectiveness of the program and the impact it will have on their stakeholders and donors. When business analytics is used to evaluate program data, nonprofits can effectively communicate the success of their initiatives and allocate resources to the correct programs and initiatives. Next, sharing the knowledge gained from business analytics using visual reports and presenting it to community members will increase the level of accountability while also building trust with supporters. Third, the transparent reporting of statistical information will encourage collaboration and fundraising from supporters, which are necessary for long-term sustainability and growth. As a result, the overall commitment to clarity and transparency will improve the engagement and trust of the stakeholders while also supporting the integrity and long-term success of industrial companies.

## REGULATORY COMPLIANCE AND ANALYTICS

Business analytics and ethics are an important part of regulatory compliance for various industries within the global market. Since regulations are becoming more advanced and complex, companies must learn to use business analytics to follow structures while also ensuring their commitment to ethical standards. In the financial services sector of the market, regulatory compliance is necessary due to the extremely sensitive nature of personal information that is gathered and collected. Next, financial companies are required to comply with government regulations, which include the Dodd–Frank Act, anti-money laundering (AML) laws, and the Payment Card Industry Data Security Standard (PCI DSS).

The Dodd–Frank Act is a US federal law that supports financial stability by improving accountability and transparency in the financial system. AML laws are regulations designed to prevent money laundering and terrorist financing by requiring financial companies to report all suspicious activities. Finally, PCI DSS is a collection of security standards created by major credit card companies to protect consumer cardholder data and reduce the chance of credit card fraud. Next, business analytics combined with ethics assists in the monitoring of transactions and in analyzing all consumer behaviors to detect irregularities or anomalies that could indicate fraudulent activities or violations of regulatory compliance. When advanced business and ethical analytics is applied, businesses can ensure they have identified and addressed all risks associated with compliance and become proactive in protecting consumer data while maintaining the integrity of their financial system.

Within the health-care sector, all companies must rely on business analytics to maintain regulatory compliance. Health-care companies need to follow all regulations and compliance standards, including HIPAA, that oversee the protection of patient data. Next, business analytics helps health-care providers audit their data handling processes to guarantee that patient information is both stored and transmitted securely. To help with this process, business analytics tools monitor the access of data and its usage patterns. This strategy will help health-care providers identify potential breaches and escalate their solution more effectively. As a result, all health-care providers can maintain their ethical obligation to protect patient privacy while also being compliant with established rules and regulations.

In the telecommunications industry, companies must also deal with compliance as it relates to privacy regulations. Next, telecommunication companies will gather large amounts of personal data for consumers, requiring a complex analytical system to be created to analyze the data. Business analytics will help telecommunications companies study their data collection practices and ensure that they communicate clearly with consumers about their usage of data and maintain the necessary levels of consent required. Finally, business analytics tools would help telecommunications companies monitor their data processing strategies to help them remain in compliance with all regulatory statutes and laws regarding consumer privacy.

Finally, the retail industry will rely on business analytics to remain in compliance with all consumer protection laws. It is necessary for all retailers to understand laws and regulations related to advertising practices, data protection, sales promotions. Next, using business analytics enables companies to analyze consumer feedback and observe compliance with established promotional guidelines while addressing any potential issues proactively instead of reactively. When the proactive approach is taken toward regulatory compliance, retailers can establish trust with consumers while following all ethical standards. As a result, a strong commitment to business analytics and ethics does not just protect the rights of the consumer but also improves the trust of the stakeholders and the integrity of the company within the market.

## Understanding Legal Frameworks Governing Data Use

Understanding legal frameworks governing data use is an important component in business analytics in several industries in the global market. To begin, health-care providers are required to follow HIPAA in the United States. The use of business analytics helps health-care providers study patient data while remaining in compliance with privacy regulations. When business analytics are used, health-care providers can track patient consent and access medical records in real time. This situation helps health-care providers identify breaches to the system or any unauthorized access as it occurs. As a result, understanding legal frameworks that govern data use helps health-care providers ensure that they respect the privacy of patients while using data effectively and efficiently to improve all outcomes.

Second, the financial service industry must meet various legal requirements that include acts and laws that protect consumer data. This situation requires financial institutions to use business analytics to determine their level of compliance with these various regulations, especially where they concern transaction reporting in customer data management. The situation requires business analytic tools to be used by organizations to help analyze large datasets and to look for outliers and anomalies so they can better detect any potential regulatory violation and fraudulent activity in the market. When compliance with legal processes is maintained, financial institutions can remain confident that they are fully protecting the data of their consumers, which will also build brand loyalty.

Third, technology companies in the tech industry must comply with many legal laws and regulations that are related to data privacy and the consent of users. Business analytics provides a process to help companies with statistical tools needed to analyze user data that follow the regulations established by the government concerning usage and consent. This situation creates a proactive approach that supports ethical business practices as businesses demonstrate to users that they truly respect privacy and their rights as they pertain to data.

Finally, retailers will experience a benefit from business analytics when it comes to the legal requirements involving data security and consumer protection. As an example, the Consumer Privacy Protection Act is a federal law focused on improving the privacy and security of consumers' personal data. These types of acts require retailers to manage consumer data responsibly and with transparency. As a result, business analytics enables retailers to monitor their sales practices, follow advertising standards, and assess consumer feedback to avoid potential risks to compliance and industry regulations.

## ETHICAL IMPLICATIONS OF PREDICTIVE ANALYTICS

Business analytics includes ethical implications of predictive analytics. Predictive analytics includes the use of historical data and statistical modeling to make predictions about future events or occurrences. While there are many advantages to this process, there are also ethical concerns, which include accountability, transparency, and bias. As we will demonstrate, various industries that rely on ethics in predictive analytics will become successful industry markets. Health-care companies that use predictive analytics can improve the outcome of patients by identifying risk factors and providing tentative measures to problems. However, ethical concerns in the development of predictive models have been created and are based on bias. The situation can cause a portion of patients to be disproportionately impacted due to their demographic grouping. To avoid the situation, health-care providers can regularly audit their data and machine learning algorithms that are used as part of the predictive analytic process to help identify potential bias to make the necessary adjustments. As a result of this approach, health-care providers can improve their level of trust between patients and providers while also making sure that all recommendations for care are based on accurate and unbiased data.

Next, financial companies in the financial services industry use protective analytics to determine the level of credit risk, personalize services, and detect fraudulent activity. However, the predictive models that are used unknowingly contain bias that would lead to the future unfair treatment of specific individuals or community members. Business analytics will need to develop a framework or system that evaluates the impact of these models on different demographic groups with an innate bias within the process. When biased action and fairness assessments are run as part of the detective analytics process, financial institutions can address ethical concerns and improve their predictive models in real time. As a result, when there is a responsible commitment by the company to business analytics and ethics, it can become more strategically aligned with the current regulatory requirements and build long-term relationships with its customers.

In the human resource sector of the global market, predictive analytics will help improve the acquisition of new talents, performance evaluation, and employee engagement. However, bias and other ethical implications can develop in the hiring process. If there is a negative attitude against a certain demographical group of people, the situation will require human resource companies to analyze the predictive models that are used in the recruiting process and performance management system to ensure that it maintains the necessary standards of fairness and transparency. When the outcomes of human resource companies are analyzed, they can properly identify any potential biases based on various demographic factors to help create a diverse and inclusive workplace.

Finally, the retail sector of the market uses predictive analytics for consumer segmentation, sales forecasting, or management. Each of these applications of predictive analytics helps improve the efficiency of the operation. However, ethical concerns or bias that are related to data privacy and consumer profiling can develop. Retailers must implement transparent communication channels of how consumer data is collected and used for predictive analytics. This process will help ensure that all consumers are informed of the process and that their data privacy is fully respected. As a result, the high level of transparency will build a higher level of trust with the consumer and will establish long-term relationships. Understanding the ethical implications of predictive analytics will ultimately contribute to trust among the various stakeholder groups and to developing sustainable business practices within the global environment.

## Discussions on Potential Ethical Dilemmas

All business analytic models contain the potential for ethical dilemmas. There are six main ethical dilemmas that can impact the use of predictive analytics and various industries within the global environment. The first is bias in data. Predictive models are only as accurate as the data on which they are trained to emulate. If historical data contains societal biases, machine learning algorithms may continue these biases in its results, leading to unfair outcomes. The situation makes it important for companies to audit and refine their datasets to ensure that predictive models are correctly trained, leading to unrepresentative and equitable data results. The second is lack of transparency. Predictive models have been accused of making it difficult for stakeholders to understand how decisions are made. The situation is due to a lack of transparency. It is necessary for companies to use business analytics to provide knowledge and insight into the decision-making process. Once the decision has been made, it must be communicated to ensure that all clients understand how the decision was made and assessed through transparency and credibility.

Third is informed consent. Ethical situations can develop when individuals are unaware that the data is being collected for predictive analysis by the company. As an example, predictive analytics can be used to identify risk situations that require a data collection process that must also respect the privacy of the individual. To avoid any ethical violation, companies can implement clear channels of communication to fully inform everyone involved of the data collection process and to place a strong emphasis on informed consent and respect for privacy. The fourth is data privacy. Predictive analytics constantly relies on large datasets that contain personal information. It is critical to ensure that the predictive model protects the privacy of the individual. Individual data can be gathered and collected to enable a company to create a balanced targeted promotion through ethical data usage. As a result, business analytics can help companies implement data protection procedures to ensure that all consumer information is protected while still being able to gain new knowledge and insight.

The fifth is accountability. Predictive analytics can support the decision-making process. However, this can cause an ethical dilemma with accountability. The use of predictive models can raise questions about accountability when someone is unfairly eliminated for consideration within a process without a human explanation. The situation makes it important for business analytics to enable organizations to transparently monitor and track outcomes to guarantee that predictive insights do not take away from fair employment practices. Finally, there is inequitable resource allocation. Predictive analytics can lead to decisions that allocate resources unfairly or unequally. This situation occurs when predictive models inaccurately prioritize the need of certain populations over others based solely on efficiency rather than actual need. When this happens, certain groups of individuals may be ignored or overlooked.

**TABLE 5.1** Potential Ethical Dilemmas

| Characteristic | Ethical Dilemmas | Resolutions |
|---|---|---|
| **Data privacy consent** | Unauthorized data collection, lack of informed consent, and privacy breaches | Implementing clear consent mechanisms, transparent privacy policies, and compliance with regulations |
| **Algorithm bias** | Discriminatory outcomes and perpetuation of existing biases | Regular bias audits, diverse datasets, and inclusive algorithm design |
| **Transparency and accountability** | Lack of clarity in data usage and insufficient accountability | Clear communication of data practices and robust accountability frameworks |
| **Data security** | Data breaches, unauthorized access and misuse of data | Strong encryption, regular security audits, and comprehensive data protection policies |
| **Resource allocation** | Inequitable distribution of resources and prioritization conflicts | Ethical guidelines for resource allocation and stakeholder engagement, fairness principles |

Business analytics needs to help companies assess and revise their current models to ensure that there is equitable resource distribution to improve the overall process and access to essential services for everyone.

Predictive analytics constantly relies on large amounts of data.

## THE ROLE OF CORPORATE SOCIAL RESPONSIBILITY

In business analytics, predictive analytics constantly relies on large amounts of data within the role of corporate social responsibility (CSR). When companies place a priority on CSR, there must be effective use of business analytics to ensure that these efforts are measurable, aligned with the expectations of stakeholders, and/or data-driven. When using business analytics correctly, businesses can better understand their impact on society, improve transparency, and maximize their resource allocation and all CSR initiatives. Within the manufacturing sector, environmental concerns are a major concern. Business analytics must be used to help companies track and determine their environmental footprint on the environment. This situation makes it necessary for manufacturing companies to analyze data that is related to waste production, resource usage, and energy consumption to help create sustainable business practices. With this new information, businesses can develop or adopt greener technologies that result in a reduction in impact to the environment and increased sustainability. Finally, by communicating these new initiatives, manufacturing companies can demonstrate their commitment to ethical business practices while meeting all regulatory requirements and exceeding stakeholder expectations.

Within the retail sector, retailers will use business analytics to determine the success of their CSR initiatives, which include community engagement programs and fair labor practices. Next, retailers will collect data on supplier compliance with ethical labor standards and then analyze the feedback from consumers about social impact initiatives. When business analytics are used by retailers in monitoring supplier performance and guaranteeing a strategic alignment with their ethical standards and beliefs, the situation will improve the level of accountability and encourage suppliers to maintain similar values. Finally, retailers can use the analysis of consumer data to identify emerging trends in behaviors and preferences for ethically sourcing products and allow them to align their inventory marketing strategies with the values of the customer.

Finally, the health-care sector will rely on business analytics and integrate them into its CSR initiatives. Health-care providers and hospitals will study data on community health needs and the effectiveness of their outreach programs. By identifying vulnerable populations and assessing health-care disparities, these institutions can design focused initiatives that align with their CSR objectives and goals. When the situation occurs, health-care providers improve community well-being and public health outcome and maintain their ethical obligations to all regulations and compliance standards. As a result, the analysis of data and feedback will help health-care providers identify potential risks and vulnerabilities and to take proactive measures to protect all consumer information to improve their level of trust and ensure a culture of social responsibility.

### How Analytics Intersects With Sustainability Efforts

There are various ways that business analytics intersects with the sustainability efforts of companies in various industries within the global market. When combining analytics with sustainability efforts, businesses can maximize their operational efficiency, reduce the amount of waste, and support new initiatives that contribute to their sustainability objectives and goals. Next, the strategic alignment improves the reputation of the business, meets all regulatory requirements, and satisfies the expectations of stakeholders. In the manufacturing industry, manufacturers will analyze data that is related to the consumption of raw materials, waste generation, and energy usage. With the use of predictive analytics, manufacturers can forecast future resource needs that enable them to adopt sustainable business practices and just-in-time manufacturing strategies. As a result, manufacturers can minimize their excess production and waste, which will ultimately lead to a lower carbon footprint on the environment.

Second, businesses in the retail industry will use business analytics to support their sustainable business practices. Retailers will use business analytics to understand consumer behavior and preferences so they can customize their inventory to include environmentally friendly products. Through the analysis of sales data and consumer preferences, retailers can identify emerging trends toward sustainable purchasing choices in the future. Next, retailers can use business analytics to maximize their supply chain through statistical analysis to ensure that their products are sourced by responsible suppliers and minimize the carbon footprint that is associated with logistics and the transportation of goods. As a result, the alignment with business analytics and sustainability efforts will benefit retailers since it will support environmentally conscious consumers while also strengthening the ethical position of the retailer in the global marketplace.

Third, companies in the energy sector will use business analytics to support their increasingly important sustainability initiatives and programs. Energy companies rely on data analytics to monitor forecasts on energy demand and consumption patterns and to maximize the integration of renewable energy sources within their daily operation. Through the analysis of data from smart grids and IOT devices, energy companies can accurately identify all inefficiencies and then implement focus on energy-saving measures to improve the process. This strategy creates a new opportunity to promote renewable technologies while reducing dependence on nonrenewable resources. As a result, energy companies can use business analytics to study the impact of their business operations on the environment while ensuring current regulatory compliance and attempting to strive for continuous improvement.

Finally, businesses in the agriculture industry will benefit from business analytics in their chase of sustainability objectives and goals. Agricultural businesses and farmers will analyze data related to water usage, crop performance, and the health of soil to promote improved and sustainable farming practices. By using these advanced statistical models, farmers can develop new data-driven fertilization and irrigation techniques, and agricultural producers can minimize the waste of resources while maximizing their ROI. This strategy guarantees that farming practices will not only be economically viable but also be environmentally responsible. Next, business analytics will help farmers determine the long-term impacts of their current practices on biodiversity and soil health to strategically align production with their sustainability goals.

As a result, the intersection of analytics and sustainability not just improves operational efficiency but instead also increases the level of trust with all stakeholder groups and contributes to the production goal of supporting responsible business practices in the global environment for future generations.

## BUSINESS ANALYTICS FUNCTION FOR ETHICS USING MICROSOFT EXCEL

In the business environment, there are many business analytical terms mentioned that play a critical role in making informed and data-driven choices that drive decisions, optimize daily operations, and develop strategic actions and initiatives. Various statistical concepts play an important role in ethics and business analytics by providing essential tools for data analysis and decision-making. Here's a detailed overview of their definition and importance and how to conduct this statistical analysis using Microsoft Excel.

### Cause-and-Effect Modeling of Data

This approach helps organizations understand the fundamental relationships between different variables that are essential in making informed decisions that directly align with ethical standards. By exploring the potential impacts of decisions, organizations can better avoid unintended threats or weaknesses.

**Steps:**

1. Organize your data into a table with independent variable(s) (the cause) in columns and the dependent variable(s) (the effect) in another column.
2. Use the Data Analysis ToolPak.
3. Select Regression from the Analysis ToolPak options, and input the data ranges for your dependent and independent variables.
4. Click OK to generate the output, which includes coefficients indicating the strength and direction of the relationship.

### Classifications of Data

Effective data classification is critical in guaranteeing that information is handled appropriately, and it enables companies to disperse data responsibly while ensuring compliance with privacy regulations and ethical standards.

**Steps:**

1. Determine the criteria for classification (i.e., age groups, revenue, products, regions, etc.).
2. Use the IF function to assign classification labels.

## Cluster Analysis

By grouping similar data points, cluster analysis is used in identifying patterns that inform ethical practices. This analysis can enhance understanding of customer needs and behaviors while promoting fair business practices in the market.

**Steps:**

1. Collect your data, and ensure it's in a numerical format for clustering.
2. Use the *k*-means clustering process by manually assigning random mean point in separate cells.
3. Calculate distances to each mean point using the Euclidean distance formula, and reassign points to clusters based on proximity.
4. Repeat the steps until the mean point stabilizes.

## Data Mining

Ethical data mining involves separating meaningful knowledge from large datasets while respecting privacy and integrity rights. Next, it allows organizations to make decisions based on comprehensive data analysis instead of relying on biased or incomplete information.

**Steps:**

1. Enter your dataset into Excel.
2. Use PivotTables to summarize key trends or patterns.
3. Apply Filters and Conditional Formatting to identify curious data subsets for easy visual identification.
4. Create charts for visual representation of the newly discovered patterns.

## Expected Present Value (EPV)

Understanding the expected present value of an investment helps companies evaluate the potential risks and returns ethically while also supporting transparency in financial reporting and decision-making.

Formula: EPV = Cash Flow / (1 + r)^n

**Steps:**

1. Use the formula EPV = Cash Flow/(1 + r)^n, where *r* is the discount rate and *n* is the time period.
2. Input = A2/(1 + B2)^C2, for a cash flow in A2, discount rate in B2, and period in C2. Drag the formula down for additional periods (A, B, and C are example cell references depending on where data is placed in the spreadsheet).

### Future Value (FV)

The estimation of future value assists organizations in planning and forecasting ethically to ensure that all potential outcomes are considered and impacts on stakeholders are assessed.

Formula: = FV(rate, nper, pmt, [pv], [type])

**Steps:**

1. Use the FV function = FV(rate, nper, pmt, [pv], [type]). For example: =FV(5%, 10, −1,000) calculates the FV of a series of payments.
2. Replace parameters depending on your specific financial circumstances.

### Internal Rate of Return (IRR)

IRR is critical when evaluating the profitability of investments. Next, ethical investment decisions are led by a clear understanding of the rate of return and allow organizations to prioritize projects that support the social good of society.

Formula: = IRR(values, guess)

**Steps:**

1. Arrange the series of cash flows in a column.
2. Use the formula =IRR(A1:A10), where *A1:A10* is an example where cell values contain your cash flows.

### Measuring Classification of Performance of Data

Performance measurement tools help ensure that organizational practices align with ethical standards by revealing how well a company meets its commitments to stakeholders.

**Steps:**

1. Define performance metrics based on the needs of your data
2. Use performance-tracking formulas (i.e., average, median, mode, etc.) to summarize.
3. Visualize with charts to compare performance across categories.

### Measuring Distance Between Financial Objects

This measurement supports ethical comparisons among financial entities and is used to improve fairness in assessments and helps avoid conflicts of interest.

**Steps:**

1. Normalize your data as required using standardized values.
2. Calculate distances using distance formulas.
3. Use consistent ranges for all financial objects to obtain meaningful metrics.

## Methods of Clustering Analysis

The use of various clustering methodologies that allow for a detailed analysis of consumer segments can lead to designing ethical marketing strategies that respect consumer rights.

**Steps:**

1. Similar procedures as cluster analysis where it defines metrics, calculating distances, and cluster items as needed.
2. Use tools like mean classification for better grouping, or use Excel's built-in clustering features if available.

## Net Present Value (NPV)

NPV is necessary in assessing the value of investments in ethical terms. By analyzing both the costs and the benefits in the present value, organizations can make informed choices that reflect their ethical commitments.

Formula: =NPV(rate, value1, value2)

**Steps:**

1. Use the formula =NPV(rate, value1, value2), where *rate* is your discount rate and *value* corresponds to cash flows over time.

## Normalizing Financial Distance Measures

Normalization assists in standardizing performance comparisons across areas to create fair evaluations free from bias that are critical for ethical assessments.

Formula: = (Value − Mean)/Standard Deviation

**Steps:**

1. Standardize your data by calculating the mean and standard deviation.
2. Use =AVERAGE(range) and =STDEV.P(range) for your dataset.
3. Normalize the data by applying the formula Normalized Value = (Value − Mean)/Standard Deviation.

## Payment (PMT)

Understanding payment structures associated with financial products and services is important to ensure transparency and fairness in offerings while strategically aligning with ethical lending practices.

Formula: =PMT(rate, nper, pv, fv, type)

**Steps:**

1. Use the PMT function to calculate loan payments. The syntax is =PMT(rate, nper, pv, fv, type).
2. Adjust factors based on loan specifics.

### Present Value (PV)

The present value analysis is essential in ensuring that future cash flows are fairly evaluated in the decision-making process and guiding organizations to operate in an ethical manner.

Formula: =PV(rate, nper, pmt, fv, type).

**Steps:**

1. Use the PV function =PV(rate, nper, pmt, fv, type).
2. Enter your values for rate, number of periods, and future cash flows.

### Rate (Internal Rate)

Evaluating rates ethically is important to measure the viability of projects from a risk-return perspective and to ensure that decisions support responsible corporate behavior.

Formula: =IRR(cash flow range)

**Steps:**

1. List out your cash flows in a column.
2. Use the =IRR(cash flow range) function.
3. Excel will determine the internal rate of return based on the cash flow range provided.

### Return on Investment (ROI)

ROI assessments lead to accountability and enable organizations to consider financial returns along with the social and ethical consequences of their investments.

Formula: =(Net Profit/Investment Cost)*100

**Steps:**

1. Calculate ROI using the formula =(Net Profit/Investment Cost)*100.
2. Enter net profit in a cell (i.e., A1) and investment cost in another cell (i.e., B1). The formula will be =(A1-B1)/B1*100 to calculate ROI as a percentage.

## REAL-WORLD EXAMPLES OF ETHICAL INSIGHTS DRIVING BUSINESS SUCCESS

### Toyota Motor Corporation

Toyota Motor Corporation used the integration of ethics and business analytics in driving their sustainable success. The company's commitment to quality and safety is evident in its comprehensive data analysis processes that are used to identify potential issues in vehicle performance. For example, the Toyota Production System uses real-time data to improve manufacturing processes and guarantees that ethical standards are followed. A primary ethical initiative is Toyota's focus on environmental sustainability. By analyzing emissions data from its vehicles, Toyota developed the hybrid Prius. The Prius significantly reduced carbon footprint compared to traditional vehicles. This decision reflects the company's commitment to eco-friendly practices and aligns itself with consumer demand for greener options. Finally, Toyota used stakeholder analysis to examine community feedback and supply chain practices to guarantee ethical sourcing and labor conditions. With this analytical knowledge, Toyota has successfully built a reputation for ethical responsibility and strengthened consumer trust and achieving long-term business success.

**Question 1**

How does the integration of ethics and business analytics contribute to Toyota's sustainable success?

Answer: The integration of ethics and business analytics is important to Toyota's sustainable success as it allows the company to make informed decisions that align with both business objectives and ethical standards. By using comprehensive data analysis processes, Toyota can identify possible issues in vehicle performance to ensure quality and safety. The Toyota Production System demonstrates this integration by using real-time data to enhance manufacturing processes while following ethical standards. This strategy not only improves operational efficiency but also supports Toyota's commitment to ethical practices and strengthens consumer trust and achieving long-term business success.

**Question 2**

In what ways has Toyota demonstrated its commitment to environmental sustainability through business analytics?

Answer: Toyota has demonstrated its commitment to environmental sustainability using business analytics by analyzing emissions data from its vehicles. This analysis led to the development of the hybrid Prius, which significantly reduces carbon footprint compared to traditional vehicles. By focusing on eco-friendly practices, Toyota aligns itself with consumer demand for greener and more environmentally friendly options. This commitment is further demonstrated in the company's continuous efforts to innovate and improve vehicle efficiency and contributed to a more sustainable future.

**Question 3**

How does stakeholder analysis play a role in Toyota's ethical sourcing and labor conditions?

Answer: Stakeholder analysis is crucial in Toyota's approach to ethical sourcing and labor conditions. By examining community feedback and supply chain practices, Toyota ensures that its operations are aligned with ethical standards. This analysis helps the company identify areas for improvement and implement strategies that guarantee ethical sourcing and fair labor conditions. By engaging with stakeholders, Toyota can address all concerns, build stronger relationships, and maintain a reputation for ethical responsibility in the market. This proactive approach not only enhances the company's image but also contributes to its long-term success by building trust and loyalty among consumers and partners.

## Johnson & Johnson

Johnson & Johnson stands out for its commitment to ethics and the effective use of business analytics to drive responsible practices. The company has long emphasized its credo and prioritized the needs of customers, employees, and communities. By implementing data analytics, Johnson & Johnson actively monitors its supply chain to ensure ethical sourcing and compliance with labor standards. One main initiative include comprehensive risk assessment programs that use data analytics to identify and reduce ethical risks related to product safety and environmental impact. This proactive approach improves product quality and reinforces consumer trust in the brand. Finally, Johnson & Johnson applies analytics to track the effectiveness of its health program, which includes community wellness programs. By analyzing health outcomes and community feedback, the company adapts its strategies to meet the changing needs of the populations it serves. With these ethical practices founded in analytical knowledge, Johnson & Johnson continues to achieve sustainable success in the health-care industry.

**Question 1**

How does Johnson & Johnson utilize data analytics to ensure ethical sourcing and compliance with labor standards in its supply chain?

Answer: Johnson & Johnson uses data analytics to constantly monitor its supply chain, ensuring ethical sourcing and compliance with labor standards. By analyzing data from various suppliers, the company can identify potential risks and areas of noncompliance. This process involves evaluating supplier performance, labor practices, and sourcing methods. The use of analytics allows Johnson & Johnson to maintain transparency and accountability within its supply chain, ensuring that all partners follow ethical standards. This approach not only mitigates risks but also strengthens the company's reputation for ethical responsibility.

**Question 2**

In what ways does Johnson & Johnson's risk assessment program contribute to product safety and consumer trust?

Answer: Johnson & Johnson's risk assessment program leverages data analytics to identify and mitigate ethical risks related to product safety and environmental impact. By continuously analyzing data on product performance, safety incidents, and environmental factors, the company can proactively address potential issues before they increase. This approach guarantees that products meet high safety standards and therefore reinforce the trust of consumers. As a result, the program's effectiveness in reducing risks and improving product quality demonstrates Johnson & Johnson's commitment to ethical practices and consumer well-being.

**Question 3**

How does Johnson & Johnson adapt its health programs to meet the changing needs of the populations it serves?

Answer: Johnson & Johnson applies analytics to track the effectiveness of its health programs, including community wellness initiatives. By studying health outcomes and gathering community feedback, the company can determine the impact of its programs and identify areas for improvement. This data-driven approach allows Johnson & Johnson to change its strategies to address the evolving needs of the populations it serves. For example, if data indicates a rise in various health issues within a community, the company can customize its programs to provide targeted interventions. As a result, this adaptability ensures that Johnson & Johnson's health initiatives remain relevant and effective and contribute to the overall well-being of the communities they serve.

## Nestlé

Nestlé demonstrates a strong commitment to ethics through business. With a focus on sustainable sourcing, the company uses data-driven insights to improve its supply chain transparency. By analyzing supplier practices, Nestlé ensures ethical standards are met, especially in sourcing raw materials that include cocoa and coffee. This commitment is reinforced by their "Nestlé Cocoa Plan," which attempts to improve the lives of cocoa farmers and promote sustainable farming practices. Next, Nestlé uses analytics to evaluate the nutritional content of its products to strategically align with its goal of promoting healthier lifestyles. By assessing consumer preferences through data analysis, the company reformulates products to reduce sugar and salt while responding to public health concerns. Finally, Nestlé engaged in community impact assessments by measuring the effectiveness of its initiatives in health and nutrition. Through these ethical practices driven by business analytics, Nestlé strengthens its reputation while achieving sustainable growth in the market.

**Question 1**

How does Nestlé use data-driven insights to enhance supply chain transparency and ensure ethical sourcing?

Answer: Nestlé employs data-driven knowledge to improve supply chain transparency by carefully analyzing supplier practices. This strategy ensures that ethical standards are constantly met, especially in the sourcing of raw materials that include cocoa and coffee. Through initiatives like the "Nestlé Cocoa Plan," the company attempts to improve the livelihoods of cocoa farmers and promotes sustainable farming practices. By using data analytics, Nestlé can monitor and verify the ethical compliance of its suppliers while reinforcing its commitment to sustainability and ethical responsibility.

**Question 2**

In what ways does Nestlé use analytics to align its product offerings with public health goals?

Answer: Nestlé uses analytics to align its product offerings with public health goals by evaluating the nutritional content of its products. Through data analytics, the company assesses consumer preferences and public health concerns, which inform its strategy to redevelop products. This includes reducing sugar and salt content to promote healthier lifestyles. By constantly analyzing nutritional data and consumer feedback, Nestlé can modify its product creations to meet changing health standards and consumer demands and supports its goal of promoting better nutrition and health.

**Question 3**

How does Nestlé measure the effectiveness of its community initiatives in health and nutrition?

Answer: Nestlé measures the effectiveness of its community initiatives in health and nutrition through community impact assessments. By collecting and analyzing data on the outcomes of its health and nutrition programs, the company can evaluate their success and areas for improvement. This data-driven method allows Nestlé to understand the impact of its initiatives on community well-being and make informed decisions to improve their effectiveness. By focusing on measurable outcomes, Nestlé can ensure that its efforts contribute positively to community health and strategically align with its ethical and sustainability goals.

## Moderna Inc.

Moderna Inc. integrated ethics and business analytics to drive success through innovative healthcare solutions. The company's commitment to transparency and ethical practices is unmistakable in its data-driven approach to vaccine development. Throughout the COVID-19 pandemic, Moderna used advanced analytics to monitor and analyze clinical trial data to ensure the safety and effectiveness of its mRNA technology while following regulatory standards. Next, Moderna employs analytics to assess supply chain integrity and ensure that raw materials and components meet ethical sourcing guidelines. This thorough process enables the company to maintain high product quality and ethical standards throughout its production processes. Finally, Moderna engages in continuous evaluation of its corporate social responsibility initiatives and analyzing community health outcomes to adapt its efforts. This data-informed strategy not only aligns with ethical commitments but also improves the trust of the public.

**Question 1**

How does Moderna Inc. use business analytics to guarantee the safety and effectiveness of its mRNA technology during the COVID-19 pandemic?

Answer: Moderna Inc. employs advanced business analytics to monitor and analyze clinical trial data to ensure the safety and effectiveness of its mRNA technology. By leveraging data-driven insights, the company can track the performance of its vaccines in real time, identify any potential safety concerns, and make informed decisions to address them promptly. This approach ensures compliance with regulatory standards and enhances the complete reliability and trustworthiness of Moderna's vaccine development process. The use of business analytics allows Moderna to maintain transparency and uphold its commitment to ethical practices that ultimately contribute to the successful deployment of its COVID-19 vaccines.

**Question 2**

In what ways does Moderna ensure ethical sourcing and supply chain integrity using analytics?

Answer: Moderna ensures ethical sourcing and supply chain integrity by employing analytics to assess the quality and ethical standards of raw materials and components used in its production processes. By analyzing data from suppliers, Moderna can verify compliance with ethical sourcing guidelines and identify any potential risks or differences. This thorough evaluation process helps maintain high product quality and ensures that all materials meet the company's ethical standards. By integrating analytics into its supply chain management, Moderna can proactively address any concerns and use this information to reinforce its commitment to ethical practices and maintaining consumer trust.

**Question 3**

How does Moderna's data-informed strategy enhance its corporate social responsibility (CSR) initiatives and public trust?

Answer: Moderna's data-informed strategy improves its corporate social responsibility (CSR) initiatives by continuously evaluating community health outcomes and adapting its efforts accordingly. By analyzing data on the impact of its initiatives, Moderna can identify areas for improvement and focus on its strategies to better meet the needs of the communities it serves. This approach aligns with the company's ethical commitments and demonstrates a genuine dedication to improving public health. By transparently sharing the results of its efforts and making data-driven adjustments, Moderna builds public trust and strengthens its reputation as a responsible and ethical health-care provider.

## CASE STUDIES ON ETHICAL SUCCESS THROUGH ANALYTICS

### Business Success Through Business Analytics

Business analytics plays a crucial role in understanding ethical trends and consumer behavior that enables organizations in the ethics industry to make more data-driven and informed decisions. Following are three examples of how ethical data and knowledge are translated into business success using analytics:

### Example 1: Ethical Solutions

Ethical Solutions is a fictional company that specializes in providing ethical compliance software to businesses. By using business analytics, Ethical Solutions has developed a platform that helps companies identify potential ethical risks in their operations. The software analyzes data from various sources, such as employee reports, financial transactions, and supply chain activities, to detect patterns that may indicate unethical behavior. The company's success is largely attributed to its ability to provide actionable insights that help businesses maintain ethical standards. For instance, Ethical Solutions' analytics can predict the likelihood of compliance breaches, allowing companies to take preventive measures. This proactive approach not only helps businesses avoid legal issues but also enhances their reputation as ethical organizations.

#### *Short-Response Questions*

1. What type of software does Ethical Solutions provide?
2. How does Ethical Solutions' platform help businesses?
3. What is one benefit of using Ethical Solutions' analytics?

### Example 2: Integral Analytics

Integral Analytics is a consultancy firm that offers ethical auditing services to corporations. By employing advanced business analytics, the company evaluates a client's ethical practices and provides detailed reports on areas needing improvement. Integral Analytics uses data from employee surveys, customer feedback, and market trends to assess a company's ethical standing.

The firm's success is driven by its comprehensive approach to ethical auditing. By providing clients with a clear understanding of their ethical strengths and weaknesses, Integral Analytics enables them to implement targeted strategies for improvement.

#### *Short-Response Questions*

1. What service does Integral Analytics provide?
2. What sources of data does Integral Analytics use for its assessments?
3. How does Integral Analytics benefit its clients?

### Example 3: Virtuous Ventures

Virtuous Ventures is a fictional start-up that focuses on developing ethical investment portfolios. By leveraging business analytics, the company identifies companies with strong ethical practices and includes them in their investment offerings. Virtuous Ventures uses data on corporate social responsibility, environmental impact, and governance practices to evaluate potential investments.

The start-up's success is attributed to its ability to attract investors who prioritize ethical considerations. By providing transparent and data-driven insights into the ethical performance of companies, Virtuous Ventures builds trust with its clients. This approach not only drives business success but also promotes ethical business practices across industries.

#### *Short-Response Questions*

1. What is the focus of Virtuous Ventures?
2. What criteria does Virtuous Ventures use to evaluate potential investments?
3. How does Virtuous Ventures build trust with its clients?

## CASE STUDY: CIRCLEOFETHICS CONSULTING

CircleOfEthics Consulting is an established leading firm dedicated to advising organizations on ethical practices and corporate social responsibility (CSR). Recognizing the high demand for transparent business operations and ethical engagement, CircleOfEthics has positioned itself as an expert in guaranteeing companies uphold ethical standards across their enterprises. In its years of operation, the company has served over 150 clients, guiding them through complex ethical situations and compliance requirements in diverse markets that include technology, finance, and manufacturing. Finally, CircleOfEthics' unique value plan is built upon comprehensive data analysis of industry trends and ethical practices.

### Business Analytics Data Tables

**TABLE 5.2** Client Engagement Metrics

| 1 | A | B | C | D |
|---|---|---|---|---|
| | Client Industry | Number of Clients | Average Consulting Fee ($) | Ethical Compliance Score (1–10) |
| 2 | Technology | 50 | 5,000 | 7.5 |
| 3 | Finance | 40 | 7,500 | 6.8 |
| 4 | Manufacturing | 30 | 4,000 | 8.2 |
| 5 | Health care | 20 | 6,000 | 7.0 |
| 6 | Retail | 10 | 4,500 | 5.5 |

**TABLE 5.3** Financial Performance Outcomes

| 1 | A | B | C | D | E |
|---|---|---|---|---|---|
| | Year | Total Revenue ($) | Total Expenses ($) | Investment ($) | Client Satisfaction Score (1–10) |
| 2 | 2021 | 600,000 | 400,000 | 200,000 | 8.5 |
| 3 | 2022 | 900,000 | 500,000 | 300,000 | 9.0 |
| 4 | 2023 | 1,200,000 | 600,000 | 250,000 | 9.5 |

### Analytics Problems Using Excel

1. Using the NPV function, calculate the net present value of CircleOfEthics' investments over three years if the discount rate is 10%.
2. Determine the IRR (internal rate of return) for the investment stream over the same three years using the IRR function.
3. Conduct a cluster analysis on the ethical compliance scores of clients across different industries to identify which sectors need more focus on ethical improvements.
4. Implement data mining techniques to classify clients based on the combination of their ethical compliance scores and consulting fees to find patterns in client behavior.
5. Calculate the return on investment (ROI) for each year based on the total revenue and total expenses, and analyze which year had the highest ROI using the formula ROI = (Total Revenue − Total Expenses)/(Total Expenses).

### Answer Key

1. *Calculating net present value (NPV).* Formula: =NPV(0.1, B2:B4)-C2-C3-C4, where *B2:B4* ranges from total revenue, and *C2:C4* for total expenses. This computes the net present value of cash flows over three years by subtracting the total initial investment.
2. *Calculating internal rate of return (IRR).* Formula: =IRR(A2:A4), where *A2:A4* captures the initial investment as a negative cash flow, followed by the positive cash flows from net revenues for 2021, 2022, and 2023. This will generate the internal rate of return for the investments made.
3. *Conducting cluster analysis.* Use the Data Analysis ToolPak and select Cluster Analysis. Define the range with ethical compliance scores, and analyze how many distinct clusters emerge and which industries show similar compliance scores, and tailor strategies accordingly.
4. *Data mining for classification.* Create a PivotTable using ethical compliance scores and consulting fees from data in Table 5.1. This analysis will reveal patterns in which combinations of score ranges correspond to specific consulting fees, helping identify client segmentation.
5. *Calculating return on investment (ROI).* For each year, calculate ROI as:
   =(B2 − C2)/C2 for 2021
   =(B3 − C3)/C3 for 2022
   =(B4 − C4)/C4 for 2023
   This calculation will reveal the ROI for each year, and you can summarize finding the highest ROI.

---

## CASE STUDY: ETHOANSWERS INC.

EthoAnswers Inc. is a consulting company specializing in helping businesses implement ethical practices and corporate social responsibility (CSR) initiatives. The company has built a reputation for guiding organizations through complex ethical dilemmas and ensuring compliance with industry standards. Recently, EthoAnswers Inc. partnered with a large manufacturing company to develop a comprehensive CSR strategy aimed at reducing environmental impact and improving labor practices. To determine the effectiveness of the CSR initiatives, EthoAnswers Inc. collected data on various metrics that included carbon emissions, employee satisfaction, and community engagement over a year. The data was analyzed to identify areas of improvement and measure the return on investment (ROI) of the implemented strategies. The following tables summarize key findings from the project:

### Analytics Problems Using Excel

1. *Classification of data.* Classify the data in Table 5.1 into different categories based on carbon emissions.
2. *Cluster analysis.* Perform a cluster analysis on the employee satisfaction and community engagement data.
3. *Data mining.* Identify patterns in the environmental impact metrics using data mining techniques.

**TABLE 5.4** Environmental Impact Metrics

| 1 | A | B | C | D |
|---|---|---|---|---|
| | **Month** | **Carbon Emissions (Tons)** | **Energy Consumption (kWh)** | **Waste Reduction (%)** |
| **2** | January | 1,200 | 50,000 | 10 |
| **3** | February | 1,150 | 48,000 | 12 |
| **4** | March | 1,100 | 46,000 | 15 |
| **5** | April | 1,050 | 44,000 | 18 |
| **6** | May | 1,000 | 42,000 | 20 |
| **7** | June | 950 | 40,000 | 22 |

**TABLE 5.5** Employee Satisfaction and Community Engagement

| 1 | A | B | C |
|---|---|---|---|
| | **Month** | **Employee Satisfaction (Out of 10)** | **Community Engagement (Hours)** |
| **2** | January | 7.5 | 100 |
| **3** | February | 7.6 | 110 |
| **4** | March | 7.8 | 120 |
| **5** | April | 8.0 | 130 |
| **6** | May | 8.2 | 140 |
| **7** | June | 8.5 | 150 |

4. *Expected present value.* Calculate the expected present value of the CSR initiatives over the next five years.
5. *Future value.* Determine the future value of the energy savings achieved.
6. *Internal rate of return.* Calculate the internal rate of return for the CSR investments.
7. Net present value. Compute the net present value of the CSR initiatives.
8. *Measuring distance between financial objects.* Measure the distance between financial metrics, such as carbon emissions and energy consumption.
9. *Payment.* Calculate the monthly payment required to fund the CSR initiatives.
10. *Present value.* Determine the present value of future community engagement benefits.
11. *Internal rate.* Calculate the internal rate of return for employee satisfaction improvements.
12. *Return on investment.* Compute the return on investment for the CSR initiatives.

## Answer Key

1. *Classification of data.* Use the IF function to classify carbon emissions: =IF(A2<1000, "Low", IF(A2<1100, "Medium", "High")).
2. *Cluster analysis.* Use the *k*-means clustering tool in Excel's Data Analysis ToolPak. Input the employee satisfaction and community engagement data.
3. *Data mining.* Use the Data Mining Add-In for Excel to identify patterns in the environmental impact metrics.

4. *Expected present value.* Use the NPV function: =NPV(rate, value1, [value2], . . .).
5. *Future value.* Use the FV function: =FV(rate, nper, pmt, [pv], [type]).
6. *Internal rate of return.* Use the IRR function: =IRR(values, [guess]).
7. *Net present value.* Use the NPV function: =NPV(rate, value1, [value2], . . .).
8. *Measuring distance between financial objects.* Use the DISTANCE function or calculate manually using the Euclidean distance formula.
9. *Payment.* Use the PMT function: =PMT(rate, nper, pv, [fv], [type]).
10. *Present value.* Use the PV function: =PV(rate, nper, pmt, [fv], [type]).
11. *Internal rate.* Use the IRR function: =IRR(values, [guess]).
12. *Return on investment.* Use the ROI formula: =(Gain from Investment − Cost of Investment)/Cost of Investment.

CHAPTER 6

# Management and Business Analytics

Management and business analytics are important in allowing organizations to make strategic and informed decisions by using knowledge that is gained from the studying of data. In today's global environment, organizations across multiple industries heavily rely on business analytics to improve efficiency, drive innovation, and maximize operations. For business analytics to be effective it must be seamlessly integrated with the management practices of the organization. As a result, the integration of business analytics and management enables organizations to achieve their objectives and goals and to remain adaptable to the changing dynamics of the market.

The main role of management and business analytics is to strategically align all organizational activities with the objectives and goals and to make sure that all decisions are made based on reliable and accurate data. Next, management works with data analysts and technology professionals to identify new opportunities for improvements to create a new strategic direction within the markets for the company based on the results of the analysis of data. The situation requires management to be capable of transforming complex datasets into actions to create a better decision-making process that can be measured by key performance metrics that benefit the organization. Finally, management is responsible for using business analytics in implementing the outcome using data focused approaches across all departments within the organization.

Next, business analytics for managers includes using techniques such as data mining, statistical analysis, and predictive modeling to study the performance of the organization, forecast future trends, and identify changes in the market. Next, managers and organizations will rely on business analytics to gain new information and knowledge to improve the experience of customers, maximize resources, and to solve current and potential problems within the internal and external environments. In the retail industry, managers use business analytics to determine consumer purchasing trends, create focus marketing campaigns, and determine the efficiency of the supply chain.

In health care, health-care providers rely on business analytics to make decisions about the allocation of resources, cost management strategies, and patient care. Next, management in the financial services industry news business analytics to improve investment strategies, detect fraud, and assess risk levels. In the manufacturing sector, managers use business analytics to streamline production processes and strengthen the supply chain management system. The situation is achieved by managers, reducing costs, increasing quality, and minimizing

DOI: 10.4324/9781003629658-6

waste using business analytics to gain a competitive advantage in the marketplace. In the technology industry, managers rely on business analytics to analyze consumer behavior, drive innovation, and improve the features of products. As a result, management and the integration of business analytics for benefits. All stakeholder groups and the organization guarantee long-term growth in the environment.

Finally, managers fully integrate and use business analytics to help ensure that data is used ethically to protect sensitive information of both the organization and the consumer. The situation requires managers to use policies and protocols to protect information and to comply with all regulatory standards and laws. The situation makes managers responsible for developing a data-focused culture. This strategy will promote collaboration between all team members and decision-makers. With the creation of a data-focused and collaborative culture, managers can guarantee that all analytical tools and resources that are used will be effective but will also ensure sustainability and long-term growth for the needs of the organization and stakeholders.

## DATA-DRIVEN DECISION-MAKING IN MANAGEMENT

Organizations rely on management to make data-driven decisions. The integration of management and business analytics is necessary for guiding organizations to long-term strategic success by making effective data-driven informed decisions. Business analytics involves the practice of collecting, analyzing, and interpreting data to determine the rights decision or action. However, management must use the results from data analytics to ensure that the objectives and goals of the organization are achieved. When management and business analytics work together, they will improve operational efficiency, improve the decision-making process, and drive performance in all industries in the global market.

When data is used to make decisions, management can respond proactively to identifying new opportunities, responding to challenges, and allocating resources efficiently. Next, management uses business analytical tools and methodologies to determine key performance indicators, address complex problems, and forecast future trends. The situation requires management to rely on data instead of personal intuition. As a result, the process of management becomes more accurate and precise due to it being based on measurable outcomes that maximize returns and minimize risks.

Management supports the use of business analytics in various industries within the global environment. First, retailers use business analytics to convert consumer data into information that helps management, improve personal marketing strategies, pricing models, and inventory planning. Next, the health-care industry uses business analytics to optimize resource allocation, improve operational efficiency, and increase the success of patient care. Third, financial companies use business analytics to detect fraud, maximize their portfolios, and conduct risk assessments so management and ensure that the organization will remain compliant and profitable.

Next, managers and business analytics in manufacturing companies use statistics to improve the performance of production, develop cost-saving measures, and reduce the amount of waste. As a result, data-driven, informed decisions in the manufacturing industry help to improve the supply chain management system by guaranteeing that all goods are delivered in a timely manner. Finally, the technology and telecommunications sectors of the global markets use business analytics to help managers identify behavior patterns of consumers, to improve the delivery of products and services, and to create new product offerings.

Management also uses business analytics to develop an organizational structure that integrates statistics into its daily processes. Managers and organizations are responsible for setting clear objectives and goals and using the necessary analytical tools to ensure success for the decision-makers. This strategy guarantees that information gained from business analytics is well thought out, actionable, and is strategically aligned with the mission and vision of the organization. Finally, managers must incorporate ethical standards and their use of business analytics to guarantee compliance and security with all federal and regulatory requirements. This situation will create transparency and trust in data sharing that is necessary for long-term success and sustainability in the market.

## Leveraging Analytics for Strategic Management Decisions

It is important for organizations to use business analytics when making strategic management decisions. Management must develop strategies using business analytics that strategically align the objectives and goals of the organization while responding to all opportunities and threats based on the changing and dynamic editions of the market. Management can use predictive analytics to anticipate future trends, behavior of consumers, and potential risks. The situation helps managers to become proactive in their planning instead of making reactive decisions. However, descriptive analytics issues by management to determine the main causes of problems provide a clear overview of current performance levels to enable them to identify areas of improvement so they can strengthen their business processes.

The use of business analytics to make strategic management decisions is seen in multiple industries. First, retail relies on his management team to use business analytics to identify pricing strategies, personalize the experience of the consumer, and adjust inventory levels to meet the changing needs of demand. Next, the management team of a health-care provider uses business analytics to focus on resource allocation, operational efficiency, and improving patient care. The use of business analytics enables health-care managers to solve problems that are related to the delivery of services.

For financial institutions, managers use business analytics to lead investment strategies, detect fraud, and analyze risk profiles by using the results to make data-driven decisions to guarantee compliance with regulatory standards and ensure long-term profitability. For manufacturing companies, managers rely on business analytics in the decision-making process to improve the production process, analyze the performance of equipment, improve the workflow of the supply chain and to reduce waste. The knowledge gained by using business analytics enables management to deliver high-quality products and to maintain cost efficiency in his business operation.

In the technology and telecommunications industries, managers use business analytics to make the decision-making process to study consumer behavior, develop new product opportunities, and monitor the performance of their system. As a result, managers within this industry to use the results to improve consumer engagement strategies, to build long-term value and dynamic markets, and to lead innovation of new products and services. Within all these industries, management must guarantee that the use of business analytics and data-driven processes are fully integrated into the process and strategy of the organization. This strategy includes the alignment of business objectives with long-term analytical goals by using tools that are capable of handling large datasets that promote collaboration between decision-makers across all departments. Finally, managers are responsible for maintaining ethical usage of data and ensuring data security and compliance with legal standards when integrating business analytics into the decision-making process.

## PERFORMANCE MANAGEMENT SYSTEMS

Business analytics is important to the performance management systems of all entrepreneurial companies. The integration of business analytics with entrepreneurial management improves the performance management systems by measuring, monitoring, and ensuring operational effectiveness that leads to innovation and strategic growth for businesses. Companies rely on business analytics to create data-driven models and business strategies to maximize the decision-making process and improve the operations of the business. The situation requires management to develop a performance management system that focuses on determining outcomes that strategically align with the objectives and goals of the organization. As a result, management and business analytics creates a dynamic and fluid approach that supports continuous improvements and adaptability for various industries within the global market.

Management focuses on solving problems, implementing innovative solutions, and identifying new opportunities that enable companies to increase their level of sustainability and to gain a competitive advantage. Managers rely on business analytics to forecast demands, identify trends, and evaluate market conditions using data-driven information. Business analytics supports management and understanding the key performance indicators and benchmarks within the performance management system to gain comprehensive understanding of how decisions made by the business impact its position within the market.

Next, business analytics acts as the backbone of the performance management system of an organization by studying data that impacts the monitoring, evaluation, and strategic processes required for success. Business analytics uses advanced statistical models and methods that include predictive modeling, statistical analysis, and visualization to interpret large and complex datasets so informed decisions and recommendations can be made. The situation enables managers to use business analytics to effectively assess efficiency, profitability, customer satisfaction, and productivity levels.

As a result, managers can customize their performance management processes to meet the needs of businesses across all industries. As a result, managers play an important role in incorporating business analytics within the culture of the organization by focusing on the importance of data in obtaining the objectives and goals of the organization. Managers use business analytics within the performance management systems to develop a strategic plan, allocate resources and to adjust workflows to meet the changing needs within their environment.

### Integrating Analytics Into Performance Evaluations

Business analytics must be integrated into performance evaluations. When business analytics is combined with the expertise of management, using statistical tools can develop a more objective, transparent, trustworthy, and actionable evaluation process to help organizations identify their strengths and weaknesses to maximize their overall performance within all industries. Business analytics supports the integration of data management into performance evaluations by developing statistical tools to measure and study the performance metrics of the individual and business. Managers must rely on this information to effectively determine efficiency, productivity, and achieve goals at both the individual and organizational level.

When business analytics are used effectively, the performance evaluations conducted by management become more measurable and focus on outcomes instead of subjective opinions. This strategy improves the level of accountability within the decision-making process. As a result, managers can use protective modeling within performance evaluations by providing real-time data into trends using dashboards and statistical modeling to guide the evaluation process and future decision-making.

As a result, the successful integration of business analytics performance evaluations requires management to develop clear key performance indicators that connect individual performance to the goals of the organization. This process will require collaboration between managers and decision-makers to implement the necessary statistical tools, design, visualization of data through dashboards, and regular reporting systems. Finally, managers will be responsible for developing the culture of transparency and trust to ensure the performance evaluations are based on ethical and accurate analytics that are aligned with the human resource policies of the organization.

## ANALYZING ORGANIZATIONAL BEHAVIOR

Business analytics is used to study the behavior of an organization within all sectors of the global environment. Business analytics is managers understand the organizational behavior required for maximizing the performance of the workforce, achieving strategic objectives and goals, and improving the flow of communication within the internal and external environments. Using a data-driven approach, business analytics assist managers in making data-informed decisions, assessing patterns of behavior, and implementing new initiatives that improve the productivity and collaboration of the organization.

Next, business analytics uses qualitative and quantitative data to break down all aspects of organizational behavior that include team dynamics, leadership effectiveness, and employee satisfaction. Managers use results of business analytics to inefficiencies within the business process, and to identify new trends. As an example, managers use business analytics to use statistical tools to conduct employee turnover, modeling, engagement scores, and sentiment analysis to help understand what drives the morale and behavior of employees within a business. By incorporating data into the organizational behavior analysis, managers can make objective decisions to understand the best solution to improve the management of the workforce.

As a result, managers play an important role in applying the results of organizational behavior analysis throughout all departments of the organization. This strategy includes implementation of customized strategies that are focused on improving productivity, employee retention, and employee satisfaction levels. Managers also are responsible for prison business analytics to acknowledge all challenges and weaknesses in leadership to improve their effectiveness in overseeing the dynamics of teams. As a result, managers are responsible for using behavioral analysis to ensure that it remains data-driven, ethical, and strategically aligns with the vision of the organization.

### Understanding Workforce Dynamics Through Data

It is important for management to understand the dynamics of the workforce through data analysis and business analytics. Using a data-driven approach enables managers within businesses to make informed decisions to maximize productivity, maintain a positive organizational culture, and strategically align the workforce with the vision and mission of businesses throughout all industries. In the retail industry, management relies on business analytics to understand the relationship between customer satisfaction and employee performance. By studying metrics that include task completion rates, consumer feedback, and sales figures, managers understand how the workforce dynamics impact the outcome of the business.

In the manufacturing industry, managers rely on business analytics to maximize the performance of teams in the production process. The situation is important in understanding the dynamics of the workforce and how it impacts timeliness, quality and level of output. Business analytics will be used by management to analyze downtime, safety compliance, and productivity to enable managers to improve the daily operational processes and to support teamwork within the company. In the health-care industry, managers use business analytics to study the efficiency of the workforce and teamwork among all health-care providers. The situation provides new information and insights for managers and to the collaborative workflows, scheduling of staff, and interactions between the patient and provider to help management improve efficiency in the delivery of services.

For financial companies, business analytics is used by managers to understand interpersonal interactions, behavior, and employee roles impact relationships with clients in the performance of an organization. The situation provides managers with information and knowledge into the dynamics of the workforce and how they can improve their decision-making process, still strategies, and employee development programs for future success. As a result, to improve the benefits of workforce dynamics, managers must analyze the data to become proactive in integrating leadership practices in human resource strategies. This process includes using performance metrics that accurately reflect business objectives and employee engagements while using feedback loops based on the analytical results of the analysis.

## OPERATIONAL EFFICIENCY ANALYTICS

Operational efficiency analytics is the process of using data to measure how effectively resources are used within an organization. Resources can include labor, time, and capital required for an organization to provide products or services to the community. Organizations rely on managers using business analytics to gain information from key performance indicators and to analyze trends to determine areas of improvement. The situation requires managers to interpret the results of the findings using business analytics to develop strategic objectives that are analytically aligned with the long-term goals. As a result, when business analytics is integrated into operational efficiency, managers can develop a process and adjust the operation that is made systematically and methodically to provide a measurable result.

In manufacturing, operational efficiency analytics is necessary for improving the production process and supply chain management system. Managers use operational efficiency analytics to study inventory turnover, defect rates, and machine usage and then use predictive modeling to determine future disruptions and to recommend preventative measures. In retail, managers use operational efficiency analytics to maximize inventory levels, improve pricing strategies, and reduce over stock or stock outs. The situation is achieved by studying consumer trends in sales performance to help managers guarantee that all resources are allocated effectively across their product lines and geographic market sectors.

In health care, operational efficiency analytics helps managers to improve the delivery of patient care using metrics that include the usage of resources, wait times, and the productivity of staff. These performance metrics help to improve the workflow process and provide higher quality service for the health-care provider. As a result, managers will help the health-care organization to reduce costs and to improve outcomes. In the finance industry, managers use operational efficiency analytics to study the exposure to risk, employee productivity, and the processing time transactions. This information is useful in the identification of new opportunities for automation of processes, improving consumer experiences, and reducing overhead costs. To fully take advantage of operational efficiency, analytics, managers and all industries must develop clear metrics that align with the objectives and goals of the organization.

## Tools for Assessing and Improving Operations

Business analytics provides organizations and managers with qualitative and quantitative tools that include predictive models, dashboards, visualization, statistical analysis, and performance tracking methodologies. These various fools help managers to determine the primary functions of daily operations, including workflow efficiency, cost effectiveness, consumer outcomes, and resource usage. By using these tools, managers can understand and interpret the operational data and determine areas that need attention or improvement. As a result of this data-driven approach, managers can become more responsible for the operational assessments of the organization, making sure that all decisions are objective, actionable and strategically aligned with the mission and vision of the business.

In the retail industry, management uses business analytics to streamline operations that include pricing strategies, supply chain, logistics, and inventory management. This process is achieved by studying trends in sales and consumer demand, studying stock levels, improving delivery efficiency times, and reducing waste. As a result, business analytics helps managers to maximize the scheduling of their workforce by studying employee productivity rates and consumer traffic patterns. For health-care providers, managers use business analytics tools to determine the process of patient care delivery and usage of resources. Analytics that must be monitored include staff productivity, equipment usage, and patient wait times to make improvements to reduce costs while maintaining high quality standards of service.

For manufacturers, managers use business analytics to assess the efficiency of production to minimize the number of defects within the process. Statistical tools that are used include predictive maintenance software that studies the performance of machine data to make predictions about potential equipment failures, optimizing output, and reducing downtime. For financial institutions, managers rely on analytical tools to analyze the speed of transactions, monitor consumer satisfaction metrics, and identify exposures to risk for the organization. As a result, managers and all industries use qualitative and quantitative data to improve the decision-making process, implement new technologies that improve customer experience, improve operational productivity, and streamline processes using clear objectives and performance benchmarks based on the goals of the business.

## PROJECT MANAGEMENT AND ANALYTICS

Project management is a process of organizing and coordinating daily tasks, resources, and stakeholders to achieve specific objectives or goals within an organization. Business analytics is used to support this process by providing statistical tools and methodologies to evaluate predicted outcomes, performance metrics, and to identify risks before they negatively impact the success of the organization's project. This situation requires managers to use forecasting models, performance tracking systems, and analytical dashboards to track and study data by monitoring the progress at every stage of the project life cycle. As a result, the integration of business analytics into project management enables managers to make real-time adjustments to current strategies and to improve the usage of resources to ensure the project is completed on schedule and without exceeding cost.

In the construction and engineering industries, project management analytics are used to track the usage of resources, evaluate risks related to delays or overruns or projects, and to assess the timelines of projects. The situation requires managers to rely on business analytics to effectively plan the allocation of resources, maximize work schedules, improve project efficiency by following specifications, and to improve all safety measures. In the manufacturing industry, project management analytics include focusing on factory upgrades, product launches, and implementation of new systems. The use of project management analytics helps managers to study work slowdowns, monitor progress, and to predict disruptions in the supply chain to guarantee the projects are run smoothly and are completed on time.

In software development and technology, project management analytics is important in ensuring the delivery of new products to consumers. In this industry, managers will use analytics to study all risk factors that can impact the testing and deployment of products. The situation will require the analysis of real-time progress based on historical data so managers can prioritize tasks, improve alignment, satisfy stakeholders and eliminate any inefficiencies within the process. In health care, project management, analytics are used to implement new medical technologies to support population health programs, and to maximize the workflow of patient care.

**TABLE 6.1** Project Analytics Used to Manage Projects, Timelines, and Resources

| Analytics | Description | Purpose |
|---|---|---|
| **Earned value management (EVM)** | Measures project performance and progress in terms of cost and schedule | Helps in tracking project budget and schedule adherence |
| **Resource utilization** | Tracks how effectively project resources are being used | Ensures optimal use of resources and identifies under- or over-utilization |
| **Schedule variance (SV)** | Compares planned progress with actual progress | Identifies delays or accelerations in the project timeline |
| **Cost variance (CV)** | Compares planned budget with actual expenditure | Detects budget overruns or savings |
| **Work velocity** | Measures the rate at which work is completed | Predicts project completion time and identifies bottlenecks |
| **Risk analysis** | Evaluates potential risks and their impact on the project | Helps in proactive risk management and mitigation |

As a result, managers and all industries use project management analytics to develop milestones and benchmarks, ensure compliance, and improve the coordination of resources. For project management analytics to successfully be implemented, managers must first define key performance indicators that are relevant to each project and become integral in the statistical method of collecting, analyzing, and reporting real-time data. This situation will guarantee that all stakeholders that are involved in the process have access to the necessary information and will develop collaboration among team members, managers, leaders, and departments that will ultimately result in a data-driven decision-making process and a higher level of accountability.

Business analytics and managing projects and timelines and resources can be used in various industries with support of different analytic methods that are demonstrated in Table 6.1.

## CHANGE MANAGEMENT THROUGH DATA INSIGHTS

Change management through data insights is the process of leading organizations through transformations that include technological upgrades, restructuring efforts, and process improvements to achieve the desired objective strategic goals established in the mission and vision of the business. Business analytics is used to improve the change management process by providing information and knowledge using data analysis that allows managers to make informed decisions to anticipate future challenges and to measure the impact of the change initiative on the organization.

Regardless of the industry, business analytics empowers all managers to analyze and interpret the results of the data as it is related to the performance of the organization, consumer behavior, and dynamics of the workforce. As an example, predictive analytics allows managers to predict the potential outcome of plan changes. However, diagnostic analytics helps managers to better understand the main cause of inefficiencies or challenges that can occur due to the transformation process. The knowledge gained by using business analytics as part of the change process helps managers to develop better strategies that prioritize initiatives and create measurable objectives and goals for the change management process.

During the implementation of the change phase, business analytics become important in monitoring and assessing progress to guarantee there is strategic alignment with the goals of the organization. Various tools are used during this process that include real-time tracking systems, performance metrics, and dashboards to help managers accurately evaluate the effectiveness of the change initiative. This strategy is achieved by managers identifying any areas that are resistant to change to redefine strategies accordingly. Next, managers within businesses are undergoing the change process. Managers can use sentiment analysis and employee engagement data to gain information into the feelings of the workforce about the change. The strategy enables managers to customize training, communication, and other support efforts to develop a smoother transition process for all industries to reduce downtime, determine satisfaction levels, and reduce risk while increasing collaboration and long-term success.

## Analytics in Facilitating Organizational Change

Business analytics is necessary and facilitates organizational change. Organizational changes include implementation of new technologies, adopting new innovative strategies, and restructuring existing processes. This strategy requires managers to conduct careful coordination of efforts to minimize disruptions to the change process. When business analytics is integrated into the change management process, managers can develop a better understanding of the anticipation of challenges and needs of the organization, monitor the impact of the change, and guarantee strategic alignment with the established objectives and goals. Within all industries of the global market, the integration of business analytics with the change management process will lead to an increase in efficiency and effectiveness for the business.

Business analytics offers the necessary statistical tools and methods to collect, analyze, and interpret data that are important to change within the organization. It is the role of managers to use this information to identify areas of improvement, develop actionable strategies, and to predict the effects of the intended change. One tool that can be used by managers is predictive analytics to predict the potential impact of the proposed changes, while then using descriptive analytics to help them understand the historical patterns and trends that may support the current decision-making process. As a result, the information collected by using business analytics will help managers to create effective change management initiatives that specifically address the challenges and opportunities facing the organization.

During the transition phase of organizational change, business analytics managers monitor progress using KPIs that include real-time reporting systems and dashboards that support continuous improvements of productivity and employee engagement. When data is analyzed during the transition phase of the change process, managers can identify bottlenecks or slowdowns and quickly adapt their strategies to respond to the emerging challenges or threats to the change initiative. As a result, information gained from the use of data analytics will improve the communication process between management, leadership, and employees by offering transparency and clarity as part of the decision-making process to explain the necessity and outcomes of the change initiative.

## BUSINESS ANALYTICS FUNCTION FOR MANAGEMENT USING MICROSOFT EXCEL

In the business environment, there are many business analytical terms mentioned that play a critical role in making informed and data-driven choices that drive decisions, optimize daily operations, and develop strategic actions and initiatives. Various statistical concepts play an important role in management and business analytics by providing essential tools for data analysis and decision-making. Here's a detailed overview of their definition and importance and how to conduct this statistical analysis using Microsoft Excel.

### Regression Assumptions

These foundational assumptions that include linearity, independence, homoscedasticity, and normality of residuals are critical in ensuring the validity of regression results. Understanding and testing these assumptions enables organizational leaders to determine the reliability of their models.

**Steps:**

1. Conduct a regression analysis using the Data Analysis ToolPak.
2. Plot the residuals against the predicted values using a scatter plot.
3. Check for nonlinear patterns to determine linearity.
4. Create a histogram of residuals to measure normality.
5. Use the F-test to check for homoscedasticity.

### Nonlinear Regression Analysis

Many real-world relationships are nonlinear. Nonlinear regression allows for the modeling of these complex relationships and provides more accurate predictions when data does not fit a straight-line pattern. This analysis is essential for leaders in industries where dynamics can drastically change in the market.

**Steps:**

1. Organize your data and choose a nonlinear model.
2. Write the formula for your model.
3. Use the Data tab, select Solver, and set your objective to minimize the difference between your predicted values and actual data.
4. Adjust changing variable cells as the coefficients in your nonlinear model.

### Confidence Intervals for Regression Coefficients

Confidence intervals provide a range of values where the actual coefficient values are most likely to appear. This analysis helps managers understand the precision of estimates and assess the reliability of relationships to improve strategic decisions.

Formula: =T.INV.2T

**Steps:**

1. Conduct a regression analysis using the Data Analysis ToolPak.
2. Get the output, which includes coefficients and their standard errors.
3. Calculate confidence intervals using the formulas:
    a. Lower Limit: Coefficient − (Critical Value * Standard Error)
    b. Upper Limit: Coefficient + (Critical Value * Standard Error)
4. Use the =T.INV.2T function to get the critical value based on your chosen confidence level.

### Best-Fit Regression Line

The best-fit line minimizes the errors between predicted and actual values. This line is essential for visualizing relationships and making quick determinations about trends in data to create an effective picture for decision-makers.

**Steps:**

1. Create a scatter plot of the data.
2. Click on a data point in the scatter plot.
3. Right-click and select Add Trendline.
4. Choose Linear and check the option to display the equation on the chart.

### Regression Analysis of Variance

This technique evaluates whether the variance explained by the regression model significantly exceeds the variance explained by random chance. This technique helps managers determine the effectiveness of their model and to guide the allocation of resources and operational strategies.

**Steps:**

1. Run a regression analysis using the Data Analysis ToolPak.
2. The ANOVA output will be included in detailing the regression SS, residual SS, and total SS.
3. Analyze the F-statistic and p-value to determine significance.

### Least-Squares Regression Analysis

This method minimizes the sum of squared differences between observed and predicted values. The importance of this technique provides a detailed framework for estimating relationships and allows managers to understand and leverage data effectively.

**Steps:**

1. Organize the data into columns.
2. Use the Data Analysis ToolPak and select Regression.
3. Specify the dependent variable (Y Range) and independent variable(s) (X Range).
4. Run the analysis to obtain regression coefficients and statistics.

### Multiple Linear Regression

By analyzing the effect of multiple independent variables on a dependent variable, multiple linear regression improves predictability and precision. This strategy is necessary for managers who must consider multiple factors simultaneously when making decisions.

**Steps:**

1. Organize your data with the dependent variable in one column and independent variables in adjacent columns.
2. Use the Data Analysis ToolPak and select Regression.
3. Specify the Y Range and multiple X Ranges.
4. Run the analysis to determine the coefficients for each independent variable.

### Modeling Relationships

Understanding and modeling the relationships between variables enable organizations to understand the underlying patterns and configurations. This knowledge can guide marketing strategies, financial forecasting, and operational improvements.

**Steps:**

1. Conduct a regression analysis.
2. Use the model to understand how changes in independent variables affect the dependent variable.
3. Visualize relationships using charts to visually communicate the results.

### Regression Models for Forecasting

These models allow for the prediction of future outcomes based on historical data and help organizations plan, prepare, and allocate resources effectively. Forecasting is necessary for inventory management, financial planning, and strategic initiatives.

**Steps:**

1. Conduct a regression analysis.
2. Use the regression equation to forecast future values based on new inputs.
3. Input new independent variable values in the regression equation.

## Regression Models for Prediction

Like forecasting, regression models predict specific outcomes based on input data. They can be influential in identifying trends and making proactive decisions that lead to business growth.

**Steps:**

1. Run a regression analysis and obtain the coefficients to create a formula with predicted Y values.
2. Enter new independent variables to calculate predictions.

## Residual Analysis

Analyzing residuals helps identify patterns that may suggest issues with the regression model that include nonlinearity or outliers. This situation ensures that models remain valid and reliable to reduce the risk of poor decision-making.

**Steps:**

1. Calculate residuals by subtracting predicted Y values from actual Y values.
2. Create a residual plot or scatter plot of residuals.
3. Check for patterns to assess the actual fit of the model.

## Simple Linear Regression

This technique provides a basic understanding of the relationship between a single independent variable and a dependent variable while also leading to a more complex analysis used to form the basis of many predictive models.

**Steps:**

1. Organize the data with the independent variable in one column and the dependent variable in another.
2. Go to the Data tab and click on Data Analysis.
3. Select Regression from the list and click OK.
4. Specify the Y Range (dependent variable) and the X Range (independent variable).
5. Configure any options you need and click OK to generate the regression statistics that will include the regression equation, R-squared value, and coefficients.

### Testing Hypotheses for Regression Coefficients

*Hypothesis testing* determines the significance of individual predictors in a regression model. This is necessary for leaders to assess which variables truly influence outcomes and improve the decision-making process.

**Steps:**

1. Run the regression analysis and study the output table that provides coefficients and their standard errors.
2. Calculate t-statistics for each coefficient using the formula t = Coefficient/Standard Error.
3. Compare the calculated t-statistic to the critical values from the t-distribution table based on the desired significance level and degrees of freedom.
4. If the absolute value of the t-statistic is greater than the critical value, you will reject the null hypothesis for that coefficient.

### Trends in Data

Identifying trends through regression analysis enables businesses to react proactively instead of being reactive. Recognition of changes in consumer behavior or market dynamics enables companies to realign their strategies efficiently.

**Steps:**

1. Plot your data in a scatter plot to visualize relationships.
2. Use a trendline by selecting any data point in the scatter plot and right-clicking to choose Add Trendline.
3. Choose the type of trendline that fits the data (i.e., linear, exponential, polynomial, etc.), and check the box to display the equation on the chart.
4. Analyze the trendline equation to understand growth patterns or declines over time.

## REAL-WORLD EXAMPLES OF MANAGEMENT INSIGHTS DRIVING BUSINESS SUCCESS

### The Walt Disney Company

With its broad use of data analytics, the Walt Disney Company has improved decision-making across various levels of the organization. A main example of this process is the use of guest data at its theme parks. By studying visitor patterns and preferences, Disney can maximize attractions, improve crowd management, and improve guest experiences. Next, Disney implements analytics for content creation and uses viewer data to guide programming decisions across its streaming service, Disney+. By studying audience metrics, the company customizes its content strategy to align with viewer interests and to ensure higher engagement and satisfaction. In financial management, Disney uses predictive analytics to forecast revenue trends and allows for strategic budgeting and investment decisions. By implementing these analytical insights, Disney not only streamlines operations but also builds a culture of informed decision-making and strongly positions them as a leader.

**Question 1**

How does the Walt Disney Company use data analytics to improve guest experiences at its theme parks?

Answer: The Walt Disney Company uses data analytics to significantly enhance guest experiences at its theme parks by studying visitor patterns and preferences. By collecting and analyzing data on how guests move through the parks, which attractions they visit, and their overall behavior, Disney can maximize the layout and operation of its parks. This strategy includes improving crowd management, reducing waiting times, and ensuring that popular attractions are accessible. Next, Disney uses this data to personalize guest experiences, offering customized recommendations and services that align with individual preferences. This data-driven approach enhances guest satisfaction and increases operational efficiency and maximizes the enjoyment of visitors.

**Question 2**

In what ways does Disney use analytics to inform its content strategy on Disney+?

Answer: Disney employs analytics to inform its content strategy on Disney+ by analyzing viewer data and audience metrics. By understanding what content connects with viewers, Disney can make informed decisions about programming that include which shows or movies to produce, continue, or discontinue. This data-driven approach allows Disney to focus its content offerings to align with viewer interest and to ensure higher levels of engagement and satisfaction. Finally, analytics helps Disney identify emerging trends and preferences and allows the company to stay ahead of the competition by delivering content that meets the evolving demands of its audience.

**Question 3**

How does predictive analytics contribute to Disney's financial management and strategic decision-making?

Answer: Predictive analytics plays an important role in Disney's financial management and strategic decision-making by forecasting revenue trends and informing budgeting and investment decisions. By analyzing historical data and market trends, Disney can predict future financial performance, allowing the company to allocate resources more effectively and make informed investment choices. This knowledge helps Disney manage risks, optimize its financial strategies, and ensure sustainable growth. Predictive analytics also allows Disney to identify potential opportunities and challenges in the market and allows the company to adapt its strategies proactively. Finally, the use of predictive analytics strengthens Disney's financial stability and supports its long-term strategic goals.

## Visa Inc.

Visa Inc. uses business analytics to improve its risk management and fraud detection processes. The company analyzes large amounts of transaction data in real time to allow it to identify and mitigate fraudulent activities swiftly to ensure the security of customer transactions. Next, Visa implements predictive analytics to understand market trends and consumer behavior. This knowledge guides strategic decision-making, allowing Visa to innovate and develop new payment solutions designed to meet the evolving needs of consumers. For example, the launch of contactless payment options was informed by data indicating a growing preference for speed and convenience. Finally, Visa's use of analytics expanded to its partnerships with merchants using data to identify spending patterns and target marketing efforts effectively. Through these analytical strategies, Visa streamlined its operations and strengthened its position as a leader in digital payments, driving growth and improving customer satisfaction in the market.

**Question 1**

How does Visa Inc. use business analytics to improve its risk management and fraud detection processes?

Answer: Visa Inc. relies on business analytics by analyzing large amounts of transaction data in real time. This strategy allows the company to quickly identify and mitigate fraudulent activities while ensuring the security of customer transactions. By using advanced algorithms and machine learning techniques, Visa can detect unusual patterns and anomalies that may indicate fraudulent behavior. This proactive use of data analytics protects consumers and also enhances Visa's reputation as a secure and reliable payment processor.

**Question 2**

In what ways does Visa Inc. use predictive analytics to drive innovation and meet consumer needs?

Answer: Visa Inc. employs predictive analytics to understand market trends and consumer behavior that guide its strategic decision-making. By analyzing data on consumer preferences and spending habits, Visa can anticipate shifts in the market and develop new payment solutions accordingly. For example, the introduction of contactless payment options was informed by data indicating a growing consumer preference for speed and convenience. The ability to predict and respond to consumer needs enables Visa to innovate regularly and maintain its competitive edge in the digital payments industry.

**Question 3**

How does Visa Inc. use analytics to enhance its partnerships with merchants and improve marketing efforts?

Answer: Visa Inc. uses analytics to analyze spending patterns and consumer behavior, which helps in effectively targeting marketing efforts. By providing merchants with insights into customer preferences and purchasing trends, Visa enables them to focus on their marketing strategies to better meet the needs of their consumers. This data-driven approach strengthens Visa's partnerships with merchants and improves consumer satisfaction by ensuring that marketing efforts are relevant and impactful. As a result of these analytical strategies, Visa maximizes its operations and reinforces its position as a leader in the digital payments market.

## Honda Motor Co. Ltd.

Honda Motor Co. Ltd. demonstrates the effective application of management and business analytics to achieve success in the automotive industry. Relying on data-driven knowledge, Honda improves its manufacturing efficiency and product development processes. For example, the company has implemented predictive analytics to optimize its supply chain to ensure the timely delivery of components while minimizing excess inventory. This approach has significantly reduced production costs and improved overall operational efficiency. Next, Honda uses consumer feedback and sales data to inform its vehicle design and features. By analyzing consumer preferences, the company can customize its models to maximize its market appeal. The introduction of the Honda Clarity series reflects this strategy since it directly responds to the growing consumer demand for eco-friendly vehicles. Finally, Honda's analytics extend to marketing strategies where data insights are used to develop targeted campaigns focused on specific demographics.

**Question 1**

How does Honda Motor Co. Ltd. use predictive analytics to enhance its supply chain management?

Answer: Honda Motor Co. Ltd. relies on predictive analytics to maximize its supply chain by ensuring the timely delivery of components while minimizing excess inventory. This data-driven approach allows Honda to predict demand accurately and adjust its supply chain operations accordingly. By analyzing historical data and market trends, Honda can forecast potential disruptions and implement strategies to mitigate them, leading the company to reduce production costs and improve operational efficiency. This proactive management of the supply chain enhances manufacturing efficiency and ensures that Honda can meet customer demands promptly.

**Question 2**

In what ways does Honda use consumer feedback and sales data to influence vehicle design and features?

Answer: Honda uses consumer feedback and sales data to customize its vehicle design and features to meet market demands. By analyzing consumer preferences and purchasing patterns, Honda identifies trends and areas for improvement in its vehicle lineup. This information guides the development of new models and the enhancement of existing ones. The introduction of the Honda Clarity series focused on eco-friendly vehicles as a direct response to the growing consumer demand for sustainable transportation options. By aligning its product offerings with consumer expectations, Honda enhances its market appeal and competitiveness.

**Question 3**

How does Honda apply data insights to develop targeted marketing strategies?

Answer: Honda uses data insights to develop marketing strategies targeted at specific demographics. By analyzing consumer data, including purchasing behavior, preferences, and demographic information, Honda can segment its audience and modify its marketing campaigns to connect with each group. This targeted approach allows Honda to deliver personalized messages and promotions that are more likely to engage potential customers. By focusing on specific demographics, Honda can efficiently dedicate marketing resources and maximize the impact of its campaigns, ultimately driving sales and strengthening brand loyalty.

## Siemens AG

Siemens AG effectively used management and business analytics to improve operational success across various market sectors. By leveraging data analytics, Siemens maximizes its manufacturing processes, especially through its Digital Industries division. The company uses real-time data to monitor machinery performance and predict maintenance needs and significantly reduce downtime and increase productivity. Next, Siemens applies analytics in its smart building solutions. By analyzing energy consumption data, the company helps clients optimize energy use and reduce operational costs. This data-driven approach not only promotes sustainability but also improves client satisfaction through improved building efficiency.

In project management, Siemens employs predictive analytics to assess project risks and the reallocation of resources. This situation enables the company to make informed decisions to ensure projects are completed on time and within budget. Through these analytical insights, Siemens AG reinforces its position as a leader in technology and engineering and drives innovation and operational excellence in the global environment.

### Question 1

How does Siemens AG use data analytics to enhance its manufacturing processes?

Answer: Siemens AG uses data analytics to optimize its manufacturing processes, particularly through its Digital Industries division. By utilizing real-time data, Siemens monitors machinery performance and predicts maintenance needs. This proactive approach significantly reduces downtime and increases productivity. The ability to anticipate maintenance requirements enables Siemens to maintain a seamless flow of production, minimize disruptions, and maximize efficiency. This data-driven strategy enhances operational success and also positions Siemens as a leader in the manufacturing sector by demonstrating a commitment to innovation and excellence.

### Question 2

In what ways does Siemens apply analytics to its smart building solutions, and what are the benefits?

Answer: Siemens applies analytics to its smart building solutions by analyzing energy consumption data. This approach helps clients optimize energy use that leads to reduced operational costs and improved building efficiency. By providing information on energy patterns, Siemens enables clients to implement energy-saving measures that contribute to their sustainability goals. The benefits of this data-driven approach include cost savings, enhanced client satisfaction, and a reduced environmental footprint. Siemens' commitment to using analytics in smart building solutions supports its dedication to promoting sustainability and delivering value to its clients.

**Question 3**

How does Siemens AG employ predictive analytics in project management, and what impact does it have on project outcomes?

Answer: Siemens AG uses predictive analytics in project management to assess project risks and reallocate resources effectively. By analyzing data related to project timelines, resource availability, and potential risks, Siemens can make informed decisions to ensure projects are completed on time and within budget. This strategic use of analytics allows Siemens to proactively anticipate challenges and adjust plans to minimize delays and costly expenditures. The impact of predictive analytics on project outcomes is significant since it enhances the company's ability to deliver successful projects that ultimately reinforce Siemens' reputation as a leader in technology and engineering.

---

## CASE STUDIES ON MANAGEMENT SUCCESS THROUGH ANALYTICS

### Business Success Through Business Analytics

Business analytics plays a crucial role in understanding management trends and consumer behavior that enables organizations in the management industry to make more data-driven and informed decisions. Following are three examples of how management data and knowledge are translated into business success using analytics:

### Example 1: Meaningful Management Solutions (MMS)

Meaningful Management Solutions (MMS) is a company that specializes in providing management consulting services to mid-sized businesses. By using advanced business analytics, MMS has developed a proprietary tool called "InsightProfessional" that helps clients optimize their operational efficiency. InsightProfesssional analyzes data from various departments, such as HR, finance, and operations, to identify bottlenecks and recommend actionable strategies for improvement. One of the main insights MMS discovered was the impact of employee engagement on productivity. By analyzing employee feedback and performance data, MMS was able to demonstrate a direct correlation between high engagement levels and increased productivity. This insight led to the development of targeted engagement programs that resulted in a 20% increase in productivity for their clients.

### Short-Response Questions

1. What is the name of the proprietary tool developed by MMS?
2. What correlation did MMS discover through their analysis?
3. By what percentage did MMS's engagement programs increase productivity for their clients?

### Example 2: Strategic Growing Partners

Strategic Growing Partners (SGP) is a management firm that focuses on helping start-ups scale effectively. SGP uses business analytics to provide insights into market trends, customer behavior, and competitive positioning. Their analytics platform, "GrowingVision," aggregates data from various sources to offer a comprehensive view of the market environment.

One significant insight SGP uncovered was the importance of agile project management in rapidly changing markets. By analyzing project timelines and outcomes, SGP found that start-ups using adaptive methodologies were able to bring products to market 25% quicker than those using traditional methods. This insight has been instrumental in advising clients to adopt agile practices, leading to quicker market entry and increased competitiveness.

### *Short-Response Questions*

1. What is the name of SGP's analytics platform?
2. What project management methodology did SGP find to be more effective in rapidly changing markets?
3. By what percentage did agile methodologies help start-ups bring products to market faster?

### Example 3: Performing Excellence Group (PEG)

Performing Excellence Group (PEG) is a company that provides management training and development programs. PEG uses business analytics to customize their training modules to the specific needs of their clients. Their analytics tool, "QualityTracker," evaluates employee performance data to identify skill gaps and training opportunities. Through their analysis, PEG discovered that personalized training programs significantly enhance employee retention rates. By customizing training to address individual skill gaps, PEG's clients experienced a 30% reduction in employee turnover. This insight has been pivotal in helping organizations retain top talent and reduce recruitment costs.

### Short-Response Questions

1. What is the name of PEG's analytics tool?
2. What impact did personalized training programs have on employee retention rates?
3. By what percentage did PEG's clients reduce employee turnover through personalized training?

## CASE STUDY: OPTICALMANAGEMENT SOLUTIONS

OpticalManagement Solutions is a management consulting company focused on providing data-driven business strategies to small and medium-sized enterprises (SMEs). The firm specializes in optimizing operational processes and improving employee performance through statistical analysis and predictive modeling. Recently, OpticalManagement serviced over 100 clients and sought to analyze various performance indicators to improve client outcomes. Finally, the management team has gathered data on various client projects to perform a detailed exploration of the relationship between consultancy duration, client satisfaction, and financial performance.

### Business Analytics Data Tables

**TABLE 6.2** Client Project Data

| 1 | A | B | C |
|---|---|---|---|
| | Project Duration (Months) | Client Satisfaction Score (1–10) | Financial Performance Improvement ($) |
| 2 | 6 | 8.0 | 50,000 |
| 3 | 12 | 9.0 | 120,000 |
| 4 | 3 | 6.5 | 30,000 |
| 5 | 8 | 7.5 | 80,000 |
| 6 | 10 | 8.5 | 110,000 |

**TABLE 6.3** Performance Analysis Data

| 1 | A | B | C | D | E |
|---|---|---|---|---|---|
| | Project ID | Marketing Spending ($) | Operational Changes (%) | Training Expenses ($) | Financial Performance Improvement ($) |
| 2 | 1 | 10,000 | 20 | 2,500 | 60,000 |
| 3 | 2 | 15,000 | 15 | 4,000 | 80,000 |
| 4 | 3 | 12,000 | 25 | 3,500 | 100,000 |
| 5 | 4 | 5,000 | 10 | 1,000 | 40,000 |
| 6 | 5 | 8,000 | 30 | 2,000 | 90,000 |

### Analytics Problems Using Excel

1. Use the REGRESSION function in Excel to analyze the relationship between project duration (months) and financial performance improvement. Determine the equation of the best-fit regression line for this simple linear regression analysis.
2. Conduct MULTIPLE LINEAR REGRESSION to analyze the impact of marketing spend, operational changes, and training expenses on financial performance improvement. Identify the coefficients and determine the confidence intervals for these coefficients.
3. Perform RESIDUAL ANALYSIS to evaluate how well the regression model predicts financial performance improvement. Calculate the residuals and create a residual plot.
4. Use ANALYSIS OF VARIANCE (ANOVA) to test the hypothesis that the regression model significantly predicts financial performance improvements.
5. How can you model the relationship between all three independent variables and financial performance improvement to forecast future projects' financial outcomes?

### Answer Key

1. *Simple linear regression analysis.* Go to the Data tab and select Data Analysis. Choose Regression and set Input Y Range to Financial Performance Improvement and Input X Range to Project Duration. Run the regression to obtain the output, which will provide

you with the regression coefficients and the equation: (Y = mx + b), where (m) is the slope and (b) is the intercept.

2. *Multiple linear regression analysis.* Go to Data Analysis and select Regression. Set Input Y Range to Financial Performance Improvement. Set Input X Range to include Marketing Spend, Operational Changes, and Training Expenses. Ensure the Output Range is designated for easier visibility, and check the Confidence Level box at 95% to see confidence intervals for the coefficients.
3. *Residual analysis.* After running the regression, copy the predicted values (Y-hat) from the regression output. Calculate residuals: Residual = (Actual) − (Predicted). Create a scatter plot of residuals versus predicted values to evaluate the model fit.
4. *Hypothesis testing using ANOVA.* In the regression output table, check the ANOVA section that provides F-statistic and p-value. Use these metrics to determine if the model significantly predicts the outcome using a significance level of 0.05 or 95%.
5. *Modeling relationships for forecasting.* Use the previously determined multiple regression equation: (Y = b_0 + b_1X_1 + b_2X_2 + b_3X_3), where *Y* is financial performance improvement, *b_0* is the intercept, and *b_1*, *b_2*, and *b_3* are the coefficients of marketing spend, operational changes, and training expenses, respectively. You can now plug in different values for the independent variables to forecast expected financial improvements for future projects.

## CASE STUDY: MANAGERPROF SOLUTIONS

ManagerProf Solutions is a management consulting firm that focuses on optimizing business processes and improving organizational efficiency. The company has helped multiple clients streamline their operations and achieve significant cost savings. Recently, ManagerProf Solutions began a project for a mid-sized manufacturing company to enhance their production efficiency and reduce operational costs. To evaluate the impact of their recommendations, ManagerProf Solutions collected data on production output, operational costs, and employee productivity over six months. The data was analyzed using various regression techniques to identify key factors influencing performance and to forecast future trends. The following tables summarize key findings from the project:

**TABLE 6.4** Production Output and Operational Costs

| 1 | A | B | C |
|---|---|---|---|
| | Month | Production Output (Units) | Operational Costs ($) |
| 2 | January | 10,000 | 50,000 |
| 3 | February | 11,000 | 52,000 |
| 4 | March | 12,000 | 54,000 |
| 5 | April | 13,000 | 56,000 |
| 6 | May | 14,000 | 58,000 |
| 7 | June | 15,000 | 60,000 |

**TABLE 6.5** Employee Productivity

| 1 | A | B | C |
|---|---|---|---|
| | **Month** | **Hours Worked** | **Units Produced per Hour** |
| **2** | January | 1,600 | 6.25 |
| **3** | February | 1,650 | 6.67 |
| **4** | March | 1,700 | 7.06 |
| **5** | April | 1,750 | 7.43 |
| **6** | May | 1,800 | 7.78 |
| **7** | June | 1,850 | 8.11 |

## Analytics Problems Using Excel

1. *Nonlinear regression analysis.* Perform a nonlinear regression analysis on the production output data.
2. *Confidence intervals for regression coefficients.* Calculate the confidence intervals for the regression coefficients.
3. *Best-fit regression line.* Determine the best-fit regression line for operational costs.
4. *Regression analysis of variance.* Conduct a regression analysis of variance (ANOVA) on the production output and operational costs.
5. *Least-squares regression analysis.* Apply least-squares regression analysis to the employee productivity data.
6. *Multiple linear regression.* Perform multiple linear regression using production output and operational costs as predictors.
7. *Modeling.* Create a model to forecast future production output based on historical data.
8. *Forecasting.* Forecast operational costs for the next six months.
9. *Residual analysis.* Conduct a residual analysis on the regression model for production output.
10. *Simple linear regression.* Perform simple linear regression on units produced per hour.
11. *Testing hypotheses for regression coefficients.* Test hypotheses for the regression coefficients in the employee productivity data.
12. *Trends in data.* Identify trends in production output and operational costs.

## Answer Key

1. *Nonlinear regression analysis.* Use the Solver tool to fit a nonlinear model to the production output data. Set the objective to minimize the sum of squared residuals.
2. *Confidence intervals for regression coefficients.* Use the LINEST function to obtain regression coefficients and their standard errors. Calculate confidence intervals using the formula Coefficient ± (Critical Value * Standard Error).
3. *Best-fit regression line.* Use the LINEST function or Regression tool in the Data Analysis ToolPak to find the best-fit line.

4. *Regression analysis of variance.* Use the ANOVA tool in the Data Analysis ToolPak to perform regression analysis of variance.
5. *Least-squares regression analysis.* Use the LINEST function to apply least-squares regression analysis to the employee productivity data.
6. *Multiple linear regression.* Use the Regression tool in the Data Analysis ToolPak to perform multiple linear regression.
7. *Modeling.* Use the FORECAST function to create a model for future production output.
8. *Forecasting.* Use the FORECAST.ETS function to forecast operational costs for the next six months.
9. *Residual analysis.* Plot residuals using the Residuals output from the regression tool, and analyze the pattern.
10. *Simple linear regression.* Use the LINEST function to perform simple linear regression on units produced per hour.
11. *Testing hypotheses for regression coefficients.* Use the T-TEST function to test hypotheses for regression coefficients.
12. *Trends in data.* Use the TREND function to identify trends in production output and operational costs.

CHAPTER 7

# Leadership and Business Analytics

Leadership combined with business analytics is necessary for all companies in today's global business environment. To be an effective leader, individuals must learn to use business analytics to make informed decisions, improve the success of the organization, and to develop strategic processes. This strategy can be applied to all industries to enable leaders to determine how information collected from business analytics issues to improve performance and to gain a competitive advantage in the market. Leadership in business analytics requires the ability to interpret large and complex datasets, and to translate them into information and actionable results.

Next, leaders within organizations are responsible for developing a mission and vision that focuses on the importance of data-driven decisions to encourage team members and stakeholders to accept analytics as part of their work culture. When a data-driven culture is developed, leaders can ensure that employees and team members understand the importance of business analytics when focusing on challenges to the operation and maximizing its performance. In the retail industry, leaders use business analytics to interpret consumer patterns of behavior to improve their overall shopping experience. Analytics that are studied by leaders include inventory data, market dynamics, and sales trends to help improve marketing strategies and to maximize product offerings to increase the overall profitability of the business.

Leadership of health-care providers use business analytics to study operational metrics and to interpret patient data to identify trends in patient care, improve outcomes, and to streamline processes. This situation requires leaders to use business analytics to reduce costs while maintaining high performance standards of patient care by collaborating with other stakeholder groups. In the finance industry, leaders use business analytics to make informed decisions about investments, assessing risk, and overall operational efficiency. The strategy requires integration of predictive analytics by leaders to anticipate changes in the market, allocate resources effectively, and to streamline processes.

Within the technology sector of the global market, leaders use business analytics to lead the development of new products and entry to new market sectors. Next, business analytics enables leaders to support the innovation of new products and services based on the identification of gaps in the market and the lack of meeting the needs of consumers. As a result, the combination of leadership with business analytics is necessary for effective management within all sectors of the global market. Leaders who use business analytics will improve the performance of the organization, maintain a competitive advantage, and develop new

DOI: 10.4324/9781003629658-7

innovations within the dynamics market environment. In a world reliant on technology, data has become an asset that leaders must continue to use and study to improve their strategic vision and to ensure the long-term success of the organization.

## THE ROLE OF LEADERSHIP IN EMBRACING ANALYTICS

The role of leadership with the embracing of business analytics within the market environment is necessary for organizations to become responsive to change and remain competitive in the global environment. Across all industries, leadership is necessary for promoting a strong culture that places an emphasis on the use of data-driven information is the main components of the strategic decision-making process to ensure operational efficiency. Within the technology sector, leaders are required to integrate business analytics into the business processes and models. Leaders use statistics to better understand consumer behavior, improve marketing strategies, and enhance the development of new products. By using business analytics, leaders of technology companies can make data-driven decisions that improve the engagement of consumers while developing new product innovations.

In the finance industry, business leaders use analytics to improve their investment strategies and mitigate risk. Financial institutions also use business analytics to study the creditworthiness of consumers, market trends, and to maximize their management of portfolios. When business analytics is incorporated into the overall operation, financial leaders can develop a more accurate forecast model to improve decision-making processes used in investing, lending, and the allocation of resources.

In the health-care industry, business leaders that rely on analytics can streamline daily operations, manage and reduce cost expenditures, and improve the care of patients. The use of business analytics requires leaders to use predictive analytics to maximize the allocation of workers, identify trends that can lead to new health-care interventions, and to anticipate the needs of patients. As a result, the leader's commitment to data-driven strategies will improve the efficiency of the organization while increasing the quality of care.

In retail, leadership of retailers use business analytics to better understand the behavior and preferences of consumers. Retail industry leaders use statistics to study consumer feedback, market trends, and purchasing data to create new focus marketing strategies and to maximize their level of inventory to improve the overall shopping experience of the consumer. Within the manufacturing industry, leaders use business analytics to improve the reduction of operational costs and to increase levels of productivity. By studying data related to the processes of production and manufacturing, leaders can streamline supply chain processes, identify inefficiencies, and implement new predictive maintenance strategies to respond to the changing dynamics of the market and to maintain operational performance.

### Encouraging a Culture of Data-Driven Decision-Making

Leaders must encourage a culture of data-driven decision-making within all organizations and industries. Leadership in business analytics is important for the development of a culture of data-driven decision-making within the business. The integration of business analytics leadership will improve the strategic capabilities of the leader, while also empowering employees in various industries to use data to improve their role within the business. In the technology sector, leaders use business analytics to prioritize the different components of the overall business strategy. The strategy focuses on the importance of data in developing new products and improving the experiences of consumers. When employees and teams are provided with the necessary information and statistical tools, technology leaders can create an environment where employees are more empowered to make data-driven and informed decisions.

In the finance sector, leadership is required to integrate business analytics into everyday operations to help develop clear strategies for the analysis of data into creating guidelines and procedures that support teams in making investment decisions in assessing risk based on quantitative measures. When analytical data is shared with employees, they can become better trained and capable of interpreting complex financial data into making more accurate predictions about the success of strategic initiatives. In health care, leaders must develop a data-driven culture as part of the decision-making process to help health-care providers understand the importance of statistics and improving operational efficiency and the care of patients. By supporting staff and using business analytics in their decisions, leadership can transform health-care providers who handle the allocation of resources in the management of patients.

In the retail industry, the role of the leader is to use business analytics that supports operational efficiency and to increase the engagement of consumers. Retail leaders must also encourage their team members to use state analytics to understand how to manage inventory, assess the preferences and behaviors of consumers, and develop focus marketing strategies.

In the manufacturing sector, leaders must influence the use of business analytics to help employees focus on continuous improvement strategies and to improve the efficiency of the daily operation. This strategy requires the implementation of data-driven practices as part of the organizational culture to inspire employees. The team members learn to identify new trends in the production process and to suggest improvements to increase productivity, become more strategically aligned with the demands of the market, and to develop cost-saving measures. As a result, leaders can motivate employees with the use of business analytics tools and methodologies to reinforce the importance of data in achieving the objectives and goals of the organization.

## LEADING THROUGH CRISIS WITH ANALYTICS

Business analytics will support leaders in managing crisis with organizations. The role of leadership in business analytics is necessary during times of crisis or unpredictability within the market. During times of uncertainty, leadership combined with business analytics provides organizations with the ability to manage uncertainties based on data-driven decisions and enables them to gain a competitive advantage in the market. Next, the use of business analytics by leaders helps them to accurately assess situations, implement strategies to address immediate challenges or threats, and to predict outcomes for long-term success.

In health care, leaders face challenges that include health-care emergencies and worldwide pandemics. By using data analytics, health-care leaders can monitor the availability of resources, understand infection rates in real time, and monitor patient outcomes. As a result, leaders using a statistical approach can improve their understanding and capability and allocate medical resources more efficiently and to manage the needs of the staff. As an example, during the COVID-19 pandemic, many health-care providers relied on business analytics to track the load of patients and the increase of infections in different geographic areas so they could allocate the necessary resources where they were needed most.

In finance, leaders use business analytics during a time of crisis to understand complex data to make informed strategic decisions and to assess the level of risk. The situation requires financial leaders to view statistics to understand the volatility of the market, changes in consumer behavior, and other emerging economic factors. By using scenario analysis and modeling, financial leaders can make data-driven decisions about credit assessments, investments, and crisis management strategies to help them maintain stability and trust among stakeholders during turbulence and changes in the market.

In the retail industry, leaders face crises related to disruptions to the supply-chain management process and sudden changes in consumer behavior. To manage these issues during a time of crisis, leaders must use business analytics to maximize inventory management, adjust pricing strategies, and to develop new focus marketing campaigns for specific consumer demographics. As an example, retailers operating during an economic downturn must use business analytics to understand the needs of consumers and to adjust their level of inventory to sustain sales volume while maintaining consumer loyalty.

In manufacturing, leaders face challenges and crises related to geopolitical issues and natural disasters. Business analytics enables leaders to gain new knowledge about the capabilities of production, potential disruptions, and vulnerabilities to the supply-chain. By studying data manufacturing, leaders can identify alternative suppliers and distributors, modify production schedules, and reduce risks to the operation. As a result, business analytics provides a proactive approach to managing crises to enable the organization to become responsive to the changing needs of the market despite facing challenges. Effective leaders in all industries will use business analytics to make informed decisions and to communicate transparently with all stakeholder groups while addressing the immediate concerns and needs in the environment to provide sustainable longevity and growth of the business.

### How Analytics Can Help Guide Organizations During Crises

Leadership and business analytics work together to lead organizations during crisis and provide the necessary statistical tools for the decision-making process and the adoption of a new strategic vision. During times of uncertainty or crisis, leaders that use business analytics would be more successful in managing resources, maintaining long-term goals, avoiding challenges and threats, and addressing the immediate objectives of the business in all industries. In the health-care industry, leaders use business analytics during natural disasters and pandemics to provide real-time data on patient outcomes, the progression of disease, and the allocation of resources to enable them to maximize the response time and improve the care of patients.

In the financial industry, leaders use business analytics during a time of crisis to determine the economic indicators and the changes in consumer behavior. The situation requires financial leaders to use business analytics to evaluate risks associated with credit ratings, market fluctuations, and investing. When leaders use scenario analysis, then they can develop a proactive and responsive business strategy to reduce the chance of loss and to increase stability. As an example, financial companies that use real-time business analytics to monitor the dynamics of the market and behaviors of consumers will become strategically capable of adapting their products and services to retain the trust and loyalty of their consumers.

In the retail industry, business analytics support leaders during a time of crisis by enabling them to understand trends and changes in consumer purchasing behavior and the need to adjust inventory levels accordingly. Next, business analytics helps leaders to identify the main products that are in demand during a time of crisis, and to ensure their inventory levels can meet the demand of consumers. As an example, if there is an unexpected disruption to the supply chain, a retail leader can use business analytics to identify alternative suppliers and to streamline the business process to ensure that they maintain the availability of the product while minimizing costs.

Finally, the manufacturing sector requires business analytics as a main component of leadership during a time of crisis to handle challenges due to geopolitical events or to breakdowns in the supply chain. Next, business analytics will help manufacturing leaders to determine the capabilities of the production process and to identify potential slowdowns within that process. This situation will require manufacturing leaders to study past data along with current trends so they can reconfigure their supply-chain management strategy and develop contingency plans. Finally, the use of business analytics helps leaders in the manufacturing industry to develop just-in-time inventory practices to improve business and to reduce disruptions to the process.

## DEVELOPING ANALYTICAL SKILLS IN LEADERS

Leadership along with business analytics is important for organizations that are attempting to develop a data-driven environment. Leaders need to use business analytics to support their strategic decisions while also working to develop analytical skills within their employees and other team members. This strategy enables organizational leaders to determine the capacity that can be gained from data-driven decisions while encouraging and supporting a culture of continuous improvement. One method is for leaders to use business analytics to develop training and other resources that improve the analytical skills of employees to enable them to gain meaningful knowledge from large and complex sets of data.

Next, leaders must develop analytical skills within their employees and teams to develop an environment where informed decision-making becomes the cultural norm. This strategy will ultimately improve the performance of the entire organization. Third, by using analytical skills, leaders can become advocates for data literacy training to ensure that all employees and team members can use business analytics in their daily work processes. Fourth, leaders must

**TABLE 7.1** The Importance of Analytics Training for Leadership

| Component | Description | Purpose |
|---|---|---|
| **Data literacy** | Understanding and interpreting data accurately | Empowers leaders to make informed decisions based on data insights |
| **Critical thinking** | Analyzing and evaluating information to solve problems | Enhances problem-solving skills and decision-making processes |
| **Statistical analysis** | Applying statistical methods to interpret data | Provides a foundation for making data-driven decisions |
| **Visualization techniques** | Using charts, graphs, and other visual tools to present data | Helps in communicating complex data clearly and effectively |
| **Predictive analytics** | Using historical data to forecast future trends | Assists in strategic planning and anticipating future challenges |
| **Decision-making models** | Frameworks for making systematic and informed decisions | Guides leaders in choosing the best course of action based on data |
| **Performance metrics** | Identifying and tracking key performance indicators (KPIs) | Monitors progress and measures success against objectives |
| **Risk management** | Assessing and mitigating potential risks using data | Ensures proactive handling of uncertainties and challenges |
| **Resource allocation** | Optimizing the distribution of resources based on data analysis | Ensures efficient use of resources to achieve project goals |
| **Continuous learning** | Encouraging ongoing education and skill development in analytics | Keeps leaders updated with the latest analytical tools and techniques |

encourage other individuals and their teams to use business analytics to become adaptable and flexible to the changing needs of the market and to prioritize their skill developments to make informed decisions used to increase consumer satisfaction and to increase sales.

Finally, leaders must develop the analytical skills of their team to identify inefficiencies and to develop training programs to support a higher level of understanding of all employees so they can make a data-driven decisions to reduce the overall costs of the business operation. With the integration of leadership in business analytics, the development of statistical analysis and skills become critical to the success of organizations across various industries. Next, leaders who use business analytics and develop analytical skills within their team will experience a higher-level decision-making process and empowerment of individuals within their individual roles of the organization. As a result, a strong commitment to business analytics and leadership will improve the performance of the organization, create adaptability and flexibility, and enable the business to become responsive to the dynamic changes within the market environment.

It is important to use analytics training for leadership. There are various components of this process that are detailed in Table 7.1.

## COLLABORATION AND COMMUNICATION THROUGH ANALYTICS

Leadership and business analytics will create collaboration and clear communication using analytics. The combination of leadership with business analytics will develop effective collaboration and communication that is necessary for organizational success in today's data focused global environments. Next, leaders who use business analytics will experience improvement in streamlined processes and improve decision-making and teamwork across various industries. In the technology sector, leaders use business analytics to support collaboration and communication among team members by using data to eliminate silos and encourage the use of cross functional teams to share information and to work toward a common goal. As a result, technology companies can work more effectively together using real-time data to develop transparency to improve productivity and generate ideas for new product innovations among diverse groups and teams.

In the finance sector, leadership will use these analytics to improve communication that is necessary for improving transparency and managing risks. Financial leaders of companies use business analytics to communicate information about investment performance, regulatory compliance, and market trends. Sharing and collaboration among teams will develop stronger strategic alignment when making informed data-driven decisions since departments work together as a single unit to address opportunities and threats that exist in the market.

In the health-care sector, leaders use business analytics to create open channels of communication between administrative teams and clinical workers. The use of business analytics and the sharing of data will enable leaders to communicate patient outcomes, resource usage rates, and other operational metrics that will be used to make informed decisions at all levels within the health-care organization. When statistical tools are used during the collaboration process, health-care leaders can improve the care of patients in the efficiency of their operations by using data dashboards and key performance indicators to determine real-time results in success.

In the retail sector, leadership uses business analytics to study sales forecasting, consumer behaviors and preferences, and inventory management. When data is shared across various departments that include sales, supply chain management, and marketing leaders can support a collaborative approach to the decision-making process. Using a collaborative approach will improve the operational efficiency of the company while also increasing the level of loyalty and satisfaction of the consumer.

Finally, leaders in the manufacturing sector use business analytics to support communication between different departments that include logistics, quality assurance, and production. Communicating and sharing real-time data will enable everyone to understand the supply chain logistics, production capabilities, and other quality metrics within the manufacturing process. As a result, leaders in all industries prioritizing data-driven information will experience an increase in teamwork, creating a more efficient decision-making process, and achieving strategic objectives and goals. The use of business analytics to encourage teamwork using data insights will provide many different aspects to success for organizations that are detailed in the table that follows.

**TABLE 7.2** How Leaders Use Business Analytics to Encourage Teamwork Using Data Insights

| Aspect | Description | Impact on Teamwork |
|---|---|---|
| **Data transparency** | Sharing data openly within the team | Builds trust and ensures everyone is on the same page |
| **Collaborative decision-making** | Using data to make collective decisions | Encourages input from all team members, fostering a sense of ownership |
| **Performance metrics** | Tracking team performance through data | Identifies strengths and areas for improvement, promoting accountability |
| **Resource allocation** | Distributing resources based on data insights | Ensures fair and efficient use of resources, reducing conflicts |
| **Predictive analytics** | Forecasting future trends and challenges | Helps teams prepare and strategize together, enhancing collaboration |
| **Feedback loops** | Using data to provide continuous feedback | Facilitates ongoing improvement and open communication |
| **Goal alignment** | Aligning team goals with data-driven insights | Ensures everyone is working toward common objectives, boosting cohesion |
| **Problem-solving** | Identifying issues and solutions through data analysis | Encourages collaborative problem-solving and innovation |

## STRATEGIC VISION AND DATA UTILIZATION

Leaders recognize that using business analytics is necessary for making informed decisions and achieving long-term objectives and goals. By integrating business analytics into their strategic vision, leaders can improve organizational and innovation in goods and services, and develop a competitive advantage across various industries. In the technology sector of the market, leaders use business analytics to make informed strategic decisions in respect to technological advancements to stay ahead of the market trends and the expectations of consumers. The situation requires leaders to use knowledge gained from business analytics based on consumer behavior and engagement metrics to improve their offering of goods and services to ultimately enhance the experience of the customer.

In the finance sector, leadership combined with business analytics assists the strategic planning process and management of risk. Financial leaders use business analytics to determine the conditions of the market and to evaluate all opportunities for lending and investment. When business analytics is combined into the strategic vision of the organization, financial leaders can make proactive decisions to adjust their portfolios, optimize the allocation of resources, and to improve the overall performance of the organization.

In the health-care sector, leadership in business analytics is necessary for improving operational efficiency of health-care providers in improving the care of patients. Health-care leaders must use business analytics to identify the usage of resources and trends in patient outcomes. The situation will help leaders to lead efforts in improving patient care and streamlining operations based on trends in the data. As a result, health-care leaders can become more committed to making informed decisions that support the mission and vision of the organization based on the results of the data.

In the retail sector, leaders will use business analytics to guide the influence of their strategic mission and vision as it relates to the understanding of the changing market dynamics and the behaviors of consumer segments of the market. This situation will require retail leaders to use advanced statistical tools to gain information related to consumer preferences, inventory levels, and sales trends to enable them to develop new marketing strategies to maximize the supply chain management process. As a result, leaders who use business analytics as part of their strategic vision will become more adaptable and flexible in responding to changes in the needs of the consumer and the conditions of the market.

Finally, the manufacturing sector of the global market requires leaders to use business analytics to improve their strategic mission and vision. This process is centered on the operational efficiency and quality improvement measures of the business. Manufacturing company leaders use data to analyze the performance of the supply chain management process and levels of production. Next, using a data-driven approach enables manufacturing leaders to reduce

**TABLE 7.3** Aligning Business Strategies with Analytical Findings

| Aspect | Description | Alignment with Analytical Findings |
|---|---|---|
| **Strategic planning** | Developing long-term goals and objectives | Uses data insights to set realistic and achievable goals |
| **Market analysis** | Evaluating market trends and competition | Incorporates data on market conditions and competitor performance |
| **Resource allocation** | Distributing resources effectively | Utilizes data to optimize resource distribution and avoid wastage |
| **Performance metrics** | Identifying key performance indicators (KPIs) | Tracks KPIs using data to measure progress and success |
| **Risk management** | Assessing and mitigating potential risks | Analyzes data to identify risks and develop mitigation strategies |
| **Decision-making** | Making informed choices based on available information | Relies on data-driven insights for accurate and timely decisions |
| **Operational efficiency** | Improving processes and workflows | Uses data to identify inefficiencies and implement improvements |
| **Customer insights** | Understanding customer needs and preferences | Leverages data to tailor strategies to customer behavior and feedback |
| **Innovation** | Encouraging new ideas and approaches | Uses data to identify opportunities for innovation and growth |
| **Continuous improvement** | Ongoing enhancement of strategies and processes | Employs data for regular review and refinement of strategies |

costs, improve the quality of products, and to identify new areas of improvement within the overall process. As a result, incorporating business analytics as part of the strategic vision of leadership will enable the business to better align their employees and team members toward a shared objective and goal of operational success.

To be successful, leadership must combine analytics with analytical findings to align business strategies. The various ways that leaders can align business strategies with analytical findings are detailed in the chart that follows.

## Empowering Teams With Data

Leadership in business analytics will be used to empower teams using data to improve the organization's performance within various industries of the global market. Next, leaders who use data analytics recognize ways to improve the capability of teams, improve the decision-making process, and to develop better outcomes based on the mission and vision of the organization. In the technology industry, leaders will integrate business analytics into the daily operations to enable them to gain real-time information about consumer behavior, performance metrics, and to identify future trends. By using a data-driven approach, technology leaders can empower their teams to make more informed decisions in real time that will ultimately result in improvements to the expectations of consumers in new product innovations.

In the finance industry, financial leaders will use business analytics to manage risks and maximize their investment capabilities. The situation requires financial managers to use analytics to analyze trends in the market, the performance of portfolios, and the behavior of clients. Next, financial leaders will use data to develop a data focused culture that guarantees individuals in the team located in various divisions or departments within the company have the necessary tools and skills to analyze data effectively to make decisions. As a result, leaders who are using a data-driven approach as part of the decision-making process will be able to respond proactively to changes in the markets and to ensure long-term growth within the market.

In the health-care industry, leaders will use business analytics to analyze the allocation of resources, the operational efficiencies of the business process, and the outcome of patients. Next, health-care leaders will provide team members with the necessary tools and skills to use analytics to interpret the data in real time. This situation will empower employees to make data-driven and evidence-based decisions to ultimately improve care for patients and to maximize the operational processes of the health-care provider.

In the retail industry, leaders will use business analytics to improve the performance of teams and to increase the engagement levels of customers. Next, retail industry leaders will use business analytics to gain information on sales trends, inventory management, and consumer preferences so employees can be empowered to make real-time decisions based on the dynamic changes in the market. As a result, the use of a data-driven strategy will provide proactive decision-making that can respond in real time to improve the satisfaction levels of the consumer and to ultimately increase the volume of sales.

The manufacturing industry requires their leaders to empower their team members to use business analytics to improve product quality and operational efficiency. Next, manufacturing

**TABLE 7.4** Tools and Practices for Data Accessibility

| Tool or Practice | Description | Benefits |
|---|---|---|
| **Self-service BI tools** | Tools like Power BI and Tableau that allow users to create reports and dashboards without needing technical expertise | Empowers employees to access and analyze data independently |
| **Data integration platforms** | Solutions that consolidate data from various sources into a unified view | Breaks down data silos and provides a comprehensive view of organizational data |
| **Cloud solutions** | Cloud-based storage and computing services for data management | Ensures scalable and secure data access from anywhere |
| **Data governance framework** | Policies and procedures to ensure data quality and security | Maintains high data quality and compliance with regulations |
| **Role-based access controls** | System that grants data access based on user roles and responsibilities | Balances data accessibility with security |
| **Data literacy programs** | Training initiatives to improve employees' ability to understand and use data | Enhances overall data competency and confidence |
| **Collaborative platforms** | Tools like Slack or Microsoft Teams for sharing data insights and collaboration | Facilitates teamwork and real-time data sharing |
| **Automated data reporting** | Systems that generate regular reports and alerts based on data | Keeps everyone informed with up-to-date information |
| **Visualization tools** | Software for creating visual representations of data | Makes complex data more accessible and understandable |
| **Feedback mechanisms** | Processes for collecting and acting on data-related feedback from employees | Continuously improves data accessibility practices based on user input |

leaders use business analytics to monitor the supply chain logistics, production processes, and other quality control measures. As a result, leaders will invest in training programs for their employees or the team members to ensure that they are skilled in analyzing operational data. This situation will create a culture of continuous improvement and empower employees to develop new solutions when inefficiencies are identified and to increase productivity. As a result, when leaders provide access to operational data and other business analytics tools, they can train their teams to make informed decisions that improve the overall performance of the organization and to develop the collaborative culture of adaptability and innovation to gain a competitive advantage in the market environment.

Finally, leaders must develop tools and practices for data accessibility for their employees and team members. There are various methods and strategies for leaders to create a culture of data usage that will improve the team's ability to use data. The decision-making processes are detailed in the chart that follows.

## BUSINESS ANALYTICS FUNCTION FOR LEADERSHIP USING MICROSOFT EXCEL

In the business environment, there are many business analytical terms mentioned that play a critical role in making informed and data-driven choices that drive decisions, optimize daily operations, and develop strategic actions and initiatives. Various statistical concepts play an important role in leadership and business analytics by providing essential tools for data analysis and decision-making. Here's a detailed overview of their definition and importance and how to conduct this statistical analysis using Microsoft Excel.

### Delphi Method

This structured communication technique gathers expert opinions to form a consensus on future trends or scenarios. In business, this method is required in strategic decision-making to incorporate diverse viewpoints, mitigate risks and biases, and validate the forecasting models.

**Steps:**

1. Create a survey in Excel to collect expert opinions on future trends.
2. Distribute the survey, collect responses, and summarize the data.
3. Use multiple rounds of analysis for incorporating feedback and refining questions in subsequent surveys until consensus has been achieved.

### Double Exponential Smoothing

This forecasting method accounts for trends in time series data by applying two smoothing constants. It is particularly useful for organizations in understanding patterns and making more accurate short-term forecasts in dynamic market environments.

**Steps:**

1. Organize the time series data in a column.
2. In a new column, input the initial smoothed value containing the average of the first few data points.
3. Input the formula for the level: Lt = α * Yt + (1 − α) * (L(t − 1) + T(t − 1)), where $\alpha$ is the smoothing constant, *Yt* is the current observation, and *T* is the trend.
4. In a new column, input the formula for the trend: Tt = β * (Lt − L(t − 1)) + (1 − β) * T(t − 1), where $\beta$ is the smoothing trend constant.
5. Use the last level and trend values to forecast future points.

## Error Metrics

*Error metrics* are quantitative measures that include mean absolute error (MAE) and root mean square error (RMSE) used to evaluate the accuracy of forecasts. In leadership, error metrics helps in assessing forecasting performance and refining methods to improve predictive capabilities of the company.

**Steps:**

1. Create a column for actual values and a column for predicted values.
2. In a new column, calculate the absolute error using the formula = ABS(A1 − B1), where *A1* is the actual value and *B1* is the predicted value.
3. For MAE, use the formula =AVERAGE(C1:Cn), where *C1:Cn* is the column with absolute errors.
4. For RMSE, calculate squared errors: =(A1 − B1)^2. And use =SQRT(AVERAGE(D1:Dn)) for the final RMSE.

## Exponential Smoothing Models

These models provide a way to forecast future values by weighing past observations with decreasing influence over time. Organizational leaders can rely on this technique for creating responsive forecasts that adjust to real-time data conditions.

Formula: = $\alpha$ * Yt + (1 − $\alpha$) * Smoothed Value (t − 1).

**Steps:**

1. Organize the historical data.
2. In a new column, input the formula for exponential smoothing: = $\alpha$ * Yt + (1 − $\alpha$) * Smoothed Value (t − 1).

## Forecast Accuracy

Ensuring the accuracy of forecasts is necessary for effective leadership to exist. Accurate forecasts allow leaders to make informed decisions regarding resource allocation, strategic initiatives, and risk management strategies.

**Steps:**

1. Calculate forecast errors in a new column using = Actual − Forecast.
2. Use the errors to compute accuracy measures like MAPE (mean absolute percentage error): =AVERAGE(ABS(Error/Actual)).

## Indexes of Forecasting

These indexes provide a numerical measure of forecast quality that assists leaders in quickly assessing the reliability of various forecasting methods. These assessments guide the selection of appropriate models for specific contexts.

**Steps:**

1. Choose appropriate accuracy measures (i.e., MAPE, MAE).
2. Create an index scale (e.g., 0 to 100) based on business standards.
3. Calculate and interpret your indexes to assess forecast quality.

## Indicators of Forecasting

These metrics provide knowledge into the underlying trends and patterns in data. Leaders use indicators to monitor performance, identify opportunities, and anticipate new challenges in the market.

**Steps:**

1. Calculate key metrics, like percentage errors, MAPE, etc.
2. Evaluate combinations of these metrics to identify performance indicators (i.e., trends, seasonality).

## Judgmental Forecasting

This approach combines expert insight and experience with quantitative data to make informed predictions. It is particularly valuable in situations where historical data may be limited or when reviewing qualitative factors is necessary.

**Steps:**

1. Organize a survey using Excel to gather information.
2. Summarize the qualitative data.
3. Integrate this qualitative forecast alongside quantitative data.

## Linear Trend Forecasting Model

This model identifies and projects future values based on historical trends. Leaders benefit from linear trend analysis by strategically planning for growth or decline based on established patterns.

**Steps:**

1. Organize data in two columns: time and value.
2. Create a scatter plot with time on the X-axis and values on the Y-axis.
3. Add a trendline, select Linear, and check Display Equation on Chart and Display R-Squared Value.
4. Use the trendline equation to forecast future values.

## Moving Average Model

This method smooths fluctuations in data by averaging values over specific periods. It enables leaders to identify underlying trends more clearly and make decisions based on longer-term insights rather than short-term volatility.

**Steps:**

1. Organize the data in a column.
2. Choose a window size.
3. In a new column, input the moving average formula: = AVERAGE(A2:A4) for a three-period moving average.

### Qualitative Forecasting

Where quantitative data is insufficient, qualitative forecasting gathers knowledge from opinions and experience. Leaders can leverage this method for strategic planning when entering new markets or launching new products.

**Steps:**

1. Gather opinions from experts using a survey.
2. Summarize the responses quantitatively and categorize them by themes.
3. Use qualitative forecasts to provide context or adjust quantitative forecasts as needed.

### Quantitative Forecasting

This approach uses historical data and statistical techniques to predict future outcomes. Leaders in data-driven environments rely on quantitative forecasts to back their strategic initiatives with empirical proof.

**Steps:**

1. Collect historical data relevant to the variable of interest.
2. Choose an appropriate quantitative method (i.e., exponential smoothing or regression).
3. Apply the chosen method using Excel formulas or tools for the dataset.

### Stationary Time Series Forecasting

This technique analyzes time series data that exhibit constant statistical properties over time. It is significant for organizational leaders looking to study and predict systems that do not show trends or seasonal patterns.

**Steps:**

1. Test for stationarity using ACF/PACF plots or the augmented Dickey–Fuller test.
2. If non-stationary, transform the data.
3. Use the transformed data to develop models for forecasting.

### Statistical Forecasting Models

Employing various statistical methodologies that include regression and time series analysis enables leaders to strengthen their forecasting capabilities with complex statistical analysis and improved decision-making.

**Steps:**

1. Organize the data in Excel.
2. Use the relevant statistical model (i.e., regression analysis, time series analysis) available in the Data Analysis ToolPak.
3. Interpret the model output to make forecasts.

### Time Series With Linear Trend Regression-Based Model

This model combines regression analysis with time series data to identify trends and predict future outcomes. Companies use this technique for specialized knowledge that reflects both historical patterns and projected pathways.

**Steps:**

1. Set up the data with time in one column and the dependent variable in another.
2. Conduct regression using the Data Analysis ToolPak and select Regression.
3. Use the regression equation output to forecast future values by inputting future time values into the equation.

## REAL-WORLD EXAMPLES OF MANAGEMENT INSIGHTS DRIVING BUSINESS SUCCESS

### Royal Dutch Shell plc

Royal Dutch Shell plc uses advanced data analytics to improve decision-making and strategic planning. For example, Shell uses predictive analytics to assess oil and gas market trends to help organizational leaders make informed investment decisions and optimize resource allocation. For sustainability, Shell analyzes environmental impact data to better align its operations with global climate goals. This commitment is evident in its transition toward renewable energy, where analytics guide the development of solar and wind projects and ensure efficient project management and effective deployment of resources. Finally, Shell emphasizes safety, using data analytics to evaluate risk factors across its operations. By analyzing incident data, the company develops proactive safety measures that are used to improve workplace safety. Through their analytical awareness, Shell establishes how effective leadership can drive innovation and operational excellence while addressing the challenges of the evolving energy market.

**Question 1**

How does Royal Dutch Shell plc use predictive analytics to enhance its investment decisions in the oil and gas sector?

Answer: Royal Dutch Shell plc uses predictive analytics to assess market trends in the oil and gas industry that is critical for making informed investment decisions. By analyzing historical data and current market conditions, Shell can forecast future trends and identify potential opportunities and risks. This strategy allows the company to optimize resource allocation while ensuring that investments are strategically placed to maximize returns. Predictive analytics also helps Shell anticipate changes in demand and supply and allows the company to adjust its strategies proactively and maintain a competitive edge in the dynamically changing energy market.

#### Question 2

In what ways does Shell integrate data analytics into its sustainability initiatives, particularly in the development of renewable energy projects?

Answer: Shell integrates data analytics into its sustainability initiatives by analyzing environmental impact data to align its operations with global climate goals. In the development of renewable energy projects that include solar and wind, Shell uses analytics to guide project planning and execution. This situation includes assessing site suitability, optimizing resource deployment, and managing project timelines effectively. By leveraging data-driven insights, Shell can ensure that its renewable energy projects are environmentally sustainable and economically feasible. This strategic use of analytics supports Shell's transition toward a more sustainable energy portfolio and demonstrates its commitment to reducing its carbon footprint.

#### Question 3

How does Shell's use of data analytics contribute to improving workplace safety across its operations?

Answer: Shell uses data analytics to enhance workplace safety by evaluating risk factors and analyzing incident data across its operations. By identifying patterns and trends in safety incidents, Shell can develop proactive safety measures and implement targeted interventions to mitigate risks. This data-driven approach allows the company to address potential issues before they result in accidents to improve the overall safety performance. Additionally, analytics enable Shell to monitor compliance with safety protocols and continuously refine its safety strategies. Through these efforts, Shell develops a culture of safety and ensures the well-being of its employees and contractors, reinforcing its reputation as a responsible and safety-conscious organization.

### BHP Group

The BHP Group has developed effective leadership through the strategic use of business analytics to improve operational efficiency and sustainability. By taking advantage of advanced data analytics, BHP maximizes its resource management across its mining operations, which enables leaders to make data-informed decisions that improve productivity and reduce costs. For example, the company analyzes equipment performance datasets to predict maintenance needs and to minimize the level of downtime and maximize outputs. In sustainability, BHP uses analytics to assess environmental impacts and to spearhead its carbon reduction strategies. By analyzing emissions data, the company can establish measurable targets that align with global climate goals and enhance its corporate responsibility. Finally, BHP employs analytics in workforce management, analyzing employee data to enhance safety protocols and training programs. This data-driven approach not only improves workplace safety but also develops a culture of continuous improvement. Through these initiatives, the BHP Group exhibits how leadership backed by analytical insights can lead to sustainable growth and operational excellence.

**Question 1**

How does the BHP Group uses data analytics to enhance operational efficiency in its mining operations?

Answer: The BHP Group uses advanced data analytics to optimize its resource management and improve operational efficiency in its mining operations. By analyzing equipment performance datasets, BHP can predict maintenance needs, which helps minimize downtime and maximize output. This proactive approach to maintenance ensures that machinery operates at peak efficiency while reducing costs and increasing productivity. The use of data analytics allows BHP to make informed decisions that enhance the overall efficiency of its mining operations, demonstrating the value of data-driven strategies in achieving operational excellence.

**Question 2**

In what ways does the BHP Group use analytics to support its sustainability initiatives?

Answer: The BHP Group employs data analytics to support its sustainability initiatives by assessing environmental impacts and leads its carbon reduction strategies. By analyzing emissions data, BHP can set measurable goals that align with global climate goals while ensuring that its operations are environmentally responsible. This data-driven approach allows BHP to track progress and make necessary adjustments to its sustainability strategies while reinforcing its commitment to corporate responsibility. Using analytics, BHP enhances its environmental performance and strengthens its reputation as a leader in sustainable mining practices.

**Question 3**

How does the BHP Group apply analytics in workforce management to improve safety and training programs?

Answer: The BHP Group applies analytics in workforce management by analyzing employee data to enhance safety protocols and training programs. By examining patterns in workplace incidents and employee performance, BHP can identify areas for improvement and develop targeted safety measures. This data-driven approach enables the company to implement effective training programs that address specific safety concerns and developing a culture of continuous improvement. As a result, BHP not only improves workplace safety but also ensures that its workforce is well-equipped to handle the challenges of the mining industry, contributing to overall operational excellence.

## Apple Inc.

Apple Inc. uses business analytics to improve product development and customer experience. Apple's leadership relies on comprehensive market analysis to understand consumer preferences and to guide the design of products like the iPhone and the MacBook. This analytical knowledge ensures that new features connect with users and thereby increases satisfaction and loyalty. Next, Apple uses analytics to maximize its supply chain management system and to balance inventory levels and demand using real-time data. This strategic approach minimizes operational costs while maintaining product availability and demonstrating effective leadership strategy in resource management. Finally, Apple studies consumer feedback and usage data to continually improve its services, such as Apple Music and the App Store. With the use of data analytics, the company not only anticipates market trends but also enhances user engagement.

**Question 1**

How does Apple Inc. use business analytics to enhance product development and customer experience?

Answer: Apple Inc. leverages business analytics to gain information about consumer preferences, which leads to the design and development of its products such as the iPhone and the MacBook. By conducting comprehensive market analysis, Apple ensures that new features identify with users to increase consumer satisfaction levels and loyalty. This data-driven approach allows Apple to anticipate consumer needs and trends while ensuring that its products remain relevant and appealing in a competitive market.

**Question 2**

In what ways does Apple Inc. apply analytics to optimize its supply chain management?

Answer: Apple Inc. uses real-time data analytics to optimize its supply chain management by balancing inventory levels with consumer demand. This strategic approach helps minimize operational costs while ensuring product availability. By analyzing data on sales trends and inventory, Apple can make informed decisions about production and distribution while demonstrating effective leadership in resource management and maintaining its reputation for efficiency and reliability.

**Question 3**

How does Apple Inc. use consumer feedback and usage data to improve its services?

Answer: Apple Inc. analyzes consumer feedback and usage data to continually enhance its services, which include Apple Music and the App Store. By studying how users interact with these services, Apple can constantly identify areas for improvement and innovation. This use of data analytics allows the company to anticipate market trends and enhance user engagement, ensuring that its services remain competitive and aligned with consumer expectations. This proactive approach improves the user experience and strengthens Apple's position in the digital services market.

## Samsung Electronics

Samsung Electronics uses advanced data analytics to enhance its product development processes. For instance, Samsung conducts extensive market research and consumer behavior analysis, allowing leaders to identify emerging trends and adapt product features accordingly. This approach has led to the successful launch of popular devices that include the Galaxy series that were created to meet consumer demands. Next, Samsung uses analytics to optimize its supply chain management using data to improve inventory control and to reduce production costs. This strategic move ensures efficient operations while maintaining high availability of products. Finally, Samsung's leadership analyzes customer feedback from various channels to refine user experience and address issues in real time. By monitoring and acting on this data, the company improves consumer satisfaction.

**Question 1**

How does Samsung Electronics use data analytics to enhance its product development processes?

Answer: Samsung Electronics uses data analytics extensively in its product development processes by conducting thorough market research and analyzing consumer behavior. This approach enables the company to identify emerging trends and adapt product features to meet consumer demands. For example, the successful launch of the Galaxy series was a direct result of understanding consumer preferences and incorporating desired features into the devices. By staying knowledgeable about market trends and consumer needs, Samsung ensures that its products remain competitive and appeal to a broad audience.

**Question 2**

In what ways does Samsung optimize its supply chain management through data analytics?

Answer: Samsung optimizes its supply chain management by using data analytics to improve inventory control and reduce production costs. By analyzing data related to supply chain operations, Samsung can make informed decisions that enhance efficiency and ensure the high availability of products. This strategy helps the company maintain a balance between supply and demand while minimizing excess inventory and reducing waste. As a result, Samsung can operate more efficiently and cost-effectively, which contributes to its overall competitiveness in the market.

**Question 3**

How does Samsung Electronics use customer feedback to improve user experience?

Answer: Samsung Electronics actively analyzes customer feedback from various channels to refine user experience and address issues in real time. By monitoring feedback, the company can identify areas for improvement and implement changes that improve the level of consumer satisfaction. This strategy enables Samsung to adapt quickly to customer needs and preferences while guaranteeing that its products and services meet or exceed expectations. As a result of continuously refining the user experience based on data-driven information, Samsung reinforces its relationship with consumers and develops brand loyalty.

## CASE STUDIES ON LEADERSHIP SUCCESS THROUGH ANALYTICS

### Business Success Through Business Analytics

Business analytics plays a crucial role in understanding leadership trends and consumer behavior that enables organizations in the leadership industry to make more data-driven and informed decisions. Following are three examples of how leadership data and knowledge are translated into business success using analytics:

### Example 1: Prophet Leaders Inc.

Prophet Leaders Inc. is a company that specializes in leadership development programs for emerging leaders in various industries. By using business analytics, they have been able to focus on their programs to meet the specific needs of their clients, resulting in significant improvements in leadership effectiveness. Next, Prophet Leaders Inc. uses data analytics to assess the leadership styles and effectiveness of their clients. By analyzing performance metrics, feedback scores, and behavioral assessments, they identify key areas for improvement. This data-driven approach allows them to customize their training modules, ensuring that each participant receives the most relevant and impactful guidance. The company has seen a 20% increase in client retention and a 20% boost in program completion rates. Their clients report a 30% improvement in leadership effectiveness, as measured by employee engagement and productivity metrics.

#### *Short-Response Questions*

1. What type of data does Prophet Leaders Inc. analyze to tailor their programs?
2. By what percentage did Prophet Leaders Inc. increase their client retention?
3. What improvement in leadership effectiveness do clients report after completing the program?

### Example 2: Leadership Creators Group

Leadership Creators Group is a consultancy that helps organizations develop strategic leadership capabilities. They employ advanced analytics to identify leadership trends and predict future leadership needs. Next, the company uses predictive analytics to forecast leadership trends and identify potential leadership gaps within organizations. By analyzing industry data, employee performance, and market trends, they provide actionable insights that help organizations prepare for future leadership challenges. Finally, Leadership Creators Group has helped clients reduce leadership turnover by 30% and increase leadership pipeline readiness by 45%. Their insights have enabled organizations to proactively address leadership gaps, resulting in more stable and effective leadership teams.

#### *Short-Response Questions*

1. What type of analytics does Leadership Creators Group use to forecast leadership trends?
2. By what percentage did Leadership Creators Group help reduce leadership turnover?
3. How much did Leadership Creators Group increase leadership pipeline readiness for their clients?

### Example 3: Dynamic Leadership Resolutions

Dynamic Leadership Resolutions offers leadership coaching and consulting services focusing on enhancing leadership skills through data-driven insights. They use analytics to measure the impact of leadership behaviors on organizational performance. The company uses analytics to correlate leadership behaviors with key performance indicators (KPIs), such as employee satisfaction, productivity, and financial performance. By identifying which leadership behaviors drive success, they provide targeted coaching to enhance these behaviors. Next, Dynamic Leadership Solutions has achieved a 40% improvement in client satisfaction and a 35% increase in leadership effectiveness scores. Their data-driven approach has enabled clients to achieve a 20% increase in overall organizational performance.

### Short-Response Questions

1. What does Dynamic Leadership Solutions correlate with key performance indicators?
2. By what percentage did Dynamic Leadership Solutions improve client satisfaction?
3. What increase in overall organizational performance did clients achieve with Dynamic Leadership Solutions?

## CASE STUDY: LEADING DYNAMICS GROUP (LDG)

Leading Dynamics Group (LDG) is a consulting firm devoted to enhancing leadership effectiveness within organizations through innovative training programs and strategies. With a focus on improving executive and team leadership skills, LDG has established itself as a thought leader in their field. Recently, the firm has conducted over 50 training sessions for various companies and collected valuable data on participant feedback and training outcomes. With a goal of leveraging this data to predict future training demands and refine their service offerings, LDG intends to implement a variety of forecasting methods using statistical and judgmental approaches.

### Business Analytics Data Tables

**TABLE 7.5** Training Session Feedback

| 1 | A | B | C | D | E |
|---|---|---|---|---|---|
| | Session ID | Month | Participation Satisfaction Score (1–10) | Number of Participants | Training Hours |
| 2 | 1 | January | 8.5 | 30 | 3 |
| 3 | 2 | February | 9.0 | 25 | 4 |
| 4 | 3 | March | 7.5 | 40 | 2 |
| 5 | 4 | April | 8.8 | 35 | 3 |
| 6 | 5 | May | 9.3 | 20 | 5 |

**TABLE 7.6** Historical Training Demand

| 1 | A | B | C | D |
|---|---|---|---|---|
| | **Month** | **Training Sessions Conducted** | **Revenue Generated ($)** | **Average Duration (Hours)** |
| 2 | January | 4 | 12,000 | 3.5 |
| 3 | February | 5 | 15,000 | 4.2 |
| 4 | March | 3 | 9,000 | 2.5 |
| 5 | April | 6 | 18,000 | 3.8 |
| 6 | May | 5 | 15,500 | 4.0 |

## Analytics Problems Using Excel

1. Use the Delphi method in Excel to gather expert forecasts for future training session demands based on historical data. Show how to aggregate the qualitative inputs and arrive at a consensus forecast.
2. Calculate the double exponential smoothing for predicting future revenue generated based on the previous months' revenues, considering an alpha value of 0.3 and a beta of 0.2 to adjust for trends.
3. Using a linear trend forecasting model, determine the forecasted number of training sessions for the next three months and calculate the forecast accuracy using error metrics such as mean absolute percentage error (MAPE).
4. Create a time series with linear trend regression–based model to analyze the relationship between the revenue generated and the number of training sessions conducted. Identify the regression equation and forecast future revenues based on this model.
5. Implement a moving average model to predict the average duration of training sessions for the next few months. What insights can be gathered from this forecasting method?

## Answer Key

1. *Using the Delphi method.* Collect expert opinions on future training demands. Create a summary table to present the range of estimates. Complete several rounds of input, and refine the results in each round until a consensus is reached. Record the final forecast in a new table.
2. *Calculating double exponential smoothing.* Set up your data with initial values: The smoothed value (S) for the forecast period equal to the first revenue value and the trend (T) as zero. Update recursively. Use these formulas in an Excel spreadsheet for relevant columns and apply them for all months.
3. *Linear trend forecasting model and forecast accuracy.* Use the LINEST function to derive the linear regression coefficients based on the number of training sessions as the independent variable and revenue generated as the dependent variable. Calculate the forecast for the next three months based on the derived regression equation. Compute MAPE. Apply the formula using the actual and forecasted values in Excel.

4. *Time series with linear trend regression–based model.* Use the regression tool in Excel, select Data Analysis, and choose Regression. Set Independent Variable (X) as the number of sessions and Dependent Variable (Y) as the revenue generated. Output will provide the regression equation (Y = mX + b), from which you can forecast future revenues.
5. *Moving average model.* Calculate the moving average by using Excel's AVERAGE function across three-month windows to smooth out short-term fluctuations. Create a new column to display these averages for insights into the trend of session durations. Analyze trends in duration data to predict future adjustments in training programs based on past averages.

## CASE STUDY: LEADINGINNOVATOR CORP.

LeadingInnovator Corp. is a company concentrating on leadership development and organizational transformation. The company has been instrumental in helping businesses cultivate effective leadership practices and develop a culture of innovation. Recently, LeadingInnovator Corp. partnered with a large technology organization to enhance their leadership training programs and improve overall employee performance. To evaluate the impact of their leadership initiatives, LeadingInnovator Corp. collected data on employee performance metrics, leadership training attendance, and employee satisfaction over a year. The data was analyzed using multiple forecasting techniques to predict future trends and measure the effectiveness of the training programs. The following tables summarize key findings from the project:

**TABLE 7.7** Employee Performance Metrics

| 1 | A | B | C |
|---|---|---|---|
| | Month | Performance Score (Out of 100) | Training Attendance (%) |
| 2 | January | 75 | 80 |
| 3 | February | 78 | 82 |
| 4 | March | 80 | 85 |
| 5 | April | 82 | 87 |
| 6 | May | 85 | 90 |
| 7 | June | 88 | 92 |

**TABLE 7.8** Employee Satisfaction

| 1 | A | B | C |
|---|---|---|---|
| | Month | Satisfaction Score (Out of 10) | Number of Feedbacks |
| 2 | January | 7.5 | 50 |
| 3 | February | 7.6 | 55 |
| 4 | March | 7.8 | 60 |
| 5 | April | 8.0 | 65 |
| 6 | May | 8.2 | 70 |
| 7 | June | 8.5 | 75 |

### Analytics Problems Using Excel

1. *Delphi method.* Use the Delphi method to forecast future employee satisfaction scores.
2. *Double exponential smoothing.* Apply double exponential smoothing to the performance score data.
3. *Error metrics.* Calculate error metrics, such as MSE, MAE, and MAPE, for the performance score forecasts.
4. *Exponential smoothing models.* Use exponential smoothing models to forecast training attendance.
5. *Forecast accuracy.* Assess the forecast accuracy of the satisfaction scores.
6. *Indexes for forecasting.* Create indexes for forecasting employee performance.
7. *Indicators of forecasting.* Identify key indicators of forecasting accuracy for training attendance.
8. *Judgmental forecasting.* Use judgmental forecasting to predict future satisfaction scores.
9. *Linear trend forecasting model.* Develop a linear trend forecasting model for performance scores.
10. *Moving average model.* Apply a moving average model to the satisfaction score data.
11. *Qualitative forecasting.* Use qualitative forecasting methods to predict future training attendance.
12. *Quantitative forecasting.* Implement quantitative forecasting techniques for performance scores.
13. *Stationary time series forecasting.* Perform stationary time series forecasting on satisfaction scores.
14. *Time series with linear trend regression–based model.* Use time series with a linear trend regression–based model to forecast performance scores.

### Answer Key

1. *Delphi method.* Gather expert opinions and use the AVERAGE function to aggregate forecasts.
2. *Double exponential smoothing.* Use the FORECAST.ETS function with the Data Analysis ToolPak.
3. *Error metrics.* Calculate MSE: =AVERAGE((Actual − Forecast)^2). Calculate MAE: =AVERAGE(ABS(Actual − Forecast)). Calculate MAPE: =AVERAGE(ABS((Actual − Forecast)/Actual)) * 100.
4. *Exponential smoothing models.* Use the FORECAST.ETS function to apply exponential smoothing.
5. *Forecast accuracy.* Compare actual and forecasted values using the FORECAST.ETS.CONFINT function.
6. *Indexes for forecasting.* Create indexes using the INDEX function to organize data for forecasting.
7. *Indicators of forecasting.* Identify indicators using correlation analysis with the CORREL function.

8. *Judgmental forecasting.* Use expert judgment and the AVERAGE function to predict future values.
9. *Linear trend forecasting model.* Use the TREND function to develop a linear trend model.
10. *Moving average model.* Apply the AVERAGE function over a moving window of data points.
11. *Qualitative forecasting.* Use qualitative methods, such as surveys and expert opinions.
12. *Quantitative forecasting.* Implement the FORECAST function for quantitative predictions.
13. *Stationary time series forecasting.* Use the STATIONARY function in the Data Analysis ToolPak.
14. *Time series with linear trend regression–based model.* Use the LINEST function to create a regression-based model.

# CHAPTER 8

# Finance and Business Analytics

Finance and business analytics play an important role in the decision-making process for organizations. The finance industry is especially impacted by using business analytics in its various market segments, which include investment management, banking, real estate, insurance, and financial services technology. Within each segment of the financial market industry, business analytics uses statistics, data analysis, and methodologies that are used to improve profitability, mitigate risk, and improve operational performance and efficiency. In the finance industry, business analytics is more than basic reporting and bookkeeping; instead, business analytics focuses on more advanced functions that include the analysis and interpretation of large sets of data to analyze trends so organizations can determine the necessary course of action to achieve their objectives and goals.

Within this industry, finance companies use business analytics to determine market conditions, maximize their investment portfolios, and predict revenue growth of current or new and emerging markets. As an example, a finance company can use predictive analytics to determine fraudulent behavior in the market. The finance company implements business analytics to conduct risk assessment when making a loan to a client. Finally, a finance company can use statistical analysis to determine fair policy premiums and to develop risk profiles for all potential transactions and investments.

One of the main functions of financial business analytics within the finance industry is to conduct and understand performance management. Performance management is achieved by companies conducting statistical analysis to understand cost structures, profitability, and sources of revenue. Through performance management, financial entities can implement data-driven improvement strategies and identify inefficiencies within their current processes. As a result, business analytics develops the proper foundation or structure for maximizing financial returns, allocating resources, and conducting strategic distributions of wealth.

Next, finance combined with business analytics will work to develop an effective risk management strategy. In today's global market, economies in various areas are unstable and lead to uncertainty for investors and clients. This situation makes it necessary for financial institutions to conduct a risk assessment to protect the company from possible financial losses or downturn. This situation will require the use of business analytics by the financial institution to create statistical models to determine all scenarios for risk to develop, determine the financial impact of projects, and to develop contingency plans. As an example, a financial

DOI: 10.4324/9781003629658-8

firm that manages assets and hedge funds can use business analytics to predict fluctuations in the market and to make the correct choices to avoid negative results to preserve the worth of the investor.

Third, financial business analytics is used as part of the decision-making process when dealing with equity financing, capital investment, and mergers and acquisitions. Knowledge that is data-driven will be used to lead investment strategies through the identification of profitable opportunities while also evaluating its success of longevity and feasibility. Fourth, financial business analytics is associated with the supporting of regulatory compliance by automating regular reporting processes and ensuring compliance with all financial laws and regulations. Fifth, financial business analytics is used to support the technology of financial firms with AI and machine learning algorithms. Finally, technology has supported the financial industry with big data capabilities to improve consumer behavior analysis and to determine the scope of financial forecasting.

## FINANCIAL MODELING AND FORECASTING TECHNIQUES

Financial modeling and forecasting techniques help various industries, including banking, investment management strategies, insurance, financial technology, and real estate. By using quantitative data analysis and other analytical tools, financial companies can improve their predictions of future financial investments, determine their level of exposure to risk, and support the strategic decision-making process. Next, financial modeling is responsible for developing mathematical models and visualization methods of data to understand the financial performance of the business. This strategy enables financial institutions to use business analytics to gain new information and knowledge from previously collected data, industry benchmarks, and market trends.

As an example, financial analytic models are used by investment bankers to evaluate the effectiveness of mergers and acquisitions, conduct a valuation of assets, and to calculate the potential repayment of debt scenarios. With the use of business analytics, financial institutions can conduct analysis in real time using predictive machine learning algorithms to ensure a more accurate projection of the outcome. Next, financial companies use forecasting models to predict the results of future investments that include expenses, revenue, cash flow, and net worth. This situation enables companies to use business analytics to implement sensitivity testing, probability-based forecasting, and scenario analysis.

As a result, there is a reciprocal relationship between financial institutions and business analytics to improve the advancements of technology of businesses. Technological advancements within this industry include AI, big data analytics, and machine learning. Using these advanced technologies enables financial institutions to develop accurate forecasts and models based on the analysis of large datasets and recognizing complex trends that were not visible through human examination. Finally, when financial technology is used by companies, predictive analytics can be performed to create new products and services based on the behavior of consumers. When risk management is integrated into business analytics, financial companies can reduce the threat of loss and predict the changes within a volatile economic market.

### Using Analytics for Accurate Financial Projections

Companies must use analytics to ensure accurate financial projections. Finance and business analytics enable businesses to make reliable financial predictions to make data-driven decisions using advanced models and predictive tools to maximize the forecasting process. The main goal of companies making financial projections is based on the detailed analysis of market variables, profitability, expenses, and revenues. Next, business analytics supports the financial projections process by studying large amounts of formless datasets, uncovering trends and patterns, developing new information for data-driven decisions. As an example, banking companies can use business analytical tools to forecast lending trends, future behavior of consumers, probabilities of credit default, and allowing financial institutions to manage risk and create effective lending policies.

Next, the integration of business analytics and technology will improve the scalability and the precision of all financial projections made by companies. These techniques include AI, machine learning algorithms, and predictive modeling to conduct a sensitivity analysis on the key performance metrics. As an example, an insurance company will use actuarial statistics to forecast expenses, claims, manage exposure to risk, and assess the premiums of revenues based on the changing dynamics of the global economy. For a real estate company, the business will depend on the analysis of rental income, property values, and the demand of the market to make secure financial development and investment decisions.

Third, business analytics supports real-time monitoring so adjustments can be made to financial projections. Real-time monitoring is required to help industries to not be negatively impacted by the volatility of the market. With the processing of real-time data, financial leaders can help their companies to stay ahead of emerging trends and any other unanticipated disruptions to the flow of business. Finally, using analytics for accurate financial projections helps to develop a risk management strategy to enable organizations to use statistics and advanced models to determine potential negative situations and scenarios so the necessary resources can be allocated to ensure success of their investment portfolios under the conditions of the economic environment.

## RISK ASSESSMENT AND MANAGEMENT IN FINANCE

Risk assessment and management in finance involve the identification and quantification of all potential threats to the financial stability of an organization. Business analytics helps financial leaders use statistics and methodologies to study large datasets and identify trends and discover hidden patterns to reduce the level of risk to the company. When financial leaders prioritize data-focused solutions, businesses can become proactive and reduce their exposure to weaknesses and threats in the market.

Next, financial leaders who conduct risk assessments and management and finance can reduce the threat to the business when the market is volatile by ensuring high-level performance in their portfolio investments. The situation is achieved using stress testing, sensitivity analysis, and scenario analysis to help organizations determine the global economic conditions of the market and the impact it will have on the value of their assets. Third, business analytics help companies to identify overexposure in various industries across the globe to help financial leaders make informed diversification strategies to improve the stability of their investment portfolio.

Third, financial leaders rely on quantitative risk models to help them determine the potential losses and to develop contingency plans and safeguards to protect themselves against threats in the market. The situation helps financial leaders to manage market related risks that include changes in value and other macroeconomic indicators that are determined by past performance data, location, and demographic trends, and to help them project future market conditions to reduce the level of risk. As a result, finance and business analytics work together to develop effective risk management strategies for companies in all sectors of the market using data-driven approaches to evaluate the level of risk that are demonstrated in the table that follows.

**TABLE 8.1** Data-Driven Approaches to Financial Risk Evaluation

| Approach | Explanation |
|---|---|
| **Big data analytics** | Utilizes large datasets from diverse sources to uncover patterns and insights, enabling more sophisticated and timely risk assessments |
| **Predictive analytics** | Employs statistical algorithms and machine learning techniques to predict future risks based on historical data, improving the accuracy of risk forecasting |
| **Machine learning (ML)** | Uses algorithms that learn from data to identify patterns and anomalies, enhancing the detection of fraud and other financial risks |
| **Artificial intelligence (AI)** | Integrates AI to automate risk assessment processes, reducing manual intervention and increasing operational efficiency |
| **Real-time data monitoring** | Continuously monitors financial data streams to detect and respond to risks as they emerge, ensuring timely mitigation |
| **Anomaly detection** | Identifies unusual patterns in data that may indicate potential risks, such as fraudulent transactions or market irregularities |
| **Credit risk modeling** | Uses advanced analytics to evaluate the creditworthiness of borrowers, helping financial institutions manage and mitigate credit risk |
| **Market risk prediction** | Analyzes market data to forecast potential market risks, aiding in the development of strategies to mitigate adverse market movements |
| **Fraud detection** | Leverages data analytics to identify and prevent fraudulent activities by recognizing suspicious patterns and behaviors |
| **Automated risk reporting** | Generates automated reports on risk metrics and compliance, improving transparency and regulatory compliance |

## INVESTMENT ANALYSIS AND PORTFOLIO MANAGEMENT

Finance and business analytics play an important role in investment analysis and management portfolios by enabling companies to make data-driven decisions, maximize investment strategies, and improve the assessment of risk. In investment analysis, finance and business analytics enable finance leaders to evaluate the performance levels and potential of financial tools, including bonds, stocks, commodities, and other alternative investments options. Next, business analytics breaks down large amounts of data that include market trends, past performance indexes, and other economic factors using statistical models, such as AI and machine learning algorithms, to provide businesses data to make informed decisions related to the selection of assets and the allocation of resources.

In portfolio management, finance combined with business analytics creates a methodical approach to developing and maintaining a well-structured portfolio that is customized to meet the objectives of the investor. Next, performance risk can be adjusted using metrics to help determine the maximization of the returns. The portfolio will be used to help reduce

**TABLE 8.2** Using Analytics to Make Informed Investment Choices

| Industry | Use of Analytics | Benefits |
|---|---|---|
| **Banking** | Predictive analytics for credit risk modeling and fraud detection | Improved risk management, reduced fraud, enhanced customer trust |
| **Insurance** | Data analytics for claim prediction and customer segmentation | Optimized pricing, better customer targeting, reduced claim costs |
| **Retail** | Sales forecasting and inventory management using business intelligence | Increased sales, efficient inventory control, better customer satisfaction |
| **Health care** | Financial analytics for cost management and investment in medical technologies | Reduced operational costs, improved patient care, strategic investment in new technologies |
| **Real estate** | Market trend analysis and property valuation using data analytics | Accurate property valuations, better investment decisions, enhanced market understanding |
| **Manufacturing** | Supply chain optimization and cost analysis using business analytics | Reduced production costs, improved supply chain efficiency, better investment in resources |
| **Technology** | Investment in R&D and innovation using predictive analytics | Enhanced product development, strategic investment in emerging technologies, competitive edge |
| **Energy** | Risk assessment and market analysis for investment in renewable energy sources | Improved risk management, strategic investment in sustainable energy, better regulatory compliance |
| **Telecommunications** | Customer behavior analysis and network optimization using data analytics | Improved customer retention, optimized network performance, strategic investment decisions |

the level of exposure of risk based on the volatility of the market. To be successful, financial leaders must conduct scenario analyses to simulate how portfolios and investments will perform under various market and economic conditions. The strategy helps financial managers to better prepare for negative scenarios in the markets that include high inflation rates, interest rate increases, and geopolitical turmoil so they can become proactive in adjusting strategies to reduce losses.

Finally, financial leaders will use business analytics and advanced technologies to provide new innovative tools. The various industries in the market that help simplify the monitoring of portfolios and investments and conduct a thorough risk evaluation of the company. As a result, finance, combined with business analytics, will create an effective investment analysis and portfolio management process to help organizations survive the changing dynamics within the financial markets. When data-driven information is used, financial leaders can improve their modeling of risk, the decision-making process, and empower businesses to achieve long-term growth and be successful in obtaining their objectives and goals by using analytics to make informed investment choices as detailed in the chart that follows.

## BUDGETING AND FINANCIAL PLANNING WITH ANALYTICS

*Budgeting* is the process of organizations allocating resources to achieve their strategic objectives and goals while reducing costs and maximizing their expenditures on assets. Financial leaders use business analytics to study past data, identify spending trends, and predict the future financial needs of the business by creating budgets that are in line with the mission and vision of the business. When business analytics are used, financial leaders can guarantee that budgets will support new initiatives for growth and also mitigate risk to the company.

Financial planning focuses on the creation of future returns on investments of stakeholders, new revenue streams, expenditures, and the overall financial outcome of the organization using information gained using business analytics. With business analytics, financial leaders within organizations can evaluate market trends and develop accurate financial forecasts to predict consumer behavior and other economic indicators to remain successful. As an example, an investment management company can use business analytics to develop a forecast to estimate the performance of the portfolio, determine future cash flows, and to allocate the right capital and resources through new diversified investment opportunities. The situation enables financial leaders to balance the level of risk with the return on investments while also ensuring strategic alignment with the long-term growth goals of the business.

Next, business analytics uses scenario analysis and sensitivity testing and financial planning and budgeting. This strategy enables financial leaders of organizations to simulate and reenact various market conditions and economic situations that can potentially impact the financial goals of the business. As an example, insurers can use business analytics to plan for natural disasters and other unexpected claims that will increase based on these events. By using business analytics, ensures can develop contingency budgets and financial planning strategies that enable them to respond dynamically to the negative developments within the environment and support the financial stability of the business and individual. As a result, business analytics helps financial leaders to determine the costs that are associated with the

**TABLE 8.3** Enhancing Budgeting Accuracy Through Data Analysis

| Method | Explanation | Benefits |
|---|---|---|
| **Historical data analysis** | Analyzing past financial data to identify trends and patterns | Provides a solid foundation for accurate budget forecasts; reduces reliance on guesswork |
| **Predictive analytics** | Using statistical models and machine learning to forecast future financial outcomes | Enhances the accuracy of budget predictions; helps anticipate financial needs and challenges |
| **Scenario planning** | Creating and analyzing different financial scenarios to prepare for various outcomes | Allows organizations to plan for uncertainties; improves flexibility and responsiveness |
| **Real-time data monitoring** | Continuously tracking financial performance and comparing it against the budget | Enables timely adjustments to the budget; ensures alignment with actual financial conditions |
| **Variance analysis** | Comparing budgeted figures with actual results to identify discrepancies | Helps in understanding the reasons for variances; improves future budgeting processes |
| **Cost–benefit analysis** | Evaluating the financial impact of different business decisions and investments | Ensures resources are allocated efficiently; supports strategic decision-making |
| **Benchmarking** | Comparing financial performance against industry standards or competitors | Identifies areas for improvement; sets realistic budget targets |
| **Automated reporting** | Generating real-time financial reports and dashboards | Increases transparency; provides quick insights for decision-makers |
| **Data visualization** | Using charts and graphs to present financial data clearly and intuitively | Enhances understanding of financial information; aids in communicating budget insights |
| **Risk assessment** | Identifying and evaluating financial risks that could impact the budget | Helps in developing risk mitigation strategies; ensures more resilient budgeting |

management and leadership process and to help identify underperforming assets to allocate resources effectively to new investment opportunities that will yield maximum results as demonstrated in Table 8.3.

## CASH FLOW ANALYSIS AND OPTIMIZATION

Finance and business analytics are important in the analysis of cash flow and the optimization process of organizations across various financial industries. This strategy is achieved when financial industries use business analytics tools to monitor, evaluate, and improve the liquidity of the cash flow process. Next, the use of business analytics supports all financial functions that include investment management, banking, real estate, insurance, and financial technology to help predict the availability of funds to achieve objectives and goals, forecast the patterns of cash flow, and identify inefficiencies and threats.

Cash flow analysis involves the study of all inflows and outflows of cash within the business to determine the level of liquidity for the organization. Business analytics will be required to monitor this process by using large amounts of data, real-time monitoring, and predictive models to accurately evaluate the trends of cash flow in and out of the organization. As an example, a banking institution uses business analytics to predict the flow of consumer deposits, the distribution of loans, and repayment schedules of clients. The strategy allows banks to identify the periods of positive and negative liquidity throughout the fiscal year so they can develop a sustainable portfolio and allocation of capital assets to remain financially stable.

Next, the optimization of cash flow is dependent on business analytics since it requires identification of all areas in business were cash is used effectively in those areas that need improvement. Only with a data-driven strategy can financial leaders use statistics to analyze the operational expenses, to streamline the payment process, and to identify future cost-saving opportunities. As an example, investment firms use business analytics to maximize the timing of the sale and purchase of assets, to maximize returns on investment, and to reduce the amount and time of unused cash deposits.

Finally, business analytics supports cash flow analysis and optimization by improving the accuracy of forecasting. Financial leaders use predictive models to predict the inflows and outflows of cash based on past market trends, historical data, and consumer behavior patterns. As an example, a real estate company can use business analytics to project the amount of income that will be gained on a rental property along with the maintenance costs. This analysis will help the real estate company to better allocate resources into plan for seasonal fluctuations of cash flow to ensure the company is not negatively impacted due to a low liquidity ratio. To be successful, financial leaders will need to use visualization tools and automation to improve the cash flow management and optimization process to make real-time decisions as detailed in the Table 8.4.

## ANALYZING FINANCIAL STATEMENTS

It is important for financial leaders of various industries to analyze financial statements. Financial statements include the balance sheet, income statement, and cash flow. These three documents provide an overall view of the organization's financial position. Next, business analytics will improve the analysis of these statements by using statistical tools and methods to process large amounts of data, uncover abnormalities, and identify trends for organizational leaders to make better financial decisions. As an example, financial statements, combined with the use of business analytics, help a banking firm to determine the soundness, liquidity, and debt-to-equity ratio of a loan applicant to see if their creditworthiness is acceptable and to minimize the risk of default.

Next, finance and business analytics will use financial statements to perform a thorough performance evaluation and ratio analysis of the organization. A ratio analysis studies the financial liquidity, profitability, and efficiency of its resources to ensure stability and future growth. As an example, investment management companies use business analytics to calculate financial ratios based on skill to create a comparison of how the different portfolios perform across multiple industries at the same time. The situation will create a monitoring capability that will determine the return on equity

**TABLE 8.4** Techniques for Improving Cash Flow Management and Optimization

| Technique | Explanation | Benefits |
|---|---|---|
| **Cash flow forecasting** | Predicting future cash inflows and outflows using historical data and predictive models | Helps anticipate shortfalls or surpluses, enabling proactive financial planning |
| **Receivables management** | Implementing automated invoice and payment tracking systems | Accelerates cash collection, reduces delays, and improves liquidity |
| **Payables optimization** | Strategically timing payments to suppliers to maintain optimal cash flow | Enhances liquidity management, avoids unnecessary interest or late fees |
| **Scenario analysis** | Evaluating different financial scenarios to prepare for various outcomes | Improves flexibility and responsiveness to financial uncertainties |
| **Real-time monitoring** | Continuously tracking cash flow metrics using advanced analytics tools | Enables timely adjustments and ensures alignment with actual financial conditions |
| **Cost control** | Identifying and reducing unnecessary expenses through detailed data analysis | Improves overall financial health and increases available cash |
| **Automated reporting** | Generating real-time financial reports and dashboards | Increases transparency and provides quick insights for decision-makers |
| **Data visualization** | Using charts and graphs to present cash flow data clearly and intuitively | Enhances understanding of financial information and aids in communicating insights |
| **Predictive analytics** | Utilizing machine learning models to forecast cash flow trends | Improves accuracy of cash flow predictions and helps in strategic planning |
| **Liquidity management** | Implementing strategies to maintain optimal levels of liquid assets | Ensures the organization can meet its short-term obligations and invest in opportunities |

(ROE) and debt to asset ratio that enables businesses to evaluate their ash performance of the companies they invest in two mitigate risk and increase the rate of return of investment (ROI).

Third, predictive analytics is used in assessing the data contained in financial statements by identifying future trends using past data. When predictive models are used, financial leaders can better understand patterns of revenue and expenses to the organization so they can forecast future earnings and predict any inconsistencies in the financial reporting system. Finally, predictive analytics and financial statements will identify potential for risk and new opportunities in real time to help the organization develop contingency plans to ensure their competitive advantage within the global environment. As a result, it is critical for financial leaders to employ business analytics to interpret the financial health and well-being of the organization. Methods for employing analytics to interpret financial health and well-being are detailed in the table that follows.

**TABLE 8.5** Employing Analytics to Interpret Financial Health and Well-Being

| Technique | Explanation | Benefits |
|---|---|---|
| **Ratio analysis** | Evaluates key financial ratios, such as liquidity, profitability, and solvency ratios | Provides insights into a company's financial stability, operational efficiency, and profitability |
| **Trend analysis** | Examines financial data over multiple periods to identify patterns and anomalies | Helps forecast future performance and detect early warning signs of financial distress |
| **Horizontal analysis** | Compares financial data across different periods to identify growth patterns and trends | Highlights long-term trends and year-over-year performance, aiding strategic decision-making |
| **Vertical analysis** | Expresses each line item in financial statements as a percentage of a base figure | Simplifies comparison across periods and between companies, aiding in benchmarking |
| **Cash flow analysis** | Analyzes inflows and outflows of cash to assess operational efficiency and liquidity | Provides insight into an organization's ability to generate cash and meet obligations |
| **Predictive analytics** | Uses statistical models and machine learning to forecast future financial outcomes | Enhances accuracy of financial predictions, supports strategic planning |
| **Scenario planning** | Evaluates different financial scenarios to prepare for various outcomes | Improves flexibility and responsiveness to financial uncertainties |
| **Benchmarking** | Compares financial performance against industry standards or competitors | Identifies areas for improvement, sets realistic targets, and enhances competitive positioning |
| **Data visualization** | Uses charts and graphs to present financial data clearly and intuitively | Enhances understanding of financial information, aids in communicating information |
| **Automated reporting** | Generates real-time financial reports and dashboards | Increases transparency, provides quick information for decision-makers |

## BUSINESS ANALYTICS FUNCTION FOR FINANCE USING MICROSOFT EXCEL

In the business environment, there are many business analytical terms mentioned that play a critical role in making informed and data-driven choices that drive decisions, optimize daily operations, and develop strategic actions and initiatives. Various statistical concepts play an important role in finance and business analytics by providing essential tools for data analysis and decision-making. Here's a detailed overview of their definition and importance and how to conduct this statistical analysis using Microsoft Excel.

## Cause-and-Effect Modeling of Data

This analytical approach helps organizations understand the relationships between different financial variables by identifying causal factors so businesses can project the impacts of potential changes and allow for improved strategic planning and risk management.

**Steps:**

1. Organize your data into two columns: one for the independent variable (cause) and one for the dependent variable (effect).
2. Go to the Data tab and click on Data Analysis.
3. Choose Regression from the options and click OK.
4. Specify the Y Range (dependent variable) and X Range (independent variable).
5. Click OK to run the regression analysis and view the output.

## Classifications of Data

Properly classifying financial data improves the ability to analyze it effectively. By grouping similar data types or categories, analysts can gain knowledge more effectively and develop targeted strategies and gain operational efficiency.

**Steps:**

1. Enter the data in a column.
2. Use the IF function to classify numeric data.

## Cluster Analysis

This technique is useful for segmenting datasets into groups that exhibit similar characteristics. In finance, cluster analysis can identify customer segments, market trends, or business units, helping customize strategies to specific groups and improve consumer engagement.

**Steps:**

1. Arrange the data in a table.
2. For manual clustering, you can use the =AVERAGE function to find centroids and =SUMSQ to calculate distances or use Excel's add-ins for clustering.

## Data Mining

This process uncovers patterns and insights within large datasets and enables financial analysts to discover hidden relationships. Data mining can lead to better predictive models and help companies understand market movements and consumer behavior.

**Steps:**

1. Select the data and go to the Insert tab.
2. Click on PivotTable, select your data range, and choose where you want to place the PivotTable.
3. Use the PivotTable Field List to analyze data dynamically by arranging fields into rows, columns, and values.

### Expected Present Value (EPV)

EPV is essential for evaluating future cash flows in today's conditions. By calculating EPV, analysts can assess the riskiness and profitability of investments that are critical for making informed investment decisions.

Formula: =Cash Flow/(1 + r)^n

**Steps:**

1. Identify cash flows in a column and discount rate.
2. In a new column, calculate EPV using the formula =Cash Flow/(1 + r)^n, where *r* is the discount rate and *n* is the time period.
3. Apply this formula for all periods, and sum the results to obtain EPV.

### Future Value (FV)

Understanding the future value of cash flows allows businesses to plan strategically for growth. FV indicates how much investment made today will grow over time and assist in financial planning and goal setting.

Formula: =FV(rate, nper, pmt, pv, type).

**Steps:**

1. Use the FV function. The syntax is =FV(rate, nper, pmt, pv, type).
2. Adjust parameters for your specific scenarios.

### Internal Rate of Return (IRR)

This metric is critical for assessing the profitability of investments or projects. By calculating IRR, finance professionals can compare the expected return of different investment opportunities and use it to support the allocation of resources.

Formula: =IRR(range)

**Steps:**

1. Arrange cash flows (including initial investment as negative) in a column.
2. Use the formula =IRR(range), where *range* corresponds to the cash flow cells.
3. Press Enter to obtain the IRR.

## Measuring Classification of Performance of Data

Performance metrics obtained from classified data help organizations evaluate their financial position. Metrics provide knowledge into operational efficiency and profitability and allow management to adjust as needed.

**Steps:**

1. Use simple metrics like averages, medians, or percentages.
2. Use formulas such as =AVERAGE(range) or =COUNTIF(range, condition) to obtain performance measures.
3. Create visualization charts to highlight performance metrics.

## Measuring Distance Between Financial Objects

Understanding the distance or difference between various financial entities or performance metrics helps identify relative strengths and weaknesses. This analysis can improve competitive strategy and market positioning.

Formula: =SQRT((A2-B2)^2 + (C2-D2)^2)

**Steps:**

1. Organize data points in a table with multiple features.
2. Use the distance formula =SQRT((A2-B2)^2 + (C2-D2)^2) to calculate the distance between objects based on their features.

## Methods of Clustering Analysis

These methods allow for in-depth market analysis that leads to improved consumer targeting and customized product offerings. By employing these methods, organizations can enhance their market strategies based on detailed consumer intelligence.

**Steps:**

1. Use sorting and filtering techniques to group data based on specified criteria.

## Net Present Value (NPV)

NPV is fundamental in investment analysis as it evaluates the profitability of an investment by considering the present value of expected cash flow. Positive NPV indicates a desirable investment opportunity and is used to make data-driven financial decisions.

Formula: =NPV(rate, value1, value2)

**Steps:**

2. Identify the cash flows in a column, starting with the initial investment as a negative number.
3. Determine the discount rate.
4. Use the NPV function =NPV(rate, value1, value2).
5. Add the initial investment to complete the NPV calculation: =NPV(rate, value1) + initial investment.

## Normalizing Financial Distance Measures

This process standardizes financial metrics and allows for fair comparisons across different units or time periods. Normalization improves analytical conclusions and supports informed decision-making.

Formula: =(Value − Mean)/StdDev

**Steps:**

1. Calculate the mean and standard deviation of your financial measures with:
    a. Mean: =AVERAGE(range)
    b. Standard Deviation: =STDEV.P(range)
2. Apply normalization using the formula = (Value − Mean)/StdDev.

## Payment (PMT)

Understanding payment structures using the PMT function is crucial for debt management and investment appraisals. It assists in evaluating the impact of payment schedules on cash flow and financial planning.

Formula: = PMT(rate, nper, pv, fv, type)

**Steps:**

1. Use the PMT function in Excel: =PMT(rate, nper, pv, fv, type).
2. Calculate the monthly payment required to repay a $ loan at?% interest over # years.
3. Adjust the inputs for your specific scenario.

## Present Value (PV)

PV calculations are critical for discounting future cash flows and enabling businesses to understand the value of future income today. This analysis is necessary when assessing investments and making financing decisions.

Formula: =PV(rate, nper, pmt, fv, type)

**Steps:**

1. Use the PV function: =PV(rate, nper, pmt, fv, type).
2. Calculate the present value of receiving $ amount in # years at a?% discount rate.
3. Input parameters as necessary for the situation.

## Rate (Internal Rate)

This rate helps assess the efficiency of investment returns. By understanding how different rates impact project viability, finance leaders can make more strategic investment choices.

Formula: =XIRR(cash_flows, dates) or =IRR(column)

**Steps:**

1. Organize your cash flows in a column.
2. Use the function =XIRR(cash_flows, dates) for non-periodic cash flows or =IRR(column) for regular cash flows.
3. Press Enter to find the internal rate of return.

## Return on Investment (ROI)

ROI calculations are essential for measuring the financial return generated from investments. This metric helps measure the effectiveness of various initiatives and guide future investment strategies.

Formula: = (Net Profit/Cost of Investment)*100

**Steps:**

1. Identify your net profit and total investment.
2. Use the formula = (Net Profit/Cost of Investment)*100.
3. Input the values in Excel to get the ROI as a percentage.

## REAL-WORLD EXAMPLES OF LEADERSHIP INSIGHTS DRIVING BUSINESS SUCCESS

### SoftBank Group Corp.

One key strategy of SoftBank Group Corp. is to use data analytics to evaluate potential investments through its Vision Fund. By analyzing market trends, growth projections, and technological advancements, SoftBank's leadership identifies promising start-ups and established companies to facilitate strategic investments that generate substantial returns.

Next, SoftBank uses financial modeling and scenario analysis to determine risks and opportunities across its diverse portfolio. This analytical approach allows the company to make informed decisions regarding investment diversification and ensure stability and growth even in unstable markets. Finally, SoftBank relies on business analytics to monitor the performance of its investments and enables timely adjustments to strategies based on real-time data. This proactive management approach helps optimize the value of its holdings. Through this use of business analytics, SoftBank Group demonstrated how finance-driven strategies advanced innovation and led to significant success in the global investment environment.

**Question 1**

How does SoftBank Group Corp. use data analytics to enhance its investment strategy through the Vision Fund?

Answer: SoftBank Group Corp. uses data analytics to improve its investment strategy by thoroughly evaluating potential investments through its Vision Fund. By analyzing market trends, growth projections, and technological advancements, SoftBank's leadership can identify promising start-ups and established companies. This data-driven approach allows the company to make strategic investments that are likely to generate substantial returns. By focusing on data analytics, SoftBank ensures that its investment decisions are informed and aligned with future market opportunities, thereby maximizing the potential for success.

**Question 2**

In what ways does SoftBank use financial modeling and scenario analysis to manage risks and opportunities within its portfolio?

Answer: SoftBank uses financial modeling and scenario analysis to effectively manage risks and opportunities across its diverse portfolio. This analytical approach allows the company to assess various market conditions and potential outcomes that enable it to make informed decisions regarding investment diversification. By understanding the potential risks and opportunities, SoftBank can create stability and growth even in unstable markets. This strategic use of analytics helps the company maximize its investment strategy and maintain a balanced portfolio that can withstand the fluctuations of the market.

**Question 3**

How does SoftBank's use of business analytics contribute to the proactive management of its investment portfolio?

Answer: SoftBank's use of business analytics plays a crucial role in the proactive management of its investment portfolio. By monitoring the performance of its investments in real time, the company can make timely adjustments to its strategies. This continuous analysis allows SoftBank to respond quickly to changes in market conditions or the performance of individual investments, optimizing the value of its holdings. This proactive approach ensures that SoftBank can capitalize on emerging opportunities and mitigate potential risks, thereby enhancing the overall success of its investment efforts.

## HSBC Holdings plc

HSBC Holdings plc uses advanced data analytics to improve risk management practices and to allow it to identify and mitigate potential financial threats. By analyzing transaction patterns and consumer data, HSBC can proactively detect fraudulent activities and safeguard both the bank and its clients. Next, HSBC uses analytics to enhance customer relationship management. By analyzing client behavior and preferences, the bank customizes its financial products and services to meet the unique needs of different consumer segments, which leads to improved satisfaction and retention rates. Finally, in its investment strategies, HSBC uses financial modeling to evaluate market conditions and economic indicators to help guide decision-making for asset management. This analytical approach guarantees that the bank remains responsive in competitive markets. Through these insights, HSBC Holdings demonstrates how effective analytics can drive informed financial decision-making and foster long-term growth and stability in the global banking landscape.

### Question 1

How does HSBC Holdings plc use data analytics to enhance its risk management practices?

Answer: HSBC Holdings plc uses advanced data analytics to significantly enhance its risk management practices by analyzing transaction patterns and consumer data. This analytical approach allows the bank to proactively detect fraudulent activities, therefore safeguarding both the bank and its clients. By identifying unusual patterns and potential threats early, HSBC can implement preventive measures to mitigate risks while ensuring the security and integrity of its financial operations. This proactive stance not only protects the bank's assets but also builds trust with its customers, reinforcing its reputation as a secure and reliable financial institution.

### Question 2

In what ways does HSBC use analytics to improve customer relationship management?

Answer: HSBC relies on data analytics to improve customer relationship management by analyzing client behavior and preferences. This detailed analysis enables the bank to customize its financial products and services to meet the unique needs of different consumer markets. By customizing offerings to align with customer expectations, HSBC improves consumer satisfaction and retention rates. This personalized approach develops stronger relationships with clients since they feel understood and valued and leads to increased loyalty and long-term engagement with the bank.

**Question 3**

How does HSBC's use of financial modeling contribute to its investment strategies?

Answer: HSBC uses financial modeling to evaluate market conditions and economic indicators, which plays a crucial role in guiding its investment strategies. By employing these analytical tools, the bank can make informed decisions regarding asset management and ensure that it remains responsive and competitive in dynamic markets. Next, financial modeling allows HSBC to simulate various scenarios and assess potential outcomes while enabling the bank to optimize its investment portfolio and capitalize on emerging opportunities. This strategic use of analytics ensures that HSBC can navigate market fluctuations effectively, developing long-term growth and stability in the global banking environment.

## China Construction Bank Corporation (CCB)

China Construction Bank Corporation (CCB) employs advanced data analytics to strengthen risk management processes. By analyzing transaction data and credit histories, CCB enhances its ability to detect potential defaults and assess borrower creditworthiness while allowing for better lending decisions. Next, CCB uses predictive analytics to identify market trends and consumer preferences that are tailored to products developed to meet changing consumer needs. This approach not only improves consumer satisfaction but also enhances competitiveness in the financial market. In investment management, CCB relies on data modeling to optimize portfolio performance and analyzes macroeconomic indicators and market conditions to guide strategic investments. Finally, the bank's knowledge of analytics supports operational efficiency by streamlining processes and reducing costs. As a result, China Construction Bank highlights how the effective use of analytics can improve successful financial outcomes and position the institution in the global banking environment.

**Question 1**

How does China Construction Bank Corporation (CCB) use data analytics to enhance its risk management processes?

Answer: China Construction Bank Corporation (CCB) employs advanced data analytics to bolster its risk management strategies by meticulously analyzing transaction data and credit histories. This analytical strategy enables CCB to enhance its ability to detect potential defaults and assess borrower creditworthiness more accurately. By using this information, the bank can make more informed lending decisions, thereby reducing the risk of financial losses. The use of data analytics in risk management not only safeguards the bank's assets but also strengthens its overall financial stability while ensuring that CCB remains a reliable institution in the global banking environment.

**Question 2**

In what ways does CCB use predictive analytics to improve its competitiveness in the financial market?

Answer: CCB uses predictive analytics to identify emerging market trends and evolving consumer preferences, which allows the bank to develop tailored financial products that meet the changing needs of its customers. By staying ahead of market changes, CCB can offer innovative solutions that enhance consumer satisfaction and loyalty. This proactive approach not only improves the bank's competitiveness but also positions it as a leader in the financial market. By continuously adapting to consumer demands, CCB ensures that it remains relevant and attractive to a diverse clientele, thereby securing its market share and driving growth.

**Question 3**

How does CCB's use of data modeling contribute to its investment management strategies?

Answer: In investment management, CCB relies on sophisticated data modeling techniques to maximize the performance of their portfolio. By analyzing macroeconomic indicators and market conditions, the bank can make strategic investment decisions that align with its financial goals. This data-driven approach allows CCB to identify lucrative investment opportunities while mitigating potential risks. Finally, the use of data modeling helps the bank diversify its investment portfolio while ensuring stability and resilience in unstable markets. Through these strategies, CCB demonstrates how the effective use of analytics can lead to successful financial outcomes and solidify its position in the global banking environment.

## Berkshire Hathaway Inc.

Berkshire Hathaway Inc. is led by Warren Buffett and uses precise data analysis to evaluate potential acquisitions and investments. By examining key financial metrics, market trends, and economic indicators, Berkshire Hathaway ensures its decisions are established through analytical knowledge and opinions. A primary example is the disciplined approach to value investing. Berkshire conducts extensive assessments of companies and analyzes financial statements and long-term performance metrics to identify undervalued assets. This analytical rigor has led to profitable investments in organizations such as Coca-Cola and American Express.

Finally, Berkshire Hathaway uses analytics to manage its large portfolio efficiently and effectively. By relying on data on risk exposure and return potential, the company maximizes its asset allocation across its subsidiaries. This strategy is used to enhance its decision-making while also leading sustainable growth. As a result, business analytics has positioned Berkshire Hathaway as a leader in the investment market by delivering consistent long-term financial success.

**Question 1**

How does Berkshire Hathaway Inc. use data analysis to make informed investment decisions?

Answer: Berkshire Hathaway Inc., under the leadership of Warren Buffett, uses precise data analysis to guide its investment decisions. The company carefully examines key financial metrics, market trends, and economic indicators to ensure that its investment choices are grounded in solid analytical knowledge. This approach is particularly evident in its disciplined value investing strategy, where Berkshire conducts thorough assessments of potential acquisitions. By analyzing financial statements and long-term performance metrics, the company identifies undervalued assets that promise substantial returns. This analytical complexity has led to successful investments in companies like Coca-Cola and American Express that highlight how data-driven decision-making can lead to profitable outcomes.

**Question 2**

What role does value investing play in Berkshire Hathaway's investment strategy?

Answer: Value investing is a foundational component of Berkshire Hathaway's investment strategy that is characterized by a disciplined approach to identifying undervalued assets. The company conducts extensive assessments of potential investments that focus on financial statements and long-term key performance metrics. This method allows Berkshire to discover new opportunities that others might overlook while ensuring that its investments are not only financially sound but also prepared for growth. The success of this strategy is evident in Berkshire's profitable investments in well-established companies, such as Coca-Cola and American Express. By following the principles of value investing, Berkshire Hathaway has consistently achieved long-term financial success and maintained its position as a leader in the investment market.

**Question 3**

How does Berkshire Hathaway manage its large portfolio to ensure sustainable growth?

Answer: Berkshire Hathaway manages its extensive portfolio by relying on data analytics to maximize asset allocation and maximize returns. The company relies on data to assess risk exposure and return potential across its subsidiaries while allowing it to make informed decisions about where to allocate resources. This strategic use of analytics ensures that Berkshire's portfolio is diversified but also aligned with its long-term growth objectives. By constantly monitoring and adjusting its investments based on data-driven insights, Berkshire Hathaway enhances its decision-making processes and maintains sustainable growth. This approach has positioned the company as a leader in the investment market and continues to deliver consistent long-term financial success.

## CASE STUDIES ON FINANCIAL SUCCESS THROUGH ANALYTICS

### Business Success Through Business Analytics

Business analytics plays a crucial role in understanding financial trends and consumer behavior that enables organizations in the finance industry to make more data-driven and informed decisions. Following are three examples of how finance data and knowledge are translated into business success using analytics:

### Example 1: Major Finance Solutions

Major Finance Solutions is a cutting-edge financial advisory firm that specializes in providing personalized investment strategies. By using advanced business analytics, Major Finance Solutions has developed a proprietary algorithm that analyzes market trends, economic indicators, and client risk profiles to offer focused investment advice. This data-driven approach has enabled the company to consistently outperform market benchmarks, attracting a growing client base of high-net-worth individuals and institutional investors. The company's success is largely attributed to its ability to integrate real-time data analytics into its decision-making processes. By continuously monitoring global financial markets and adjusting strategies accordingly, Major Finance Solutions ensures that its clients' portfolios are optimized for maximum returns. Finally, the firm puts strong emphasis on transparency, providing clients with detailed reports and insights into their investment performance.

#### *Short-Response Questions*

1. What is the primary tool Major Finance Solutions uses to provide personalized investment strategies?
2. How does Major Finance Solutions ensure its clients' portfolios are optimized?
3. What aspect of Major Finance Solutions' service is emphasized to build client trust?

### Example 2: Zenith Financial Analytics

Zenith Financial Analytics is a leading provider of financial data analytics services to banks and financial institutions. The company has developed a comprehensive analytics platform that aggregates and analyzes large amounts of financial data to identify patterns and trends. This platform enables clients to make informed decisions regarding credit risk assessment, fraud detection, and customer segmentation. Zenith's success is driven by its commitment to innovation and accuracy. The company invests heavily in machine learning and artificial intelligence to enhance its analytics capabilities while ensuring that clients receive the most accurate information. By providing a competitive edge in risk management and customer knowledge, Zenith Financial Analytics has become a necessary partner for many financial institutions.

#### Short-Response Questions

1. What type of platform has Zenith Financial Analytics developed?
2. What technologies does Zenith invest in to enhance its analytics capabilities?
3. How does Zenith Financial Analytics provide a competitive edge to its clients?

### Example 3: RedWave Investment

RedWave Investment is an investment firm focused on sustainable and socially responsible investing. The firm uses business analytics to evaluate the environmental, social, and governance (ESG) performance of potential investments. By integrating ESG data with traditional financial metrics, RedWave Investment identifies opportunities that align with its clients' values while delivering strong financial returns. The firm's analytics-driven approach has resonated with a growing number of investors who prioritize sustainability. RedWave Capital's success is further reinforced by its commitment to transparency and accountability, providing clients with regular updates on the impact of their investments. This approach not only enhances client satisfaction but also contributes to the firm's reputation as a leader in ethical investment.

### *Short-Response Questions*

1. What type of investment does RedWave Investment focus on?
2. How does RedWave Investment integrate ESG data into its investment decisions?
3. What has contributed to RedWave Investment's reputation as a leader in ethical investing?

## CASE STUDY: FINANCIALTECH INNOVATIONS INC.

FinancialTech Innovations Inc. is a cutting-edge financial technology firm that specializes in developing data-driven financial solutions for businesses. The company attempts to improve decision-making processes through intelligent analytics and predictive modeling. With a diverse portfolio including investment analytics, personal finance management applications, and risk assessment tools, FinancialTech Innovations has positioned itself as the main player in the financial sector. Recently, the company wanted to analyze customer data and investment performance to improve service offerings and optimize product development strategies.

### Business Analytics Data Tables

**TABLE 8.6** Investment Performance Metrics

| 1 | A | B | C | D | E |
|---|---|---|---|---|---|
| | Investment Type | Initial Investment ($) | Final Value ($) | Duration (Years) | Annual Cash Flows ($) |
| 2 | Equities | 50,000 | 75,000 | 5 | 10,000 |
| 3 | Bonds | 30,000 | 40,000 | 5 | 5,000 |
| 4 | Real estate | 70,000 | 100,000 | 10 | 8,000 |
| 5 | Start-ups | 20,000 | 25,000 | 3 | 6,000 |
| 6 | Mutual funds | 40,000 | 50,000 | 5 | 7,000 |

**TABLE 8.7** Customer Feedback Data

| 1 | A | B | C | D | E |
|---|---|---|---|---|---|
| | Customer ID | Age Group | Investment Type | Satisfaction Score (1–10) | Investment Amount ($) |
| 2 | 1 | 18–25 | Equities | 8 | 5,000 |
| 3 | 2 | 26–35 | Bonds | 9 | 3,000 |
| 4 | 3 | 36–45 | Real estate | 7 | 15,000 |
| 5 | 4 | 46–55 | Start-ups | 6 | 10,000 |
| 6 | 5 | 56–65 | Mutual funds | 8 | 12,000 |

## Analytics Problems Using Excel

1. Using cause-and-effect modeling of data, analyze how customer age groups and investment types influence satisfaction scores. Create a model to depict this relationship using Excel functions.
2. Calculate the net present value (NPV) of each investment type using the annual cash flow figures, the duration of the investments, and a discount rate of 8%. Interpret the results, and determine which investments are the most favorable.
3. Implement cluster analysis to classify customers based on their satisfaction scores and investment amounts. Identify the optimal number of clusters using methods such as the elbow method, and visualize the clusters in a scatter plot.
4. Estimate the internal rate of return (IRR) for each investment type, and determine which offers the best return potential. Compare these returns with the investment amounts to measure profitability effectively.
5. Use data mining techniques to assess which investment types correlate most strongly with high customer satisfaction scores, and present findings that can enhance product offerings.

## Answer Key

1. *Cause-and-effect modeling of data.* Set up a scatter plot using "Age Group" as the independent variable (X) and "Satisfaction Score" as the dependent variable (Y). Use Excel functions such as LINEST to derive the regression line and interpret the coefficients to understand the influence of age and investment type on satisfaction scores.
2. *Calculating net present value (NPV).* Set up a spreadsheet with cash flows based on annual cash flows for the given duration and apply =NPV(0.08, cash_flow_range) − initial_investment. Identify which investments have positive NPV values, indicating potential profitability.
3. *Implementing cluster analysis.* Use the Data Analysis ToolPak and select Clustering, and input satisfaction scores and investment amounts. Use the elbow method by plotting the number of clusters against the explained variance. Identify where the variance levels off, indicating an optimal number of clusters. Create a scatter plot to visualize the identified clusters.
4. *Estimating internal rate of return (IRR).* Use the IRR formula as follows: R = IRR(values). Input the initial investment as a negative value, followed by the cash flows for each year. Determine which investment provides the highest IRR percentage by analyzing the calculated values.
5. *Using data mining techniques.* Create a correlation matrix in Excel using the CORREL function to analyze the relationship between investment types and satisfaction scores. Summarize findings in a report that quantifies which investment types have the highest correlation to customer satisfaction scores, potentially revealing market opportunities.

---

## CASE STUDY: FUTUREFINANCE INNOVATIONS LTD.

FutureFinance Innovations Ltd. specializes in developing financial technology solutions for businesses and consumers. The company has rapidly grown by offering innovative products such as mobile payment systems, investment platforms, and financial analytics tools.

Recently, FutureFinance Innovations Ltd. started on a project to enhance their investment platform by integrating advanced data analytics and predictive modeling to improve investment decision-making. To evaluate the impact of their new features, FutureFinance Innovations Ltd. collected data on user engagement, investment returns, and platform performance over six months. The data was analyzed using various financial modeling techniques to identify key factors influencing user behavior and to forecast future returns. The following tables summarize key findings from the project:

**TABLE 8.8** User Engagement and Investment Returns

| **1** | **A** | **B** | **C** |
|---|---|---|---|
| | **Month** | **Active Users** | **Average Investment Return (%)** |
| **2** | January | 10,000 | 5.0 |
| **3** | February | 11,000 | 5.2 |
| **4** | March | 12,000 | 5.4 |
| **5** | April | 13,000 | 5.6 |
| **6** | May | 14,000 | 5.8 |
| **7** | June | 15,000 | 6.0 |

**TABLE 8.9** Platform Performance Metrics

| 1 | **A** | **B** | **C** |
|---|---|---|---|
| | **Month** | **Transactions Processed** | **System Downtime (Hours)** |
| 2 | January | 50,000 | 2 |
| 3 | February | 55,000 | 1.8 |
| 4 | March | 60,000 | 1.6 |
| 5 | April | 65,000 | 1.4 |
| 6 | May | 70,000 | 1.2 |
| 7 | June | 75,000 | 1.0 |

## Analytics Problems Using Excel

1. *Cause-and-effect modeling.* Identify the cause-and-effect relationship between active users and investment returns.
2. *Cluster analysis.* Perform a cluster analysis on the platform performance metrics.
3. *Data mining.* Use data mining techniques to uncover patterns in user engagement data.
4. *Expected present value.* Calculate the expected present value of future investment returns.
5. *Future value.* Determine the future value of the average investment returns.
6. *Internal rate of return.* Calculate the internal rate of return for the investment platform enhancements.

7. *Measuring classification of performance data.* Classify the performance data into distinct categories based on system downtime.
8. *Net present value.* Compute the net present value of the investment platform enhancements.
9. *Normalizing financial measures.* Normalize the financial measures for transactions processed.
10. *Payment.* Calculate the monthly payment required to fund platform enhancements.
11. *Present value.* Determine the present value of future transactions processed.
12. *Internal rate.* Calculate the internal rate of return for user engagement improvements.
13. *Return on investment.* Compute the return on investment for platform enhancements.

## Answer Key

1. *Cause-and-effect modeling.* Use the CORREL function to find the correlation between active users and investment returns. Use the LINEST function to model relationships.
2. *Cluster analysis.* Use the k-means clustering tool in Excel's Data Analysis ToolPak. Input the platform performance metrics.
3. *Data mining.* Use the Data Mining Add-In for Excel to identify patterns in user engagement data.
4. *Expected present value.* Use the NPV function: =NPV(rate, value1, [value2], . . .).
5. *Future value.* Use the FV function: =FV(rate, nper, pmt, [pv], [type]).
6. *Internal rate of return.* Use the IRR function: =IRR(values, [guess]).
7. *Measuring classification of performance data.* Use the IF function to classify system downtime: =IF(A2<1.5, "Low", IF(A2<2, "Medium", "High")).
8. *Net present value.* Use the NPV function: =NPV(rate, value1, [value2], . . .).
9. *Normalizing financial measures.* Use the STANDARDIZE function to normalize transactions processed: =STANDARDIZE(x, mean, standard_dev).
10. *Payment.* Use the PMT function: =PMT(rate, nper, pv, [fv], [type]).
11. *Present value.* Use the PV function: =PV(rate, nper, pmt, [fv], [type]).
12. *Internal rate.* Use the IRR function: =IRR(values, [guess]).
13. *Return on investment.* Use the ROI formula: = (Gain from Investment − Cost of Investment)/Cost of Investment.

CHAPTER 9

# Accounting and Business Analytics

Accounting and business analytics are two important functions to create the framework of the organization's strategic and financial decision-making processes. When combined, accounting and business analytics create accurate reporting of key performance metrics, financial data, and the potential for operational improvements and opportunities within the global environment. Next, accounting and business analytics support each other by providing a clear understanding of the situation and information and resources for organizations to succeed in a data-driven environment.

*Accounting* is a systematic method of recording, classifying, and summarizing financial data to provide stakeholders with a trustworthy and transparent visualization of the financial position of the organization. The main goal of the accounting process is to ensure compliance with federal laws and regulations and other reporting standards that include the Generally Accepted Accounting Principles (GAAP) and the Financial Reporting Standards (IFRS). GAAP is the collection of accounting rules and standards used primarily in the United States that is monitored by the Financial Accounting Standards Board (FASB) and the Governmental Accounting Standards Board (GASB). IFRS is a set of accounting standards developed by the International Accounting Standards Board (IASB) and is instituted in more than 140 jurisdictions worldwide.

Next, accounting is an important tool within the decision-making process. Organizational leaders and managers rely on the information provided in financial statements to make strategic decisions that will directly impact the investments, operations, and growth of the business. Third, accounting and business analytics are necessary for sharing the financial health and well-being of the organization and its overall performance with all internal and external stakeholder groups, including creditors, regulators, and investors.

When business analytics is integrated into the accounting process, the ability to produce accurate financial reports and operational analysis increases. This situation is due to the use of advanced statistical and analytical tools that empower accountants to manage large amounts of data, to automate routine, monetary processes, and to predict the financial outcomes more accurately in the future. As a result of this process, businesses can use accounting combined with business analytics to determine trends in late payments and inventory expenses to determine the maximization of stocking levels while reducing waste and cost.

DOI: 10.4324/9781003629658-9

Finally, accounting and business analytics supports various businesses to guarantee there is financial transparency and trust across all market sectors. First, public accounting companies provide financial services that include tax preparation, consulting, and auditing to help companies comply with all laws and regulations. Second, corporate accounting departments focus on the internal processes of a business that include governance and budgeting. Third, forensic accounting uses investigative techniques and methods to detect fraud. Finally, governmental accounting provides financial services to help all businesses within the public sector of the market.

## INTRODUCTION TO ANALYTICS IN ACCOUNTING

The main goal of accounting is to maintain systematic and methodical records to help individuals and businesses ensure compliance with all financial regulations. Next, accounting provides reporting mechanisms of accurate data for both internal and external stakeholders. The process of accounting supports the effective allocation of resources, processes, and profitability levels and helps identify areas for improved control and cost management strategies. This strategy becomes the basis for making data-driven and informed decisions by creating financial statements, including the balance sheet, income statement, and cash flow, to enable managers to make the most beneficial decision for future growth and sustainability within the market.

Next, accounting is an important tool to provide trust and transparency within the channels of communication to regulatory agencies, investors, and creditors. Accounting industries will provide industries within various sectors of the markets with resources that include public accounting, corporate accounting, auditing, governmental accounting, and forensic accounting. Each area of accounting will use business analytics to improve the decision-making process. Business analytics techniques that are used include predictive modeling and data visualization methods for interpreting data. Accounting and business analytics will improve the traditional methods of financial reporting through an automated process to identify threats, inefficiencies, and to understand new trends that previously were identified.

The integration of business analytics in the accounting process has changed how businesses measure, analyze, and predict the financial performance of the company. In public accounting companies, there has been an increase in using business analytics to conduct comprehensive audits. Next, corporate accounting has used business analytics to improve its budgeting and reporting processes. Third, forensic accounting uses business analytics to monitor and track any irregularities within the financial activity of a business or individual. Finally, governmental accounting uses business analytics to improve its resource allocation and transparency with stakeholders. As a result, the integration of business analytics with accounting will enable organizations to gain a greater level of efficiency, accuracy, and teacher planning within all industries of the global market.

The role of and methods of analytics in modern accounting practices is explained in the table that follows.

**TABLE 9.1** The Role of Analytics in Modern Accounting Practices

| Role of Analytics | Explanation | Methods |
|---|---|---|
| **Enhanced decision-making** | Provides deeper insights into financial data, aiding strategic decisions | Predictive analytics: uses historical data to forecast future financial outcomes |
| **Improved accuracy** | Reduces errors in financial reporting and auditing | Data visualization: transforms complex datasets into comprehensible visual formats |
| **Efficiency in processes** | Streamlines accounting processes, reducing manual effort | Automated reporting: generates real-time financial reports and dashboards |
| **Fraud detection** | Identifies anomalies and suspicious activities | Anomaly detection: uses algorithms to detect unusual patterns in financial data |
| **Compliance and governance** | Ensures adherence to regulatory standards like GAAP and IFRS | Continuous auditing: provides ongoing assurance through real-time analytics |
| **Cost management** | Helps in identifying and reducing unnecessary expenses | Cost–benefit analysis: evaluates the financial impact of business decisions |
| **Risk management** | Assesses and mitigates financial risks | Scenario planning: evaluates different financial scenarios to prepare for various outcomes |
| **Performance monitoring** | Tracks financial performance against benchmarks and goals | Benchmarking: compares financial performance against industry standards |
| **Strategic planning** | Supports long-term financial planning and investment decisions | Trend analysis: examines financial data over multiple periods to identify patterns |

## FINANCIAL AUDITING AND COMPLIANCE

Accounting and business analytics are used in financial auditing and compliance for all businesses. When used together, accounting and business analytics provide accurate financial reporting and compliance with laws and regulations and detect risks and threats to the business. The situation creates a high level of trust, integrity, and operational efficiency for the company. Next, accounting provides the system or process for analyzing data to evaluate the return on investments of all financial activities of the business. Accounting and auditing are used to study the financial statements and reporting practices to make sure that businesses are following all regulations, laws, and internal company policies.

Next, business analytics is used to improve the auditing and compliance process by using data-driven models to study all transactions, predict risk, and identify emerging trends and patterns. Next, financial auditing involves the analysis of large amounts of data to look for anomalies in outliers and to review the accuracy of financial reports of the business. This situation relies on analytical tools that include AI in machine learning algorithms to provide simplified visualization of data to communicate the results to all stakeholder groups.

For public accountants, business analytics is used to enable auditors to prioritize areas that need further examination and to conduct risk-based auditing. For corporate accountants, business analytics improves the levels of control for internal compliance while enabling real-time monitoring and reporting. Third, forensic accountants require advanced business analytical tools to find fraudulent activities within the accounting process. Finally, governmental accountants use business analytics to improve the maximization of resource allocation and transparency in the budgeting process to enhance accuracy and accountability as detailed in the table that follows.

**TABLE 9.2** Using Analytics to Enhance Accuracy and Accountability

| Aspect | Explanation | Methods |
|---|---|---|
| **Accuracy in financial reporting** | Ensures financial statements are precise and error-free | Data validation: uses algorithms to check for inconsistencies and errors in financial data |
| **Accountability in decision-making** | Provides transparent and traceable data for informed decisions | Audit trails: maintains detailed records of all financial transactions and changes |
| **Fraud detection** | Identifies and prevents fraudulent activities | Anomaly detection: uses machine learning to spot unusual patterns in financial data |
| **Compliance with regulations** | Ensures adherence to financial standards like GAAP and IFRS | Automated compliance checks: continuously monitor transactions for regulatory compliance |
| **Efficiency in processes** | Streamlines accounting processes, reducing manual effort | Automated reporting: generates real-time financial reports and dashboards |
| **Enhanced forecasting** | Improves the accuracy of financial predictions | Predictive analytics: uses historical data to forecast future financial outcomes |
| **Performance monitoring** | Tracks financial performance against benchmarks and goals | Benchmarking: compares financial performance against industry standards |
| **Cost management** | Identifies and reduces unnecessary expenses | Cost–benefit analysis: evaluates the financial impact of business decisions |
| **Risk management** | Assesses and mitigates financial risks | Scenario planning: evaluates different financial scenarios to prepare for various outcomes |
| **Transparency in reporting** | Provides clear and accessible financial information | Data visualization: uses charts and graphs to present financial data clearly and intuitively |

## FORENSIC ACCOUNTING AND FRAUD DETECTION

Accounting and business analytics are important in fraud detection and forensic accounting since they provide accountants with the ability to analyze complex financial data, identify abnormalities and irregularities, and detect fraudulent activities in real time. Forensic accounting is responsible for conducting a thorough financial investigation using data analysis to protect assets, guarantee the integrity of the business, and support legal requirements and compliance regulations. This situation requires forensic accountants to use business analytical methodologies to detect fraud more efficiently and effectively to improve trust and transparency with all stakeholder groups.

Next, forensic accounting relies on detailed explanation of financial records to identify fraudulent activities, misappropriated funds, and other discrepancies. Financial accounting also provides financial knowledge to support the legal processes by developing databased evidence and information that can be used in the assessment of an organization, regulatory inquiries, and legal litigation. Finally, financial accounting requires the ability to detect anomalies and to trace all financial transactions across different platforms and frameworks so the accountants can evaluate the vulnerabilities of the internal control system of the business. As a result, forensic accountants contribute to accountability of the financial system of the business by focusing on organizational policies, unethical practices, and breaches to the system.

Forensic accountants use analytical techniques for identifying fraudulent activities within the business. The methods used by forensic accountants are detailed in Table 9.3.

## COST MANAGEMENT AND ANALYSIS

Accounting and business analytics are required in the analysis of the cost management of an organization. Business analytics integrated within the accounting process consists of the analysis of cost management by helping businesses understand how to manage their expenses, effectively allocate resources, and maximize operational performance. Next, cost management involves processes of monitoring, assessing, and controlling costs to guarantee profitability. However, cost analysis will also focus on providing accountants with information related to trends, opportunities for improvement, and inefficiencies and threats to the business. As a result, the relationship between business analytics and accounting exists to improve the accuracy of all accounting processes of cost management analysis for various accounting industries in the global market.

As part of the accounting process, cost management is required to keep detailed records of all financial transactions and reporting of the organization. Cost accounting then focuses specifically on monitoring and analyzing expenditures that are associated with daily operations, supply chain management activities, and production. By categorizing indemnifying costs that include variable, direct, fixed, and indirect, accounting and

**TABLE 9.3** Analytics Techniques for Identifying Fraudulent Activities

| Analytical Method | Explanation | Benefits |
|---|---|---|
| **Data mining** | Extracts useful information from large datasets to identify patterns and anomalies | Enhances the detection of fraudulent activities and financial irregularities |
| **Ratio analysis** | Compares financial ratios over different periods to identify inconsistencies | Helps detect manipulation and unusual financial behavior |
| **Benford's law** | Analyzes the frequency distribution of digits in numerical data | Identifies anomalies that may indicate fraudulent activities |
| **Regression analysis** | Examines relationships between variables to identify unusual trends | Helps in understanding the factors contributing to financial anomalies |
| **Time series analysis** | Analyzes data points collected or recorded at specific time intervals | Detects trends, cycles, and seasonal variations in financial data |
| **Network analysis** | Studies relationships and interactions within data to identify suspicious connections | Helps uncover complex fraud schemes involving multiple entities |
| **Text analytics** | Analyzes textual data from emails, documents, and social media for keywords and patterns | Identifies potential fraud indicators and supports investigations |
| **Visualization tools** | Uses charts and graphs to present data clearly and intuitively | Enhances the understanding of complex data and communicates findings effectively |
| **Predictive analytics** | Uses historical data and machine learning to predict future fraudulent activities | Improves the ability to anticipate and prevent fraud |
| **Forensic data analytics (FDA)** | Combines various analytical techniques to investigate financial crimes comprehensively | Provides a holistic approach to detecting and investigating fraud |

cost management can develop new knowledge into the allocation of monies in the profitability of the company. Next, cost management accounting systems within an organization are used to develop budgets, study variances and changes, and implement new cost control measures.

Within the various accounting industries, cost management will vary in size and responsibility based on the needs of the organization. First, corporate accounting departments will be involved in the analysis of costs to monitor operational budgets, improve the bottom line, and to reduce waste and inefficiencies. Next, public accountants will help clients to evaluate their cost structures and to reduce expenses. Third, government accounting focuses on using cost control measures to ensure that taxpayer funds are used efficiently and effectively to provide services to the community. Finally, forensic accounting is used to analyze the cost structures in history to uncover fraud or irregularities within the accounting process. Within all accounting industries, each level of accounting will employ analytics to control and reduce costs. These methods are detailed in Table 9.4.

**TABLE 9.4** Employing Analytics to Control and Reduce Costs

| Accounting Type | Methods of Analytics | Benefits |
|---|---|---|
| **Corporate accounting departments** | Cost allocation: assigns costs to specific departments, products, or projects using methods like activity-based costing (ABC) | Ensures accurate cost distribution, identifies cost-saving opportunities. |
| | Predictive analytics: forecasts future costs based on historical data | Enhances budgeting accuracy, anticipates financial needs |
| | Variance analysis: compares actual costs to budgeted costs to identify discrepancies | Helps understand reasons for variances, improves future budgeting processes |
| | Automated reporting: generates real-time financial reports and dashboards | Provides quick insights for decision-makers (increased transparency) |
| **Public accountants** | Cost intelligence: uses multidimensional cost and profitability modeling solutions | Provides valuable insights for faster, more confident decision-making |
| | Benchmarking: compares financial performance against industry standards | Identifies areas for improvement, sets realistic targets |
| | Scenario analysis: evaluates different financial scenarios to prepare for various outcomes | Improves flexibility and responsiveness to financial uncertainties |
| | Predictive modeling: anticipates course corrections and manages costs | Enhances strategic cost management and profitability |

## REAL-TIME FINANCIAL REPORTING

In real-time financial reporting, business analytics and accounting have developed a methodical process for organizations to access, analyze, and communicate financial data to stakeholders at the time it is created. Next, real-time reporting is important in today's dynamic and changing global environment. This situation makes the accuracy of real-time information important to organizational decision-makers so they can quickly respond to new emerging threats and opportunities. As a result, the integration of accounting and business analytics will create a methodical process that provides high-quality real-time reporting of data to improve the financial management and operational planning processes.

In the past, accounting primarily focused on periodic reporting that includes monthly, quarterly, and annual financial statements. However, financial real-time reporting focuses on the ability of organizations to help instant access to information and to receive continual updates on changes. This strategy greatly improves the decision-making process by eliminating delays within the communication process and availability of data. Next, accounting functions that include transaction recording, budget monitoring, and financial reporting, require access to real-time data to improve the relevance and accuracy of the performance assessment management process. By using automated accounting systems, financial information is collected and processed in an efficient manner that provides real-time updated information to leaders and team members, so they remain accountable to other regulatory entities and the communities they serve. Finally, it allows them to make data informed decisions and actions.

Corporate accounting departments require real-time information to monitor budgets, cash flows, and to guarantee compliance with internal policies and procedures. Next, public accounting companies require real-time data to create reports that provide financial information and support services to their clients. Governmental accounting agencies use real-time accounting practices to develop trust and transparency of all public spending. Finally, forensic accountants require real-time financial reporting to monitor and track fraudulent activities as they occur. As a result, each type of accounting process requires technologies that enable up-to-date financial insights so data-driven and informed decisions can be made. These technologies used by accounting agencies are detailed in Table 9.5.

## AUTOMATION IN ACCOUNTING PROCESSES

The combination of business analytics and accounting has led to new advancements in the automation of the accounting process. The automation of the accounting process relies on advanced technologies to streamline the traditional manually operated tasks associated with financial data, to maximize efficiency, and to improve accuracy in the financial management strategy of the organization. The automation of the accounting process has reduced the amount of human error while also enabling accounting leaders to focus on new analytical and strategic responsibilities within the organization. The situation is seen in all accounting industries, including corporate accounting, public accounting, mental accounting, and forensic accounting, where the automation of workflows and processes has led to the support of better decision-making.

First, accounting is the framework upon which automation is developed by including the process of transaction recording, financial reporting, auditing, budget preparation, and the management of payroll. In the past, these tasks have required a large amount of time and effort to ensure that the high level of detail was achieved. When using technology and automation, these tools can eliminate repetitive manual tasks and increase the level of accuracy in the data reporting process. Next, accountants will rely on technology and automation to create batch processing of transactions, streamline the reporting of compliance to its stakeholders and overseeing agencies, and to create financial statements that include the balance sheet, income statement, and cash flow. Finally, automation of the accounting process will provide real-time reconciliation reports that are required for review that can be completed in seconds, where the process would take weeks under manual review.

For corporate accounting, automation technology reduces the time required to complete routine tasks that include expense tracking, compliance reporting, and payroll processing. The situation enables corporate accounts to focus on budgeting and strategic planning, instead of these repetitive tasks. For public accounting companies, technology and automation improves the accounting process by using software to conduct tax preparation, data analysis of audits, and to improve all other financial services for clients. Third, governmental accountants use

**TABLE 9.5** Technologies Enabling Up-to-Date Financial Insights

| Accounting Type | Technologies | Explanation | Benefits |
|---|---|---|---|
| **Corporate accounting departments** | AI and machine learning: automates routine tasks and enhances predictive analytics | Improves accuracy and efficiency in financial forecasting and reporting | Reduces manual effort, enhances decision-making, and improves operational efficiency |
| | Blockchain: provides secure and transparent transaction records | Ensures data integrity and enhances audit trails | Reduces risk of fraud, improves compliance, and enhances trust |
| | Cloud computing: offers scalable and accessible financial data storage | Facilitates real-time access to financial information | Enhances collaboration, reduces IT costs, and improves data accessibility |
| **Public accountants** | Data analytics: uses advanced analytical tools to uncover patterns and insights | Enhances accuracy of financial reporting and compliance | Improves decision-making, identifies inefficiencies, and supports proactive planning |
| | Blockchain: ensures transparent and tamperproof financial records | Enhances audit efficiency and compliance | Improves trust, reduces fraud risk, and ensures accurate recordkeeping |
| | AI and machine learning: analyzes large datasets for fraud detection | Identifies anomalies and suspicious activities | Enhances fraud detection, improves accuracy, and reduces manual effort |
| **Governmental accounting agencies** | AI-driven insights: uses AI for document processing and predictive analytics | Rapidly reviews and extracts data, detects anomalies, and provides real-time insights | Improves efficiency, enhances accuracy, and supports compliance |
| | Specialized accounting systems: tailored systems for government-specific needs | Guides auditors through complex regulations and standards | Ensures compliance, improves accuracy, and enhances audit efficiency |
| | Cloud-based reporting: provides real-time access to financial data | Facilitates timely and accurate financial reporting | Enhances transparency, improves collaboration, and reduces IT costs |
| **Forensic accountants** | AI and machine learning: analyzes vast datasets for fraud detection | Identify suspicious transactions and anomalies | Enhances efficiency, improves accuracy, and supports proactive fraud detection |
| | Blockchain: traces cryptocurrency transactions and provides tamperproof records | Offers transparency and traceability in financial investigations | Reduces fraud risk, enhances trust, and improves compliance |
| | Data analytics and visualization tools: presents complex data in interactive formats | Identifies trends and patterns indicative of fraud | Enhances understanding, improves communication, and supports investigations |

**TABLE 9.6** The Impact of Analytics-Enhanced Automation

| Accounting Type | Impact of Analytics-Enhanced Automation | Benefits |
|---|---|---|
| **Corporate accounting** | Efficiency and accuracy: automates routine tasks, such as data entry, reconciliations, and financial reporting | Reduces human error, speeds up processes, and allows accountants to focus on strategic activities |
| | Predictive analytics: forecasts future financial outcomes based on historical data | Enhances budgeting accuracy and financial planning |
| | Real-time monitoring: provides up-to-date financial insights through continuous data tracking | Improves decision-making and responsiveness to market changes |
| **Public accounting** | Compliance and reporting: automates compliance checks and generates real-time reports | Ensures adherence to regulations, reduces audit risks, and enhances transparency |
| | Data analytics: uses advanced tools to uncover patterns and insights in financial data | Improves accuracy of financial reporting and supports proactive planning |
| | Fraud detection: identifies anomalies and suspicious activities through machine learning | Enhances fraud detection and reduces manual effort |
| **Governmental accounting** | Cost allocation and compliance: optimizes cost distribution and ensures compliance with regulations | Enhances accuracy, reduces error rates, and improves audit preparedness |

technology and automation to monitor public expenditure and to ensure regulatory compliance. Finally, forensic accountants use business analytics and automated accounting technology tools to analyze large sets of data to improve the risk management process and investigate fraudulent activities in real time. The impact of analytics enhanced automation by each accounting industry is detailed in Table 9.6.

## BUSINESS ANALYTICS FUNCTION FOR ACCOUNTING USING MICROSOFT EXCEL

In the business environment, there are many business analytical terms mentioned that play a critical role in making informed and data-driven choices that drive decisions, optimize daily operations, and develop strategic actions and initiatives. Various statistical concepts play an important role in accounting and business analytics by providing essential tools for data analysis and decision-making. Here's a detailed overview of their definition and importance and how to conduct this statistical analysis using Microsoft Excel.

## Accounting Principles

Fundamental accounting principles, such as the Generally Accepted Accounting Principles (GAAP) or the International Financial Reporting Standards (IFRS), ensure accuracy, consistency, and transparency in financial reporting. Following these principles is critical for maintaining stakeholder trust and ensuring compliance.

**Steps:**

1. List the applicable accounting principles or standards (e.g., GAAP, IFRS).
2. Create a list in Excel to ensure compliance with each principle during financial reporting and data entry.

## Accounts Payable Ratio

This ratio measures how well a company can pay off its short-term liabilities with its accounts payable. It is important in assessing financial efficiency and liquidity, which enables organizations to manage their cash flow effectively.

Formula: = Average Accounts Payable/COGS

**Steps:**

1. Gather data on average accounts payable and cost of goods sold (COGS).
2. Use the formula = Average Accounts Payable/COGS.

## Accounts Receivable Ratio

This metric indicates how efficiently a company collects its receivables. A high accounts receivable ratio suggests effective credit management, which is essential in maintaining cash flow and financial stability.

Formula: = Accounts Receivable/Total Credit Sales

**Steps:**

1. Gather data on average accounts receivable and total credit sales.
2. Use the formula = Accounts Receivable/Total Credit Sales.

## Accruals

Accrual accounting recognizes revenues and expenses when they occur, regardless of when cash transactions happen. Understanding accruals is important for accurate financial reporting and to better reflect an organization's financial position.

Formula: =Expense*Time Period

**Steps:**

1. List the expenses and the corresponding accrual periods.
2. Calculate total accruals by using the formula =Expense*Time Period.

## Assumption Modeling

This process involves creating models based on various assumptions to project future financial performance. It helps companies understand potential risks and opportunities needed to better guide data-driven and informed decision-making.

**Steps:**

1. List key variables and their potential values (i.e., sales growth rates, etc.).
2. Create input cells for each assumption.
3. Build a model that uses those assumptions in a calculation.

## Business Principles

Core business principles provide a foundation for operational strategies and ethical decision-making. They steer interactions with stakeholders and shape corporate culture and governance.

**Steps:**

1. Write down the business principles in a column.
2. Assign a rating or checklist next to each principle for assessment.

## Cash Budgeting

Effective cash budgeting entails planning for the inflows and outflows of cash to ensure liquidity. It is critical for maintaining operational stability and supporting strategic initiatives.

Formula: =SUM(Inflows) − SUM(Outflows)

**Steps:**

1. Create a table listing all cash inflows and outflows for a specific period (monthly, quarterly).
2. Input total cash inflows and outflows in Excel.
3. Use this formula to calculate net cash flow: =SUM(Inflows) − SUM(Outflows).

## Current Ratio

This liquidity ratio assesses an organization's ability to pay short-term debts with its current assets. It is a key indicator of financial health that helps organizations make informed operational and financial decisions.

Formula: =Current_Assets_Cell / Current_Liabilities_Cell

where Current_Assets_Cell and Current_Liabilities_Cell

**Steps:**

1. Gather data on current assets and current liabilities.
2. Use the formula Current Assets/Current Liabilities.

## Data Validation

Guaranteeing data quality through validation processes is crucial in accounting analytics. Accurate data supports reliable analysis and reporting while preventing errors that can mislead decision-makers.

**Steps:**

1. Select the cells you want to restrict.
2. Go to the Data tab and select Data Validation.
3. Set criteria (i.e., whole numbers, lists).

## Debt-to-Equity Ratio

This ratio evaluates the relative proportion of shareholders' equity and debt used to finance a company's assets. It is important for assessing financial leverage and soundness to guide investment and financing strategies.

Formula: =Total Liabilities/Shareholders' Equity.

**Steps:**

1. Gather total liabilities and shareholders' equity.
2. Use the formula =Total Liabilities/Shareholders' Equity.

## Facilities Resource Allocation

The efficient allocation of resources, including facilities, is critical for maximizing operations and optimizing productivity. This ensures that resources are used in line with strategic goals.

**Steps:**

1. List resources and priorities (e.g., budget allocation).
2. Calculate total resources allocated to each facility using formulas.
3. For each facility, input this formula to sum up resources allocated =SUM(value 1:value 2).

## Goal Seek

This Excel function allows users to find necessary input values to achieve a desired output. It is useful in financial modeling and forecasting and is used to support decision-making about financial targets.

**Steps:**

1. Go to the Data tab, and click on What-If Analysis, then select Goal Seek.
2. Set the cell you want to change to achieve a specific value.
3. Define the target cell with the desired value and where to change it.

## Gross Profit

Analyzing gross profit provides knowledge of an organization's profitability related to its sales. It is essential for evaluating operational efficiency and helps inform pricing strategies.

Formula: =Total Revenue − COGS

**Steps:**

1. Gather data for total revenue and cost of goods sold (COGS).
2. Use the formula = Total Revenue − COGS.

## Historical Data Modeling

Using historical financial data enables predictive modeling and trend analysis. This informs future performance expectations and assists in strategic planning and risk management.

**Steps:**

1. Set up a table with historical data (i.e., sales over months).
2. Use Excel's charting features to visualize the trend.
3. Create a regression model using the Data Analysis ToolPak.

## Influence Diagrams

These visual representations of relationships between variables help stakeholders understand the complex decision-making process. They are beneficial in scenario planning and evaluating potential outcomes.

**Steps:**

1. List the variables impacting decisions.
2. Define relationships in a flow chart format using shapes and arrows in Excel.

### Inventory Turnover Ratio

This metric measures how efficiently a company manages its inventory. High turnover rates indicate effective inventory management that is important for maximizing cash flow and reducing costs.

Formula: =COGS/Average Inventory

**Steps:**

1. Gather data on cost of goods sold (COGS) and average inventory.
2. Use the formula COGS/Average Inventory.

### Investment Decision Analysis

This involves evaluating the potential returns and risks associated with various investment opportunities. It is necessary for resource allocation and long-term financial planning.

**Steps:**

1. Create a table listing potential investments with corresponding returns and risks.
2. Use weighted averages or scenario analysis in tables to evaluate each option's potential.

### Logic Principles

Logical reasoning supports financial analysis and decision-making and drives consistency and analytics in assessments.

**Steps:**

1. Create a flowchart in Excel to represent logical flows of decisions.
2. Use logical functions (IF, AND, OR) to represent decision criteria in calculations.

### Net Profit

As a key performance indicator, net profit measures overall profitability after all expenses. It is critical in evaluating financial performance and informing strategic business decisions.

Formula: = Total Revenue − Total Expenses

**Steps:**

1. Gather total revenue and total expenses.
2. Use the formula = Total Revenue − Total Expenses.

## Portfolio Allocation

This involves diversifying investments to maximize returns while mitigating risk. Effective portfolio allocation is necessary for optimizing asset performance and achieving financial goals.

**Steps:**

1. List assets and their corresponding values/investment proportions.
2. Calculate the percentage of each asset relative to the total portfolio =A1/SUM(variable 1:variable 2) to include all portfolio investments.

## Project Management Planning

Understanding financial implications in project management guarantees that projects are executed within budget and aligned with strategic objectives to improve the use of resources.

**Steps:**

1. Create a table for project tasks, start and end dates, and resources.
2. Use Gantt charts to illustrate schedules, and insert a bar chart for visualization.

## Purchasing Decision Analysis

This analysis aids in evaluating the costs and benefits associated with procurement decisions to enhance cost efficiency and supplier relationships.

**Steps:**

1. List options and their costs and benefits.
2. Use a decision matrix where you score each option against criteria and then sum the scores.

## Quick Ratio (Acid Test)

This ratio assesses an organization's liquidity position more thoroughly by excluding inventory from current assets. It provides a better picture of financial longevity and short-term wealth.

Formula: = (Current Assets − Inventory)/Current Liabilities

**Steps:**

1. Gather current assets and inventory.
2. Use the formula = (Current Assets − Inventory)/Current Liabilities).

### Return on Assets (ROA)

This metric measures how effectively a company uses its assets to create a profit. It is necessary for assessing operational efficiency and making investment decisions.

Formula: = Net Income/Average Total Assets

**Steps:**

1. Gather total net income and average total assets.
2. Use the formula =Net Income/Average Total Assets.

### Return on Equity (ROE)

ROE evaluates a company's profitability relative to shareholders' equity. It is important in measuring financial performance and comparing organizations in the same industry.

Formula: =Net Income/Shareholders' Equity

**Steps:**

1. Gather net income and shareholders' equity.
2. Use the formula =Net Income/Shareholders' Equity.

### Scenario Manager

This Excel tool enables users to create and evaluate different financial scenarios based on changing assumptions. It assists strategic planning by enabling decision-makers to explore potential outcomes based on different variables, helping assess risks and opportunities.

**Steps:**

1. Go to the Data tab and select What-If Analysis, then choose Scenario Manager.
2. Click Add to create a new scenario.
3. Define the changing cells and the scenario values.
4. Click OK and repeat to add multiple scenarios.
5. Use Show to view the effects of each scenario on the calculations.

### Staffing Decision Analysis

Analyzing staffing decisions involves evaluating the cost-effectiveness of hiring, training, and managing personnel. It ensures that organizations maximize human resources in alignment with strategic goals to optimize productivity and performance.

**Steps:**

1. Create a table with roles, salaries, and projected outcomes (performance metrics).
2. Use Excel functions like SUM, AVERAGE, and other statistical analysis to assess staffing costs and benefits.
3. Use a decision matrix to evaluate the effect of each role on overall performance.

### What-If Analysis

This analytical tool allows companies to simulate different scenarios and their potential impacts on financial performance. It generates informed decision-making by enabling leaders to understand how changes in assumptions or external factors could affect outcomes.

**Steps:**

1. Set up a spreadsheet with variables that could change and their respective formulas.
2. Use the Data tab and select What-If Analysis to use tools like Goal Seek or Scenario Manager.
3. For Goal Seek, specify the cell you want to achieve a certain value, set the desired value, and identify the cell to adjust.

## REAL-WORLD EXAMPLES OF ACCOUNTING INSIGHTS DRIVING BUSINESS SUCCESS

### Sony Corporation

Sony Corporation uses advanced data analytics to modernize its financial reporting processes and to enable real-time access to important financial information. This strategy allows Sony to make timely and informed decisions regarding investments and the allocation of resources. One example is Sony's implementation of predictive analytics to forecast sales and revenue trends across its various divisions, which include gaming and entertainment. By analyzing historical data and market conditions, the company can effectively allocate budgets to ensure that resources are directed toward high-potential areas. Finally, Sony uses data analytics in cost management to identify inefficiencies and reduce operational costs. This analytical knowledge has enabled the company to improve its profitability margins.

**Question 1**

How does Sony Corporation use data analytics to enhance its financial reporting processes?

Answer: Sony Corporation employs advanced data analytics to modernize its financial reporting processes while providing real-time access to critical financial information. This approach allows Sony to make real-time and informed decisions regarding investments and resource allocation. By integrating data analytics into its financial systems, Sony can quickly analyze financial performance across its various divisions, which include gaming and entertainment. This capability not only improves the accuracy and efficiency of financial reporting but also supports strategic decision-making by providing insights into financial health and potential areas for growth.

**Question 2**

In what ways does Sony use predictive analytics to forecast sales and revenue trends?

Answer: Sony uses predictive analytics to forecast sales and revenue trends by analyzing historical data and current market conditions. This situation involves examining past sales performance, consumer behavior, and external economic factors to predict future trends. Next, Sony can effectively allocate budgets and resources to high-potential areas while ensuring that its divisions include gaming and entertainment and are well-positioned to capitalize on market opportunities. This strategic use of predictive analytics helps Sony maintain a competitive edge by anticipating market demands and adjusting its strategies accordingly.

**Question 3**

How does Sony control data analytics for cost management and operational efficiency?

Answer: Sony controls data analytics for cost management by identifying inefficiencies and reducing operational costs. Through a detailed analysis of operational data, Sony can determine areas where resources are being misused or where processes can be streamlined. This analytical approach enables the company to implement cost-saving measures without compromising quality or productivity. By continuously monitoring and optimizing its operations, Sony improves its profitability margins and guarantees that it remains competitive in the global market. As a result of this, a focus on efficiency and cost management is necessary in sustaining long-term growth and financial stability.

## McDonald's Corporation

McDonald's Corporation relies on advanced data analytics to streamline its financial processes and improve accuracy in budgeting and forecasting. By analyzing historical sales data and market trends, McDonald's can predict demand more accurately and optimize inventory management and reduce food waste. Next, McDonald's uses real-time data analytics in its pricing strategy. The company conducts market analyses to understand regional price sensitivities, which allows it to adjust menu prices and promotional offers as needed. This dynamic pricing approach maximizes revenue while maintaining customer satisfaction. Finally, McDonald's uses analytics to assess the performance of its franchises, relying on key performance indicators to identify areas for improvement. This information supports franchisee training and development while ensuring consistent operational standards across locations.

**Question 1**

How does the McDonald's Corporation utilize data analytics to enhance its inventory management and reduce food waste?

Answer: The McDonald's Corporation employs advanced data analytics to improve its inventory management and minimize food waste by analyzing historical sales data and market trends. By using this information, McDonald's can accurately predict demand for its products while allowing the company to optimize inventory levels. This predictive capability ensures that each restaurant location is stocked with the right amount of ingredients, reducing the likelihood of overstocking or understocking. Next, McDonald's can minimize food waste, which not only contributes to cost savings but also supports the company's sustainability goals. This strategic use of data analytics in inventory management demonstrates McDonald's commitment to operational efficiency and environmental responsibility.

**Question 2**

In what ways does McDonald's use real-time data analytics to inform its pricing strategy?

Answer: McDonald's employs real-time data analytics to refine its pricing strategy by conducting comprehensive market analyses to understand regional price sensitivities. By analyzing data on consumer behavior, competitor pricing, and economic conditions, McDonald's can adjust menu prices and promotional offers to align with local market dynamics. This dynamic pricing approach enables the company to maximize revenue while maintaining customer satisfaction. Next, McDonald's offers region-specific promotions or adjusts prices based on local demand fluctuations. This data-driven pricing strategy ensures that McDonald's remains competitive and responsive to consumer needs, ultimately enhancing its profitability and competitive advantage in the market.

**Question 3**

How does McDonald's use analytics to support franchisee performance and ensure consistent operational standards?

Answer: McDonald's uses analytics to assess the performance of its franchises by relying on key performance indicators (KPIs) to identify areas for improvement. By analyzing data on sales, customer satisfaction, and operational efficiency, McDonald's can determine specific challenges faced by individual franchise locations. This information is used to customize training and development programs for franchisees while ensuring they have the necessary tools and knowledge to enhance their operations. Finally, McDonald's uses analytics to monitor compliance with its operational standards to guarantee consistency across all locations. This data-driven approach not only supports franchisee success but also maintains the brand's reputation for quality and service excellence.

## Boeing Company

The Boeing Company uses advanced data analytics to streamline its financial reporting processes to ensure accuracy and timely information for decision-making. Through the comprehensive analysis of project costs and budgets, Boeing can better manage its large-scale aerospace projects. Next, Boeing uses predictive analytics in supply chain management. By analyzing historical data and market trends, the company maximizes its inventory levels and mitigates risks associated with material shortages. This strategy reduces costs and enhances production efficiency. Finally, Boeing uses analytics to monitor the financial performance of its various divisions and to identify key performance metrics required to drive profitability. This data-driven process allows the leadership team to make informed decisions regarding resource allocation and investment strategies.

**Question 1**

How does the Boeing Company use data analytics to improve its financial reporting processes?

Answer: The Boeing Company uses advanced data analytics to enhance its financial reporting processes by ensuring accuracy and providing timely information for decision-making. By conducting comprehensive analyses of project costs and budgets, Boeing can effectively manage its large-scale aerospace projects. This approach allows the company to maintain financial transparency and accountability, necessary for stakeholders and investors. The use of data analytics in financial reporting also enables Boeing to identify trends and anomalies, ensuring that financial statements reflect the true financial health of the company. This capability supports strategic planning and resource allocation, which ultimately contributes to Boeing's overall financial stability and growth.

**Question 2**

In what ways does Boeing apply predictive analytics to its supply chain management?

Answer: Boeing applies predictive analytics to its supply chain management by analyzing historical data and market trends to optimize inventory levels and mitigate risks associated with material shortages. This strategy allows Boeing to anticipate demand fluctuations and adjust its supply chain operations by reducing costs and enhancing production efficiency. By leveraging predictive analytics, Boeing can predict potential disruptions and implement contingency plans to ensure a steady flow of materials. This proactive approach not only minimizes downtime and production delays but also strengthens relationships with suppliers and customers by ensuring the timely delivery of products.

**Question 3**

How does Boeing use analytics to monitor the financial performance of its divisions?

Answer: Boeing uses analytics to monitor the financial performance of its various divisions by identifying key performance metrics that drive profitability. Through data-driven analysis, Boeing's leadership team can assess the financial health of each division and make informed decisions regarding resource allocation and investment strategies. This process involves evaluating revenue streams, cost structures, and market conditions to determine areas of strength and opportunities for improvement. By continuously monitoring these metrics, Boeing can ensure that its divisions operate efficiently and contribute positively to the company's overall financial success. This analytical approach supports strategic decision-making and helps Boeing maintain its competitive edge in the aerospace industry.

## Philips N.V.

Philips N.V. implements advanced data analytics to streamline financial reporting processes and allow for accurate and well-timed insights that inform decision-making across its varied health-care, consumer lifestyle, and lighting divisions. Next, Philips implements predictive analytics to manage its inventory more effectively. By studying sales trends and market demand, Philips reduces excess stock and minimizes costs while ensuring that products remain available to meet customer needs. Finally, Philips implements business analytics to evaluate the profitability of various product lines to identify areas of strength and opportunities for improvement. This insight supports strategic resource allocation and helps the company prioritize investments in high-growth areas.

### Question 1

How does Philips N.V. use data analytics to enhance its financial reporting processes?

Answer: Philips N.V. employs advanced data analytics to streamline its financial reporting processes, ensuring that knowledge is both accurate and timely. By integrating data analytics into its financial systems, Philips can immediately access and analyze financial data across its diverse divisions, including health care, consumer lifestyle, and lighting. This capability enables the company to generate real-time financial reports that inform strategic decision-making. The use of analytics in financial reporting helps Philips identify trends, forecast future financial performance, and make informed decisions regarding investments and resource allocation. This data-driven approach not only enhances the accuracy of financial reports but also supports the company's overall strategic objectives.

### Question 2

In what ways does Philips N.V. apply predictive analytics to improve inventory management?

Answer: Philips N.V. relies on predictive analytics to optimize its inventory management processes. By analyzing sales trends and market demand, Philips can accurately forecast future product needs, reducing the risk of overstocking or stock outputs. This approach allows the company to maintain optimal inventory levels, minimizing costs associated with excess stock while ensuring that products are readily available to meet consumer demand. Predictive analytics enables Philips to respond quickly to changes in market conditions, adjust inventory levels accordingly, and improve overall supply chain efficiency. This strategic use of data analytics not only reduces operational costs but also enhances customer satisfaction by ensuring product availability.

### Question 3

How does Philips N.V. use business analytics to evaluate the profitability of its product lines?

Answer: Philips N.V. uses business analytics to assess the profitability of its various product lines by identifying areas of strength and opportunities for improvement. By analyzing financial data, market trends, and consumer preferences, Philips can determine which product lines are performing well and which may require strategic adjustments. This information allows the company to dedicate resources effectively, prioritize investments in high-growth areas, and develop strategies to enhance the profitability of underperforming products. Business analytics provides Philips with a comprehensive understanding of its product portfolio, which enables the company to make informed decisions that drive growth and profitability across its diverse divisions.

## CASE STUDIES ON ACCOUNTING SUCCESS THROUGH ANALYTICS

### Business Success Through Business Analytics

Business analytics plays a crucial role in understanding accounting trends and consumer behavior that enables organizations in the accounting industry to make more data-driven and informed decisions. Following are three examples of how accounting data and knowledge are translated into business success using analytics:

#### Example 1: BalancePro Solutions

BalancePro Solutions is an accounting firm that specializes in providing comprehensive accounting services to small and medium-sized enterprises (SMEs). By using advanced business analytics, BalancePro has been able to offer focused financial information that helps their clients optimize cash flow and reduce operational costs. Next, BalancePro implemented a complex analytics platform that integrates real-time financial data from various sources. This platform allows the firm to conduct detailed cash flow analysis, identify spending patterns, and predict future financial trends. By analyzing this data, BalancePro provides clients with actionable information that includes identifying periods of high expenditure and suggesting cost-saving measures. Finally, the firm uses predictive analytics to forecast future cash flow scenarios while enabling clients to make informed financial decisions. The use of business analytics has enabled BalancePro to improve client satisfaction and retention. Clients have reported a 10% reduction in unnecessary expenses and a 5% improvement in cash flow management. This success has positioned BalancePro as a leader in the accounting industry while attracting new clients and increasing revenue by 20% over the past year.

#### *Short-Response Questions*

1. What type of businesses does BalancePro Solutions primarily serve?
2. What specific financial aspect does BalancePro focus on in optimizing their clients?
3. By what percentage did BalancePro's clients improve their cash flow management?

#### Example 2: AccurateTraking Analytics

AccurateTraking Analytics is a firm that offers specialized services in forensic accounting and fraud detection. By leveraging business analytics, AccurateTraking has developed a reputation for uncovering financial discrepancies and preventing fraud. Next, AccurateTraking uses advanced data mining techniques and machine learning algorithms to analyze large volumes of financial transactions. This strategy allows the firm to detect anomalies and patterns indicative of fraudulent activity. The firm also employs predictive analytics to assess the likelihood of future fraud occurrences, providing clients with proactive measures to safeguard their financial assets. Finally, using business analytics, AccurateTraking has successfully identified and prevented numerous fraud cases, saving clients millions of dollars. The firm's expertise in fraud detection has led to a 40% increase in client acquisition as businesses seek to protect themselves from financial misconduct. AccurateTraking's innovative approach has also earned them industry recognition and several awards for excellence in forensic accounting.

### *Short-Response Questions*

1. What specialized service does AccurateTraking Analytics provide?
2. What technology does AccurateTraking use to detect fraudulent activity?
3. By what percentage did AccurateTraking increase its client acquisition?

### Example 3: GreenTree Accounting

GreenTree Accounting is a firm that focuses on sustainability and environmental accounting. By integrating business analytics, GreenTree helps clients measure and improve their environmental impact while maintaining financial health. Next, GreenTree uses analytics tools to track and report on clients' carbon footprints, energy consumption, and waste management. The firm provides detailed reports that highlight areas for improvement and suggest strategies for reducing environmental impact. Third, GreenTree uses scenario analysis to evaluate the financial implications of adopting sustainable practices, helping clients balance environmental goals with profitability. Finally, GreenTree's commitment to sustainability has resonated with environmentally conscious businesses, leading to a 40% increase in client base. Clients have successfully reduced their carbon emissions by 15% on average, while also achieving cost savings through more efficient resource use. GreenTree's innovative approach has positioned them as a leader in the niche market of environmental accounting.

### *Short-Response Questions*

1. What is the primary focus of GreenTree Accounting?
2. What type of analysis does GreenTree use to evaluate the financial implications of sustainable practices?
3. By what percentage did GreenTree increase its client base?

## CASE STUDY: EXACTITUDE ACCOUNTING SOLUTIONS (EAS)

Exactitude Accounting Solutions (EAS) is an accounting company that provides comprehensive financial services, including bookkeeping, tax preparation, auditing, and financial consulting. Serving a diverse clientele ranging from small family-owned businesses to larger corporations, EAS prides itself on delivering precise financial reports and strategic knowledge. Recently, the firm sought to improve its financial management practices by analyzing key financial ratios, cash flow, and client accounts. Finally, to optimize their financial strategy, EAS uses various Excel tools and functions to model financial scenarios and evaluate performance metrics over time.

### Business Analytics Data Tables

**TABLE 9.7** Financial Ratios

| 1 | A | B |
|---|---|---|
| | **Financial Metric** | **Value** |
| 2 | Current assets ($) | 300,000 |
| 3 | Current liabilities ($) | 200,000 |
| 4 | Long-term debt ($) | 100,000 |
| 5 | Total equity ($) | 500,000 |
| 6 | Net profit ($) | 120,000 |
| 7 | Gross profit ($) | 200,000 |
| 8 | Accounts payable ($) | 50,000 |
| 9 | Accounts receivable ($) | 80,000 |
| 10 | Inventory ($) | 70,000 |
| 11 | Total revenue ($) | 450,000 |

**TABLE 9.8** Monthly Cash Budgeting

| 1 | A | B | C | D |
|---|---|---|---|---|
| | **Month** | **Cash Inflow ($)** | **Cash Outflow ($)** | **Ending Cash Balance ($)** |
| 2 | January | 100,000 | 90,000 | 10,000 |
| 3 | February | 120,000 | 95,000 | 35,000 |
| 4 | March | 110,000 | 100,000 | 45,000 |
| 5 | April | 130,000 | 115,000 | 60,000 |
| 6 | May | 125,000 | 110,000 | 75,000 |

### Analytics Problems Using Excel

1. Calculate the accounts payable and accounts receivable ratios using the financial metrics provided to assess the company's efficiency in managing its payables and receivables.
2. Use what-if analysis to determine the effect of increasing monthly cash inflows by 10% in the upcoming month. Implement Goal Seek to find out what cash outflow would allow the firm to maintain a target ending cash balance of $70,000.
3. Determine the firm's debt-to-equity ratio and current ratio and interpret the results to evaluate the company's financial stability and liquidity. Implement an influence diagram to illustrate the relationships among assets, liabilities, and equity.

4. Calculate the inventory turnover ratio to assess how efficiently PAS manages its inventory. Suggest operational improvements based on this ratio.
5. Implement scenario manager to analyze how changes in cash inflows and outflows would impact the firm's overall liquidity. Create scenarios for the best case, worst case, and most likely case to visualize financial outcomes.

### Answer Key

1. *Calculating accounts payable and accounts receivable ratios.*
   Accounts Payable Ratio: (50,000)/(450,000) = 0.1111 or 11.11%
   Accounts Receivable Ratio: (80,000)/(450,000) = 0.1778 or 17.78%
   Use simple formulas in the corresponding cells to reflect these calculations.
2. *What-if analysis and goal seek.* In a new cell, increase the relevant cash inflow by 10%: New Cash Inflow = Cash Inflow * 1.1. Use Goal Seek: Go to Data → What-If Analysis → Goal Seek. Set "Set cell" to the ending cash balance cell, "To value" to $70,000, and "By changing cell" to the cash outflow cell for the next month.
3. *Calculating debt-to-equity and current ratios.*
   Debt-to-Equity Ratio: (100,000)/(500,000) = 0.2
   Current Ratio: (300,000)/(200,000) = 1.5
   Create an influence diagram by using shapes and arrows in Excel to show the relationship between assets, liabilities, and equity.
4. *Calculating inventory turnover ratio.*
   Inventory Turnover Ratio: (Cost of Goods Sold)/(Average Inventory)
   Recommend increasing market demand forecasting for efficient inventory management.
5. *Implementing scenario manager.* Prepare the current sheet to hold different values for cash inflows and outflows. Go to Data → What-If Analysis → Scenario Manager, add various scenarios, and determine cash flows for each. Compare results in a summary report to gauge potential impacts on liquidity based on chosen scenarios.

---

### CASE STUDY: ACCURACY ACCOUNTING SERVICES

Accuracy Accounting Services is an accounting firm that provides comprehensive fiscal management solutions to small and medium-sized enterprises (SMEs). The company has built a reputation for delivering accurate and timely financial reports, helping clients make informed business decisions. Recently, Accuracy Accounting Services started a project for a retail client to optimize their financial operations and improve overall profitability. To evaluate the financial well-being of the client, Accuracy Accounting Services collected data on key financial metrics, including accounts payable, accounts receivable, inventory levels, and profitability over six months. The data was analyzed to identify areas for improvement and develop strategies for better fiscal management. The following tables summarize key findings from the project:

**TABLE 9.9** Financial Metrics

| 1 | A | B | C | D | E |
|---|---|---|---|---|---|
| | **Month** | **Accounts Payable ($)** | **Accounts Receivable ($)** | **Inventory ($)** | **Net Profit ($)** |
| **2** | January | 50,000 | 70,000 | 100,000 | 20,000 |
| **3** | February | 55,000 | 75,000 | 105,000 | 22,000 |
| **4** | March | 60,000 | 80,000 | 110,000 | 24,000 |
| **5** | April | 65,000 | 85,000 | 115,000 | 26,000 |
| **6** | May | 70,000 | 90,000 | 120,000 | 28,000 |
| **7** | June | 75,000 | 95,000 | 125,000 | 30,000 |

**TABLE 9.10** Liquidity and Profitability Ratios

| 1 | A | B | C | D | E |
|---|---|---|---|---|---|
| | **Month** | **Current Ratio** | **Quick Ratio** | **Gross Profit ($)** | **Return on Assets (%)** |
| **2** | January | 2.2 | 1.5 | 50,000 | 10 |
| **3** | February | 2.3 | 1.6 | 55,000 | 11 |
| **4** | March | 2.4 | 1.7 | 60,000 | 12 |
| **5** | April | 2.5 | 1.8 | 65,000 | 13 |
| **6** | May | 2.6 | 1.9 | 70,000 | 14 |
| **7** | June | 2.7 | 2.0 | 75,000 | 15 |

## Analytics Problems Using Excel

1. *Accounts payable ratio.* Calculate the accounts payable ratio for each month.
2. *Accounts receivable ratio.* Determine the accounts receivable ratio for each month.
3. *Accruals.* Record the monthly accruals based on financial metrics.
4. *Assumption modeling.* Create an assumption model to forecast future financial metrics.
5. *Cash budgeting.* Develop a cash budget for the next six months.
6. *Current ratio.* Verify the current ratio for each month.
7. *Data validation.* Implement data validation to ensure accurate data entry.
8. *Debt-to-equity ratio.* Calculate the debt-to-equity ratio for each month.
9. *Facilities resource allocation.* Allocate resources for facility management based on financial data.
10. *Goal Seek.* Use Goal Seek to determine the required sales to achieve a target net profit.
11. *Gross profit.* Calculate the gross profit for each month.
12. *Influence diagram.* Create an influence diagram to visualize financial relationships.

13. *Inventory turnover rate.* Determine the inventory turnover rate for each month.
14. *Net profit.* Verify the net profit for each month.
15. *Portfolio allocation.* Allocate investment portfolios based on financial performance.
16. *Purchasing decision analysis.* Analyze purchasing decisions based on financial metrics.
17. *Acid test (quick ratio).* Verify the quick ratio for each month.
18. *Return on assets.* Calculate the return on assets for each month.
19. *Return on equity.* Determine the return on equity for each month.
20. *Scenario manager.* Use Scenario Manager to analyze different financial scenarios.
21. *Staffing decision analysis.* Analyze staffing decisions based on financial data.
22. *What-if analysis.* Perform a what-if analysis to evaluate the impact of changes in financial metrics.

## Answer Key

1. *Accounts payable ratio.* Use the formula Accounts Payable/Net Sales. Example: =B2/Net Sales.
2. *Accounts receivable ratio.* Use the formula Accounts Receivable/Net Sales. Example: =C2/Net Sales.
3. *Accruals.* Record monthly accruals using the SUM function. Example: =SUM(B2:B7).
4. *Assumption modeling.* Create assumptions and use the FORECAST function. Example: =FORECAST(x, known_y's, known_x's).
5. *Cash budgeting.* Develop a cash budget using the SUM and IF functions. Example: =SUM(B2:B7) − IF(condition, value_if_true, value_if_false).
6. *Current ratio.* Use the formula: Current Assets/Current Liabilities. Example: =Current Assets/Current Liabilities.
7. *Data validation.* Implement data validation using the Data Validation tool in Excel.
8. *Debt-to-equity ratio.* Use the formula Total Debt/Total Equity. Example: =Total Debt/Total Equity.
9. *Facilities resource allocation.* Allocate resources using the SUM and IF functions. Example: =SUM(B2:B7) − IF(condition, value_if_true, value_if_false).
10. *Goal seek.* Use the Goal Seek tool in Excel to determine required sales. Example: Data > What-If Analysis > Goal Seek.
11. *Gross profit.* Use the formula Net Sales − Cost of Goods Sold. Example: = Net Sales − Cost of Goods Sold.
12. *Influence diagram.* Create an influence diagram using shapes and connectors in Excel.
13. *Inventory turnover rate.* Use the formula Cost of Goods Sold/Average Inventory. Example: =Cost of Goods Sold/((Beginning Inventory + Ending Inventory)/2).
14. *Net profit.* Verify net profit using the formula Total Revenue − Total Expenses. Example: = Total Revenue − Total Expenses.
15. *Portfolio allocation.* Allocate portfolios using the SUM and IF functions. Example: =SUM(B2:B7) − IF(condition, value_if_true, value_if_false).
16. *Purchasing decision analysis.* Analyze purchasing decisions using the IF and SUM functions. Example: =IF(condition, value_if_true, value_if_false).

17. *Acid test (quick ratio).* Use the formula (Current Assets − Inventory)/Current Liabilities. Example: =(Current Assets − Inventory)/Current Liabilities.
18. *Return on assets.* Use the formula Net Income/Total Assets. Example: = Net Income/Total Assets.
19. *Return on equity.* Use the formula Net Income/Shareholder's Equity. Example: =Net Income/Shareholder's Equity.
20. *Scenario Manager.* Use the Scenario Manager tool in Excel to analyze different scenarios. Example: Data > What-If Analysis > Scenario Manager.
21. *Staffing decision analysis.* Analyze staffing decisions using the IF and SUM functions. Example: =IF(condition, value_if_true, value_if_false).
22. *What-if analysis.* Perform a what-if analysis using the Data > What-If Analysis tool in Excel.

# CHAPTER 10

# Human Resources and Business Analytics

Human resources (HR) combined with business analytics is necessary in developing a successful strategy for all industries within the global environment. HR defines the department within an organization that is responsible for managing all aspects related to its employees. This function includes recruitment and hiring, training and development, employee relations, compensation and benefits, and compliance. When business analytics is combined with HR, HR analysts become responsible for managing the employees and workforce of the company. Since people are the most asset of a company, the management of employees using business analytics is critical to ensure longevity and the success of a business. When business is integrated in HR analytics, HR departments can develop information to support operational growth and improve the performance of employees.

The main function of HR is to provide organizations with workforce planning, employee relations, talent management, regulatory compliance, and the administration of benefits. Next, HR must retain and recruit new individuals to enter the workforce of the organization to create a strong internal work environment. Third, HR must focus on the alignment of objectives of the employees with the overall goals of the organization. As a result, the use of data-driven decisions based on statistical analysis through business analytics is required for the company to become more empowered within its market segment.

Business analytics in HR allows all forms of data to be collected, analyzed, and interpreted by the workforce so everyone can make more informed data-driven decisions. Next, the use of business analytics in HR creates the ability to predict future performance, identify new and emerging trends, and change from reactive to a proactive approach to handing opportunities and threats in the market. As an example, an HR analyst can monitor the engagement of employees, minimize turnover rates, and improve job satisfaction by understanding all factors that influence individual performance rates. By using predictive analytics, the HR analyst will use statistical tools for training, recruitment, and succession planning.

Next, business analytics relies on the use of key performance indicators (KPIs) that include employee absenteeism, diversity metrics, time-to-hire, and retention rates. With access to this data, HR analysts can identify areas of need within the organization to help improve overall efficiency and to streamline the recruitment process. There are many industries that rely on HR analytics to perform workforce management that include health care, education, technology, manufacturing, government, retail, hospitality, finance, and other professional services.

DOI: 10.4324/9781003629658-10

Finally, in today's global environment the integration of HR and business analytics is important in developing a competitive workforce. Next, HR and business analytics work together to enable the organization to become flexible and adaptable to anticipated challenges and opportunities within dynamic markets. As a result, the relationship between HR and analytics requires a detailed statistical analysis of data to improve the morale of employees, develop short-term objectives and long-term goals, and align all workforce strategies to improve the success of the organization. Within these various industries, HR analytics must support the culture, requirements, technology, and compliance standards as demonstrated in Table 10.1.

**TABLE 10.1** HR Function and Talent Acquisition in Various Industries

| Industry | HR Analytics Focus | Key Applications | Challenges Addressed |
|---|---|---|---|
| **Health care** | Predictive analysis for talent management | Forecasting attrition risks, selecting high-performance job applicants, analyzing engagement, productivity | Recruitment and retention, succession planning, engaging in a diverse workforce |
| **Education** | Optimizing workforce management and institutional success | Analyzing faculty perceptions, performance appraisals, research initiatives, training and development | Performance management, talent development, creating a thriving academic ecosystem |
| **Technology** | Improving workforce performance through data analysis | Understanding patterns in turnover, hiring times, investment in employee development | Making informed decisions, planning future initiatives |
| **Manufacturing** | Optimizing workforce efficiency and safety | Reducing accidents, predicting/preventing turnover, identifying skills gaps and training needs | Labor shortages, high turnover, rising compensation costs |
| **Government** | Using data to improve organizational performance | Identifying predictors of performance, understanding performance changes, foreseeing future impacts | Enhancing efficiency and effectiveness |
| **Retail** | Tackling workforce retention and optimizing scheduling | Understanding workforce trends, improving recruitment, enhancing performance and productivity | High turnover rates, labor cost control, forecasting workforce needs |
| **Hospitality** | Enhancing operations by predicting demand and adjusting staffing | Efficient staffing management, reducing labor costs, improving guest satisfaction | Efficient staffing, labor cost management, guest experience personalization |
| **Finance** | Gathering, analyzing, and reporting HR data | Understanding employee performance, optimizing payroll and benefits, improving hiring processes | Budget planning, workforce optimization, financial aspects of HR management |
| **Professional services** | Improving decision-making through data analysis | Descriptive, diagnostic, predictive, and prescriptive analytics for recruitment, performance management | Enhancing recruitment, performance management, workforce planning, reducing turnover |

## USING DATA TO IMPROVE RECRUITMENT PROCESSES

Data can be used to improve the recruitment processes of businesses in the global market. In the global market, HR analytics has become an integral part of using data in useful ways to improve the efficiency of the recruitment process by attracting top talented individuals and strengthening the decision-making process. When combined, business analytics and HR functions will change from the traditional approach of hiring that is based on intuition of the hiring manager to a more data-driven approach that chooses the candidate based on performance metrics. Using a data-driven approach will lead to a higher level of accuracy in choosing the correct candidate for the position since the result is based on analytics and not personal feelings. As a result, the change from a traditional to a data-driven approach has been implemented in the recruitment processes of businesses in various industries and markets.

With business analytics, data is used to enable HR analysts to gather, model, and interpret data that is related to the workforce so companies can develop a better understanding of their recruitment process. As an example, by analyzing past hiring data the company can identify new patterns and trends associated with the success rate of individuals, time-to-fill positions, and effectiveness of job applications. The analysis of this data will help HR analysts to improve the recruitment process by reducing downtime and delays in hiring a new candidate to fill a vacant position. As a result, the new trends gained from conducting the data analysis will support the identification of work slowdowns or stoppages, reduce delays, and improve efficiency using predictive analytics related to employee turnover, seasonal demands for hiring, and sustainable business growth.

Next, HR analytics study the recruitment process by optimizing the evaluation of candidates. This analysis focuses on skills, values, resumes, interviews, and past performance measures. When these areas are properly analyzed, the HR analyst can better fill open positions with the correct candidate based on their matching of skills and requirements due to the post-hire performance feedback loops. By following and tracking metrics, HR analysts can study the conversion success rate of successful applicants to those that are mismatched in the position they were hired to fill. As a result, the use of business analytics provides an increase in the accuracy of recruitment over time to ultimately reduce hiring errors and turnover costs within the acquisition process.

Finally, HR analytics is important in the health care, technology, finance, manufacturing, retail, and education industries. Within each industry, there is a unique need for hiring qualified individuals to perform specific functions. This situation makes access to relevant and useful data important for each type of business. In health care and education, hiring and recruiting must ensure compliance with licensing and certification regulations. In technology, HR will use statistical models to focus on candidates that have unique skill sets in software development or programming. In the retail and hospitality industries, HR analysts will need data analytics to assist in seasonal, temporary, and high-volume staffing during the fiscal year.

## PERFORMANCE ANALYTICS IN EMPLOYEE EVALUATION

HR and business analytics use data-driven methods and models to gauge the performance levels of individuals using key performance metrics as part of the employee evaluation process. With the use of business analytics, HR analysts can strategically align employee performance objectives with the overall goals of the organization. Next, HR analytics can lead to new areas for growth within the internal and external environment of the organization. This situation creates a new method for developing a data-driven process to improve the development of the employees and the productivity of the workplace.

Next, performance analytics are used to predict the effectiveness and efficiency of every employee and how they collectively contribute to the goals and vision of the company. HR analysts will use business analytics and statistical modeling to gather, sort, and analyze data from KPIs based on goal achievement, employee productivity, project completion, and attendance and absentee rates. By conducting this analysis, HR analysts will be capable of determining employees that need additional support, high-performing employees, and team performance trends. While this strategy is used to reward top talented employees, it also is used to develop focused training and development programs to assist everyone.

Finally, one of the major benefits of integration of business analytics into HR performance evaluations is the ability of the company to eliminate individual assessments based on subjection. In only using qualitative feedback, managers are making choices based on intuition and gut feelings. However, when quantitative measures and feedback are used, HR managers can develop a comprehensive and inclusive understanding of how the employee is performing using benchmarks and other metrics. As a result of using advanced analytics, various new metrics and methods can be used for assessing employee performance that are detailed in the table that follows.

## EMPLOYEE ENGAGEMENT AND SATISFACTION ANALYSIS

By combining HR and business analytics, organizations can develop new strategies to improve employee engagement and satisfaction analysis. This strategy will also identify areas of improvement, determine employee dissatisfaction levels, and create a positive work culture and environment. Next, employee engagement and satisfaction analysis create a more motivated workforce by increasing employee retention levels, morale, and productivity. Employee engagement is the commitment employees have related to their workplace and their individual objectives and organizational goals. Factors used in this analysis include compensation, development opportunities, work conditions, and organizational culture.

When HR is combined with business analytics, organizations can provide more information besides subjective information. Instead, organizations can offer employees quantifiable data and results. This new information will be used to identify new and emerging trends and

**TABLE 10.2** Metrics and Methods for Assessing Employee Performance

| Metric/Method | Description | Application | Industry Examples |
|---|---|---|---|
| **Time to hire** | Measures the time taken to fill job vacancies | Evaluates recruitment efficiency and speed | Health care, technology, retail |
| **Acceptance rate** | Percentage of job offers accepted by candidates | Indicates attractiveness of job offers and effectiveness of recruitment strategies | Education, government, professional services |
| **Cost per hire** | Total cost incurred to recruit a new employee | Assesses recruitment budget efficiency | Manufacturing, finance, hospitality |
| **Employee turnover rate** | Percentage of employees leaving the organization | Identifies retention issues and workforce stability | Health care, retail, government |
| **Performance appraisals** | Regular evaluations of employee performance | Provides feedback and identifies areas for improvement | Education, technology, professional services |
| **Training and development** | Investment in employee skill enhancement | Measures effectiveness of training programs and employee growth | Manufacturing, finance, hospitality |
| **Employee engagement** | Level of employee involvement and enthusiasm | Assesses overall job satisfaction and organizational commitment | Health care, retail, government |
| **Productivity metrics** | Measures the output and efficiency of employees | Evaluates individual and team performance | Technology, manufacturing, professional services |
| **Diversity metrics** | Measures diversity within the workforce | Assesses inclusiveness and representation in hiring and promotions | Education, government, finance |
| **Absenteeism rate** | Percentage of days employees are absent | Identifies patterns and causes of absenteeism | Health care, retail, hospitality |
| **360-degree feedback** | Comprehensive feedback from peers, subordinates, and supervisors | Provides a holistic view of employee performance | Technology, professional services, government |
| **Management by objectives (MBO)** | Setting specific objectives for employees to achieve | Aligns individual goals with organizational objectives | Education, finance, manufacturing |
| **Employee net promoter score (eNPS)** | Measures employee satisfaction and likelihood to recommend workplace | Indicates overall employee satisfaction and loyalty | Health care, retail, hospitality |
| **Succession planning** | Identifying and developing future leaders | Ensures leadership continuity and prepares for future organizational needs | Government, professional services, technology |
| **HR cost analytics** | Analysis of HR-related costs and their impact on the organization | Helps in budget planning and optimizing HR expenditures | Finance, manufacturing, hospitality |

to assist the business to develop data-driven decisions to increase its competitiveness in the market. Next, HR and business analytics will work together to develop metrics to determine absenteeism, overtime, and turnover rates by collecting feedback from employee surveys about their level of productivity and role within the organization.

Finally, the implementation of employee engagement and satisfaction analysis establishes the segmentation of data for targeted interventions. This situation is achieved by segmenting and dividing data by demographics, position, team, and department. When data is broken down into subgroups, HR analysts can better understand the hiring process for employee onboarding so that HR can redesign training programs to improve satisfaction levels using predictive analytics to reduce risk, burnout, and employee attrition. This situation is used to improve the understanding of employee morale through analytics, as seen in Table 10.3.

## LEARNING AND DEVELOPMENT ANALYTICS

HR analytics is important for organizations developing learning and development (L&D) analytics. *L&D analytics* is the process of enabling companies to have the ability to assess, measure, and maximize training programs within a company to improve the success of the workplace. This collaborative approach using L&D analytics helps HR departments guarantee that the learning programs used by companies are strategically aligned with the objectives and goals of the business, produce measurable results, and develop the skill set of employees. As a result, the use of analytics combined with HR will lead to an improvement in employee performance levels and long-term success.

Next, L&D analytics will study data that is associated with employee training and development efforts. Next, HR analytics analyze skill acquisition, training participation rates of employees, knowledge retention, and post-training performance that must be considered when determining the effectiveness of current programs. As an example, HR will benefit from business analytics by determining if an employee is applying the new skills, they learned during a recent training program and can also establish if the new skills that were gained translate into improved performance in the workplace.

Finally, business analytics enables HR to identify the skill gaps of employees within the business by analyzing employee performance data comparing current and future job requirements. Next, HR will be responsible for designing focused L&D to find critical gaps in the process. As an example, technology companies experience rapid innovations that require employees to remain current and aware of new technologies, analytical tools, and programming languages to help improve the quality of training or to offer new specific training. This strategy will create personalized training to improve the service skills, foundational knowledge, management, and leadership skills to help individuals become fully engaged in the workplace by measuring the effectiveness of training programs as detailed in the table that follows.

**TABLE 10.3** Understanding Employee Morale Through Analytics

| Metric/Method | Description | Application | Benefits |
|---|---|---|---|
| **Employee engagement surveys** | Regular surveys to gauge employee satisfaction and engagement levels | Collects feedback on workplace environment, leadership, and job satisfaction | Identifies areas for improvement, enhances engagement, boosts morale |
| **Sentiment analysis** | Analyzing employee communications (emails, chats) for sentiment | Uses natural language processing to understand employee emotions and attitudes | Provides real-time insights into employee mood, helps address issues promptly |
| **Pulse surveys** | Short, frequent surveys to monitor employee sentiment | Tracks changes in morale over time, identifies trends and immediate concerns | Enables quick responses to emerging issues, maintains continuous engagement |
| **360-degree feedback** | Comprehensive feedback from peers, subordinates, and supervisors | Provides a holistic view of employee performance and interpersonal relationships | Enhance self-awareness, fosters a culture of continuous improvement |
| **Employee net promoter score (eNPS)** | Measures employee satisfaction and likelihood to recommend workplace | Indicates overall employee satisfaction and loyalty | Helps gauge employee advocacy, identifies areas for organizational improvement |
| **Absenteeism rate** | Percentage of days employees are absent | Identifies patterns and causes of absenteeism | Helps address underlying issues affecting morale, improves attendance |
| **Real-time employee evaluation** | Frequent check-ins and feedback sessions | Provides timely feedback and recognition, monitors performance and engagement | Enhances employee satisfaction, improves performance, reduces disengagement |
| **Exit interview** | Interviews with departing employees to understand reasons for leaving | Collects insights into employee experiences and reasons for turnover | Helps identify systemic issues, improves retention strategies |
| **Social media monitoring** | Analyzing employee posts on social media platforms | Understands employee sentiment and public perception of the workplace | Provides insights into employee morale outside of formal channels, helps address concerns |
| **Predictive analytics** | Using historical data to predict future employee behavior | Forecasts turnover, engagement levels, and morale trends | Enables proactive management of employee morale, reduces turnover |
| **Training and development programs** | Investment in employee skill enhancement | Measures effectiveness of training programs and employee growth | Improves job satisfaction, enhances morale, fosters career development |

**TABLE 10.4** Measuring the Effectiveness of Training Programs

| Metric/Method | Description | Application | Benefits |
|---|---|---|---|
| **Training completion rate** | Percentage of employees who complete the training program | Evaluates engagement and commitment to training | Identifies areas for improvement, ensures training goals are met |
| **Knowledge retention** | Assessment of how well employees retain information post-training | Measures effectiveness of training content and delivery | Ensures employees can apply learned skills, improve training methods |
| **Behavior change** | Observing changes in employee behavior after training | Evaluates practical application of training | Demonstrates real-world impact, enhances performance |
| **Performance improvement** | Measuring improvements in job performance post-training | Assesses the direct impact of training on employee productivity | Validates training effectiveness, boosts organizational performance |
| **Employee feedback** | Collecting feedback from employees on training programs | Gauges satisfaction and perceived value of training | Identifies strengths and weaknesses, improves future training initiatives |
| **ROI (return on investment)** | Calculating the financial return from training investments | Measures of cost-effectiveness and financial impact of training | Justifies training expenditures, optimizes budget allocation |
| **Training engagement** | Monitoring participation and interaction during training sessions | Evaluates engagement levels and interest in training | Enhances training delivery, increases participation |
| **Skill assessments** | Testing employees' skills before and after training | Measures skill acquisition and improvement | Ensures training objectives are met, identifies skill gaps |
| **Completion time** | Time taken by employees to complete training programs | Evaluates efficiency and pacing of training | Optimizes training duration, improves scheduling |
| **Certification rates** | Percentage of employees earning certifications post-training | Measures of achievement and recognition of training | Validates skill acquisition, enhances employee credentials |
| **Training satisfaction** | Surveys to measure employee satisfaction with training programs | Gauges overall satisfaction and effectiveness | Improves training content and delivery, enhances employee morale |
| **Learning transfer** | Assessing how well employees apply learned skills to their job | Evaluates practical application and impact of training | Ensures training relevance, enhances job performance |
| **Absenteeism rate** | Monitoring absenteeism rates post-training | Identifies impact of training on employee attendance | Reduces absenteeism, improves engagement and morale |
| **Peer reviews** | Feedback from colleagues on employee performance post-training | Provides a comprehensive view of training impact | Enhances collaboration, validates training effectiveness |
| **Training cost analysis** | Analyzing costs associated with training programs | Evaluates cost-efficiency and budget allocation | Optimizes training investments, improves financial planning |

## DIVERSITY AND INCLUSION ANALYTICS AND METRICS FOR PROMOTING DIVERSITY IN THE WORKPLACE

Diversity and inclusion analytics focus on workplace data to evaluate the equity, inclusion, and representation of employees from different backgrounds and demographics. There are various performance indicators and metrics that can be used to determine demographics, promotion rates, diversity within departments, employee sentiment, and pay equity. These metrics will help companies gain knowledge about all levels within the hierarchy of the company. This strategy enables companies and HR departments to collect, track, and interpret data to identify performance gaps, trends, and patterns.

To promote diversity in the workplace, organizations must use advanced analytics to identify roadblocks in the current system of hiring candidates from different backgrounds and cultures within all levels of the organization. When demographic data is analyzed, HR analysts can determine the level of diversity or underrepresentation of salary earnings and leadership positions. As an example, a business analytical study of diversity can provide information demonstrating that female employees are hired and have a high ratio of employment in a company but do not hold senior positions to make strategic decisions. As a result of the analysis, the company can conduct performance reviews of all female candidates and implement a new re-evaluation process and to develop mentorship programs that are focused on specific groups to help provide equity and equality within the company based on historical data.

## ATTRITION PREDICTION AND RETENTION STRATEGIES

Attrition prediction in HR analytics involves using data and statistical methods to predict which employees are likely to leave the organization. The use of this predictive approach helps HR departments take proactive measures to improve employee retention and maintain a stable workforce. Once the attrition rate has been determined, retention strategies to maintain employees can be developed. Retention strategies are created by using business analytics to assist HR in developing effective retention programs, including leadership development, training development and opportunities, employee recognition programs, and mentorship initiatives. As a result, HR analytics will conduct attrition prediction and retention strategies and use business analytics to minimize turnover rates using the methods detailed in the tables that follow.

## BUSINESS ANALYTICS FUNCTION FOR HUMAN RESOURCES USING MICROSOFT EXCEL

In the business environment, there are many business analytical terms mentioned that play a critical role in making informed and data-driven choices that drive decisions, optimize daily operations, and develop strategic actions and initiatives. Various statistical concepts play an important role in human resources and business analytics by providing essential tools for data analysis and decision-making. Here's a detailed overview of their definition and importance and how to conduct this statistical analysis using Microsoft Excel.

**TABLE 10.5** Using Analytics to Minimize Turnover Rates

| Aspect | HR Analytics Application | Key Metrics/Methods | Benefits |
|---|---|---|---|
| **Turnover rates** | Identifying patterns and trends in employee turnover | • Turnover rate: percentage of employees leaving the organization<br>• Exit interviews: insights from departing employees<br>• Employee engagement surveys: gauging satisfaction and engagement levels | • Pinpoints areas of concern<br>• Develops targeted strategies<br>• Reduces recruitment and training costs |
| **Attrition predictions** | Forecasting which employees are likely to leave | • Predictive modeling: using historical data to predict future attrition<br>• Sentiment analysis: analyzing employee communications for sentiment<br>• Performance metrics: evaluating job performance and satisfaction | • Proactive risk management<br>• Improves retention<br>• Maintains a stable workforce |
| **Retention strategies** | Implementing data-driven strategies to retain employees | • Employee feedback: collecting feedback through surveys and reviews<br>• Career development: offering training and growth opportunities<br>• Recognition and rewards: regularly acknowledging employee contributions | • Enhances employee satisfaction<br>• Boosts morale and loyalty<br>• Reduces turnover rates |

**TABLE 10.6** Detailed Comparison of Turnover Rates, Attrition Predictions, and Retention Strategies

| Aspect | Turnover Rates | Attrition Predictions | Retention Strategies |
|---|---|---|---|
| **Data collection** | Historical turnover data, exit interviews, engagement surveys | Historical data, sentiment analysis, performance metrics | Employee feedback, career development data, recognition and rewards data |
| **Analysis techniques** | Trend analysis, pattern identification | Predictive modeling, machine learning algorithms, sentiment analysis | Feedback analysis, career path mapping, reward system evaluation |
| **Proactive measures** | Targeted retention initiatives, improving work environment | Identifying at-risk employees, addressing dissatisfaction, enhancing engagement | Personalized career plans, regular check-ins, wellness programs |
| **Outcome** | Reduced turnover rates, improved employee satisfaction | Improved retention, stable workforce, proactive management | Enhanced employee morale, increased loyalty, reduced turnover rates |

## Absenteeism Rate

This metric measures the frequency of employee absences and is an indicator of workforce engagement and morale. High absenteeism rates can signal issues such as job dissatisfaction or health problems, prompting managers to investigate underlying causes and implement strategies to improve morale and attendance.

Formula: =(Number of Days Absent/Total Workdays)*100

**Steps:**

1. Gather data on the total workdays available and the number of days absent.
2. Calculate the absenteeism rate using the formula =(Number of Days Absent/Total Workdays)*100.

## Average Tenure of Employees

Tracking the average tenure helps organizations understand employee loyalty and retention trends. A longer average tenure can indicate a positive work environment and effective retention strategies, while a shorter tenure may show potential issues in company culture or employee satisfaction.

**Steps:**

1. List the hire dates for each employee in a column.
2. Use the formula to calculate each employee's tenure in years =DATEDIF(C2, TODAY(), "Y").
3. Find the average tenure in a new cell using =AVERAGE(variable 1:variable 2), which contains the tenure values derived from the preceding formula.

## Calculating the Overtime Rate

Understanding overtime rates is necessary in controlling labor costs and assessing employee workload and productivity. Frequent overtime can indicate staffing shortages or operational inefficiencies that will determine the allocation of resources and staffing strategies.

Formula: =Regular Hourly Rate*Overtime Multiplier*1.5

**Steps:**

1. Identify regular hourly wage and total hours worked.
2. Define the overtime rate (typically 1.5 times the regular pay).
3. Use the formula =Regular Hourly Rate*Overtime Multiplier*1.5.

## Cost per Hire

This metric provides insight into the efficiency and effectiveness of the recruiting process. By calculating the total costs involved in hiring (i.e., advertising, time spent interviewing), organizations can evaluate and streamline their recruitment strategies to attract talent more cost-effectively.

Formula: =Total Output/Total Hours Worked

**Steps:**

1. Gather total recruitment costs (advertising, interviews, etc.) and number of hires.
2. Use the formula =Total Recruiting Costs/Number of Hires.

## Diversity Ratio

Measuring diversity within the workforce is essential in developing an inclusive environment and in enhancing innovation. A higher diversity ratio can lead to a wider range of perspectives, which can improve decision-making and enhance organizational performance.

Formula: =(Employees from Diverse Backgrounds/Total Employees)*100

**Steps:**

1. Identify the number of employees from diverse backgrounds and total employees.
2. Use the formula =(Employees from Diverse Backgrounds/Total Employees)*100.

## Employee Productivity

Productivity metrics assess the efficiency of employees in completing tasks relative to predefined goals. Tracking productivity provides insights into performance and helps managers identify high achievers, address underperformance, and allocate resources effectively.

Formula: =Total Output/Total Hours Worked

**Steps:**

1. Collect data on total output (sales, completed projects) and total hours worked.
2. Use the formula =Total Output/Total Hours Worked.

## Employee Turnover Rate

This metric indicates the rate at which employees leave an organization. High turnover rates can be costly and disruptive, prompting a closer examination of workplace conditions, management practices, and employee engagement strategies.

Formula: =(Number of Employees Who Left/Average Number of Employees)*100

**Steps:**

1. Collect data on the number of employees who left in a period and the average number of employees during that period.
2. Use the formula =(Number of Employees Who Left/Average Number of Employees)*100.

### Retention Rate

The retention rate complements the turnover rate and helps assess the effectiveness of employee engagement and satisfaction initiatives. High retention rates are revealing of a supportive work environment, which is necessary in maintaining organizational knowledge and minimizing recruitment costs.

Formula: =(1 − (Employee Turnover/Number of Employees at Start))*100

**Steps:**

1. Use the total number of employees at the start of the period and the number of employees who stayed throughout the period.
2. Use the formula =(1 − (Employee Turnover/Number of Employees at Start))*100.

### Return on Investment (ROI) for Employee Training

Evaluating the ROI on training programs helps organizations understand the financial benefits of investing in employee development. A positive ROI indicates that training efforts are effectively improving employee skills and contributing to organizational success.

Formula: =((Benefits from Training − Cost of Training)/Cost of Training)*100

**Steps:**

1. Gather data on the total cost of training and the benefits gained from that training (i.e., increased productivity).
2. Use the formula =((Benefits from Training − Cost of Training)/Cost of Training)*100.

### Salary Increase Percentage

Tracking salary increases allows organizations to assess their compensation strategies relative to industry standards and employee performance. Understanding salary trends is crucial in maintaining competitive positioning and improving employee satisfaction and retention.

Formula: =((New Salary − Original Salary)/Original Salary)*100

**Steps:**

1. Identify the original salary and the new salary.
2. Use the formula =((New Salary − Original Salary)/Original Salary)*100.

## REAL-WORLD EXAMPLES OF HUMAN RESOURCES (HR) INSIGHTS DRIVING BUSINESS SUCCESS

### Bristol–Myers Squibb Company

Bristol–Myers Squibb Company relies on data analytics to identify talent acquisition trends that enable HR leaders to make informed decisions about recruitment strategies. By analyzing applicant data, Bristol–Myers can update its hiring processes and ensure a better fit between candidate skills and organizational needs. Next, Bristol–Myers employs predictive analytics to assess employee engagement and retention. By analyzing survey data and performance metrics, HR can identify potential turnover risks and develop targeted initiatives to improve employee satisfaction rates. This proactive approach strengthens organizational culture while also enhancing productivity. Finally, the company also uses analytics to evaluate the effectiveness of training programs and to measure their impact on employee performance and development.

**Question 1**

How does Bristol–Myers Squibb use data analytics to enhance its talent acquisition strategies?

Answer: Bristol–Myers Squibb leverages data analytics to improve its talent acquisition strategies by analyzing applicant data to identify trends and patterns. This approach allows HR leaders to make informed decisions about recruitment strategies while ensuring a better alignment between candidate skills and organizational needs. By analyzing data such as candidate qualifications, application sources, and hiring timelines, the company can optimize its recruitment processes. This data-driven strategy improves the quality of hires and enhances the efficiency of the recruitment process, ultimately leading to a more skilled and cohesive workforce.

**Question 2**

In what ways does Bristol–Myers Squibb utilize predictive analytics to improve employee engagement and retention?

Answer: Bristol–Myers Squibb employs predictive analytics to improve employee engagement and retention by analyzing survey data and performance metrics. This analysis helps HR identify potential turnover risks and develop targeted initiatives to improve employee satisfaction. By understanding factors that contribute to employee disengagement or dissatisfaction, the company can implement proactive measures, such as focused development programs, recognition initiatives, and work–life balance improvements. This strategic use of predictive analytics strengthens organizational culture and increases productivity by retaining top talent and reducing turnover costs.

### Question 3

How does Bristol–Myers Squibb assess the effectiveness of its training programs using data analytics?

Answer: Bristol–Myers Squibb evaluates the effectiveness of its training programs through data analytics by measuring their impact on employee performance and development. By collecting and analyzing data on employee performance before and after training, the company can assess the return on investment of its training initiatives. Key performance metrics, such as skill acquisition, productivity improvements, and career progression, are used to determine the success of training programs. This analytical approach enables Bristol–Myers Squibb to continuously refine its training offerings while ensuring they are aligned with both employee development goals and organizational objectives and ultimately leading to a more competent and competitive workforce.

## Caterpillar Inc.

Caterpillar Inc. implements data analytics to optimize its talent acquisition processes and employs advanced algorithms to analyze candidate profiles and improve the recruitment process. This analytical approach enables Caterpillar to identify candidates who not only meet the technical requirements but also align with the company's culture. Next, Caterpillar uses analytics to assess employee performance and engagement. By analyzing employee feedback and performance data, HR can identify areas needing attention and implement targeted development programs while enhancing employee satisfaction and retention. Finally, the company focuses on workforce planning using predictive analytics to anticipate future labor needs based on market trends and project demands. This proactive approach guarantees that Caterpillar maintains a skilled workforce ready to meet evolving industry challenges within the market.

### Question 1

How does Caterpillar Inc. use data analytics to enhance its talent acquisition process?

Answer: Caterpillar Inc. relies on data analytics to refine its talent acquisition process by employing advanced algorithms to analyze candidate profiles. This approach enables the company to identify candidates who not only possess the necessary technical skills but also align with the company's cultural values. By integrating data analytics into recruitment, Caterpillar can streamline its hiring process, reduce time to hire, and improve the quality of new hires. This strategy guarantees that the company attracts and retains top talent that is necessary for maintaining its competitive advantage in their industry.

### Question 2

In what ways does Caterpillar use analytics to improve employee performance and engagement?

Answer: Caterpillar uses data analytics to improve employee performance and engagement by analyzing employee feedback and performance data. This analysis helps HR identify areas that require attention, including skill gaps or low engagement levels. By understanding these areas, Caterpillar can implement new development programs and initiatives focused on improving employee satisfaction and retention levels. This data-driven approach improves individual performance and contributes to a more motivated and productive workforce to ultimately benefit the organization.

**Question 3**

How do predictive analytics support workforce planning at Caterpillar Inc.?

Answer: Predictive analytics plays a crucial role in workforce planning at Caterpillar Inc. by allowing the company to anticipate future labor needs based on market trends and project demands. By analyzing historical data and forecasting future requirements, Caterpillar can proactively plan for changes in workforce demand while ensuring that it has the right number of skilled employees available when needed. This strategy helps the company avoid labor shortages or surpluses, maximize resource allocation, and maintain operational efficiency, thereby positioning Caterpillar to effectively meet dynamic challenges within the industry.

## Deere & Company

Deere & Company relies on data analytics to refine its recruitment process, analyzing candidate characteristics and performance metrics to identify top talent that aligns with its strategic goals. This data-driven approach improves the process of hiring and ensures that Deere attracts individuals with the right skills and cultural fit. Next, Deere relies on analytics to monitor employee engagement and performance. By evaluating employee surveys and productivity data, HR identifies trends and areas for improvement, enabling the company to implement targeted initiatives that enhance job satisfaction and retention. Finally, in workforce planning, Deere applies predictive analytics to anticipate future labor needs based on market data and project requirements. As a result, this proactive strategy ensures that the company maintains a skilled workforce capable of meeting industry demands.

**Question 1**

How does Deere & Company use data analytics to enhance its recruitment process?

Answer: Deere & Company uses data analytics to refine its recruitment process by analyzing candidate characteristics and key performance metrics. This approach allows the company to identify top talent that aligns with its strategic goals. By focusing on both technical skills and cultural fit, Deere ensures that new hires are not only capable of performing their roles effectively but also positively contributing to the company culture. This data-driven recruitment strategy enhances the quality of hires, reduces turnover, and supports the company's long-term objectives by building a workforce to meet its strategic needs.

**Question 2**

In what ways does Deere & Company use analytics to monitor and improve employee engagement and performance?

Answer: Deere & Company employs analytics to monitor employee engagement and performance by evaluating data from employee surveys and key productivity metrics. This analysis helps HR identify trends and areas that require attention while enabling the implementation of targeted initiatives to enhance job satisfaction and retention. By understanding the factors that influence employee morale and productivity, Deere can develop programs and policies that address specific needs, leading to a more motivated and committed workforce. This strategy improves individual performance and contributes to the overall success of the organization.

**Question 3**

How do predictive analytics support workforce planning at Deere & Company?

Answer: Predictive analytics plays a crucial role in workforce planning at Deere & Company by allowing the organization to anticipate future labor needs based on market data and project requirements. By analyzing trends and forecasting demand, Deere can successfully address potential skill gaps and ensure that it has the best talent in place to meet industry demands. This strategic approach to workforce planning helps the company maintain a competitive edge by ensuring that it is always prepared to respond to changes in the market. Finally, it supports efficient resource allocation and minimizes the risks associated with labor shortages or surpluses.

## Lockheed Martin Corporation

Lockheed Martin Corporation employs advanced data analytics to optimize its talent acquisition strategy by analyzing hiring patterns and candidate data to identify the most effective recruitment channels. This strategy allows Lockheed Martin to attract top talent aligned with its mission and values. Next, Lockheed Martin uses analytics to monitor employee engagement and retention rates. By evaluating feedback from employee surveys and performance data, HR identifies trends and potential issues, enabling the implementation of focused initiatives to improve workplace culture and employee job satisfaction. Finally, the company relies on predictive analytics in workforce planning by assessing future skill needs based on industry trends and project demands. This strategy ensures that Lockheed Martin maintains a skilled workforce capable of meeting evolving challenges in defense and aerospace.

**Question 1**

How does the Lockheed Martin Corporation use data analytics to enhance its talent acquisition strategy?

Answer: The Lockheed Martin Corporation uses advanced data analytics to refine its talent acquisition strategy by analyzing hiring patterns and candidate data. This approach allows the company to identify the most effective recruitment channels while ensuring that they attract top talent who align with the company's mission and values. By effectively using data analytics, Lockheed Martin can maximize its recruitment processes to make them more efficient and focused. This strategy helps in attracting candidates with the right skills and cultural fit and enhances the overall quality of hires, contributing to the company's long-term success in the defense and aerospace sectors.

**Question 2**

In what ways does Lockheed Martin use analytics to improve employee engagement and retention?

Answer: Lockheed Martin uses analytics to monitor employee engagement and retention by evaluating feedback from employee surveys and performance data. This data-driven approach helps HR identify trends and potential issues within the workplace. By understanding these patterns, the company can implement focused initiatives aimed at improving workplace culture and employee job satisfaction. These initiatives may include targeted development programs, enhanced communication strategies, and adjustments to workplace policies. As a result, Lockheed Martin can develop a more positive work environment that leads to a higher employee satisfaction level and reduced turnover rates.

**Question 3**

How do predictive analytics support workforce planning at Lockheed Martin?

Answer: Lockheed Martin relies on predictive analytics in workforce planning by assessing future skill needs based on industry trends and project demands. This strategy enables the company to anticipate changes in the labor market and adjust its workforce accordingly. By understanding the skills that will be in demand, Lockheed Martin can focus on recruiting and developing employees who possess these capabilities. This ensures that the company maintains a skilled workforce capable of meeting evolving challenges in the defense and aerospace markets. Finally, predictive analytics helps Lockheed Martin allocate resources more effectively while ensuring that they are prepared for future projects and industry shifts.

## CASE STUDIES ON HUMAN RESOURCE (HR) SUCCESS THROUGH ANALYTICS

### Business Success Through Business Analytics

Business analytics plays a crucial role in understanding HR trends and consumer behavior that enables organizations in the HR industry to make more data-driven and informed decisions. Following are three examples of how HR data and knowledge are translated into business success using analytics:

### Example 1: AvailableTalent Solutions

AvailableTalent Solutions is a leading HR consultancy firm that specializes in talent acquisition and management. By using advanced business analytics, AvailableTalent has developed a proprietary algorithm that predicts employee turnover with remarkable accuracy. This knowledge allows their clients to proactively address potential retention issues while reducing turnover rates by an average of 25%. Next, the company's analytics platform integrates data from employee surveys, performance reviews, and external market trends to provide a comprehensive view of employee satisfaction and engagement. This comprehensive approach enables AvailableTalent to offer customized recommendations to improve workplace culture and employee satisfaction, ultimately leading to enhanced productivity and reduced recruitment costs.

### *Short-Response Questions*

1. What is the primary focus of AvailableTalent Solutions?
2. By what percentage did AvailableTalent Solutions help reduce turnover rates?
3. What types of data does AvailableTalent integrate to provide insights?

### Example 2: CommunityPulse Analytics

CommunityPulse Analytics is an innovative HR tech company that has revolutionized the way organizations understand employee engagement. By employing machine learning algorithms, CommunityPulse analyzes real-time data from various communication platforms, such as emails and instant messaging, to gauge employee sentiment and engagement levels. This real-time analysis allows companies to identify and address issues as they arise, rather than waiting for annual surveys. As a result, CommunityPulse clients have reported a 25% increase in employee engagement scores and a significant improvement in team collaboration and morale.

### *Short-Response Questions*

1. What technology does CommunityPulse Analytics use to understand employee engagement?
2. How much did CommunityPulse clients increase their employee engagement scores?
3. What type of data does CommunityPulse analyze to gauge employee sentiment?

### Example 3: VisionaryHR Inc.

VisionaryHR Inc. is a forward-thinking HR consultancy firm that focuses on diversity and inclusion (D&I) strategies. By leveraging business analytics, VisionaryHR has developed a D&I dashboard that provides organizations with insights into their workforce composition and diversity metrics. The dashboard uses data visualization to highlight areas where diversity is lacking and suggests actionable strategies to improve inclusivity. Clients of VisionaryHR have seen a 15% increase in diverse hires and a more inclusive workplace culture that has been linked to higher innovation and creativity within teams.

### *Short-Response Questions*

1. What is the primary focus of VisionaryHR Inc.?
2. By what percentage did VisionaryHR clients increase their diverse hires?
3. What tool does VisionaryHR use to provide insights into workforce composition?

## CASE STUDY: HUMAN RESOURCES INNOVATIONS LTD.

Human Resources Innovations Ltd. is a leading human resources consulting firm dedicated to improving workforce management for businesses across various industries. The company provides a wide range of services that include talent acquisition, employee training, and performance management. Recently, HR Innovations has developed several analytical tools designed to help organizations maximize their employee management practices and improve retention rates. Finally, the firm has recognized the importance of data-driven decisions in managing their clients' human resources effectively.

### Business Analytics Data Tables

**TABLE 10.7** Employee Metrics

| 1 | A | B | C | D | E | F | G | H |
|---|---|---|---|---|---|---|---|---|
| | Employee ID | Hire Date | Salary ($) | Termination Date | Overtime Hours | Hours Worked | Training Hours | Performance Score (1–10) |
| 2 | 1 | 1/10/2018 | 55,000 | 6/14/2022 | 80 | 2,080 | 20 | 8 |
| 3 | 2 | 3/15/2019 | 60,000 | 1/20/2023 | 40 | 1,950 | 15 | 9 |
| 4 | 3 | 5/22/2020 | 50,000 | | 50 | 2,100 | 25 | 7 |
| 5 | 4 | 7/18/2021 | 70,000 | | 60 | 2,000 | 10 | 6 |
| 6 | 5 | 9/1/2022 | 65,000 | | 30 | 1,800 | 30 | 9 |

**TABLE 10.8** Employee Diversity and Training Data

| 1 | A | B | C | D | E |
|---|---|---|---|---|---|
| | Department | Employees | Minority Representation (%) | Total Training Cost ($) | ROI on Training (%) |
| 2 | Engineering | 15 | 20 | 12,000 | 150 |
| 3 | Marketing | 10 | 30 | 8,000 | 175 |
| 4 | Sales | 20 | 25 | 15,000 | 200 |
| 5 | Human resources | 8 | 50 | 5,000 | 125 |
| 6 | Operations | 25 | 15 | 10,000 | 100 |

### Analytics Problems Using Excel

1. Calculate the absenteeism rate and employee turnover rate for Human Resource Innovations Ltd., and derive insights from these metrics.
2. Using the data, determine the average tenure of employees within the company, and interpret the significance of this length of service on the business.

3. Evaluate the cost per hire based on the number of employees hired, factoring in the total training costs and employee turnover.
4. Analyze the diversity ratio within the different departments, and suggest strategies to improve minority representation in departments with lower rates.
5. Assess employee productivity through performance score and correlation to training hours. Calculate the salary increase percentage for high-performing employees needing motivation based on their performance scores.

### Answer Key

1. *Calculating absenteeism rate and employee turnover rate.* Absenteeism rate is calculated by taking the total number of absent days and dividing by the total number of available workdays for all employees.
   Employee Turnover Rate: = ((Number of Terminations)/(Average Number of Employees))*100
   Use the COUNTIF function for counting terminations in Excel.
2. *Calculating average tenure of employees.* Create a new column that calculates the tenure for each employee. For current employees, use Tenure = (Today's Date) − (Hire Date). For terminated employees: Tenure = (Termination Date) − (Hire Date). Average this value across the employee dataset using the AVERAGE function.
3. *Calculating cost per hire.* Cost per Hire = (Total Training Cost)/(Number of New Hires). Total new hires identified from the dataset can be derived analogously from the length of service and divided by the total training cost accordingly.
4. *Assessing diversity ratio.* Diversity Ratio = ((Minority Representation)/(Total Employees))*100. Document the results in a table format in Excel. Strategy suggestions may include targeted recruitment from diverse candidate pools or mentorship programs.
5. *Analyzing employee productivity and salary increase percentage.* Employee productivity can be correlated with training hours using the CORREL function in Excel. Salary Increase Percentage = ((New Salary) − \(Old Salary))/(\text(Old Salary)) *times 100. Create conditions to apply salary increases for those with performance scores above a certain threshold, and calculate resulting values.

---

### CASE STUDY: EXCELLENCEINHR INC.

ExcellenceinHR Inc. is a human resources consulting firm that focuses on maximizing HR practices for businesses of all sizes. The company has helped various organizations improve their employee engagement, retention, and overall productivity. Recently, ExcellenceinHR Inc. partnered with a large retail company to enhance their HR strategies and address issues related to employee turnover and absenteeism. To evaluate the impact of their recommendations, ExcellenceinHR Inc. collected data on various HR metrics, including absenteeism rates, employee turnover, and productivity, over six months. The data was analyzed to identify trends and measure the effectiveness of the implemented strategies. The following tables summarize key findings from the project:

**TABLE 10.9** Employee Metrics

| 1 | A | B | C | D | E |
|---|---|---|---|---|---|
| | **Month** | **Absenteeism Rate (%)** | **Average Tenure (Years)** | **Overtime Rate (%)** | **Employee Turnover Rate (%)** |
| **2** | January | 5.0 | 3.5 | 10 | 12 |
| **3** | February | 4.8 | 3.6 | 9 | 11 |
| **4** | March | 4.6 | 3.7 | 8 | 10 |
| **5** | April | 4.4 | 3.8 | 7 | 9 |
| **6** | May | 4.2 | 3.9 | 6 | 8 |
| **7** | June | 4.0 | 4.0 | 5 | 7 |

**TABLE 10.10** Recruitment and Training Metrics

| 1 | A | B | C | D | E | F | G |
|---|---|---|---|---|---|---|---|
| | **Month** | **Cost per Hire ($)** | **Diversity Ratio (%)** | **Employee Productivity (Units/Hour)** | **Retention Rate (%)** | **ROI for Employee Training (%)** | **Salary Increase (%)** |
| **2** | January | 3,000 | 30 | 50 | 85 | 10 | 2 |
| **3** | February | 2,900 | 32 | 52 | 86 | 12 | 2.5 |
| **4** | March | 2,800 | 34 | 54 | 87 | 14 | 3 |
| **5** | April | 2,700 | 36 | 56 | 88 | 16 | 3.5 |
| **6** | May | 2,600 | 38 | 58 | 89 | 18 | 4 |
| **7** | June | 2,500 | 40 | 60 | 90 | 20 | 4.5 |

## Analytics Problems Using Excel

1. *Absenteeism rate.* Calculate the average absenteeism rate over the six months.
2. *Average tenure of employees.* Determine the average tenure of employees for each month.
3. *Overtime rate.* Calculate the monthly overtime rate.
4. *Cost per hire.* Compute the total cost per hire for the six months.
5. *Diversity ratio.* Analyze the trend in diversity ratio over the six months.
6. *Employee productivity.* Calculate the average employee productivity for each month.
7. *Employee turnover rate.* Determine the monthly employee turnover rate.
8. *Retention rate.* Calculate the retention rate for each month.
9. *Return on investment for employee training.* Compute the ROI for employee training for each month.
10. *Salary increase percentage.* Analyze the trend in salary increase percentage over the six months.

### Answer Key

1. *Absenteeism rate.* Use the AVERAGE function: =AVERAGE(B2:B7).
2. *Average tenure of employees.* Use the AVERAGE function: =AVERAGE(C2:C7).
3. *Overtime rate.* Use the SUM function to calculate monthly overtime rate: =SUM(D2:D7).
4. *Cost per hire.* Use the SUM function: =SUM(B2:B7).
5. *Diversity ratio.* Use the TREND function to analyze the trend: =TREND(C2:C7).
6. *Employee productivity.* Use the AVERAGE function: =AVERAGE(D2:D7).
7. *Employee turnover rate.* Use the SUM function to calculate monthly turnover rate: =SUM(E2:E7).
8. *Retention rate.* Use the AVERAGE function: =AVERAGE(E2:E7).
9. *Return on investment for employee training.* Use the ROI formula: =(Gain from Investment − Cost of Investment)/Cost of Investment.
10. *Salary increase percentage.* Use the TREND function to analyze the trend: = TREND(G2:G7).

CHAPTER **11**

# Supply Chain and Distributor Analytics

Supply chain and distributor analytics function in modern industries within the global environment. Next, supply chain and distributor analytics influence the strategy-making process along with operational efficiency. Supply chain management focuses on the entire process, including the production and distribution of goods that are transformed from raw materials to the end customer. This process requires a strong and reliable network of suppliers, manufacturers, warehouses, transportation, and retailers. For effective supply chain management to exist, products must be delivered at the right time, at the right quantity, and at the lowest cost point possible. This situation will ensure that the company can reduce waste while maximizing customer satisfaction.

Business analytics becomes a part of supply chain management by studying the techniques used to support the decision-making process within a manufacturing company. By analyzing data that has been collected through multiple stages of the supply chain, manufacturers can identify trends, predict future demands, and optimize their daily business processes. As a result, supply chain and distributor analytics provide a data-driven approach to reduce costs, improve performance, and streamline daily operations. Within the supply chain and distributor industries, business analytics will be used to maximize inventory levels, improve supplier performance, and predict demand in the future based on the changes in the market.

Finally, supply chain and distributor analytics support the collaborative process among their various stakeholder groups within the supply chain and distribution channels. The situation is achieved through the sharing of knowledge and information so that suppliers, distributors, and retailers can better align their business strategies to ensure that the necessary level of supply and demand is met within the market. Next, collaboration through business analytics can improve customer satisfaction levels by guaranteeing the availability of products that arrive to retailers or customers in a timely fashion. As a result, the relationship between supply chain and distributors, combined with business analytics, will enable manufacturers in today's global environment to become flexible and adapt to the changing demands of consumers to create sustainable growth.

## SUPPLY CHAIN PERFORMANCE METRICS

Supply chain management involves the collaboration and coordination of all business processes necessary to convert raw materials and finished products so they can be

DOI: 10.4324/9781003629658-11

delivered to retailers and, ultimately, consumers within the market. This strategy requires a network of synchronous activities that include sourcing, production, warehousing, transportation, and distribution of materials and products. Within this process, distributors become the main intermediaries that manage the transportation of goods between the manufacturer, the retailer, and then the consumer. As a result, this process requires reliance on business analytics to create a systematic process that supports data-driven decision-making.

By using business analytics, manufacturing companies can identify new patterns related to the behavior and preferences of consumers along with new trends in the market. This situation is made possible through supply chain performance metrics. Supply chain performance metrics are analytical tools that measure the efficiency and effectiveness of the supply chain operation. Performance metrics that are measured include inventory turnover, lead time, and order accuracy to ensure that consumer satisfaction has been achieved and can be measured using reliable indicators.

In distributor industries, performance metrics are used to explain the efficiency of the distribution channels or networks. Metrics to evaluate this process include order fulfillment rates, transportation costs and delivery performance to enable distributors to determine the effectiveness of the current business operation. Through a regular analysis of these performance metrics, distributors can reduce costs, mitigate risk, improve service levels, and optimize their logistics throughout the market. As a result, the integration of supply chain management, distributor functions, business analytics, and performance metrics will create a data-driven structure that leads to operational excellence and efficiency. Supply chain and distributor companies that take advantage of the collaboration of these elements will become more responsive in the dynamic and competitive global environment to increase the value they offer to their customers.

## Key Indicators for Evaluating Supply Chain Effectiveness

There are key indicators in evaluating supply chain effectiveness using business analytics. To determine the effectiveness of supply chain operations, companies must rely on a variety of key performance indicators. These metrics and indicators will produce quantifiable results that enable businesses to conduct a comprehensive assessment of their supply chain. Common key performance indicators for the supply chain management process follow:

- *Order fulfillment rate.* Measures the percentage of consumer orders that are completed and delivered on time. The higher the fulfillment rate, the more responsive and efficient the supply chain.
- *Inventory turnover.* Determines how often inventory is sold over time. The higher the turnover rate, the more effective the inventory management process, and the more holding costs are minimized.
- *Lead time.* Measures the amount of time required for order placement delivery to occur. When there are shorter lead times, customer satisfaction is increased due to the continuous operation within the supply chain process.

- *Cost per order.* A metric that determines the total cost associated with processing the delivery of an order. This KPI identifies areas for efficiency improvements and cost reduction.
- *Supplier performance.* Studies the quality and reliability of suppliers to guarantee that companies work with distributors to meet their current standards, necessary for maintaining supply chain efficiency.

When business analytics tools are used to monitor KPIs, suppliers and distributors can develop a full understanding of the performance of their supply chain management process. However, this process will require a continuous evaluation of these performance indicators to ensure that companies remain capable of identifying strengths, weaknesses, opportunities, and threats to streamline processes and make data-driven decisions to improve their competitive advantage within the global environment.

## INVENTORY MANAGEMENT ANALYTICS

Supply chain and distributor analytics involve all aspects that are involved in the sourcing, production, and delivery of materials and goods throughout the supply chain management process. Within this process, distributors act as the connection required to manage the flow of production from manufacturer to retailers to consumers. Next, distributors have several responsibilities, including warehousing, family distribution of goods, and inventory control, which is required in maintaining customer satisfaction and product availability within the market. As a result, an effective inventory management is necessary in reducing holding costs while also meeting the demand of consumers. It is this reason that predictive business analytics is required to provide data analysis and statistical modeling to determine new inventory patterns, changes in consumer behavior, and sales trends.

Next, within the supply chain and distributor industries, inventory management, analytics will support various key functions that include demand forecasting, inventory optimization, supplier management, cost analysis, and performance monitoring detailed in the table that follows.

**TABLE 11.1** Inventory Management Analytics for Supply Chain and Distributor

| Metrics | Supply Chain | Distributor |
|---|---|---|
| **Demand forecasting** | High accuracy in predicting demand | Moderate accuracy in predicting demand |
| **Inventory optimization** | Optimal stock levels maintained | Adequate stock levels maintained |
| **Supplier management** | Effective supplier relationships | Good supplier relationships |
| **Cost analysis** | Detailed cost tracking and analysis | Basic cost tracking and analysis |
| **Performance management** | Continuous performance monitoring | Periodic performance monitoring |

**TABLE 11.2** Techniques for Optimizing Inventory Level

| Techniques | Supply Chain | Distributor |
|---|---|---|
| **Demand forecasting** | Predicting future demand accurately | Estimating future demand based on trends |
| **Inventory management systems** | Automated systems for tracking inventory | Manual or semi-automated inventory tracking |
| **Just-in-time (JIT) inventory** | Minimizing inventory holding costs | Reducing excess inventory |
| **Safety stock optimization** | Determining optimal safety stock levels | Setting safety stock based on historical data |
| **Supplier collaboration** | Working closely with suppliers | Maintaining good supplier relationships |

As a result, combination and integration of supply chain management, distributors, and business analytics greatly improve inventory management analytics. When these elements are combined and used together, companies can maximize their inventory processes. Second, businesses will become proactive in the changing demands of the market. Third, a combination of these elements ultimately leads to higher levels of consumer satisfaction within the global environment. As a result of this process, businesses can develop a competitive advantage within their current or new and emerging markets.

### Techniques for Optimizing Inventory Level

There are various techniques used in optimizing inventory levels within the supply chain and distribution as part of the supply chain management process. To optimize inventory levels, business analytics is required to take full advantage of advanced data analytics to allow companies to gain information and knowledge of their inventory performance strategies, the market trends, and the buying patterns of consumers. There are several key factors used by business analytics to assist companies in optimizing their inventory levels. These key factors include demand forecasting, inventory management systems, just-in-time inventory, safety stock, optimization, and supplier collaboration, which are detailed in Table 11.2.

## SUPPLIER PERFORMANCE EVALUATION

Supplier performance evaluation is determined by the success of the supply chain management system and all activities that are related to the managing of the flow of goods and services from raw materials to the end consumer. While distributors act as intermediaries and handle the logistical components of moving products from manufacturer to the consumer, effective supply chain management also relies on strong relationships with suppliers to make the supply chain successful. The situation is achieved by using business analytics integrated into the evaluation process. As a result of this integration, businesses can make data-driven and informed decisions to guarantee optimal management and the selection of suppliers.

There are five main components of the supplier performance evaluation process. The first is performance metrics. Performance metrics create KPIs necessary for evaluating supplier performance that include product quality, lead times, on-time delivery rates, cost effectiveness, and responsiveness. Second, data-driven insights study data that has been collected from various suppliers. So companies can develop new knowledge into the reliability and performance of suppliers by uncovering patterns that can indicate potential risks that include quality issues and frequent delays of shipments.

The third component is benchmarking. Benchmarking is a business analytics tool that allows companies to compare performance against competitors or industry standards. This comparison enables companies to identify high-performing suppliers along with those who need improvement to ensure the highest level of effectiveness in the supply chain. The fourth component is supplier scorecards that create a comprehensive analysis of the performance of suppliers based on the compilation of data metrics that provide a complete assessment of every individual supplier.

The final component is collaboration and communication. This analysis is important to determine the performance of a supplier and to develop effective communication with all suppliers in the process. When performance information is shared, businesses can directly engage with suppliers in open discussions about potential risks and areas requiring improvement within the process. As a result of these components, a strong relationship will be formed between supply chain management, suppliers, and distributors with supportive business analytics to enable everyone to make data-driven decisions and to become more strategically aligned within the delivery of goods and services.

## Data-Driven Approaches to Assess Supplier Reliability

There are data-driven approaches to assess supplier reliability. These data-driven approaches include performance metrics, addictive analytics, real-time monitoring, risk assessment, and root cause analysis. Performance metrics include on-time delivery rates, quality of production, order accuracy, and response times. Predictive analytics studies the past behavior of suppliers so companies can identify trends to predict future issues, delays, or quality defects. Real-time monitoring is the capability to identify deviations from normal performance standards in real time, including defect rates and late deliveries.

Risk assessments study all geographic and social economic influences, historical performance, and financial stability that can directly cause issues with the reliability of suppliers. Finally, cause analysis allows businesses to analyze data to identify the underlying reasons that contribute to all performance problems that are related to the processes, materials used, or external conditions to the supplier. As a result of these analytical tools, companies can better understand all the causes and reasons to develop a more focused strategy based on open communication and process improvements to correct specific issues.

The approaches to assess supplier reliability using business analytics and data-driven approaches are provided in the chart that follows.

**TABLE 11.3** Data-Driven Approaches to Assess Supplier Reliability

| Approaches | Supply Chain | Distributor |
|---|---|---|
| **Key performance indicators (KPIs)** | Tracking supplier performance using KPIs | Evaluating supplier performance with KPIs |
| **Predictive analytics** | Using historical data to predict supplier reliability | Analyzing trends to forecast supplier reliability |
| **Real-time monitoring** | Monitoring supplier activities in real time | Tracking supplier operations in real time |
| **Risk assessment** | Assessing potential risks associated with suppliers | Evaluating risks related to suppliers |
| **Root cause analysis** | Identifying the root causes of supplier issues | Determining the root causes of supplier problems |

## DEMAND FORECASTING IN SUPPLY CHAINS

Demand forecasting is an important component optimizing the efficiency and effectiveness across supply chains in various industries that rely on supply chain management, distributors, and business analytics. Demand forecasting is an important component of supply chain management that is used to directly influence the multiple operational activities of the company. With demand forecasting, businesses can predict future product demand and align their manufacturing, procurement, and distribution strategies appropriately. The situation requires a relationship between demand forecasting, supply chain management, and business analytics to develop a conducive environment for the maximization of inventory levels and an improved delivery of services.

There are various elements in supply chains that include optimizing inventory levels, enhancing resource allocation, improving customer satisfaction, mitigating risk, and collaboration and communication. First, demand forecasting enables businesses to maintain the necessary level of inventory to reduce the risk of stock outs or experiencing excess and surplus of goods. This situation develops the balance required to minimize holding costs while also guaranteeing that products are available to meet the changing needs of consumers. Within this process, distributors play a critical role in effectively managing these inventory levels based on the forecasted levels of demand.

Second, enhancing resource allocation is conducted through the accurate demand forecasts accompanies to allocate resources more effectively and efficiently to support their strategic initiatives. When companies understand fluctuations in future demand, they can accurately modify and adjust their production schedules, logistics plans, and workforce allocation. As a result, suppliers and distributors can develop a proactive approach that minimizes waste and maximizes the usage of resources.

Third, improving customer satisfaction will require demand forecasting to enable companies to guarantee timely availability of products to the consumer market. The situation is necessary for the improvement of order fulfillments and consumer satisfaction levels. As a result, achieving consumer expectations about the availability of products or services will improve brand loyalty and competitiveness from the global market.

Fourth, mitigating risks is based on businesses using analytics to study past sales data to determine all external factors that directly influence demand that include economic conditions and seasonal demand levels of goods and services. When these components are understood, companies will become better prepared to manage unexpected changes and fluctuations in the environment. As a result, businesses in all industries can develop and implement contingency plans to reduce potential risks to their supply chain management system.

Finally, collaboration and communication as part of the supply chain management process will guarantee that all stakeholder groups, including suppliers and distributors, are strategically aligned with the predicted demand forecasts. As a result of this collaborative alignment, suppliers and distributors will experience improvement in communication channels that allow for real-time adjustments to delivery schedules and the production of goods and services. As a result, the combination of these factors will allow companies in various industries within the global market to improve their daily operations, address the needs of the consumer, improve the allocation of resources, reduce risk, prove operational efficiency, and gain a competitive advantage over their competitors.

## Employing Analytics to Predict Consumer Demands

All companies contained in the various industries of the global market that rely on a supply chain management system must employ analytics to predict consumer demands. This process requires several methods within business analytics to empower the prediction of consumer demands by a company. The first method is data collection and integration. In today's global environment, supply chains create large amounts of data from multiple sources, including inventory levels, market trends, sales transactions, and interactions with customers. Business analytics is required to integrate this data into the supply chain management system to enable companies to develop a comprehensive understanding of their daily operations and to predict the future demands of consumers.

The second method is historical trend analysis. Historical trend analysis analyzes past sales data using statistical methods to enable companies to identify new trends and patterns that can directly influence future consumer behavior. As a result, this analysis provides companies with the ability to anticipate changes in consumer demand and make adjustments to the current strategies to meet these new developments. The third method is predictive modeling. This type of modeling uses advanced analytics techniques that include AI and machine learning algorithms to create predictive models to predict the future demand of consumers based on external factors and historical data. As a result, predictive modeling takes into account all variables that include changes in the demographics, economic indicators, and competitive environments to create a better prediction of consumer demands.

The fourth method is real-time analytics. Real-time analytics provides companies with the ability to study data in real time so they can quickly respond to changes in consumer behaviors and preferences or dynamics in the market. Through constantly monitoring the performance of sales and inventory levels, companies can improve their demand predictions and make immediate changes to their distribution and production strategies.

The final method is collaboration with distributors. Collaboration with distributors improves accuracy in demand predictions through the sharing of sales data, market intelligence, and inventory levels to both the manufacturer and the distributor. The ability to share data will help both manufacturers and distributors strategically align their supply chain strategies. As a result, improved communication channels will guarantee that all stakeholder groups are working toward a shared common goal of meeting consumer demand more effectively and efficiently in the market.

## LOGISTICS OPTIMIZATION TECHNIQUES

There are various logistics optimization techniques as part of business analytics in the supply chain management process. These optimization techniques include route optimization, inventory management, demand forecasting, and performance monitoring. First, route optimization includes the statistical analysis of historical shipping data, geographical information, and traffic patterns to determine the most efficient roots for the transportation of materials or goods. When delivery routes are optimized, companies can reduce their consumption of fuel, lower transportation costs, and minimize delivery times.

Next, inventory management requires effective maximization of logistics to create an effective inventory management system. Using business analytics, companies are provided with knowledge of their current levels of inventory, demand forecast, and turnover rates that enable them to maintain the necessary level of stock on hand. When her levels and logistical capabilities of the business are to be aligned, the company can reduce carrying costs while also ensuring the availability of products to consumers.

Third, demand forecasting is necessary for logistics planning. Through the analysis of past sales data and market trends, business analytics support companies by anticipating changes in demand. These new data-driven insights will enable businesses to accurately adjust their logistic strategy so they can increase or decrease their capacity of transportation for materials or goods depending on the projected need.

Fourth, performance monitoring requires the use of key performance indicators that include delivery times, accuracy of orders, and cost per shipment to determine the performance of the logistics operation. When these metrics are evaluated, the supplier or distributor can identify potential slowdowns and other areas for improvement within process required to enhance the efficiency of the daily operation.

Finally, supplier and distributor collaboration involves the sharing of information among supply chain partners to maximize logistics process. When information and data are shared, suppliers, distributors, and manufacturers can work together to align their logistics operations more effectively. As a result of this collaborative process, all three contributors can work together to better plan and execute their logistic strategy to reduce costs and improve service.

### Using Data to Enhance Logistics and Transportation Strategies

Data can be used to enhance logistics and transportation strategies using various methods of business analytics to drive improvements that include route optimization, predictive analytics, real-time tracking and visibility, cost management and reduction, and collaboration with suppliers and distributors. Round optimization relies on the analysis of past data in advanced analytics to help companies maximize transportation routes. When factors such as delivery windows, traffic patterns, and fuel costs are analyzed, the business can reduce transit time to improve the efficiency of deliveries.

Predictive analytics uses predictive modeling to forecast transportation needs based on past trends and seasonal demand of materials and goods. These forecasts enable businesses to predict changes and shipment volumes to allow them to adjust their logistics operation more proactively to plan for additional transportation capacity during peak seasons of the year, while preventing interruptions in the service.

Real-time tracking uses business analytics to identify real-time tracking systems for shipments. This situation gives companies the ability to understand the status of deliveries to ensure timely responses to any unpredictable delays, like issues caused by changes to the route. Factors that must be studied include costs related to fuel, warehousing, and freight. As a result of real-time tracking, companies can maintain transparency and develop trust within their supply chain management process while improving consumer communication and reliability services.

Cost management and reduction is a business analytics function that examines transportation costs in detail to identify new opportunities for cost savings. When these expenditures are analyzed, the cost of fuel, warehousing, and freight can be determined to renegotiate contracts with suppliers and distributors to maximize shipping methods. As a result of this process, the company can create a more efficient operational budget and allocation of resources.

Finally, collaboration with suppliers and distributors requires the sharing of data between supply chain partners to improve the planning of transportation of goods and services. Through collaboration, shared analysis demand forecasts or levels can be conducted to enable all parties to develop a unified logistics approach that will lead to more efficient transportation. As a result of collaboration with suppliers and distributors, the supply chain management process will become more adaptable, flexible, and responsive to the changing needs of the market.

## RISK MANAGEMENT IN SUPPLY CHAINS

Risk management is an important function for suppliers and distributors in supply chains. There are several ways in which business analytics will support supply chain risk management, which include risk identification, assessments, predictive analytics, scenario planning, supply chain visibility, supplier and distributor collaboration. *Risk identification assessment* is the analytical process of collecting and analyzing data from various sources to help the company identify any potential risk within the supply chain. Potential risks to the supply chain include geopolitical issues, market changes, supplier reliability, and natural disasters. By analyzing the chance or impact of potential risk, suppliers and distributors can place priorities on risks and manage them accordingly.

Second, *predictive analytics* use predictive modeling to forecast any potential disruptions in the supply chain based on past trends or historical data. Examples of the interruption supply chains include transportation challenges, economic downturns, or natural disasters. By using predictive analytics, suppliers and distributors can become proactive in mitigating risk and minimizing the impact of disruptions in the supply chain management system.

Third, *scenario planning* is the process of simulating chances or events of risk in evaluating the potential impact on the performance of the supply chain management process. With this approach, companies can develop contingency plans to help guarantee that they are fully prepared to respond effectively to unexpected situations in real time instead of being reactive to their competitors in the market.

Fourth, supply chain visibility is necessary for effective risk management. Using business analytics, suppliers and distributors are given the capability of tracking inventory levels, order status, and shipment locations in real time. The situation creates a higher level of transparency that enables a business to effectively identify any potential issues that arise and to implement corrective action to minimize potential disruptions based on data-driven analysis.

Finally, supplier and distributor collaboration develops strong relationships that are important for the management in the mitigation of risk. By sharing data and information that are related to all factors of risk, suppliers and distributors can work together to develop effective risk mitigation strategies. As a result, the partnership between supplier and distributor will improve the communication process and strengthen the ability of the supply chain management system to overcome obstacles and changes in the market. As a result, all these factors will create a comprehensive approach to mitigate risk disruptions while also providing some supply chain management system of companies in various industries to ensure operational continuity and to meet the changing demands and behaviors of customers.

## Data Analytics for Identifying and Mitigating Supply Chain Risks

Data analytics is required in identifying and mitigating supply chain risks. When identifying and mitigating supply chain risks, an integrated approach must be used to enable companies to develop a stronger and reliable supply chain, improve decision-making, and guarantee operational continuity in the dynamic and changing global environment. There are various techniques used to integrate and identify supply chain risks, including data collection, ratio, risk assessment, predictive modeling, scenario analysis, real-time monitoring, alerts, and collaboration and communication. First, data collection and integration is an important component of business analytics since it allows for data from various sources to be studied, including market trends, internal operations, and supplier performance. By analyzing these datasets, suppliers and distributors can develop a more comprehensive understanding of their supply chain, which will lead to the identification of risk.

Second, risk assessment requires the use of advanced analytics by companies to determine the potential of risks associated with different suppliers, distributors, and other logistics partners. Next, risk assessment is achieved by studying past data to help companies identify new patterns and trends that were directly related to previous disruptions. This information can include trends related to quality failures and late deliveries. As a result, risk assessments enable companies to prioritize the risk management strategies based on the potential and chance of impacting the supply chain management system based on the identified risks.

Third, predictive modeling will be used to study predictive analytics that forecast potential supply chain disruptions. When past trends and external variables that include natural disasters, geopolitical factors, and economic indicators are studied, the company can anticipate future challenges and develop a proactive strategy. As a result, predictive modeling will lead to more informed decision-making and help the supplier and distributor become more prepared to deal with potential risks within the global environment.

Fourth, scenario analysis helps suppliers and distributors simulate scenarios related to various risks and evaluate the potential of their impact on the daily operation of the supply chain management system. This strategy enables companies to understand how different risks might affect or impact the performance of the supply chain, also providing the ability to develop contingency plans that are customized to meet the specific risk scenarios that have been developed.

Fifth, real-time monitoring and alerts using advanced analytics will provide continuous monitoring of all supply chain activities in real time to detect various risk factors. When companies implement real-time monitoring and alerts, all deviations from the expected level of performance are identified. The situation enables the company to respond quickly to emerging issues, risks that include transportation disruptions or delays by suppliers to help minimize the impact on the daily operation.

Finally, collaboration and communication are important in identifying and mitigating supply chain risks. When there are enhanced data sharing capabilities among suppliers, distributors, and other supply chain partners, everyone will experience improvements in communication about the potential risks to the process. When suppliers and distributors work closely together, both entities can work collaboratively to develop effective risk management strategies and to adjust their supply chain management operation, which is needed to mitigate the identified risks. As a result, using data analytics, predictive modeling, scenario analysis, real-time monitoring, and collaboration and communication, suppliers and distributors can strengthen their supply chain strategies to overcome risks and uncertainties in a constantly dynamic and changing global business environment and all types of industries.

## BUSINESS ANALYTICS FUNCTION FOR SUPPLY CHAIN AND DISTRIBUTION USING MICROSOFT EXCEL

In the business environment, there are many business analytical terms mentioned that play a critical role in making informed and data-driven choices that drive decisions, optimize daily operations, and develop strategic actions and initiatives. Various statistical concepts play an important role in supply chain and distribution and business analytics by providing essential tools for data analysis and decision-making. Here's a detailed overview of their definition and importance and how to conduct this statistical analysis using Microsoft Excel.

### Blended Models in Linear Optimization

These models combine different types of optimization techniques to enhance decision-making. In supply chain management, blended models allow businesses to address complex problems, such as inventory management and logistics optimization, that lead to improved overall performance.

**Steps:**

1. Define your problem and identify the different types of optimizations you will employ.
2. Set up separate sheets in Excel for each modeling type (i.e., linear model in one sheet, nonlinear in another).
3. Use the results from one model as input data for another model.

## Constraints of Linear Optimization

Understanding constraints is necessary as they define the limitations or restrictions within which optimization must occur. In supply chain analytics, constraints can include budget limits, resource availability, and production capabilities. Properly identifying and managing these constraints ensures that solutions are practical and applicable in real-world scenarios.

**Steps:**

1. Identify all relevant constraints (i.e., resource limits, budget caps).
2. In Excel, create a table or list outlining each constraint clearly, alongside its mathematical expression.
3. Ensure these constraints are established in the model you will optimize using Solver.

## Developing Linear Optimization Models

Creating these models involves defining variables, objectives, and constraints that accurately represent the business problem. In supply chain management, this process allows organizations to simulate different scenarios and identify optimal solutions for production scheduling, transportation, and inventory control.

**Steps:**

1. Define your objective function in a cell.
2. List decision variables in adjacent cells.
3. Set constraints in separate cells using formulas to reflect specific limits.
4. Ensure the objective function cell references the decision variables and constraints.

## Graphing Linear Optimization Models

The visual representation of linear optimization models helps in understanding the possible region defined by constraints and the potential solutions. By graphing these models, decision-makers can quickly assess impacts, visualize trade-offs, and communicate findings to stakeholders effectively.

**Steps:**

1. Input your constraints as equations (using slopes) in a format suitable for graphing.
2. Use the Insert tab and choose Scatter to plot the constraints.
3. Highlight the reasonable region defined by the intersection of constraints.
4. Mark the objective function line to visualize where it intersects the feasible region.

## Linear Optimization

This technique is used to maximize or minimize a linear objective function subject to linear constraints. It is important in supply chain decision-making, which enables businesses to achieve the optimal use of resources, maximize profits, or minimize costs in areas like transportation and warehousing.

**Steps:**

1. Establish an objective function to maximize or minimize.
2. List all constraints in terms of decision variables.
3. Use the Solver tool to optimize your model based on these parameters.

## Objectives of Linear Optimization

Clearly defined objectives guide the optimization process. In supply chains, objectives may include optimizing transportation costs, maximizing production efficiency, or improving service levels. Aligning objectives with wider business goals ensures that optimization efforts contribute to overall organizational success.

**Steps:**

1. Write down your primary objective in a dedicated cell.
2. Ensure this objective is included in the function being optimized using Solver.

## Solver and Alternative Optimal Solution

The Solver tool in Excel provides solutions to optimization problems that include the identification of alternative optimal solutions. Recognizing multiple solutions can provide flexibility in decision-making, which allows businesses to adapt strategies based on changing conditions or constraints.

**Steps:**

1. Set up your linear optimization model and run Solver (Data tab > Solver).
2. After finding an optimal solution, check the option for "Sensitivity Report" or "Answer Report."
3. Review the report to see if alternative solutions exist and how changes in constraints might yield different optimal values.

## Solver and Infeasibility

An *infeasibility* occurs when no solution meets all constraints. Understanding this concept is critical in identifying when adjustments to constraints or objectives may be needed. In supply chain management, addressing infeasibility ensures that operational plans can be realistically implemented.

**Steps:**

1. Run Solver, and if you receive an "infeasible" message, review the constraints.
2. Check to ensure no constraints contradict each other and that they accurately reflect real-world limits.
3. Adjust or loosen constraints as necessary to achieve feasibility.

## Solver and Unbound Solution

An unbound solution arises when the optimization model lacks upper or lower bounds for the objective function. Recognizing unbounded solutions is crucial to determining necessary constraints to develop possible and actionable plans for resource allocation.

**Steps:**

1. Set up the optimization model and attempt to run Solver.
2. If you receive a message about an "unbounded" solution, then check your constraints.
3. Ensure you have defined the necessary upper or lower bounds for your decision variables to avoid them being unbounded.

## Solver and Unique Optimal Solution

Identifying a unique optimal solution is important as it indicates the most efficient use of resources given the specified constraints. In supply chain applications, unique solutions can improve operational effectiveness and streamline processes.

**Steps:**

1. Use Solver to find the optimal solution.
2. Look for a message that confirms the solution is unique, or review the sensitivity report to identify multiple optimal values.
3. If multiple optimal solutions exist, analyze the probability of each to determine the best course of action.

## Solver Function in Excel

The Solver function is a key tool for running linear optimization scenarios within Excel, allowing users to create and analyze models easily. Its integration with Excel empowers supply chain managers to make data-driven decisions quickly and efficiently.

**Steps:**

1. Navigate to the Data tab and choose Solver.
2. Set the objective by selecting a cell and choosing whether to maximize, minimize, or achieve a specific value.
3. Define the variable cells that Solver can change.
4. Add constraints by clicking on Add in the Solver dialog box.
5. Click Solve to find the optimal solution.

### Variables of Linear Optimization

Variables represent the decision options within the optimization model. Understanding how to define and manipulate these variables allows businesses to tailor solutions to specific supply chain challenges, optimizing areas like production allocation, inventory levels, and transportation routes.

**Steps:**

1. In your Excel spreadsheet, designate a section or column for the decision variables. These can include quantities of products to produce, amounts of resources to allocate, or any other quantifiable elements.
2. Clearly label each decision variable in the adjacent column for easy reference.
3. Input initial values for each decision variable, which can be estimates or zeros to start.
4. Ensure that your objective function and constraints reference these decision variable cells.

## REAL-WORLD EXAMPLES OF SUPPLY CHAIN AND DISTRIBUTOR INSIGHTS DRIVING BUSINESS SUCCESS

### Volkswagen Group

The Volkswagen Group engages in advanced data analytics to optimize its global supply chain and allows real-time monitoring of inventory levels and production schedules. This data-driven approach enables Volkswagen to respond quickly to changes in market demand, reducing lead times and minimizing excess inventory. Next is Volkswagen's implementation of predictive analytics in demand forecasting. By analyzing historical sales data and market trends, Volkswagen can accurately predict future demand for specific models and components while ensuring that production aligns with consumer preferences. Finally, Volkswagen uses data analytics to assess supplier performance, allowing the company to identify potential risks and make informed decisions about partnerships. By a thorough monitoring of supply chain metrics, Volkswagen ensures high quality and timely delivery of components.

### Question 1

How does the Volkswagen Group use advanced data analytics to optimize its global supply chain, and what are the benefits of this approach?

Answer: The Volkswagen Group employs advanced data analytics to optimize its global supply chain by enabling the real-time monitoring of inventory levels and production schedules. This data-driven approach allows Volkswagen to quickly respond to changes in market demand that help in reducing lead times and minimizing excess inventory. The benefits of this approach include improved efficiency in production and distribution processes, cost savings from reduced inventory holding, and improved consumer satisfaction due to the real-time delivery of products. By leveraging data analytics, Volkswagen can maintain a competitive edge in the automotive industry by ensuring that its supply chain operations are flexible and responsive to market dynamics.

### Question 2

In what ways does Volkswagen implement predictive analytics for demand forecasting, and how does this impact production alignment with consumer preferences?

Answer: Volkswagen relies on predictive analytics for demand forecasting by analyzing historical sales data and market trends. This strategy allows the company to accurately predict future demand for specific models and components. By understanding these demand patterns, Volkswagen can adjust its production schedules to align with consumer preferences while ensuring that the right products are available at the right time. This strategy helps with meeting customer expectations and optimizes resource allocation and reduces waste. Finally, the impact of predictive analytics on production alignment is significant since it enables Volkswagen to produce vehicles that are in high demand to maximize sales and market share.

### Question 3

How does Volkswagen use data analytics to assess supplier performance, and what are the implications for supply chain management?

Answer: Volkswagen uses data analytics to assess supplier performance by monitoring various supply chain metrics, such as delivery times, quality of components, and reliability of suppliers. By analyzing this data, Volkswagen can identify potential risks and areas for improvement in its supplier relationships. This analytical assessment allows the company to make informed decisions about partnerships while ensuring that it collaborates with suppliers who meet its standards for quality and reliability. The implications for supply chain management are important since this approach improves the overall efficiency and effectiveness of the supply chain. Finally, data analytics ensures high-quality and timely delivery of components, reduces the risk of disruptions, and creates collaborative relationships with suppliers, contributing to Volkswagen's success in the automotive market.

## ExxonMobil Corporation

ExxonMobil Corporation relies on advanced data analytics to optimize its supply chain operations to allow for real-time monitoring of inventory levels and logistics. This analytical approach allows ExxonMobil to respond in real time to fluctuations in market demand and adjusts production schedules accordingly. Next, ExxonMobil uses predictive analytics in forecasting oil and gas production. By analyzing geological data and past production trends, ExxonMobil can correctly predict future output to make informed decisions about resource allocation and investment. Finally, ExxonMobil implements analytics to evaluate supplier performance, allowing the company to mitigate risks associated with the procurement process. By analyzing supplier data, ExxonMobil identifies potential disruptions and proactively addresses them to enhance efficiency, reduce costs, and improve overall performance in the energy market.

**Question 1**

How does ExxonMobil use advanced data analytics to optimize its supply chain operations, and what are the benefits of real-time monitoring?

Answer: ExxonMobil uses advanced data analytics to enhance its supply chain operations by enabling real-time monitoring of inventory levels and logistics. This approach allows the company to quickly respond to changes in market demand while ensuring that production schedules are adjusted as necessary. The benefits of real-time monitoring include reduced lead times, minimized excess inventory, and improved operational efficiency. By having immediate access to data, ExxonMobil can make informed decisions that strategically align with current market conditions and lead to cost savings and enhanced customer satisfaction.

**Question 2**

In what ways does ExxonMobil use predictive analytics in forecasting oil and gas production, and how does this impact resource allocation and investment decisions?

Answer: ExxonMobil uses predictive analytics by analyzing geological data and past production trends to forecast future oil and gas output. This capability allows the company to make informed decisions regarding resource allocation and investment. By correctly predicting production levels, ExxonMobil can optimize its exploration and extraction activities, ensuring that resources are efficiently allocated. This strategic approach not only maximizes production potential but also minimizes risks associated with overproduction or the underutilization of resources, leading to more effective investment strategies and improved financial performance.

**Question 3**

How does ExxonMobil implement analytics to evaluate supplier performance, and what are the advantages of identifying potential disruptions in the procurement process?

Answer: ExxonMobil uses data analytics to assess supplier performance by analyzing various metrics related to supplier reliability, quality, and delivery times. By identifying potential disruptions in the procurement process, ExxonMobil can proactively address issues before they impact daily operations. The advantages of this analytical approach include enhanced efficiency, reduced costs, and improved overall performance in the energy market. By maintaining strong supplier relationships and guaranteeing a reliable supply chain, ExxonMobil can mitigate risks, maintain production continuity, and defend its reputation of delivering high-quality products to its customers.

## Samsung SDI

Samsung SDI uses data analytics to streamline its supply chain processes to guarantee the immediate delivery of raw materials and components essential for production. This analytical approach allows Samsung SDI to maintain efficient inventory levels while reducing costs associated with excess stock. Next, Samsung SDI uses predictive analytics to forecast demand for electric vehicle batteries. By analyzing market trends and consumer behavior data, Samsung SDI can adjust its production schedules to align with anticipated demand fluctuations while enabling the company to respond proactively to market changes. Finally, Samsung SDI analyzes supplier performance through data-driven metrics by identifying areas of improvement and potential risks within its supply chain. This knowledge improves collaboration and reliability among its suppliers and distributor channels.

**Question 1**

How does Samsung SDI use data analytics to optimize its supply chain processes, and what are the benefits of this approach?

Answer: Samsung SDI uses data analytics to modernize its supply chain processes by ensuring the immediate delivery of raw materials and components essential for production. This analytical approach allows the company to maintain efficient inventory levels, reducing costs associated with excess stock. By leveraging real-time data, Samsung SDI can monitor inventory levels and logistics while enabling them to respond swiftly to changes in demand. The benefits of this approach include improved operational efficiency, cost savings, and the ability to meet production targets without overstocking, which is necessary in maintaining a competitive edge in the market.

**Question 2**

In what ways does Samsung SDI apply predictive analytics to forecast demand for electric vehicle batteries, and how does this impact their production strategy?

Answer: Samsung SDI applies predictive analytics by analyzing market trends and consumer behavior data to forecast demand for electric vehicle batteries. This involves examining historical sales data, market growth projections, and consumer preferences to anticipate future demand fluctuations. Next, Samsung SDI can adjust its production schedules to align with anticipated demand while ensuring that they can meet market needs without overproducing. This proactive strategy enables the company to respond effectively to market changes, maximize resource allocation, and maintain a balance between supply and demand to improve their market responsiveness and competitiveness.

**Question 3**

How does Samsung SDI's analysis of supplier performance contribute to improved collaboration and reliability within its supply chain?

Answer: Samsung SDI analyzes supplier performance through data-driven metrics to identify areas for improvement and potential risks within its supply chain. By evaluating supplier data, the company can pinpoint inefficiencies, assess the reliability of suppliers, and address any issues that may occur. This knowledge enables Samsung SDI to create improved collaboration with suppliers by setting clear expectations and performance standards. Improved supplier performance leads to more reliable delivery of components, reduced risk of disruptions, and enhanced overall supply chain efficiency. This collaborative approach strengthens relationships with suppliers and ensures a more resilient and responsive supply chain.

## NVIDIA Corporation

The NVIDIA Corporation relies on data analytics to optimize its supply chain processes while enabling real-time visibility to inventory levels and production schedules. This capability allows NVIDIA to immediately respond to changes in demand within the highly competitive graphics processing unit (GPU) market. A notable example is the application of predictive analytics to forecast component availability and manage supplier relationships. By analyzing historical data and market trends, NVIDIA can anticipate potential shortages or delays in component delivery, allowing proactive measures to mitigate risks. Next, NVIDIA implements analytics to optimize its logistics operations by assessing transportation routes and costs to improve distribution efficiency. This data-driven approach supports the timely delivery of products to customers worldwide. Through these analytical insights, the NVIDIA Corporation demonstrates how effectively managed supply chain strategies can drive innovation and meet growing customer demands in an evolving market.

### Question 1

How does the NVIDIA Corporation use data analytics to optimize its supply chain processes, and what are the benefits of real-time visibility on inventory levels and production schedules?

Answer: The NVIDIA Corporation leverages data analytics to enhance its supply chain processes by providing real-time visibility on inventory levels and production schedules. This capability allows NVIDIA to quickly respond to changes in demand within the competitive GPU market. By having immediate access to inventory data, NVIDIA can make informed decisions about production adjustments while ensuring that they meet market demands without overproducing. This approach minimizes excess inventory and reduces lead times while enhancing the overall operational efficiency. Finally, the benefits of this real-time visibility include improved resource allocation, reduced waste, and the ability to maintain a competitive edge by quickly adapting to changes in the market.

### Question 2

In what ways does NVIDIA apply predictive analytics to manage supplier relationships and forecast component availability, and what are the potential outcomes of these practices?

Answer: NVIDIA applies predictive analytics by analyzing historical data and market trends to forecast component availability and manage supplier relationships effectively. This approach allows NVIDIA to anticipate potential shortages or delays in component delivery while allowing the company to take proactive measures to mitigate risks. By maintaining strong supplier relationships and having a clear understanding of component availability, NVIDIA can ensure a steady supply of necessary materials necessary to meet production targets. Finally, the potential outcomes of these practices include enhanced supply chain resilience, reduced risk of production disruptions, and the ability to maintain consistent product quality and delivery schedules.

**Question 3**

How does NVIDIA's use of data analytics in logistics operations contribute to improved distribution efficiency, and what impact does this have on customer satisfaction?

Answer: NVIDIA uses data analytics to optimize its logistics operations by assessing transportation routes and costs, which leads to improved distribution efficiency. By analyzing data related to shipping routes, delivery times, and transportation expenses, NVIDIA can identify the most cost-effective and timely methods for distributing its global products. This data-driven approach ensures that products are delivered to consumers promptly while reducing delays and enhancing the overall customer experience. The impact on consumer satisfaction is important since it includes timely delivery, which is a critical factor in customer loyalty and brand reputation. By constantly meeting or exceeding customer expectations, NVIDIA strengthens its competitive market advantage and develops long-term customer relationships.

---

## CASE STUDIES ON SUPPLY CHAIN AND DISTRIBUTOR SUCCESS THROUGH ANALYTICS

### Business Success Through Business Analytics

Business analytics plays a crucial role in understanding supply chain & distributor trends and consumer behavior that enables organizations in the supply chain & distributor industry to make more data-driven and informed decisions. Following are three examples of how supply chain & distributor data and knowledge are translated into business success using analytics:

### Example 1: Modernized Logistics Inc.

Modernized Logistics Inc. is a leading supply chain company that specializes in optimizing transportation routes for its clients. By implementing advanced business analytics, Modernized Logistics has significantly reduced delivery times and costs. The company uses predictive analytics to anticipate potential disruptions in the supply chain, including weather conditions and traffic congestion, while allowing them to reroute shipments proactively. This approach has resulted in a 20% increase in on-time deliveries and a 15% reduction in transportation costs.

#### *Short-Response Questions*

1. What type of analytics does Modernized Logistics use to anticipate disruptions?
2. By what percentage did Modernized Logistics increase on delivery times?
3. What was the reduction in transportation costs achieved by Modernized Logistics?

### Example 2: Globalization Distributors Network (GDN)

Globalization Distributors Network (GDN) is a supply chain company that focuses on inventory management for retail clients. GDN has implemented a sophisticated analytics platform that provides real-time insights into inventory levels across multiple locations. By analyzing sales trends and customer demand patterns, GDN can optimize stock levels, reducing excess inventory by 15% and minimizing stockouts by 20%. This strategy has led to improved customer satisfaction and increased sales for their clients.

### *Short-Response Questions*

1. What does GDN's analytics platform provide insights into?
2. By what percentage did GDN reduce excess inventory?
3. How much did GDN minimize stockouts?

### Example 3: Effective Supply Solutions (ESS)

Effective Supply Solutions (ESS) is a distributor that specializes in streamlining the procurement process for manufacturing companies. ESS uses data analytics to evaluate supplier performance and negotiate better terms. By analyzing historical data and supplier metrics, ESS has improved supplier reliability by 30% and reduced procurement costs by 18%. This strategic use of analytics has improved the overall efficiency of their clients' supply chains.

### *Short-Response Questions*

1. What does ESS use data analytics to evaluate?
2. By what percentage did ESS improve supplier reliability?
3. What was the reduction in procurement costs achieved by ESS?

## CASE STUDY: GLOBAL SELL CHAIN SOLUTIONS INC.

Global Sell Chain Solutions Inc. (GSS) is a company specializing in supply chain management and distribution of services for consumer electronics. GSS has rapidly grown into a major player in the industry while providing a comprehensive range of services that include inventory management, transportation logistics, and supplier negotiations. Recently, the company was presented with the challenge of optimizing its distribution strategy across multiple suppliers while minimizing costs and maintaining delivery effectiveness. To achieve this goal, GSS implemented linear optimization models using Excel's Solver tool to identify cost-effective distribution strategies.

### Business Analytics Data Tables

**TABLE 11.4** Supplier Cost Structure

| 1 | A | B | C | D |
|---|---|---|---|---|
| | Supplier | Cost per Unit ($) | Monthly Supply Capacity (Units) | Minimum Order Quantity (Units) |
| 2 | Supplier A | 15 | 1,000 | 200 |
| 3 | Supplier B | 12 | 1,500 | 300 |
| 4 | Supplier C | 10 | 2,000 | 400 |
| 5 | Supplier D | 14 | 1,200 | 259 |

**TABLE 11.5** Demand Forecast

| 1 | A | B |
|---|---|---|
| | Month | Demand Requirements (Units) |
| 2 | January | 2,500 |
| 3 | February | 3,200 |
| 4 | March | 3,500 |
| 5 | April | 3,000 |

### Analytics Problems Using Excel

1. Develop a linear optimization model that determines the optimal order quantities from each supplier to minimize overall costs while meeting demand and adhering to supplier constraints. What are the objectives of this optimization model?
2. Use Excel's Solver function to find the unique optimal solution for the allocation of orders across suppliers. What constraints must be included in this optimization model, and how can Solver be used to identify infeasibility or unbounded solutions?
3. After deriving the initial solutions, assess the sensitivity of the model by graphing the optimal solution. How can alternative solutions be explored, and what implications do changes in supply costs or demand forecasts have for the linear optimization results?

### Answer Key

1. *Developing a linear optimization model.* Set up a cell for total cost, the objective function, which is the sum of products of the unit costs and order quantities from each supplier:
   Total Cost = (Cost per Unit) * (Order Quantity)
   Define the decision variables for the order quantities.
   The objective of the model is to minimize total cost while ensuring that the total ordered units meet or exceed demand across all months, along with ensuring each supplier's order conforms to minimum and maximum capacity.
2. *Using Excel's Solver function.* Go to Data > Solver, then set the objective to minimize the total cost cell. Add constraints:

   a. Total units from all suppliers must meet or exceed the monthly demand.
   b. Order quantities must be greater than or equal to each supplier's minimum order quantity.
   c. Order quantities must be less than or equal to the suppliers' maximum supply capacities.

   Click Solve to identify the optimal solution.
   If the Solver indicates infeasibility, check the constraints to ensure that they are realistically aligned with supplier capacities.
   For unbounded solutions, review constraints to prevent unlimited solutions, particularly around costs or demands.

3. *Assessing and graphing sensitivity of the model.* After obtaining the optimal solution, you can use the Excel graphing tools to plot the cost versus order quantities for visual analysis. To discover alternative solutions, adjust the cost per unit for one or more suppliers and re-run the Solver to see how the new constraints affect the allocation. Use data tables or Scenario Manager to understand how changes impact costs and supply arrangements. Understand that changes in demand will necessitate adapting order quantities, prompting a new Solver run, allowing exploration of sensitivity and responsiveness in supply chain strategies.

## CASE STUDY: SUPPLYCHAINDISTRIBUTION SOLUTIONS INC.

SupplyChainDistribution Solutions Inc. specializes in optimizing supply chain and distribution networks for businesses across multiple industries. The company has helped numerous clients streamline their logistics operations, reduce costs, and improve delivery times. Recently, SupplyChainDistribution Solutions Inc. partnered with a large manufacturing firm to improve their distribution network and address issues related to inventory management and transportation costs. To evaluate the impact of their recommendations, SupplyChain-Distribution Solutions Inc. collected data on key supply chain metrics that include inventory levels, transportation costs, and delivery times over six months. The data was analyzed using linear optimization techniques to identify the most efficient distribution strategies. The following tables summarize key findings from the project:

**TABLE 11.6** Inventory and Transportation Costs

| 1 | A | B | C |
|---|---|---|---|
| | **Month** | **Inventory Level (Units)** | **Transportation Costs ($)** |
| **2** | January | 10,000 | 50,000 |
| **3** | February | 11,000 | 52,000 |
| **4** | March | 12,000 | 54,000 |
| **5** | April | 13,000 | 56,000 |
| **6** | May | 14,000 | 58,000 |
| **7** | June | 15,000 | 60,000 |

**TABLE 11.7** Delivery Times and Customer Satisfaction

| 1 | A | B | C |
|---|---|---|---|
| | **Month** | **Average Delivery Time (Days)** | **Customer Satisfaction (%)** |
| **2** | January | 5 | 80 |
| **3** | February | 4.8 | 82 |
| **4** | March | 4.6 | 84 |
| **5** | April | 4.4 | 86 |
| **6** | May | 4.2 | 88 |
| **7** | June | 4.0 | 90 |

## Analytics Problems Using Excel

1. *Blended models in linear optimization.* Create a blended model to optimize inventory levels and transportation costs.
2. *Constraints of linear optimization.* Identify and apply constraints to the linear optimization model.
3. *Graphic linear optimization models.* Develop a graphic linear optimization model for delivery times.
4. *Linear optimization.* Perform linear optimization to minimize transportation costs.
5. *Solver and alternative optimal solution.* Use Solver to find alternative optimal solutions for inventory management.
6. *Solver and infeasibility.* Analyze infeasibility issues in the optimization model using Solver.
7. *Solver and unbound solution.* Address unbound solutions in the optimization model using Solver.
8. *Solver and unique optimal solution.* Find the unique optimal solution for minimizing delivery times using Solver.
9. *Solver function in Excel.* Utilize the Solver function in Excel to optimize customer satisfaction.
10. *Variables of linear optimization.* Define and manipulate variables in the linear optimization model.

## Answer Key

1. *Blended models in linear optimization.* Use the Solver tool to create a blended model. Set the objective to minimize transportation costs while maintaining optimal inventory levels.
2. *Constraints of linear optimization.* Define constraints, such as maximum inventory levels and budget limits. Example: Inventory <= 15,000 and Transportation Costs <= $60,000.
3. *Graphic linear optimization models.* Use Excel charts to visualize the optimization model. Plot delivery times against customer satisfaction.
4. *Linear optimization.* Use the Solver tool to minimize transportation costs. Set the objective function and constraints.
5. *Solver and alternative optimal solution.* Use Solver to find alternative solutions. Example: Data > Solver > Options > Allowable Increase/Decrease.
6. *Solver and infeasibility.* Analyze infeasibility by checking constraints and adjusting the model. Example: Data > Solver > Options > Show Infeasibility Report.
7. *Solver and unbound solution.* Address unbound solutions by setting realistic constraints. Example: Data > Solver > Options > Show Unbound Solution Report.
8. *Solver and unique optimal solution.* Find the unique optimal solution using Solver. Example: Data > Solver > Options > Show Unique Optimal Solution.
9. *Solver function in Excel.* Utilize Solver to optimize customer satisfaction. Example: Data > Solver > Set Objective > Maximize.
10. *Variables of linear optimization.* Define variables such as inventory levels and transportation costs. Manipulate variables using Solver to achieve optimal results.

CHAPTER 12

# Risk Mitigation Through Analytics

*Risk mitigation* is a process of developing strategies and implementing actions that are designed to reduce the impact of potential risks on an organization. Next, the process of risk mitigation involves identifying, assessing, and prioritizing tasks so that coordinated efforts can be made to minimize, monitor, and control the probability of a negative impact on events. The situation makes risk mitigation an important component of an organization strategy across various industries, including finance, health care, manufacturing, information technology, and instruction.

In finance, risk management is necessary to prevent losses and to guarantee that the firm meets all compliance standards and regulations established by the government. When financial companies use risk analytics, they possess the ability to monitor credit risk, operational risks, and market fluctuations. In health care, health-care providers reduce the level of risk involved with the maintenance of patient safety, guaranteeing compliance with regulations, and their supply chain management system. This situation requires the continual use of data analytics to monitor operational efficiencies and improvement of patient outcomes.

In the manufacturing industry, companies will experience risks that are related to the disruption of their supply chain process, compliance, and safety hazards. The situation makes it important for manufacturing companies to reduce risk using strategies that protect their assets and streamline their business operations. In the information technology sector, IT companies experience risks, such as cybersecurity threats and identity theft, that can lead to severe consequences for both the business and the user. As a result, IT companies must develop a risk management process to identify potential vulnerabilities in their system along with protecting sensitive data of the consumer.

In the construction industry, construction companies face multiple risks that include contractual, financial, and safety dangers. The situation requires construction companies to implement effective management practices to avoid cost overruns or project delays. For each of these industries, business analytics is required to develop a systematic process and analysis to enable businesses to make data-driven decisions to improve the outcome of the company. The use of business analytics includes descriptive, predictive, and prescriptive analytics, which enable the company to use historical data to predict future trends in the market. When dealing with mitigating risk, business analytics will help identify risks, quantify risks, optimize strategies, and provide continuous improvements for the business.

DOI: 10.4324/9781003629658-12

Identifying risks relies on data analysis to determine potential risks by detecting patterns in outliers and daily operational procedures along with financial data. Quantifying risks uses business analytics to provide quantitative measures that enable companies to determine the chance and impact of identified risks while leading to more informed, knowledgeable decisions and actions. Optimizing strategies is supported by business analytics by allowing companies to develop effective risk mitigation strategies that are customized to the specific needs and risk profiles of the industry. Finally, continuous improvements are used by business analytics to create an ongoing cycle of monitoring improvements of risk management processes to guarantee that companies can adapt to the changing risks within their sector in the global market. As a result, there is a symbiotic relationship between risk mitigation and business analytics that empower companies to become proactive to address environmental challenges and to improve performance levels across all industries within the global environment.

## UNDERSTANDING BUSINESS RISKS

*Risk mitigation* is an organizational process that is used to reduce the negative impact of potential risks. By identifying, assessing, and prioritizing risks, measures can be implemented to reduce the chance of impact on future events. This situation has made the role of risk mitigation important in various industries, including finance, health care, manufacturing, information technology, and construction. In the finance sector, risk mitigation is used in managing investment risks, regulatory compliance, and credit risks using a quantitative model to determine market conditions and to protect against unpredictable volatility in the environment.

In the health-care sector, companies face risks related to data privacy, regulatory compliance, and patient safety that require effective risk mitigation strategies that include cybersecurity and compliance training to protect both patients and organizational data. The manufacturing sector must understand risks that are associated with equipment failures, workplace safety, and disruptions. Risk assessment tools and preventative maintenance practices can be used by manufacturing companies to improve safety and reduce downtime.

In the information technology sector, companies face the threat of data breaches, system vulnerabilities, and cybersecurity threats. This situation makes it necessary for IT companies to implement comprehensive security protocols and to constantly monitor their systems to reduce the threat of these risks and to protect sensitive data. Finally, the construction sector implements risk mitigation strategies so they can improve their focus on regulatory compliance, financial concerns, and safety. Construction companies that use risk assessments and protocols can better identify potential threats, manage project budgets, and implement safety protocols.

To understand business risks, companies must implement business analytics to develop a systematic process to study and determine potential threats and their implications. This situation requires business analytics to help the company develop risk identification and risk quantification, improve the strategic decision-making process, and perform continuous monitoring. Risk identification is an analytic tool that discovers potential risks for the analysis and review of data and to look for patterns and anomalies to help the company before the level of risk increases. Risk quantification is a statistical method that quantifies risk by providing a numerical assessment of the chance of impact of that event. This situation enables companies to prioritize risks based on their potential effect on the financial and operational performance of the business.

The strategic decision-making process requires data-driven information to enable companies to develop and form strategies to reduce the chance of identified risks. The situation requires business analytics to help develop focused approaches based on the industry standards, contexts, and risk profiles. Finally, the continuous monitoring process is the use of ongoing business analytics strategies to enable companies to monitor dynamic environments while guaranteeing that real-time adjustments to risk management strategies can be made to respond to changes in the markets and emerging threats. As a result, using business analytics and strategic knowledge will enable companies in various industries to effectively minimize risks while improving their operational performance and ensuring sustainable growth in the market.

### Types of Risks Organizations Face in Today's Market

There are various types of risks that organizations face in today's market. The most common types of risks that organizations face today include operational risks, market risks, regulatory risks, cybersecurity risk, and reputational risks. *Operational risks* are those that develop from internal business processes, human error, or systems. For effective risk management strategies to exist, they must involve the implementation of comprehensive monitoring systems and improving the efficiency of the company's operations. Next, *market risks* develop changes in the economic environment. Economic environmental changes include pricing, competition, and consumer demand levels. The situation requires business analytics to play an important role in making informed strategic decisions and forecasting future trends in the environment.

*Regulatory risks* can develop when companies face new challenges and comply with constantly changing regulations and laws within the environment. The situation makes it necessary for companies in various industries to remain informed and to adapt using business analytics to manage these regulatory and compliance risks accordingly. Next, *cybersecurity risks* develop when businesses must identify and address risks that are associated with cyberattacks and data breaches. With an increased use of technology in the global environment, companies must continually monitor and provide quick responses to minimize the impact of potential threats. As a result, the understanding and addressing of various risks can enable companies in all industries to improve their competitive position and become resilient to weaknesses and threats to provide sustainable growth within the market.

## RISK ASSESSMENT AND ANALYTICS FRAMEWORKS

Companies in various industries must learn to implement risk assessments and to develop analytics frameworks. In the finance industry, risk mitigation is necessary in managing the market, operational risks, and credit. The situation requires financial companies to manage risk by developing statistical models to forecast potential losses and to implement strategies for hedging and diversification to fully protect their monetary assets. In the health-care industry, health-care providers face risks associated with data security, regulatory compliance, and patient safety. The situation makes risk assessments an important part of the strategic process that will require the health-care provider to conduct regular audits, develop incident response plans, and provide employee training to reduce the negative impact of risk and to protect sensitive patient information.

In the manufacturing sector, risk assessment and analytics are required to develop a framework or process to eliminate risks that are associated with equipment failures, workplace safety, and supply chain disruptions. When risk assessments are implemented, manufacturing companies can identify threats and vulnerabilities and can create a contingency plan that guarantees that the business operation will be seamless and not negatively impacted, while still maintaining safety compliance standards. Information technology companies are vulnerable to cybersecurity threats and system attacks. The situation requires IT companies to implement risk mitigation strategies that include system audits, employee training, and advanced security measures to protect their digital data from potential hackers and breaches.

In the construction industry, companies face risks that include finance, safety hazards, and regulatory compliance. As a result, comprehensive risk assessment is required to develop safety protocols that are implemented to reduce the risk of projects being delayed, and so budgets will not face a financial downturn. To be successful, business analytics will require several key factors that include data collection, risk identification, risk quantification, and decision-making, which can be seen in the table that follows.

**TABLE 12.1** Risk Assessment and Analytics Frameworks

| Feature | Business Analytics | Risk Assessment |
|---|---|---|
| **Data collection** | Involves gathering data from various sources, such as internal databases, surveys, and external data, to uncover patterns and insights | Involves identifying potential hazards and risks from various sources, including internal processes, external events, and human factors |
| **Risk identification** | Uses data analysis to identify trends and anomalies that could indicate potential business opportunities or threats | Focus on identifying and documenting potential risks that could influence the success of a project or business |
| **Risk quantification** | Uses statistical methods to predict and quantify business outcomes, often involving predictive modeling | Quantifies risks by assessing their likelihood and impact, often using qualitative and quantitative methods |
| **Decision-making** | Supports decision-making by providing knowledge and recommendations based on data analysis | Supports decision-making by evaluating risks and determining appropriate measures to mitigate or influence them |

### Approaches for Evaluating Potential Risks Through Data

There are different approaches for evaluating potential risks through data and business analytics in the various industries that make up the global market. The first approach is data collection. *Data collection* is the first step in the process of risk evaluation that requires the collection of important data from various sources, including market trends, history of incidents, and key performance metrics. The collection of data will provide the foundation for developing an effective business analysis using statistics. The second approach is to identify patterns. The identification of patterns enables companies to determine correlations and trends in the collected dataset. When these correlations and trends are understood, companies can identify new emerging risks that were not previously identified.

The third approach is quantifying risks. This approach requires an analytical model to determine potential risks by estimating their chance and impact on the current business process. Various techniques can be used. To help companies quantify how various factors can impact the outcome of events and to help prioritize each risk appropriately based on a numerical value. The fourth approach is informed decision-making. Knowledge that is gained from business analytics will provide organizations. The capability to make data-driven and informed decisions about the risk mitigation strategies. When all areas of threat and vulnerability are understood, companies can then begin to allocate the necessary resources and to implement the necessary measures for protection against those risks.

The final approach is continuous monitoring. Within this approach, organizations will need to use business analytics to monitor all risk factors on a continuous basis. This strategy will provide real-time analysis that will be used to support quick adjustments to current strategies of the business. As a result of this process, continuous monitoring will ensure that all companies remain adaptable and flexible in responding to the changing and dynamic risks within the market. As a result, the combination of risk mitigation and business analytics provides organizations with the comprehensive approach in evaluating all potential risks and threats through data analysis to help reduce negative impact and to provide sustainable growth for all industries within the global market.

## PREDICTIVE ANALYTICS FOR RISK MANAGEMENT

Predictive analytics for risk management is used by various industries within the global environment. For each industry, we need to understand the important role of business analytics and predictive analytics. While business analytics improves the risk management process by developing new knowledge that is gained from the analysis of data, predictive analytics uses past data and statistical algorithms to predict potential outcomes and risks. The situation requires the implementation of risk identification, risk assessment, informed decision-making, continuous improvement, and scenario planning.

Risk identification is achieved by companies using business analytics to determine potential risks through the analysis of trends and patterns contained within their datasets. This situation enables companies to focus on the most critical and threatening risks that can impact on their daily operations and long-term profitability. Risk assessments use predictive models

**TABLE 12.2** Techniques for Anticipating and Managing Risks

| Feature | Business Analytics | Techniques for Anticipating and Managing Risks |
|---|---|---|
| **Data analysis** | Involves examining data to identify trends, patterns, and insights to inform business decisions | Involves analyzing data to identify potential risks and their impact on business operations |
| **Predictive modeling** | Uses historical data and statistical techniques to forecast future business outcomes | Uses historical data and statistical models to predict potential risks and their likelihood |
| **Risk prioritization** | Focuses on identifying key business opportunities and challenges based on data insights | Involves assessing and ranking risks based on their potential impact and likelihood |
| **Informed decision-making** | Supports decision-making by providing data-driven insights and recommendations | Supports decision-making by evaluating risks and determining appropriate mitigation strategies |
| **Continuous monitoring** | Involves the continual analysis of business processes to ensure optimal performance and compliance | Involves continuous tracking of risk factors to detect and respond to emerging threats |

to help companies quantify and prioritize risks based on their potential impact within their environment. Third, informed decision-making is achieved with the use of predictive analytics to gain new knowledge to make informed strategic decisions. As a result of this process, companies can develop effective risk mitigation strategies that are customized to meet the anticipated threats and challenges in the environment while also maximizing response time and allocating resources.

Fourth, continuous improvements rely on companies using predictive analytics to support their continuous monitoring of risk within their internal and external environments. Finally, scenario planning is a component of predictive analytics that enables companies to simulate various risk situations within the environment. As a result of this approach, businesses can identify all potential outcomes and prepare companies in various industries to implement the appropriate measures and responses to the situation. When business analytics is combined with the mitigation of risk, predictive analytics can develop a comprehensive process for effective risk management to reduce threats and ensure sustainable growth.

There are techniques for anticipating and managing risks. These techniques include data analysis, predictive modeling, risk prioritization, informed decision-making, and continuous monitoring. Each of these techniques is identified in detail in the Table 12.2.

## CRISIS MANAGEMENT AND DATA UTILIZATION

Crisis management and data utilization are an important part of the risk management process for all industries within the global environment. The key components of business analytics within risk mitigation and crisis management include data-driven insights, crisis management, planning, real-time monitoring, performance evaluation, and enhancing communication. First, data-driven insights are achieved when companies use business analytics to study past data to identify trends and uncover new patterns that may indicate potential for risk. The situation will provide companies with the ability to make proactive decisions and to support their risk mitigation strategies.

Second, crisis management planning helps to create a plan for simulating various risk scenarios based on past or historical data. The situation allows companies to prepare for potential crises or threats by determining how various factors can impact the daily operation while also anticipating the necessary response. Third, real-time monitoring requires business analytics to enable companies to monitor all risk factors in the sustainability of the organization on a continual basis. The usage of real-time data will guarantee that organizations can identify emerging issues more efficiently while also facilitating a quick response and plan for intervention.

Next, performance evaluation occurs after a risk or crisis to the company. Business analytics will offer the necessary knowledge for evaluating the effectiveness of a company's response strategy to a threat. This situation will be used to support the future planning of the business and to help the company to improve its approach to crisis management and risk mitigation. Finally, enhancing communication requires the effective use of data to help guarantee that clear communication channels are used during a time of crisis to communicate accurately and effectively with all stakeholder groups. As a result, a high level of transparency and trust is created that is necessary for ensuring all responses are coordinated around a single strategic initiative to reduce threats and risks.

## How Analytics Aids in Crisis Preparedness and Response

Business analytics is used to aid in crisis preparedness and response for all industries within the global market. Various methodologies are used to improve crisis preparedness and response, including data analysis for risk identification, predictive analytics, scenario simulation, and post-crisis evaluation. Data analysis risk application involves the collection and analysis of data to identify potential threats and trends within a business. By using past data, companies can determine all potential vulnerabilities that can lead to a crisis in the future.

Next, predictive analytics use statistical models to enable companies to forecast and predict the chance of potential crises in the future. By studying external factors in past incidents, businesses can develop a proactive response process to minimize and reduce the impact of identified risks. The third methodology is scenario simulation. This methodology develops simulations of various crisis scenarios that are based on past data. As a result, scenario simulation helps companies to better understand potential outcomes and develop a crisis response plan that can be implemented when it is needed most.

Fourth, real-time monitoring uses key performance indicators and risk factors to analyze the situation as it occurs. This strategy requires a continuous analysis of data to provide companies with the ability to detect outliers and anomalies to the daily business process so a rapid response can be used during emerging crisis events. Finally, post-crisis evaluation is used to develop new knowledge for evaluating the effectiveness of the crisis response. Companies can analyze and determine what strategies and methods worked best in which need improvement. As a result of this process, the post-crisis evaluation will be used for future mitigation of risk and crisis management plans.

## REGULATORY RISKS AND COMPLIANCE ANALYTICS

Regulatory risks and compliance analytics are a major component in the business environment of all industries. The mitigation of risk can be seen in the finance, health care, manufacturing, information technology, and pharmaceuticals industries. In finance, organizations must deal with regulatory risks that are associated with compliance statutes. As a result, financial risk mitigation strategies include the analysis of risk assessments, regular audits, and implementing strong internal control measures to prevent financial penalties and noncompliance with regulations.

In health care, providers must follow strict regulations and guidelines that are directly related to patient care standards, billing practices, and data privacy. The role of risk mitigation is involved in developing a comprehensive compliance program, implementing data security measures, and training staff to minimize the risk of regulatory violations were data breaches. In manufacturing, firms have risks that are related to safety standards, supply chain, compliance, and environmental regulations. The situation requires an effective risk mitigation strategy that supports safety training, the assessment of suppliers, and compliance audits to guarantee that all regulations are being followed and potential for risk and liabilities are reduced.

In information technology, businesses face risks related to data protection laws and regulations. The situation requires IT companies to develop a risk mitigation strategy that includes access control policies, data encryption, and ongoing compliance training for personnel to avoid any regulatory challenges. Finally, and pharmaceuticals companies must follow strict regulations and guidelines that oversee the development of new drugs, testing, approval, and marketing. As a result, a risk mitigation strategy is needed. That includes regular audits, compliance with the Food and Drug Administration (FDA), and documentation practices of all trials and tests. For companies in all industries, the role of business analytics and regulatory risks in compliance will include a data-driven process, the use of predictive analytics, auditing and reporting, and developing a continuous improvement process to ensure compliance with all future regulations.

### Using Analytics to Maintain Regulatory Standards

Business analytics are used to maintain regulatory standards. Next, business analytics will vastly improve the ability to maintain regulatory standards using methods that include identifying compliance steps, monitoring compliance and real-time predictive analytics, streamlining reporting processes, and continuous improvement. Identifying compliance gaps helps companies study compliance-related data while helping identify gaps in all areas of threat or vulnerabilities. By identifying gaps, new trends and patterns can be visualized to help businesses determine where current compliance strategies are failing.

Second, monitoring compliance in real time is a statistical tool that supports the continuous monitoring of key performance indicators that are related to regulatory standards by all governing bodies. As a result, companies can quickly determine abnormalities or deviations from regular compliance practices and can implement real-time corrective actions to correct the problem. Third, predictive analytics helps organizations predict potential compliance challenges and threats through the identification of past patterns and trends in the data. By analyzing and understanding past events and behaviors, businesses can implement proactive strategies that will be used to mitigate risks before they increase in nature.

Next, streamlining reporting processes requires the use of compliance reporting. Compliance reporting helps make it easier for companies to collect and gather data that is necessary when submitting documentation. As a result, developing automated reporting fully helps increase efficiency in meeting reporting deadlines while reducing errors. Finally, continuous improvement uses data analytics to help companies evaluate the effectiveness of their current compliance strategies on a regular basis. By evaluating program performance, businesses can improve the strategies and enhance their compliance to regulatory standards.

## INSURANCE RISK ASSESSMENT

Business analytics and insurance risk assessment are necessary in maximizing pricing strategies and improving the overall risk management process for companies in the global market. In the insurance market, risk mitigation is necessary for accurate underwriting and claims management. Next, insurers must conduct a thorough assessment to identify and categorize risks that are associated with various insurance policies so they can provide the necessary coverage at competitive rates while also minimizing losses. In health care, health-care providers must mitigate risk using strategies that include conducting regular risk audits, fomenting comprehensive safety protocols, and ensuring compliance with government regulations, such as HIPAA. As a result, these risk mitigation and insurance risk assessment practices will reduce the amount of liabilities while guaranteeing high-quality care for patients.

In the construction industry, businesses must conduct insurance risk assessments to support safety training and project management to reduce the chance of exposure to threats and to improve operational efficiency. In manufacturing, manufacturers must conduct a comprehensive risk assessment and develop preventative maintenance programs to guarantee compliance with federal regulations are met, and there are safeguards to the production process. Finally, IT companies must reduce the level of risk by implementing complete security measures that include continuous monitoring and employee training to protect sensitive and valuable information. For each of these industries, it is necessary for them to use business analytics to complete the main aspects of data gathering, risk identification and quantification, predictive modeling, claims management, and continuous improvements.

### Analytics Applications in the Insurance Sector

Within the insurance sector, the application of analytics is important to all businesses. First, risk mitigation is the process of identifying, assessing, and implementing strategies to reduce potential risk that could negatively impact a company. This strategy is important for various industries, including insurance, health care, manufacturing, construction, and information technology. First, the insurance sector is involved in underwriting, claims management, and pricing. The situation requires insurance companies to develop systematic processes to determine risks to the policyholder while guaranteeing that coverage is both price-competitive and adequate for the client.

In the health-care sector, providers will require risk mitigation strategies to ensure compliance with regulations, minimize liabilities, maintain high standards of care, and develop quality control processes to reduce the level of insurance payouts for failures or mistakes involving patient care. The manufacturing sector must conduct continual risk assessments to develop preventative measures to reduce disruptions to daily operation while increasing the efficiency of production.

In construction, there are various risks that include regulatory, safety hazards, and delays to projects. The situation requires risk mitigation strategies that focus on safety training, following government regulations, and developing detailed project planning to help reduce costs and guarantee the delivery of projects to the customer. Finally, the IT sector faces threats to compliance standards and through cybersecurity threats. As a result, IT risk mitigation strategies must include constant security assessments combined with employee training to guarantee the protection of their system and of sensitive information.

There are many factors included within business analytics to improve the insurance sector's ability to conduct statistical analysis and risk assessment. The first factor is data collection and analysis that is necessary for understanding and developing risk profiles to make data-driven business decisions. The second factor is risk assessments which helps insurers to determine the chance of claims and financial impacts of noncompliance while also providing a more knowledgeable underwriting decision process. The third factor is predictive modeling that uses analytics to understand potential claims to the insurer and to help them determine appropriate premiums and adequate funds for future payouts based on those filed claims.

The fourth factor is fraud detection. Fraud detection requires the analysis of patterns and outliers related to claims data so insurers can accurately identify any unusual activity that may determine fraudulent behavior. As a result, the strategy provides a proactive approach to reducing fraud and minimizing financial losses. The final factor is customer insights that study the behaviors and preferences of consumers. When the needs of consumers are understood, companies can customize their products and services to meet their needs and to improve retention and satisfaction levels while increasing the results of their sales strategies. As a result, the information gained from business analytics must be used to proactively reduce risk so companies in all industries can improve their decision-making process and gain a competitive advantage in the global environment.

## BUSINESS ANALYTICS FUNCTION FOR RISK MITIGATION USING MICROSOFT EXCEL

In the business environment, there are many business analytical terms mentioned that play a critical role in making informed and data-driven choices that drive decisions, optimize daily operations, and develop strategic actions and initiatives. Various statistical concepts play an important role in risk mitigation and business analytics by providing essential tools for data analysis and decision-making. Here's a detailed overview of their definition and importance and how to conduct this statistical analysis using Microsoft Excel.

### Binomial Distributions

This distribution models scenarios with two possible outcomes that include success or failure. In risk analysis, binomial distributions enable companies to estimate the probability of certain events occurring, which is especially useful for forecasting risks associated with binary outcomes.

Formula: = BINOM.DIST

**Steps:**

1. Identify the number of trials (*n*), probability of success (*p*), and the number of successes (*k*).
2. Use the formula P(X = k) = binom(n)(k)(p^k)(1 − p)^(n − k).
3. In Excel, use the BINOM.DIST function and replace *k*, *n*, and *p* with your specific values.

### Exponential Distributions

This distribution is useful for modeling time until an event occurs, including waiting times, or failure rates. Understanding exponential distributions assists in assessing risks related to time-sensitive processes like equipment failures or customer service delays and allows organizations to implement proactive measures to mitigate associated risks.

Formula: = EXPON.DIST

**Steps:**

1. Identify the rate parameter ($\lambda$), which is the inverse of the mean.
2. Use the formula for the cumulative distribution function (CDF): P(X leq x) = 1 − e^(−lambda x).
3. In Excel, use the EXPON.DIST function and replace *x* and *lambda* with your specific values.

### Generating Random Variates

This technique involves creating random samples from specified distributions. Generating random variates is critical for simulations and in modeling scenarios in risk management. It enables organizations to test various risk scenarios and outcomes to provide knowledge of the potential impacts of uncertain variables.

Formula: =BINOM.INV(n, p, RAND()) and =−LN(RAND())/lambda

**Steps:**

1. For a binomial distribution, use =BINOM.INV(n, p, RAND()).
2. For exponential distribution use =−LN(RAND())/lambda, where *lambda* is the rate parameter.

## Normal Distributions

Normal distribution describes many natural phenomena. In risk mitigation, understanding and applying normal distributions help businesses identify typical behavior and calculate probabilities for outcomes that are distributed around a mean. This analysis aids in evaluating risks and making data-driven predictions.

Formula: =NORM.DIST(x, mean, standard_dev, TRUE)

**Steps:**

1. Identify the mean ($\mu$) and standard deviation ($\sigma$).
2. Use the formula for the cumulative distribution function =NORM.DIST(x, mean, standard_dev, TRUE), where *x* is the value for which you want to calculate the probability.

## Probability Distribution

Probability distributions represent the possibility of various outcomes. Analyzing probability distributions enables organizations to assess potential risks effectively and helps them quantify uncertainty and decide on appropriate risk management strategies based on empirical data.

**Steps:**

1. Create a frequency table with possible outcomes in one column.
2. Calculate probabilities for each outcome based on the data.
3. Use the SUM function to ensure the total probabilities equal 1.

## Random Sampling

This process ensures that observations or data points are collected in a way that accurately represents the entire population. Random sampling is critical for risk assessment since it enables organizations to evaluate risks based on unbiased data and leads to more reliable forecasts and decision-making.

Formula: =RAND() and =INDEX

**Steps:**

1. Identify the range of data you want to sample from.
2. Use the RAND function to generate random numbers: =RAND().
3. Use the INDEX function to select items based on generated random numbers.

## Systems Simulation for Product Development

Systems simulation uses models to imitate real-world processes and allows organizations to analyze the effects of different variables on outcomes. In risk mitigation, simulations help companies identify potential issues in product development cycles, assess risks associated with various design choices, and optimize processes before implementation.

**Steps:**

1. Model the key variables in the product development process.
2. Use random variates to simulate outcomes.
3. Set up a table to run multiple iterations of the simulation using Excel's built-in functions and random number generation methods.

### Uniform Distributions

This distribution represents scenarios where all outcomes are equally probable. Understanding uniform distributions assists companies in analyzing risks where there is no apparent bias toward any outcome. This can be particularly useful in situations such as quality control or evaluating performance metrics under uniform operating conditions.

Formula: =UNIFORM.DIST and =IF(x < a, 0, IF(x > b, 1, (x − a)/(b − a)))

**Steps:**

1. Define the minimum (*a*) and maximum (*b*) values.
2. Use the formula for the uniform distribution probability =UNIFORM.DIST function for probability.
3. Use the formula =IF(x < a, 0, IF(x > b, 1, (x − a)/(b − a))).

## REAL-WORLD EXAMPLES OF RISK MITIGATION INSIGHTS DRIVING BUSINESS SUCCESS

### LVMH Moët Hennessy Louis Vuitton

LVMH Moët Hennessy Louis Vuitton uses data analytics to assess potential risks across its supply chain, from the sourcing of materials to their distribution. By analyzing market trends and supplier performance, LVMH can identify vulnerabilities and implement proactive measures to ensure uninterrupted operations. Next, LVMH relies on analytics to forecast changes in demand for luxury products. By understanding customer behavior and market dynamics, LVMH can modify production levels and inventory management as needed, while minimizing the risks associated with overproduction or stockouts. Finally, LVMH uses analytics to monitor and respond to risks related to brand reputation and compliance. By analyzing consumer feedback and social media sentiment, the company can immediately address potential issues to protect its significant brand image.

**Question 1**

How does LVMH Moët Hennessy Louis Vuitton use data analytics to manage risks within its supply chain?

Answer: LVMH uses data analytics to carefully assess and manage risks throughout its supply chain, including sourcing materials for distribution. By analyzing market trends and supplier performance data, LVMH can identify potential vulnerabilities that may interrupt operations. This proactive approach allows the company to implement measures that ensure continuity and efficiency. If a particular supplier shows signs of unreliability, LVMH can quickly use alternative sources or adjust its procurement strategies to mitigate potential disruptions. This strategic use of data analytics not only protects the supply chain but also enhances the overall resilience of LVMH's operations.

**Question 2**

In what ways does LVMH use analytics to forecast demand for its luxury products?

Answer: LVMH leverages data analytics to correctly forecast demand for its luxury products by analyzing customer behavior and market dynamics. By examining historical sales data, consumer preferences, and new market trends, LVMH can predict changes in demand and adjust production levels accordingly. This capability helps the company maintain optimal inventory levels while reducing the risks associated with overproduction or stockouts. During peak shopping seasons or in response to fashion trends, LVMH can increase production of high-demand items while scaling back on less-popular products to ensure that supply strategically aligns with consumer demand.

**Question 3**

How does LVMH use data analytics to protect its brand reputation and ensure compliance?

Answer: LVMH uses data analytics to monitor and respond to risks related to brand reputation and compliance by analyzing consumer feedback and social media opinion. This real-time analysis allows the company to immediately identify and address potential issues that could harm its brand image. If negative feedback about a product or service begins to trend on social media, LVMH can investigate the main cause and implement corrective actions to resolve the issue. Finally, by monitoring compliance-related data, LVMH ensures that its operations follow the industry regulations and standards to protect its reputation as a leading luxury brand.

## Berkshire Hathaway Inc.

Berkshire Hathaway Inc. implements complex data analytics to evaluate potential risks associated with its various investments, ranging from insurance to manufacturing. This analytical approach enables Berkshire Hathaway to identify vulnerabilities and make informed decisions that improve the resilience of its operations. Next, the company uses predictive modeling in the insurance sector. By analyzing vast amounts of historical claims data, Berkshire can assess risk factors and set appropriate premiums while reducing the likelihood of unexpected losses. Finally, Berkshire Hathaway relies on analytics to monitor the performance of its subsidiaries by identifying trends that might indicate potential financial or operational risks. This proactive monitoring allows for early intervention and strategic adjustments within their market sector.

**Question 1**

How does Berkshire Hathaway Inc. use data analytics to manage risks across its diverse investment portfolio?

Answer: Berkshire Hathaway Inc. employs complex data analytics to evaluate potential risks associated with its wide range of investments that span industries such as insurance, manufacturing, and others. By analyzing data from various sources, the company can identify vulnerabilities within its operations and investment strategies. This analytical approach enables Berkshire Hathaway to make informed decisions that improve the resilience of its diverse portfolio. By assessing market trends and financial indicators, the company can anticipate economic shifts and adjust its investment strategies as needed to minimize potential losses and maximize returns.

**Question 2**

In what ways does predictive modeling benefit Berkshire Hathaway's insurance sector?

Answer: Predictive modeling plays a crucial role in Berkshire Hathaway's insurance sector by enabling the company to analyze vast amounts of historical claims data. This analysis helps in assessing risk factors and setting appropriate premiums for policyholders. By correctly predicting the chance of claims, Berkshire Hathaway can reduce the chances of unexpected losses while ensuring financial stability. Finally, predictive modeling allows the company to customize its insurance products to meet the specific needs of different consumer segments to improve consumer satisfaction levels and competitiveness in the insurance market.

**Question 3**

How does Berkshire Hathaway use data analytics to monitor the performance of its subsidiaries?

Answer: Berkshire Hathaway relies on data analytics to continuously monitor the performance of its subsidiaries. By analyzing financial and operational data, the company can identify trends that may denote potential risks or opportunities for improvement. This proactive monitoring enables early intervention and strategic adjustments while ensuring that subsidiaries remain competitive and financially stable. If a subsidiary shows signs of declining performance, Berkshire Hathaway can investigate the root causes and implement corrective measures, including optimizing operations or reallocating resources to enhance overall performance and maintain market leadership.

## Northrop Grumman Corporation

The Northrop Grumman Corporation integrates advanced data analytics to assess and manage risks in complex projects to ensure compliance with regulatory standards and enhance operational efficiency. Next is Northrop Grumman's application of analytics to anticipate supply chain disruptions. By analyzing historical data related to supplier performance and market conditions, the company can identify potential risks and develop contingency plans to promote the timely delivery of critical components for its projects. Finally, Northrop Grumman uses analytics to evaluate cybersecurity vulnerabilities across its systems. By continuously monitoring data traffic and threat intelligence, the company can quickly identify and address potential breaches and protect sensitive information and maintain its operational integrity.

**Question 1**

How does the Northrop Grumman Corporation use data analytics to manage risks in complex projects and ensure compliance with regulatory standards?

Answer: The Northrop Grumman Corporation uses advanced data analytics to manage risks in its complex projects by systematically assessing potential vulnerabilities and ensuring compliance with regulatory standards. By integrating data from various sources, the company can identify areas of concern early in the project life cycle. This proactive approach allows Northrop Grumman to implement corrective measures before issues escalate, thereby maintaining project timelines and budgets. Finally, the use of analytics helps the company stay aware of evolving regulatory requirements while ensuring that all projects adhere to the necessary legal and industry standards. This situation enhances operational efficiency while also protecting the company's reputation and trust of stakeholders.

**Question 2**

In what ways does Northrop Grumman apply analytics to anticipate and mitigate supply chain disruptions?

Answer: Northrop Grumman applies analytics to anticipate and mitigate supply chain disruptions by analyzing historical data related to supplier performance and market conditions. By using predictive analytics, the company can identify patterns and trends that may indicate potential risks, including supplier delays or market volatility. This information enables Northrop Grumman to develop contingency plans that include diversifying its supplier base or adjusting inventory levels to ensure the real-time delivery of critical components. The ability to anticipate disruptions and respond proactively helps the company maintain the continuity of its operations and meet project deadlines, which are necessary in the defense and aerospace sectors, where Northrop Grumman operates.

**Question 3**

How does Northrop Grumman use data analytics to evaluate and address cybersecurity vulnerabilities?

Answer: Northrop Grumman uses data analytics to evaluate and address cybersecurity vulnerabilities by continuously monitoring data traffic and threat intelligence across its systems. The company uses advanced analytics tools to detect abnormalities and potential threats in real time, allowing for immediate identification and response to cybersecurity incidents. By analyzing patterns in data traffic and integrating threat intelligence from various sources, Northrop Grumman can prioritize vulnerabilities and allocate resources effectively to mitigate risks. As a result, this proactive approach protects sensitive information and ensures the integrity and reliability of the company's operations, which are essential given the sensitive nature of its work in defense and aerospace.

## BAE Systems plc

BAE Systems plc implements advanced data analytics to identify and evaluate risks associated with its complex projects while ensuring compliance with regulations and enhancing project resilience. Next, BAE Systems' use of analytics to assess supply chain vulnerabilities. By analyzing supplier performance data and external market trends, the company can learn to expect potential disruptions and develop contingency strategies to ensure an uninterrupted production of critical defense systems. Finally, BAE Systems implements analytics to bolster cybersecurity measures. By continuously monitoring network activity and analyzing threat intelligence, the organization can detect and respond to potential cyberthreats while providing safeguards to sensitive information and operational reliability.

### Question 1

How does BAE Systems plc use advanced data analytics to manage risks in its complex projects, and what are the benefits of this approach?

Answer: BAE Systems plc employs advanced data analytics to manage risks by systematically identifying and evaluating potential threats and vulnerabilities in its complex projects. This approach involves analyzing vast amounts of data related to project parameters, regulatory requirements, and operational conditions. Next, BAE Systems can ensure compliance with regulations and enhance the resilience of its projects. The benefits of this approach include improved decision-making, reduced chances of project delays or failures, and enhanced ability to adapt to changing conditions. Finally, this proactive risk management strategy ultimately leads to more efficient and successful project outcomes.

### Question 2

In what ways does BAE Systems use analytics to assess and reduce supply chain vulnerabilities, and what impact does this have on its operations?

Answer: BAE Systems uses analytics to assess supply chain vulnerabilities by analyzing supplier performance data and external market trends. This strategy involves evaluating historical data on supplier reliability, delivery times, and quality of materials, along with monitoring market conditions that could affect supply chain stability. By identifying potential disruptions, BAE Systems can develop contingency strategies that include diversifying suppliers or adjusting inventory levels to ensure uninterrupted production of critical defense systems. This data-driven approach improves operational efficiency, reduces the risk of production delays, and guarantees that BAE Systems can meet its commitments to consumers and stakeholders.

### Question 3

How do BAE Systems implement analytics to enhance its cybersecurity measures, and what are the key outcomes of this strategy?

Answer: BAE Systems implements analytics to enhance its cybersecurity measures by continuously monitoring network activity and analyzing threat intelligence. This strategy involves using advanced algorithms and machine learning techniques to detect unusual patterns or anomalies in data traffic that may indicate potential cyberthreats. Next, BAE Systems can quickly identify and respond to security breaches while protecting sensitive information and maintaining operational reliability. The primary outcomes of this strategy include a strengthened cybersecurity posture, reduced risk of data breaches, and increased confidence among clients and partners in the security of BAE Systems' operations.

## CASE STUDIES ON RISK MITIGATION SUCCESS THROUGH ANALYTICS

### Business Success Through Business Analytics

Business analytics plays a crucial role in understanding risk mitigation trends and consumer behavior that enables organizations in the risk mitigation industry to make more data-driven and informed decisions. Following are three examples of how risk mitigation data and knowledge are translated into business success using analytics:

### Example 1: SafeProtect Analytics

SafeProtect Analytics specializes in providing comprehensive risk assessment solutions for financial institutions. By using advanced predictive analytics, SafeProtect identifies potential financial risks, such as credit defaults and market volatility. The company employs machine learning algorithms to analyze historical data and predict future trends while allowing clients to make informed decisions about their investment portfolios. Next, SafeProtect's success is driven by its ability to offer real-time risk assessment dashboards that provide clients with a clear view of their risk exposure. This transparency enables financial institutions to adjust their strategies proactively, minimizing potential losses. Finally, SafeProtect's insights have helped clients optimize their capital allocation, leading to improved financial performance.

#### *Short-Response Questions*

1. What type of risks does SafeProtect Analytics focus on?
2. How does SafeProtect Analytics provide real-time risk assessment?
3. What is one benefit clients have experienced from SafeProtect's insights?

### Example 2: PerilShield Solutions

PerilShield Solutions is a leader in the manufacturing sector and provides risk mitigation strategies to enhance operational efficiency. The company uses data analytics to identify potential supply chain disruptions and equipment failures. By analyzing data from IoT devices and historical maintenance records, PerilShield predicts when machinery is likely to fail and recommends preventive maintenance schedules. This proactive approach has significantly reduced downtime and maintenance costs for clients. PerilShield's knowledge has also enabled manufacturers to streamline their supply chains by identifying alternative suppliers and optimizing inventory levels, ensuring uninterrupted production.

### *Short-Response Questions*

1. What sector does PerilShield Solutions primarily serve?
2. How does PerilShield Solutions predict machinery failures?
3. What is one outcome of PerilShield's risk mitigation strategies for manufacturers?

### Example 3: CyberSafety Dynamics

CyberSafety Dynamics specializes in cybersecurity risk mitigation for large enterprises. The company employs advanced analytics to detect and respond to cyberthreats in real time. By analyzing network traffic patterns and user behavior, CyberSafety identifies anomalies that may indicate a security breach. CyberSafety's knowledge has enabled enterprises to enhance their cybersecurity posture by implementing targeted security measures. The company's analytics-driven approach has reduced the incidence of data breaches and minimized the impact of cyberattacks, safeguarding sensitive information and maintaining client trust.

### *Short-Response Questions*

1. What type of risk does CyberSafety Dynamics focus on?
2. How does CyberSafety Dynamics detect potential security breaches?
3. What is one benefit enterprises have gained from CyberSafety's information?

## CASE STUDY: RISKGUARDIAN SOLUTIONS

RiskGuardian Solutions is a company that specializes in providing risk management and mitigation services to small and medium-sized enterprises (SMEs). Understanding that each business faces unique risks, RiskGuardian uses sophisticated statistical models to analyze potential risks and develop tailored mitigation strategies. In its initial year of operation, the company focused on improving its service offering through systematic simulations to identify vulnerabilities in various sectors, including manufacturing, health care, and finance. Using Excel for probability modeling and simulations, RiskGuardian set out to provide its clients with actionable information.

### Business Analytics Data Tables

**TABLE 12.3** Risk Assessment Metrics

| 1 | A | B | C | D |
|---|---|---|---|---|
| | Risk Factor | Probability (%) | Impact ($) | Risk Score (Probability × Impact) |
| 2 | Supply chain distribution | 40 | 50,000 | 2,000,000 |
| 3 | Cybersecurity breaches | 30 | 100,000 | 3,000,000 |
| 4 | Regulatory changes | 20 | 25,000 | 500,000 |
| 5 | Market fluctuations | 10 | 70,000 | 700,000 |

### Analytics Problems Using Excel

1. Use binomial distribution to model the likelihood of experiencing supply chain disruptions, given that historical data shows such disruptions have occurred in 40% of the cases. Use the normal distribution to estimate the impact on total risk score.
2. Implement random sampling techniques using the RANDBETWEEN function to generate random variates for risk factors across several scenarios. How can this model help simulate various risk mitigation strategies?
3. Assess exponential distribution to estimate the time between potential disruptions in the supply chain and apply systematic simulation to evaluate risk over multiple iterations. What insights does this provide for strategic planning and resource allocation?

### Answer Key

1. *Modeling with binomial distribution and normal distribution.* To calculate the probability of experiencing a supply chain disruption: =BINOM.DIST(k, n, p, cumulative), where *k* is the number of disruptions, *n* is the total number of observations, *p* is the probability (0.4), and cumulative is set to FALSE for exact probability.
   To estimate the impact on total risk score, calculate the impact using a normal distribution: =NORM.INV(RAND(), mean, standard deviation).
   Use appropriate mean and standard deviation values based on past risk score data.
2. *Implementing random sampling for risk factors.* For each simulation, use the RANDBETWEEN function to randomly assign values for each risk factor. Multiply by the corresponding impact to generate random variates for risk factors. Total risk score can be calculated for each scenario using the SUM function across the columns representing risk scores.
3. *Using exponential distribution for disruption timing.* The EXPON.DIST function can model the time between disruptions with the formula =EXPON.DIST(x, lambda, cumulative), where *x* is the time and *lambda* could represent the average rate of disruption events per period.
   For systematic simulations, copy down the formula across multiple rows corresponding to different simulations to understand the distribution of risk over time.
   Analyze how often disruptions might occur based on historical data and the calculated average times.

---

### CASE STUDY: RISKDEFENDER SOLUTIONS

RiskyDefender Solutions is a firm focusing on risk mitigation strategies for businesses across various sectors. The firm has developed a reputation for helping clients identify, assess, and manage risks effectively. Recently, RiskDefender Solutions partnered with a large technology firm to enhance their risk management practices and ensure the stability of their product development processes. To evaluate the impact of their risk mitigation strategies, RiskDefender Solutions collected data on key risk metrics, including the probability of equipment failure, the frequency of production delays, and the impact of these risks on overall productivity. The data was analyzed using various probability distributions and simulation techniques to identify potential risk factors and develop strategies to mitigate them. The following tables summarize key findings from the project:

**TABLE 12.5** Equipment Failure and Production Delays

| 1 | A | B | C |
|---|---|---|---|
| | Month | Equipment Failure Probability (%) | Production Delays (Hours) |
| 2 | January | 5 | 10 |
| 3 | February | 4 | 8 |
| 4 | March | 6 | 12 |
| 5 | April | 7 | 14 |
| 6 | May | 5 | 10 |
| 7 | June | 4 | 8 |

**TABLE 12.6** Risk Impact on Productivity

| 1 | A | B | C |
|---|---|---|---|
| | Month | Productivity Loss (Units) | Financial Impact ($) |
| 2 | January | 500 | 10,000 |
| 3 | February | 400 | 8,000 |
| 4 | March | 600 | 12,000 |
| 5 | April | 700 | 14,000 |
| 6 | May | 500 | 10,000 |
| 7 | June | 400 | 8,000 |

## Analytics Problems Using Excel

1. *Binomial distributions.* Calculate the probability of equipment failure occurring at least once in a month.
2. *Exponential distributions.* Determine the time between equipment failures using exponential distribution.
3. *Generating random variates.* Generate random variates for production delays.
4. *Normal distributions.* Analyze the distribution of productivity loss using normal distribution.
5. *Probability distribution.* Create a probability distribution for financial impact.
6. *Random sampling.* Perform random sampling to estimate the average production delay.
7. *Systems simulation for product development.* Simulate the impact of equipment failure on product development.
8. *Uniform distributions.* Use uniform distribution to model the variability in production delays.

## Answer Key

1. *Binomial distributions.* Use the BINOM.DIST function: =BINOM.DIST(number_s, trials, probability_s, cumulative). Example: =BINOM.DIST(1, 30, 0.05, TRUE).

2. *Exponential distributions.* Use the EXPON.DIST function: =EXPON.DIST(x, lambda, cumulative). Example: =EXPON.DIST(1, 0.05, TRUE).
3. *Generating random variates.* Use the RAND function to generate random numbers. Example: =RAND().
4. *Normal distributions.* Use the NORM.DIST function: =NORM.DIST(x, mean, standard_dev, cumulative). Example: =NORM.DIST(500, 550, 100, TRUE).
5. *Probability distribution.* Create a probability distribution using the FREQUENCY function. Example: =FREQUENCY(data_array, bins_array).
6. *Random sampling.* Use the RANDBETWEEN function to perform random sampling. Example: =RANDBETWEEN(1, 12).
7. *Systems simulation for product development.* Use the Data Analysis ToolPak to simulate the impact of equipment failure. Example: Data > Data Analysis > Random Number Generation.
8. *Uniform distributions.* Use the UNIFORM.DIST function: =UNIFORM.DIST(x, a, b, cumulative). Example: =UNIFORM.DIST(1, 0, 1, TRUE).

CHAPTER 13

# Business Types and Their Analytical Approaches

The role of various business types in business analytics is important in today's global market. Business analytics involving various business types provides knowledge and information that will be used to lead the decision-making process and improve the operational efficiency of businesses. First, it is necessary to understand the various business types that range from small companies to large corporations. This understanding of diverse business types provides a clear understanding of how business analytics can be customized to meet the specific needs of companies in various industries.

The first business type is small and medium enterprises (SMEs). SMEs are companies that serve niche or local markets. Next, SMEs do not have the same number of resources in larger companies but can use business analytics to identify consumer trends, maximize marketing strategies, and streamline business operations. With the use of business analytics, SMEs can compete effectively and efficiently to improve their overall profitability within the market.

The second type of business is start-ups. Start-ups are innovative businesses that are in their beginning stages and use business analytics to identify new market opportunities and consumer preferences. Next, start-ups primarily focus on data-driven strategies and real-time experimentation to maximize their growth potential. As a result, start-ups rely on business analytics to change their product and service offerings based on real-time feedback from consumers in the market.

The third type of business is corporations. *Corporations* are large companies that operate on a national, international, or global scale. Next, corporations have teams dedicated to business analytics and use sophisticated systems to perform statistical analysis on large amounts of data. As a result, corporations rely on business analytics to conduct risk management, performance management, and strategic planning to remain competitive in their current or new and emerging markets.

The final type of business is nonprofits. Nonprofits use business analytics to determine the effectiveness of their current program. Next, business analytics are used by nonprofits to maximize the allocation of resources. As a result, the analysis of data using business analytics will determine the needs of the community along with their outcomes so nonprofits can guarantee that their current strategy and initiatives align with their mission and vision to improve delivery of services.

DOI: 10.4324/9781003629658-13

In the retail sector, business analytics is used to understand consumer preferences, maximize supply chain management process, and manage inventory levels. Next, retailers use business analytics to develop a market basket analysis to improve the experience of the consumer by personalizing product and service recommendations. In the health-care sector, business analytics improves patient care outcomes and operational efficiency. Through the analysis of data, health-care providers can identify new trends to maximize treatment protocols, reduce expenses, and improve the disease management process.

In the finance sector, business analytics is used to identify risk, detect fraud, and ensure regulatory compliance. This strategy requires predictive modeling to enable banks, credit unions, and other financial investment firms to predict trends in the market and the behavior of consumers. In the manufacturing sector, manufacturing firms use business analytics to improve processes, conduct predictive maintenance, and ensure quality control. By studying production data, manufacturing companies can improve the quality of products, while reducing their amount of downtime.

Finally, the technology sector uses business analytics to lead to the development of new products and services. Next, business analytics is used to drive innovation and to understand the engagement of all users and clients. As a result, technology companies use machine learning algorithms, AI, and big data analytics to develop a more comprehensive understanding of the consumer environment. As a result, there is a direct relationship between the various types of businesses and the functions of business analytics to develop data-driven information to improve business operations, increase growth in the market, and improve consumer satisfaction for all industries.

## ANALYZING VARIOUS BUSINESS MODELS AND THE IMPORTANCE OF ANALYTICS ACROSS DIFFERENT BUSINESS STRUCTURES

The differentiation of various business types in the use of business analytics will lead to important data-driven decision-making across all organizational structures. This situation makes it important for business leaders to understand how business analytics must be fully integrated with the different types of businesses that enable companies to improve consumer experiences, maximize operations, and achieve their strategic objectives and goals. First, SMEs must use business analytic tools to maximize marketing strategies, reduce operational inefficiencies, and improve their financial management strategies. With the use of business analytics, SMEs can gain the ability to compete effectively against larger firms in the market.

Second, start-ups require business analytics to help remain innovative and flexible within the diverse market. The situation requires start-ups to use business analytics to improve their business models and determine the opportunities of the market. Using data analysis, start-ups can change their product and service offerings in real time while developing focus marketing strategies to meet the needs and preferences of the consumers. As a result, this data-driven strategy will reduce the level of risk associated with new ventures and initiatives while supporting longevity and sustainable growth in the environment.

Third, corporations are large companies that use business analytics to manage large-scale operations to evaluate the performance of multiple ventures at one time. By using business analytics, corporations can study and analyze large sets of data to make informed strategic decisions, identify market trends, and maximize the allocation of resources. As a result, business analytics helps corporations make decisions that are supported by data instead of intuition, while also improving their competitive advantage over their competitors.

Fourth, nonprofits use business analytics to determine the impact of their programs and to maximize their funding strategies. By studying community needs and demographic data, nonprofits can dedicate resources more effectively and efficiently to improve the outcomes of current and future programs. As a result, they had analytics will empower nonprofits to communicate their effectiveness and efficiency to all stakeholder groups while improving their community outreach initiatives.

Various industries that use business analytics include retail, health care, finance, manufacturing, and technology. Retail companies use business analytics study data to customize the shopping experience of customers while also improving sales and consumer loyalty. Healthcare providers use business analytics to improve workflows, identify emerging trends, and increase success of treatment outcomes for patients to improve their service delivery within the community. Finance companies rely on business analytics to predict market trends and improve the decision-making process when it comes to making loan approvals and investments to clients. Fourth, manufacturing companies use business analytics to study production data to reduce waste, predict maintenance needs, and improve productivity. Finally, technology companies use business analytics to guide the development of new innovative products and solutions that meet the demands of the consumer and increase customer satisfaction levels.

## START-UP ANALYTICS VS. ESTABLISHED ENTERPRISES

There is a difference in business analytics compared to start-up analytics versus established enterprises. In the retail sector, business analytics is used in understanding consumer preferences and behaviors while also maximizing inventory management. Start-up companies will use analytics to focus on niche markets, while established retail companies will use business analytics to manage supply chains and improve the loyalty of consumer programs, by providing personalized experiences based on the data. In the health-care sector, start-ups will use business analytics to develop new technologies, like personalized medicine and telehealth, to deliver customized health-care solutions based on patient data. However, established healthcare providers use business analytics across various departments to improve the delivery of care and streamline all administrative processes and procedures.

In the finance sector, start-up companies will use business analytics to develop new and innovative financial technology solutions that provide customized and focused financial services based on the analysis of data. Established finance companies will use business analytics to detect fraud, perform risk assessments, and ensure regulatory compliance using predictive modeling to improve the decision-making process of leadership. In manufacturing, start-ups use business analytics to streamline the process of production and to develop a just-in-time inventory system. However, established manufacturing companies use business analytics to conduct quality control, maximize their supply chain, and conduct predictive maintenance to improve their overall productivity while reducing overhead costs.

Finally, technology start-up companies will use business analytics to focus on rapid innovation of products and services within the market. Next, start-ups will use business analytics to monitor and track the engagements of customers and to confirm if it is of the product and service offerings to the needs of the market. However, established technology companies use business analytics to maximize their product and service offerings, redefine consumer experiences, and to understand the current and future trends of the markets to guarantee long-term sustainability and growth.

## Distinctions in Analytical Needs Between Business Types

There are distinctions in analytical needs between the various types of businesses. In the retail industry, SMEs focus on the basic sales data and feedback from consumers to make informed decisions about inventory management and marketing promotions. However, established retail companies use business analytics to follow consumer preferences over time to maximize their supply chain management system. Next, established retail companies use predictive analytics to anticipate future demands and to improve their operational efficiencies in the market.

In the health-care industry, start-ups rely on business analytics to drive innovation and development of new patient care solutions. The situation revolves around the use of real-time data to customize and personalize products and services. However, established health-care providers use business analytics to streamline daily operations, manage the outcome of patients, and support the compliance with all federal regulations. As a result, the focus of established health-care providers integrates data from different departments into a single comprehensive perspective to make more informed decisions.

In the finance industry, start-ups study consumer data to develop focused and customized financial services to their clients. However, established finance companies use business analytics to monitor compliance. Next, established finance companies use business analytics to ensure accurate regulatory reporting, to develop sophisticated modeling and data management systems, and to detect fraud.

In the manufacturing industry, smaller manufacturing companies will use business analytics to improve production scheduling, while established manufacturers will use statistical analysis to conduct predictive maintenance and ensure a high level of quality control. As a result, established manufacturers require a high level of efficiency and a reduction of costs to remain an established enterprise within the market.

Finally, technology start-up firms rely on business analytics before product and service development based on the feedback and engagement of users. However, established technology companies use business analytics to study large amounts of user data and to identify new emerging trends. As a result, established technology companies use business analytics to maximize their product and service offerings to adjust the scale to mee the needs of the current market. As a result, business analytics can be customized to meet the needs of small, large, or other various business types to provide meaningful knowledge that will be used to increase growth, competitive advantage, and operational efficiency.

## B2B VS. B2C ANALYTICS APPROACHES

There are both business-to-business (B2B) and business-to-consumer (B2C) approaches to business analytics. The distinction between B2B and B2C business analytics demonstrates how different business models require customized analytical models. As a result, the differentiation between B2B and B2C enables organizations across various industries to maximize their performance and to improve their relationships with the consumer market. The different analytics approaches by B2B and B2C are compared in the table that follows.

B2B analytics helps businesses of various sizes and types to focus on pipeline analytics, account base marketing, and consumer relationship management. Next, B2B analytics supports the understanding of customer lifetime value, customer acquisition costs, and the duration of sales cycles. As a result, using a data-driven approach helps B2B businesses to improve their sales strategies with information and knowledge based on consumer preferences and behaviors. As a result, B2B analytics helps various business types maximize their consumer relationships and lead generations to developing new innovations and markets.

B2C analytics helps companies focus on understanding the preferences and behavior of consumers that lead to an increase in sales and levels of engagement. Next, B2C analytics studies metrics that include brand loyalty, consumer satisfaction, and purchasing trends. The situation helps companies use B2C analytics to perform segmentation analysis and predictive analytics to develop personalized and customized marketing strategies. As a result, industries like e-commerce, retail, and hospitality will benefit from the B2C analytics approach since

**TABLE 13.1** B2B vs. B2C Analytics Approaches

| Feature | B2B Analytics | B2C Analytics |
|---|---|---|
| **Customer focus** | Focuses on understanding the needs and behaviors of other businesses | Focuses on understanding the needs and behaviors of individual consumers |
| **Sales cycle** | Usually involves longer sales cycles, often months or years | Typically involves shorter sales cycles, often days or weeks |
| **Data sources** | Uses data from CRM systems, business transactions, and industry reports | Utilizes data from social media, website analytics, and consumer surveys |
| **Metrics** | Key metrics: lead generation, conversion rates, and customer lifetime value | Key metrics: customer acquisition cost, churn rate, and average order value |
| **Decision-making** | Decisions often driven by data on business performance and market trends | Decisions often driven by data on consumer preferences and buying behavior |
| **Challenges** | Challenges: complex decision-making processes and longer relationship-building | Challenges: high competition and rapidly changing consumer preferences |
| **Opportunities** | Opportunities for personalized marketing and long-term partnerships | Opportunities for mass marketing and quick feedback loops |

**TABLE 13.2** Tailoring Analytics Strategies to Customer Types

| Industry | Customer Types | Business Analytics Strategies |
|---|---|---|
| **Retail** | Individual consumers | Focuses on understanding consumer preferences, optimizing inventory, and personalizing marketing |
| **Health care** | Patients, health-care providers | Utilizes data to improve patient outcomes, optimize operations, and drive innovation in treatments |
| **Finance** | Individual investors, businesses | Employs predictive analytics for risk management, investment strategies, and customer intelligence |
| **Technology** | Businesses, end users | Leverages data to drive product development, enhance user experience, and support digital transformation |
| **Hospitality** | Travelers, guests | Uses analytics for personalized guest experiences, dynamic pricing, and operational efficiency |

it enables companies to create focused marketing promotions into maximizing their levels of inventory based on current market.

### Tailoring Analytics Strategies to Customer Types

It is important to customize and tailor analytics strategies to customer types. The diversity of various business types in the use of business analytics plays a critical role in the development and customization of analytical strategies that are used effectively to meet the unique needs of consumers. The situation makes it important for various industries to understand, design, and implement business analytical approaches that increase consumer satisfaction, enhance customer engagement, and improve brand loyalty.

The various types of businesses include SMEs, start-ups, established enterprises and large corporations. By using business analytics, various business types can improve their level of consumer engagement and satisfaction levels while providing personalized experiences that increase growth and brand loyalty across different industries within the global environment. Industries that must tailor analytic strategies to their customer types include retail, health care, finance, technology, and hospitality detailed in the Table 13.2.

## NONPROFIT ORGANIZATIONS AND ANALYTICS

Nonprofit organizations use business analytics to ensure that their goals are focused on social impact and community engagement instead of creating profit for the business. Next, business analytics plays an important role in allowing nonprofits to accurately measure and determine the level of effectiveness and maximize business operations against for-profit companies. One method is through program evaluation. Nonprofits use business analytics to determine the outcome of their programs. This strategy is achieved through the collection of data based on the engagement of participants, progress, and satisfaction levels, which help the company determine effectiveness and identify areas for improvement. As a result, business analytics helps ensure that all resources are allocated appropriately, and the functions of the business will have a maximum impact and improve delivery of service.

The second method is fundraising strategies. Business analytics is important in developing unreasoning strategies for nonprofit organizations by analyzing data from donors. By studying donor data, nonprofits can divide their market segment based on preferences, patterns, and trends. Next, understanding the behavior of donors will enable nonprofits to customize their outreach programs and to create focused marketing promotions that directly connect with the specific donor groups. As a result, nonprofits can use funding strategies to increase donor contributions and support.

The third method is community needs assessment. Nonprofits will use business analytics to determine the needs of the community and to identify gaps in service. The situation is achieved by the analysis of demographic data and feedback from the community. Next, nonprofits will be able to fully understand the threats and challenges in the communities they serve, and to enable them to design new programs that specifically address any potential issues or risks.

The fourth method is collaboration and partnerships. Nonprofits typically engage in partnerships with other businesses and organizations to increase their impact on the community they serve. Business analytics is used to develop these elaborations by identifying shared objectives and goals within the target population. As a result of this process, business analytics leads to effective collaboration and joint initiatives between business types. As a result, various business types combined with business analytics are necessary for the success of nonprofits and all other sectors within the global market.

## How Analytics Can Improve Impact Measurement and Operations

Business analytics can improve the impact measurements and operations of nonprofits in all various business types. There are several practices related to business analytics that must be adopted by nonprofits to help them measure the outcome of success of their initiatives in real time. Using business analytics will help determine the impact of measurements within nonprofits across various business types. The first impact measurement is program evaluation. Program evaluation helps nonprofits determine the effectiveness of the programs using a systematic method. This strategy is achieved by collecting and studying data on the outcome of programs, the satisfaction of participants, and engagement levels so nonprofits can quickly identify which initiatives are successful and which are not. As a result, a feedback loop is created, providing nonprofits with continuous information about improvements and increased accountability for all stakeholder groups.

The second impact measurement is resource allocation. Business analytics will help nonprofits to become more effective in their allocation of resources by studying data that is related to program outcomes and costs. This analysis will help nonprofits understand its ROI from all its various initiatives. Next, business analytics will provide nonprofits with new information and knowledge to help accurately allocate funding resources more effectively to guarantee that they are used to support programs with the highest impact on the community.

The third impact measurement is donor analytics. Donor analytics helps to understand the behavior of donors when conducting fundraising efforts and initiatives. By using business analytics, nonprofits can divide their donor base based on the identification of patterns and through the customization of marketing communication and promotions. As a result, the donor analytics help to increase engagement of donors while supporting the nonprofits capability of collecting the necessary funds for future initiatives.

The final impact measurement is community needs assessment. Nonprofits will use business analytics to initiate a thorough assessment of the needs of the community. By studying demographic data and other metrics, nonprofits can gain a better understanding of the challenges that are faced within the target market populations. As a result, nonprofits that use business analytics will be able to effectively design new programs that support the genuine needs and preferences of the community. Business analytics assist nonprofits within all various business types by developing operational effectiveness in improving the impact of their programs on the community they serve while developing trust and transparency among all stakeholder groups.

## FRANCHISE MODELS AND PERFORMANCE METRICS

Franchise models and performance metrics provide businesses with a quick way to expand by providing them with the right to use a brand and operational model to independent owners. This strategy will lead to a clear understanding of performance metrics while guaranteeing consistency and profitability across geographic locations within the global market. First, business analytics will be used to determine brand consistency. Franchisors will use business analytics to study consumer feedback and other operational metrics to guarantee that all the franchise locations are following the same brand standard. As a result of this analysis, brand consistency analytics will help build trust with consumers and increase loyalty to the brand.

Next, performance metrics will be used to develop key performance indicators that are important for evaluating the success of the franchise. KPIs will include consumer retention rates, operational efficiency, and sales growth to help both the franchise and the franchisee to monitor the progress and identify all areas requiring changes or improvements. As a result, business analytics and KPIs will provide metrics at the regional, national, and global level when making strategic decisions or acting.

Third, market expansion is used within the business analytics process to support growth of a franchise by properly identifying potential new territories for the business. This situation is achieved by studying consumer behavior, market trends, and demographic data, so the franchisor can make data-driven and informed decisions about where to dedicate resources for new location openings. As a result of this process, market expansion through business analytics leads to a higher chance of success for the new location and overall business.

Franchise models are used in various industries. In the restaurant industry, franchises use business analytics to monitor consumer preferences, inventory management, and the performance of menu items. In the retail industry, business analytics is used to assess sales data across various locations and to create focused marketing campaigns and optimized inventory levels using a data-driven approach. In the service industry, franchises will monitor customer satisfaction and operational efficiency using detailed performance metrics to help the francise maintain a high level of quality and to retain customers.

## E-COMMERCE ANALYTICS

Business analytics combined with various business types is critical in the industry of e-commerce. While online shopping continues to increase, it is important for all various business types to understand consumer behavior, operational efficiencies, and new trends in the market to maintain a competitive advantage. The situation requires various business types across all industries to use data analytics to improve their e-commerce strategies, enhance the experience of the customer, and maximize performance.

For SMEs, e-commerce provides a new opportunity to expand into wider markets without incurring higher overhead costs associated with physical store locations. Next, business analytics helps these companies monitor and analyze consumer purchasing patterns and website traffic and to determine the effectiveness of marketing promotions and campaigns. By using analytical tools, SMEs can make more informed decisions about their promotional strategies and product and service offerings to improve their competitive advantage in the e-commerce sector and online environment.

Next, start-ups will use e-commerce is the main method to channel sales. For these various types of businesses, business analytics is important for scalability and rapid growth in the environment. Next, the use of A/B testing will be used to evaluate pricing strategies, webpage designs, and marketing communications. Next, start-ups can analyze the engagement of users using metrics to improve their marketing efforts while also ensuring that they are focusing on the right target audience. As a result, effective business analytics will enable start-ups using e-commerce analytics to adapt and become flexible in the market based on information from data and on feedback from the consumer.

Third, established enterprises and large corporations that have e-commerce frameworks use business analytics to maximize their efficiency and effectiveness of their operation. Next, data that is collected from sales transactions, supply chain, logistics, and interactions of consumers will be compiled for a comprehensive analysis of the success of the company. As a result of e-commerce, business analytics establish enterprises and large corporations contract the lifetime value of consumers and develop predictive models for inventory management into improving the personalization of marketing promotions to increase sales and retention of consumers.

There are various components included in e-commerce analytics that will be used to support the business practices and behaviors of companies in various industries. The first component is customer insight. E-commerce analytics will provide information about the knowledge of customers that include buying behaviors, browsing patterns, and demographics that are necessary to understand who the target population is and what they want. So companies can customize the product offering to meet the specific needs. The second component is conversion rate optimization (CRO). CRO is a process of studying conversion rates to allow businesses to determine how effective the online store front turns browsers into actual buyers. Metrics used during this strategy include checkout efficiency and online cart abandonment rates. The final component is inventory management. E-commerce analytics will monitor inventory levels by forecasting demand and tracking sales trends. This situation will help businesses to maintain the right number of products at a specific time, causing a reduction in stock outs or overstock that will directly impact the level of profitability.

Industries where e-commerce analytics are used include retail, travel and hospitality, and consumer electronics. In the retail industry, e-commerce analytics helps businesses identify product placements on virtual shells, customize promotions to segments of the market, and identify trends in consumer purchasing behavior. In the travel and hospitality industry, e-commerce analytics improves pricing strategies by studying changes in demand that are used to help businesses determine the quality of their service offerings based on consumer reviews and feedback. Finally, the consumer electronics market uses e-commerce analytics to analyze and understand market trends and product performance and to identify new opportunities of selling or cross-selling products based on the preferences and behaviors of consumers.

## Specific Analytical Techniques for Online Businesses

There are specific analytical techniques that can be used by online businesses in various industries. For SMEs, companies want to make the most out of their limited resources. This situation requires companies to use business analytics to develop techniques to make future decisions based on historical data and patterns in consumer behavior. As a result of business analytics, e-commerce SMEs can modify their marketing campaigns and improve their level of inventory to support the current trends in the market. As an example, an online jewelry store may study sales patterns and trends to determine peak purchasing seasons throughout the year so customized marketing promotions that directly connect with the interests of the consumer at that time can be developed.

For start-ups, e-commerce companies succeed based on innovation and quick adaptation to the needs of the market. These e-commerce companies use predictive analytics to predict trends and behaviors of the consumer market. As an example, a business may use in e-commerce framework to study visitor data to predict which products will see an increase in demand based on the seasonal purchasing patterns in the past. This strategy enables the start-up company to maximize their level of inventory and marketing strategies. The start-up company can also use A/B testing to enable them to develop new website designs and online marketing strategies to best meet the needs of their target audience.

Finally, established enterprises and large companies in the e-commerce industry will use business analytics to evaluate various situations and scenarios to determine the maximum strategies for increasing sales and consumer satisfaction. As an example, an international retailer will use prescriptive analytics to create a complex machine algorithm to study data from all regions to develop focused marketing emotions for specific demographic groups of consumers. As a result, the company can use machine learning algorithms and AI to personalize the experiences of the consumer, recommending new products and services based on the historical purchasing behavior of the buyer.

There are various analytical techniques and online businesses. The first technique is customer segmentation. Customer segmentation is important in e-commerce, since it allows companies to categorize and break down their consumer base into specific categories or attributes that include demographics or purchasing behaviors. By using clustering algorithms, businesses can create focus marketing campaigns that directly connect with specific groups of consumers.

The second technique is turned analysis. In e-commerce, understanding consumer retention rates is necessary for online businesses. By using logistic regression analysis, and other techniques, companies can identify the factors that contribute to the churn or turnover rates and then implement new strategies to improve the loyalty of consumers. This strategy is especially important for e-commerce companies that offer subscription-based services.

The third technique is sentiment analysis. *Sentiment analysis* is the process of studying consumer feedback and reviews using natural language processing (NLP) protocols and techniques. Next, NLP helps e-commerce companies determine the feelings and thoughts of consumers about specific products and services. As a result of this analysis, e-commerce companies can make more informed decisions about the development of products and the improvement of consumer services.

The application of these analytical techniques can be seen in e-commerce, travel and hospitality, and digital marketing agencies' services of the global market. In the e-commerce sector, retailers must use predictive analytics to predict consumer demand and manage their inventory levels accordingly. The use of predictive analytics will guarantee that the retailer meets the expectations of the customer without overstocking or understocking shelves. Next, the travel and hospitality sectors use business analytics by using consumer segmentation methodologies to customize pricing and service offers based on the preferences of the traveler during a specific time. Finally, digital marketing agencies use these analytical techniques to conduct A/B testing and sentiment analysis to target potential consumers and to improve their marketing strategies based on real-time feedback from individuals in the market. As a result, the combination of various business types with business analytics provides e-commerce companies with the ability to use specific statistical methods that assist in overcoming challenges to their operational process.

## BUSINESS ANALYTICS FUNCTION FOR DIFFERENT BUSINESS TYPES USING MICROSOFT EXCEL

In the business environment, there are many business analytical terms mentioned that play a critical role in making informed and data-driven choices that drive decisions, optimize daily operations, and develop strategic actions and initiatives. Various statistical concepts play an important role in different business types and business analytics by providing essential tools for data analysis and decision-making. Here's a detailed overview of their definition and importance and how to conduct this statistical analysis using Microsoft Excel.

### Binary Variable Optimization Model

This model uses binary variables (0 or 1) to represent decisions in scenarios where options are mutually exclusive. In economics, binary models are necessary for making yes or no decisions, like launching a new product or entering a market. They help in outlining complex problems with flexibility, allowing for precise optimization under constraints.

**Steps:**

1. Set up your data listing the binary variables (0 or 1) for each product in one column.
2. In another column, list the profits associated with each product.
3. Create a formula to calculate total profit based on binary selection using = SUMPRODUCT(A#:A#, B#:B#), where *A#* contains binary selection and *B#* contains profits.
4. Open Solver by going to Data > Solver.
5. Set the objective to maximize the total profit cell.
6. Add constraints to ensure the binary decision variables are assigned as 0 or 1.
7. Click "Solve."

### General Integer Variables Optimization Model

This model extends binary variables to include integers and allows for the representation of decision variables that can take on whole number values. It is essential for situations where fractional solutions do not make sense, like allocating resources or determining production quantities by a company. By using integer programming, organizations can maximize complex scenarios involving discrete choices.

**Steps:**

1. List decision variables in one column (i.e., quantities of resources).
2. Set up an objective function to maximize or minimize in another cell.
3. In Solver, define the objective cell and set it to maximize or minimize.
4. Add any constraints (i.e., total resource availability) to ensure the decision variables are set as integers.
5. Click "Solve."

### Integer Optimization

Integer optimization is significant for problems requiring whole number solutions. This analysis is important in logistical operations, budget allocations, and portfolio selections and ensures that solutions are practical and implementable. Integer optimization techniques lead to effective planning in scenarios where resources or decisions cannot be divided.

**Steps:**

1. Input the objective function and decision variables.
2. Open Solver and use the same setup as before.
3. Select "integer" for the relevant variable cells in the Solver parameters.
4. Click "Solve" to find the optimal integer solution.

## Nonlinear Optimization

Many real-world economic scenarios involve nonlinear relationships between variables. Nonlinear optimization models help in maximizing or minimizing objectives subject to nonlinear constraints. These models are important in maximizing production technologies, usage of resources, and financial portfolio risks, and in providing knowledge of complex economic activities.

**Steps:**

1. Set up the objective function that includes nonlinear elements.
2. In Solver, set the objective to maximize or minimize this nonlinear function.
3. Open Solver and add any relevant constraints as necessary.
4. Click "Solve" to obtain the optimal solution.

## Nonlinear Pricing Model

This model determines optimal pricing strategies when revenue generation is influenced by nonlinear demand structures. It is particularly useful in markets where pricing affects buyer behavior differently at various levels. This situation can lead to better revenue management and pricing strategies that align with consumer response patterns.

**Steps:**

1. Create a table with price ranges and associated demand or revenue.
2. Use a formula to calculate total revenue based on price and demand.
3. Define the objective in Solver to maximize revenue.
4. Set constraints if there are any restrictions on pricing.
5. Click "Solve."

## Non-Smoothing Optimization Model

Non-smoothing techniques handle optimization problems where the objective function may have sudden changes. These models are important in applications like project scheduling or resource allocation in environments characterized by immediate changes or distinct segments and ensure a responsive and effective decision-making process.

**Steps:**

1. Set up your optimization model.
2. Identify objectives and constraints by remembering the sudden changes.
3. Use integer or binary constraints as needed.
4. Use Solver to analyze the model and obtain optimal conditions.

## Quadratic Optimization Model

Quadratic optimization incorporates quadratic functions in the objective or constraints. This type of modeling is frequently used in resource allocation problems where there are increasing or decreasing returns to scale. It allows for understanding trade-offs between competing objectives and the market dynamics of cost, revenue, and risk.

**Steps:**

1. Set up the objective function in quadratic form: C = ax^2 + bx + c.
2. Open Solver and enter the quadratic function as the objective.
3. Add constraints relevant to your specific problem.
4. Click "Solve."

## Smoothing Optimization Model

Smoothing optimization techniques deal with problems that require minimizing the impact of noise or variability in data. These models are necessary in making decisions based on uncertain or fluctuating information and improve forecasting accuracy and operational reliability in economic settings.

**Steps:**

1. Set up the data to include variables with smoothing considerations.
2. Define the objective function to minimize variability.
3. Use Solver and specify constraints related to the smoothing parameters.
4. Click "Solve."

## Supply Chain Optimization Models

Supply chain optimization is necessary for improving efficiency, reducing costs, and enhancing service levels. These models help in making informed decisions regarding inventory management, transportation logistics, supplier selection, and production planning. Effective supply chain optimization leads to improved operational performance and consumer satisfaction.

**Steps:**

1. Create a model that includes cost factors like production, transportation, and inventory costs.
2. Input the relationships and constraints.
3. Use Solver to define objectives.
4. Add constraints associated with supply chain limits.
5. Click "Solve" to find the optimal solution for the supply chain model.

## REAL-WORLD EXAMPLES OF INSIGHTS OF VARIOUS BUSINESS TYPES DRIVING BUSINESS SUCCESS

### Nestlé S.A.

Nestlé S.A. implements advanced data analytics to better understand consumer preferences and market trends that allow it to innovate and customize products that meet evolving consumer demands. Next is Nestlé's use of analytics in product development. By analyzing purchasing patterns and consumer feedback, the company identifies gaps in the market and creates new products that include plant-based offerings that accommodate health-conscious consumers. This data-driven approach has led to a significant growth in its portfolio. Finally, Nestlé uses supply chain analytics to optimize logistics and inventory management. By monitoring real-time data, the company can improve efficiency, reduce costs, and minimize waste in its operations.

**Question 1**

How does Nestlé S.A. use advanced data analytics to understand consumer preferences and market trends, and what impact does this have on product innovation?

Answer: Nestlé S.A. uses advanced data analytics to gain insights into consumer preferences and market trends by analyzing vast amounts of data from various sources that include social media, sales data, and consumer feedback. This analytical approach allows Nestlé to identify emerging trends and shifts in consumer behavior while enabling the company to innovate and customize products that align with evolving consumer demands. By recognizing the growing interest in health-conscious and plant-based diets, Nestlé has expanded its product offerings to include plant-based alternatives. This data-driven strategy helps Nestlé stay ahead of market trends and develop product innovation to lead to a more varied and competitive product portfolio.

**Question 2**

In what ways does Nestlé use analytics in product development, and how has this approach contributed to the company's growth?

Answer: Nestlé employs analytics in product development by examining purchasing patterns and consumer feedback to identify market gaps and opportunities for new product introductions. By understanding what consumers are buying and their feedback on existing products, Nestlé can customize its product development strategies to meet specific consumer needs. This approach has been effective in the creation of health-focused products, such as plant-based offerings, that cater to the increasing demand for healthier food options. Finally, Nestlé has experienced significant growth in its product portfolio since it continuously adapts to consumer preferences and expands its market reach.

**Question 3**

How does Nestlé S.A. maximize its supply chain operations using data analytics, and what benefits does this bring to the company?

Answer: Nestlé S.A. maximizes its supply chain operations by using data analytics to monitor real-time data related to logistics and inventory management. By analyzing this data, Nestlé can enhance operational efficiency, reduce costs, and minimize waste. Real-time monitoring allows the company to adjust inventory levels based on demand fluctuations while ensuring that products are available when needed without overstocking. Finally, analytics help Nestlé streamline transportation routes and improve distribution efficiency to lead to cost savings and a more sustainable supply chain. These benefits improve Nestlé's operational performance and contribute to its overall competitiveness in the global market.

## Biogen Inc.

Biogen Inc. relies on advanced data analytics to enhance its research and development processes and to drive innovation in treatments for neurological diseases. Next, Biogen uses real-world data analytics to study patient outcomes. By analyzing extensive patient data from clinical trials and post-marketing studies, Biogen gains knowledge of treatment effectiveness and patient populations that may benefit from their therapies. This approach informs clinical strategy and enhances drug development timelines. Finally, Biogen employs analytics in its supply chain management. By using predictive analytics to assess demand for its products, the company maximizes inventory levels and improves distribution efficiency to ensure timely delivery to health-care providers.

### Question 1

How does Biogen Inc. use advanced data analytics to enhance its research and development processes for neurological diseases?

Answer: Biogen Inc. leverages advanced data analytics to improve its research and development (R&D) processes, especially around neurological diseases. By integrating large datasets from various sources, including genomic data, clinical trial results, and scientific literature, Biogen can identify potential drug targets more efficiently. This data-driven approach enables the company to prioritize promising compounds and maximize clinical trial designs to ultimately increase the development of innovative treatments. Finally, data analytics helps in identifying biomarkers that can predict patient responses to develop personalized treatment approaches and improve overall value.

### Question 2

In what ways does Biogen use real-world data analytics to study patient outcomes, and how does this impact their clinical strategy?

Answer: Biogen implements real-world data analytics to gain knowledge of patient outcomes by analyzing extensive datasets from clinical trials and post-marketing studies. This approach enables the company to assess the effectiveness of their therapies in diverse patient populations and real-world settings. By understanding how treatments perform outside controlled clinical environments, Biogen can refine its clinical strategies, identify new therapeutic opportunities, and enhance drug development timelines. This data-driven information assists in the customization of treatments to specific patient groups by improving overall patient care and treatment success rates.

**Question 3**

How does Biogen implement predictive analytics in its supply chain management to ensure the efficient distribution of its products?

Answer: Biogen uses predictive analytics in its supply chain management to optimize inventory levels and enhance distribution efficiency. By analyzing historical sales data, market trends, and health-care provider demand, the company can predict future product needs with greater accuracy. This predictive capability allows Biogen to maintain optimal inventory levels while reducing the risk of stockouts or overproduction. Finally, this strategy enables the company to streamline its distribution processes while ensuring the timely delivery of products to health-care providers and ultimately improving patient access to essential therapies to deliver high-quality care.

## Medtronic plc

Medtronic plc employs advanced data analytics to enhance product development and improve patient outcomes in areas such as cardiovascular and diabetes care. Next, Medtronic uses analytics to monitor the performance of its medical devices in real time. By collecting data from connected devices, the company analyzes patient responses and device effectiveness. This information drives product enhancements and informs clinicians about patient adherence and potential issues to lead to a more proactive care management process. Finally, Medtronic implements analytics in supply chain optimization. By determining demand forecasts and inventory levels, the company guarantees that essential devices are available when and where needed, reducing lead times and minimizing waste.

**Question 1**

How does Medtronic plc use advanced data analytics to enhance product development and improve patient outcomes, particularly in cardiovascular and diabetes care?

Answer: Medtronic plc leverages advanced data analytics to drive innovation in product development and improve patient outcomes, especially in the fields of cardiovascular and diabetes care. By analyzing large datasets from clinical trials and real-world patient interactions, Medtronic can identify patterns and insights that inform the design and functionality of their medical devices. This data-driven approach enables the company to customize their products to better meet the needs of patients while ensuring that devices are not only effective but also user-friendly. Finally, by understanding patient outcomes through data, Medtronic can continuously refine their products to improve efficiency and safety to develop improved health outcomes for patients.

**Question 2**

In what ways does Medtronic use real-time analytics to monitor the performance of its medical devices, and how does this benefit both clinicians and patients?

Answer: Medtronic employs real-time analytics to monitor the performance of its medical devices by collecting and analyzing data from connected devices. This continuous data flow enables the company to assess device effectiveness and patient responses in real time. For clinicians, this strategy means having access to up-to-date information about patient obedience and potential issues while enabling them to make informed decisions and provide proactive care management. For patients, this process translates to improved health outcomes, as potential problems can be identified and addressed in real time. The knowledge gained from real-time analytics also drives product enhancements to ensure that Medtronic's devices remain at the head of medical technology.

**Question 3**

How does Medtronic implement analytics in its supply chain optimization, and what are the benefits of this approach?

Answer: Medtronic implements analytics in its supply chain optimization by using data-driven techniques to predict demand and manage inventory levels. By analyzing historical sales data, market trends, and other relevant factors, Medtronic can accurately predict the demand for its medical devices. This situation ensures that essential devices are available when and where they are needed while reducing lead times and minimizing waste. The benefits of this approach include improved efficiency in the supply chain, cost savings from reduced inventory holding, and enhanced consumer satisfaction due to the real-time availability of products. Finally, this analytics-driven supply chain strategy supports Medtronic's mission to deliver high-quality medical solutions to patients in the global environment.

## Honeywell International Inc.

Honeywell International Inc. implements data analytics to improve product innovation and operational efficiency while also driving growth in multiple business segments. Next, Honeywell uses data analytics in its aerospace division. By analyzing flight data and maintenance records, Honeywell can predict equipment failures and optimize maintenance schedules for aircraft. This strategy reduces downtime for airlines while enhancing safety and customer satisfaction. Finally, in the building technologies sector, Honeywell uses analytics to improve energy management solutions. By analyzing energy consumption patterns, the company provides clients with information to optimize energy usage that ultimately results in significant cost savings and a reduction in the impact on the environment.

**Question 1**

How does Honeywell International Inc. use data analytics to enhance product innovation and operational efficiency across its business segments?

Answer: Honeywell International Inc. uses data analytics to drive product innovation and operational efficiency by integrating advanced analytical tools across its various business segments. In its aerospace division, Honeywell studies flight data and maintenance records to predict equipment failures and maximize maintenance schedules. This proactive analytical approach reduces aircraft downtime, improves safety, and strengthens consumer satisfaction. In the building technologies sector, Honeywell uses analytics to assess energy consumption patterns, which allow clients to maximize energy usage. This strategy results in significant cost savings and reduces environmental impact. By inserting data analytics into its operations, Honeywell can continuously innovate and improve efficiency, ultimately driving growth and maintaining a competitive edge in the market.

**Question 2**

In what ways does Honeywell's aerospace division benefit from the application of data analytics?

Answer: Honeywell's aerospace division benefits significantly from the application of data analytics by enhancing predictive maintenance and operational efficiency. By analyzing large amounts of flight data and maintenance records, Honeywell can accurately predict potential equipment failures before they develop. This predictive capability allows airlines to schedule maintenance more effectively while minimizing unexpected downtime and ensuring aircraft are operational when needed. Finally, the use of data analytics helps improve safety standards by identifying and proactively addressing potential issues. As a result, airlines experience increased reliability and customer satisfaction, while Honeywell strengthens its reputation as a leader in aerospace technology.

**Question 3**

How does Honeywell's use of data analytics in the building technologies sector contribute to energy management and environmental sustainability?

Answer: In the building technologies sector, Honeywell relies on data analytics to enhance energy management and promote environmental sustainability. By analyzing energy consumption patterns, Honeywell provides clients with actionable insights to maximize their energy usage. This data-driven approach enables businesses to implement energy-saving measures that result in significant cost reductions and a lower carbon footprint. Next, Honeywell's analytics solutions help clients identify inefficiencies and make informed decisions about energy consumption to contribute to a more sustainable building operation. By prioritizing energy efficiency and sustainability, Honeywell supports its clients' environmental goals and reinforces its commitment to creating innovative solutions that benefit both the economy and the planet.

## CASE STUDIES ON THE SUCCESS OF VARIOUS BUSINESS TYPES THROUGH ANALYTICS

### Business Success Through Business Analytics

Business analytics plays a crucial role in understanding the trends of various business types and consumer behavior that enables organizations in the marketing industry to make more data-driven and informed decisions. Following are three examples of how the various types of business data and knowledge are translated into business success using analytics:

### Example 1:

NewTech Innovations is a company specializing in renewable energy solutions. By using business analytics, they have been able to optimize their supply chain and improve their product range. NewTech Innovations implemented advanced analytics to monitor and predict energy consumption patterns. By analyzing data from smart grids and IoT devices, they identified peak usage times and optimized their energy distribution accordingly. This not only reduced waste but also improved customer satisfaction by ensuring a reliable energy supply. Finally, they used predictive analytics to forecast equipment maintenance needs, reducing downtime and operational costs.

#### *Short-Response Questions*

1. What type of data did NewTech Innovations analyze to optimize energy distribution?
2. How did predictive analytics benefit NewTech Innovations in terms of equipment maintenance?
3. What was one of the outcomes of optimizing energy distribution for NewTech Innovations?

### Example 2: PositiveHealth Pharmaceuticals

PositiveHealth Pharmaceuticals is a company that develops and distributes pharmaceutical products. They have leveraged business analytics to enhance their research and development processes. By employing data analytics, PositiveHealth Pharmaceuticals was able to analyze clinical trial data more efficiently. They identified patterns and correlations that led to faster drug development cycles. Finally, they used market analytics to understand consumer needs and preferences, allowing them to customize their product offerings and marketing strategies effectively. As a result, this approach resulted in a significant increase in market share and customer loyalty.

#### *Short-Response Questions*

1. What type of data did PositiveHealth Pharmaceuticals analyze to speed up drug development?
2. How did market analytics benefit PositiveHealth Pharmaceuticals?
3. What was one of the outcomes of PositiveHealth Pharmaceuticals' use of business analytics?

### Example 3

UrbanLifestyle Retail is a fashion retail company that has used business analytics to enhance customer experience and streamline operations. Next, UrbanLifestyle Retail implemented customer analytics to gain insights into shopping behaviors and preferences. By analyzing purchase history and social media interactions, they personalized marketing campaigns and improved inventory management. This led to a more engaging shopping experience and reduced overstock and stockouts. Finally, they used location analytics to maximize store layouts and staffing, further enhancing operational efficiency.

### *Short-Response Questions*

1. What type of analytics did UrbanLifestyle Retail use to understand shopping behaviors?
2. How did UrbanLifestyle Retail benefit from analyzing purchase history and social media interactions?
3. What operational aspect did UrbanLifestyle Retail optimize using location analytics?

## CASE STUDY: DIVERSITY ORGANIZATIONAL SOLUTIONS INC. (DOS)

Diversity Organizational Solutions Inc. (DOS) is a consulting firm whose focus is in providing customized business solutions across various industries that include manufacturing, retail, and technology. The firm focuses on optimizing operational efficiencies, enhancing supply chain management, and developing pricing strategies. As part of its commitment to data-driven decision-making, DBS has invested in advanced analytics and optimization strategies to help its clients improve profitability and reduce costs. During its initial year of operation, the company was determined to streamline its service offerings and enhance profitability through a series of optimization models implemented in Excel.

### Business Analytics Data Tables

**TABLE 13.3** Optimization Variables

| 1 | A | B | C | D | E |
|---|---|---|---|---|---|
| | Variable | Type | Lower Bound | Upper Bound | Coefficient |
| 2 | Unit production (X1) | Integer | 100 | 500 | 25 |
| 3 | Unit price (X2) | Binary | 0 | 1 | 50 |
| 4 | Marketing budget (X3) | General integer | 1,000 | 5,000 | 10 |
| 5 | Inventory level (X4) | Continuous | 50 | 1,000 | 15 |

**TABLE 13.4** Constraints and Objectives

| 1 | A | B | C | D |
|---|---|---|---|---|
| | Constraint Description | Coefficient (LHS) | Inequality | Right-Hand Side (RHS) |
| 2 | Product capacity | 1 × 1 + 2 × 2+ 0.5 × 3 | ≤ | 1,200 |
| 3 | Budget constraint | 3 × 1 + 2 × 3 | ≤ | 30,000 |
| 4 | Minimum inventory requirement | 1 × 4 | ≥ | 200 |
| 5 | Demand requirement | 0.3 × 1 + 0.5 × 3 | = | 800 |

### Analytics Problems Using Excel

1. Use a binary variable optimization model to optimize the unit price and determine how it affects overall profitability. How can this binary approach be effectively translated in Excel?

2. Construct a quadratic optimization model to analyze the impact of production quantity on the overall profit while considering diminishing returns. How can we express this in an Excel optimization framework using the defined coefficients?
3. Apply a nonlinear optimization model using the available data to ensure that all constraints are respected while maximizing profit. Discuss how to integrate these optimization techniques with Excel Solver to arrive at a feasible solution.

## Answer Key

1. *Binary variable optimization model.* Create the decision variable for unit price (*X2*) in a specific cell in Excel. Use the binary constraint to ensure that units of price are either 0 or 1. In the Solver configuration, set *X2* as a binary variable under "Decision Variables." Set the objective function to maximize profit. Go to Data > Solver, set the objective to maximize, and include constraints for availability.
2. *Quadratic optimization model.* In Excel, express profit as a quadratic function that considers production levels: Profit = 25X1 − 0.1X1^2 − (total costs).
   Define the total costs function linearly based on production and other expenses as described in the provided coefficient table. Go to Solver, set the objective to maximize the profit cell while setting constraints according to inventory and capacity. Ensure the solver is set to "GRG Nonlinear" under the options to handle the quadratic nature.
3. *Nonlinear optimization model.* Calculate the nonlinear profit or cost function considering all variables and constraints established. Include constraints that represent capacity limitations, budget constraints, and minimum inventory requirements using the provided coefficient data.
   Create a generalized objective function in Excel: Maximize Profit = f(X1, X2, X3, X4)). Open Solver and set it to find the maximum profit while adhering to the defined constraints. Choose the method suitable for nonlinear problems, such as "GRG Nonlinear." Review Solver's output for optimal values and adjust as required to ensure feasibility under the constraints.

## CASE STUDY: OPTIMAXBIZ SOLUTIONS

OptiMaxBiz Solutions is a company that provides optimization consulting services to businesses across various industries, including manufacturing, retail, and logistics. The company has built a reputation for helping clients improve their operational efficiency and profitability through advanced optimization techniques. Recently, OptiMaxBiz Solutions partnered with an e-commerce company to maximize their supply chain and pricing strategies, aiming to reduce costs and enhance customer satisfaction. To evaluate the impact of their optimization strategies, OptiMaxBiz Solutions collected data on key metrics, including inventory levels, transportation costs, and product pricing over six months. The data was analyzed using various optimization models to identify the most efficient strategies for managing the supply chain and setting prices. The following tables summarize key findings from the project:

**TABLE 13.5** Supply Chain Metrics

| 1 | A | B | C | D |
|---|---|---|---|---|
| | **Month** | **Inventory Level (Units)** | **Transportation Costs ($)** | **Delivery Time (Days)** |
| **2** | January | 10,000 | 50,000 | 5 |
| **3** | February | 11,000 | 52,000 | 4.8 |
| **4** | March | 12,000 | 54,000 | 4.6 |
| **5** | April | 13,000 | 56,000 | 4.4 |
| **6** | May | 14,000 | 58,000 | 4.2 |
| **7** | June | 15,000 | 60,000 | 4.0 |

**TABLE 13.6** Pricing and Revenue Metrics

| 1 | A | B | C | D |
|---|---|---|---|---|
| | **Month** | **Product Price ($)** | **Units Sold** | **Revenue ($)** |
| **2** | January | 20 | 5,000 | 100,000 |
| **3** | February | 21 | 5,200 | 109,200 |
| **4** | March | 22 | 5,400 | 118,800 |
| **5** | April | 23 | 5,600 | 128,800 |
| **6** | May | 24 | 5,800 | 139,200 |
| **7** | June | 25 | 6,000 | 150,000 |

## Analytics Problems Using Excel

1. *Binary variable optimization model.* Create a binary variable optimization model to determine whether to increase inventory levels each month.
2. *General integer variables optimization model.* Develop a general integer variables optimization model for transportation costs.
3. *Integer optimization.* Perform integer optimization to minimize delivery times.
4. *Nonlinear optimization.* Apply nonlinear optimization to maximize revenue.
5. *Nonlinear pricing model.* Develop a nonlinear pricing model for product prices.
6. *Non-smoothing optimization model.* Use a non-smoothing optimization model to optimize inventory levels.
7. *Quadratic optimization model.* Create a quadratic optimization model for transportation costs.
8. *Smoothing optimization model.* Implement a smoothing optimization model for delivery times.
9. *Supply chain optimization model.* Develop a supply chain optimization model to minimize costs and maximize efficiency.

### Answer Key

1. *Binary variable optimization model.* Use the Solver tool to create a binary variable model. Set the objective to minimize costs with binary variables for inventory decisions. Example: Data > Solver > Set Objective > Minimize.
2. *General integer variables optimization model.* Use the Solver tool to develop an integer variables model. Set the objective to minimize transportation costs with integer constraints. Example: Data > Solver > Set Objective > Minimize.
3. *Integer optimization.* Use the Solver tool to perform integer optimization. Set the objective of minimizing delivery times with integer constraints. Example: Data > Solver > Set Objective > Minimize.
4. *Nonlinear optimization.* Use the Solver tool to apply nonlinear optimization. Set the objective to maximize revenue with nonlinear constraints. Example: Data > Solver > Set Objective > Maximize.
5. *Nonlinear pricing model.* Use the Solver tool to develop a nonlinear pricing model. Set the objective of optimizing product prices with nonlinear constraints. Example: Data > Solver > Set Objective > Maximize.
6. *Non-smoothing optimization model.* Use the Solver tool to create a non-smoothing optimization model. Set the objective to optimize inventory levels with non-smoothing constraints. Example: Data > Solver > Set Objective > Minimize.
7. *Quadratic optimization model.* Use the Solver tool to create a quadratic optimization model. Set the objective to minimize transportation costs with quadratic constraints. Example: Data > Solver > Set Objective > Minimize.
8. *Smoothing optimization model.* Use the Solver tool to implement a smoothing optimization model. Set the objective of optimizing delivery times with smoothing constraints. Example: Data > Solver > Set Objective > Minimize.
9. *Supply chain optimization model.* Use the Solver tool to develop a supply chain optimization model. Set the objective to minimize costs and maximize efficiency with supply chain constraints. Example: Data > Solver > Set Objective > Minimize.

CHAPTER 14

# The World of Technology and Their Analytical Approaches

Technology has become an important component in business analytics in today's global environment. Technology acts as the main source of data collection, storage, processing, and analysis that allows companies to gain new knowledge and information about their consumers, operations, and trends in the market. While technology is a tool, business analytics uses these technological advancements to study data, identify patterns and trends, and improve the strategic decision-making process for all industries within the global market. For technology industries, the use of business analytics is critical to their success. Companies in the technology industry include information technology, telecommunications, health care, finance, and manufacturing. Each of these companies relies on the use of data to maximize their daily business processes and improve the delivery of goods and services to the consumer market. In the health-care industry, health-care providers use business analytics to predict the needs of patients, provide treatment recommendations, and reduce the amount of time it takes to complete administrative tasks, which ultimately leads to better patient care and lower costs.

In the information technology sector, businesses use analytics to improve the performance of software, improve the experience of the user, and streamline the management of projects. By studying consumer behaviors and interactions, telecommunication companies can customize services or products to meet the developing needs while also ensuring higher customer satisfaction rates. Next, telecommunications companies rely on statistics and analytics to maximize their network, determine consumer turnover rates, predict product life cycles, and develop focused marketing strategies.

In the finance sector, companies use business analytics to determine the level of risk and potential for new opportunities using data-based models. By studying past data and market trends, financial companies can develop new strategies that reduce the level of risk, while also capitalizing on the conditions of the market. As a result, business analytics supports the development of risk assessment techniques that are generated through machine algorithms and other technologies that enable businesses to predict potential swings in the economy so they can adjust their investment strategies accordingly.

In the manufacturing sector, companies will use business analytics in real time to monitor data to improve their supply chain efficiency, predict equipment failures, and manage

DOI: 10.4324/9781003629658-14

their inventory levels. Next, business analytics leads to predictive maintenance schedules for manufacturers. Predictive maintenance analytics provides manufacturing companies with the ability to maintain their operational continuity while reducing downtime. As a result, these companies can optimize the allocation of resources and increase their level of productivity in the market.

Finally, technological advancements, including AI and machine learning, have transformed business analytics by producing advanced tools for the more complex analysis of data. When businesses use these advanced technologies, they become capable of using sophisticated methodologies and models to gain a better understanding of the situation so more informed decisions can be made. The result? The ability of businesses across various industries to visualize data through dashboards and other interactive methods to make it easier for decision-makers to interpret the results and to develop logic and reasoning to act in real time.

## DATA ANALYSIS MODEL

The role of technology in business analytics in today's global environment is directly connected to the optimization of business operations and to improving the decision-making process. First, technology provides the framework to collect, store, process, and analyze data. Next, business analytics transforms the raw data into meaningful information that is used to drive strategic initiatives and companies across various industries. When technology and business analytics are combined, they provide companies with a higher level of understanding about their environments so they can anticipate future market trends and respond more effectively to the needs of the consumer.

In technology companies, information technology and analytics are used to improve software solutions, reduce downtime, and improve the user experience. The situation is made possible through the studying of user feedback and behavior. Based on the data, information technology companies improve their products and services to better align the demands of the market. As a result, business analytics supports the identification of new opportunities and inefficiencies software development cycles so the company can maximize its resource allocation that will ultimately result in lower cost savings and increased productivity. Next, the telecommunications market uses technological analytics to maximize network performance, reduce turnover rates, and manage relationships with their consumers. This situation is achieved through the analysis of call data, market trends, and customer preferences, so these companies can develop focused market strategies and improve their service offerings to consumers. As a result, a data-driven strategy not only improves consumer satisfaction levels but also increases consumer retention and brand loyalty.

Third, financial institutions use data analytic models to study credit risk, identify investment opportunities, and detect fraudulent activities. With the use of predictive analytics, financial companies can analyze historical data to predict future market conditions. As a result, these businesses can make more informed decisions based on data and information to reduce potential risks while maximizing profitability. Fourth, manufacturing companies use business analytics to improve their production processes and supply chain management strategies. Within this industry, business analytics can predict equipment failures, improve logistics operations, and maximize the maintenance schedules of equipment. Using a proactive analysis approach will reduce downtime, which ultimately leads to increased overall productivity. As a result, manufacturing companies will become more competitive within their market sector based on the data analysis model.

The data analysis model uses various methods and techniques that are necessary for leaders to make effective decisions. Descriptive analytics provides information about historical data that helps companies to better understand past performance. However, predictive analytics uses statistical models and machine learning algorithms to predict future trends and consumer behaviors in the market. Finally, prescriptive analytics recommend actions that are based on predictive insight and information. As a result of these three models, companies in various industries can make data informed decisions that are more strategically aligned with their objectives and goals. Finally, the integration of AI, machine learning, and big data technologies have changed the business analytics environment. By using advanced algorithms and data visualization tools, companies can use large datasets to gain deeper knowledge and understanding of their choices and actions so they can become more responsive in their business strategies.

## Data Collection Techniques and Usage

With the increase of data in various industries and market sectors, organizations rely more heavily on technology and analytical models to drive growth and performance using data-driven methods. For technological companies, data collection is extremely important. Various methods used by these companies to collect data include interviews, surveys, Internet of Things devices, and web scraping. By using these methods, technological companies can collect information about operational efficiency, market trends, and consumer behavior. As a result, this information becomes important in improving the development of software products, improving the user experience, and creating more focused marketing strategies.

Like technological companies, telecommunications companies collect data through network monitoring systems and consumer feedback. Techniques used in this industry include real-time analytics based on consumer usage to prove their delivery of services. The situation will result in higher consumer satisfaction levels for the company. As a result, analyzing network traffic data and call quality metrics will enable telecommunications companies to maximize their infrastructure and to determine downtime and maintenance needs to improve user experience.

In the health-care sector, health-care providers with electronic health records (HER) and surveys from patients. Both methods provide valuable information on operational efficiencies and the care of patients. Next, health-care analytics can identify new trends in patient outcomes, improve the streamlining of administrative tasks and functions, and maximize processes for treatment. The situation will ultimately reduce costs, create better resource management structures, and improve patient satisfaction levels for the health-care provider.

Financial institutions use various data collection techniques that include credit scoring models and transaction analysis to assess risk and make data-driven lending decisions. When financial behavior in market trend patterns is analyzed, the company can reduce risks that are associated with lending and investing to clients. As a result, predictive analytics divide financial institutions, the capability to anticipate fluctuations in the market into becoming flexible and adapt their current strategies as necessary.

Finally, manufacturing companies use business analytics technologies, including automated production systems and sensors, that help monitor equipment performance and product quality in real time. With the use of business analytics to collect data, manufacturing companies can improve their predictive maintenance strategies to reduce the level of risk to equipment failure. As a result, manufacturing firms can improve their overall production efficiency and effectiveness. As a result, companies in various industries in the global market can use technology and business analytics to analyze data quickly and accurately while breaking down complex patterns to gain a higher level of understanding in the decision-making process.

## IMPLEMENTING BUSINESS ANALYTIC SOLUTIONS

Technology is the foundation of business analytics. With technology, business analytics can begin the data collection process, store information, process data, and analyze the results. With new advancements in AI, cloud computing, and big data technologies, businesses can efficiently collect and analyze data from various sources. The situation gives companies the ability to process large amounts of data in real time while immediately responding to changing conditions in the market and consumer preferences. As an example, companies in the information technology sector use analytics to improve software development and to monitor user interactions with their platforms and applications. With the use of business intelligence tools, information technology companies can maximize resource allocation, improve user experience, and identify blockages in performance. As a result, analytical knowledge is used to develop more flexible and adaptable development cycles and better products that meet the demand of consumers.

In telecommunications, companies use business analytics to analyze customer relationship management strategies and maximize network efficiency. The situation is achieved by analyzing call data records and consumer feedback to help businesses identify the main causes of service disruptions and to create a focused marketing strategy that appeals to their clientele. As a result, predictive analytics issues predict consumer retention levels, customer satisfaction levels, and the turnover of consumers in the target market. In the health-care sector, providers use analytical solutions to implement new strategies based on patient data, treatment protocols, and resource management. With predictive models, health-care providers can predict patient discharge and admission relationships. This situation enables health-care providers to deliver better care and to prepare for the demand of the current environment.

Financial institutions integrate business analytic tools into their business strategies by analyzing past data market trends that are used to make data-driven investment decisions. As a result, this information is used to create new solutions that allow banks and credit unions to determine credit risk more accurately while identifying fraudulent behaviors and transactions in real time to improve trust, transparency, and integrity. Finally, manufacturing companies implement business analytic solutions to study data in real time about their production lines. This situation enables manufacturing firms to maximize their maintenance schedules and to identify inefficiencies in the process. Using a proactive approach also minimizes the downtime of the equipment and improves the overall productivity of the company. As a result, successful implementation of business analytic solutions requires companies in all industries to create a data-driven culture, invest where required, and to guarantee that employees are trained and equipped with the necessary skills so the company can achieve its objectives and goals.

## Choose the Right Platform

The combination of technology and business analytics empowers companies in all industries to better understand their markets, improve consumer experiences, and maximize operational efficiencies. This situation makes it important for companies to choose the right platform for technology and business analytics to succeed. First, IT companies use advanced technological tools and analytics to study performance issues, develop products that align more with the needs of the consumer, and understand the behavior of customers. The ability to quickly respond to changes in trends in the markets is necessary in maintaining an advantage in the global environment.

Second, telecommunications companies must choose a platform that maximizes network performance, while also managing consumer relationships more effectively. With the use of a data analysis framework, call records in consumer interactions can be studied to help the business develop focused promotions, implement retention strategies, and identify any potential disruptions to service. As a result, predictive analytics will assist these businesses to predict turnover rates of products and consumers so they can take proactive measures that improve the loyalty of clients. Third, health-care providers must choose a business analytic framework that studies patient data and provides operational performance metrics to help the company

**TABLE 14.1** Factors for Choosing the Right Platform

| Factor | Description | Importance |
|---|---|---|
| **Ease of use** | User-friendly interface and intuitive design for all user types | High – ensures quick adoption and efficient use by all employees |
| **Integration capabilities** | Ability to seamlessly integrate with existing systems and data sources | High – facilitates comprehensive data analysis and smooth workflow |
| **Scalability** | Capacity to handle growing data volumes and user demands | High – supports future growth and increased data complexity |
| **Analytical features** | Advanced analytics capabilities, like predictive modeling and real-time tracking | High – provides deeper insights and better decision-making |
| **Support and training** | Availability of customer support and training resources | Medium – ensures users can effectively utilize the platform and resolve issues |
| **Cost** | Overall cost includes subscriptions, hidden fees, and maintenance | Medium – must fit within budget while offering good value |

improve their quality of care, allocate resources more effectively, and reduce the amount of time it takes to complete administrative processes.

In the finance market, the proper framework to be used is one that assesses investment strategies and risk management processes. It is important for all financial companies to use technology and business analytics to reduce fraud, analyze market trends, and assess the credit worthiness of lending and borrowing decisions for clients. When data-driven information is used to make decisions, banks, credit unions, and other investments firms can maximize their portfolios. As a result of this process, financial institutions can increase their level of trust and transparency with their consumers.

When selecting the right business analytics platform, there are several factors that must be considered by companies in all industries of the global market. These factors are seen in the chart that follows.

## INTEGRATION OF ANALYTICS WITH EXISTING IT INFRASTRUCTURE

Business analytics must be integrated with existing IT infrastructure in all industries within the global environment. With the use of the analysis of past data and current market trends, companies in all industries can make data-informed decisions that reduce risk and increase profitability. By integrating analytics with existing IT infrastructure, businesses can optimize their overall value of data to help improve the accessibility and flow of data within the organization when taking into consideration all factors required in effectively combining technology with business analytics.

The first factor to consider is compatibility. Companies must choose an analytic solution that is compatible with their existing systems. These existing systems include customer relationship management software, databases, and enterprise resource planning systems. By ensuring compatibility, enhancement and data sharing will help to minimize disruptions to the daily business process. The second factor is data quality and consistency. This process ensures that the collection of data from various sources is consistent and accurate. Next, data quality and consistency involve the implementation of data governance policies to maintain quality across the various platforms within the organization.

The third factor is scalability. Scalability is the process of selecting the correct analytical tools that can increase or decrease with the growth of the business. When data volume increases the chosen analytic solution can conduct a more complex analysis without the degradation of performance. The fourth factor is user training and adoption. It is important for companies to train employees on how to use the advanced analytics will tools so they can become more effective within their existing environment. The situation will enable the business to promote a culture of data-driven decision-making that requires familiarity with the technology and a high level of user engagement.

The final factor is security and compliance. Security and compliance guarantee that the integration of technology and analytics follows the existing security standards and data privacy regulations that have been established. This situation is necessary for companies when dealing with sensitive data in consumer privacy rights. As a result, the integration of analytics into existing IT infrastructure in all industries in the global market will optimize the use of data while also providing the business with a competitive advantage within their market due to a more informed decision-making process to support their strategic initiatives.

## FUTURE TRENDS IN BUSINESS ANALYTICS AND TECHNOLOGY

There are future trends in business analytics and technology in all industries within the global environment. For the information technology sector, companies use analytics to improve the user experience, refine software development processes, and support more efficient project management initiatives. This situation is made possible by examining application performance metrics and user engagement data to adjust its current strategy based on data-driven information. Second, the telecommunications sector heavily uses business analytics to focus on network optimization and improve relationships with its customers. With technology and business analytics, telecommunications companies can determine service quality, identify areas for improvement, and monitor network traffic. As a result, telecommunications companies can use the new information found in the existing data to develop focused marketing strategies to improve the retention levels of consumers and increase brand satisfaction and loyalty.

In the health-care sector, health-care providers use business analytics to analyze operational efficiency and patient outcomes. The situation requires health-care providers to carefully study patient data to identify emerging trends in treatment effectiveness, to improve clinical decision-making, and allocate resources more efficiently. With the use of predictive analytics, health-care providers can also maximize staffing levels and forecast patient admission rates to develop a better resource and care management system. For the financial

**TABLE 14.2** Future Trends in Business Analytics and Technology

| | Description | Impact |
|---|---|---|
| **Artificial intelligence (AI) and machine learning (ML)** | Transforms business analytics through predictive analytics, natural language processing, and automation | Enhanced decision-making, automation of complicated tasks, and improved accuracy in insights |
| **Augmented analytics** | Integrates AI and ML to automate data research, model selection, and insight generation | Democratizes data analysis, allowing non-technical users to gain knowledge and make data-driven decisions |
| **Real-time analytics** | Analyzes data as soon as it's generated, providing immediate insights and actions | Enables quick decision-making, increases operational efficiency, and improves customer experiences |
| **Cloud computing** | Moves data analytics to the cloud, offering scalable resources and powerful analytical tools | Mitigates costs, improves scalability, and allows for more efficient data processing and storage |
| **Focus on data privacy and ethics** | Highlights ethical data collection, storage, and usage, ensuring compliance with regulations | Develops consumer trust, protects personal information, and avoids legal issues |

sector, firms must analyze compliance, investment strategies, and risk management with the support of technology and business analytics. Next, financial firms will need to implement advanced analytical methodologies to assess credit risk, analyze market trends, and detect fraudulent behaviors and activities in real time. As a result, using a data-driven approach provides all of these industries to make more informed decisions that reduce risk, maximize profit, provide transparency, and increase trust and support from consumers within their market segment.

Finally, there are several future trends in business analytics technology that are shaping the global environment. These future trends are seen in the chart that follows.

## BUSINESS ANALYTICS FUNCTION FOR INFORMATION TECHNOLOGY USING MICROSOFT EXCEL

In the business environment, there are many business analytical terms mentioned that play a critical role in making informed and data-driven choices that drive decisions, optimize daily operations, and develop strategic actions and initiatives. Various statistical concepts play an important role in information technology and business analytics by providing essential tools for data analysis and decision-making. Here's a detailed overview of their definition and importance and how to conduct this statistical analysis using Microsoft Excel.

### Availability

This metric indicates the uptime of systems and services, essential in ensuring uninterrupted business operations and in maintaining consumer satisfaction. High availability equals greater trust and reliability in information technology services.

Formula: = (Total Uptime/(Total Uptime + Total Downtime))*100

**Steps:**

1. Open Excel and create a new spreadsheet.
2. In cell A1, type "Total Uptime."
3. In cell B1, enter the value of total uptime.
4. In cell A2, type "Total Downtime."
5. In cell B2, enter the value of total downtime.
6. In cell A3, type "Availability (%)."
7. In cell B3, enter the formula =(B1/(B1+B2))*100
8. Press Enter to see the availability percentage.

### Cost Per User

Understanding the cost encountered for each user helps organizations in budgeting, allocating resources, and optimizing expenditures in relation to user engagement and satisfaction.

Formula: = Total Cost/Total Users

**Steps:**

1. In cell A4, type "Total Cost."
2. In cell B4, enter the value.
3. In cell A5, type "Total Users."
4. In cell B5, enter the number.
5. In cell A6, type "Cost Per User."
6. In cell B6, enter the formula =B4/B5.
7. Press Enter to calculate the cost per user.

### Data Growth Rate

This metric highlights how quickly an organization's data is expanding, informing data management strategies, storage requirements, and analytics capabilities required to handle that growth efficiently.

Formula: = ((New Data Size − Old Data Size)/Old Data Size)*100

**Steps:**

1. In cell A7, type "Old Data Size."
2. In cell B7, enter the old size.
3. In cell A8, type "New Data Size."
4. In cell B8, enter the new size.
5. In cell A9, type "Data Growth Rate (%)."
6. In cell B9, enter the formula =((B8-B7)/B7)*100.
7. Press Enter to get the growth rate.

### Equipment Life Cycle Replacement Strategy

Having a clear replacement strategy ensures that outdated equipment is continually upgraded, maintaining performance and technological relevance, while also preventing increased costs associated with repairs.

**Steps:**

1. Outline criteria in a separate sheet.
2. Consider factors such as usage, cost of downtime, and technology trends.

### Expected Value Strategy

This strategic context evaluates potential outcomes of decisions based on expected values and enables organizations to prioritize initiatives that offer the greatest potential return on investment (ROI).

Formula: = (Probability of Outcome1*Value of Outcome1) + . . . + (Probability of OutcomeN*Value of OutcomeN)

**Steps:**

1. In column A, list potential outcomes.
2. In column B, add their probabilities.
3. In column C, input their corresponding values.
4. In cell B13, enter the formula =SUMPRODUCT(value:1, value:2).
5. Press Enter to calculate the expected value.

## Formation of Decision Problems

Structuring decision-making challenges is necessary for analytical transparency and enables organizations to break down complex situations into manageable components for more effective resolution.

**Steps:**

1. Define and list different scenarios with varying inputs.
2. Add scenarios and use the Scenario Manager to add and manage scenarios.
3. Compare results to generate summary reports to compare outcomes across scenarios.

## Frequency of Software Errors

Monitoring software errors helps identify areas for improvement in software development and maintenance practices that ultimately lead to enhanced system reliability and user satisfaction.

Formula: = Total Software Errors/Total Time

**Steps:**

1. In cell A14, type "Total Software Errors."
2. In cell B14, enter the number of errors.
3. In cell A15, type "Total Time."
4. In cell B15, enter the time frame used for observation.
5. In cell A16, type "Error Frequency."
6. In cell B16, enter the formula =B14/B15.
7. Press Enter to see the frequency.

## Mean Time Between Failures (MTBF)

This reliability measure provides knowledge of system performance and durability and leads to maintenance schedules and information required in making investments in new technologies.

Formula: = Total Operational Time/Total Number of Failures

**Steps:**

1. In cell A17, type "Total Operational Time."
2. In cell B17, enter the operational time.
3. In cell A18, type "Total Number of Failures."
4. In cell B18, enter the value.
5. In cell A19, type "MTBF."
6. In cell B19, enter the formula =B17/B18.
7. Press Enter to get MTBF.

## Mean Time to Repair (MTTR)

Understanding MTTR helps organizations measure the efficiency of their response to incidents and influences IT support strategies and improvement initiatives.

Formula: = Total Repair Time/Total Number of Repairs

**Steps:**

1. In cell A20, type "Total Repair Time."
2. In cell B20, enter the total repair time.
3. In cell A21, type "Total Number of Repairs."
4. In cell B21, enter the number of repairs.
5. In cell A22, type "MTTR."
6. In cell B22, enter the formula =B20/B21.
7. Press Enter to obtain the MTTR value.

## Network Efficiency

This metric assesses how well network resources are used and how it impacts the overall productivity and potential upgrades or optimizations in network infrastructure.

Formula: = (Total Data Transmitted/Total Data Sent)*100

**Steps:**

1. In cell A23, type "Total Data Transmitted."
2. In cell B23, enter the data transmitted.
3. In cell A24, type "Total Data Sent."
4. In cell B24, enter the total data sent.
5. In cell A25, type "Network Efficiency (%)."
6. In cell B25, enter the formula =(B23/B24)*100.
7. Press Enter to see the network efficiency percentage.

## Probability for Maximizing Strategies

Evaluating the probability of successful outcomes from various strategies helps decision-makers prioritize actions that align with business objectives and goals.

**Steps:**

1. To assess this probability analytically, consider the probabilities of each strategy's success based on past performance.
2. Use collected data in a separate sheet for more complex calculations.

## Probability of Decisions With Conflicting Objectives

This metric assists organizations in addressing trade-offs between competing goals while ensuring that the chosen strategies sufficiently address key stakeholder interests.

**Steps:**

1. List conflicting objectives in column A.
2. In column B, provide corresponding probabilities of achieving those objectives based on historic data or expert judgment.
3. Aggregate the probabilities to reflect the chance of success given the conflicts using Excel functions like SUM or AVERAGE.

## Probability Outcomes for Decision Strategies

Understanding the probabilities associated with decision-making strategies guides informed choices while helping to mitigate risks and use resources more effectively.

Formula: = (Number of Successful Outcomes/Total Outcomes)

**Steps:**

1. In cell A26, type "Number of Successful Outcomes."
2. In cell B26, input the number.
3. In cell A27, type "Total Outcomes."
4. In cell B27, input the total outcomes.
5. In cell A28, type "Probability of Success."
6. In cell B28, enter the formula =B26/B27.
7. Press Enter to find the success probability

## Project Completion Ratio

Tracking project completion ratios reveals the proportion of projects finished on time and within budget and highlights the efficiency and effectiveness in the project management processes.

Formula: = (Number of Completed Projects/Total Projects) × 100

**Steps:**

1. In cell A29, type "Number of Completed Projects."
2. In cell B29, enter the number.
3. In cell A30, type "Total Projects."
4. In cell B30, enter the total number of projects.
5. In cell A31, type "Project Completion Ratio (%)."
6. In cell B31, enter the formula =(B29/B30)*100.
7. Press Enter to get the completion ratio.

## Return on Investment (ROI) for IT Projects

Assessing ROI enables organizations to quantitatively measure the financial benefits of IT investments to develop smarter data-driven budget decisions and resource allocations.

Formula: = (Net Profit/Cost of Investment) × 100

**Steps:**

1. In cell A32, type "Net Profit."
2. In cell B32, enter the profit.
3. In cell A33, type "Cost of Investment."
4. In cell B33, enter the investment cost.
5. In cell A34, type "ROI (%)."
6. In cell B34, enter the formula =(B32/B33)*100.
7. Press Enter to see the ROI.

## Usage Rate of Resources

Monitoring resource usage ensures optimal performance while allowing organizations to recognize underused assets and adjust strategies accordingly for improved efficiency.

Formula: = (Resource Used/Total Available Resources) × 100

**Steps:**

1. In cell A35, type "Resource Used."
2. In cell B35, input the resource used.
3. In cell A36, type "Total Available Resources."
4. In cell B36, enter the total available.
5. In cell A37, type "Usage Rate (%)."
6. In cell B37, enter the formula =(B35/B36)*100.
7. Press Enter to calculate the usage rate.

## REAL-WORLD EXAMPLES OF INFORMATION TECHNOLOGY (IT) INSIGHTS DRIVING BUSINESS SUCCESS

### Facebook Inc. (Meta Platforms)

Facebook Inc. (Meta Platforms) relies on data analytics to understand user behavior, which is used to support product development and targeted advertising strategies. Next, Facebook uses machine learning algorithms to analyze user interactions and preferences. By processing large amounts of data, the company customizes content and advertisements to individual users, which increases user engagement and satisfaction. This data-driven approach allows businesses to reach their target audiences more effectively while enhancing advertising ROI. Finally, Meta Platforms implements data analytics to improve its platform security. By analyzing traffic patterns and user data, the company can identify and mitigate potential threats to ensure a safer experience for millions of users worldwide.

**Question 1**

How does Facebook use data analytics to enhance user engagement and satisfaction through its product development and advertising strategies?

Answer: Facebook uses data analytics to gain knowledge into user behavior, preferences, and interactions on its platform. By using machine learning algorithms, the company processes large amounts of data to customize content and advertisements for individual users. This personalized approach increases user engagement by presenting relevant content and enhances user satisfaction by providing a more focused experience. Finally, businesses benefit from this strategy as it allows them to reach their target audiences more effectively to improve their advertising return on investment (AROI). Finally, the continuous analysis of user data enables Facebook to improve its algorithms and maintain an active platform that adapts to changing user needs and preferences.

**Question 2**

In what ways does Facebook's use of machine learning algorithms contribute to its targeted advertising strategies?

Answer: Facebook's use of machine learning algorithms is central to its targeted advertising strategies. These algorithms analyze user interactions, preferences, and demographic information to create detailed user profiles. By understanding the interests and behaviors of its users, Facebook can deliver highly focused advertisements that are likely to connect with individual users. This focused precision increases the effectiveness of advertising campaigns that enable businesses to reach potential customers who are genuinely interested in their products or services. As a result, there is a higher engagement rate with ads, improved conversion rates, and a stronger ROI for advertisers.

**Question 3**

How does Meta Platforms implement data analytics to improve platform security and ensure a safer user experience?

Answer: Meta Platforms uses data analytics to improve its platform security by continuously monitoring network activity and analyzing user data for potential threats. By examining traffic patterns and user behavior, the company can identify anomalies that may indicate security breaches or other malicious activities. Next, advanced analytics tools help in detecting and responding to cyberthreats in real time, allowing Meta to mitigate risks before they impact users. Finally, the company uses threat intelligence to stay informed about emerging security challenges and to develop predictive measures to protect sensitive information, to ensure that users can enjoy a safer experience on the platform by developing trust and reliability among its global users.

## Intel Corporation

Intel Corporation relies on advanced data analytics to improve its chip design, manufacturing processes, and supply chain management. Next, Intel applies analytics in its semiconductor fabrication facilities. By analyzing production data in real time, the company can identify potential issues to optimize the manufacturing process and reduce waste. This approach results in higher-quality products and improved cost efficiency. Finally, Intel uses data analytics to predict market trends and demand for its products. By analyzing customer feedback and competitive landscapes, the company strategically aligns its research and development efforts with market needs to ensure the timely introduction of cutting-edge technologies.

### Question 1

How does Intel Corporation use data analytics to improve its semiconductor fabrication processes, and what are the benefits of this approach?

Answer: Intel Corporation employs data analytics in its semiconductor fabrication facilities by analyzing production data in real time. This strategy allows the company to identify potential issues early in the manufacturing process while enabling timely interventions to optimize operations. The benefits of this approach include reduced waste, improved cost efficiency, and the production of higher-quality semiconductor products. By relying on data analytics, Intel can maintain a competitive edge in the market by ensuring that its manufacturing processes are both efficient and effective, leading to better performance and reliability of its products.

### Question 2

In what ways does Intel use data analytics to predict market trends and demand for its products, and how does this influence its research and development efforts?

Answer: Intel uses data analytics to predict market trends and demand by analyzing customer feedback, purchasing patterns, and competitive markets. This data-driven approach allows Intel to gain knowledge into consumer preferences and emerging technologies that are used to support its research and development strategies. By strategically aligning its R&D efforts with market needs, Intel can ensure the timely introduction of cutting-edge technologies that meet consumer demands. Finally, this strategic alignment enhances Intel's product offerings and strengthens its position as a leader in the semiconductor industry.

**Question 3**

Discuss the role of data analytics in Intel's supply chain management and the impact it has on the company's operational efficiency.

Answer: Data analytics plays a crucial role in Intel's supply chain management by providing real-time insights into logistics, inventory levels, and demand forecasts. By monitoring and analyzing this data, Intel can maximize its supply chain operations, leading to improved efficiency and reduced costs. The use of predictive analytics helps Intel anticipate demand fluctuations and adjust its inventory while minimizing waste and ensuring that products are delivered to market in a timely fashion. Finally, this enhanced operational efficiency reduces lead times and guarantees that Intel can meet consumer demands effectively to maintain high levels of customer satisfaction.

## China Mobile Ltd.

China Mobile Ltd. uses business analytics in the information technology and telecommunications sectors to ensure significant growth and customer engagement. The company uses advanced data analytics to maximize its network performance and improve their consumer experiences. Next, China Mobile's use of data analytics is to manage network traffic. By analyzing user data and traffic patterns in real time, the company can dynamically allocate resources to guarantee peak service quality while reducing latency and enhancing consumer satisfaction during prime usage times. Finally, China Mobile implements analytics to modify its marketing strategies. By analyzing consumer behavior and preferences, the company can develop focused promotions and personalized services to increase user retention and sales for sustainability and long-term growth.

**Question 1**

How does China Mobile Ltd. use data analytics to enhance network performance and consumer experiences?

Answer: China Mobile Ltd. uses advanced data analytics to optimize its network performance and improve consumer experiences by analyzing user data and traffic patterns in real time. This strategy allows the company to dynamically allocate network resources while ensuring peak service quality and reducing delays during peak demand periods. Next, China Mobile can improve consumer satisfaction while providing a stable and reliable service experience even during peak usage times. This strategic use of data analytics improves network efficiency and strengthens consumer loyalty and engagement.

**Question 2**

In what ways does China Mobile Ltd. use data analytics to manage network traffic effectively?

Answer: China Mobile Ltd. uses data analytics to manage network traffic by constantly monitoring user data and traffic patterns. This real-time analysis enables the company to identify bottlenecks and allocate resources vigorously to maintain optimal service quality. By reducing latency and ensuring consistent performance, China Mobile can improve consumer satisfaction during peak usage times. As a result, this proactive management of network traffic through data analytics guarantees that the company can meet the demands of its large consumer base while maintaining high service standards.

**Question 3**

How does China Mobile Ltd. implement data analytics to refine its marketing strategies?

Answer: China Mobile Ltd. uses data analytics to improve its marketing strategies by analyzing consumer behavior and preferences. This analysis allows the company to develop customized promotions and personalized services that identify individual users. By understanding consumer needs and preferences, China Mobile can create more effective marketing campaigns that increase user retention and drive sales. This data-driven approach enhances consumer satisfaction and supports the company's sustainability and long-term growth by guaranteeing that marketing efforts are strategically aligned with consumer expectations and market trends.

## Oracle Corporation

Oracle Corporation relies on data analytics to improve its cloud services and database management systems and to provide significant value to its customers. Next, Oracle uses machine learning algorithms in its cloud applications. By analyzing enormous datasets, Oracle enables organizations to gain predictive insights that drive decision-making and improve operational efficiency. This strategy enables companies to proactively address challenges and optimize their business processes. Finally, Oracle implements analytics to improve consumer experience through personalized service offerings. By studying consumer interaction data, the company customizes solutions that meet their specific needs, which ultimately lead to increased levels of user satisfaction and brand loyalty.

**Question 1**

How does Oracle Corporation use data analytics to improve its cloud services and database management systems?

Answer: Oracle Corporation uses data analytics to significantly improve its cloud services and database management systems by integrating advanced analytical tools and machine learning algorithms. Next, these technologies enable Oracle to process and analyze large amounts of data efficiently while providing organizations with analytical knowledge, which is crucial for informed decision-making. As a result, Oracle helps businesses maximize their operations, improve performance, and reduce costs. The ability to forecast trends and potential issues before they develop enables companies to address challenges while ensuring stable and more efficient business processes.

**Question 2**

In what ways does Oracle use machine learning algorithms to benefit organizations using its cloud applications?

Answer: Oracle implements machine learning algorithms within its cloud applications to offer organizations predictive knowledge, which leads to strategic decision-making and operational efficiency. By analyzing large datasets, these algorithms can identify patterns and trends that are not immediately apparent to human analysts. This capability enables businesses to predict market changes, consumer behavior, and operational challenges, which enables them to adapt quickly and effectively. Finally, organizations can maximize their business processes, mitigate risks, and take advantage of new opportunities that will lead to improved performance and competitive advantage.

**Question 3**

How does Oracle implement data analytics to improve consumer experience and foster brand loyalty?

Answer: Oracle implements data analytics to improve consumer experience by personalizing service offerings based on consumer interaction data. By analyzing how consumers interact with their products and services, Oracle can customize solutions to meet specific consumer needs and preferences. This personalized and unique approach increases user satisfaction and develops brand loyalty since consumers are more willing to remain with a brand that understands and caters to their individual requirements. Finally, by continuously analyzing consumer feedback and behavior, Oracle can make data-driven improvements to its product offerings while ensuring that they remain important and valuable to their consumer markets.

## CASE STUDIES ON INFORMATION TECHNOLOGY (IT) SUCCESS THROUGH ANALYTICS

### Business Success Through Business Analytics

Business analytics plays a crucial role in understanding IT trends and consumer behavior that enables organizations in the IT industry to make more data-driven and informed decisions. Following are three examples of how IT data and knowledge are translated into business success using analytics:

### Example 1: WaveTech Solutions

WaveTech Solutions is an IT company specializing in cloud computing services. By using advanced business analytics, WaveTech has been able to optimize its resource allocation and improve service delivery. The company uses predictive analytics to anticipate client needs and adjust their cloud resources accordingly while ensuring optimal performance and cost efficiency. This proactive approach has led to a 25% increase in client satisfaction and a 10% reduction in operational costs.

### *Short-Response Questions*

1. What type of services does WaveTech Solutions specialize in?
2. How has WaveTech Solutions improved client satisfaction?
3. What percentage reduction in operational costs has WaveTech achieved?

### Example 2: CyberITGuard

CyberITGuard Innovations is an IT company focused on cybersecurity solutions. The company employs business analytics to monitor and analyze data from various sources to detect potential security threats. By implementing machine learning algorithms, CyberITGuard can identify patterns and anomalies that indicate cyberthreats, allowing them to respond quickly. This has resulted in a 30% decrease in security breaches for their clients and has positioned CyberITGuard as a leader in proactive cybersecurity measures.

### *Short-Response Questions*

1. What is the primary focus of CyberITGuard Innovations?
2. How does CyberITGuard Innovations detect potential security threats?
3. What is the percentage decrease in security breaches achieved by CyberITGuard?

### Example 3: DataFlow Dynamics

DataFlow Dynamics is an IT company that provides data analytics and business intelligence services. By leveraging big data analytics, DataFlow helps businesses make informed decisions by providing information on market trends and consumer behavior. The company uses real-time data processing to deliver information used to enable clients to adapt quickly to market changes. This approach has led to a 30% increase in client revenue and a 30% improvement in decision-making efficiency.

### *Short-Response Questions*

1. What services does DataFlow Dynamics offer?
2. How does DataFlow Dynamics help businesses make informed decisions?
3. What improvement has DataFlow achieved for its clients?

---

## CASE STUDY: TECHRESOLUTIONS INC.

TechResolutions Inc. is an information technology company dedicated to providing innovative software solutions and IT consulting services to businesses across various market sectors. The company prides itself on its ability to improve operational efficiency through technology and offering services like cloud computing, cybersecurity, and system integration. Recently, TechResolutions experienced critical operational challenges related to resource allocation, equipment life cycle management, and software reliability. To improve its performance metrics and strategic decision-making, the company incorporated advanced analytical techniques using Excel to monitor and optimize their IT processes.

## Business Analytics Data Tables

**TABLE 14.3** IT Resource and Performance Metrics

| 1 | A | B |
|---|---|---|
| | **Metric** | **Value** |
| 2 | Cost per user ($) | 150 |
| 3 | Data growth rate (%) | 25 |
| 4 | Mean time between failures (MTBF) | 300 hours |
| 5 | Mean time to repairs (MTTR) | 5 hours |
| 6 | Frequency of software errors | 12 per month |
| 7 | Project completion ratio (%) | 85 |
| 8 | Return on investment (ROI) (%) | 20 |

**TABLE 14.4** Equipment Life Cycle and Resource Usage

| 1 | A | B | C | D | E |
|---|---|---|---|---|---|
| | **Equipment Type** | **Initial Cost ($)** | **Replacement Cost ($)** | **Lifespan (Years)** | **Usage Rate (%)** |
| 2 | Servers | 20,000 | 5,000 | 5 | 60 |
| 3 | Networking devices | 15,000 | 3,000 | 4 | 70 |
| 4 | Workstation | 3,000 | 1,000 | 3 | 80 |
| 5 | Backup systems | 10,000 | 2,000 | 6 | 50 |

## Analytics Problems Using Excel

1. Evaluate the cost per user for TechResolutions while considering the return on investment (ROI) of IT projects. How can Excel be used to calculate an expected value strategy regarding future investment decisions?
2. Use the mean time to repair (MTTR) and mean time between failures (MTBF) to assess network efficiency in relation to equipment life cycle strategies. How can this information influence the equipment life cycle replacement strategy to maximize uptime?
3. Analyze the probability outcomes of decision strategies based on software error frequency and the project completion ratio. How do conflicting objectives affect the decision-making process, and how can the formation of decision problems be structured in Excel?

## Answer Key

1. *Calculation of cost per user and ROI.* Calculate total IT costs: Total IT Cost = (Number of Users) × (Cost per User). Replace "Number of Users" with relevant data. The formula for ROI can be established as:
   ROI = ((Net Profit))/(Total Investment)) × 100
   In Excel, set up cells for each variable, and apply the formulas to calculate current and projected ROI. Use =IF() statements to define ranges of expected values based on investment ranges as part of the decision strategy evaluation.
2. *Assessment of network efficiency and equipment life cycle.* Calculate network efficiency as Network Efficiency = ((MTBF))/(\text(MTBF)) + (MTTR). Create a formula in Excel: + (MTBF)/(MTBF + MTTR). Evaluate the life cycle strategy by comparing the total cost of ownership (Initial Cost + Replacement Cost) against the expected return, including uptime improvements determined from enhanced reliability with lower frequency of software errors. Assess if current equipment aligns with the expected usage rate, and suggest a replacement timeline.
3. *Probability outcomes and decision strategies.* For assessing probabilities of error frequency impacts, employ the basic probability formula: Error = (Frequency of Errors)/(Total Tests). Set up in Excel with respective values in dedicated cells. To evaluate the impact of conflicting objectives on the project completion ratio, consider using a weighted scoring model in Excel: Weighted Score = (Weight_1 Score_1 + Weight_2 * Score_2)/(Total Weights).
   Apply scenario analysis using Excel's What-If Analysis to visualize potential decision outcomes and configure achievable goals across conflicts.

## CASE STUDY: TECHOPTIMIZATION INC.

TechOptimization Inc. is an IT consulting firm that focuses on optimizing technology infrastructure and improving network efficiency for businesses. The company has helped numerous organizations enhance their IT systems, reduce costs, and improve overall performance. Currently, TechOptimization Inc. has partnered with a management services

**TABLE 14.5** IT System Metrics

| 1 | A | B | C | D | E |
|---|---|---|---|---|---|
| | Month | System Availability (%) | Cost per User ($) | Data Growth Rate (%) | Frequency of Software Errors |
| **2** | January | 99.0 | 150 | 5 | 10 |
| **3** | February | 99.2 | 145 | 5.5 | 9 |
| **4** | March | 99.4 | 140 | 6 | 8 |
| **5** | April | 99.6 | 135 | 6.5 | 7 |
| **6** | May | 99.8 | 130 | 7 | 6 |
| **7** | June | 99.9 | 125 | 7.5 | 5 |

**TABLE 14.6** Network and Project Metrics

| 1 | A | B | C | D | E | F | G |
|---|---|---|---|---|---|---|---|
| | Month | Mean Time Between Failures (Hours) | Mean Time to Repair (Hours) | Network Efficiency (%) | Project Completion Ratio (%) | ROI for IT Projects (%) | Usage Rate of Resources (%) |
| 2 | January | 500 | 2 | 85 | 80 | 10 | 70 |
| 3 | February | 550 | 1.8 | 86 | 82 | 12 | 72 |
| 4 | March | 600 | 1.6 | 87 | 84 | 14 | 74 |
| 5 | April | 650 | 1.4 | 88 | 86 | 16 | 76 |
| 6 | May | 700 | 1.2 | 89 | 88 | 18 | 78 |
| 7 | June | 750 | 1.0 | 90 | 90 | 20 | 80 |

company to upgrade their IT infrastructure while focusing on improving system availability, reducing software errors, and maximizing resource usage. To evaluate the impact of their recommendations, TechOptimization Inc. collected data on key IT metrics, including system availability, cost per user, data growth rate, and frequency of software errors over six months. The data was analyzed to identify trends and measure the effectiveness of the implemented strategies. The Tables 14.5 and 14.6 summarize key findings from the project:

## Analytics Problems Using Excel

1. *Availability.* Calculate the average system availability over the six months.
2. *Cost per user.* Determine the total cost per user for the six months.
3. *Data growth rate.* Analyze the trend in data growth rate over the six months.
4. *Equipment life cycle replacement plan.* Develop an equipment life cycle replacement plan based on the mean time between failures.
5. *Expected value strategy.* Calculate the expected value of reducing software errors.
6. *Frequency of software errors.* Determine the monthly frequency of software errors.
7. *Mean time between failures.* Calculate the average mean time between failures.
8. *Mean time to repair.* Determine the average mean time to repair.
9. *Network efficiency.* Analyze the trend in network efficiency over the six months.
10. *Probability for maximizing strategies.* Calculate the probability of achieving maximum network efficiency.
11. *Probability of decisions with conflicting objectives.* Analyze the probability of decisions with conflicting objectives for IT projects.
12. *Probability of outcomes for decision strategies.* Determine the probability of outcomes for different decision strategies.
13. *Project completion ratio.* Calculate the average project completion ratio.
14. *Return on investment for IT projects.* Compute the ROI for IT projects for each month.
15. *Usage rate of resources.* Analyze the trend in usage rate of resources over the six months.

## Answer Key

1. *Availability.* Use the AVERAGE function: =AVERAGE(B2:B7).
2. *Cost per user.* Use the SUM function: =SUM(C2:C7).
3. *Data growth rate.* Use the TREND function to analyze the trend: =TREND(D2:D7).
4. *Equipment life cycle replacement plan.* Use the IF function to develop a replacement plan: =IF(E2>600, "Replace", "Keep").
5. *Expected value strategy.* Use the SUMPRODUCT function to calculate expected value: =SUMPRODUCT(probabilities, values).
6. *Frequency of software errors.* Use the SUM function to determine monthly frequency: = SUM(E2:E7).
7. *Mean time between failures.* Use the AVERAGE function: =AVERAGE(B2:B7).
8. *Mean time to repair.* Use the AVERAGE function: =AVERAGE(C2:C7).
9. *Network efficiency.* Use the TREND function to analyze the trend: =TREND(D2:D7).
10. *Probability for maximizing strategies.* Use the PROB function to calculate probability: =PROB(range, probabilities, lower_limit, upper_limit).
11. *Probability of decisions with conflicting objectives.* Use the BINOM.DIST function: =BINOM.DIST(number_s, trials, probability_s, cumulative).
12. *Probability of outcomes for decision strategies.* Use the NORM.DIST function: =NORM.DIST(x, mean, standard_dev, cumulative).
13. *Project completion ratio.* Use the AVERAGE function: =AVERAGE(E2:E7).
14. *Return on investment for IT projects.* Use the ROI formula: =(Gain from Investment − Cost of Investment)/Cost of Investment.
15. *Usage rate of resources.* Use the TREND function to analyze the trend: =TREND(G2:G7).

CHAPTER **15**

# The Global Analytic Approach of Regional and International Management

Business analytics plays an important role in the global analytical approach of regional and international management. The combined role of global, regional, and international management with business analytics is necessary in the interconnected economy to enable managers and leaders to develop strategies, maximize operations, and increase their competitive advantage in various industries. First, it is important to define each of these roles. *Global management* is the process of managing operations that cross national boundaries. Next, global management uses strategies that are customized to meet the needs of diverse markets, regulatory environments, and economic conditions and to accommodate all cultural diversities that exist. As a global manager, individuals must possess a complete understanding of international trade laws, cross-cultural communication, and global supply chain processes. Examples of global management industries include pharmaceuticals and technology that require businesses to identify emerging trends across market segments, perform metrics analysis, and guarantee compliance with international trade standards.

*Regional management* focuses on specific geographic areas within the global market. Next, regional management attempts to support the unique characteristics and needs of these regions. This type of management strategy has the primary focus of addressing the dynamics of the local market while aligning them with their overall corporate strategies. Examples of regional management industries include retail, logistics, and hospitality, since they must adapt their business operations to the local regulations and preferences of the area. Finally, *regional managers* who use business analytics to collect information about consumer behavior and regional economic conditions and to effectively allocate resources to meet market demand. As a result, regional managers will use a localized approach to remain responsive to the changes in the market to develop long-term relationships with their stakeholder groups.

International management combines global and regional business practices by focusing primarily on managing operations and resources in different countries around the world. Next, international managers must overcome the complexities of doing business in diverse cultural and legal environments. This situation is essential in international marketing when it comes to human resource practices and collaborating with local businesses and governments. Examples of international management industries include manufacturing, telecommunications, and

DOI: 10.4324/9781003629658-15

finance, since they rely on a global distance operation for cost-effectiveness and business efficiency. As a result of business analytics combined with international management, managers can analyze the market entry strategies of new sectors and determine performance levels across different markets and the changes in value of currency and improve their decision-making capabilities.

In global management, regional management, and international management business analytics are used within all levels of management. Next, business analytics provides necessary methodologies and statistical tools that are required to change raw data into actionable information. This process relies on data collection, statistical analysis, and predictive modeling to allow companies to anticipate future trends, maximize operational efficiency, and to better understand consumer preferences. In all these various industries, business analytics supports data-driven strategies that are used to make informed decisions and to help companies gain a competitive advantage in their market segments.

## IMPORTANCE OF ANALYTICS IN REGIONAL AND INTERNATIONAL MANAGEMENT

In regional and international management, business analytics plays an important role. First, business analytics helps global management to oversee their business operations, which extend beyond national borders. Next, business analytics will require global managers to develop a comprehensive approach to balancing the needs of the market, government regulations, and diverse cultures. The situation will make it necessary for global managers to become skilled in international trade laws and supply chain management. Industries with this process that are seen the most include pharmaceuticals, consumer goods, and technology, since it is important for individuals to identify emerging trends, ensure compliance, and evaluate market performance when making informed strategic decisions.

In regional management, business analytics focuses primarily on specific geographic areas and then customizes its business strategies to meet local demand while also aligning its processes with broader corporate goals. At the regional management level, business analytics supports industries that include hospitality, logistics, and retail, where it is important to understand the needs of the local market and the nuances that are involved. Next, regional managers must use business analytics to gain new knowledge and information about the behavior of consumers, allocate resources effectively, and track economic changes. As a result, the focus of regional management will be improving the responsiveness of the business to changes in the market while also ensuring that organizations remain competitive against the competition.

Finally, business analytics supports international management by developing a connection between global and regional management strategies. This process oversees business operations in various countries while also dealing with complex legal and cultural environments contained within them. International managers in human resource management, international marketing, and those attempting to form partnerships with local countries must understand the needs and values of the people. Industries that include telecommunications, manufacturing, and finance rely on international management business analytics to analyze important data that is necessary for evaluating market entry strategies, changes in currency, improving decision-making process, and developing key performance metrics to determine the level of success.

As a result, business analytics and regional and international management is paramount to the success of industry leaders. Business analytics will convert large amounts of data into meaningful information. The strategy will enable organizations to make informed data-driven decisions. In regional management, business analytics will help to identify the preferences of local consumers, market trends, and allow the business to customize marketing strategies to improve the engagement of the customer. However, in international management, business analytics will be used to analyze the dynamics of the regulatory environments in the various countries the business operates, so we can maintain a successful operation and experience long-term sustainable growth.

## Comparative Analysis of Regional Management Styles

Comparative analysis is an important business analytic tool that applies to the styles of regional management. In global management, managers are required to gain a comprehensive understanding of international regulations, global market trends, and cultural and diverse sensitivities of the community. Next, global managers will need to balance local responsiveness with global efficiency. Industries experiencing the situation include consumer goods, pharmaceuticals, and technology to streamline their operations and optimize their presence in the market. With the help of business analytics, global management companies can develop data-driven information that will support corporate strategies and provide benchmarking performance measures across all markets.

In regional management, the focus is on specific geographic areas that require localized business strategies that reflect the diverse and unique characteristics of each market segment. Next, regional management is necessary in industries that include logistics, retail, and hospitality, where the preferences of consumers and regulatory compliance can change drastically from one area to the next. This situation requires regional managers to adopt a wider range of corporate strategies to meet the local expectations while also taking advantage of their understanding of the market dynamics with the assistance of business analytics. As a result, business analytics will provide knowledge and insight into all regional economic measures, competitive environment, and trends of the customers that allow managers to make informed decisions that improve their entrance into new and emerging markets while maintaining operational efficiency.

In international management, business analytics will combine regional and global business practices that must be managed across various countries at the same time. International managers must be familiar with cross-border operations, cultural differences, diverse market conditions, and legal environments. Industries within the international management style include manufacturing, finance, and telecommunications since they require strategic alignment across many markets around the world. As a result, business analytics will play an important part in analyzing the needs of the environment so that managers can develop better entry-level strategies, assess risk, and improve operational performance.

Finally, it is important to remember that when analyzing comparative regional management styles, distinct approaches will develop based on economic and cultural factors. An example is, in Asian countries, management styles will place a strong focus on elective decision-making and consensus building among the stakeholders. However, for Western nations, such as the United States and the Great Britain, the focus will be on assertiveness and individualism. Finally, in South American and Latin markets, the management style focuses on personal connections and networking and is relationship-oriented. As a result, it is important to understand these variations of regional management styles that are combined with business analytics so the business customizes management strategies effectively and efficiently so they can improve their engagement production levels within their market environments.

## DATA SOURCES FOR IDENTIFYING KEY SOURCES OF DATA FOR ANALYSIS

Within business analytics, there are various data sources used in identifying key sources of data for analysis. In today's global economy, the roles of global, regional, and international management have become interconnected with one another. Within all levels of management, it is important for companies to identify and use the correct data sources for business analysis. Next, each management level operates in a unique environment and supports different economic sectors in cultures. This situation will provide a strong influence on the data that is used to develop acquisition strategies. In global management, aligning business strategies with global trends is paramount to the success of the business and can only be done through the comprehensive analysis of large datasets that rely on macroeconomic indicators and international trade statistics.

Next, regional management must have a broader understanding of the regional markets related to their specific geographic areas. This situation makes important regional managers use business analytics to help adapt their current strategies to meet the local preferences and demands of the consumer. Resources used as part of the business analytic process include regional, industry associations and governmental economic reports. As a result, the industries most impacted by regional management include agriculture or energy. Third, international managements rely on business analytics to adapt to various regions based on their cross-border operations and distinctions within the markets.

Pharmaceutical and finance companies are most impacted by international management styles and use resources that include multinational databases and financial performance indices, to ensure that their business operation alliance with both the local requirements and it is overarching corporate strategy. As a result, business analytics provides each management style with the ability to transform data into useful information through data mining, machine learning, and predictive analytics to help businesses in all industries to uncover new patterns and trends that will guide the decision-making process.

### Interpreting Global Trends Using Data

Business analytics is important in the interpretation of global trends by using all available data sources. The global environment is strongly influenced by the various roles of global, regional, and international management styles and their inclusion of business analytics. All these components must work together to accurately interpret the global trends and gain new meaning or insight from existing data sources that are required to improve the strategic decision-making process across all industries. From global management, individuals must rely on comprehensive data and statistical analysis to discover patterns across different regions and markets. As an example, the technology company must analyze the engagement metrics of global users and industry developments to forecast future demand and to develop new product innovations.

Next, regional management industries must focus on adapting global ideas to better meet the needs of the regions it serves. This situation can cause the business to operate differently from one country to the next or even from one locality to another. As an example, an automotive company can analyze local economic conditions, consumer preferences, and sales data to help improve the launch of a new product in its marketing campaigns. To be successful, the automotive company must rely on the data that has been analyzed from regional market research and demographic studies to ensure the marketing campaign and product meet the needs of the target audience and respond quickly to changes in demand.

Third, international management industries are primarily concerned with cross-border business operations while also understanding localized business practices. Industries impacted the most by international management include financial companies, where it is important to comply with all international regulations. This situation requires financial businesses to accurately interpret data to remain competitive in the market. Next, international managers will need to take advantage of investment trends, regulatory changes, and global economic forecasts to make improved decisions that strategically align with both short-term objectives and long-term regional and global requirements.

Within all three levels of management, business analytics is an important tool that is used to convert large amounts of data into decisions or actions based on the use of advanced statistical methodologies. When statistical analysis is used, all industries can conduct data visualization, predictive modeling, and identify global trends that will impact future of their business strategy. As a result, the combination of global, regional, and international management along with business analytics is necessary for interpreting global trends through the use of data analysis. With this integrated approach, businesses, and all industries can become empowered to understand weaknesses and threats, and to take advantage of their strengths and opportunities to increase their competitive advantage within the environment. With the effective use of business analytics, companies have the capability to strategically align their objectives and goals with regional and global markets to increase their level of sustainable growth and product innovation.

## THE ROLE OF CULTURAL CONSIDERATIONS IN DATA INTERPRETATION

The role of cultural considerations and data interpretation is important to all levels of management styles when using business analytics. In the overseeing of worldwide operations, global management relies on business analytics to understand the social, political, and economic environments contained within the market. The situation requires global managers to systematically analyze data to identify emerging trends that can impact the organizations on an international level. As an example, a consumer goods company will need to consider the cultural preferences of the community when analyzing sales data. As a result of the understanding of cultural preferences, the company can then begin to influence buying behavior and improve product development and marketing campaigns that are directly focused on their targeted consumer markets.

Regional managers and companies will need to understand geographic areas around the world. The situation requires regional managers to adapt the business analytics to take into consideration the languages, values, and tastes of the communities. As an example, a hotel chain must study consumer feedback and booking patterns differently in various regions so they can adjust their promotional strategies and services to better align with the local expectations and customs. However, international managements companies will place a stronger emphasis on cross-border operations that consider the cultural differences in each sector. As an example, a multinational bank will use business analytics to determine the local cultural information when developing regional financial products and services that directly connect with the appropriate clientele

As a result, business analytics provides all the necessary tools to develop detailed data interpretation with the use of statistical and predictive modeling. To be successful, businesses in all industries must examine data trends and develop cultural awareness of their consumers. If cultural factors are ignored, business analytics can lead to the misuse of data in a misinterpretation of the results. As an example, a technology company that is attempting to study user engagement across different countries that does not consider the different levels of technology adoption and usage will experience incorrect data when developing their products and marketing campaigns due to a lack of understanding of the cultural dynamics within the area. As a result, it is very important for all industries and management styles to understand the context of the data and to implement cultural considerations when interpreting the results.

## The Impact of Global Analytics on Decision-Making

Through business analytics, there is a global impact on decision-making. In global management, the overseeing of business operations across various markets requires managers to deal with diverse regulatory, economic, and cultural environments. The situation requires managers to develop strategies that both align with global demand and market trends. By implementing global analytics, managers can identify all encompassing patterns, changes in consumer behavior patterns, and new or emerging market opportunities. As an example, a global retailer can study sales data from different regions to determine which products connect best with consumers within a specific area. As a result, the use of a data-driven approach will enable the retailer to allocate the correct resources and to customize his product offering to meet global demand.

Next, regional management will need to understand the nuances in consumer preferences in specific geographic areas. Regional managers must also understand the economic conditions and competitive environments within each geographic location. As an example, regional automotive companies can use data related to changes in demographics, market conditions, and government regulations to maximize production and its marketing strategies. By using business analytics in a data-driven approach, the regional automotive company can develop a regional understanding to improve consumer engagement to increase its position within the market.

Third, international managements must develop a corporate strategy that aligns with its overall vision, along with the realities of the local environment, through cross-border operations. The situation makes it important for international managers to use business analytics to understand the various trends that are impacting the different regions it operates in, so they can interpret the context of local business practices. As an example, a multinational technology firm can use business analytics to determine the adoption rates of its global software so we can improve its product offering based on user need and the regional technology infrastructure of the area.

Finally, business analytics uses advanced statistical methodologies and data visualization tools to transform and make sense of large datasets. By using global analytics, decision-makers, and all industries can understand new and emerging trends that were previously unknown using regional analysis. As an example, health-care providers can use global data to identify trends of health care or outbreaks so they can better allocate resources across different regions and to develop new informed treatment protocols to become more effective in responding to global health situations. As a result, all industries will benefit from global analytics as part of the decision-making process to develop sustainable growth initiatives and to gain a competitive advantage within the global environment.

## FUTURE OPPORTUNITIES AND CHALLENGES IN GLOBAL ANALYTICS

There are both future opportunities and challenges in global analytics. As companies expand their foothold in the global environment, they will experience both opportunities and challenges when using global analytics to improve strategies across various industries or markets. First, global management must oversee business operations in multiple countries. At the same time, the situation requires an understanding of the diverse cultures and markets within all areas. Next, global managers will need to analyze large datasets to identify trends that can impact their level of performance and corporate strategy. As an example, consumer goods companies can use data related to purchasing habits throughout different regions to maximize their product offerings and marketing strategies. This situation enables consumer goods companies to gain new information about the markets to enable their business to maintain a competitive advantage in a rapidly changing environment.

Regional management must use regional data analytics to enable managers to customize their strategic approaches to meet the needs of the economy and local consumer preferences. As an example, a hospitality business will study consumer feedback, seasonal trends, and occupancy rates to improve its operational strategies. With the development of a new localized approach, the hospitality company can develop long-term relationships with consumers and respond in real time to changes in demand within the market. However, international management will use international analytics to gain a better understanding of global trends that are associated with the specifics of each region it operates in. As an example, an international finance company can use data to determine the volatility of the market based on consumer behavior in various market segments. This strategy will enable the international finance company to improve strategic investment decisions to develop a comprehensive approach to improve its level of risk management while maximizing opportunities across different regions at the same time.

As a result, business analytics provides statistical tools to develop the identification of trends, to conduct predictive modeling, to develop key performance metrics, and to improve the decision-making process throughout all management levels of various industries. However, today's global environment will require companies to become more reliant on global analytics, which will also require them to address the threat and challenges of data privacy regulations and cybersecurity risks to help ensure the protection and safety of consumer data.

In the future, new opportunities in global analytics will include the use of machine learning to improve data analysis and predictive modeling capabilities. The benefits of these technologies will be of help in streamlining the daily operations of businesses and in enabling companies to anticipate changes in the markets more accurately and effectively. However, there will also be challenges to global analytics in the future due to the complex nature of global data sources. Next, there will also be new ethical implications for the usage of data companies.

Organizations everywhere will need to place a strong priority on sustainable business practices and data management. This situation will need to ensure regulatory compliance with the different international regulations around the world. As a result, they will need to be collaborated between global, regional, and international management along with business analytics for companies in all industries to remain successful in the modern business environment. When business analytics tools and strategies are used effectively and efficiently, organizations and industries everywhere can benefit from new opportunities while reducing risk to help lead the way for sustained growth and innovation.

## BUSINESS ANALYTICS FUNCTION FOR INTERNATIONAL BUSINESS USING MICROSOFT EXCEL

In the business environment, there are many business analytical terms mentioned that play a critical role in making informed and data-driven choices that drive decisions, optimize daily operations, and develop strategic actions and initiatives. Various statistical concepts play an important role in international business and business analytics by providing essential tools for data analysis and decision-making. Here's a detailed overview of their definition and importance and how to conduct this statistical analysis using Microsoft Excel.

### Adjusted Return on Investment (ROI)

This metric provides an advanced measure of profitability by accounting for various factors like investment risk or changes in financing structure. It helps organizations determine the true return on investment and leads to better investment decisions and comparisons across different projects.

Formula: = (Net Profit/Initial Investment)*100

**Steps:**

1. Open Excel and create a new spreadsheet.
2. In cell A1, type "Net Profit."
3. In cell B1, enter the net profit value.
4. In cell A2, type "Initial Investment."
5. In cell B2, enter the investment amount.
6. In cell A3, type "Adjusted ROI (%)."
7. In cell B3, enter the formula =(B1/B2)*100.
8. Press Enter to see the adjusted ROI percentage.

### Break-Even Analysis

This analysis determines the point at which total revenues equal total costs and provides knowledge of the minimum sales required to avoid financial losses. It is critical for pricing strategies, understanding profit margins, and making informed operational decisions related to cost control.

Formula: =Fixed Costs/(Selling Price per Unit − Variable Cost per Unit)

**Steps:**

1. In cell A4, type "Fixed Costs."
2. In cell B4, enter the fixed costs.
3. In cell A5, type "Selling Price per Unit."
4. In cell B5, enter the selling price.
5. In cell A6, type "Variable Cost per Unit."
6. In cell B6, enter the variable cost.
7. In cell A7, type "Break-Even Point (Units)."
8. In cell B7, enter the formula =B4/(B5 − B6).
9. Press Enter to obtain the break-even point in units.

### Cash Flow From Foreign Operations

Evaluating cash flow generated from international activities is necessary in understanding the financial stability of global operations. This analysis assists in assessing the sustainability of foreign investments and their impact on overall cash flow management.

Formula: = Cash Inflows − Cash Outflows

**Steps:**

1. In cell A8, type "Cash Inflows."
2. In cell B8, enter the total cash inflows from foreign operations.
3. In cell A9, type "Cash Outflows."
4. In cell B9, enter the total cash outflows.
5. In cell A10, type "Cash Flow from Foreign Operations."
6. In cell B10, enter the formula =B8 − B9.
7. Press Enter to see the cash flow.

## Exchange Rate Calculation

Accurate exchange rate calculations are essential for businesses engaged in international trade. They affect pricing strategies, revenue recognition, and profitability analysis by determining how currency changes impact profits and costs associated with foreign transactions.

Formula: = Amount in Original Currency * Exchange Rate

**Steps:**

1. In cell A11, type "Amount in Original Currency."
2. In cell B11, enter the amount.
3. In cell A12, type "Exchange Rate."
4. In cell B12, enter the exchange rate.
5. In cell A13, type "Total Amount in New Currency."
6. In cell B13, enter the formula =B11*B12.
7. Press Enter to convert the amount.

## Foreign Tax Rate Comparison

Comparing tax rates across different countries helps companies maximize their tax planning strategies. Understanding the variances can lead to informed data-driven decisions about locations for expansion, investment structures, and overall financial planning.

**Steps:**

1. Create a new table, starting in cell A1, where you compare different foreign tax rates.
2. In column A, list country names.
3. In column B, enter the respective tax rates.
4. Input the country names and tax rates in subsequent rows.
5. Analyze the data to determine which country has the highest and lowest tax rates.

## Global Market Share

This metric is critical to evaluating an organization's position in a competitive market. By analyzing global market share, companies can evaluate growth opportunities, monitor market dynamics, and develop strategies to improve their competitive advantage.

Formula: = (Company Sales/Total Market Sales)*100

**Steps:**

1. In cell A17, type "Company Sales."
2. In cell B17, enter the sales amount.
3. In cell A18, type "Total Market Sales."
4. In cell B18, enter the total market sales.
5. In cell A19, type "Global Market Share (%)."
6. In cell B19, enter the formula =(B17/B18)*100.
7. Press Enter to see the market share percentage.

## International Trade Ratio

This ratio evaluates the relationship between a country's exports and imports. Analyzing this ratio provides knowledge into a nation's economic stability, trade balance, and dependency on foreign markets and guides policymaking and business strategy.

Formula: = (Exports/Imports)

**Steps:**

1. In cell A20, type "Exports."
2. In cell B20, enter the exports value.
3. In cell A21, type "Imports."
4. In cell B21, enter the imports value.
5. In cell A22, type "International Trade Ratio."
6. In cell B 22, enter the formula =B20/B21.
7. Press Enter to calculate the international trade ratio.

## Net Present Value (NPV) in Different Currencies

NPV is a main metric for assessing the profitability of investments. When calculated in various currencies, it allows organizations to evaluate investment opportunities across different countries and consider the local market conditions, risks, and expected returns.

Formula: = Σ (Cash Flow/(1 + r)^n), where $r$ = discount rate and $n$ = period

**Steps:**

1. In cell A23, type "Cash Flow."
2. In column B, list the cash flows for each year.
3. In cell A26, type "Discount Rate."
4. In cell B26, enter the discount rate.
5. In cell A27, type "NPV."
6. In cell B27, enter the formula =NPV(B26, B23:B25).
7. Press Enter to obtain the NPV for the cash flows.

## Price Adjustments for Inflation

Adjusting prices for inflation is important in maintaining purchasing power and ensuring profitability. This analysis helps companies set appropriate pricing strategies to indicate real economic conditions and consumer behavior.

Formula: =Original Price*(1 + Inflation Rate)

**Steps:**

1. In cell A28, type "Original Price."
2. In cell B28, enter the original price.
3. In cell A29, type "Inflation Rate."
4. In cell B29, enter the inflation rate.
5. In cell A30, type "Adjusted Price."
6. In cell B30, enter the formula =B28*(1 + B29).
7. Press Enter to calculate the adjusted price considering inflation.

## Weighted Average Cost of Capital (WACC)

WACC is a crucial measure that reflects the average cost of financing an organization's operations through debt and equity. Understanding WACC helps organizations assess investment opportunities, evaluate project viability, and make strategic financial decisions that optimize the value of shareholders.

Formula: = (E/V*Re) + (D/V*Rd*(1 − Tc)), where *E* is the market value of equity, *D* is the market value of debt, *V* is the sum of E and D, *Re* is the cost of equity, *Rd* is the cost of debt, and *Tc* is corporate tax rate

**Steps:**

1. In cell A31, type "Market Value of Equity (E)."
2. In cell B31, enter the value.
3. In cell A32, type "Market Value of Debt (D)."
4. In cell B32, enter the value.
5. In cell A33, type "Cost of Equity (Re)."

6. In cell B33, enter the rate.
7. In cell A34, type "Cost of Debt (Rd)."
8. In cell B34, enter the rate.
9. In cell A35, type "Corporate Tax Rate (Tc)."
10. In cell B35, enter the rate.
11. In cell A36, type "Total Value (V)."
12. In cell B36, enter the formula =B31 + B32.
13. In cell A37, type "WACC."
14. In cell B37, enter the formula =(B31/B36*B33) + (B32/B36*B34*(1 − B35)).
15. Press Enter to calculate WACC.

## REAL-WORLD EXAMPLES OF GLOBAL, REGIONAL, AND INTERNATIONAL INSIGHTS DRIVING BUSINESS SUCCESS

### Pfizer Inc.

Pfizer Inc. relies on advanced analytics to improve its research and development processes and to drive innovation in drug discovery and development across its international markets. Next, Pfizer uses data analytics to analyze clinical trial results in real time. By assessing patient data globally, the company can identify new trends and make informed adjustments to trials based on data to expedite the development of necessary medications and vaccines. This strategy has proven to be invaluable, especially during the development of COVID-19 and other pandemic vaccines. Finally, Pfizer implements analytics for market access strategies by analyzing regional health-care data to understand pricing and reimbursement strategies. This information enables the company to streamline its approach to various markets while ensuring effective distribution and access to medications.

**Question 1**

How does Pfizer Inc. use data analytics to enhance its research and development processes, particularly in drug discovery and development?

Answer: Pfizer Inc. uses advanced data analytics to significantly improve its research and development processes by analyzing large datasets from clinical trials and other research activities. This approach enables the company to identify patterns and trends that may not be readily apparent through traditional strategies. By integrating data from various sources, Pfizer can streamline the drug discovery process while identifying potential drug candidates more efficiently and predicting their effectiveness and safety profiles. As a result, this data-driven strategy accelerates the development timeline but also reduces costs and increases the likelihood of successful outcomes in the development of new drugs.

**Question 2**

In what ways has Pfizer's use of real-time data analytics during clinical trials accelerated the development of medications and vaccines, especially during the COVID-19 pandemic?

Answer: During the COVID-19 pandemic, Pfizer's use of real-time data analytics played a crucial role in expediting the development of vaccines. By continuously analyzing patient data from global clinical trials, Pfizer can quickly identify trends and make informed decisions about trial adjustments. Next, this real-time analysis allowed the company to maximize trial designs, improve patient recruitment strategies, and ensure the collection of high-quality data. As a result, Pfizer was able to fast-track the development and approval process for its COVID-19 vaccine and demonstrated the importance of data analytics in responding to all urgent public health needs.

#### Question 3

How does Pfizer implement data analytics to inform its market access strategies, and what benefits does this bring to the company and its consumers?

Answer: Pfizer implements data analytics to inform its market access strategies by analyzing regional health-care data, including pricing, reimbursement policies, and patient demographics. This analysis allows Pfizer to focus its market entry strategies on the specific needs and conditions of each region while ensuring that its products are accessible and affordable to the target populations. By understanding the distinctions of different markets, Pfizer can maximize its pricing strategies, bargain for better reimbursement terms, and improve distribution networks. As a result, this approach enhances Pfizer's competitive edge and ensures that patients worldwide have timely access to essential medications to ultimately improve health outcomes and customer satisfaction.

### Anheuser–Busch InBev SA/NV

Anheuser–Busch InBev SA/NV uses data analytics to maximize its supply chain and improve marketing strategies across diverse markets. Next, Anheuser–Busch InBev's use of data analytics helps it to better understand consumer preferences and trends in different regions. By analyzing purchasing behavior and market data, the company adapts its product offerings and marketing campaigns to resonate with local tastes to increase brand loyalty and sales. Finally, the company uses data analytics to optimize production and distribution processes. By monitoring inventory levels and global consumer demand, Anheuser–Busch InBev can adjust production schedules to minimize waste and guarantee quick delivery to retailers and suppliers.

#### Question 1

How does Anheuser–Busch InBev utilize data analytics to enhance its supply chain management?

Answer: Anheuser–Busch InBev leverages data analytics to optimize its supply chain by closely monitoring inventory levels and global consumer demand. By analyzing this data, the company can modify its production schedules to minimize waste and ensure efficient resource allocation. This approach not only reduces costs but also guarantees the timely delivery of products to retailers and suppliers and improves the overall supply chain efficiency. The use of predictive analytics allows the company to anticipate demand fluctuations and respond proactively to ensure that production and distribution processes are aligned with market needs.

#### Question 2

In what ways does Anheuser–Busch InBev use data analytics to tailor its marketing strategies across different regions?

Answer: Anheuser–Busch InBev uses data analytics to gain insights into consumer preferences and trends in various regions. By analyzing purchasing behavior and market data, the company can change its product offerings and marketing campaigns to align with local tastes and cultural nuances. This focused approach helps increase brand loyalty and sales by ensuring that marketing efforts identify with the specific preferences of consumers in each market. The ability to customize marketing strategies based on data-driven insights enables Anheuser–Busch InBev to effectively engage with diverse consumer bases and maintain a competitive edge in the global market.

**Question 3**

How does data analytics contribute to Anheuser–Busch InBev's understanding of consumer preferences and trends?

Answer: Data analytics plays a crucial role in Anheuser–Busch InBev's ability to understand consumer preferences and trends by providing detailed knowledge of purchasing behaviors and market dynamics. By analyzing large sets of data, the company can identify emerging trends and shifts in consumer preferences that allow it to adapt its product offerings accordingly. Next, this data-driven approach allows Anheuser–Busch InBev to stay ahead of market trends and ensure that its products meet the changing and dynamic needs of consumers. Finally, the knowledge gained from data analytics informs the development of new products and marketing strategies that help the company maintain its relevance and appeal in a competitive industry.

## Verizon Communications Inc.

Verizon Communications Inc. implements business analytics to improve network performance, enhance customer experience, and maximize operations. Next, Verizon's application of data analytics is required in predicting network demand by users. By analyzing usage patterns and customer data, the company can proactively manage bandwidth allocation to ensure high-quality service during peak times. This strategy improves user satisfaction and reduces the overall cost of operations. Finally, Verizon uses geographic information systems (GIS) analytics to identify market opportunities in various regions. Through the examination of demographic and usage data, the company can strategically invest in infrastructure development where demand is projected to grow and allows for more efficient allocation of resources.

**Question 1**

How does Verizon Communications Inc. use data analytics to enhance its network performance and customer experience?

Answer: Verizon Communications Inc. uses data analytics to significantly improve its network performance and customer experience by predicting network demand. By analyzing usage patterns and consumer data, Verizon can proactively manage bandwidth allocation while ensuring high-quality service during peak times. Next, this approach not only improves user satisfaction by reducing instances of network congestion and service interruptions but also optimizes operational costs. By anticipating demand, Verizon can allocate resources more efficiently and can maintain a complex and reliable network that meets customer expectations.

**Question 2**

In what ways does Verizon use geographic information systems (GIS) analytics to identify market opportunities?

Answer: Verizon implements geographic information systems (GIS) analytics to identify and capitalize on market opportunities by examining demographic and usage data across various regions. This analysis allows Verizon to strategically invest in infrastructure development in areas where demand is projected to expand. By understanding the geographic distribution of potential consumers and their service needs, Verizon can efficiently dedicate resources to ensure that network growth and upgrades are focused on regions with the highest growth potential. This strategic approach not only maximizes return on investment but also improves service availability and quality for customers in those areas.

**Question 3**

How does Verizon's use of data analytics contribute to cost reduction in its operations?

Answer: Verizon's use of data analytics contributes to cost reduction in its operations by enabling more efficient bandwidth management and resource allocation. By predicting network demand through the analysis of usage patterns and consumer data, Verizon can maximize its bandwidth allocation to reduce the need for expensive over-provisioning of network resources. Finally, GIS analytics helps Verizon identify the most promising regions for infrastructure investment while ensuring that capital expenditures are directed toward areas with the highest potential for growth and return. As a result, this focused approach minimizes waste and maximizes the efficiency of Verizon's operational expenditures, which will ultimately lead the company to reduced costs.

## Novartis International AG

Novartis International AG relies on analytics to improve drug development and to significantly reduce the time taken to bring new treatments to the market. By analyzing patient data and market trends across various regions, Novartis customizes its drug offerings to meet local health needs and improve its competitiveness in new markets. Finally, Novartis relies on business analytics to maximize supply chain operations while ensuring the timely worldwide delivery of medications. The implementation of machine learning algorithms allows for the real-time monitoring of product demand and inventory levels while minimizing waste. As a result, the company's commitment to analytics has improved its investments in digital health programs that were used to further support the improvement of patient outcomes and operational efficiency in the pharmaceutical industry.

**Question 1**

How does Novartis International AG utilize analytics to enhance its drug development process and reduce time-to-market for new treatments?

Answer: Novartis International AG relies on advanced analytics to focus its drug development process by analyzing large amounts of patient data and market trends. This approach allows the company to identify potential drug candidates more efficiently and customize their development to meet specific health needs in various regions. By using predictive analytics,

Novartis can anticipate future challenges in clinical trials and make data-driven decisions to accelerate the development process. This strategy not only reduces the time-to-market for new treatments but also guarantees that the drugs are more effectively aligned with patient needs to improve the overall success rate of new drug launches.

**Question 2**

In what ways does Novartis customize its drug offerings to improve competitiveness in new markets?

Answer: Novartis customizes its drug offerings by analyzing regional patient data and market trends to understand the specific health needs and preferences of different populations. This data-driven approach enables the company to alter its product portfolio to better serve local markets while ensuring that its offerings are relevant and competitive. By customizing its drugs to address prevalent health issues in specific regions, Novartis can improve its market penetration and brand loyalty. Finally, this strategy enables the company to allocate resources more efficiently so the company can focus on areas with the highest potential for growth and impact.

**Question 3**

How does the implementation of machine learning algorithms benefit Novartis's supply chain operations?

Answer: The implementation of machine learning algorithms significantly enhances Novartis's supply chain operations by enabling the real-time monitoring of product demand and inventory levels. These algorithms can predict fluctuations in demand, allowing the company to adjust its production schedules and distribution strategies accordingly. This proactive strategy minimizes waste and ensures that medications are delivered promptly to meet global demand. Finally, machine learning helps optimize logistics and resource allocation, reducing operational costs and improving overall efficiency. By integrating these advanced technologies into its supply chain, Novartis can develop a large and responsive supply chain that supports its commitment of delivering high-quality medications to its global market.

## CASE STUDIES ON GLOBAL, REGIONAL, AND INTERNATIONAL SUCCESS THROUGH ANALYTICS

### Business Success Through Business Analytics

Business analytics plays a crucial role in understanding global, regional, and international business trends and consumer behavior, which enables organizations in the global, regional, and international business industry to make more data-driven and informed decisions. Following are three examples of how global, regional, and international business data and knowledge are translated into business success using analytics:

### Example 1: GlobalConnections Solutions

GlobalConnections Solutions is a multinational corporation specializing in telecommunications infrastructure. With operations in over 50 countries, the company provides seamless connectivity solutions to businesses and consumers worldwide. Next, GlobalConnections

Solutions utilized business analytics to optimize its network infrastructure. By analyzing data from various regions, the company identified areas with high demand for bandwidth and potential network congestion. This knowledge allowed them to strategically invest in infrastructure upgrades, ensuring reliable service and reducing downtime. Predictive analytics helped anticipate future demand trends, enabling proactive capacity planning. Finally, the strategic use of analytics led to a 20% increase in customer satisfaction due to improved service reliability. Furthermore, the company saw a 15% reduction in operational costs by optimizing resource allocation. These improvements strengthened GlobalConnections's market position and increased its global market share.

### *Short-Response Questions*

1. What was the primary focus of GlobalConnections Solutions' business analytics efforts?
2. How did business analytics impact customer satisfaction for GlobalConnections Solutions?
3. What was the percentage reduction in operational costs achieved by GlobalConnections Solutions?

### Example 2: Regional Hub

Regional Hub is a logistics and distribution company operating across the Southeast. The company specializes in providing efficient supply chain solutions to regional businesses. Next, Regional Hub implemented advanced analytics to streamline its supply chain operations. By analyzing transportation routes, warehouse operations, and delivery schedules, the company identified inefficiencies and bottlenecks. This data-driven approach enabled them to optimize routes, reduce delivery times, and improve inventory management. Finally, the use of analytics resulted in a 25% reduction in delivery times and a 30% improvement in inventory turnover rates. These enhancements not only increased customer satisfaction but also reduced operational costs, allowing Regional Hub to offer competitive pricing and expand its client base.

### *Short-Response Questions*

1. What specific areas did Regional Hub focus on to streamline its operations?
2. What was the percentage reduction in delivery times achieved by Regional Hub?
3. How did the improvements in inventory turnover rates impact Regional Hub's business?

### Example 3: InternationalMarketing Insights

InternationalMarketing Insights is a market research firm providing strategic insights to businesses looking to expand internationally. The company offers data-driven analysis to help clients understand global market trends and consumer behavior. Next, InternationalMarketing Insights uses big data analytics to provide clients with comprehensive market reports. By analyzing consumer data, economic indicators, and competitive landscapes, the firm offers actionable information on emerging markets. This situation enables clients to make informed decisions about market entry strategies and product localization. Finally, the analytics-driven approach allows InternationalMarketing Insights to deliver highly accurate market forecasts, resulting in a 50% increase in client retention. Clients report a 45% improvement in market entry success rates, attributing their success to the firm's insights.

### *Short-Response Questions*

1. What type of analytics did InternationalMarketing Insights use to provide market reports?
2. How did the use of analytics impact client retention for InternationalMarketing Insights?
3. What improvement in market entry success rates did clients of InternationalMarketing Insights experience?

## CASE STUDY: GLOBAL TRANSACTIONS INNOVATIONS (GTI)

Global Transactions Innovations (GTI) is a multinational corporation specializing in international trade and logistics solutions. The company has expanded its operations to Europe, Asia, and South America while enabling the movement of goods and services across borders. With a strong emphasis on using technology and data to improve supply chain efficiency, GTI seeks to maximize its global market share while managing the complexities of international business operations. Recently, the company attempted to evaluate its performance and investment strategies globally through several financial metrics.

### Business Analytics Data Tables

**TABLE 15.1** Financial Performance Metrics

| 1 | A | B | C | D | E |
|---|---|---|---|---|---|
| | **Metric** | **Q1 2023** | **Q2 2023** | **Q3 2023** | **Q4 2023** |
| 2 | Revenue of foreign operations ($) | 500,000 | 600,000 | 550,000 | 700,000 |
| 3 | Costs from foreign operations ($) | 300,000 | 350,000 | 320,000 | 400,000 |
| 4 | Exchange rate (1 USD to local currency) | 0.85 | 0.82 | 0.80 | 0.78 |
| 5 | Foreign exchange rate (%) | 15 | 15 | 15 | 15 |

**TABLE 15.2** Investment and Market Data

| 1 | A | B | C | D | E |
|---|---|---|---|---|---|
| | **Region** | **Investment ($)** | **Weighted Average Cost of Capital (%)** | **Expected Return on Investment (%)** | **Break-Even Point ($)** |
| 2 | North America | 1,000,000 | 10 | 12 | 900,000 |
| 3 | Europe | 750,000 | 8 | 10 | 700,000 |
| 4 | Asia | 500,000 | 7 | 11 | 450,000 |
| 5 | South America | 300,000 | 9 | 10 | 250,000 |

### Analytics Problems Using Excel

1. Calculate the adjusted return on investment (ROI) for each region, considering both the foreign tax rate and the weighted average cost of capital. How can these calculations help prioritize investment decisions in different regions?
2. Conduct a break-even analysis for each of the regions to determine when GTI would begin to profit from its investments. What is the significance of break-even points in financial planning?
3. Use the net present value (NPV) function in Excel to assess the cash flow from foreign operations in different currencies. How can you effectively calculate NPV considering the varying exchange rates and forecasted cash flows?

### Answer Key

1. *Adjusted return on investment calculation.* The adjusted ROI formula is:
   Adjusted ROI = ((Expected Return − Foreign Tax))/(Weighted Average Cost of Capital).
   In Excel, create a formula for each region based on the values.
   = (Expected Return − (Investment × Foreign Tax Rate))/Investment
   This strategy allows GTI to evaluate which regions provide the most favorable returns considering financing costs and tax implications.
2. *Break-even analysis.* The break-even point can be determined using the formula Break-Even Point = ((Fixed Costs)/(Selling Price per Unit)) − (Variable Cost per Unit). The relevant data points may necessitate approximating total costs and revenues by creating estimates for fixed costs and the average unit sale price in Excel. Specify any assumptions in the cells, and use Excel's data validation features to restrict input errors. Focus on the break-even analysis to explain its importance in ensuring profitability.
3. *Net present value calculation.* Use the NPV formula, where *CF_t* is the cash flow at time *t* and *r* is the discount rate, which can vary by region. In Excel, set up the cash flows and apply the NPV function considering the corresponding exchange rates: = NPV(Exchange_Rate, Cash_Flows). This analysis will help GTI evaluate the financial feasibility of each region's investments while considering currency fluctuations.

---

### CASE STUDY: GLOBALTRADING DYNAMICS

GlobalTrading Dynamics is an organization that specializes in international trade and logistics and helps businesses expand their operations across global markets. The company has established a strong presence in multiple regions, including North America, Europe, and Asia. Recently, GlobalTrading Dynamics partnered with a medium-sized manufacturing organization to maximize their international trade operations while focusing on improving cash flow from foreign operations, managing exchange rate fluctuations, and increasing global market share.

To evaluate the impact of their strategies, GlobalTrading Dynamics collected data on key financial metrics, including cash flow from foreign operations, exchange rates, and global market share over six months. The data was analyzed to identify trends and measure the effectiveness of the implemented strategies. The following tables summarize key findings from the project:

**TABLE 15.3** Financial Metrics

| 1 | A | B | C | D |
|---|---|---|---|---|
| | **Month** | **Cash Flow From Foreign Operations ($)** | **Exchange Rate (USD/EUR)** | **Foreign Tax Rate (%)** |
| **2** | January | 500,000 | 1.10 | 25 |
| **3** | February | 520,000 | 1.12 | 24 |
| **4** | March | 540,000 | 1.11 | 23 |
| **5** | April | 560,000 | 1.13 | 22 |
| **6** | May | 580,000 | 1.12 | 21 |
| **7** | June | 600,000 | 1.10 | 20 |

**TABLE 15.4** Market Metrics

| 1 | A | B | C | D |
|---|---|---|---|---|
| | **Month** | **Global Market Share (%)** | **International Trade Ratio** | **Weighted Average Cost of Capital (%)** |
| **2** | January | 10 | 1.5 | 8 |
| **3** | February | 10.5 | 1.6 | 7.8 |
| **4** | March | 11 | 1.7 | 7.6 |
| **5** | April | 11.5 | 1.8 | 7.4 |
| **6** | May | 12 | 1.9 | 7.2 |
| **7** | June | 12.5 | 2.0 | 7.0 |

## Analytics Problems Using Excel

1. *Adjusted return on investment.* Calculate the adjusted return on investment for foreign operations.
2. *Break-even analysis.* Perform a break-even analysis for international trade operations.
3. *Cash flow from foreign operations.* Determine the total cash flow from foreign operations over the six months.
4. *Exchange rate calculations.* Calculate the average exchange rate over the six months.
5. *Foreign tax rate comparison.* Compare the foreign tax rates for each month.
6. *Global market share.* Analyze the trend in global market share over the six months.
7. *International trade ratio.* Calculate the average international trade ratio.
8. *Net present value in different currencies.* Compute the net present value of cash flows in different currencies.
9. *Price adjustment.* Determine the price adjustment needed based on exchange rate fluctuations.
10. *Weighted average cost of capital.* Calculate the weighted average cost of capital for each month.

## Answer Key

1. *Adjusted return on investment.* Use the formula Adjusted ROI = (Net Profit from Foreign Operations − Foreign Taxes)/Investment. Example: =(B2 − (B2 * D2/100))/Investment.
2. *Break-even analysis.* Use the formula Break-Even Point = Fixed Costs/(Selling Price per Unit − Variable Cost per Unit). Example: =Fixed Costs/(Selling Price − Variable Cost).
3. *Cash flow from foreign operations.* Use the SUM function: =SUM(B2:B7).
4. *Exchange rate calculations.* Use the AVERAGE function: =AVERAGE(C2:C7).
5. *Foreign tax rate comparison.* Use the IF function to compare tax rates: =IF(D2<D3, “Lower”, “Higher”).
6. *Global market share.* Use the TREND function to analyze the trend: =TREND(B2:B7).
7. *International trade ratio.* Use the AVERAGE function: =AVERAGE(C2:C7).
8. *Net present value in different currencies.* Use the NPV function: =NPV(rate, value1, [value2], . . .). Convert cash flows to different currencies using exchange rates.
9. *Price adjustment.* Use the formula Adjusted Price = Original Price * Exchange Rate. Example: =Original Price * C2.
10. *Weighted average cost of capital.* Use the formula WACC = (E/V * Re) + ((D/V * Rd) * (1 − Tax Rate)). Example: = (Equity/(Equity + Debt) * Cost of Equity) + ((Debt/(Equity + Debt) * Cost of Debt) * (1 − Tax Rate)).

# Appendix 1: How to Perform Data Analytics Using Microsoft Excel

## DATA ANALYTICS

Data analytics in Excel involves using the software's functions, tools, and features to collect, process, and analyze data to uncover insights and support decision-making. Following are key types of data analytics conducted using Excel accompanied by examples of how each analytic can be performed.

### Descriptive Analytics

This type of analysis involves summarizing historical data to understand what has happened in past events.

Example: Using PivotTables

**How to Conduct:**

1. Select your data range, then go to the Insert tab and click on PivotTable.
2. Drag fields to the Rows and Values areas to summarize data.
3. You can also use the Design tab to format your PivotTable for better readability.

### Diagnostic Analytics

This focuses on understanding why something happened by looking at the data trends and patterns.

Example: Using Charts

**How to Conduct**

1. Select your data, then go to the Insert tab and select a chart type (like line, bar, or scatter plot).
2. Analyze the resulting chart to identify trends or patterns (e.g., if sales dropped in a specific month, check for correlations with external factors).

## Predictive Analytics

Predictive analytics involves using historical data to forecast future outcomes.

Example: Using the Forecast Sheet

**How to Conduct**

1. Select a range of data.
2. Go to the Data tab and choose Forecast Sheet.
3. Configure the forecast options, and let Excel generate a forecast chart which displays predicted trends based on historical data.

## Prescriptive Analytics

This type provides recommendations based on data analysis.

Example: Using Solver

**How to Conduct**

1. Set up the objective function and constraints in a worksheet.
2. Go to the Data tab, click on Solver, and define your goal.
3. Run Solver to find the optimal solution based on your defined criteria and constraints.

## Exploratory Data Analysis (EDA)

EDA is used to analyze datasets to summarize their main characteristics, often with visual methods.

Example: Using Conditional Formatting and Data Visualization

**How to Conduct**

1. Highlight your data range, go to the Home tab, and select Conditional Formatting to highlight data points.
2. Create a heat map, color scale, or icon set to visualize the distribution of data.

## Text Analysis

This involves analyzing and extracting insights from text data.

Example: Using Text Functions

**How to Conduct**

1. Use functions such as TEXTJOIN, LEFT, RIGHT, or MID to manipulate and analyze textual data.
2. Utilize COUNTIF or SEARCH functions to analyze the event of specific words or phrases.

## DATA VISUALIZATION

Data visualization in Excel is a method of representing data graphically to enable understanding and analysis. Next, it allows users to identify patterns, trends, and knowledge through visual representations that include charts, graphs, tables, and sparklines. By converting raw data into visual presentations, it improves communication and interpretation to make it easier to develop important and valid conclusions.

### Sample Data Table

Following is a sample table of data that we will use for our visualizations:

| 1 | A | B | C |
|---|---|---|---|
| | Month | Product A Sales | Product B Sales |
| 2 | January | 150 | 200 |
| 3 | February | 180 | 150 |
| 4 | March | 220 | 300 |
| 5 | April | 200 | 250 |
| 6 | May | 250 | 270 |
| 7 | June | 300 | 300 |
| 8 | July | 280 | 320 |
| 9 | August | 320 | 290 |
| 10 | September | 310 | 330 |
| 11 | October | 350 | 360 |
| 12 | November | 400 | 350 |
| 13 | December | 450 | 400 |
| 14 | January | 380 | 420 |
| 15 | February | 420 | 400 |
| 16 | March | 480 | 450 |
| 17 | April | 500 | 460 |
| 18 | May | 540 | 490 |
| 19 | June | 580 | 500 |
| 20 | July | 600 | 550 |
| 21 | August | 630 | 580 |

## Chart Types and How to Create Them

*Column Chart*

Used to compare sales across months for various products.

**How to Create**

1. Select the data range (A1:C21).
2. Go to the Insert tab, click on Column Chart, and choose a Clustered Column.
3. Customize the chart with titles and labels.

**Example**

**APPENDIX FIGURE 1**

*Bar Chart*

Like column charts but presents data horizontally.

**How to Create**

1. Select the data range and choose Bar Chart from the Insert tab.
2. This format works well for long month names.

**Example**

**APPENDIX FIGURE 2**

*Line Chart*

Ideal for displaying trends over time.

**How to Create**

1. Select the data range, go to Insert, and select Line Chart.
2. This chart helps visualize sales trends for each product over the months.

**Example**

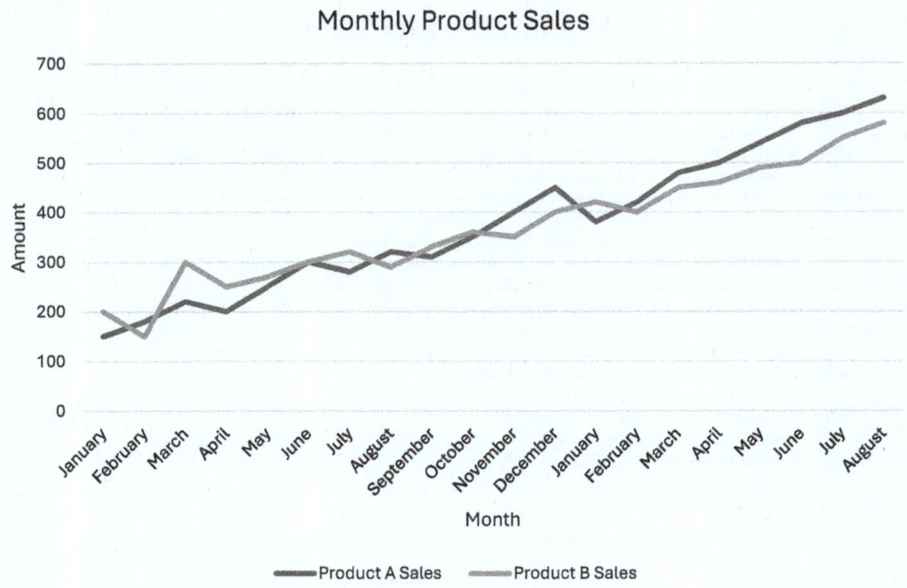


**APPENDIX FIGURE 3**

*Pie Chart*

Useful for showing the percentage share of total sales by product in a specific month.

**How to Create**

1. Select the sales data for a specific month (e.g., January), select Insert, and then Pie Chart.
2. Customize the chart to display percentages.

**Example**

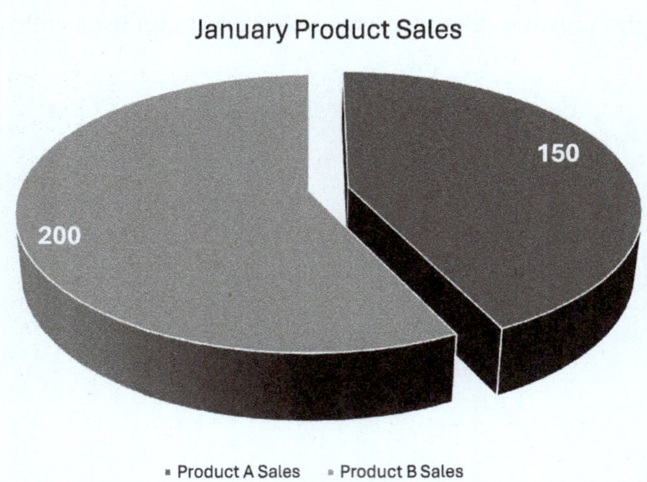


**APPENDIX FIGURE 4**

*Scatter Plot*

Useful in identifying correlations between sales of Product A and Product B.

**How to Create**

1. Select Product A's and Product B's sales data for the months.
2. Go to Insert and choose Scatter Chart.

**Example**

**APPENDIX FIGURE 5**

*Area Chart*

Like line charts but highlights the volume under the line.

**How to Create**

1. Select the data range and choose Area Chart from the Insert menu.

**Example**

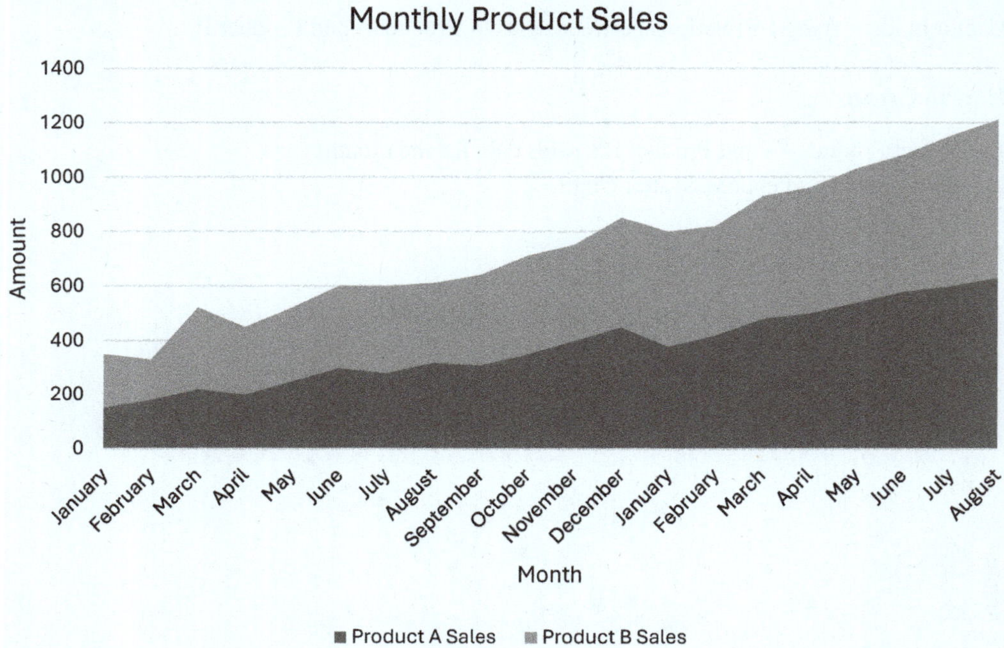


**APPENDIX FIGURE 6**

## Creating a PivotTable and PivotChart

*PivotTable*

A PivotTable summarizes the data and helps analyze the sales figures across products and months.

**How to Create**

1. Select the entire dataset, go to the Insert tab, and choose PivotChart.
2. In the dialog box, choose to place the PivotTable in a new worksheet.
3. Drag a data field to Axis (Categories), Columns, and Values.

*Example of a PivotTable and PivotChart*

1. *Setting up the PivotTable.*
   - After selecting the data and creating a PivotTable, a new worksheet will open.
   - In the PivotTable Fields pane, drag "Month" to the Rows area, and drag "Product A Sales" and "Product B Sales" to the Values area.

2. *Resulting PivotTable and PivotChart.*

| Row Labels | Sum of Product A Sales | Sum of Product B Sales |
|---|---|---|
| January | 530 | 620 |
| February | 600 | 550 |
| March | 700 | 750 |
| April | 700 | 710 |
| May | 790 | 760 |
| June | 880 | 800 |
| July | 880 | 870 |
| August | 950 | 870 |
| September | 310 | 330 |
| October | 350 | 360 |
| November | 400 | 350 |
| December | 450 | 400 |
| **Grand Total** | **7540** | **7370** |

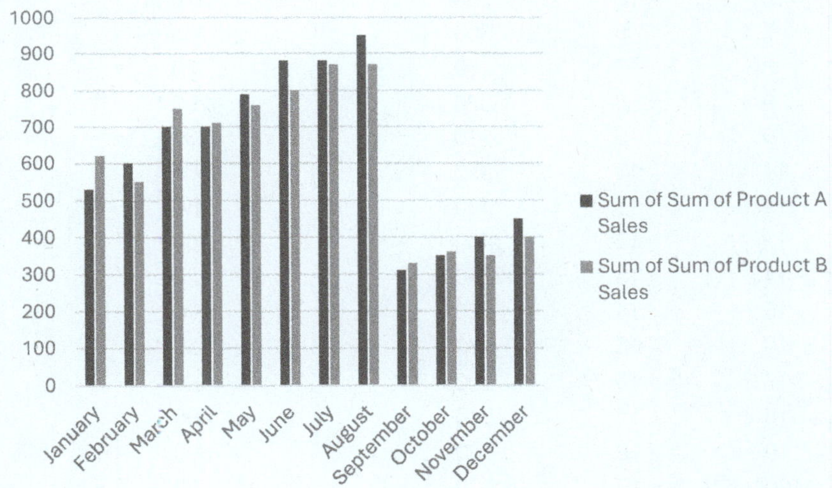


**APPENDIX FIGURE 7**

## PivotTable and PivotChart Notes

- You can also apply filters, such as filtering by months or product sales, to analyze specific segments of data.
- The right-click option is for sorting or formatting your PivotTable and PivotChart to improve clarity.

## DESCRIPTIVE STATISTICS

*Descriptive statistics* in Excel refers to the various methods used for summarizing and analyzing the primary features of a dataset. This type of analysis provides simple summaries about the sample and the measures of the data and can include characteristics such as mean, median, mode, standard deviation, variance, range, and more.

### Sample Data Table

Following is a sample table of data to demonstrate the use of descriptive statistics:

| 1 | A | B | C |
|---|---|---|---|
| | ID | Product A Sales | Product B Sales |
| 2 | 1 | 150 | 200 |
| 3 | 2 | 180 | 150 |
| 4 | 3 | 220 | 300 |
| 5 | 4 | 200 | 250 |
| 6 | 5 | 250 | 270 |
| 7 | 6 | 300 | 300 |
| 8 | 7 | 280 | 320 |
| 9 | 8 | 320 | 290 |
| 10 | 9 | 310 | 330 |
| 11 | 10 | 350 | 360 |
| 12 | 11 | 400 | 350 |
| 13 | 12 | 450 | 400 |
| 14 | 13 | 380 | 420 |
| 15 | 14 | 420 | 400 |
| 16 | 15 | 480 | 450 |
| 17 | 16 | 500 | 460 |
| 18 | 17 | 540 | 490 |
| 19 | 18 | 580 | 500 |
| 20 | 19 | 600 | 550 |
| 21 | 20 | 630 | 580 |

### How to Use the Data Analysis Tool for Descriptive Statistics in Excel

**Step-by-Step Procedure**

1. *Enable the Data Analysis ToolPak.*
    - Go to the File tab.
    - Click on Options.
    - In the Excel Options dialog box, select Add-Ins.

- In the Manage box, select Excel Add-ins and click Go.
- Check Analysis ToolPak and click OK.

2. *Perform descriptive statistics.*
   - Click on the Data tab in the Ribbon.
   - Select Data Analysis found in the Analysis group.
   - From the list of tools, select Descriptive Statistics and click OK.
3. *Input data range*
   - In the Input Range box, select the range of your data. For this example, use **B1:C1**.
   - Check the Labels in First Row box since headers are included in your selection.
4. *Select output options.*
   - You can choose Output Range to place the results in a specific cell location or select New Worksheet to display results in a new sheet. It is recommended that you place your Output Range next to your dataset for easier analysis.
5. *Select the summary statistics.*
   - Check Summary Statistics.
   - The "confidence level" for mean is already set to 95%, or .05. Unless otherwise stated in the problem, leave this option as is.
   - Click OK.

## Example Output and Interpretation

Following is an illustrative summary of what the output might look like:

| Product A Sales | | Product B Sales | |
|---|---|---|---|
| Mean | 377 | Mean | 368.5 |
| Standard Error | 32.49372409 | Standard Error | 25.60093543 |
| Median | 365 | Median | 355 |
| Mode | #N/A | Mode | 300 |
| Standard Deviation | 145.3163518 | Standard Deviation | 114.4908638 |
| Sample Variance | 21116.84211 | Sample Variance | 13108.15789 |
| Kurtosis | −1.026057637 | Kurtosis | −0.515102727 |
| Skewness | 0.204551468 | Skewness | 0.073016011 |
| Range | 480 | Range | 430 |
| Minimum | 150 | Minimum | 150 |
| Maximum | 630 | Maximum | 580 |
| Sum | 7540 | Sum | 7370 |
| Count | 20 | Count | 20 |

### Explanation of Results

1. *Count.* The total number of observations for Product A and Product B sales (20 for both products).
2. *Sum.* The total sales over the dataset. For Product A, the sum is 9,910. For Product B, the sum is 9,830.
3. *Mean.* Average sales for Product A, which is 495.5, and Product B, which is 491.5. This amount is calculated as the sum divided by the count.
4. *Standard error.* An estimate of the variability of the sample mean. Lower values typically indicate more precise estimates.
5. *Median.* The middle value that separates the higher half from the lower half of the sales dataset. In this example, the amount is 400 for both products.
6. *Mode.* The value that appears most frequently. In this example, there may be no repeated values for both products. While Product B has a value of 300, Product A has no value, or N/A.
7. *Standard deviation.* A measure of the amount of variation or dispersion in a set of values. Product A has a standard deviation of 135.76, which indicates more variability compared to Product B, whose standard deviation is 98.85.
8. *Variance.* The square of the standard deviation. It quantifies the degree of spread in the sales data.
9. *Minimum.* The smallest value. In this example, the value is 150 for both Products A and B.
10. *Maximum.* The largest value. In this example, Product A's largest value is 630, while Product B's largest value is 580.
11. *Range.* The difference between the maximum and minimum values. In this example, Product A's value is 480, while the value for Product B is 430. These values indicate the spread or dispersion of the sales data.

## PROBABILITY DISTRIBUTION AND DATA MODELING IN EXCEL

*Probability distribution* is a statistical function that describes the likelihood of each potential outcome in each sample. Next, it provides insight into how probabilities are distributed over the possible values of a random variable. Probability distribution contains several types of probability distributions that include binomial, normal, Poisson, and more. *Data modeling* is the process of creating a data model to represent complex real-world data structures and relationships. In Excel, data modeling frequently involves organizing data into tables and establishing relationships between variables that can be used for analysis, forecasting, and visualization of the data.

## Sample Data Table

Following is a sample table of data illustrating sales figures for two products over four months.

| 1 | A | B | C |
|---|---|---|---|
| | **Month** | **Product A Sales** | **Product B Sales** |
| 2 | January | 150 | 200 |
| 3 | February | 180 | 150 |
| 4 | March | 220 | 300 |
| 5 | April | 200 | 250 |
| 6 | May | 250 | 270 |
| 7 | June | 300 | 300 |
| 8 | July | 280 | 320 |
| 9 | August | 320 | 290 |
| 10 | September | 310 | 330 |
| 11 | October | 350 | 360 |
| 12 | November | 400 | 350 |
| 13 | December | 450 | 400 |
| 14 | January | 380 | 420 |
| 15 | February | 420 | 400 |
| 16 | March | 480 | 450 |
| 17 | April | 500 | 460 |
| 18 | May | 540 | 490 |
| 19 | June | 580 | 500 |
| 20 | July | 600 | 550 |
| 21 | August | 630 | 580 |

## Using Excel for Probability Distribution

As an example, we will demonstrate how to calculate probabilities using the normal distribution for Product A Sales.

### Step-by-Step Procedure

1. *Calculate mean and standard deviation.*
   - Place the following formulas in any empty cells below the dataset for Product A:
     - **Mean: =AVERAGE(B2:B21)** (to calculate the average sales for Product A)
     - **Standard deviation: =STDEV.P(B2:B21)** (to calculate the standard deviation for Product A)

| | |
|---|---|
| **Mean** | 377 |
| **Standard Deviation** | 141.6368596 |

2. *Calculate probability for a given sales value.*

   - Now we want to find the probability that Product A sales will be less than 400.
   - Use the **NORM.DIST** function. Formula: **=NORM.DIST(400, Mean, Standard Deviation, TRUE).**
   - Replace "Mean" and "Standard Deviation" with their respective cell references.

| **Normal Distribution** | 0.564499489 |
|---|---|

3. *Visualize the normal distribution.*

   - To create a normal distribution curve, create a range of values (X values) around the mean (i.e., from 100 to 800).
   - Calculate the normal distribution for each X value using the **NORM.DIST** function.
   - Use these values to plot a chart (Insert > Chart > Scatter with Smooth Lines).

| A | B | | **Mean** | **377** |
|---|---|---|---|---|
| Month | Product A Sales | Normal Distribution | **Standard Deviation** | **141.6368596** |
| January | 150 | 0.000779769 | **Normal Distribution** | **0.564499489** |
| February | 180 | 0.00107066 | | |
| March | 220 | 0.001523788 | | |
| April | 200 | 0.001290083 | | |
| May | 250 | 0.001884291 | | |
| June | 300 | 0.00242972 | | |
| July | 280 | 0.002227858 | | |
| August | 320 | 0.002597559 | | |
| September | 310 | 0.002518508 | | |
| October | 350 | 0.00276594 | | |
| November | 400 | 0.002779763 | | |
| December | 450 | 0.002466328 | | |
| January | 380 | 0.002816024 | | |
| February | 420 | 0.002689797 | | |
| March | 480 | 0.002162212 | | |
| April | 500 | 0.001931845 | | |
| May | 540 | 0.001452585 | | |
| June | 580 | 0.001008494 | | |
| July | 600 | 0.000815548 | | |
| August | 630 | 0.000571318 | | |

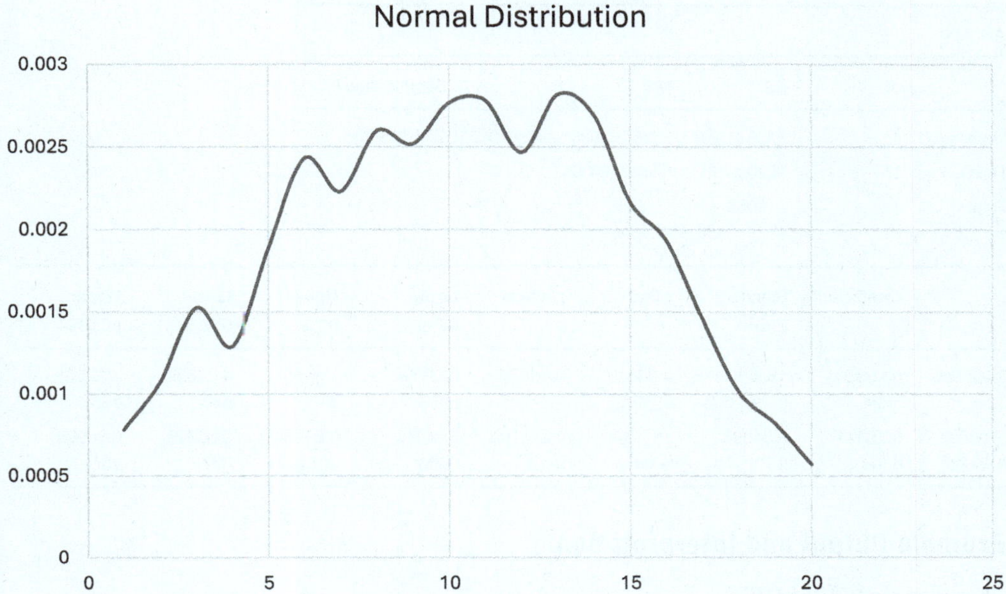


**APPENDIX FIGURE 8**

## Using Excel for Data Modeling

1. *Organize your data.* Ensure that your dataset is structured properly in columns (like our sample table) to represent various variables.
2. *Create a table.* Select your data and go to the Insert tab and choose Table.
3. *Use data analysis.* If you want to create a regression model (for example, predicting Product B sales based on Product A sales):
   - Go to Data > Data Analysis > Regression.
   - Set your "Input Y Range" to Product B sales and "Input X Range" to Product A sales.
   - Check labels and select an output range.
   - Click OK.

SUMMARY OUTPUT

| Regression | Statistics |
|---|---|
| Multiple R | 0.968996606 |
| R-Square | 0.938954423 |
| Adjusted R-Square | 0.935563002 |
| Standard Error | 29.06286882 |
| Observations | 20 |

| ANOVA | | | | | |
|---|---|---|---|---|---|
| | df | SS | MS | F | Significance F |
| Regression | 1 | 233851.2938 | 233851.2938 | 276.8616569 | 2.24615E-12 |
| Residual | 18 | 15203.7062 | 844.6503442 | | |
| Total | 19 | 249055 | | | |

| | Coefficients | Standard Error | t Stat | p-value | Lower 95% | Upper 95% | Lower 95.0% | Upper 95.0% |
|---|---|---|---|---|---|---|---|---|
| Intercept | 80.6806 7394 | 18.4781 8164 | 4.36626 6959 | 0.00037 2236 | 41.8594 5488 | 119.501 893 | 41.8594 5488 | 119.501 893 |
| Product A Sales | 0.76344 6488 | 0.04588 2513 | 16.6391 6034 | 2.24615 E-12 | 0.66705 0906 | 0.85984 2071 | 0.66705 0906 | 0.85984 2071 |

## Example Output and Interpretation

*Output from NORM.DIST*

When calculating the probability of sales being less than 400, you might get a result like 0.65.

Interpretation: This means there is a 65% chance that the sales for Product A will be less than 400 units based on the dataset's characteristics.

## Output from Regression Analysis

The regression output includes coefficients, *R*-squared value, and statistical significance (*p*-values).

### Example Coefficients

- Intercept: 100 is the expected value of Product B sales, while Product A sales is zero.
- Coefficient for Product A is 0.75 for every additional unit of Product A sold, while Product B sales are expected to increase by 0.75 units.
- *R*-squared: For Product A, the *R*-squared value is 0.938954422934284, or 94%, which means that there is a high correlation. Product B might read 0.85 to suggest that approximately 85% of the variability in Product B Sales can be explained by Product A Sales.

## Detailed Summary of Functions and Outputs

*Probability Distribution Outputs*

1. *Mean.* Represents the average for Product A Sales. When the calculation yields 392.5, it indicates that, on average, Product A sold approximately 392 units.
2. *Standard deviation.* Measures the spread of sales data around the mean. A standard deviation of 135 means most sales figures fall to within 135 units of the average. This result indicates an excellent level of dispersion in sales.
3. *NORM.DIST output.* The result from this calculation indicates the probability that a randomly selected sale will be less than 400 units. For example, a value of 0.65 shows that 65% of the time that sales will be below this level.

*Data Modeling Outputs: Analysis Output*

1. *Intercept.* The expected value of Product B's sales when Product A's sales are zero. This may not have practical significance, but it is necessary for statistical modeling.
2. *Coefficient for product A.* Indicates the relationship between Product A and Product B sales. A coefficient of 0.75 means that for each unit increase in Product A, Product B is expected to increase by 0.75 units.
3. *R-squared.* A value of 0.85 implies a strong positive correlation and means that 85% of the variance in Product B's sales is accounted for by Product A's sales. This indicates a strong relationship within the data model.

## SAMPLING AND ESTIMATION IN EXCEL

*Sampling* is a statistical technique used to select a subset of individuals or observations from a larger population. Next, sampling helps in making assumptions or estimates about the population based on the sample data. *Estimation* refers to the process of assuming the value of an unknown parameter based on sample statistics, such as the population mean. There are two types of estimates. The first type is point estimates, which use single values. The second type is interval estimates, which use a range of values along with a confidence level (90%, 95%, or 99%).

### Sample Data Table

Following is a sample table of data representing sales data for two products over various months:

| 1 | A | B | C |
|---|---|---|---|
| | Month | Product A Sales | Product B Sales |
| 2 | January | 150 | 200 |
| 3 | February | 180 | 150 |
| 4 | March | 220 | 300 |
| 5 | April | 200 | 250 |
| 6 | May | 250 | 270 |
| 7 | June | 300 | 300 |
| 8 | July | 280 | 320 |
| 9 | August | 320 | 290 |
| 10 | September | 310 | 330 |
| 11 | October | 350 | 360 |
| 12 | November | 400 | 350 |
| 13 | December | 450 | 400 |
| 14 | January | 380 | 420 |
| 15 | February | 420 | 400 |
| 16 | March | 480 | 450 |
| 17 | April | 500 | 460 |
| 18 | May | 540 | 490 |
| 19 | June | 580 | 500 |
| 20 | July | 600 | 550 |
| 21 | August | 630 | 580 |

## Using Excel for Sampling and Estimation

*Step 1: Random Sampling*

We can draw a simple random sample of five observations from the dataset using the Data Analysis ToolPak.

1. *Select your data.* Highlight the range A1:C21.
2. *Generate random sample.*
    - Go to the Data tab, then select Data Analysis.
    - From the list, select Sampling and click OK.
    - In the Sampling dialog box, set the input range to include your sales data (i.e., B2:C21). Choose Random for the sampling method. Set sample size to 5. Specify an output range or choose to have it in a new worksheet.
3. *Output.* Click OK to see a random sample selected from the data.

| Month | Product A Sales | Product B Sales | Random Samples |
|---|---|---|---|
| January | 150 | 200 | **450** |
| February | 180 | 150 | **400** |
| March | 220 | 300 | **280** |
| April | 200 | 250 | **420** |
| May | 250 | 270 | **400** |
| June | 300 | 300 | |
| July | 280 | 320 | |
| August | 320 | 290 | |
| September | 310 | 330 | |
| October | 350 | 360 | |
| November | 400 | 350 | |
| December | 450 | 400 | |
| January | 380 | 420 | |
| February | 420 | 400 | |
| March | 480 | 450 | |
| April | 500 | 460 | |
| May | 540 | 490 | |
| June | 580 | 500 | |
| July | 600 | 550 | |
| August | 630 | 580 | |

*Step 2: Estimation*

To estimate the mean and confidence intervals using the sample data:

1. *Mean and standard deviation for the sample.*
    - Mean: =AVERAGE(D2:D6) (or the column the sample data is located).
    - Standard Deviation: =STDEV.S(D2:D6).

| Random Samples | |
|---|---|
| 450 | |
| 400 | |
| 280 | |
| 420 | |
| 400 | |
| **390** | **Mean** |
| **64.80740698** | **Standard Deviation** |

2. *Confidence interval calculation.*

   - The formula for the confidence interval can be calculated using the following steps:

     - Choose a confidence level (standard is 95% with a z-score of 1.96).
     - Calculate the t-critical value using the T.INV.2T function:

       t = T.INV.2T(0.05, n − 1), where *n* is the sample size
       t = T.INV.2T(0.05, 40 − 1) = 2.02269092

3. *Calculate margin of error.* Use the formula Margin of Error = z-score (t) *(Standard Deviation/sqrt n) =1.96*(64.80740698/sqrt(40)) = 20.0840235.
4. *Construct confidence interval.*

   - Lower Limit: Mean − Margin of Error.
   - Upper Limit: Mean + Margin of Error.

## Example Output and Interpretation

Assuming our random sample produces the following Product A sales:

| Sample Sales |
|---|
| 150 |
| 200 |
| 250 |
| 300 |
| 400 |

1. *Mean calculation.* Mean = (150 + 200 + 250 + 300 + 400)/5 = 260.
2. *Standard deviation calculation.* Standard Deviation = STDEV.S(D2:D6), assuming the sample data is in cells D2 to D6 or where your sample data is located. We also assume it calculates to approximately 100.
4. *T-critical value.* For a 95% confidence level and a sample size of 5, the degrees of freedom = n(5 − 1) = 4. The formula would be t = T.INV.2T(0.05, 4)/2.776.
5. *Margin of error calculation.* Margin of Error = z-score (t) *(Standard Deviation/sqrt n) = 2.776*(100)/sqrt(/)) = approximately 124.58.
6. *Confidence interval.*
   Lower Limit = Mean − Margin of Error = 260 − 124.58 = 135.42
   Upper Limit = Mean + Margin of Error = 260 + 124.58 = 384.58

### Final Results Interpretation

1. *Mean of sample.* The average sales for the sampled data is 260 units. This value indicates the central tendency of the sales for the Product A in our random sample.
2. *Standard deviation.* A standard deviation of approximately 100 suggests there is a high level of variability around the mean sales figure in our sample data.
3. *Confidence interval.* The confidence interval for the mean sales from our sample is approximately (135.42, 384.58). This means there is 95% confidence that the true population mean of Product A sales lies between these two values.

## STATISTICAL INFERENCE IN EXCEL

*Statistical inference* is the process of drawing conclusions about a population based on a sample taken from that specific population. This method allows the analyst to estimate population parameters, test hypotheses, and make predictions. There are various methods of statistical inference, which include confidence intervals and hypothesis testing.

### Sample Data Table

Following is a sample table of data representing sales data for two products over time:

| 1 | A | B | C |
|---|---|---|---|
| | Month | Product A Sales | Product B Sales |
| 2 | January | 150 | 200 |
| 3 | February | 180 | 150 |
| 4 | March | 220 | 300 |
| 5 | April | 200 | 250 |
| 6 | May | 250 | 270 |
| 7 | June | 300 | 300 |
| 8 | July | 280 | 320 |
| 9 | August | 320 | 290 |
| 10 | September | 310 | 330 |
| 11 | October | 350 | 360 |
| 12 | November | 400 | 350 |
| 13 | December | 450 | 400 |
| 14 | January | 380 | 420 |
| 15 | February | 420 | 400 |
| 16 | March | 480 | 450 |
| 17 | April | 500 | 460 |
| 18 | May | 540 | 490 |

| 1 | A | B | C |
|---|---|---|---|
| | Month | Product A Sales | Product B Sales |
| 19 | June | 580 | 500 |
| 20 | July | 600 | 550 |
| 21 | August | 630 | 580 |

## Using Excel for Statistical Inference

To demonstrate statistical inference, the following must be performed:

1. Estimate the mean and create a confidence interval for Product A sales.
2. Conduct a hypothesis test to see if the average sales of Product A is significantly different from a specified value (i.e., test if the average sales vary greatly from 300).

*Step 1: Estimate the Mean and Create a Confidence Interval*

1. *Calculate the mean and standard deviation.*
   Formula:

   Mean: =AVERAGE(B2:B21) (or column where Product A sales are located).
   Standard Deviation: =STDEV.S(B2:B21)

   | Mean | 368.5 |
   |---|---|
   | Standard Deviation | 114.4908638 |

2. *Calculate confidence interval.* Assume there is a 95% or 0.05 confidence interval.

   Sample size ($n$): =COUNT(B2:B21) = 20
   T-critical value: Use =T.INV.2T(0.05, n − 1), where $n$ is from the previous
   Margin of error: = z-score (t) *(Standard Deviation/sqrt n)
   Confidence Interval:

   Lower Limit: Mean − Margin of Error
   Upper Limit: Mean + Margin of Error

*Step 2: Conduct a Hypothesis Test*

1. *Set up the null and alternative hypotheses.*

   Null hypothesis ($H_0$): The population mean of Product A sales is 300 (H0: $\mu = 300$).
   Alternative hypothesis ($H_1$): The population mean of Product A sales is not equal to 300 (H1: $\mu \neq 300$).

2. Conduct the t-test. Go to the Data tab and select Data Analysis. Choose t-Test: Two-Sample Assuming Equal Variances. In the dialog box, for input range, select the range for Product A and B sales. Set hypothesized mean to 300. For output range, specify where to display the results. Click OK.

| t-Test: Two-Sample, Assuming Equal Variances | | |
|---|---|---|
| | *Product A Sales* | *Product B Sales* |
| Mean | 377 | 368.5 |
| Variance | 21116.84211 | 13108.15789 |
| Observations | 20 | 20 |
| Pooled variance | 17112.5 | |
| Hypothesized mean difference | 300 | |
| df | 38 | |
| t-stat | −7.046635843 | |
| P(T<=t) one-tail | 1.06348E-08 | |
| t Critical one-tail | 1.68595446 | |
| P(T<=t) two-tail | 2.12696E-08 | |
| t Critical two-tail | 2.024394164 | |

## Example of Outputs and Interpretation

*Confidence Interval Results*

Assuming calculations yield:

Mean: 400
Standard Deviation: 100
Sample Size ($n$): 20
T-Critical Value: = 2.086 (for 19 degrees of freedom at 95% confidence)
Margin of Error: = 2.086*(100/sqrt(20)) = 46.68
Confidence Interval:

Lower Limit: = 400 − 46.68 = 353.32
Upper Limit: = 400 + 46.68 = 446.68

*Interpretation:* The result is that we are 95% confident that the true population mean of Product A sales falls between 353.32 and 446.68.

*Hypothesis Test Results*

Assuming the t-test results produce the following:

t-stat: 4.57

The calculated t-statistic is 4.57, which indicates how many standard deviations the sample mean is away from the hypothesized mean (300).

P-value: 0.0005

The p-value of 0.0005 is much smaller than the common alpha level of 0.05. This result means we reject the null hypothesis.

Degrees of Freedom (df): 19

*Conclusion:* There is considerable evidence to suggest that the average sales for Product A are not equal to 300 at the 95% confidence level.

# Appendix 2: Sample Case Studies Using Microsoft Excel

## THE PROBLEM-SOLVING PROCESS IN DATA AND BUSINESS ANALYTICS

There are steps in the problem-solving process using data analytics as a main component of business analytics. Problem-solving in business analytics using data analytics typically follows a structured approach that can be defined in various steps and logical orders that include recognizing the problem, defining the problem, structuring the problem, analyzing the problem, interpreting results and making decisions, and implementing a solution. With each step, data analytics relies on the use of Microsoft Excel functions and tools that include the following:

### Recognize the Problem

*Excel Formulas/Functions/Tools:* Use functions =IF, =COUNTIF, or =SUMIF to identify variances or patterns in the data. Visualizations are achieved with charts, PivotTables, and PivotCharts to help envision the problem.

### Define the Problem

*Excel Formulas/Functions/Tools:* Create a clear definition by summarizing data using functions =SUM, =AVERAGE, =MEAN, =MEDIAN, or =MODE to establish the significance of the issue. Creating PivotTables and PivotCharts can help in summarizing the key points of the problem.

### Structure the Problem

*Excel Formulas/Functions/Tools:* Implement brainstorming techniques and tools like SWOT analysis or PESTLE analysis that can be categorized and organized in Excel tables. Functions include =VLOOKUP and =INDEX/MATCH to link data points that provide context to the problem.

### Analyze the Problem

*Excel Formulas/Functions/Tools:* Perform statistical analysis using =AVERAGE, =STDEV, and =CORREL for understanding relationships between variables. More complex and detailed analyses can use the Data Analysis function for regression analysis, ANOVA, and hypothesis testing.

### Interpret Results and Make Decisions

*Excel Formulas/Functions/Tools:* Use visualization tools and summary statistics to interpret results clearly and accurately. Functions include =PMT, =NPV, and =IRR, which can aid in evaluating choices quantitatively.

### Implement a Solution

*Excel Formulas/Functions/Tools:* Create action plans using structured tables and track progress with conditional formatting and sparklines. Use project management strategies, managing tasks, deadlines, and responsible individuals using features like Gantt charts in Excel.

Excel is a powerful tool that can enable data manipulation, analysis, and visualization, to make it easier for the organization to gain insights and knowledge and to support the decision-making process. Next, Excel provides documentation using data-driven strategies to create a well-structured report or presentation to support the implementation phase once decision has been made. Finally, the combination of analytical functions, visualizations, and structured data manipulation in Excel will greatly enhance and support the analytical process in business problem-solving for the organization.

## CASE STUDY EXAMPLES

### Case Study: Market4Excellence Inc.

Market4Excellence Inc. (M4EI) is a marketing LLC specializing in digital marketing strategies for small to medium-sized businesses (SMBs) in the United States. MEI has a diverse consumer portfolio ranging from local service businesses to e-commerce start-up ventures. Currently, M4EI faces challenges in consumer retention and satisfaction, prompting leadership and management to analyze their marketing strategies. This example examines how data analytics can help identify performance issues and suggest potential actions to improve the organization's overall marketing strategy.

#### *Data Tables*

Three key datasets were collected that represent M4EI's marketing campaign results over the last six months.

**CONSUMER CAMPAIGN PERFORMANCE**

| Consumer Name | Campaign Type | Impressions | Clicks | Conversions | Consumer Satisfaction (1–10) |
|---|---|---|---|---|---|
| Consumer A | Social media | 20,000 | 300 | 45 | 8 |
| Consumer B | Email | 15,000 | 230 | 20 | 5 |
| Consumer C | PPC | 25,000 | 400 | 90 | 7 |
| Consumer D | SEO | 30,000 | 450 | 70 | 9 |

**MONTHLY CLICK-THROUGH RATE (CTR)**

| 1 | A | B | C | D | D |
|---|---|---|---|---|---|
| | Month | Total Impressions | Total Clicks | CTR (%) | CTR (%) |
| 2 | January | 150,000 | 1,200 | 0.80 | = C2/B2*100 |
| 3 | February | 160,000 | 1,400 | 0.88 | = C3/B3*100 |
| 4 | March | 140,000 | 1,350 | 0.96 | = C4/B4*100 |
| 5 | April | 145,000 | 1,500 | 1.03 | = C5/B5*100 |
| 6 | May | 155,000 | 1,600 | 1.03 | = C6/B6*100 |
| 7 | June | 165,000 | 1,620 | 0.98 | = C7/B7*100 |

**CONSUMER RETENTION RATES**

| Consumer Name | Retained (Y/N) | Months With M4EI | Campaigns Launched |
|---|---|---|---|
| Consumer A | Y | 6 | 3 |
| Consumer B | N | 4 | 1 |
| Consumer C | Y | 5 | 2 |
| Consumer D | Y | 6 | 4 |

**MARKETING SPEND VS. REVENUE GENERATED**

| Campaign Type | Marketing Expenditures | Revenue Generated |
|---|---|---|
| Social media | $5,000 | $30,000 |
| Email | $3,000 | $8,000 |
| PPC | $7,000 | $75,000 |
| SEO | $4,000 | $20,000 |

## IDENTIFYING PATTERNS AND VARIANCES

Use the =IF function to determine if a consumer satisfaction score is below an acceptable level, indicating possible retention risk for the organization. For this example, we will use 6 as our at-risk level.

=IF(F2<6, "At Risk", "Satisfactory")

Use the =COUNTIF function to count the number of consumers retained compared to those who are not:

=COUNTIF(B2:B5, "Y") for the number of retained consumers
=COUNTIF(B2:B5, "N") for the number of lost consumers

Use the =SUMIF function to sum up the revenues generated by campaigns exceeding a certain marketing spend:

=SUMIF(B2:B5, ">4000", C2:C5) for the total revenue from campaigns with spend > $4000

## VISUALIZATIONS

A *bar chart* can be created to display consumer satisfaction scores by consumers.

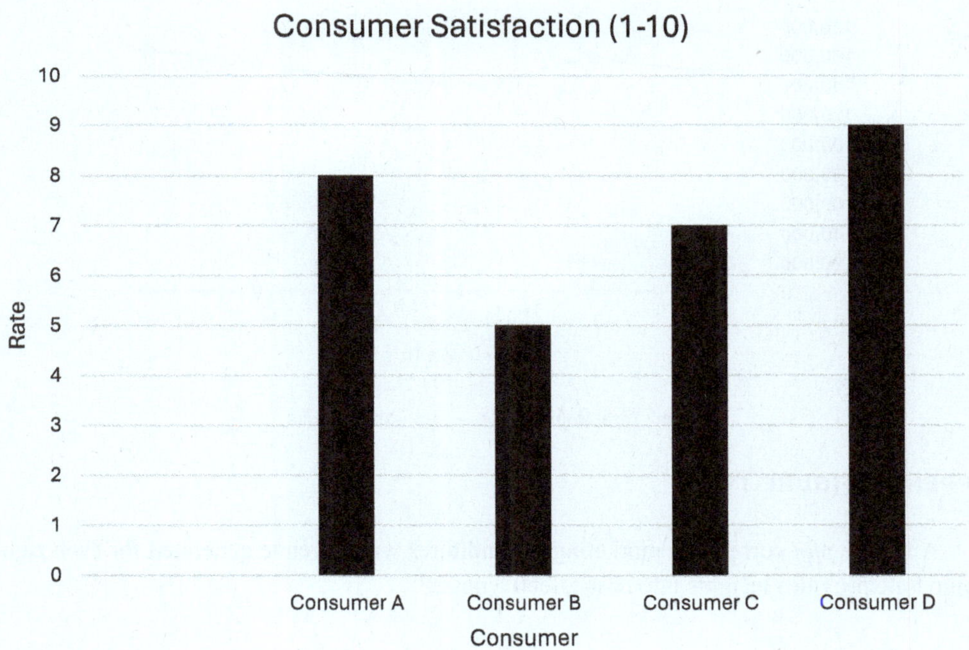


**APPENDIX FIGURE 9**

A *pie chart* could illustrate the proportion of retained vs. lost consumers.

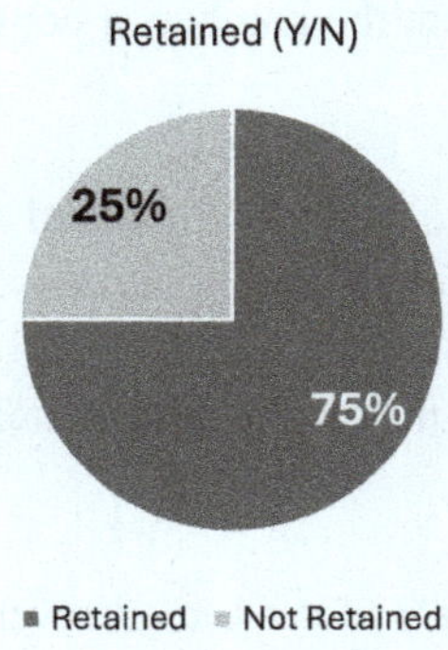


**APPENDIX FIGURE 10**

A *line graph* could show the trend of CTR over the months to visualize performance changes.

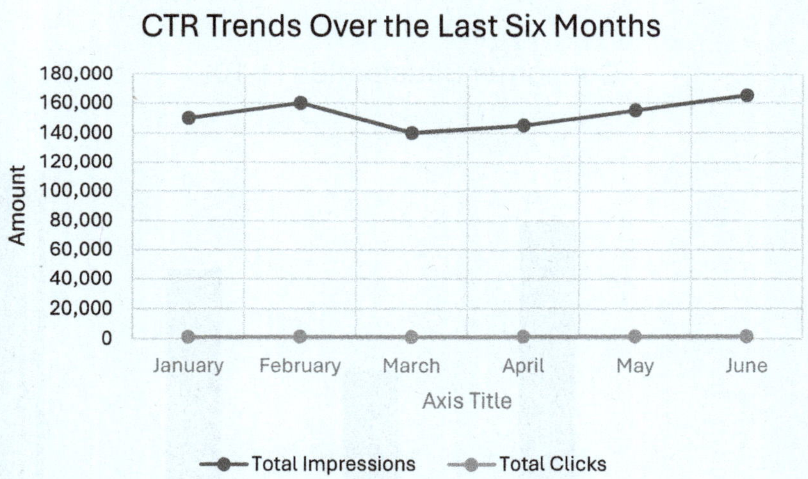


**APPENDIX FIGURE 11**

A *scatter plot* correlating marketing expenditures with revenue generated for each campaign type provides insights into cost-effectiveness.

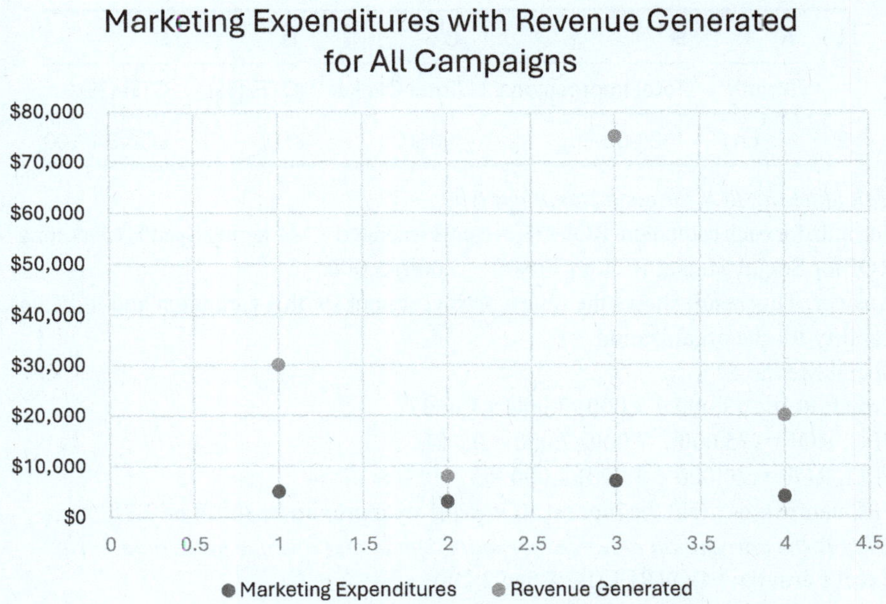


**APPENDIX FIGURE 12**

## BUSINESS ANALYTICS OPEN-ENDED QUESTIONS

1. *Calculate the average consumer satisfaction score.*
   Formula: =AVERAGE(F2:F5)
   Answer: Calculate the average to understand overall consumer sentiment.
   Using the scores (8, 5, 7, 9): =AVERAGE(8, 5, 7, 9) = 7.25.
   The average satisfaction is 7.25.
2. *Determine the retention rate.*
   Formula: =(COUNTIF(B2:B5, "Y")/COUNTA(A2:A5))*100
   Answer: This calculates the percentage of retained consumers out of the total number of consumers.
   Consumers retained 3, and lost 1.
   = (3/4) × 100 = 75%
   Retention rate is 75%.
3. *What is the click-through rate (CTR) for March?*
   Formula: = (Total Clicks in March/Total Impressions in March) × 100
   Using the data, it will be: = (1,350/140,000) × 100 = 0.9643%
   Answer: The CTR for March is approximately 0.96%.

| 1 | A | B | C | D | D |
|---|---|---|---|---|---|
| | Month | Total Impressions | Total Clicks | CTR (%) | CTR (%) |
| 2 | March | 140,000 | 1,350 | 0.96 | =C4/B4*100 |

4. *Calculate the ROI for each campaign type.*
   Formula for each campaign: ROI = (Revenue Generated − Marketing Spend)/Marketing Spend
   ROI for Social Media: ROI = (30,000 − 5,000)/5,000 = 5
   Answer: This result shows the return on investment for this campaign and indicates profitability for the organization.
   Social Media: 5
   Email: ROI = (8,000 − 3,000)/3,000 = 1.6667
   PPC: ROI = (75,000 − 7,000)/7,000 = 9.7143
   SEO: ROI = (20,000 − 4,000)/4,000 = 5
   PPC campaigns yield the highest ROI, with an approximate result of 9.71.
5. *What is the correlation between marketing spend and revenue generated?*
   Excel Formula: =CORREL(B2:B5, C2:C5)
   Answer: The correlation coefficient reveals the strength of the relationship between marketing expenditure and revenue generated.
   Assume we get the value, for example, 0.85, indicating a strong positive correlation. However, if we get a value of, say, .10, this would indicate a weak correlation. The closer to 1, the stronger the positive correlation. The closer to 0, the weaker the correlation.
6. *Recommendation question:* Based on the analysis, which campaign type should the company prioritize for new consumers? Why?
   Answer: Consumers may find that PPC campaigns bring the highest revenue relative to expenditures. This situation suggests that PPC should be prioritized by the organization. To improve new consumer acquisition, PPC campaigns should be selected due to their high ROIs and effectiveness in generating revenue, although they have higher upfront costs.

## Case Study: Summit Business Solutions

Summit Business Solutions is a company based in New York. The company specializes in digital business solution services, including social media management, SEO optimization, and content marketing. Over the past few years, Summit has experienced unreliable growth that has generated concerns regarding customer retention and operational effectiveness. The management team has decided to investigate this issue further by focusing on consumer satisfaction and billable hours.

### *Data Summary*

To analyze Summit's situation, the following dataset has been constructed. This dataset tracks 25 consumers, detailing their:

- Monthly spending on marketing services
- Duration of their contracts

- Number of campaigns executed
- Satisfaction ratings

| 1 | A | B | C | D | E |
|---|---|---|---|---|---|
| | Consumer ID | Monthly Spending | Contract Duration (Months) | Number of Campaigns | Satisfaction Rating (1–10) |
| 2 | 1 | $500 | 12 | 8 | 7 |
| 3 | 2 | $700 | 8 | 6 | 6 |
| 4 | 3 | $300 | 15 | 5 | 8 |
| 5 | 4 | $1,000 | 5 | 10 | 5 |
| 6 | 5 | $200 | 20 | 4 | 9 |
| 7 | 6 | $800 | 10 | 7 | 4 |
| 8 | 7 | $600 | 6 | 8 | 6 |
| 9 | 8 | $1,500 | 3 | 15 | 3 |
| 10 | 9 | $400 | 18 | 5 | 10 |
| 11 | 10 | $1,200 | 7 | 9 | 5 |
| 12 | 11 | $750 | 11 | 12 | 6 |
| 13 | 12 | $300 | 22 | 8 | 7 |
| 14 | 13 | $600 | 4 | 7 | 2 |
| 15 | 14 | $900 | 9 | 10 | 5 |
| 16 | 15 | $350 | 16 | 4 | 9 |
| 17 | 16 | $450 | 17 | 2 | 7 |
| 18 | 17 | $950 | 2 | 14 | 1 |
| 19 | 18 | $550 | 19 | 6 | 8 |
| 20 | 19 | $750 | 13 | 5 | 6 |
| 21 | 20 | $1,100 | 1 | 8 | 4 |
| 22 | 21 | $360 | 14 | 3 | 10 |
| 23 | 22 | $850 | 8 | 6 | 5 |
| 24 | 23 | $500 | 12 | 13 | 3 |
| 25 | 24 | $650 | 10 | 9 | 8 |
| 26 | 25 | $1,300 | 9 | 11 | 7 |

## DATA ANALYSIS

1. *Calculate summary statistics.* To assess the extent of the issue, we will summarize the data using various functions.
   Total Monthly Spending: =SUM(500 + 700 + . . . + 650 + 1,300) = $17,560
   Average Monthly Spend: =AVERAGE(C2:C26) = $702
   Mean Satisfaction Rating: =SUM(F2:F26)/25 = 6.04
   Median Contract Duration: =MEDIAN (F2:F26) = 6
   Mode of Satisfaction Ratings: =MODE(F2:F26) = 7

## CREATING PIVOTTABLES AND PIVOTCHARTS

To effectively summarize the primary aspects of the data and to visualize the trends, a PivotTable and PivotChart can be created in Excel or a similar spreadsheet application. The PivotChart created from this data can visually represent the average monthly spend against the contract duration. This chart can help identify whether higher rates correspond with longer contracts and higher satisfaction ratings. The PivotTable and PivotChart can be structured based on the following data:

| 1 | A | B | C | D |
|---|---|---|---|---|
| | **Contract Duration (Months)** | **Average Monthly Spending** | **Total Campaigns** | **Average Satisfaction Rating** |
| 2 | 1 | $1,100 | 8 | 4 |
| 3 | 2 | $950 | 14 | 1 |
| 4 | 3 | $1,500 | 15 | 3 |
| 5 | 4 | $600 | 7 | 2 |
| 6 | 5 | $1,000 | 10 | 5 |
| 7 | 6 | $600 | 8 | 6 |
| 8 | 7 | $1,200 | 9 | 5 |
| 9 | 8 | $700 | 6 | 5 |
| 10 | 9 | $1,450 | 17 | 6 |
| 11 | 10 | $800 | 8 | 5 |
| 12 | 11 | $750 | 12 | 6 |
| 13 | 12 | $800 | 9 | 7 |
| 14 | 13 | $750 | 5 | 6 |
| 15 | 14 | $400 | 3 | 10 |
| 16 | 15 | $300 | 4 | 8 |
| 17 | 16 | $350 | 4 | 9 |
| 18 | 17 | $450 | 2 | 7 |
| 29 | 18 | $550 | 6 | 8 |
| 20 | 19 | $750 | 5 | 6 |
| 21 | 20 | $1,100 | 8 | 4 |
| 22 | 21 | $360 | 3 | 10 |
| 23 | 22 | $850 | 6 | 5 |
| 24 | 23 | $500 | 13 | 3 |
| 25 | 24 | $650 | 9 | 8 |
| 26 | 25 | $1,300 | 11 | 7 |

## CREATING A PIVOTTABLE AND PIVOTCHART

- Go to Insert and select PivotChart.
- Input Table/Range.
- Choose where you want the PivotChart to be placed.
- Click OK.
- In the PivotChart Fields, select the following:
    - Filters
    - Legend (Series)
    - Axis (Categories)
    - Values

For this example, we will select the following:

Filters: Consumer ID
Legend (Series): Satisfaction Rating (1–10)
Axis (Categories): Number of Campaigns
Values: Monthly Spending

Consumer ID (All)

| Sum of Monthly Spending / Row Labels | 1 | 2 | 3 | 4 | 5 | 6 | 7 | 8 | 9 | 10 | Grand Total |
|---|---|---|---|---|---|---|---|---|---|---|---|
| 2 | | | | | | | $450 | | | | $450 |
| 3 | | | | | | | | | | $360 | $360 |
| 4 | | | | | | | | | $550 | | $550 |
| 5 | | | | | | $750 | | $300 | | $400 | $1,450 |
| 6 | | | | | $850 | $700 | | $550 | | | $2,100 |
| 7 | | $600 | | $800 | | | | | | | $1,400 |
| 8 | | | | $1,100 | | $600 | $800 | | | | $2,500 |
| 9 | | | | | $1,200 | | | $650 | | | $1,850 |
| 10 | | | | | $1,900 | | | | | | $1,900 |
| 11 | | | | | | | $1,300 | | | | $1,300 |
| 12 | | | | | | $750 | | | | | $750 |
| 13 | | | $500 | | | | | | | | $500 |
| 14 | $950 | | | | | | | | | | $950 |
| 15 | | | $1,500 | | | | | | | | $1,500 |
| **Grand Total** | **$950** | **$600** | **$2,000** | **$1,900** | **$3,950** | **$2,800** | **$2,550** | **$1,500** | **$550** | **$760** | **$17,560** |

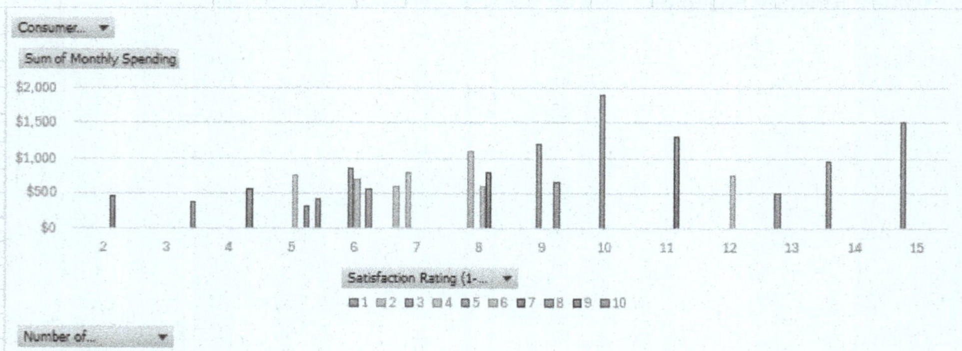


**APPENDIX FIGURE 13**

## ANALYSIS OF KEY ISSUES

Upon reviewing the data and visuals:

- *Satisfaction ratings.* Most consumers have a rating below 6, and more specifically the consumers with contract durations between 2 and 5 months.
- *Revenue vs. campaign results.* High spending does not always result in high satisfaction. Consumers who spend less have high satisfaction scores.

## QUESTIONS FOR ANALYSIS

1. What is the total revenue generated from consumers with a satisfaction rating above 7?
   Consumers: 3 (Consumer 3, 5, and 9) with spending of $300, $200, and $400.
   Total revenue = 300 + 200 + 400 = 900
2. How many consumers have a contract duration of more than 12 months?
   Consumers: 12 (Consumer 3, 5, 9, 12, 15, 16, 18, 19, 21, 22, 24)
   Total count = 10
3. What is the median monthly spending of all consumers?
   Sort by monthly spending (200, 300, 350, 360, 400, 450, 500, 500, 550, 600, 600, 650, 700, 750, 800, 850, 900, 1,000, 1,100, 1,200, 1,300, 1,500)
   Midpoint values (12th and 13th) are $650 and $700.
   ($650 and $700)/2 = 675
   Or
   =MEDIAN(B2:B2) = 675
4. What percentage of consumers are dissatisfied (rating below 5)?
   Consumers with ratings below 5: (Consumers 6, 8, 13, 17, 20, and 23) = 6
   Percentage dissatisfied = 6/25*100 = 24%
   Around 24% of consumers have a rating below 5.
5. Is there a correlation between the number of campaigns executed and satisfaction rating?
   =CORREL(C2:C26,D2:D26) = −0.57293
   A correlation coefficient of −0.57293 indicates a negative relationship between two variables. As one variable increases, the other will decrease. The value is close to −1, which suggests a strong negative linear relationship. As a result, a correlation of −0.57293 suggests that while there is a relationship between the two variables, it is not perfect, and there are other factors influencing this relationship.
6. What is the average spending of consumers who executed more than ten campaigns?
   Consumers with >10 campaigns: Consumers 4, 9, 14, 22, 25 (corresponding campaigns: 10, 15, 10, 11).
   Total consumers with >10 campaigns = 5
   Corresponding consumer spending: $1,000, $400, $900, $850, and $1,300
   Average spending = ($1,000 + $400 + $900 + $850 + $1,300)/5 = 690

### Case Study: Vision Economics LLC

Vision Economics LLC specializes in integrated economics solutions. Vision Economics LLC has shown consistent growth in revenue and consumer acquisition over the past few years. However, the leadership team has observed a decline in consumer satisfaction and an increase in consumer turnover. This situation has led to market concerns about long-term sustainability and competitive advantage in the business environment. To better understand the company's situation, a SWOT analysis will need to be conducted along with a related financial data analysis to improve future performance.

### *Data Summary*

The following data tables will provide the background for Vision Economics LLC's current market standing.

**CONSUMER SATISFACTION SURVEY**

| 1 | A | B | C | D | E |
|---|---|---|---|---|---|
| | Consumer ID | Satisfaction Score (1–10) | Services Used | Contract Status | Monthly Spending |
| 2 | 1 | 8 | SEO | Active | $1,200 |
| 3 | 2 | 5 | PPC | Active | $800 |
| 4 | 3 | 9 | Content | Active | $1,500 |
| 5 | 4 | 4 | Event | Inactive | $600 |
| 6 | 5 | 6 | SEO, PPC | Active | $950 |
| 7 | 6 | 7 | SEO | Active | $1,100 |
| 8 | 7 | 3 | Social media | Inactive | $500 |
| 9 | 8 | 10 | PPC | Active | $2,000 |
| 10 | 9 | 2 | Content | Inactive | $400 |
| 11 | 10 | 6 | Social media | Active | $1,000 |

**FINANCIAL OVERVIEW**

| 1 | A | B | C | D |
|---|---|---|---|---|
| | Year | Total Revenue | Operating Costs | Net Profit |
| 2 | YEAR 1 | $500,000 | $350,000 | $150,000 |
| 3 | YEAR 2 | $600,000 | $400,000 | $200,000 |
| 4 | YEAR 3 | $700,000 | $550,000 | $150,000 |
| 5 | YEAR 4 | $650,000 | $500,000 | $150,000 |

**SERVICE PERFORMANCE**

| 1 | A | B | C | D |
|---|---|---|---|---|
| | Service Type | Total Consumers | Average Satisfaction Score | Overall Revenue |
| 2 | SEO | 5 | 7.0 | $5,950 |
| 3 | PPC | 4 | 6.5 | $5,200 |
| 4 | Content | 3 | 6.0 | $4,800 |
| 5 | Event | 1 | 4.0 | $600 |
| 6 | Social Media | 2 | 3.0 | $1,500 |

**MARKET TRENDS DATA**

| 1 | A | B | C |
|---|---|---|---|
| | Trend | Impact Level (1–5) | Opportunity Level (1–5) |
| 2 | Digital transformation | 5 | 4 |
| 3 | Competition | 4 | 2 |
| 4 | Economic conditions | 3 | 3 |
| 5 | Customer preferences | 5 | 5 |
| 6 | Technological advancements | 4 | 4 |

**SWOT ANALYSIS TABLE**

| Strengths | Weaknesses | Opportunities | Threats |
|---|---|---|---|
| Established brand reputation | Decreasing consumer satisfaction | Growing demand for digital marketing | Increased competition |
| Diverse service offerings | High consumer churn rate | Adoption of new technologies | Economic downturn |
| Experienced team of marketers | Insufficient market research | Expansion into new markets | Rapid changes in consumer behavior |
| Strong digital presence | Inconsistent quality of service | Collaboration with tech firms | Price sensitivity among consumers |

## USING FUNCTIONS

1. *Count of active vs. inactive consumers.* To analyze the number of active versus inactive consumers:
   =COUNTIF(Consumer_Satisfaction_Survey!D:D, "Active") = 6
   =COUNTIF(Consumer_Satisfaction_Survey!D:D, "Inactive") = 4
2. *Lookup for consumer satisfaction scores.* To find the satisfaction score for a given consumer (i.e., consumer 3), the VLOOKUP formula will return the satisfaction score of consumer ID 3.
   =VLOOKUP(excel =VLOOKUP(3, Consumer_Satisfaction_Survey!A:E, 2, FALSE) = 9
3. *Retrieve monthly spend using INDEX/MATCH.* To find the monthly spend for a specific consumer using INDEX and MATCH, the INDEX/MATCH formula will retrieve the monthly spending for Consumer ID 5.
   =INDEX(Consumer_Satisfaction_Survey!E:E, MATCH(5, Consumer_Satisfaction_Survey!A:A, 0)) = 950

## IDENTIFYING KEY ISSUES

Based on the financial overview, it is evident that while revenue had been increasing up to year 3, there was a dip in year 4. Combined with the consumer satisfaction scores with several scores below the average, Vision Economics LLC must address both the quality of service and consumer relations to sustain growth and market share.

## BUSINESS ANALYTICS OPEN-ENDED QUESTIONS

1. What is the overall consumer satisfaction average?
   =AVERAGE(Consumer_Satisfaction_Survey!B:B) = 6.1
   The average satisfaction score is approximately 6.1.
2. How many services were provided to consumers with a satisfaction score below 5?
   =COUNTIF(Consumer_Satisfaction_Survey!B:B, "<5") = 3
   There are three services provided to dissatisfied consumers.
3. What is the percentage increase in total revenue from year 1 to year 2?
   =(\$600,000 − \$500,000)/\$500,000 × 100 = 20%
4. What is the average profit margin for the company over the last four years?
   Calculating profit margin for each year:
   Year 1: \$150,000/\$500,000 × 100 = 30%
   Year 2: \$200,000/\$600,000 × 100 = 33.33%
   Year 2: \$150,000/\$700,000 × 100 = 21.43%
   Year 3: \$150,000/\$650,000 × 100 = 23.08%
   To find the average profit margin:
   = (30 + 33.33 + 21.43 + 23.08)/4 = 26.95%
5. How many consumers use the SEO service, and what is their average satisfaction score?
   =COUNTIF(Service_Performance!A:A, "SEO") = 5
   =AVERAGEIF(Consumer_Satisfaction_Survey!C:C, "SEO", Consumer_Satisfaction_Survey!B:B) = 7.0
   There are five consumers using the SEO service, with an average satisfaction score of 7.0.
6. What is the correlation between satisfaction scores and monthly spend?
   =CORREL(Consumer_Satisfaction_Survey!B:B, Consumer_Satisfaction_Survey!E:E) = −0.35
   The correlation coefficient of −0.35 shows a weak negative correlation between satisfaction scores and monthly spending. The assumption is that higher spending does not directly correlate with higher satisfaction.

## Case Study: B2C Branding LLC

### *Company Overview*

B2C Branding LLC specializes in brand consulting and social media management. After experiencing steady revenue growth in its early years, B2C Branding is now facing internal challenges within its environment regarding staff productivity and overall consumer satisfaction. As the leadership and management team attempt to understand these issues, they will use statistical analysis to gain insights from consumer data and performance metrics.

### *Consumer Performance Data*

The following dataset tracks key performance indicators (KPIs) from 25 consumers, which include their monthly spend on marketing services, satisfaction scores, and the number of campaigns executed.

| 1 | A | B | C | D |
|---|---|---|---|---|
| | Consumer ID | Monthly Spend | Satisfaction Score (1–10) | Number of Campaigns |
| 2 | 1 | $800 | 8 | 5 |
| 3 | 2 | $1,200 | 7 | 4 |
| 4 | 3 | $1,500 | 9 | 6 |
| 5 | 4 | $600 | 5 | 3 |
| 6 | 5 | $900 | 6 | 4 |
| 7 | 6 | $2,000 | 10 | 8 |
| 8 | 7 | $300 | 4 | 2 |
| 9 | 8 | $700 | 5 | 3 |
| 10 | 9 | $1,000 | 8 | 5 |
| 11 | 10 | $1,100 | 6 | 4 |
| 12 | 11 | $1,800 | 9 | 7 |
| 13 | 12 | $2,200 | 10 | 9 |
| 14 | 13 | $400 | 3 | 2 |
| 15 | 14 | $500 | 4 | 2 |
| 16 | 15 | $1,600 | 7 | 5 |
| 17 | 16 | $2,500 | 9 | 10 |
| 18 | 17 | $1,300 | 8 | 4 |
| 19 | 18 | $650 | 5 | 3 |
| 20 | 19 | $2,000 | 9 | 6 |
| 21 | 20 | $750 | 4 | 3 |
| 22 | 21 | $850 | 6 | 4 |
| 23 | 22 | $1,400 | 8 | 5 |
| 24 | 23 | $1,200 | 7 | 4 |
| 25 | 24 | $1,500 | 6 | 5 |
| 26 | 25 | $1,700 | 8 | 6 |

## STATISTICAL ANALYSIS

1. **Statistical Functions**
   **Average Monthly Spending**: =AVERAGE(B2:B26) = $1,218
   **Standard Deviation of Monthly Spending**: =STDEV(B2:B26) = 592.99
   **Correlation Between Monthly Spending and Satisfaction Score**: =CORREL (B2:B26,C2;C26) = 0.86
2. **Regression Analysis**
   **Regression Formula:** The regression equation can be derived as follows: [y = mx + b] Where:
   $y$ = satisfaction score
   $m$ = slope of the line (change in satisfaction score per additional dollar spent)
   $x$ = monthly spending
   $b$ = y-intercept
   Use the Data Analysis tool in Excel. Go to the Data tab and select Data Analysis. Select Regression and click OK.
   Enter Y Range: (Satisfaction Score)
   Enter X Range: (Monthly Spending)
   Select Output Range

SUMMARY OUTPUT

| Regression | Statistics |
|---|---|
| Multiple R | 0.864201475 |
| R-Square | 0.746844189 |
| Adjusted R-Square | 0.735837414 |
| Standard Error | 1.03519059 |
| Observations | 25 |

ANOVA

| | df | SS | MS | F | Significance F |
|---|---|---|---|---|---|
| Regression | 1 | 72.7127502 | 72.7127502 | 67.85313849 | 2.58813E-08 |
| Residual | 23 | 24.6472498 | 1.071619557 | | |
| Total | 24 | 97.36 | | | |

| | Coefficients | Standard Error | t Stat | p-value | Lower 95% | Upper 95% | Lower 95.0% | Upper 95.0% |
|---|---|---|---|---|---|---|---|---|
| Intercept | 3.264829253 | 0.480874145 | 6.789363266 | 6.34089E-07 | 2.270065294 | 4.259593212 | 2.270065294 | 4.259593212 |
| Monthly Spend ($) | 0.00293528 | 0.00035634 | 8.237301651 | 2.58813E-08 | 0.002198134 | 0.003672425 | 0.002198134 | 0.003672425 |

$R^2$ = .7468, meaning that there is a high correlation between variables.

3. **Scatter Plot Chart**

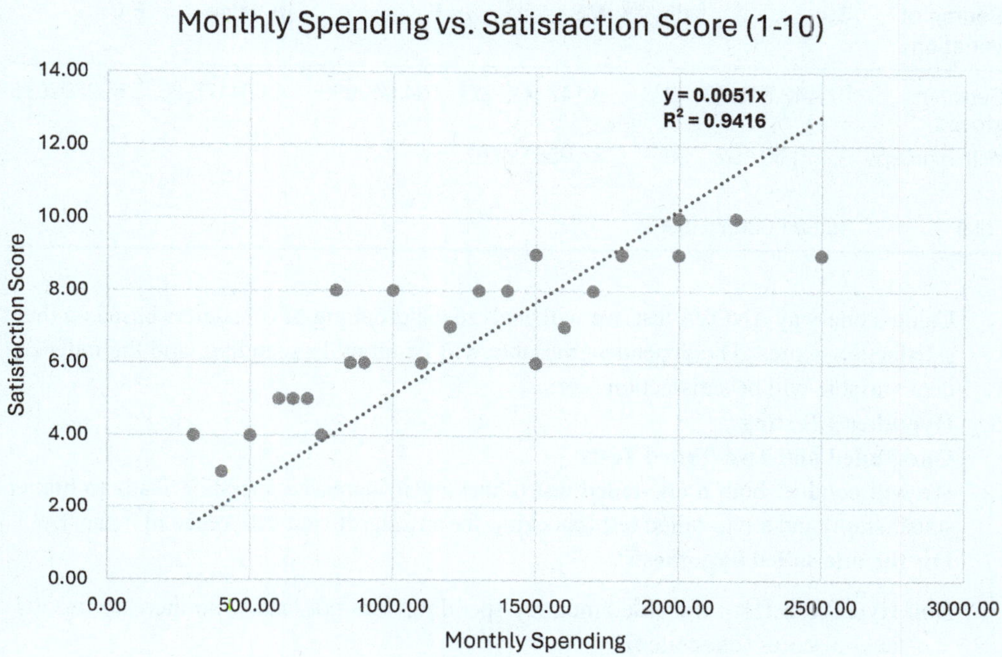


**APPENDIX FIGURE 14**

4. **ANOVA**
   State your hypothesis.
   Null Hypothesis ($H_0$): Mean consumer spending is the same across all satisfaction levels.
   Alternative Hypothesis ($H_1$): At least one satisfaction level has a different mean monthly spending.

Anova: Single Factor

SUMMARY

| Groups | Count | Sum | Average | Variance |
|---|---|---|---|---|
| Consumer ID | 25 | 325 | 13 | 54.16666667 |
| Monthly spend ($) | 25 | 30,450 | 1,218 | 351,641.6667 |
| Satisfaction score (1–10) | 25 | 171 | 6.84 | 4.056666667 |
| Number of campaigns | 25 | 119 | 4.76 | 4.356666667 |

ANOVA

| Source of Variation | SS | df | MS | F | p-value | F Crit |
|---|---|---|---|---|---|---|
| Between groups | 27,443,718.83 | 3 | 9,147,906.277 | 104.0408964 | 4.68417E-30 | 2.699392598 |
| Within groups | 8,440,901.92 | 96 | 87,926.06167 | | | |
| Total | 35,884,620.75 | 99 | | | | |

Using a one-way ANOVA test, we will analyze the grouping of consumers based on their satisfaction scores. The dependent variable will be monthly spending, and the independent variable will be satisfaction score.

5. **Hypothesis Testing**

**One-Tailed and Two-Tailed Tests**

We will conduct both a one-tailed test (checking if increased spending leads to higher satisfaction) and a two-tailed test (checking for any significant difference in means).

**For the one-tailed hypothesis:**

Null Hypothesis ($H_0$): Increased monthly spending does not lead to an increase in satisfaction scores (one-tailed).

Alternative Hypothesis ($H_1$): Increased monthly spending leads to higher satisfaction scores (one-tailed).

**For the two-tailed hypothesis:**

Null Hypothesis ($H_0$): There is no difference in satisfaction scores based on spending.

Alternative Hypothesis ($H_1$): There is a difference in satisfaction scores based on spending.

The significance level ($\alpha$) can be set at 0.05 (95%).

## DATA ANALYSIS SUMMARY

Here's a summarized analysis based on our data:

Average Spending: $1,218

Standard Deviation: $592.99

Correlation Between Spending and Satisfaction: 0.86 indicates a relative to strong positive correlation.

Regression: After computing the necessary statistics and applying ANOVA, if the p-value is less than $\alpha$ (0.05), we reject the null hypothesis.

## BUSINESS ANALYTICS OPEN-ENDED QUESTIONS

1. What is the average satisfaction score of consumers who spend more than $1,000?
   This function calculates the average satisfaction score for consumers who spend more than $1,000.
   =AVERAGEIF(A2:A26, ">1000", C2:C26)
2. How does the standard deviation of satisfaction scores inform us about the variability in consumer satisfaction?
   The standard deviation gives perceptions into the variability of satisfaction scores. A high standard deviation suggests that the consumers' satisfaction levels are widely spread out. When the standard deviation is high, the data shows inconsistent satisfaction levels.
3. What is the predicted satisfaction score for a consumer spending $1,400 based on the regression analysis?
   Using regression coefficients taken, we can assume ($m = 0.003$) and ($b = 3$):
   y = 0.003*$1,400 + 3 = 4.2.
   The predicted satisfaction score for a consumer spending of $1,400 would be approximately 4.2.
4. Is there a significant difference in monthly spending across different satisfaction levels based on ANOVA results?
   If the p-value correlated with ANOVA is less than 0.05, we can conclude that there is a significant difference in monthly spending across different satisfaction levels.
5. If we want to increase consumer satisfaction by at least one point, how much more should we advise consumers to spend on average?
   If the regression analysis indicates a direct increase in satisfaction score with spending:
   Increase in Spending = 1/0.0015 = $666.67.
   Therefore, consumers would need to spend approximately $667 more.
6. Given a correlation of 0.68, what recommendations can be made to improve consumer satisfaction through spending?
   Since there is a positive correlation coefficient of 0.68, it is recommended for consumers to increase their monthly marketing budgets. The data shows that higher spending typically correlates with higher satisfaction and provides incentives to consumers to consider an increased investment in marketing services.

### Case Study: Reputable Investors Corp.

#### *Company Overview*

Reputable Investors Corp. is an investment company that has quickly grown its consumer base and reputation by relying on data-driven strategies and innovative investment campaigns. However, as Reputable Investors Corp. operates in a competitive landscape, the management team is assessing new project investments to improve its services further and to deliver better results for its consumer base.

### *Investment Proposals*

The following dataset demonstrates the cash flows associated with three different investment project proposals over a five-year period.

| 1 | A | B | C | D | E | F | G |
|---|---|---|---|---|---|---|---|
| | Project ID | Initial Investment | Year 1 Cash Flow | Year 2 Cash Flow | Year 3 Cash Flow | Year 4 Cash Flow | Year 5 Cash Flow |
| 2 | 1 | $10,000 | $3,000 | $4,000 | $3,500 | $2,000 | $1,500 |
| 3 | 2 | $15,000 | $5,000 | $6,000 | $7,000 | $6,500 | $6,000 |
| 4 | 3 | $25,000 | $10,000 | $15,000 | $12,000 | $8,000 | $5,000 |

## STATISTICAL ANALYSIS USING EXCEL

### Summary Statistics

1. **Total Initial Investment:** =SUM(B2:B4) = $50,000
2. **Total Cash Flow Over Five Years for Each Project:**
   - Project 1: =SUM(C2:G2) = $14,000
   - Project 2: =SUM(C3:G3) = $30,500
   - Project 3: =SUM(C:4:FG) = $50,000
3. **Average Annual Cash Flows for Each Project:**
   - Project 1: =AVERAGE(C2:G2) = $2,800
   - Project 2: =AVERAGE(C3:G3) = $6,100
   - Project 3: =AVERAGE(C4:G4) = $10,000

## FINANCIAL EVALUATION FUNCTIONS

1. *PMT function.* To calculate the annual payment of a loan based on a constant interest rate and fixed payments for the investment needs. Assuming an annual interest rate of 10% for a period of five years:
   =PMT(0.10, 5, − $50,000) = $13,189.87
   *NPV function.* To calculate the net present value (NPV) of each project's cash flows, the NPV function takes into account the time value of money: =NPV(Interest Rate, Cash Flow Range) − Initial Investment).
   Assuming an annual interest rate of 10%:
   For Project 1: =NPV(0.10, C2:G2) − B2 = $5,315.33
   For Project 2: =NPV(0.10, C2:G2) − B2 = $14,461.34
   For Project 3: =NPV(0.10, C2:G2) − B2 = $24,960.25

2. *IRR function.* To determine the internal rate of return (IRR) for each project: =IRR(Cash Flow Range)
   For Project 1: =IRR(A2:G2) = $11,400
   Approximately between 10 and 12%
   For Project 2: =IRR(A2:G2) = $18,050
   Approximately between 14 and 16%
   For Project 3: =IRR(A2:G2) = $30,000
   Approximately between 8 and 10%

By reviewing the annual cash flows, management can determine how quickly each project will start generating returns. Projects with higher NPVs and IRRs are generally more desirable and indicate better long-term profitability and return on investment.

## EXCEL VISUALIZATION TOOLS

### Creating Charts

To provide visual insights into the financial evaluation, the following charts can be created:

1. **Bar Chart** for Total Cash Flows

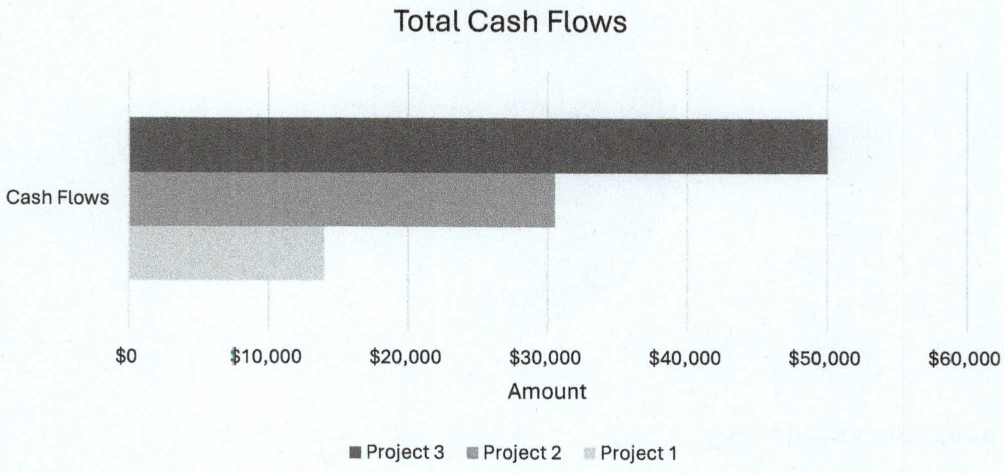


APPENDIX FIGURE 15

2. **Line Chart** for Cash Flows Over Time

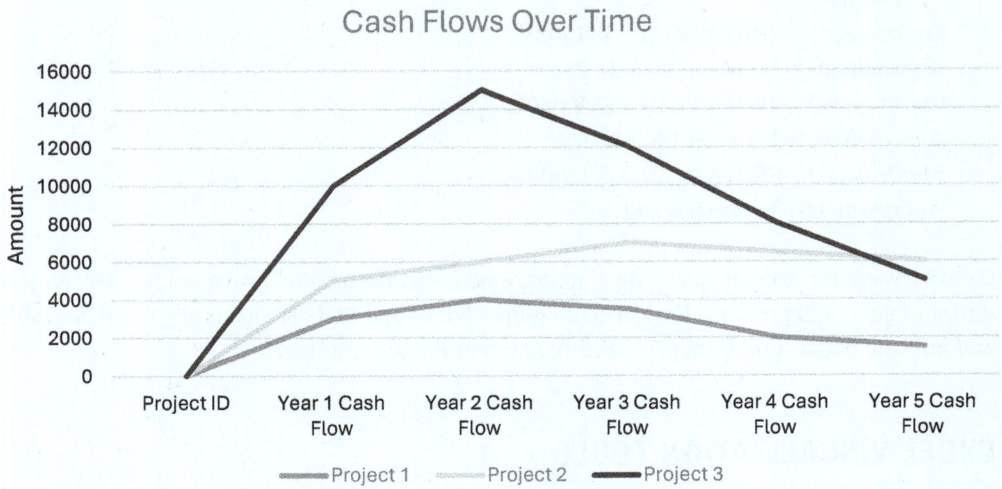


**APPENDIX FIGURE 16**

3. **Pie Chart** for Investments

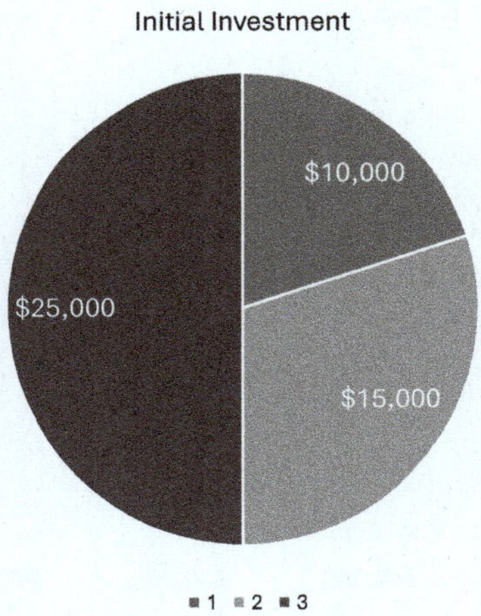


**APPENDIX FIGURE 17**

## EXPECTED PROJECT EVALUATIONS

By entering the respective cash flow data from the projects into the formulas and visualizations described, the leadership and management team can communicate the financial consequences of each investment proposal. Here is a breakdown of what they could find:

## PROJECT 1

NPV might yield a positive value but is potentially lower than the other two projects. IRR could fall below the company's required rate of return of 10%.

## PROJECT 2

Higher annual cash flows could denote a more stable and gradual increase in returns and will feature a higher NPV and IRR compared to Project 1.

## PROJECT 3

Despite a high initial investment, the cash flows in the first two years may yield the highest IRR and NPV, which suggest a higher return over time despite risks due to the diminishing cash flows in later years.

## BUSINESS ANALYTICS QUESTIONS FOR ANALYSIS

1. What is the project with the highest NPV, and what does this imply about its viability? Which project has the lowest risk based on the IRR and investment return?
   For Project 1: =NPV(0.10, C2:G2) − B2 = $5,315.33
   For Project 2: =NPV(0.10, C2:G2) − B2 = $14,461.34
   For Project 3: =NPV(0.10, C2:G2) − B2 = $24,960.25
   The project with the highest NPV indicates the best investment opportunity as it maximizes shareholder wealth. Project 3 has the highest value of $24,960.25.
   Which project has the lowest risk based on the IRR and investment return?
   For Project 1: =IRR(A2:G2) = $11,400
   Approximately between 10 and 12%
   For Project 2: =IRR(A2:G2) = $18,050
   Approximately between 14 and 16%
   For Project 3: =IRR(A2:G2) = $30,000

Approximately between 8 and 10%
Project 3 has the highest IRR, with a value of $30,000 and an NPV value of $24,960.25.
Project 3 is the lowest-risk option for the company.

2. How do the annual cash flows vary from year to year across all projects, and what trends can we observe?
   Use **STDEV** on the cash flows to understand variability.
   Project 1 =STDEV(C2:G2) = $1,037
   Project 2 =STDEV(C3:G3) = $742
   Project 3 =STDEV(C4: G4) = $3,808
   **Trend Analysis**: Over time, Project 3 has the highest value of $3,808.
3. What would be the impact on NPV if the discount rate increased to 12%?
   For Project 1: =NPV(0.12, C2:G2) − B2 = $5,414.44
   For Project 2: =NPV(0.12, C2:G2) − B2 = $14,165.87
   For Project 3: =NPV(0.12, C2:G2) − B2 = $24,683.34
   This analysis can indicate how sensitive the projects are to changes in the cost of capital.
4. How much total profit can the company expect from each project over the investment period?
   Total Profit = Total Cash Inflows − Initial Investment
   =SUM(Cash Flow Range) − Initial Investment
   =SUM(C2:G4) − $50,000 = $44,500
5. If Project 1's cash flows were to drop by 20% annually, how would that affect its NPV and IRR?
   Original Cash Flow for Project: =SUM(C2:G2) = $11,400
   New Cash Flow for Project 1: =$11,400*.80 = $9,120
   The net present value of Project 1 would decrease in value.
6. What is the impact of cash flow drops on NPV and IRR?
   There will be a significant drop in the cash flows of all projects that affect the overall return on investment (ROI) and expectations of the investors.

## Case Study: WeGiveUtheBusiness Corp.

### *Company Overview*

WeGiveUtheBusiness Corp. is a market research firm that specializes in providing solutions, including SEO, online marketing, and content creation. With a growing portfolio of clients, WeGiveUtheBusiness recognizes the necessity of coordinated project management and effective tracking systems to streamline their business operations and maximize effectiveness and efficiency. Despite steady growth, WeGiveUtheBusiness has experienced delays in project timelines and challenges in task assignments. To reduce these issues, the leadership team has decided to implement a structured project management approach using tools like Gantt charts and conditional formatting in Excel for progress tracking. The corporation has developed an action plan that includes deadlines, tasks, and assigned individuals to ensure accountability.

### ***Project Management Plan***

*Data Overview*

The following dataset represents various marketing projects at WeGiveUtheBusiness and details the tasks, deadlines, team assignments, and status updates:

| 1 | A | B | C | D |
|---|---|---|---|---|
| | **Project ID** | **Task** | **Deadline** | **Responsible Individual** |
| 2 | 1 | Market research | 04-15-2023 | Alice |
| 3 | 1 | Content development | 04-20-2023 | Bob |
| 4 | 1 | Social media strategy | 04-25-2023 | Carol |
| 5 | 1 | Campaign launch | 05-01-2023 | Dave |
| 6 | 2 | SEO audit | 04-10-2023 | Eve |
| 7 | 2 | Keyword research | 04-12-2023 | Frank |
| 8 | 2 | On-page optimization | 04-18-2023 | Grace |
| 9 | 2 | Performance monitoring | 04-30-2023 | Henry |
| 10 | 3 | Consumer consultation | 04-05-2023 | Iris |
| 11 | 3 | Design mockups | 04-15-2023 | Jack |
| 12 | 3 | Approval from consumer | 04-20-2023 | Kim |
| 13 | 3 | Finalize design | 04-25-2023 | Lily |
| 14 | 4 | Email marketing setup | 04-14-2023 | Mike |
| 15 | 4 | Create content | 04-20-2023 | Nate |
| 16 | 4 | Scheduling campaign | 04-28-2023 | Oscar |
| 17 | 4 | Launch campaign | 05-03-2023 | Paul |
| 18 | 5 | Event planning | 05-10-2023 | Quinn |
| 19 | 5 | Promotion strategy | 05-15-2023 | Rachel |
| 20 | 5 | Confirm venue | 05-18-2023 | Steve |
| 21 | 5 | Execute event | 05-20-2023 | Tina |
| 22 | 6 | Video production | 05-01-2023 | Uma |
| 23 | 6 | Editing and post-production | 05-10-2023 | Vic |
| 24 | 6 | Distribute content | 05-15-2023 | Will |
| 25 | 6 | Performance analytics | 05-20-2023 | Xena |
| 26 | 7 | Consumer follow-up | 05-05-2023 | Yara |
| 27 | 7 | Testimonials collection | 05-10-2023 | Zach |
| 28 | 7 | Case study development | 05-15-2023 | Abbi |
| 29 | 7 | Review and launch | 05-20-2023 | Ben |

## GANTT CHART FOR PROJECT MANAGEMENT

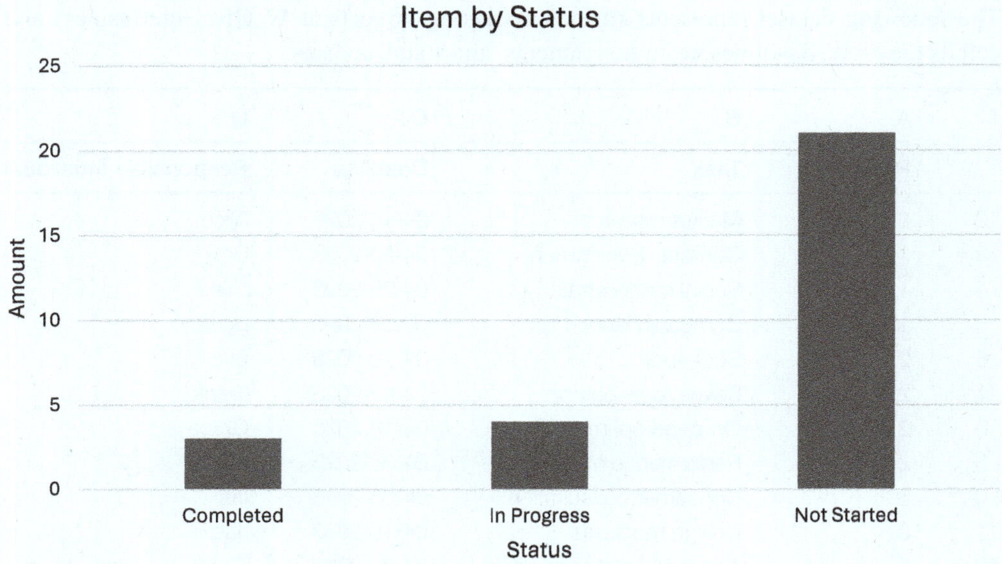


**APPENDIX FIGURE 18**

## ACTION PLANS

To organize tasks effectively and track progress, an action plan is created as follows:

| Action Item | Assigned To | Deadline | Status | Comments |
|---|---|---|---|---|
| Market research | Alice | 04-15-2023 | In Progress | Drafting report |
| Content development | Bob | 04-20-2023 | Not Started | Waiting for research |
| Social media strategy | Carol | 04-25-2023 | Not Started | Initial ideas planned |
| Campaign launch | Dave | 05-01-2023 | Not Started | Need inputs from all teams |
| SEO audit | Eve | 04-10-2023 | Completed | Report shared |
| Keyword research | Frank | 04-12-2023 | In Progress | Analyzing trends |
| On-page optimization | Grace | 04-18-2023 | Not Started | Scheduled for next week |
| Performance monitoring | Henry | 04-30-2023 | Not Started | Meeting with consumer |
| Consumer consultation | Iris | 04-05-2023 | Completed | Feedback received |
| Design mockups | Jack | 04-15-2023 | In Progress | First draft shared |
| Approval from consumer | Kim | 04-20-2023 | Not Started | Pending sign-off |
| Finalize design | Lily | 04-25-2023 | Not Started | Awaiting approval |
| Email marketing setup | Mike | 04-14-2023 | Completed | Template ready |
| Create content | Nate | 04-20-2023 | Not Started | Content strategy needed |

(*Continued*)

**Continued**

| Action Item | Assigned To | Deadline | Status | Comments |
|---|---|---|---|---|
| Scheduling campaign | Oscar | 04-28-2023 | Not Started | Awaiting final details |
| Launch campaign | Paul | 05-03-2023 | Not Started | Timeline to be confirmed |
| Event planning | Quinn | 05-10-2023 | Not Started | Researching venues |
| Promotion strategy | Rachel | 05-15-2023 | Not Started | To discuss in team meeting |
| Confirm venue | Steve | 05-18-2023 | Not Started | Venue options checked |
| Execute event | Tina | 05-20-2023 | Not Started | Logistics to be finalized |
| Video production | Uma | 05-01-2023 | In Progress | Filming scheduled |
| Editing and post-production | Vic | 05-10-2023 | Not Started | Based on filming progress |
| Distribute content | Will | 05-15-2023 | Not Started | Awaiting approval |
| Performance analytics | Xena | 05-20-2023 | Not Started | Plan to be outlined |
| Consumer follow-up | Yara | 05-05-2023 | Not Started | Follow-up email drafted |
| Testimonials collection | Zach | 05-10-2023 | Not Started | Awaiting responses |
| Case study development | Abbi | 05-15-2023 | Not Started | Data gathering process |
| Review and launch | Ben | 05-20-2023 | Not Started | Final presentation preparation |

## CONDITIONAL FORMATTING

To visually track the progress of these tasks, Excel's conditional formatting feature can be applied. Color-coded tasks based on their status:

- **Red** for "Not Started"
- **Yellow** for "In Progress"
- **Green** for "Completed"

| Action Item | Assigned To | Deadline | Status | Comments |
|---|---|---|---|---|
| Market research | Alice | 04-15-2023 | In Progress | Drafting report |
| Content development | Bob | 04-20-2023 | Not Started | Waiting for research |
| Social media strategy | Carol | 04-25-2023 | Not Started | Initial ideas planned |
| Campaign launch | Dave | 05-01-2023 | Not Started | Need inputs from all teams |
| SEO audit | Eve | 04-10-2023 | Completed | Report shared |
| Keyword research | Frank | 04-12-2023 | In Progress | Analyzing trends |
| On-page optimization | Grace | 04-18-2023 | Not Started | Scheduled for next week |
| Performance monitoring | Henry | 04-30-2023 | Not Started | Meeting with consumer |
| Consumer consultation | Iris | 04-05-2023 | Completed | Feedback received |
| Design mockups | Jack | 04-15-2023 | In Progress | First draft shared |
| Approval from consumer | Kim | 04-20-2023 | Not Started | Pending sign-off |
| Finalize design | Lily | 04-25-2023 | Not Started | Awaiting approval |

**Continued**

| Action Item | Assigned To | Deadline | Status | Comments |
|---|---|---|---|---|
| Email marketing setup | Mike | 04-14-2023 | Completed | Template ready |
| Create content | Nate | 04-20-2023 | Not Started | Content strategy needed |
| Scheduling campaign | Oscar | 04-28-2023 | Not Started | Awaiting final details |
| Launch campaign | Paul | 05-03-2023 | Not Started | Timeline to be confirmed |
| Event planning | Quinn | 05-10-2023 | Not Started | Researching venues |
| Promotion strategy | Rachel | 05-15-2023 | Not Started | To discuss in team meeting |
| Confirm venue | Steve | 05-18-2023 | Not Started | Venue options checked |
| Execute event | Tina | 05-20-2023 | Not Started | Logistics to be finalized |
| Video production | Uma | 05-01-2023 | In Progress | Filming scheduled |
| Editing and post-production | Vic | 05-10-2023 | Not Started | Based on filming progress |
| Distribute content | Will | 05-15-2023 | Not Started | Awaiting approval |
| Performance analytics | Xena | 05-20-2023 | Not Started | Plan to be outlined |
| Consumer follow-up | Yara | 05-05-2023 | Not Started | Follow-up email drafted |
| Testimonials collection | Zach | 05-10-2023 | Not Started | Awaiting responses |
| Case study development | Abbi | 05-15-2023 | Not Started | Data gathering process |
| Review and launch | Ben | 05-20-2023 | Not Started | Final presentation preparation |

## TRACKING WITH WHISKER PLOT

A box plot can summarize the distribution of project deadlines, providing insight into deadlines across various projects. This helps identify outliers and understand the expected completion time for individual tasks or projects.

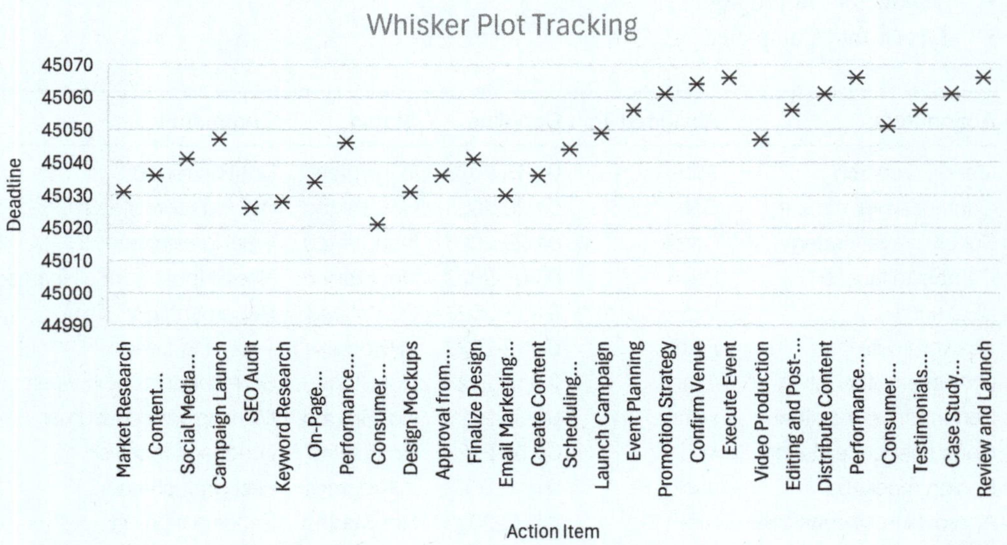


**APPENDIX FIGURE 19**

Through Gantt charts, box plots, and conditional formatting, the leadership team can identify potential blockages and can work to ensure that tasks are completed on schedule while maintaining high-quality standards for consumers. The ongoing tracking of progress, combined with performance metrics, allows WeGiveUtheBusiness to adapt to changing circumstances and empower their employees for increased productivity.

## Case Study: HR People Innovations Inc.

### *Company Overview*

HR People Innovations Inc. is a resource consulting company specializing in talent acquisition, employee retention strategies, and organizational development. The company has grown significantly by providing services to various industries that include information technology, health care, economics, and finance. HR People Innovations has a client-centric model, but recent economic challenges and a competitive job market have caused HR People Innovations Inc. to re-evaluate its strategic approach to maintain sustainable growth within their market environment.

### *Business Environment Challenges*

- *Increased competition.* The HR consulting market is flooded with new entrants offering similar services.
- *Changing workforce dynamics.* The rise of remote work has altered traditional hiring processes.
- *Client retention.* Businesses are becoming selective about HR service providers and are demanding better value and results.

### *Goals*

- Increase client acquisition by 15% in the next year.
- Improve client retention rates by implementing new engagement strategies.
- Develop an all-inclusive training program to improve employee satisfaction and skill sets.

### *Action Plan*

**ACTION PLAN FOR HR INNOVATIONS INC.**

| 1 | A | B | C | D |
|---|---|---|---|---|
| | **Action Item** | **Responsible Party** | **Start Date** | **End Date** |
| 2 | Market analysis | Marketing team | 01-01-2024 | 01-15-2024 |
| 3 | Update service offerings | Product development team | 01-16-2024 | 03-01-2024 |
| 4 | Launch client feedback survey | HR team | 03-02-2024 | 03-15-2024 |
| 5 | Create employee training program | HR and training team | 03-16-2024 | 04-30-2024 |
| 6 | Develop strategic partnerships | Business development | 05-01-2024 | 06-30-2024 |
| 7 | Monitor and evaluate results | Management team | 07-01-2024 | 07-30-2024 |

## TRACKING PROGRESS AND WHAT-IF ANALYSIS

HR people Innovations Inc. plans to track the progress of its action plan utilizing a combination of performance metrics and forecast sheets in Excel. Following is a dataset representing key performance metrics for the action plan:

## DATA TABLE SHOWING MONTHLY METRICS

| 1 | A | B | C | D |
|---|---|---|---|---|
| | Month | New Clients Acquired | Client Retention Rate (%) | Employee Satisfaction Score |
| 2 | Jan. 24 | 10 | 85 | 75 |
| 3 | Feb. 24 | 12 | 84 | 77 |
| 4 | Mar. 24 | 9 | 86 | 80 |
| 5 | Apr. 24 | 15 | 87 | 82 |
| 6 | May 24 | 20 | 88 | 85 |
| 7 | Jun. 24 | 18 | 89 | 88 |
| 8 | Jul. 24 | 22 | 90 | 90 |
| 9 | Aug. 24 | 25 | 91 | 92 |
| 10 | Sep. 24 | 20 | 92 | 91 |
| 11 | Oct. 24 | 30 | 93 | 93 |
| 12 | Nov. 24 | 28 | 94 | 95 |
| 13 | Dec. 24 | 35 | 95 | 96 |

## WHAT-IF ANALYSIS

HR Innovations Inc. can conduct a what-if analysis to evaluate the impact of various scenarios on its performance goals. Key scenarios could include:

- Increasing marketing spending to attract more clients
- Introducing innovative technologies to improve employee satisfaction

## MATH AND OPEN-ENDED QUESTIONS

1. What is the average client retention rate for the first half of the year (January 24 to June 24)?
   =AVERAGE(C2:C7) = 86.50 or 86.50%
2. Calculate the total number of new clients acquired from January 24 to December 24.
   =SUM(B2:B13) = 244 new clients

3. If HR Innovations Inc. increases its employee training budget by 20% and retains a client satisfaction score of 90%, how might this impact new client acquisitions?
   A potential increase in employee training could lead to higher employee satisfaction and improved services that can attract more clients. If employee satisfaction positively affects client perception, a forecast can be conducted to estimate a higher client acquisition rate.
4. What is the total increase in employee satisfaction from January 24 to December 24?
   Satisfaction in December 24 − Satisfaction in January 24 = 96 − 75 = 21
5. If the company implements a referral strategy that leads to a 50% increase in clients from the average acquired in the first six months, how many new clients should they expect?
   The average new clients acquired from January 24 to June 24 are 10 + 12 + 9 + 15 + 20 + 18.
   =AVERAGE(B2:B7) = 14 new clients
   A 50% increase would result in 14 + (0.5 × 14) = 14 + 7 = 21 new clients.
6. If HR Innovations Inc. wants to achieve a client retention rate of 96% by December 24, what percentage increase from their current average (which is 89% for June 24) would that require?
   The percentage increase:
   New Rate − Current Rate × Current Rate × 100
   = (96 − 89) × (89) × 100 = 7.87%
   To achieve a client retention rate of 96%, a 7.87% increase from the current average retention rate is required.

# Index

Note: Numbers in **bold** indicate tables and numbers in *italics* indicate figures on the corresponding page.